Direct Marketing

Direct Marketing

AN INTEGRATED APPROACH

William J. McDonald, Ph.D.
Hofstra University

New Thinking—An International
Direct Marketing Agency

Irwin
McGraw-Hill

Boston Burr Ridge, IL Dubuque, IA Madison, WI New York San Francisco St. Louis
Bangkok Bogotá Caracas Lisbon London Madrid
Mexico City Milan New Delhi Seoul Singapore Sydney Taipei Toronto

Irwin/McGraw-Hill

A Division of The **McGraw-Hill** *Companies*

Vice president and editorial director: *Michael W. Junior*
Publisher: *Gary Burke*
Executive editor: *Stephen M. Patterson*
Editorial coordinator: *Andrea L. Hlavacek-Rhoads*
Senior marketing manager: *Colleen J. Suljic*
Project manager: *Robert A. Preskill*
Production supervisor: *Madelyn Underwood*
Senior designer: *Crispin Prebys*
Photo Research Coordinator: *Sharon Miller*
Compositor: *Carlisle Communications, Ltd.*
Typeface: *10/12 Times Roman*
Printer: *R. R. Donnelley & Sons Company*

DIRECT MARKETING: AN INTEGRATED APPROACH

Photo permissions and other credits appear at the end of this book.

This book is printed on acid-free paper.

1 2 3 4 5 6 7 8 9 0 DOC/DOC 9 0 9 8 7

ISBN 0-256-19783-0

Library of Congress Cataloging-in-Publication Data

McDonald. William J.
Direct marketing : an integrated approach / William J. McDonald.
p. cm. -- (Irwin/McGraw-Hill series in marketing)
Includes bibliographical references and index.
ISBN 0-256-19783-0 (alk. paper)
1. Direct Marketing 2. Direct marketing--Case studies.
I. Title. II. Series.
HF415.126.M395 1998
658.8′4--dc21 97-27343

http://www.mhcollege.com

Irwin McGraw-Hill Series in Marketing

Alreck & Settle
THE SURVEY RESEARCH HANDBOOK, 2/E

Anderson, Hair & Bush
PROFESSIONAL SALES MANAGEMENT, 2/E

Arens
CONTEMPORARY ADVERTISING, 6/E

Bearden, Ingram & LaForge
MARKETING: *PRINCIPLES & PERSPECTIVES*, 2/E

Bearden, Ingram & LaForge
MARKETING INTERACTIVE, 1/E

Belch & Belch
INTRODUCTION TO ADVERTISING AND PROMOTION: *AN INTEGRATED MARKETING COMMUNICATIONS APPROACH*, 4/E

Bernhardt & Kinnear
CASES IN MARKETING MANAGEMENT, 7/E

Berkowitz, Kerin, Hartley & Rudelius
MARKETING, 5/e

Bowersox & Closs
LOGISTICAL MANAGEMENT, 1/E

Bowersox & Cooper
STRATEGIC MARKETING CHANNEL MANAGEMENT, 1/E

Boyd, Walker & Larreche
MARKETING MANAGEMENT: *A STRATEGIC APPROACH WITH A GLOBAL ORIENTATION*, 3/E

Cateora
INTERNATIONAL MARKETING, 9/E

Churchill, Ford & Walker
SALES FORCE MANAGEMENT, 5/E

Churchill & Peter
MARKETING, 2/E

Cole & Mishler
CONSUMER AND BUSINESS CREDIT MANAGEMENT, 11/E

Cravens
STRATEGIC MARKETING, 5/E

Cravens , Lamb & Crittenden
STRATEGIC MARKETING MANAGEMENT CASES, 5/E

Crawford
NEW PRODUCTS MANAGEMENT, 5/E

Dillon, Madden & Firtle
ESSENTIALS OF MARKETING RESEARCH, 2/E

Dillon, Madden & Firtle
MARKETING RESEARCH IN A MARKETING ENVIRONMENT, 4/E

Dobler, Burt, & Lee
PURCHASING AND MATERIALS MANAGEMENT: *TEXT AND CASES*, 6/E

Douglas & Craig
GLOBAL MARKETING STRATEGY, 1/E

Etzel, Walker & Stanton
MARKETING, 11/E

Faria, Nulsen & Roussos
COMPETE, 4/E

Futrell
ABC'S OF RELATIONSHIP SELLING, 5/E

Futrell
FUNDAMENTALS OF SELLING, 5/E

Gretz, Drozdeck & Weisenhutter
PROFESSIONAL SELLING: A CONSULTATIVE APPROACH, 1/E

Guiltinan & Paul
CASES IN MARKETING MANAGEMENT, 1/E

Guiltinan, Paul & Madden
MARKETING MANAGEMENT STRATEGIES AND PROGRAMS, 6/E

Hasty & Reardon
RETAIL MANAGEMENT, 1/E

Hawkins, Best & Coney
CONSUMER BEHAVIOR, 7/E

Hayes, Jenster & Aaby
BUSINESS TO BUSINESS MARKETING, 1/E

Johansson
GLOBAL MARKETING, 1/E

Johnson, Kurtz & Scheuing
SALES MANAGEMENT: *CONCEPTS, PRACTICES & CASES*, 2/E

Kinnear & Taylor
MARKETING RESEARCH: *AN APPLIED APPROACH*, 5/E

Lambert & Stock
STRATEGIC LOGISTICS MANAGEMENT, 3/E

Lambert, Stock, & Ellram
FUNDAMENTALS OF LOGISTICS MANAGEMENT, 1/E

Lehmann & Winer
ANALYSIS FOR MARKETING PLANNING, 4/E

Lehmann & Winer
PRODUCT MANAGEMENT, 2/E

Levy & Weitz
RETAILING MANAGEMENT, 3/E

Levy & Weitz
ESSENTIALS OF RETAILING, 1/E

Loudon & Della Bitta
CONSUMER BEHAVIOR: *CONCEPTS & APPLICATIONS*, 4/E

Lovelock & Weinberg
MARKETING CHALLENGES: *CASES AND EXERCISES*, 3/E

Mason, Mayer & Ezell
RETAILING, 5/E

Mason & Perreault
THE MARKETING GAME!

McDonald
DIRECT MARKETING, 1/E

Meloan & Graham
INTERNATIONAL AND GLOBAL MARKETING CONCEPTS AND CASES, 2/E

Monroe
PRICING, 2/E

Moore & Pessemier
PRODUCT PLANNING AND MANAGEMENT: *DESIGNING AND DELIVERING VALUE*, 1/E

Oliver
SATISFACTION: *A BEHAVIORAL PERSPECTIVE ON THE CONSUMER*, 1/E

Patton
SALES FORCE: A SALES MANAGEMENT SIMULATION GAME, 1/E

Pelton, Strutton & Lumpkin
MARKETING CHANNELS: *A RELATIONSHIP MANAGEMENT APPROACH*, 1/E

Perreault & McCarthy
BASIC MARKETING: A GLOBAL MANAGERIAL APPROACH, 12/E

Perreault & McCarthy
ESSENTIALS OF MARKETING: *A GLOBAL MANAGERIAL APPROACH*, 7/E

Peter & Donnelly
A PREFACE TO MARKETING MANAGEMENT, 7/E

Peter & Donnelly
MARKETING MANAGEMENT: *KNOWLEDGE AND SKILLS*, 5/E

Peter & Olson
CONSUMER BEHAVIOR AND MARKETING STRATEGY, 4/E

Peter & Olson
UNDERSTANDING CONSUMER BEHAVIOR, 1/E

Quelch
CASES IN PRODUCT MANAGEMENT, 1/E

Quelch, Dolan & Kosnik
MARKETING MANAGEMENT: TEXT & CASES, 1/E

Quelch & Farris
CASES IN ADVERTISING AND PROMOTION MANAGEMENT, 4/E

Quelch, Kashani & Vandermerwe
EUROPEAN CASES IN MARKETING MANAGEMENT, 1/E

Rangan
BUSINESS MARKETING STRATEGY: *CASES, CONCEPTS & APPLICATIONS*, 1/E

Rangan, Shapiro & Moriarty
BUSINESS MARKETING STRATEGY: *CONCEPTS & APPLICATIONS*, 1/E

Rossiter & Percy Stanton, Spiro, & Buskirk
MANAGEMENT OF A SALES FORCE, 10/E

Sudman & Blair
MARKETING RESEARCH: *A PROBLEM-SOLVING APPROACH*, 1/E

Thompson & Stappenbeck
THE MARKETING STRATEGY GAME, 1/E

Ulrich & Eppinger
PRODUCT DESIGN AND DEVELOPMENT, 1/E

Walker, Boyd & Larreche
MARKETING STRATEGY: *PLANNING AND IMPLEMENTATION*, 2/E

Weitz, Castleberry & Tanner
SELLING: BUILDING PARTNERSHIPS, 3/E

Zeithaml & Bitner
SERVICES MARKETING, 1/E

Brief Contents

Contents

3. Segmentation and Target Marketing 62

4. Direct Marketing and Technology 78

5. Database Marketing 92

6. List Selection and Management 112

Preface

Few people have heard of America Online's (AOL) Jan Brandt, but if you have ever received an AOL trial diskette, you have seen the results of her masterful direct marketing activities. As senior vice president of marketing at AOL, Brandt helped make the nationally known online service into a household word in just a few years. How did she do it? The answer is direct marketing.

Brandt, named the number one sales and marketing executive in the United States in 1997 by the technology magazine *Upside,* used her direct marketing background and skills to orchestrate an avalanche of trial AOL software targeted at owners of personal computers. What started with inserts in computer magazines, evolved into bundling with new computers, direct mail, direct response print ads, television, and much more, including packaging diskettes with Omaha Steaks and with airplane snacks on commuter flights. To try AOL using a diskette, all a person needs to do is install the software on a personal computer and connect to a local AOL phone number to begin the service trial period.

Direct marketing includes *direct mail* which disseminates messages via the postal service as letters, postcards, leaflets, catalogs, and coupons; *mail order,* which includes advertisements in various media to which prospective customers can respond by making a phone call, sending in a postcard, or use some other mechanism; *direct response* television and radio ads; print ads in magazines, and newspapers placements where customer orders come through the mail or by the telephone or via online ordering services such as AOL.

Direct marketing is growing in strength because it is *interactive* in that marketers and prospective customers engage in two-way communications. Direct marketing activities give the target market of the communication an opportunity to respond. That response or non-response related information is used in planning the next direct marketing program.

THE GROWTH OF DIRECT MARKETING

In 1995, direct marketing produced sales of $1.1 trillion. Consumer (household) sector sales account for 54 percent of that total and business-to-business selling the other 46 percent. Consumer sector sales in direct marketing represented nearly 9 percent of all U.S. retail sales. Real yearly increases in direct marketing activity have averaged 5 percent over the last 20 years, outpacing the real average growth of gross national product (GNP) over the same period by about 100 percent. While traditional retail sales growth grew an average of about 5 percent per year in the 1980s, mail-order sales increased by an average of 10 percent.

A very wide range of products and services are bought direct, ranging from jewelry to meat to airline tickets. Some companies depend almost exclusively on direct marketing to sell their product and services, including such well known firms as the Franklin Mint (mail order), Home Shopping Network (home shopping channel), and NordicTrack (mail order, direct response television, infomercials, and direct response print). Other firms are also heavily involved in direct marketing activities, but those efforts are not the only way they appeal to the buying public. They use both traditional, general mass marketing approaches and direct marketing in combination with other forms of selling. Included are general merchandisers such as J.C. Penney and Montgomery Wards which publish and distribute catalogs targeted at specific market segments to sell tools, clothing, or others lines of items; insurance firms such as the Travelers group which make extensive use of telemarketing and direct mail; mutual fund companies such as Charles Schwab and Fidelity Investments that use direct mail, direct response print, and telemarketing to sell their line of investment services; and American Express, which relies on a combination of image-oriented, mass-market advertising, direct response television, and direct mail, including monthly bill stuffers with merchandise offers for its credit card holders.

THE DEATH OF MASS MEDIA ADVERTISING

In contrast to direct marketing's rapid growth, general, mass media advertising is dying. Advertising agencies are restructuring to accommodate a harsher advertising climate and flat agency income. As a result, advertising agencies have had to lay off employees. This is all happening because direct marketing is stealing business from traditional advertising. The main reason for advertising's impending demise is the emergence of new technologies that fuel the growth of direct marketing, which thrives on the fragmentation of media and markets, empowering consumers and business because of all the targeted product and service offers available to select from. In the place of traditional mass media advertising, a new communications environment is also developing around new media, which is high capacity, interactive, and multimedia. The result is a new era of marketer-customer interactions. Because of the speed of technological innovation, the new media advertising and marketing environment that results will attain prominence faster than did mass media advertising in the 1960s, 1970s, and 1980s.

THIS BOOK

This book is designed to assist you in understanding and organizing the process of management decision making and activities required to plan and implement direct marketing programs. It provides a systematic approach to the study of direct marketing by emphasizing the scope of direct marketing and the nature of what direct marketers do. Therefore, there are few abstract theories in this book, although theory is used when it helps to explain or structure a real-world process.

This book provides a thorough coverage of the direct marketing field. Each chapter includes descriptions of important direct marketing concepts and applications, the related major managerial decision issues, and examples of direct marketing by numerous firms. Those examples and applications are about a wide range of consumer, and business-to-business direct marketing efforts for both products and services.

The 10 cases at the end of this book are designed to enhance your understanding of direct marketing and excite you about those aspects of direct marketing not usually conveyed well by textbook reading alone. The cases also play an important role because they allow you to work on direct marketing problems for actual firms, and, thereby, to develop an appreciation for the types of business issues facing direct marketers. The cases help to develop the analysis and decision-making skills necessary for success in the field of direct marketing.

The cases represent a broad range of direct marketing situations. Because the cases are comprehensive, most can to fit into any topic of a course on direct marketing. They are long and complex enough to require some analysis depth, but not so long and complex as to be overly burdensome.

This book is augmented by a computer program designed to provide a visually interesting and structured environment in which to do a case analysis. The program also helps in developing analysis and decision-making skills by presenting you with the options direct marketers must consider when creating a plan.

Note that the program should be installed in the directory C:\DMPAS, which is the default location. If you decide to put it another location, that may cause printing problems. See the readme.txt file in the DMPAS program directory or go to the web site http://www.newthinking.com/dmpas for more information on fixing a printing problem.

All of the chapters and cases in this book were written by the author based on numerous public and private sources and experiences. They make significant use of information published in such business periodicals as *Advertising Age, Adweek, Business Week, Catalog Age, Direct Marketing, Direct, The Economist, Forbes, Fortune, Marketing News, Target Marketing,* and *Telemarketing.* In particular, I would like to thank Henry Hoke publisher of *Direct Marketing* for allowing me to adapt articles from his magazine into this text. Additionally, the contents of this text also reflect my own work in direct marketing as the general manager of *New Thinking* (**http://www.newthinking.com**), an international direct marketing agency with clients in the United States and Europe. I would like to acknowledge influences from textbooks on direct marketing and general marketing that I used over the years before developing this book, and thank my colleagues at Hofstra University. I would like to thank the following reviewers for their invaluable feedback: Reid P. Claxton, East Carolina University; James W. Camerius, Northern Michigan University; Paul Cohen, Castleton State College; Richard A. Hamilton, University of Missouri-Kansas City; John B. Harris, Virginia State University; Richard C. Leventhal, Metropolitan State College of Denver; Dennis Pitta, University of Baltimore; James D. Porterfield, Pennsylvania State University; and Denise D. Schoenbachler, Northern Illinois University. I would finally like to thank the staff of Irwin/McGraw-Hill for their work in the development and production of this text: Stephen M. Patterson, Andrea Hlavacek-Rhoads, Robert A. Preskill, Crispin Prebys, Madelyn Underwood, and Sharon Miller.

William J. McDonald, Ph. D.

CHAPTER 1

Introduction to Direct Marketing

OBJECTIVES

1. To explain the nature and scope of direct marketing.
2. To examine the ways in which direct marketing differs from the image-oriented advertising so common in the media today.
3. To preview the media of direct marketing and show how they operate in conjunction with direct marketing efforts designed to sell products and services.
4. To examine the major factors that have contributed to the growth in direct marketing activities.
5. To describe direct marketing's special competencies and explain how they contribute to the success of direct marketing efforts.

INTRODUCTION

This book is about a field of marketing promotion and selling called direct marketing. It describes the strategy planning and execution activities associated with this growing form of marketing, which focuses on motivating buyers to place orders through the mail or some other nonstore channel such as the telephone. In recent decades, direct marketing has been remarkably successful in the United States and Europe, particularly as new technologies have emerged to assist firms in the distribution of information and goods. Most important has been the development of computer-generated mailing lists of potential customers, pinpointed as to income, occupation, interests, or any of a number of other characteristics that define a target market.

Today direct marketing is conducted through numerous media, including mail, telephone, print, television, radio, and such new vehicles as infomercials, home shopping networks, and the Internet. Regardless of the medium, the goal of direct marketing is always a response; a successful offer persuades prospects to return a coupon or dial a telephone number or place an order online using a personal computer (PC).

Historically, direct marketing has been called by other names, including direct mail, mail order, or direct response. Today these areas are recognized as aspects of direct marketing. *Direct mail* disseminates messages via the postal service as letters, postcards, leaflets, catalogs, and coupons. *Mail order* includes advertisements in various media to which prospects can respond by making a phone call, sending in a postcard, or using some other mechanism. This behavior is a *direct response* to television ads, print ads in magazines, and newspaper placements where customer orders come through the mail or by the telephone or by online ordering services such as Prodigy or America Online. In broadcast media, such as television and radio, watchers or listeners are encouraged to call a number immediately to place an order or make an inquiry for more information.

A committee of the Direct Marketing Association (DMA), a trade association, developed the most widely accepted definition of direct marketing:

> Direct marketing is an interactive system of marketing which uses one or more advertising media to effect a measurable response and/or transaction at any location.

There are three key elements of this definition: First, direct marketing is *interactive* in that marketer and prospective customer engage in two-way communication. In other types of marketing, a "general marketer" provides the target audience with a one-way communication of information (or an emotional theme), but the audience is not encouraged to respond via a telephone call or by returning a coupon. In contrast, direct marketing activities give the target market of the communication an opportunity to respond. That response, or nonresponse-related information, can then be used in planning the next direct marketing program.

Second, all direct marketing activities are significantly more *measurable* than traditional general advertising and sales promotion. A response, or lack thereof, can be associated with each catalog mailing, each direct-response television advertisement, or each direct mail piece. Direct marketers use direct marketing databases of stored purchase behavior and other information about individuals and households to analyze customer characteristics and plan new campaigns. These databases are the foundation of effective direct marketing. They allow the direct marketer to identify the specific communication that prompted a response, which provides an opportunity to know exactly which communication the customer responded to and the nature of that response, including whether it was a sale or a request for more information.

Third, activities connected with direct marketing communications can take place at *any location.* It is not necessary for prospects to come into a retail store or to be visited by a salesperson. The contact can be made by mail, over the phone, by fax, or online via a PC.

From a company perspective, direct marketing is an efficient way to promote and sell products and services because it has a record of proven profitability, it addresses the growing concern over accountability in how marketing dollars are spent, it allows careful use of a firm's resources in an age of downsized firms, and it is particularly good at reaching fragmented markets with special needs.

Direct marketing and general marketing (or general advertising) are distinguishable by what each is attempting to accomplish. While direct marketing seeks to make a prospect order an item or request more information immediately, general marketing focuses on changing attitudes and building loyalty through appeals based on facts or emotion. With general advertising, the viewer or reader is expected to develop a positive orientation toward a product or service so that on some later date he or she will make a purchase.

Unlike general marketing or image-oriented advertising, direct marketing works well for firms of all sizes. Direct marketing is particularly suited to the objectives and tasks associated with promoting small businesses. Any entrepreneur with enough money to place an ad in a magazine encouraging people to call an 800 number can build that small investment into a personal fortune if he or she is selling something people really want to buy. There are many success stories about aggressive direct marketers investing their savings into businesses that have grown from nothing into nationally recognized companies. This book contains many examples of such success stories.

1-800-FLOWERS[1]

The famous Long Island florist 1-800-FLOWERS is a prime example of a very successful direct marketing company. The firm has been growing fast and now has annual sales between $80 and $100 million. It is still one of the leaders in using direct-response television and telemarketing to generate sales for local retailers.

A pioneer direct marketer named Jim McCann started it all. You can see him hosting his own television commercials for 1-800-FLOWERS, which appear over and over again right before gift-giving holidays. To send a gift of flowers, you call the 800 number in the ad; the flowers are delivered by a local retailer within the giftee's zip code.

The parent of 1-800-FLOWERS, Teleway, is a marketing utility. The company creates, schedules, and runs direct-response advertising designed to generate orders for a network of 2,500 U.S. retail florists called BloomNet. Teleway receives orders from around the world in one of three telemarketing centers. Within three minutes, each order is transmitted to a PC at the florist nearest the recipient's address. The florist makes up the bouquet from specifications and color photos in a manual. Teleway charges $8.95 for each transaction plus 20 percent of the sale.

McCann has also expanded beyond the flower business with television commercials that display 1-800-BASKETS, 1-800-GROWERS, 1-800-GOODIES, and 1-800-CANDIES. These are extensions that fit easily into the firm's growing product line. All are successful, but BASKETS is the most productive of the group. In addition to television, the firm uses direct mail and radio to market its products. Direct mail is sent to consumer segments in a 1.5-million-customer file, and radio is used to generate orders from people at work or in their cars. Those who place flower orders may receive a four-color postcard offering gift baskets, candy, or Florida oranges. The response channel is always through the phone via an 800 number. A sample ad is shown in Exhibit 1.1.

EXHIBIT 1.1 1-800-Flower Advertising

SCOPE OF DIRECT MARKETING

A 1995 estimate of direct marketing sales puts the value of the industry at around $1.1 trillion. Consumer (household) sector sales account for 54 percent of that total, or $594.4 billion, with the remainder, $498.1 billion, due to business-to-business selling (see Chapter 15). Consumer sector sales in direct marketing represent nearly 9 percent of all U.S. retail sales. However, growth in direct marketing is of relatively recent origin. Real yearly increases in direct marketing activity have averaged 5 percent over the last 20 years, outpacing the real average growth of gross national product (GNP) over the same period by about 100 percent. While traditional retail sales grew by an average of about 5 percent per year in the 1980s, mail-order sales increased by an average of 10 percent.

Table 1.1 shows the value of direct marketing sales by media, including trend numbers from 1990 to 1996 and a forecast for the year 2000. The table indicates that business-to-business growth has consistently outpaced consumer sales in the 1990s. Exhibit 1.2 shows the amount spent on merchandise or services ordered by mail or phone in a 12-month period. Note that the majority of spending is above the $100 amount. Table 1.2 shows the number of items ordered by mail or phone in a 12-month period. It is clear that consumers buy a very wide range of items, though magazines and clothing stand out the most.

As you study the industry numbers describing the size of the direct marketing industry, however, keep in mind that they are widely disputed because the value of direct marketing activities is based on estimates. U.S. Census Bureau data

TABLE 1.1. U.S. Direct-Marketing-Driven Sales by Medium and Market (billions of dollars)*
Business-to-business sales growth will consistently outpace consumer sales growth throughout the 1990s.

	1990	1994	1995	1996	2000	Growth 1990–1995	Growth 1995–2000
Direct mail	**250.0**	**333.2**	**356.1**	**382.9**	**517.3**	**7.3%**	**7.8%**
Consumer	164.6	214.0	225.7	239.8	308.6	6.5	6.5
Business-to-business	85.4	119.2	130.4	143.0	208.7	8.8	9.9
Telephone marketing	**272.8**	**356.1**	**385.6**	**421.4**	**599.1**	**7.2**	**9.2**
Consumer	117.2	150.2	159.3	171.0	230.7	6.3	7.7
Business-to-business	155.6	205.9	226.3	250.4	368.3	7.8	10.2
Newspaper	**105.6**	**123.6**	**137.0**	**148.8**	**204.3**	**5.3**	**8.3**
Consumer	68.4	77.5	84.9	91.1	119.9	4.4	7.1
Business-to-business	37.2	46.1	52.2	57.7	84.4	7.0	10.1
Magazine	**43.7**	**55.1**	**60.7**	**66.4**	**92.0**	**6.8**	**8.7**
Consumer	23.0	28.4	30.9	33.3	44.1	6.1	7.4
Business-to-business	20.7	26.7	29.9	33.1	48.0	7.6	9.9
Television	**49.6**	**64.4**	**72.7**	**81.0**	**121.9**	**7.9**	**10.9**
Consumer	31.2	39.3	43.8	48.2	69.5	7.0	9.7
Business-to-business	18.3	25.1	28.9	32.8	52.4	9.6	12.6
Radio	**18.0**	**23.6**	**25.5**	**27.8**	**38.9**	**7.2**	**8.8**
Consumer	10.6	13.5	14.4	15.5	20.8	6.3	7.6
Business-to-business	7.5	10.1	11.1	12.3	18.0	8.2	10.2
Other	**40.4**	**51.0**	**55.0**	**59.2**	**78.2**	**6.4**	**7.3**
Consumer	27.4	33.4	35.6	37.8	47.6	5.4	6.0
Business-to-business	13.0	17.6	19.4	21.3	30.6	8.3	9.5
Total	**780.1**	**1,007.0**	**1,092.6**	**1,187.5**	**1,651.6**	**7.0**	**8.6**
Consumer	**442.4**	**556.3**	**594.4**	**636.9**	**841.2**	**6.1**	**7.2**
Business-to-business	**337.7**	**450.7**	**498.1**	**550.7**	**810.4**	**8.1**	**10.2**

*These numbers have not been inflation adjusted—they represent current (nominal) dollars.
Note: Due to rounding, totals may not exactly equal the sum of each column.
Source: DMA Report—Economic Impact: U.S. Direct Marketing Today, 1995.

significantly understate the size of the industry because the bureau classifies business units according to their primary activity. For example, even though a department store has sales via direct mail and telephone orders, it is classified as a retail store and all its sales volume is credited to that category. What is not in dispute is the importance of direct marketing in a marketplace where technological

EXHIBIT 1.2. Total Amount Spent on Merchandise and Services Ordered by Mail or Phone

The Study of Media and Markets is a syndicated study based on a stratified multistage area probability sample of 22,468 adults in 1993 and 22,051 in 1994, interviewed between the months of June and May. The product usage and buying behavior data was gathered through self-administered questionnaires and personal interviews.

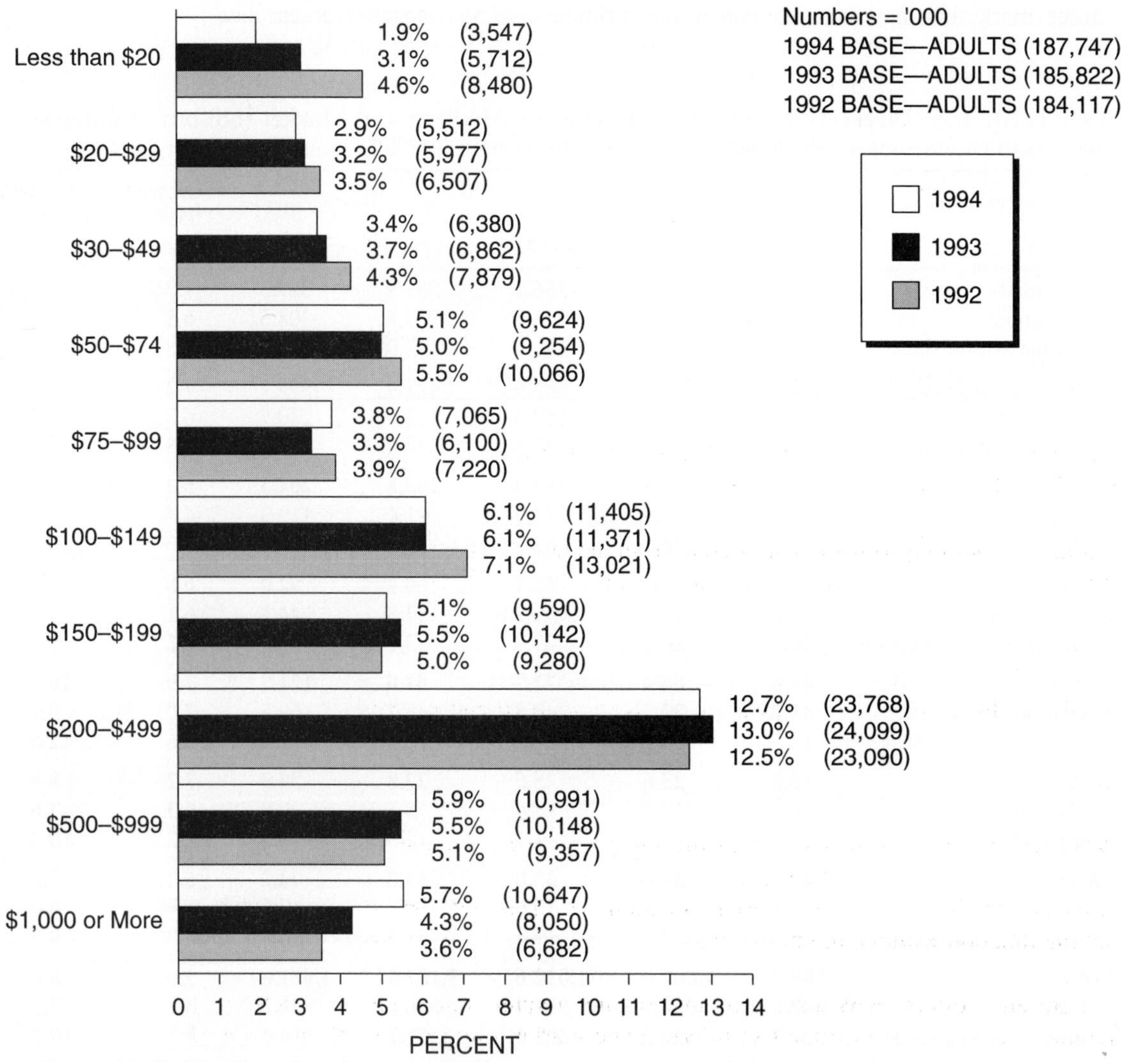

Results are based on extrapolations made for entire U.S. population base for that year.

Source: Simmons Market Research Bureau: 1992, 1993, and 1994 Study of Media and Markets.

advances and the trend toward personalization (bringing market segmentation as close to the individual as possible) are making a major impact on how goods and services are sold.

Some companies depend almost exclusively on direct marketing to sell their products and services. Well-known firms that specialize in direct marketing include Franklin Mint (mail order), Home Shopping Network (home shopping channel), and NordicTrack (mail order, direct-response television, infomercials, and direct-response print). There are extended discussions about each of these firms in cases at the back of this book.

Some firms have heavy involvement in direct marketing activities but also use other means to appeal to the buying public, including traditional marketing approaches. These firms include general merchandisers such as J.C. Penney and Montgomery Ward, which publish and distribute catalogs targeted at specific market segments to sell tools, clothing, or other product lines; insurance firms such as the Travelers Group, which makes extensive use of telemarketing and direct mail; mutual fund companies such as Charles Schwab and Fidelity Investments (see Case 6 at the end of this book), which use direct mail, direct-response print, and telemarketing to sell their line of investment services; and American Express, which relies on a combination of image-oriented advertising, direct-response television, and direct mail, including monthly bill stuffers with merchandise offers for its credit card holders.

DIRECT MARKETING'S SPECIAL COMPETENCIES

Direct-response advertising, like other forms of promotion, seeks to persuade people to buy products or services. However, there are some things that direct marketing does much better than general marketing. Virtually all of direct marketing's special competencies derive from the fact that the communications are directed at specific individuals and not at mass markets via mass media. This includes the combination of advertising and selling into a single function, the prominence of customer service, the ability to precisely target individuals, and the ability to create personalized messages that call for immediate action. Finally, the results of direct marketing campaigns can be monitored and measured.

Combinations of Advertising and Selling

Although direct marketers use paid messages in the mass media, as do general advertisers, they do more than general advertisers because they attempt to elicit a response. In the process, the communication performs both an advertising and selling function without an intermediary. For example, a direct-response print ad is designed to make a sale without the help of a salesperson or a store.

Because direct marketing activities do not require intermediaries such as retailers, they reduce or eliminate intermediate markups and potentially increase profits. However, direct marketers spend proportionately more in media to compensate for the absence of personal selling and retailing. These expenditures generally range from 10 to 30 percent of sales, depending on the media involved.

TABLE 1.2. Items Ordered by Mail or Phone

The Study of Media and Markets is a syndicated study based on a stratified multistage area probability sample of 22,468 adults in 1993 and 22,051 in 1994, interviewed between the months of June and May. The product usage and buying behavior data were gathered through self-administered questionnaires and personal interviews. The results below were then projected to reflect the entire adult U.S. population, estimated to be 185,822,000 in 1993, and 187,747,000 in 1994.

	By Mail or Phone		*By Mail*		*By Phone*	
	000	%	000	%	000	%
Auto accessories	**6,505***	**3.5**	**4,110**	**2.2**	**2,797**	**1.5**
	5,188	2.8	3,294	1.8	2,182	1.2
Cookbooks	**7,669**	**4.1**	**6,747**	**3.6**	**1,005**	**0.5**
	8,186	4.4	6,797	3.7	1,498	0.8
Children's books	**9,968**	**5.3**	**8,877**	**4.7**	**1,777**	**0.9**
	11,570	6.2	10,152	5.5	1,950	1.0
Other books	**11,116**	**5.9**	**9,622**	**5.1**	**2,402**	**1.3**
	11,892	6.4	10,388	5.6	2,174	1.2
Greeting cards	**5,957**	**3.2**	**5,218**	**2.8**	**823**	**0.4**
	6,189	3.3	5,744	3.1	637	0.3
Stationery	**3,674**	**2.0**	**3,209**	**1.7**	**512**	**0.3**
	4,198	2.3	3,869	2.1	415	0.2
Cosmetics	**5,517**	**2.9**	**3,243**	**1.7**	**2,597**	**1.4**
	6,498	3.5	4,099	2.2	2,751	1.5
Records	**3,978**	**2.1**	**3,477**	**1.9**	**670**	**0.4**
	4,884	2.6	3,985	2.1	1,251	0.7
Prerecorded audio cassette tapes	**11,019**	**5.9**	**9,284**	**4.9**	**2,108**	**1.1**
	9,677	5.2	8,051	4.3	1,937	1.0
Prerecorded videotapes	**8,540**	**4.5**	**6,222**	**3.3**	**2,758**	**1.5**
	7,363	4.0	5,272	2.8	2,407	1.3
Stereo equipment	**1,432**	**0.8**	**981**	**0.5**	**554**	**0.3**
	1,784	1.0	1,175	0.6	717	0.4
Computer hardware	**2,152**	**1.1**	**965**	**0.5**	**1,436**	**0.8**
	2,205	1.2	1,035	0.6	1,458	0.8
Computer software	**4,293**	**2.3**	**2,081**	**1.1**	**2,857**	**1.5**
	4,187	2.3	2,779	1.5	2,187	1.2
Other electronic equipment	**2,039**	**1.1**	**995**	**0.5**	**1,177**	**0.6**
	2,911	1.6	1,784	1.0	1,267	0.7
Magazines	**32,399**	**17.3**	**28,984**	**15.4**	**5,116**	**2.7**
	30,191	16.2	27,922	15.0	3,499	1.9
Photo processing	**5,491**	**2.9**	**5,285**	**2.8**	**231**	**0.1**
	5,874	3.2	5,565	3.0	442	0.2
Food	**7,774**	**4.1**	**4,974**	**2.7**	**3,164**	**1.7**
	7,633	4.1	5,322	2.9	2,699	1.5
Shoes or boots	**9,224**	**4.9**	**5,212**	**2.8**	**4,843**	**2.6**
	8,298	4.5	5,122	2.8	3,722	2.0
Costume jewelry	**4,682**	**2.5**	**3,378**	**1.8**	**1,700**	**0.9**
	5,356	2.9	3,921	2.1	1,826	1.0
Clothing	**33,908**	**18.1**	**19,928**	**10.6**	**19,590**	**10.4**
	32,719	17.6	20,053	10.8	17,701	9.5
Curtains, bedspreads, linens	**10,203**	**5.4**	**4,918**	**2.6**	**5,731**	**3.1**
	10,417	5.6	5,762	3.1	5,315	2.9
Needlecraft kits and supplies	**3,940**	**2.1**	**3,294**	**1.8**	**940**	**0.5**
	4,420	2.4	3,738	2.0	862	0.5

(continued)

TABLE 1.2. (continued) Items Ordered by Mail or Phone

	By Mail or Phone		*By Mail*		*By Phone*	
	000	%	000	%	000	%
Dolls (collectible type)	**2,473**	**1.3**	**1,915**	**1.0**	**715**	**0.4**
	2,911	1.6	2,412	1.3	645	0.3
Toys	**7,015**	**3.7**	**4,139**	**2.2**	**3,754**	**2.0**
	8,507	4.6	5,457	2.9	3,809	2.0
Sporting goods	**4,348**	**2.3**	**2,492**	**1.3**	**2,419**	**1.3**
	4,792	2.6	2,837	1.5	2,607	1.4
Gardening equipment tools	**2,013**	**1.1**	**1,310**	**0.7**	**864**	**0.5**
	2,839	1.5	2,073	1.1	942	0.5
Workshop tools	**3,500**	**1.9**	**2,407**	**1.3**	**1,504**	**0.8**
	3,473	1.9	2,302	1.2	1,600	0.9
Coins (numismatic)	**1,330**	**0.7**	**1,195**	**0.6**	**138**	**0.1**
	1,567	0.8	1,175	0.6	510	0.3
Medallions, commemorative	**4,187**	**2.3**	**3,737**	**2.0**	**667**	**0.4**
plates, etc.	3,587	2.0	3,008	1.6	775	0.4
Figurines (porcelain, pewter,	**2,505**	**1.3**	**2,135**	**1.1**	**406**	**0.2**
bronze, etc.)	2,791	1.5	2,204	1.2	728	0.4
Furniture	**2,266**	**1.2**	**1,157**	**0.6**	**1,178**	**0.6**
	2,180	1.2	1,155	0.6	1,114	0.6
Cookware and kitchen	**7,317**	**3.9**	**4,722**	**2.5**	**2,963**	**1.6**
	8,059	4.3	5,769	3.1	2,606	1.4
Small appliances	**2,244**	**1.2**	**1,154**	**0.6**	**1,181**	**0.6**
	4,110	2.2	2,663	1.4	1,614	0.9
Banking information	**3,517**	**1.9**	**1,547**	**0.8**	**2,286**	**1.2**
	6,324	3.4	2,847	1.5	3,895	2.1
Stocks, bonds, mutual funds	**4,252**	**2.3**	**1,762**	**0.9**	**2,838**	**1.5**
	5,748	3.1	2,757	1.5	3,622	1.9
Investment information/	**3,204**	**1.7**	**2,279**	**1.2**	**1,155**	**0.6**
newsletter	3,730	2.0	2,424	1.3	1,511	0.8
Credit cards	**10,510**	**5.6**	**8,345**	**4.4**	**3,068**	**1.6**
	11,240	6.0	9,250	5.0	2,920	1.6
Insurance	**3,760**	**2.0**	**2,357**	**1.3**	**1,683**	**0.9**
	5,407	2.9	2,958	1.6	2,756	1.5
Real estate information	**2,607**	**1.4**	**1,106**	**0.6**	**1,711**	**0.9**
	2,811	1.5	1,613	0.9	1,603	0.9
Travel information	**12,952**	**6.9**	**7,862**	**4.2**	**7,026**	**3.7**
	13,924	7.5	7,722	4.2	7,889	4.2
Educational programs	**2,922**	**1.6**	**1,709**	**0.9**	**1,528**	**0.8**
	3,312	1.8	2,247	1.2	1,376	0.7
Trees, plants, seeds	**7,705**	**4.1**	**6,685**	**3.5**	**1,504**	**0.8**
	8,693	4.7	7,884	4.2	1,564	0.8
Vitamins	**4,485**	**2.4**	**3,096**	**1.6**	**1,604**	**0.9**
	4,879	2.6	3,831	2.1	1,228	0.7
Other items (not listed)	**13,933**	**7.4**	**9,287**	**4.9**	**7,262**	**3.9**
	12,244	6.6	7,617	4.1	7,012	3.8
Don't know/no answer	**12,282**	**6.5**	**9,070**	**4.8**	**17,880**	**9.5**
	13,123	7.1	11,259	6.1	19,158	10.3

*Boldface = 1994; Lightface = 1993
Source: Simmons Market Research Bureau: 1993 and 1994 Study of Media and Markets.

Customer Service

Customer service plays an important role in direct marketing. For most firms, customer loyalty is an important issue because companies make money from a repetitive pattern of purchases rather than from just one sale. An emphasis on customer service, including order fulfillment functions, is important as a mechanism for encouraging regular interactions between the direct marketer and the customer. A popular idea now in direct marketing called relationship marketing places an emphasis on building long-term relationships with customers.

Precision Targeting

Direct marketing communications are frequently aimed at individuals. This is particularly true of direct-mail and telemarketing campaigns based on the use of segmented lists that come from information contained in databases. Such communications are addressed to individuals who represent viable prospects for a product or service. Targeted marketing reduces the waste inherent in many other types of communications.

Personalization

In direct marketing communications, individual consumers should be addressed by name, while business prospects should be addressed by name and title. However, the ability to personalize extends beyond the use of names; information from a database may be used to produce a specific appeal based on a consumer's personal characteristics and/or past purchase behavior.

For example, in its magazine *American Rifleman,* the National Rifle Association (NRA) includes election-specific information that tells the member who to vote for by congressional district and state. On the front of some of its catalog mailings, Viking Office Products prints offers that are personalized according to what the addressee purchased during the previous several months.

Call for Immediate Action

Direct marketing offers differ from those of general marketing in that their copy calls for specific and immediate action. The prospect is encouraged to place an order or request more information by calling a number or sending in a card.

Measurement

Direct marketing activities have an advantage over general marketing activities in the area of performance tracking. Campaigns can be monitored to determine if they are successful, and knowing precisely what worked and what did not allows direct marketers to select the most effective way to sell their goods and services. Also, the ability to measure the results of campaigns precisely makes possible the testing of major elements in any offering, which leads to a more efficient allocation of marketing resources.

Tracking performance allows direct marketers to analyze relationships between customer characteristics and buyer behavior in their database. These databases contain records of transactions that can be used to evaluate program performance and to select prospects for selling appeals. Chapter 5 of this book contains a discussion of the benefits direct marketers derive from applying database technologies to their marketing efforts.

REASONS FOR THE GROWTH OF DIRECT MARKETING

Three major factors have contributed to the growth in direct marketing: changes in American lifestyles and demographics, an evolving economy and international competition, and technological advances and innovations. All three factors are changing how businesses operate and how consumers live. These changes represent long-term macroenvironmental trends that are outside the control of any individual or firm.

Changing Lifestyles and Demographics

From knowing the age distribution of the population as of a certain date, and estimates of births and deaths, direct marketers can reliably predict the size of various age groups in the future. And, because age correlates with key events such as college attendance, marriage, and childbearing, it is one of the most frequently used predictors of coming changes in purchasing behavior. By monitoring changes in the number and composition of households at each stage in the family life cycle, direct marketers can also predict buying behaviors that depend on a combination of age, marital status, and the presence of children. The family life cycle describes the various stages in the formation, growth, and decline of the family unit and the effect of time passage on consumption. For example, in the future, with relatively fewer young married couples, there may be fewer sales of small appliances, furniture, and linens. When fewer children arrive, purchases of insurance, baby foods, washers, and dryers will decrease. Large families (three or more children), while declining in importance, account for 20 percent of the dollars spent for food, clothing, and education in the United States and 8 percent of all housing and entertainment.

These estimates of marketplace buyer behavior have clear implications for direct marketers. For example, the 77 million baby boomers in the United States are approaching middle age, a period when they can expect to have substantial purchasing power. In the years ahead, this group will affect the sales of such products as clothing, home furnishings, travel, educational services, and insurance. At the same time, the number of people ages 35 to 44 increased 26 percent, to 43 million in 1997. The purchasing power of this latter group will grow by $195 billion, to $939 billion.

In recent years, the increase in the number of women in the workforce has changed women's roles as homemakers and consumers. It has increased the demand for convenience foods and appliances, automobiles (a second car), child care services, and cosmetics. Today, women buy 45 percent of new cars sold in the United States and influence the purchase of another 40 percent.

With lifestyles that place a premium on time use, consumers are also interested in quicker and easier ways to shop, including the ability to order from the home. For example, convenience is a major reason for shopping by mail, which allows consumers to do less traveling and searching. Because personal safety while shopping is also an issue for some consumers, buying products and services direct is a way to avoid the growing dangers associated with going to retail outlets.

An Evolving Economy and International Competition

Today's boom in international trade and competition is affecting both how businesses operate and the quality of life in nearly every country. In South Korea, foreign demand has stimulated a tripling of manufacturing output over the past decade; in Malaysia, rising incomes from new factories have led Toys "R" Us Inc. to open two new stores; and in Spain, exports have more than doubled since the fall of fascism.

Yet in some ways rising prosperity seems to be eluding the United States, once the economic leader of the world. The Japanese and Germans are bringing technological advances to the market faster and more cheaply than Americans. The country that invented mass production can no longer compete for routine manufacturing jobs against such low-wage countries as Taiwan and Mexico. Imports seem to have permanently staked out a big share of the U.S. market.

The hot U.S. industries of the 1980s—computers, finance, retailing, and defense—are now cutting workers. Real wages and salaries have stagnated since the early 1970s, and Americans are carrying a staggering burden of national and personal debt. While the U.S. standard of living is still among the highest in the world, rivals are catching up fast.

Direct marketers are particularly concerned about how the changing fortunes of the U.S. economy and labor may influence the ability of consumers and businesses to purchase their goods and services. If American consumers have substantially less money to spend, or if American businesses are in very tight competitive situations, their spending patterns will change accordingly. Also, as more and more firms from other countries enter the U.S. market to compete, additional pressures are placed on American direct marketers to improve their offerings or face extinction.

Technological Advances and Innovations

Technology is an important agent of change in today's business and society. It is becoming possible to shop from the comfort of one's living room, using a telephone or a PC to order merchandise. The media options available to the direct marketer are growing exponentially as a result of new transmission technologies and economics associated with particular media.

Technological advances, particularly in computer power and communications, are transforming the direct marketing industry. A revolution is occurring in the ways direct marketers promote and sell their goods and services. This is influencing how products and services are marketed to consumers and businesses, who are now targeted and marketed to via a variety of mail, broadcast media, and telephone solicitations.

However, because of changes in lifestyles and markets, direct marketers must now divide consumers and businesses into significantly more segments in order to effectively manage markets using the new technologies. The growth of databases to store and manage information substantially increases firms' ability to divide potential customers into those specific market segments, providing an enhanced capability to match products with markets. The use of demographics or socioeconomic characteristics can help a firm identify target audiences. Outside lists can be matched with those of customers and prospects, eliminating duplication in mailings and telephone calls. Computer databases track customer contacts and orders, allowing direct marketers to maintain tighter control over their operations.

The number and nature of media formats are also being transformed by emerging communications technologies. The advent of cable television, the growth of radio, the proliferation of magazines, and the emergence of the Internet together have led to a significant fragmentation of nearly all media. At the same time, a few nonelectronic transformations have been occurring in the media world. Direct-response techniques have been fused with mass media delivery. Television has expanded beyond the home to an array of different locations, from schools to airports to supermarkets.

With all these changes, competition among firms is also being transformed. Firms can no longer prosper without plans to address the needs of a multitude of market segments using the latest and most sophisticated marketing tools. The firms that are better able to target and reach multiple niches will enjoy greater profits and increasing sales.

WHAT CAN BE SOLD VIA DIRECT MARKETING?

Today almost any product or service can be sold through direct marketing. Items currently being offered range from television sets to meat, and the list of items is expanding daily. What these items have in common is that they are convenient to purchase and have offers that reduce any perceived risks associated with making the purchase. For example, clothing is sold with a money-back guarantee, as are exercise machines, computers, and videotapes.

However, not all products and services are considered well suited for direct marketing. Those that are very perishable, that sell for very little, or that are not readily transportable are not normally thought of as candidates for distribution through direct marketing. For example, six-packs of Coca-Cola have such a low unit-selling price that it would be unprofitable to sell them direct. Similarly, many food products that are cooked before consumption are not practical candidates for selling direct. While pizzas work in direct marketing because of their high profit margins, the same cannot be said for Big Macs and fries. In contrast, most products that are sold direct have relatively high unit sales prices and profit margins. Examples include computers, office supplies (which are usually sold in large-order sizes), and contact lenses (see Exhibit 1.3). Note, however, that some marketers believe that almost anything can be sold direct and that all it takes is some innovation in how a product or service is handled or bundled or produced.

Innovations at Lens Express

Lens Express is an innovative firm that has found a unique way to distribute what many consider a product not well suited for direct marketing. Although controversial, the firm has been extremely successful. It sells a growing line of contact lenses and eye-related products through mail order. The Lens Express catalog, a 24-page, glossy, four-color digest, features well-known brands of lenses such as Acuvue by Johnson & Johnson, Ciba Vision, Bausch & Lomb, Wesley Jessen, Barnes Hind, CooperVision, and Allergan Optical, along with saline solution, lens lubricant, and lens cases.

Before Lens Express came onto the scene, optometrists and ophthalmologists held a virtual monopoly on the replacement contact lens market. And, as is the case with monopolies, it was the consumers, some 25 million American contact lens wearers, who suffered through high prices, long waiting periods, and time-consuming doctors' appointments that in many cases were unnecessary.

Eight years and 10 million replacement lenses later, Florida-based Lens Express has grabbed 2 to 3 percent of a $2-billion-a-year industry. That is a considerable dent for a market that remained level for five years. And, although eye doctors are fighting Lens Express and its competitors, it appears that the consumers have spoken. At the very least, the company has opened the public's eyes about the low basic cost of replacement lenses.

Lens Express has created and filled its own niche. Sales in its first year were $500,000 and have been growing by leaps and bounds. Gross sales doubled every year for the past five years, to roughly $45 million in 1993, with sales doubling again in 1994. The staff includes in-house doctors, telephone sales and fulfillment representatives, and marketing personnel.

Customers are encouraged to join the Lens Express Discount Club at $25 for three years or $40 for five years. Members receive a free pair of sunglasses with their first offer and are entitled to additional discounts of 15 percent on future purchases. About 98 percent of Lens Express customers purchase memberships.

The majority of Lens Express leads are generated by direct-response television advertisements on national cable networks such as CNN, A&E, and VH-1. The firm developed a series of three ads featuring actress/model Linda Carter, a contact lens wearer known for her distinctive eyes. Each of the ads (in 30-, 60-, 90- and 120-second versions) offers the free catalog and touts savings of up to 50 percent, overnight delivery via Federal Express, and a full money-back guarantee.

"I trust these baby blues to Lens Express," says Carter in one commercial. In another, she reminisces about how she tore a contact lens the day before her wedding and went through the ceremony with only one lens. See Exhibit 1.3 for a direct-response ad version of the Linda Carter campaign.

EXHIBIT 1.3. Direct-Response Ad: Lens Express

Welcome to Lens Express!
America's #1 Vision Care Service
Save on Eye Exams, Eyeglasses, Contacts!
Over 500,000 Lenses In Stock
All Lenses 100% Guaranteed
Over 10 Million Lenses Sold!
We Have In Stock:
Acuvue
Ciba Vision
Bausch & Lomb
Wesley Jessen
Pilkington Barnes Hind
CooperVision
Ocular Sciences
American Hydron
And Others
1-800-666-LENS
International (305) 422-8181
LENS EXPRESS INC.
"With Lens Express, I have fresh new lenses delivered to my door–even if I'm 3,000 miles from home. They free up my time–that's important to me." –Lynda Carter

According to Roberts and Berger,[3] general marketing involves managing product, price, promotion, and place—better known as the four Ps. For direct marketing, the following variables are associated with making program decisions:

Offer	Timing/sequencing
Creative	Customer service
Media	

These decision variables are discussed briefly below and in detail in subsequent chapters in this book.

Offer

The offer is the complete proposition made to a prospective customer by the firm selling the good or service. It includes the product or service, the positioning of the product or service in terms of needs or benefits, the price of the offering, any risk-reduction mechanisms such as a money-back guarantee, and any bonuses or price discounts available to the buyer.

The Elvis plate advertisement from the Bradford Exchange (see Exhibit 1.4) offers consumers the opportunity to purchase a commemorative item honoring Elvis's 1968 comeback special.

EXHIBIT 1.4. A Sample Offer

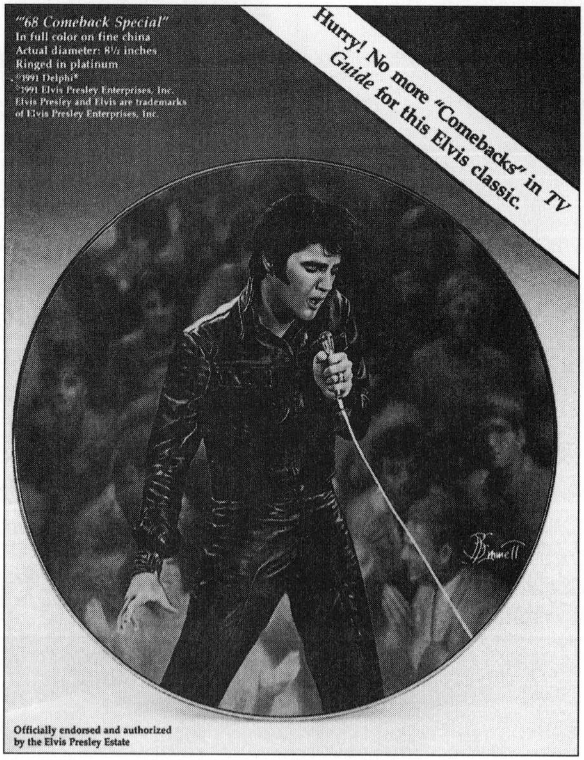

"'68 Comeback Special"
In full color on fine china
Actual diameter: 8½ inches
Ringed in platinum
©1991 Delphi®
©1991 Elvis Presley Enterprises, Inc.
Elvis Presley and Elvis are trademarks of Elvis Presley Enterprises, Inc.
Hurry! No more "Comebacks" in TV Guide for this Elvis classic.
Officially endorsed and authorized by the Elvis Presley Estate

Creative

The creative component includes the copy platform, graphic design elements, involvement techniques, and production considerations such as personalization. The benefit-oriented copy in the Elvis offer (Exhibit 1.4) addresses consumer interest in Elvis memorabilia and the possibility of making money as the value of the plate increases (as it has in the case of previous Elvis plates). The graphics are crisp and nostalgic in feeling, with illustrations designed to stimulate readers' memories of the "young Elvis" and perhaps their own youth. Although the *TV Guide* print advertisement is not personalized, it does convey a sense of personal appeal and urgency in its copy and response card.

Media

The media used by direct marketers include all those used by general marketers as well as direct mail, telephone, and online services. Direct-response print and television advertising are particularly effective in generating responses to complex offers that contain items which can be displayed visually. One measure of the success of the Bradford Exchange's plates series is the proliferation of such offerings in other *TV Guide* issues, women's magazines, and on television.

EXHIBIT 1.4. A Sample Offer, *Continued*

Send no money now. To acquire "'68 Comeback Special" at its $24.75 issue price – backed by our 365-day money-back guarantee – simply fill out and mail the coupon below or write to us at: The Bradford Exchange, 9345 Milwaukee Avenue, Chicago, Illinois 60648. You will be billed in two convenient monthly installments.

But don't delay. The time to get "'68 Comeback Special" is now – *before* it has a chance to increase in value.

*As cited in the Bradford Exchange Market Report, Volume III-3.

Order Form
The Bradford Exchange
9345 Milwaukee Avenue
Chicago, IL 60648

Please respond by: June 30, 1991

YES. Please enter my buy-order for "'68 Comeback Special," first issue in the *Elvis Presley: In Performance* series. *Limit: one plate per customer.*

I understand that I need SEND NO MONEY NOW. I will pay for "'68 Comeback Special" in two convenient monthly installments of $12.37* each, the first being billed before shipment.

X
Signature

Mr. Mrs. Ms. (Circle One) Name (Please Print) ( ) Telephone

Address

City State Zip

*Plus a total of $3.19 postage and handling, and sales tax where applicable.
The plate price in Canada is $37.75.

5451-E92411

EXHIBIT 1.4. A Sample Offer, *Continued*

Own a historic first issue. "'68 Comeback Special" captures the excitement and magic that was Elvis Presley in performance. Created by noted artist Bruce Emmett, this depiction of the King of Rock and Roll is a landmark first issue in a series devoted exclusively to dramatic portrayals of notable Elvis performances. And it bears the hallmark of Delphi, at the leading edge in contemporary plate concepts.

A potentially valuable limited edition. Because of its intrinsic appeal, "'68 Comeback Special" is expected to generate unusually high interest among knowledgeable collectors. To assure acquisition of this exciting work of art at issue price, we suggest that you order your plate now.

©1991 BGE

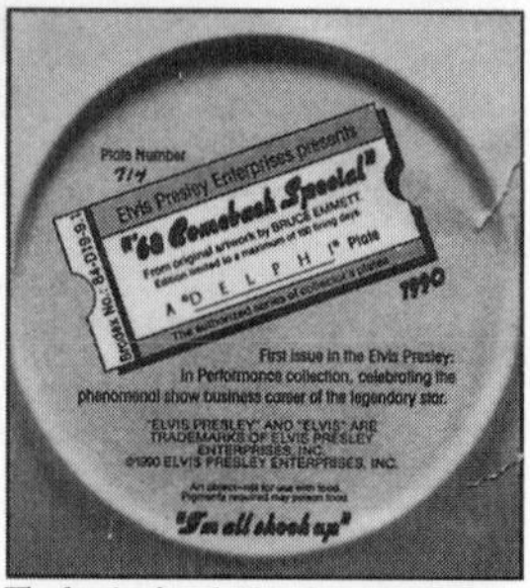

The back of each "'68 Comeback Special" plate bears the legend above, which testifies to its authenticity as part of this historic limited-edition.

Mail your order form today.

EPJ-529

NO POSTAGE
NECESSARY
IF MAILED
IN THE
UNITED STATES

BUSINESS REPLY MAIL
FIRST CLASS MAIL PERMIT NO. 73554 CHICAGO, ILLINOIS

POSTAGE WILL BE PAID BY ADDRESSEE

The Bradford Exchange
Trading Floor
9345 Milwaukee Avenue
Chicago, Illinois 60648-9960

Timing/Sequencing

Timing and sequencing of direct marketing communications determine whether the product or service is offered once or as part of a campaign, that is, as a one-shot message or as multiple messages. Also at issue is whether a campaign should be on intermittently (a method called pulsing) or continuously, as well as how often the communication should be repeated.

Customer Service

The importance of customer service cannot be overstated because it leads to strong customer franchise and loyalty. Satisfaction with service is a prime consideration in customers' repurchase decisions. In fact, many direct marketers consider expenditures on customer service as an investment. The types of customer service that build businesses include speedy and accurate order fulfillment; prompt and satisfactory handling of customer inquiries and complaints; and a guaranteed return policy. Other important elements of a firm's customer service are toll-free telephone numbers, money-back guarantees, and the acceptance of credit cards. Such services can overcome customer resistance to buying by direct-response media.

At least part of the success of Lands' End, a major cataloger, has been attributed to its customer-oriented marketing philosophy. This orientation is reflected in prompt service supported by personal attention and quick responses to orders and complaints. Phone calls are answered quickly, and nearly all orders are shipped within 24 hours. A well-trained and dedicated staff, a sophisticated computer support system, and a well-stocked distribution center facilitate this level of service.

DIRECT MARKETING MEDIA

An advertisement is defined as direct when it either stimulates a direct order, generates a qualified lead that can result in a sale, or drives store traffic that results in sales. As an example, out of direct advertising's $14.1 billion contribution to television's $38.1 billion advertising revenue for 1995, almost $10 billion is termed lead generation. (Lead generation is discussed in more detail later in this chapter; see p. 29.)

Virtually all media can be used to transmit direct marketing offers. While both general marketers and direct marketers use many of the same media, the direct marketer uses and evaluates their effectiveness differently. Later chapters in this book will explain how to develop and implement direct marketing programs in each of the major media.

The Contribution of Direct Marketing Media

In the United States, the cost of direct marketing advertisements totaled $134 billion in 1995, accounting for about 57.1 percent of all U.S. media spending ($234.5 billion). In 1996, direct marketing cost $143.3 billion (see Table 1.3). In

TABLE 1.3. The 1996 Impact of Direct Marketing by Advertising Medium

	1996		*2000*	
Advertising Medium	Percent	Billions	Percent	Billions
Telephone	40	$ 58.0	41	$ 78.9
Direct mail	23	32.9	22	41.8
Television	11	15.5	12	23.0
Newspapers	10	14.5	10	19.1
Magazines	5	7.3	5	9.6
Radio	3	4.4	3	5.9
Other	8	10.8	7	13.6
Total	100	$143.4	100	$191.9

Source: Adapted from Direct Marketing Association, *Statistical Fact Book 1996* (New York: Direct Marketing Association, 1996), p. 322.

1995, direct marketing advertisements generated some 7 percent of combined U.S. consumer and business-to-business sales. On the consumer side in 1995, direct marketing produced 12.1 percent of sales (some $594.4 billion out of $4.9 trillion) and generated about 4.7 percent of total business-to-business sales ($498.1 billion of $10.6 trillion).

By the year 2000, the total percentage will rise one point as consumer sales from direct marketing grow 7.2 percent annually and business-to-business sales expand to 10.2 percent. Consumer-targeted direct advertising in television will grow to $23 billion by the year 2000, when 51 percent of the direct-advertising volume will be business-to-business. By the year 2000, it will have some 56.2 percent of direct marketing's total projected $191.7 billion contribution to the U.S. economy.

Estimates are that telephone marketing is the largest advertising medium in the United States today, with some $58 billion spent on outgoing calls for selling purposes and on incoming calls for purchases and customer service (see Table 1.3). Of the $143.4 billion spent on direct marketing during 1996, telephone marketing accounted for the bulk. The popularity of the telephone as the tool of direct advertisers will continue as postal rates rise. Direct mail is next in spending, followed by television. Direct mail accounted for an estimated $32.9 billion expenditures in 1996 and should reach $41.8 billion in the year 2000.

Telemarketing

As noted previously, the telephone is the largest of the direct marketing media. Telemarketing is indispensable for the marketing of many consumer and business products. Telemarketing makes use of the latest technologies, including communications hardware and software, database technology, in-bound and out-bound WATS, call centers, and autodialers. Telephone marketing comprises the integrated and systematic application of telecommunications and information-processing technologies with management systems to optimize the marketing communications mix used by a company to reach its customers. It is well planned; it does not consist of making a series of hit-or-miss telephone calls. Rather, it is a carefully thought-out and controlled activity in which the persons or companies called have been identified as actual or potential members of the firm's target market. Telemarketing retains personalized customer interaction while simultaneously attempting to better meet customer needs and improve the firm's cost effectiveness.

Telephone marketing is most often used as part of an integrated marketing communications program. Only rarely is it used as a stand-alone medium. One of the key advantages of telephone marketing is that it allows a business to build and maintain its customer relationships. Interaction with the customer or prospect is personal, even though it is not face-to-face.

Direct-Mail Marketing

Direct mail includes individual mailings of brochures and other offers as well as catalogs containing many pages of merchandise. Nearly 15,000 firms in the United

States are primarily in the business of selling products and services by mail. However, this figure does not include many companies for which selling by mail is not the main distribution channel but that still do a large volume of business via direct marketing. Table 1.4 shows the 10 largest worldwide direct marketing firms as measured by 1994 mail-order sales volume. The list contains both well-known firms and those that are less visible because they are primarily direct-mail marketers.

Individual Mailings

Individual mailings represent a very widely used (and often resented) form of direct marketing communication. They generally emphasize a single product or service such as an offer to sell a mutual fund or a computer software package. The development and execution of strategies involving one or more individual mailings will be discussed in Chapter 9.

Catalogs

Although catalogs are described separately here, they are one of the most widely used forms of direct mail. Catalogs contain a line of merchandise, usually with a specialty focus, although some contain an array of general merchandise. Catalogs are used extensively by both consumer goods and business-to-business marketers. The issues involved in the development and management of catalogs are discussed in Chapter 10.

As one of today's most progressive retailers, Bloomingdale's has achieved considerable success with catalog mailings to its carefully managed database of credit card holders and prospects. Targeted mailings promote store traffic on

TABLE 1.4. The 10 Largest Worldwide Mail-Order Companies in 1994

Rank	Company Name	Mail-Order Sales ($ millions)	Type of Merchandise
1	United Services Automobile Association	5,250.2	Insurance, general merchandise
2	Tele-communications	4,530.1	Cable TV
3	Time Warner	4,321.1	Books, cable TV, magazines
4	J. C. Penney	4,178.0	General merchandise, insurance
5	American Association of Retired Persons	2,853.3	Health insurance, magazines
6	Gateway 2000	2,701.2	Business supplies
7	Dell Computer	2,585.0	Business supplies
8	GEICO	2,476.3	Insurance
9	Reader's Digest	2,422.1	Books, collectibles, magazine subscriptions, general merchandise
10	Comcast Cable	2,247.5	Cable TV, general merchandise

Source: Adapted from Direct Marketing Association, *Statistical Fact Book 1996* (New York: Direct Marketing Association, 1996), p. 36.

special occasions and maintain a special relationship with the company's clientele. Bloomingdale's customers are in general affluent (making in excess of $50,000 a year) and extremely loyal. They are the kind of busy people who build a relationship with a store's name and even with its sales associates. And, while their mailboxes are often cluttered, Bloomingdale's customers are extremely receptive to the company's mailings.

Bloomingdale's mailings (some 500,000 at a time) go to customers in specific circumstances. In the case of semiannual furniture promotions, for example, new movers who relocate into a store's trading area are selected. Because Bloomingdale's customers tend to be upwardly mobile (from an apartment to a house or from a small house to a larger house), they often purchase better and better furniture as they move along in life. Unlike other categories, such as cosmetics, furniture departments see few impulse sales. Purchasing decisions for furniture are made over the course of months, the data show, and direct mail is an effective way to bring the customer through the door to take a look. For this kind of promotion, Bloomingdale's uses a database to find those consumers most likely to purchase big-ticket items such as cabinets, dressers, armoires, and upholstered chairs and sofas, and sends them a 24-page, full-color catalog of its newest offerings. Although the catalog does feature some smaller items, such as decorative lamps and pillows, the thrust of the semiannual campaign is the large items, or case goods, which require shipping.

Direct-Response Television

A direct-response television commercial is more like a direct-mail package than it is like an ordinary television commercial. Both direct mail and direct-response television ask for an immediate decision from individuals. Thus, direct-response advertisements are nothing like the mainstream television commercials designed to address a crowd. The mass-market advertisements tell us to drink Dr Pepper or eat at Burger King; they communicate to consumers in the aggregate. In contrast, direct-response television aims to talk directly to a more specialized target audience and contains a telephone number to encourage viewers to place orders or request more information.

There are several important uses of television in direct marketing: direct response and support advertising; infomercials; and home shopping channels. Like any other direct-response medium, television can be used for sales or lead generation. It also has a special capability to increase the sales or number of leads generated by advertising in other media such as direct mail or magazines.

A good example of a well-targeted commercial in which the advertiser clearly knows its audience is the 90-second spot for *Sport Illustrated for Kids.* The ad's copy encourages parents to order a subscription to the magazine so that their children will read more and do better in school. The ad itself contains testimonials from parents and educators about the value of reading and the benefits of enjoying sports as a vehicle to achievement in later life. Each testimonial is given by a person close up to the camera who speaks directly to the watcher, providing the impression of one person talking to another. An 800 number is repeated several times during this direct-response commercial.

Along with direct-response advertisements, infomercials are beginning to dominate television programming. When the television guide says "paid programming," you know the "show" is really an infomercial: a half-hour commercial that resembles a regular show. You can expect to see demonstrations of gadgets, celebrity spokespersons, and testimonials. Testimonials, as well as appearances by celebrities, are favorite tools for persuasion. Infomercials are appearing increasingly outside their usual late-night time slots and blending into entertainment programming. Local independent stations and network affiliates now air infomercials on weekends and during prime time.

Direct-Response Print Media

Direct-response print is another major direct marketing medium. It usually involves the placement of an advertisement in a magazine, newspaper, or some other similar medium. A direct-response space advertisement always includes at least one reply mechanism. For example, the book club and investment fund ads (Exhibits 1.5 and 1.6) feature cutouts for mailing.

Magazines

Direct-response advertising in magazines is used by a wide variety of product and service marketers. The two advertisements in Exhibits 1.5 and 1.6 on pages 24 and 25 appeared in the same issue of *U.S. News* (August 22, 1994). However, the objectives and target market strategies of these two companies are quite different. The book club ad appears to be aimed at people who enjoy history and reading. The investment information ad, which features many statistics and much small print, offers the opportunity to call or write for more information about the Templeton Foreign Fund.

Newspapers

Newspapers, too, are an important medium for many direct marketers. Once the dominant mass medium, newspapers have found competition, especially from television, to be intense in recent years.

Numerous factors have contributed to the decline of newspapers as the primary medium for conveying both national and local news. Network and, more recently, cable television have assumed first place as providers of news for a majority of consumers, and radio is able to respond more quickly than print to fast-moving events. Magazines, increasing in number and ever more targeted in their editorial matter, also provide competition for newspapers.

Specialty Print Media Advertisements

Newspapers and magazines are vehicles for distributing a variety of preprinted *inserts.* These items are frequently four-color printings on glossy paper stock. Direct marketers use inserts to get the attention of consumers, ideally resulting in a request for more information, a telephone order, or the redemption of a coupon.

Bind-in and *blow-in* advertisements, usually in the form of postal reply cards, are found in most magazines (see Exhibit 1.7 on page 26). These cards may support an adjacent advertisement, for example, an advertisement for a computer software package. Usually the card invites the reader to send away for additional

EXHIBIT 1.5. Direct-Response Print Advertising: Book Club

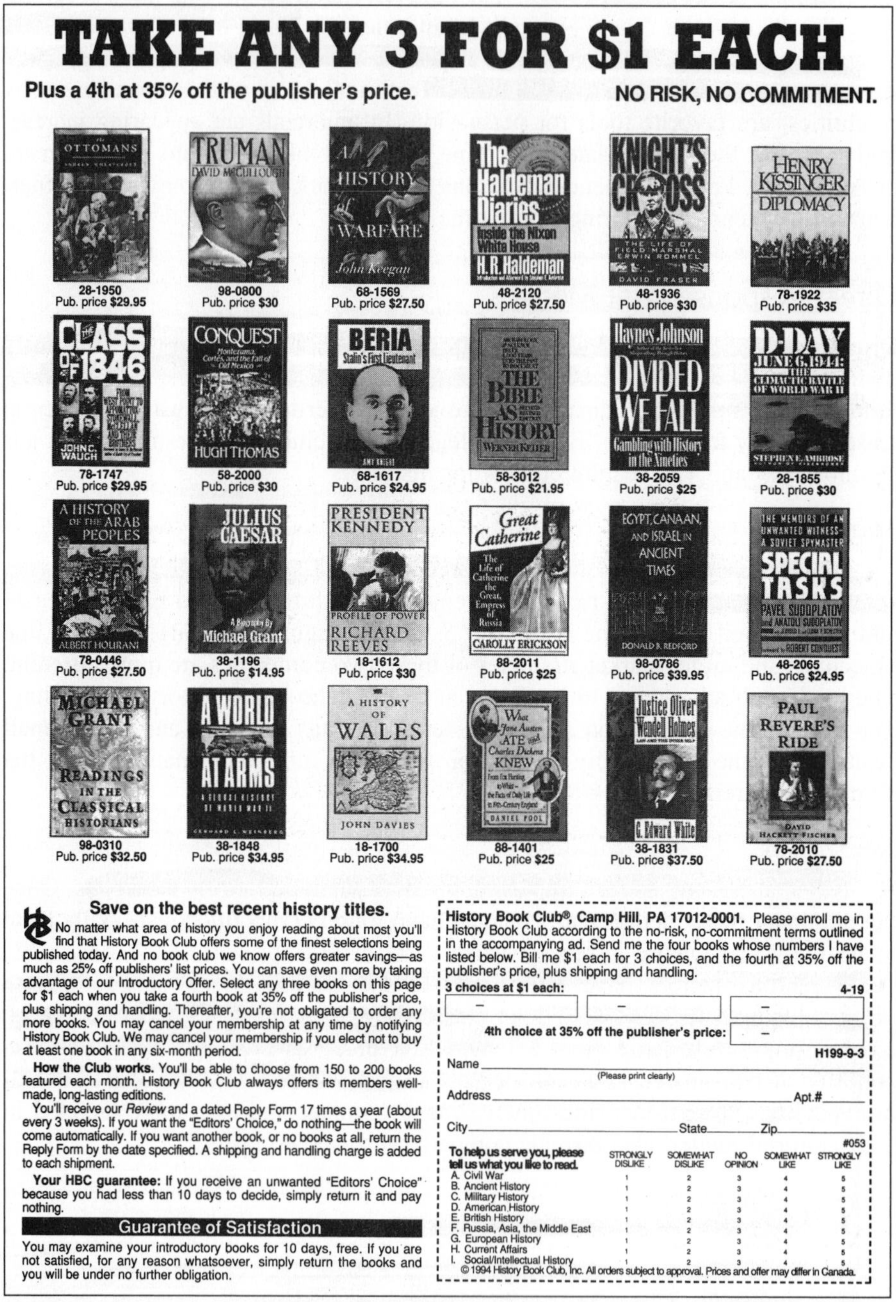
TAKE ANY 3 FOR $1 EACH
Plus a 4th at 35% off the publisher's price.
NO RISK, NO COMMITMENT.
28-1950 Pub. price $29.95
98-0800 Pub. price $30
68-1569 Pub. price $27.50
48-2120 Pub. price $27.50
48-1936 Pub. price $30
78-1922 Pub. price $35
78-1747 Pub. price $29.95
58-2000 Pub. price $30
68-1617 Pub. price $24.95
58-3012 Pub. price $21.95
38-2059 Pub. price $25
28-1855 Pub. price $30
78-0446 Pub. price $27.50
38-1196 Pub. price $14.95
18-1612 Pub. price $30
88-2011 Pub. price $25
98-0786 Pub. price $39.95
48-2065 Pub. price $24.95
98-0310 Pub. price $32.50
38-1848 Pub. price $34.95
18-1700 Pub. price $34.95
88-1401 Pub. price $25
38-1831 Pub. price $37.50
78-2010 Pub. price $27.50
Save on the best recent history titles.
No matter what area of history you enjoy reading about most you'll find that History Book Club offers some of the finest selections being published today. And no book club we know offers greater savings—as much as 25% off publishers' list prices. You can save even more by taking advantage of our Introductory Offer. Select any three books on this page for $1 each when you take a fourth book at 35% off the publisher's price, plus shipping and handling. Thereafter, you're not obligated to order any more books. You may cancel your membership at any time by notifying History Book Club. We may cancel your membership if you elect not to buy at least one book in any six-month period.
How the Club works. You'll be able to choose from 150 to 200 books featured each month. History Book Club always offers its members well-made, long-lasting editions.
You'll receive our Review and a dated Reply Form 17 times a year (about every 3 weeks). If you want the "Editors' Choice," do nothing—the book will come automatically. If you want another book, or no books at all, return the Reply Form by the date specified. A shipping and handling charge is added to each shipment.
Your HBC guarantee: If you receive an unwanted "Editors' Choice" because you had less than 10 days to decide, simply return it and pay nothing.
Guarantee of Satisfaction
You may examine your introductory books for 10 days, free. If you are not satisfied, for any reason whatsoever, simply return the books and you will be under no further obligation.
History Book Club®, Camp Hill, PA 17012-0001. Please enroll me in History Book Club according to the no-risk, no-commitment terms outlined in the accompanying ad. Send me the four books whose numbers I have listed below. Bill me $1 each for 3 choices, and the fourth at 35% off the publisher's price, plus shipping and handling.
3 choices at $1 each:
4-19
4th choice at 35% off the publisher's price:
H199-9-3
Name
(Please print clearly)
Address
Apt.#
City
State
Zip
#053
To help us serve you, please tell us what you like to read.
STRONGLY DISLIKE
SOMEWHAT DISLIKE
NO OPINION
SOMEWHAT LIKE
STRONGLY LIKE
A. Civil War 1 2 3 4 5
B. Ancient History 1 2 3 4 5
C. Military History 1 2 3 4 5
D. American History 1 2 3 4 5
E. British History 1 2 3 4 5
F. Russia, Asia, the Middle East 1 2 3 4 5
G. European History 1 2 3 4 5
H. Current Affairs 1 2 3 4 5
I. Social/Intellectual History 1 2 3 4 5
© 1994 History Book Club, Inc. All orders subject to approval. Prices and offer may differ in Canada.

EXHIBIT 1.6. Direct-Response Print Advertising: Investment Information

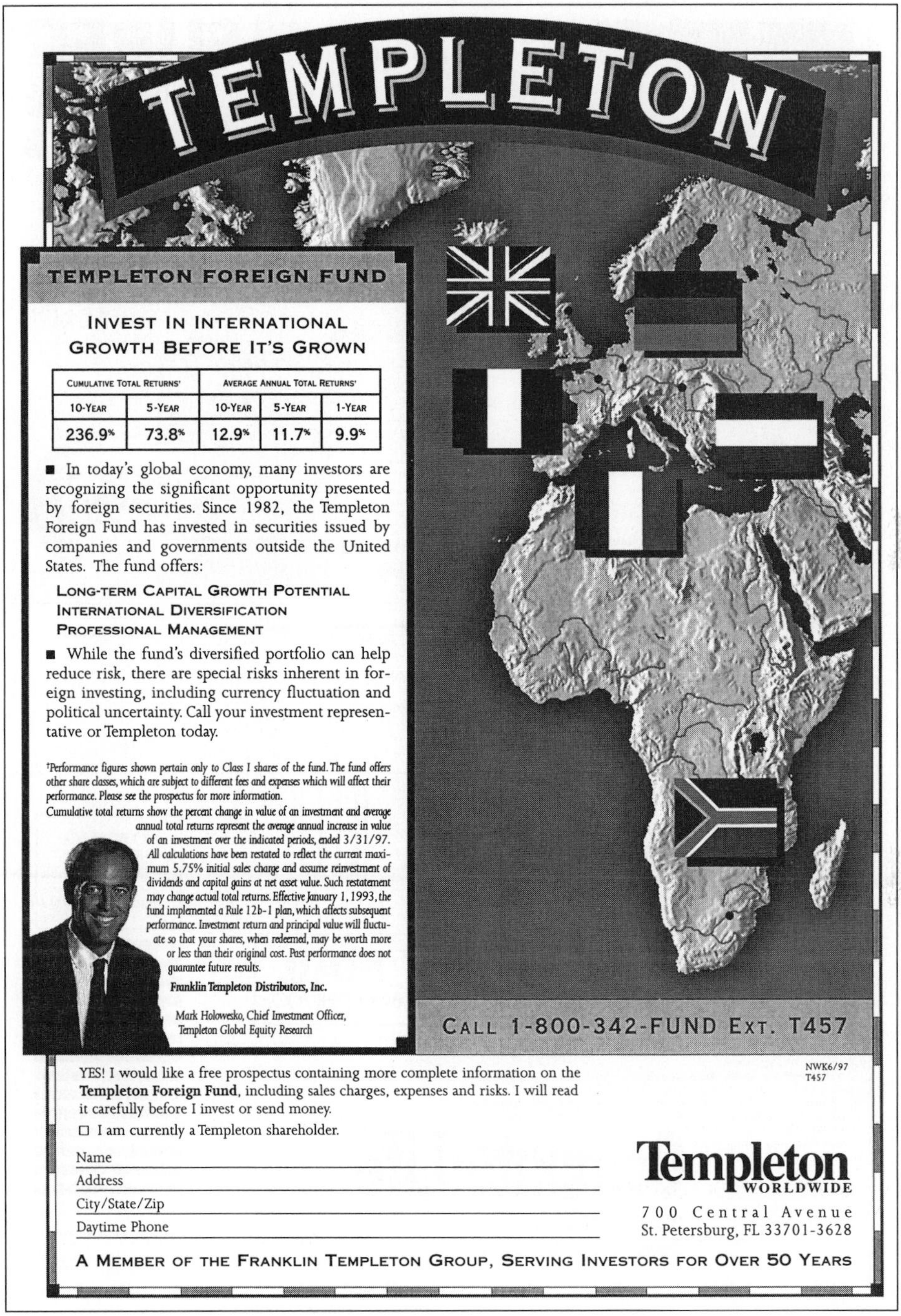
TEMPLETON
TEMPLETON FOREIGN FUND
INVEST IN INTERNATIONAL GROWTH BEFORE IT'S GROWN
CUMULATIVE TOTAL RETURNS† | AVERAGE ANNUAL TOTAL RETURNS†
10-YEAR | 5-YEAR | 10-YEAR | 5-YEAR | 1-YEAR
236.9% | 73.8% | 12.9% | 11.7% | 9.9%
■ In today's global economy, many investors are recognizing the significant opportunity presented by foreign securities. Since 1982, the Templeton Foreign Fund has invested in securities issued by companies and governments outside the United States. The fund offers:
LONG-TERM CAPITAL GROWTH POTENTIAL
INTERNATIONAL DIVERSIFICATION
PROFESSIONAL MANAGEMENT
■ While the fund's diversified portfolio can help reduce risk, there are special risks inherent in foreign investing, including currency fluctuation and political uncertainty. Call your investment representative or Templeton today.
†Performance figures shown pertain only to Class I shares of the fund. The fund offers other share classes, which are subject to different fees and expenses which will affect their performance. Please see the prospectus for more information.
Cumulative total returns show the percent change in value of an investment and average annual total returns represent the average annual increase in value of an investment over the indicated periods, ended 3/31/97. All calculations have been restated to reflect the current maximum 5.75% initial sales charge and assume reinvestment of dividends and capital gains at net asset value. Such restatement may change actual total returns. Effective January 1, 1993, the fund implemented a Rule 12b-1 plan, which affects subsequent performance. Investment return and principal value will fluctuate so that your shares, when redeemed, may be worth more or less than their original cost. Past performance does not guarantee future results.
Franklin Templeton Distributors, Inc.
Mark Holowesko, Chief Investment Officer, Templeton Global Equity Research
CALL 1-800-342-FUND EXT. T457
YES! I would like a free prospectus containing more complete information on the Templeton Foreign Fund, including sales charges, expenses and risks. I will read it carefully before I invest or send money.
NWK6/97
T457
☐ I am currently a Templeton shareholder.
Name
Address
City/State/Zip
Daytime Phone
Templeton
WORLDWIDE
700 Central Avenue
St. Petersburg, FL 33701-3628
A MEMBER OF THE FRANKLIN TEMPLETON GROUP, SERVING INVESTORS FOR OVER 50 YEARS

EXHIBIT 1.7. Blow-in Advertisements

ComputerLife™ subscription
SUPER SAVINGS
Yes! Send me Computer Life, the totally different Computer Magazine. And rush me my FREE Gaming MegaPac CD-ROM, loaded with fantasy/adventure games, classic arcade games, flight simulators and more!
☐ One year (12 issues) just $14.97. I SAVE 58%
☐ Two years (24 issues) only $27.94. I SAVE 61%
NAME PLEASE PRINT 5ND59
COMPANY
ADDRESS
CITY/STATE/ZIP
☐ PAYMENT ENCLOSED. ☐ BILL ME LATER.
Annual newsstand price $35.88. Non-U.S. add US$16 per year; Canadian GST included.
Free CD-ROM will be shipped upon payment.
12 ISSUES ONLY $35.88. $14.97
24 ISSUES ONLY $71.76. $27.94
ComputerLife
39 Great
ComputerLife
GAMING MEGAPAC

For fastest service, visit our Website —
http://subscribe.computerlife.com/order
NO POSTAGE NECESSARY IF MAILED IN THE UNITED STATES
BUSINESS REPLY MAIL
FIRST-CLASS MAIL PERMIT NO. 66 BOULDER, CO
POSTAGE WILL BE PAID BY ADDRESSEE
ComputerLife™
PO Box 55880
Boulder, CO 80323-5880

information, request a sales call, or place an order. Frequently, the cards are stand-alone advertisements for a subscription to a magazine. Bind-ins are stapled into the magazine, and blow-ins are literally blown into magazines by specialized machinery. Blow-ins may be more noticeable than bind-ins but are more easily lost.

Most trade journals, and some general-interest magazines, contain reader service cards, known as *bingo cards* (see Exhibit 1.8). The reader uses these cards to send away for additional information about products and services described in magazine advertisements. However, bingo cards tend to attract many respondents who are merely information seekers, not potential purchasers.

Direct-Response Radio

The use of radio as a direct-response or support medium is similar to the use of television, but radio has the special ability to reach people as they pursue their daily lives in their cars or at work where television viewing is not practical.

Radio was not traditionally considered a strong medium for direct-response marketing, because people usually listen to the radio while they are doing something else. It is generally not convenient for consumers to stop what they are doing, find a pencil and paper, and write down an address or a telephone number. And, by the time they find the pencil and paper, the ad may be over.

EXHIBIT 1.8. A Bingo Card

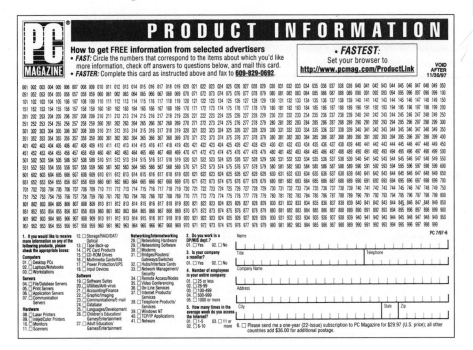

PC MAGAZINE®

PRODUCT INFORMATION

How to get FREE information from selected advertisers

- ***FAST:*** Circle the numbers that correspond to the items about which you'd like more information, check off answers to questions below, and mail this card.
- ***FASTER:*** Complete this card as instructed above and fax to **609-829-0692**.

• ***FASTEST:***
Set your browser to
http://www.pcmag.com/ProductLink

VOID AFTER 11/30/97

001 002 003 004 005 006 007 008 009 010 011 012 013 014 015 016 017 018 019 020 021 022 023 024 025 026 027 028 029 030 031 032 033 034 035 036 037 038 039 040 041 042 043 044 045 046 047 048 049 050
051 052 053 054 055 056 057 058 059 060 061 062 063 064 065 066 067 068 069 070 071 072 073 074 075 076 077 078 079 080 081 082 083 084 085 086 087 088 089 090 091 092 093 094 095 096 097 098 099 100
101 102 103 104 105 106 107 108 109 110 111 112 113 114 115 116 117 118 119 120 121 122 123 124 125 126 127 128 129 130 131 132 133 134 135 136 137 138 139 140 141 142 143 144 145 146 147 148 149 150
151 152 153 154 155 156 157 158 159 160 161 162 163 164 165 166 167 168 169 170 171 172 173 174 175 176 177 178 179 180 181 182 183 184 185 186 187 188 189 190 191 192 193 194 195 196 197 198 199 200
201 202 203 204 205 206 207 208 209 210 211 212 213 214 215 216 217 218 219 220 221 222 223 224 225 226 227 228 229 230 231 232 233 234 235 236 237 238 239 240 241 242 243 244 245 246 247 248 249 250
251 252 253 254 255 256 257 258 259 260 261 262 263 264 265 266 267 268 269 270 271 272 273 274 275 276 277 278 279 280 281 282 283 284 285 286 287 288 289 290 291 292 293 294 295 296 297 298 299 300
301 302 303 304 305 306 307 308 309 310 311 312 313 314 315 316 317 318 319 320 321 322 323 324 325 326 327 328 329 330 331 332 333 334 335 336 337 338 339 340 341 342 343 344 345 346 347 348 349 350
351 352 353 354 355 356 357 358 359 360 361 362 363 364 365 366 367 368 369 370 371 372 373 374 375 376 377 378 379 380 381 382 383 384 385 386 387 388 389 390 391 392 393 394 395 396 397 398 399 400
401 402 403 404 405 406 407 408 409 410 411 412 413 414 415 416 417 418 419 420 421 422 423 424 425 426 427 428 429 430 431 432 433 434 435 436 437 438 439 440 441 442 443 444 445 446 447 448 449 450
451 452 453 454 455 456 457 458 459 460 461 462 463 464 465 466 467 468 469 470 471 472 473 474 475 476 477 478 479 480 481 482 483 484 485 486 487 488 489 490 491 492 493 494 495 496 497 498 499 500
501 502 503 504 505 506 507 508 509 510 511 512 513 514 515 516 517 518 519 520 521 522 523 524 525 526 527 528 529 530 531 532 533 534 535 536 537 538 539 540 541 542 543 544 545 546 547 548 549 550
551 552 553 554 555 556 557 558 559 560 561 562 563 564 565 566 567 568 569 570 571 572 573 574 575 576 577 578 579 580 581 582 583 584 585 586 587 588 589 590 591 592 593 594 595 596 597 598 599 600
601 602 603 604 605 606 607 608 609 610 611 612 613 614 615 616 617 618 619 620 621 622 623 624 625 626 627 628 629 630 631 632 633 634 635 636 637 638 639 640 641 642 643 644 645 646 647 648 649 650
651 652 653 654 655 656 657 658 659 660 661 662 663 664 665 666 667 668 669 670 671 672 673 674 675 676 677 678 679 680 681 682 683 684 685 686 687 688 689 690 691 692 693 694 695 696 697 698 699 700
701 702 703 704 705 706 707 708 709 710 711 712 713 714 715 716 717 718 719 720 721 722 723 724 725 726 727 728 729 730 731 732 733 734 735 736 737 738 739 740 741 742 743 744 745 746 747 748 749 750
751 752 753 754 755 756 757 758 759 760 761 762 763 764 765 766 767 768 769 770 771 772 773 774 775 776 777 778 779 780 781 782 783 784 785 786 787 788 789 790 791 792 793 794 795 796 797 798 799 800
801 802 803 804 805 806 807 808 809 810 811 812 813 814 815 816 817 818 819 820 821 822 823 824 825 826 827 828 829 830 831 832 833 834 835 836 837 838 839 840 841 842 843 844 845 846 847 848 849 850
851 852 853 854 855 856 857 858 859 860 861 862 863 864 865 866 867 868 869 870 871 872 873 874 875 876 877 878 879 880 881 882 883 884 885 886 887 888 889 890 891 892 893 894 895 896 897 898 899 900
901 902 903 904 905 906 907 908 909 910 911 912 913 914 915 916 917 918 919 920 921 922 923 924 925 926 927 928 929 930 931 932 933 934 935 936 937 938 939 940 941 942 943 944 945 946 947 948 949 950
951 952 953 954 955 956 957 958 959 960 961 962 963 964 965 966 967 968 969 970 971 972 973 974 975 976 977 978 979 980 981 982 983 984 985 986 987 988 989 990 991 992 993 994 995 996 997 998 999

PC 7/97-6

1. If you would like to receive more information on any of the following products, please check the appropriate boxes:

Computers
01. ☐ Desktop PCs
02. ☐ Laptops/Notebooks
03. ☐ Workstations

Servers
04. ☐ File/Database Servers
05. ☐ Print Servers
06. ☐ Application Servers
07. ☐ Communication Servers

Hardware
08. ☐ Laser Printers
09. ☐ Inkjet/Color Printers
10. ☐ Monitors
11. ☐ Scanners
12. ☐ Storage/RAID/DAT/Optical
13. ☐ Tape Back-up
14. ☐ PC Card Products
15. ☐ CD-ROM Drives
16. ☐ Multimedia Cards/Kits
17. ☐ Power Protection/UPS
18. ☐ Input Devices

Software
19. ☐ Software Suites
20. ☐ Utilities/Anti-virus
21. ☐ Accounting/Finance
22. ☐ Graphic/Imaging
23. ☐ Communications/E-mail
24. ☐ Database
25. ☐ Languages/Development
26. ☐ Children's Education/Games/Entertainment
27. ☐ Adult Education/Games/Entertainment

Networking/Internetworking
28. ☐ Networking Hardware
29. ☐ Networking Software
30. ☐ Modems
31. ☐ Bridges/Routers/Gateways/Switches
32. ☐ Hubs/Interface Cards
33. ☐ Network Management/Security
34. ☐ Remote Access/Nodes
35. ☐ Video Conferencing
36. ☐ On-Line Services
37. ☐ Internet Products/Services
38. ☐ Telephone Products/Services
39. ☐ Windows NT
40. ☐ TCP/IP Applications
41. ☐ Netware

2. Do you work in a DP/MIS dept.?
01. ☐ Yes 02. ☐ No

3. Is your company a reseller?
01. ☐ Yes 02. ☐ No

4. Number of employees in your entire company:
01. ☐ 25 or less
02. ☐ 26-99
03. ☐ 100-499
04. ☐ 500-999
05. ☐ 1000 or more

5. How many times in the average week do you access the Internet?
01. ☐ 1-5 03. ☐ 11 or more
02. ☐ 6-10

Name

Title Telephone

Company Name

Address

City State Zip

6. ☐ Please send me a one-year (22-issue) subscription to PC Magazine for $29.97 (U.S. price); all other countries add $36.00 for additional postage.

EXHIBIT 1.8. A Bingo Card, *Continued*

However, even in the television era, radio has shown itself to be an effective direct-response medium that does have advantages to offer direct marketers. One attraction is radio's ability to reach highly segmented audiences. Some products have an obvious affinity to radio or, more accurately, to people on the move who are heavy radio listeners. Mattresses, flowers, paging systems, and cellular telephones have been sold successfully by direct-response radio.

Database Marketing

Database marketing uses individually addressable marketing media and channels (such as mail, telephone, and the sales force) to deliver highly targeted offers to customers and prospects. Firms can stay close to their target market by compiling and keeping a permanent record of all customer and prospect communications and buyer behavior. This helps improve all future contacts and makes possible more realistic planning of all of a firm's marketing activities.

Database marketing works by creating information about individual customer offers, inquiries, and orders. That information is used to analyze response patterns and to create target products and services; it also helps identify those customers most likely to buy new products and services, thereby increasing sales effectiveness. This growing form of direct marketing is the subject of Chapter 5.

Successful marketing efforts are built on specific, measurable objectives. Direct marketing programs or campaigns are not exceptions. Roberts and Berger[4] describe four broad types of objectives appropriate for direct marketing efforts:

1. Product or service sales.
2. Lead generation.
3. Lead qualification.
4. Customer relationship building and maintenance.

Product or Service Sales

The most common objective of direct marketing programs is to sell products or services. Some direct marketers are first concerned with producing well-qualified leads (prospective customers) for their field salespeople and subsequently with selling. Lead generation efforts are more common in business-to-business direct marketing (the subject of Chapter 15), where requests for additional information may also be used to qualify prospects—by answering questions or engaging in other behaviors, prospects indicate their intention to buy, thereby becoming "qualified prospects." The two-step process of qualification or additional information requests is also common for consumer products direct marketing, by which expensive or complex services such as insurance policies are sold.

Lead Generation

The key to lead generation is understanding the three keys: media investment, relationship investment, and actions. Lead generation involves a combination of targeted communications delivered at one time with the goal of generating a response. Multimedia lead generation involves the use of several lead-generating tools simultaneously. It is difficult to achieve because most marketing communications are created and executed as stand-alone programs by managers in separate departments. Multimedia lead generation requires that all communications deliver the same message with the same desired action by the target. The communications include all of the media used to deliver the message to the market from broadcast through telemarketing and sales contacts. If two or more media are used, they must deliver a consistent message and ask for a specific action to qualify as direct marketing multimedia. If the message is not consistent and the action requested is not the same, the media are being used for advertising or promotional purposes, but not direct-response multimedia lead generation. Most companies design an advertising campaign as an "umbrella" to serve as "background music" in "positioning" the company or its products. Marketing goes to market with a direct-mailed frequent-user program. Sales promotion hits trade shows and on-pack with a discount or load-up program. This is multimedia chaos, not multimedia marketing.

Lead Qualification

Lead qualification is designed to screen out bad leads or nonserious prospects. For college programs, for example, this involves ensuring that those who are interested in what the schools have to offer are in fact qualified to attend. Lead qualification normally is used to disqualify bad leads or to grade leads according to some criteria.

Customer Relationship Building and Maintenance

The direct marketing activities of colleges and universities illustrate how various types of communications are used to build relationships with prospective students. Colleges big and small are bombarding high school students with highly targeted messages in hopes of maintaining successful recruitment and tuition income. With a decreasing number of high school seniors and a dwindling undergraduate student base, colleges are competing to maintain enrollment numbers. Many colleges are realizing the effectiveness of direct marketing and are using targeted mailings that include informative glossy brochures, catalogs, interactive disks, and videos. They are also using direct-response ads, telemarketing, and other marketing resources to capture a share of the student pool.

Schools are identifying potential students based on ethnicity, household income, zip codes, and other factors. List rentals and purchases of student selections are on the upswing, as recruiters are always seeking the upper hand. With costs today ranging from $20,000 to $80,000+ for a four-year degree, colleges are like any other big business trying to close a sale on a high-ticket item in a very competitive marketplace.

Direct mail works and is still cheaper than most other means of acquiring students. Schools want a name and address to target when seeking new students. The average college-bound student receives more than 200 unsolicited mailings during high school; the student who is a good scholar and/or participates in many extracurricular activities can expect an additional 50 pieces.

Sending large quantities of colorful direct mail can result in a 20 percent response if a mailing is sent to students who have not heard of an institution. Schools need to sell a prospect; they often emphasize prestige, what is special about the college and its programs, and the feeling that the potential student will fit in.

For example, Texas Tech University, a college in Lubbock with 21,000 students, purchases search lists to target students with mailings detailing the campus and its program offerings. The school also began sending a video to prospective students in the fall of 1990. Tech's freshman classes usually number about 3,500 students, who come from all 50 states and 48 foreign territories. During the school year (approximately September to June), Tech distributes about 70,000 catalogs/brochures, all of which contain a reply card used to request more information or to inquire about a campus visit. After all the campus fairs and direct-mail replies are totaled, the response rate for some information is close to 50 percent.

Because Tech has increased academic standards and implemented more minority and specialty student targeting, the school has not felt the impact of the decline in college-age students as severely as some other schools have. For the future, Tech will be developing more focused booklets and information guides so that students with different needs get specific information just for them. The Texas Tech video has proved quite popular and successful, but it must be continually updated as the campus grows and program offerings and requirements change.

NEW DIRECT MARKETING APPROACHES

Online, Internet, and Videotex Direct Marketing

Online, Internet, and videotex are three of the emerging electronic media that are achieving widespread acceptance among direct marketers. Such online services as Prodigy and America Online offer subscribers shopping, communications, and news services. These systems have graphical user interfaces, making it easy to shop from a variety of vendors, and they provide customers with a wide range of products at prices comparable to those in retail outlets. They are accessible via a local phone call 24 hours a day, seven days a week.

The Internet, particularly the World Wide Web, is gaining mass-market acceptance. Although the audience on the Internet is small by television or magazine standards, it still numbers in the tens of millions and is growing rapidly. Some estimate that there are hundreds of thousands of consumer goods and business-to-business marketers on the Internet. Their Web sites are designed to entertain, to inform, and to sell. While Internet commerce is small compared to what occurs in traditional channels of promotion and distribution, the possibilities are nearly endless for firms willing to place catalogs, brochures, and other similar material on the Web so that customers can conveniently place orders for goods at better-than-retail-store prices.

Videotex applications include displays of daily schedules in hotels, flight information in airports, and listings of specials in supermarkets. Businesses can display large amounts of information and merchandise through this medium, guaranteeing it a significant role in the future of direct marketing.

Relationship Marketing[5]

For many years, direct-response marketers have struggled to find more effective and reliable ways to achieve an elusive goal: building and sustaining customer loyalty over an extended period of time. Many efforts have often been narrowly labeled as frequency marketing, database marketing, or relationship marketing. But creating and sustaining a lasting bond between a consumer and a product or service is a far more complex, interactive, and dynamic process than such reductive terms would suggest. It involves more than collecting data about customers and then selling to them. It involves entering into a relationship with customers, giving them a sense of satisfaction with the purchase decision they have made, letting them know that the firm recognizes and values their business, and showing them the firm understands their needs and will respond to their concerns.

The objective is to make them feel special—needed and wanted not just as consumers or prospects but as individuals. These efforts should be viewed as the process of managing customer relationships over an extended period of time. Many companies now sense that they may have focused too much time, effort, and marketing dollars on building brand awareness and acquiring new customers while neglecting the relatively small investment required to maximize the profit potential of their existing customer base.

Many leading U.S. marketers are starting to realize how important long-term relationships are to their profitability, and how much can be gained by cultivating existing relationships in addition to building new ones.

Like the implicit rules that guide personal relationships, the relationship management principles are grounded in such old-fashioned values as respect, openness, and trust. It is the skillful application of these values to every aspect of the customer relationship, through thoughtful strategic planning, imaginative database management, and informed creative executions, that is the heart of relationship management.

The fundamentals of relationship management include building the framework for relationships, establishing relationships, developing an ongoing dialogue, maximizing the value of relationships, rewarding loyalty, and sustaining relationships. To effectively manage the development of long-term relationships, a firm needs to create the basic building blocks that support all subsequent interactions. If it does not have a current customer database and an ongoing means of capturing new names, the process should begin there.

Home Shopping Shows

A big direct marketing story of the 1980s was the emergence of home shopping shows (see the Home Shopping Network case at the end of this book). This innovate electronic merchandising is changing the way America buys. The potential is there to sell large volumes of merchandise through a whole new type of direct marketing outlet. From a modest beginning in the mid-1980s, home shopping channels have grown to include audiences of millions all over the world. This form of televised selling moves hundreds of millions of dollars in merchandise yearly, including assortments of jewelry, electronics, designer fashions, appliances, tools, housewares, and gifts. Every item offered is available for immediate shipment. The channels use entertainment in an effort to make the shopping experience an attractive leisure-time activity.

These channels range from the Home Shopping Network (HSN), which tends to serve a broad lower-middle-class audience, to the more upscale QVC Network. Both networks broadcast live 24 hours a day and present their viewers with a wide array of retail items at good prices. HSN offers a never-ending stream of merchandise, including branded merchandise and specially manufactured products. Each item appears for a few minutes to encourage viewers to make a buying decision. HSN's television hosts prod viewers to call and participate in the show. Contests and prizes generate excitement and keep programming lively. Home shopping shows carefully track customer purchases. HSN stores data from the entire relationship between the firm and each member within its database. This allows HSN to ensure customer satisfaction and to continue to provide the kind of merchandise and programming necessary to keep viewers tuned in and buying.

SUMMARY

The most widely accepted definition of direct marketing was developed by a committee of the Direct Marketing Association (DMA), a trade association:

> Direct marketing is an interactive system of marketing which uses one or more advertising media to effect a measurable response and/or transaction at any location.

According to this definition, direct marketing is *interactive* in that marketer and prospective customer engage in two-way communication; it gives the target market of the communication an opportunity to respond; and that response or nonresponse-related information can then be used in planning later direct marketing programs.

Direct-response advertising, like other forms of promotion, seeks to persuade people to buy products or services. Virtually all the special competencies of direct marketing derive from the fact that the communications are directed at specific individuals and not at mass markets via mass media. These include the combination of advertising and selling into a single function, the prominence of customer service, the ability to precisely target individuals, and the ability to create personalized messages that call for immediate action. The results of direct marketing campaigns can be monitored and measured.

Three major factors have contributed to the growth in direct marketing: changes in American lifestyles and demographics, an evolving economy and international competition, and technological advances and innovations. All three factors are transforming how businesses operate and how consumers live.

Virtually any medium can be used to transmit direct marketing offers. The most common media include television, radio, magazines, the telephone, and the mail. While some of these media are used by both general marketers and direct marketers, the direct marketer uses and evaluates the effectiveness of each medium differently.

Successful marketing efforts are built on specific, measurable objectives. Direct marketing programs or campaigns are not exceptions. The four broad types of objectives appropriate for direct marketing efforts are product or service sales, lead generation, lead qualification, and customer relationship building and maintenance.

REVIEW QUESTIONS

1. What is meant by the term *direct marketing,* and what is it designed to do? In what ways is direct marketing different from the image-oriented advertising so common in the media today?
2. What are the media of direct marketing? How does each one operate in conjunction with direct marketing efforts designed to sell products and services?
3. What are the major factors that have contributed to the growth in direct marketing activities?
4. What are direct marketing's special competencies? How do those special competencies contribute to the success of direct marketing efforts?

5. What are the four broad types of objectives appropriate for direct marketing efforts? What specifically is each designed to do?

6. What is relationship marketing? What are home shopping shows? What is each designed to accomplish? In what ways are these new forms of direct marketing similar to or different from other forms of direct marketing?

NOTES

1. Adapted from Henry R. Hoke, "1-800-FLOWERS Blossoms as Premier Marketing Utility," *Direct Marketing,* March 1993, pp. 28–30.
2. Adapted from Greg Gattuso, "Marketing Vision," *Direct Marketing,* February 1994, pp. 24–26.
3. Mary Lou Roberts and Paul D. Berger, *Direct Marketing Management* (Englewood Cliffs, NJ; Prentice Hall, 1989) pp. 5–8.
4. Ibid, pp. 9–10.
5. Adapted from Harold M. Brierley, "The Art of Relationship Management," *Direct Marketing,* May 1994, pp. 25–26.

SOURCES

Baker, Stephn, and Geri Smith. "The Mexican Worker." *Business Week,* April 19, 1993, pp. 84–92.

Bernstein, Aaron, et al. "What Happened to the American Dream?" *Business Week,* August 19, 1991, pp. 80–85.

Boyd, Harper W., and Orville C. Walker. *Marketing Management.* Homewood, IL: Richard D. Irwin, 1990.

Braun, Harvey. "Guess Who's Watching?" *Direct Marketing,* July 1993, pp. 21–23.

Brierley, Harold M. "The Art of Relationship Management." *Direct Marketing,* May 1994, pp. 25–26.

Claxton, Reid P. "Customer Safety: Direct Marketing's Under-Marketed Advantage." *Journal of Direct Marketing* 9, Winter 1995, pp. 67–78.

_______. "Retail Shopping Safety and the Direct Marketing Alternative: Exploring Student Perceptions." *Journal of Direct Marketing* 9, 1995, pp. 68–75.

"Customer Rapport." *Direct Marketing,* January 1994, p. 46.

Direct Marketing Association. *Statistical Fact Book 1996.* New York: Direct Marketing Association, 1996.

Emerick, Tracy. "The Multimedia Mix." *Direct Marketing,* June 1993, pp. 20–22.

Endicott, R. Craig. "Direct Ads Spur 12% Of Consumer Sales." *Advertising Age,* October 9, 1995, p. 34.

Fierman, Jaclyn. "What Happened to the Jobs?" *Fortune,* July 12, 1993, pp. 40–41.

Fishman, Arnold. "International Mail Order Overview." *Direct Marketing,* October 1992, pp. 28–32.

Garland, Susan B., et al. "Those Aging Boomers." *Business Week,* May 20, 1991, pp. 106–112.

Gattuso, Greg. "Marketing Vision." *Direct Marketing,* February 1994, pp. 24–26.

Hoke, Henry R. "1-800-FLOWERS Blossoms as Premier Marketing Utility." *Direct Marketing,* March 1993, pp. 28–30.

Holtz, Herman. *Databased Marketing.* New York: Wiley and Sons, 1992.

JOHNSON, CLAUDE A. "Winning Back Customers through Database Marketing." *Direct Marketing,* November 1994, pp. 36–37.

KATZENSTEIN, HERBERT, AND WILLIAMS S. SACHS. *Direct Marketing.* 2nd ed. New York: MacMillan, 1992.

KLUES, JACJ M., AND JAYNE ZENALT SPITTLER. "A Media Planner's Guide to the Future." In *Beyond 2000: The Future of Direct Marketing,* ed. Jerry I. Reitman. Lincolnwood, IL: NTC Business Books, 1994, pp. 79–95.

LABICH, KENNETH. "Four Possible Futures." *Fortune,* January 25, 1993, pp. 40–48.

MANDEL, MICHAEL J., AND CHRISTOPHER FARRELL. "How to Get America Growing Again." *Business Week,* Special Issue on Reinventing America, 1992, pp. 22–44.

MCDONALD, WILLIAM J. "Home Shopping Channel Customer Segments: A Cross-Cultural Perspective." *Journal of Direct Marketing* 9, Autumn 1995, pp. 57–67.

O'REILLY, BRIAN. "Preparing for Leaner Times." *Fortune,* January 27, 1992, pp. 40–47.

PEPPERS, DON, AND MARTHA ROGERS. "The End of Mass Marketing." *American Demographics,* Marketing Tools Supplement, March/April 1995, pp. 42–47+.

RICHMAN, LOUIS S. "The Truth about the Rich and Poor." *Fortune,* September 21, 1992, pp. 134–46.

________. "Bringing Reason to Regulation." *Fortune,* October 19, 1992, pp. 94–96.

ROBERTS, MARY LOU, AND PAUL D. BERGER. *Direct Marketing Management.* Englewood Cliffs, NJ: Prentice Hall, 1989.

ROSENBLOOM, BERT. *Direct Selling Channels.* New York: Haworth Press, 1992.

RUST, ROLAND T., AND RICHARD W. OLIVER. "The Death of Advertising." *Journal of Advertising* 23, 4, December 1994, pp. 71–77.

SPIERS, JOSEPH. "Let's Get Real about Taxes." *Fortune,* October 19, 1992, pp. 78–81.

SROGE, MAXWELL. *The United States Mail Order Industry.* Lincolnwood, IL: NTC Business Books, 1994.

STONE, BOB. *Successful Direct Marketing Methods.* 5th ed. Lincolnwood, IL: NTC Books, 1995.

SUSMAN, ANDREW. "Switching the Channel." *Direct Marketing,* January 1993, pp. 44–46, 70.

"Those Amazin' Infomercials." *Consumer Reports,* January 1995, p. 10.

VERITY, JOHN W., AND RUSSELL MITCHELL. "A Trillion-Byte Weapon." *Business Week,* July 31, 1995, pp. 80–81.

"Will New Technology Change the Marketing Rules?" *Direct Marketing,* October 1994, pp. 14–19, 40.

WITEK, JOHN. *Response Television.* Lincolnwood, IL: NTC Business Books, 1992.

WOFTAS, GARY W. "School Daze." *Direct Marketing,* September 1991, pp. 28–32.

ZIN, LAURA, ET AL. "Move Over, Boomers." *Business Week,* December 14, 1992, pp. 74–82.

CHAPTER 2

Direct Marketing Strategies

OBJECTIVES

1. To understand the primary purpose of a firm's marketing strategy and the steps that must be taken to develop that strategy.
2. To understand why having a sustainable competitive advantage is important in direct marketing.
3. To examine the major areas included in a comprehensive strategic marketing plan and what each is designed to do.

INTRODUCTION

The decision-making factors of offer, creative, media, and customer service discussed in Chapter 1 are key to the short-term planning process for direct marketing, but direct marketers must also take a longer-term perspective on their business. This involves strategic planning, which is designed to help companies cope with competition and marketplace change over a span of several years.

The primary purposes of a firm's marketing strategy are to allocate resources effectively, coordinate activities, and accomplish specific goals. Accordingly, managers articulate the desired direction for a product or service based on profit objectives and the efficient allocation of resources. They also make decisions during all phases of the planning process about what is to be accomplished, how it is to be accomplished, and how it all will occur given the firm's strengths and weakness. In doing so, managers must evaluate the problems, opportunities, and threats facing the firm, as well as the firm's competitive advantages. Firms seek competitive advantages through well-integrated marketing programs that coordinate the production, pricing, promotion, and distribution of their product or service offerings. (These four elements—product, price, promotion, and distribution—are often referred to as the marketing mix.)

Strategic marketing decisions are often complex. There are four major reasons for this complexity:

1. *A large number of factors influence market outcomes.* When marketing managers introduce a new offering or reposition a product or service, a large number of factors determine the success or failure of their effort. Competitive reactions, changing economic conditions, and the willingness of consumers to try something new all influence ultimate sales and profitability.

2. *Many factors that influence market outcomes are not controllable by marketing management.* For example, changes in consumer preferences or increased competition can adversely affect a marketing manager's plans. Changes in national or international economic conditions will also affect product or service sales and profitability.
3. *Factors affecting the outcome of marketing plans lack stability.* Consumer preferences, economic conditions, or other uncontrollable factors can change rapidly, over relatively short periods of time. Technology changes quickly in some markets, like that for personal computers, where major new products appear regularly. These changes can have serious adverse impacts on a firm's sales and profits.
4. *Responses to the allocation of marketing resources are not linear.* Numerous underlying forces make for nonlinear responses to marketing moves. Frequently the end result is diminishing returns for resource allocations. The so-called S-curve describes the relationship between many marketing efforts and their eventual results. For example, doubling a product's or service's advertising budget rarely increases sales by a commensurate amount; the actual impact is usually much more modest.

In addition to having a high degree of complexity, marketing decisions frequently involve significant financial risks. For example, the introduction of a new product may require funding in the multimillion-dollar range. For some firms, the amount at risk may comprise their entire revenue stream for the last several years.

Marketing decisions also have significant impact beyond the marketing department. In a marketing-driven firm, the approval of marketing budgets and plans determines the budgeting for other functional areas like manufacturing and human resources. Thus, in fitting the organization to the business environment, strategic marketing management provides the firm with direction and influences production, financial, and human resource requirements. While the consequences should be explicitly stated when the marketing plan is approved, the decisions still represent commitments that frequently detract from the other activities of a functional area. Normally, these production and human resource departments are considered cost centers, while only marketing has the dual role of revenue generation and cost management.

LANDS' END

Lands' End, Inc., is a good example of a firm that has successfully developed and implemented direct marketing strategies in a highly competitive market but that also continues to face challenges as it makes marketing decisions. From the company's founding in 1963, its sales grew to about $992 million in 1995, making Lands' End one of the nation's largest merchants selling almost exclusively through a direct-mail catalog. Sales continued to increase through 1997's fiscal year to $1.119 billion. (Exhibit 2.1 shows a sample catalog cover.) During 1995, Lands' End saw growth in all its operations, with new business areas, international sales, and specialty catalogs leading the way. This sales growth was driven primarily by increases in catalog circulation. Some 191 million catalogs were

EXHIBIT 2.1. Lands' End Catalog Cover

mailed in 1995, 23 percent more than in 1994. Much of the circulation increase was due to a prospecting program established to add new customers in advance of the postal-rate and paper-price increases anticipated for 1996. However, the sales growth generated by the primary and prospecting catalogs was not as strong as the firm had hoped. In fiscal year 1997, Lands' End delivered 211 million full-price catalogs.

In fiscal 1995, Lands' End's business operations produced some mixed results. The $992 million sales figure reached in 1995 was a 14 percent increase from 1994's $870 million in sales (see Exhibit 2.2). However, profitability for the year was disappointing. Fiscal 1995 net income was $36.1 million, down 17 percent from the $43.7 million earned in 1994 (see Exhibit 2.3). Net income decreased again in 1996 to $30.6 million only to rise again in 1997 to $51 million. Gross profit for 1995 was 42.7 percent of net sales, rising 1.6% from the prior fiscal year, but this profit increase was mainly due to lower costs in domestic and offshore merchandise sourcing. Lands' End also negotiated price reductions with its domestic vendors and shifted some manufacturing offshore in order to maintain its value positioning.

Despite the mixed results of 1995 sales, Lands' End continued to focus attention on its catalog business, which generates the bulk of the firm's sales and profits. In addition, the firm increased efforts in international expansion of its catalog businesses in Japan and Europe. By 1997, the company reported that their increase in sales was mainly due to growth in specialty and international business as well as some growth in their core business.

Many companies create catalogs with appealing merchandise, compelling benefits, generous services, and reasons to buy, but few companies select a combination of attributes that clearly differentiates their offering from that of competitors, nor do they emphasize their offering consistently in a creative way and achieve an emotional connection with their customers. The most successful companies use their brand identity to emphasize their key attributes and to reinforce lasting relationships with their customers.

The centerpiece of Lands' End's brand identity is its catalog. It is produced with what the firm calls an editorial approach. Individual catalogs frequently contain large half- or full-page descriptions for key products designed to be interesting, appealing, and original. In addition, some pages are devoted to editorials, essays, and commentary about a variety of subjects related to product usage and typical customer lifestyles.

Lands' End reinforces its brand identity by being a customer-service-oriented company. This is reflected in prompt service and personal attention from a dedicated staff, fast shipping, a sophisticated computerized operating system, and

EXHIBIT 2.2. Lands' End Sales Figures: 1991–95*

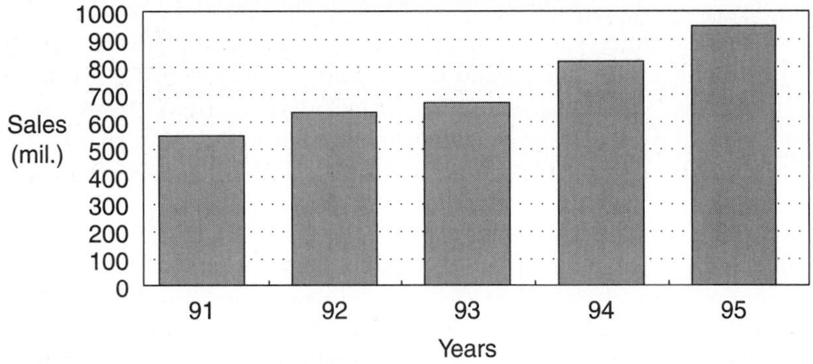

Source: Lands' End 1995 annual report.
*By fiscal year 1997, sales increased to $1.119 billion.

EXHIBIT 2.3. Lands' End Income, 1991–95*

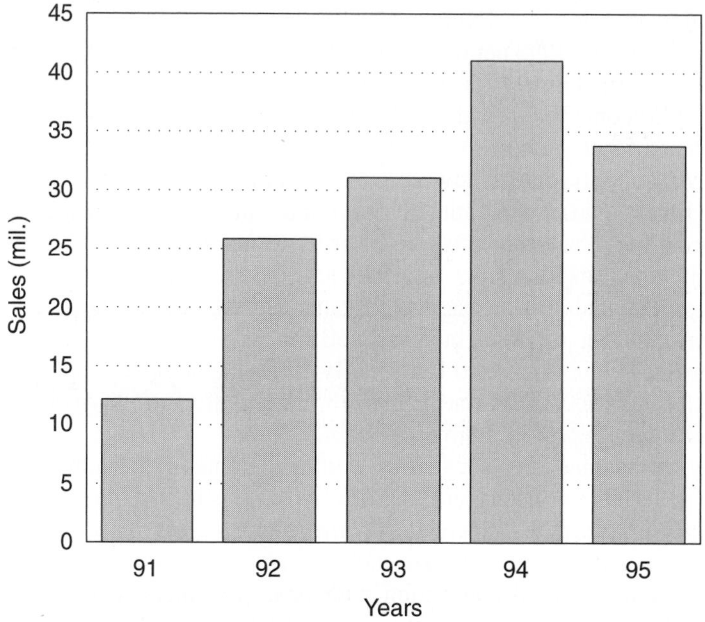

Source: Lands' End 1995 annual report.
*In 1996, net income dipped to 30.6 million, rising again in 1997 to $51 million.

a huge distribution center to handle customer orders. Lands' End's marketing and service philosophy is summed up in its "Principles of Doing Business" (see Exhibit 2.4). These widely published principles form the basis for the firm's operations.

Lands' End maintains its brand identity by concentrating on traditional clothing and other products that are functional, well made, and durable. It does not promote fashion or fad clothing. Accordingly, Lands' End's catalog offers basic product lines such as knit shirts, sweaters, sport shirts, trousers, and soft luggage, along with gift items, children's clothing, and sheets and towels. All goods are purchased from independent manufacturers except for soft luggage, which is manufactured at the firm's own facilities. U.S. manufacturers supply approximately 80 percent of Lands' End's merchandise. The remainder is purchased from overseas manufacturers, mostly in the United Kingdom, Asia, and Europe. To ensure that products are produced to Lands' End's quality standards at reasonable prices, buyers and quality-assurance personnel develop rigid product specifications, including the fibers, fabric construction, and manufacturing sources for each item. They are also responsible for the styling and quality features of the products.

THE NATURE OF STRATEGIC MARKETING

Strategic firms such as Lands' End are successfully working their way through the complex, dynamic selling environments in which they operate. They arrive at their

EXHIBIT 2.4. Lands' End's "Principles of Doing Business"

Principle 1. We do everything we can to make our products better. We improve material, and add back features and construction details that others have taken out over the years. We never reduce the quality of a product to make it cheaper.

Principle 2. We price our products fairly and honestly. We do not, have not, and will not participate in the common retail practice of inflating mark-ups to set up a future phony "sale."

Principle 3. We accept any return, for any reason, at any time. Our products are guaranteed. No fine print. No arguments. We mean exactly what we say GUARANTEED. PERIOD.

Principle 4. We ship faster than anyone we know of. We ship items in stock the day after we receive the order. At the height of the last Christmas season the longest time an order was in the house was 36 hours, excepting monograms which took another 12 hours.

Principle 5. We believe that what is best for our customers is best for all of us. Everyone here understands that concept. Our sales and service people are trained to know our products, and to be friendly and helpful. They are urged to take all the time necessary to take care of you. We even pay for your call, for whatever reason you call.

Principle 6. We are able to sell at lower prices because we have eliminated middlemen; because we don't buy branded merchandise with high protected mark-ups; and because we have placed our contracts with manufacturers who have proven they are cost conscious and efficient.

Principle 7. We are able to sell at lower prices because we operate efficiently. Our people are hard-working, intelligent, and share in the success of the company.

Principle 8. We are able to sell at lower prices because we support no fancy emporiums with their high overhead. Our main location is in the middle of a 40-acre cornfield in rural Wisconsin. We still operate our first location in Chicago's Near North tannery district.

strategies only after careful consideration of numerous issues associated with the planning process.

Planning takes place at several levels in the strategically managed firm. At the corporate level, strategic planning establishes broad directions to guide all parts of the organization. At the next level down, *strategic marketing planning* is done for individual business units within the firm. Finally, at the lowest level, plans are developed for individual functions within each operating unit based on the requirements of the strategic marketing plan.

When direct marketing's role in the overall effort is minor, its plan can be formulated after the business units' overall marketing plan is drawn up, often without the participation of direct marketing personnel. In such cases the plan for direct marketing may even be treated as an afterthought. In large consumer goods companies, direct marketing is usually a small part of the overall budget.

When direct marketing is an important part of the marketing mix, or is closely interwoven with other marketing approaches, it is planned concurrently with the business's other marketing efforts. But when the main focus of a business's marketing effort is direct marketing, all planning revolves around direct-marketing-related issues and opportunities, including the direct-response tools needed to achieve the operating unit's objectives.

In reality, most direct marketing firms are relatively small operations—individual businesses with one or more product lines rather than members of large corporations. In this book, we focus primarily on what the marketing function must do to contribute to the success of the typical direct marketing firm. In that sense, this chapter emphasizes strategic marketing planning for individual business units. This sets the stage for the remainder of the book, which focuses on the specifics of direct marketing planning, that is, the operational planning for the direct marketing function and the specific marketing plans for individual products and services and the support they require from such functions as manufacturing and finance.

If the firm has more than one direct marketing business, individual business units within the firm are identified by their relationship with an external market (as opposed to an internal one) and have a distinct group of customers and competitors. These individual business units constitute separate sales and profit centers managed by individuals with bottom-line responsibilities.

SUSTAINABLE COMPETITIVE ADVANTAGE

Strategic marketing planning involves achieving and sustaining a *competitive advantage,* where long-run above-average performance is achieved by satisfying customers better than the competition does. Thus, sustainable competitive advantage is a core concept in strategic marketing management. The strategic marketing process involves the identification of factors that make a firm's offerings unique in the eyes of its targeted customers on attributes those customers value in their purchase decision making.

The result is a competitive advantage. This distinctive advantage reflects a way of doing business that can be sustained over time in the face of competition. Distinctive competencies are the things a business does especially well; they may include lowest delivered cost, a differentiated offering, and a protected niche. Such competencies can work in combination or operate individually to provide a firm with its competitive advantage. However, if a firm's distinctive competencies do not matter to its target market, they have little meaning in terms of the firm's future sales and profits.

Economies of scale and tight financial controls frequently result in the lowest costs; both are usually achieved through considerable effort over time. Differentiated offerings are usually the result of creating a strong brand image; maintaining a full line of merchandise that reflects superior value and satisfies customer needs in the product category; developing innovative products not available from the competition; creating productive and cost-effective ways of reaching prospects, such as highly refined mailing lists; and providing outstanding customer service.

Protected niches of sufficient size and purchasing power, and of little interest to most competitors in a market, may form the basis for a very profitable direct marketing business. Firms with the products and skills to exploit such opportunities can establish a hold on a portion of the market that competitors will find difficult to break. The Sharper Image is an example of niche marketing in the catalog area. The company's merchandise mix is composed primarily of electronics, luxury household goods, and personal care products. As mentioned earlier, Lands' End occupies a unique market position with its strong brand identity, exemplified by the firm's catalog merchandise and editorial approach to individual products. Lands' End's superior customer service also provides the firm with a competitive advantage because attention to customers is such an important aspect of company operations.

The strategic objectives of a firm should reflect long-term goals and the types of effort required to develop distinctive competencies. Policies for functional areas such as marketing, production, and finance form the basis for strategy implementation. They also ensure that all functions and various related subfunctions will be coordinated with one another in support of the strategy. When a firm has more than one business unit, having those business units support and complement one another creates synergy. Thus, a multiple-unit organization can achieve an overall impact that is greater than the sum of the impacts of each individual unit.

THE STRATEGIC MARKETING PLANNING PROCESS

Strategic marketing planning is a formal method for considering alternative courses of action. It is useful to large and small companies alike because it provides a road map for the future and standards by which to evaluate a firm's performance. A strategic marketing plan is not *a* marketing plan, but it does include individual marketing plans for the products and services that are the responsibility of the business unit creating the strategic plan.

As outlined in Exhibit 2.5, a comprehensive strategic marketing plan includes five major areas: the situation analysis; the delineation of problems, opportunities, and threats; the setting of objectives; the description of alternative marketing strategies; and decisions concerning recommended courses of action, with implementation and monitoring plans. Within this framework, the decision section contains marketing plans for specific products and services; these plans follow from the preceding sections in the strategic marketing plan and reflect the strategic direction of the business as outlined in the objectives and evaluation of alternatives. However, before such a comprehensive strategic marketing plan can be developed, a firm must first determine what business it is in and what it is trying to accomplish in that business, including the customer need it intends to fulfill, the nature of its product offerings and intended product-market, and the business's distinctive competence or competitive advantage in that product-market.

EXHIBIT 2.5. A Comprehensive Strategic Marketing Plan Outline

1. Situation analysis
   - A. Extent of demand
   - B. Nature of demand
   - C. Strategy analysis
   - D. Life-cycle stage
   - E. Macroenvironmental trends
   - F. International issues
   - G. Strengths and weaknesses
   - H. Nature of competition
2. Problems, opportunities, and threats
   - A. Problems
   - B. Opportunities
   - C. Threats
3. Objectives
4. Alternatives
   - A. Marketing alternatives
   - B. Evaluation of alternatives
5. Decision
   - A. Recommendations
   - B. Implementation
   - C. Monitoring

While all strategic marketing plans have similar formats, the steps vary among companies. Each firm has different ways of combining resources, adapting policies, and acting on its plans. The following sections describe the basic elements of the strategic marketing plan outlined in Exhibit 2.5 and the processes associated with formulating that plan.

1. Situation Analysis

The situation analysis produces a synopsis and evaluation of a firm's current situation, which then leads to an identification of problems, opportunities, and threats. This helps the direct marketer to prepare alternatives and to make specific decisions about what to do next, including recommendations and performance monitoring. The situation analysis interprets and shows the relevance of important firm information, providing a diagnostic rather than a descriptive background for proceeding with the specifics of the overall plan.

The firm's situation determines the breadth and depth of an appropriate situation analysis. A given firm may require a situation analysis that is different from those of other firms because of the information available or because of unique potential alternatives.

The situation analysis includes a thorough and comprehensive assessment of the overall market; a profiling of present and potential customers; an examination of marketing objectives and strategies (including the marketing mix of product, price, promotion, and distribution); product life-cycle considerations; a detailed review and assessment of macroenvironmental trends; a specification of international issues, particularly those relating to competitive considerations; an analysis of the firm's and competitors' major strengths and weaknesses; and a delineation of the basis on which other firms in the market compete for the attention and sales of potential customers.

A. Extent of Demand

Understanding the extent of demand in a market involves defining the actual or potential size of that market and making estimates of future sales potential. This is a quantitative exercise because it provides information on the unit and dollar sales demand for a category of products or services.

To understand the extent of demand, the firm needs to estimate the size of the market in units and dollars now and in the future. It also needs to estimate competitor market shares and trends in market size, and to study forecasts of market segment growth, usually for the next five years, for the segments in which the firm competes. Finally, the firm must consider differences in demand at the primary (category) and selective (product- or service-specific) demand levels and to make assumptions about related trends.

Lands' End operates in the highly competitive catalog market. In 1995, Lands' End ranked 4th among the 10 largest general merchandise and apparel catalog retailers in the United States. Today, catalog firms in the United States mail between 14 and 15 billion catalogs a year. The largest firms in catalog marketing include J. C. Penney in first place, followed by Fingerhut, Spiegel, and Lands' End. In recent years, large general merchandise catalogs have done poorly while more focused specialty catalogs have done well.

Lands' End is part of a catalog apparel industry that accounts for approximately 12 percent of all apparel sales. The firm holds a 4 to 5 percent share of that market, making it one of the nation's largest direct marketers. However, although catalog apparel was once a fast-growing market, there has been a recent slowdown due to market saturation, competition from such diverse sources as home shopping networks, and declining consumer discretionary income. Higher postage and paper costs have also reduced profits.

B. Nature of Demand

To determine the nature of demand, the firm identifies buyers and their purchase decision-making process by consumer or industrial market segment. That includes specifics about how those purchases are influenced by factors external to the customer, including any joint decision making that may occur in families or business organizations. The key to conducting this analysis is to think about implications for alternative marketing strategies.

SEGMENTATION. A good starting point for analyzing the nature of demand is an examination of the appropriate target market(s). Proper identification of the target market is a key part of strategic planning. Firms should be interested in whether certain segments of the market, along with the total market, are growing. Can the market be meaningfully segmented into several homogeneous groups with respect to what they want and how they buy? Is the firm's segment of the market large enough to support the product or service?

The firm should look at the buyer segment's demographics, psychological characteristics, and decision-making processes in the context of influences from family, friends, society, and organizations. The firm should also examine if and how the market has been segmented by competitors and on what basis those segmentations were made, including the identification of which segments are the largest and which have the most potential. What key competitors serve each customer group? Are any segments currently not being served? Can the firm successfully serve those segments? (Chapter 3 of this book contains a comprehensive discussion of market segmentation.)

Lands' End knows that, among catalog merchandise buyers, women outnumber men, 58 percent to 42 percent. However, among those who never buy through catalogs, there are just as many men as women. The percentage of married consumers is higher among the catalog shoppers; some 57 percent are married, compared to only 45 percent of noncatalog shoppers. Breaking down the two groups by age, larger percentages of catalogers are in the age ranges 25–34, 35–44, and 45–54. Catalog shoppers are better educated, with more than two-thirds having attended college. On the other hand, only a little more than half of those who never buy through catalogs have attended college. Catalog shoppers are more likely to be professionals, business managers, and secretaries, while noncatalogers are more likely to be factory workers, laborers, drivers, and salespersons. More than half of those who regularly buy through catalogs earn between $30,000 and $99,000 annually, while only about 38 percent of those who never buy through catalogs earn in that range.

DECISION MAKING. The firm needs to determine the *who, what, where, when, why,* and *how* of the purchase decision. How do buyers (consumer or industrial) go about purchasing products or services? What are the main types of attitudes and behavior patterns? Also, the firm needs to identify the number of sources buyers consider in the decision-making process; the degree of overt information seeking in connection with decision making; the degree of brand awareness and loyalty; the sources of product or service information; and who makes the purchase decision—men, women, children, the whole family, purchasing agents, or buying committees.

Is the choice an individual or group decision, and who influences the decision maker(s)? How frequently is the purchase decision made or repeated? What is the buyer's involvement in the decision-making process? What is the risk or uncertainty level associated with the purchase, and what are the consequences of making a poor choice? What are the rationales for purchase behavior? Do they tend to be practical or emotional? What needs do buyers satisfy by purchasing the product or service? What other important sources of information do buyers use to make a decision, and what criteria do they use to evaluate products or services?

Decision making in the apparel catalog market is based on such factors as ease of catalog use, convenience, company reputation, merchandise variety, good value in the offerings, catalog attractiveness, the perception of low financial risk in making a purchase, and merchandise uniqueness. When customers make purchasing decisions, they select among a set of products. A catalog's image communicates its distinctive positioning to customers and prospects, which encourages them to believe that a catalog contains items that will satisfy their needs. At a basic level, apparel purchases are motivated by a need for clothing. At a psychological level, the motivation is to purchase apparel that fulfills a need for status, self-esteem, or social acceptance. Over time, customers learn preferences for catalogs based on the desirability of the attributes of those catalogs.

C. Strategy Analysis

An understanding of the firm's own strategy and the strategies of major competitors is an important aspect of the situation analysis. The way to start is by delineating the objectives and related successes of each marketing strategy.

MARKETING STRATEGY. As the firm analyzes the strategy of each company in its product-market, it should address a series of specific questions about itself and its major competitors: Does the firm (or major competitor) have an integrated marketing strategy made up of individual product, price, promotion, and distribution strategies? Is the role selected for each marketing mix element consistent with the overall program objectives, and does it properly complement other mix elements? Are adequate resources available to carry out the marketing strategy? Are resources committed to target markets according to the importance of each?

PRODUCT STRATEGY. Is the product mix geared to the needs the firm seeks to address for each product-market? What branding strategy is being used? Are products properly positioned against competing brands? Does the firm have a sound approach to product planning and management, and is marketing involved in product decisions? Are additions to, modifications of, or deletions from the product mix needed to make the firm more competitive in the marketplace? Is the performance of each product and specific product offering evaluated regularly?

DISTRIBUTION STRATEGY. Has the firm selected the type of direct marketing approaches appropriate to each of its products or services? Is the extent of its focus on those direct marketing alternatives consistent with the products or services it offers? How well does each distribution alternative reach its target market? How is each of the distribution alternatives managed? What improvements are needed? Are desired customer service levels reached, and are the costs of doing this acceptable?

Remember from Chapter 1 that direct marketing includes many alternative ways to distribute a product or service to a firm's target market. A direct marketer may distribute via catalogs, the mail, or direct-response television ads, to name just a few of the alternatives.

PRICING STRATEGY. What roles does price have in the marketing mix? Does price play an active or passive role in the product or service positioning? How responsive is each market target to price variations? How do the firm's price strategy and tactics compare to those of its competition? Are there indications that changes are needed in pricing strategy or tactics?

PROMOTION STRATEGY. Is the creative strategy consistent with the positioning for the product or service being sold? What promotional alternatives should be used for the product or service to achieve cost-effective communication with the target market? Does the copy in the firm's brochures, catalogs, and letters effectively convey the intended message?

D. Life-Cycle Stage

The marketer needs to make explicit assumptions about where a product or service market is in its life cycle. This is important because the effectiveness of specific marketing options, including the product, price, promotion, and distribution alternatives, tend to vary by stages of that life cycle.

The catalog market in which Lands' End competes is generally considered mature. However, some particular niches are growing much faster than others, implying that the maturity of the market is more a function of the products and services offered by groups of catalogs than of the catalog as a direct marketing tool. In other words, the life-cycle stage is about what is being sold rather than how it is being sold.

E. Macroenvironmental Trends

Six components of the macroenvironment are critical from a marketing perspective: the sociocultural, demographic, political and legal, technological, economic, and competitive environments (Exhibit 2.6). While each environment is conceptually distinct, they all interact in complex ways. For example, government actions on tax policy affect economic growth and the distribution of incomes, and technological changes influence the nature of competition among firms.

THE SOCIOCULTURAL ENVIRONMENT. This sociocultural environment represents the cultural, attitudinal, and behavioral aspects of the market. Changes in this environment tend to be more evolutionary than revolutionary; they occur between generations more than they do among individuals from a given generation. Of particular interest to direct marketers are changes in individual values, family structure, leisure-time activities, and expectations about the future. Such changes affect the sale of personal care products; the personal selling of insurance services; the direct-mail marketing of political candidates; and sales of products and services in almost every other area of social, economic, and political life.

EXHIBIT 2.6. Macroenvironmental Areas

1. Sociocultural environment
2. Demographic environment
3. Political and legal environment
4. Technological environment
5. Economic environment
6. Competitive environment

The sales of such firms as Lands' End are particularly influenced by what individuals value and what lifestyles are popular. Any clothing cataloger must offer the merchandise consumers want. However, predicting what they will want at some future point is very difficult. Lands' End must closely follow cultural, attitudinal, and behavioral trends for indication about influences on clothing purchases.

THE DEMOGRAPHIC ENVIRONMENT. Changing demographics are a major influence on all aspects of American society. Of particular interest to direct marketers are the emerging profiles of age, income, and social structure in the United States because they each directly affect consumer and industrial markets for products and services.

The major demographic force that will affect the U.S. economy in the years ahead is the maturing of the well-educated, sophisticated, and relatively well-to-do baby boomers. This demographic trend offers companies the opportunity to develop new products and services catering to the needs of this portion of the population.

International competition (which includes other factors, such as technology) is driving changes in income and social class structure. In a 1993 U.S. Senate committee hearing on the North American Free Trade Agreement (NAFTA), Lester C. Thurow, the dean of the Harvard Business School, described the plight of the U.S. labor force in a very competitive international environment by characterizing the top one-third of all U.S. workers as "world class" and the other two-thirds as "positively third world." He predicted that the future will bring an end to the "American labor premium" because of low-wage competition from workers in other countries. He believes that the majority of the U.S. labor force does not warrant a wage rate higher than that paid to comparable workers in Korea or Mexico. For these U.S. workers, real wages will systematically fall over the next 10 to 20 years, as they have done for the last 15 years.

The dean's scenario is widely accepted in government and academia as a major reason for the declining incomes and lower living standards of less-skilled workers in the United States. It is also consistent with theories about the way the nation's social class structure is changing. The message is that the U.S. middle class is in decline and that the future class structure of the United States will resemble that of third world countries, with the highly educated and trained at the top, a relatively small number in the middle, and the majority of the population at the bottom. Those who analyze this phenomenon say that the top group will be about 25 percent of households, while the bottom will represent close to 65 percent, with the remaining 10 percent in the middle. According to this analysis, the majority of the current middle class is downwardly, not upwardly, mobile.

Direct marketers should be particularly concerned about the implications of a changing income distribution and social class structure. If the middle class has substantially less money to spend, the impact will be felt by all businesses serving that group. Firms will have to change their targeting to more upscale consumers or lower their sights to the growing numbers of less affluent buyers.

Like many other firms selling clothing items to an essentially middle-class target market, Lands' End must pay close attention to how people spend their after-tax income. With substantially less money, the middle class will make fewer clothing purchases, particularly of the typically leisure-oriented items offered by Lands' End. The firm also needs to be concerned about the aging of its customer base, particularly baby boomers, because people buy less clothing as they age and because the generation following the boomers is significantly smaller. The generation X group will be a considerably less attractive market than the boomers because they will have less disposable income.

THE POLITICAL AND LEGAL ENVIRONMENT. The political and legal environment includes all the factors controlled by public authorities, interest groups, and other forces that operate within the legislative arena. These factors define the regulatory environment within which businesses must operate. The political and legal process has the ability to impose mandatory constraints on a firm's operations and the behavior of consumers. As with any other external force, the political and legal environment presents both opportunities and threats to a firm. Major elements of this environment that have a potential impact on direct marketing activities are government regulation and consumer protection legislation.

THE TECHNOLOGICAL ENVIRONMENT. Technology is the driving force behind the development of many products and services. A dramatic acceleration has occurred in the identification of commercially viable technologies. The time between idea, invention, and commercialization is decreasing.

Direct marketing is a technological-intensive business. Advances in computer power and capabilities have a major influence on how the industry markets its products and services. Chapter 4 of this book contains a comprehensive discussion of the technological trends affecting direct marketing today.

Like most direct marketers, Lands' End has benefited from the technology revolution. The use of computerized databases is the wave of the future in direct marketing. As the costs associated with this technology drop, Lands' End, like other firms, is capitalizing on its ability to create highly detailed customer records. It is also developing databases of noncustomers who represent prospects at which it intends to direct its marketing efforts.

THE ECONOMIC ENVIRONMENT. The economic environment in the United States is undergoing dramatic transformations. Some of the changes are attributable to the recent recession, but the most important ones are actually systemic. The developed countries, including the United States, Canada, and the Western European nations, are "averaging" their economies (and standards of living) with those of the less developed world. Worldwide technological change is also resulting in more worker productivity and therefore less of a need for workers, causing massive social and economic dislocations.

Years ago the majority of the world's population worked on farms; next, few worked on farms but many labored in manufacturing-related activities; today, few are on farms or in manufacturing but many are in service jobs (which tend to be lower paid than those in manufacturing). If current predictions hold true, in the near future many people will not work at all because it only takes a finite number of workers (many of whom may be in the third world) to serve the total consumer population of the globe. In fact, the largest growth segment of "workers" in the United States consists of people who "do nothing," including those who have retired, were forced to retire early, or just cannot find another job. And, of those who do work, many are underemployed.

With this fundamental structural transformation, what new postindustrial world will emerge? Because so much depends on the answers, social and economic forecasters across the United States are developing scenarios for the future. Governments and major corporations base long-range plans on such scenarios. While there are many possible futures, most forecasters adhere to one of four alternatives.

First, a small minority of forecasters say that the remainder of the 1990s will bring a full-scale boom, with unemployment declining and economic growth averaging 5 to 6 percent annually. These optimists base much of their analysis on the economy's current strengths, particularly the low interest and inflation rates.

Second, the most optimistic futurists predict that the U.S. economy will be lifted to unprecedented heights as the baby-boom generation reaches its peak spending years. Historically, good times have arrived as each new generation has progressed up a predictable curve of earning and spending, until its consumption peaks between the ages of 45 and 49. The inevitable result of the 78-million-strong baby boomers, now between the ages of 28 and 46, will be a significant increase in consumer demand. Those dramatic changes are also possible because a surge of new technologies and a wave of innovations will join the baby boomers' spending power.

Third, some forecasters are convinced that the United States will emerge from the 1990s far stronger than its current global competitors. Many of these forecasters are particularly negative on Japan's prospects, citing that country's limited natural resources and rigid social structure. They see enhanced U.S. competitiveness leading to strong export gains and higher corporate profits.

Fourth, however, most of the forecasters take only a moderately bullish view. According to their scenario, the U.S. economy is likely to produce a steady annual growth rate of slightly more than 2 percent, which will increase to slightly under 3 percent by the end of the 1990s.

While Lands' End cannot know which of these four futures is the correct one, it must plan its business activities with some expectation about what will happen. Every marketing plan is a bet on a particular future. This is true because some scenario of the future serves as the premise for the plan and includes assumptions about how consumers will behave, how the economy will operate, and what competitors will do.

THE COMPETITIVE ENVIRONMENT. Competition both in the United States and internationally is intense. The United States no longer enjoys competitive advantages in many of the industries it once dominated. Competition among firms for customers and market share is resulting in major shakeouts. New and innovative products play a critical role in satisfying consumer needs, which is key to a firm's survival.

Even as the United States enters its postrecession recovery, there is good reason to believe that the upturn is not curing what ails the economy and the U.S. labor market. This relatively negative outcome is traceable to global competition. In the 1980s, manufacturing companies fought most of America's international competitiveness battles. The result was not favorable, as is evident in the U.S. electronics, steel, and automotive industries.

Yet as America saw the decline of its smokestack industries, many analysts pointed to the potential of the service sector. Banks, retailers, insurance companies, telecommunications giants, and airlines were all viewed as industries with great competitive strength and potential. These industries were expected to more than compensate for the steady decline of the factory sector. The hope was for a smooth transition to a postindustrial era, and initially those hopes seemed well founded. During the 1980s, service companies generated about 18 million new jobs, accounting for 96 percent of total employment growth.

Unfortunately, as the pressures of global competition spread from capital-intensive manufacturing companies to people-intensive service organizations, American workers faced a painful reality. For the factory sector, cost-cutting measures have ranged from layoffs and plant closings to improved inventory control and outsourcing. For service industries, restructuring has focused on a reduction of white-collar labor expenses, the single largest component of the service sector's cost structure.

While Lands' End competes with dozens of firms, it is in most direct competition with such companies as L. L. Bean. Other competitors include apparel-focused J. Crew (men's and women's clothing) and mass cataloger J. C. Penney, which maintains both major retail operations and catalog lines.

F. International Issues

Direct marketing firms need to delineate the international issues relevant to their business and marketing activities. Such delineation should include a discussion of products and services from international competitors and any changes in international market opportunities, including shifts in demand and international competitive trends.

The vast majority of direct marketers in the United States are inwardly focused, but some are beginning to make major moves abroad. Direct marketers such as the home shopping channels have found receptive audiences in such diverse places as the United Kingdom and Japan. Lands' End is among a small but growing number of U.S. catalogers that have tried to make inroads into the European market. This interest in Europe appears to have less to do with the lowering of trade barriers than with the slow growth prospects of the U.S. catalog market. In Asia, Lands' End is among some 15 U.S. catalogers that have succeeded in penetrating the Japanese market. Competitor L. L. Bean has also met with success in Japan by offering high-quality products that have a unique U.S. appeal and carry a money-back guarantee.

G. Strengths and Weaknesses

After delineating international issues, the next step in the strategic marketing plan is to identify the firm's internal strengths and weaknesses and the strengths and weaknesses of major competitors. These attributes should first emerge in the initial stages of the situation analysis. The direct marketing firm takes all the information it has analyzed in developing the previous parts of the situation analysis and uses it to develop a profile of its strengths and weaknesses and those of competitors. It also examines each of its functional areas such as finance and human resources, and identifies those functions that are strong or weak. For example, a company may be weak in marketing but strong in manufacturing.

Questions covered in the strengths-and-weaknesses analysis should include the following: Does the firm and its key competitors have the skills and experience to perform the functions necessary to compete in their product or service category? To answer this question, a firm must look closely at each of the following:

Marketing skills.

Production skills.

Management skills.

Financial skills.

Research and development skills.

How do the firm's skills compare with those of competitors? Does the firm have the funds to support an effective direct marketing program across all these areas?

Lands' End is a particularly savvy marketer. However, the firm also exhibits strengths in other functional areas. It is a well-managed company with a focused product line and a strong customer-service orientation. This has led to a loyal customer following and a strong image versus the competition.

H. Nature of Competition

The key to evaluating the present and future nature of competition is to understand how buyers evaluate alternative products and services relative to their needs by considering what factors in a market are critical to success and whether the firm is strong in those areas. The firm's probability of success with a target market depends on whether its business strengths (i.e., distinctive competencies) not only match the key success requirements for operating in a market but also exceed those of its competitors. The best-performing company will be the one that is strong on what customers value and that can sustain the differential advantage of its competencies over time. Having competence is not enough; the firm must use its superior competence to attain a sustainable competitive advantage.

The key factors in Lands' End's success include its attractive and innovative catalog, its internally developed mailing list, and its order-fulfillment and customer-service activities. These attributes are particularly attractive to the firm's loyal base of affluent, college-educated, and professional or managerial customers.

2. Problems, Opportunities, and Threats

In the second major step of the strategic marketing plan, the firm prepares a definite analysis of *key* problems, opportunities, and threats identified during the situation analysis.

A. Problems

A major pitfall in defining problems occurs when symptoms are confused with problems. Such things as declining sales, declining profits, and increasing costs are symptoms that are often incorrectly identified as problems. Firms can avoid incorrectly defining a symptom as a problem by thinking in terms of causes and effects.

Problems are causes, and symptoms are effects. For example, a firm might list two problems as "Sales are down" and "Profits are declining." But that would not be correct; decreases in sales and profits are symptoms. Answering the following questions identifies the real problems: Why are sales declining? Why are profits dropping? The key word is *why*. Sales may be declining because product quality is low, and profit reductions may occur because of increasing pressure on prices from competitors and higher promotion expenses designed to answer comparative claims by a major rival. The firm needs to keep asking why until it has identified the root problem(s) and not just another symptom. Even then, it is often necessary to break the problem down into its component parts.

If the firm identifies two or more major problems, it must ask itself whether or not the problems are related enough to be considered as one central problem. If, however, the firm determines that the problems are not directly associated with one another, it should rank them in order of importance and address them in that order. Many firms find that although their problems do not appear to be closely linked, the solutions are related; one solution may solve multiple problems.

Lands' End faces a complex set of problems in the United States that result mostly from the changing nature of the clothing catalog market. Chief among those problems is competitive pressures on sales and profits. It is involved in a protracted struggle to keep its customer base and to protect its profitability as U.S. consumers have more catalog options to choose from and less disposable income to spend on clothing.

B. Opportunities

One of the major purposes of the situation analysis is to discern opportunities. A marketing opportunity is an attractive arena for marketing action in which the firm would enjoy a competitive advantage. The firm should classify each opportunity according to its attractiveness and the probability of its success.

However, firms should not confuse identifying opportunities with taking action. A firm can recognize an opportunity but not take any action related to it. For example, a large market for a product may exist; this is an opportunity. However, a firm may decide not to compete in that market due to a lack of resources or skills or to the existence of strong competition.

It is one thing to identify attractive opportunities in the environment; it is another to have the necessary competencies to succeed with those opportunities. The analysis of firm strengths and weaknesses or competencies in the marketing, financial, manufacturing, and organizational areas forms the basis for determining whether opportunities can and should be pursued. Of course, not all factors are equally important for succeeding in a business or with a new marketing opportunity. The firm should ask the following types of questions about potential opportunities: Will pursuing the opportunity allow the firm to expand its core business(es)? Exploit new market segments? Widen product range? Extend a differentiation advantage? Diversify into new growth businesses? Expand into foreign markets? Apply research and development skills in new areas? Enter new, related businesses? Apply brand-name equity in new areas?

Lands' End's main opportunities are probably in the international marketplace. The U.S. domestic market is saturated with catalog offerings in an environment with a stagnant population and limited economic growth. If the firm wants to expand its U.S. operations, it may find opportunities in new catalog lines or in new ways of distributing its current line of products.

C. Threats

A threat is a challenge posed by an unfavorable trend or development in the environment external to the firm that would lead, in the absence of purposeful marketing action, to an erosion of the firm's position. The various identified threats should be classified according to their seriousness and their probability of occurrence. Among the many potential threats to a firm are increased foreign or domestic competition, changing consumer tastes, new or substitute products, new forms of competition, changes in demographics, changes in economic trends, government legislation, economic changes such as a recession, and slower market growth.

The threats to Lands' End are primarily in the U.S. marketplace. Growing competition and a stagnant consumer market are leading to market-share battles, which drive down profit margins and eliminate all but the most well-managed firms. Given that Lands' End has shown itself to be a strong competitor in the past, there is every reason to believe it will survive in the future; however, a protracted battle for survival is no marketer's dream situation.

3. Objectives

Before marketing alternatives can be developed, the firm needs to specify some overall objectives. These objectives should be specific and should point to where the firm wants to be at a particular time in the future, usually in five years. If the objectives are not explicitly stated, the firm will need to speculate about them because they are the standards against which the success or failure of a strategy is evaluated.

When constructing or modifying objectives, the firm should be sure they are measurable, as well as feasible and attainable. Moreover, because strategic marketing is futuristic, and no one can predict the future with complete accuracy, objectives should always be adaptable to changing conditions in an organization or industry.

Objectives are usually classified in terms of sales, market share growth, and/or financial targets. For example, a firm may decide that it needs to grow sales by 10 percent per year for each of the next five years, with a market-share growth of five points at the end of that five-year period. At the same time, this direct marketer could expect after-tax profits to increase by 12 percent annually. Other objectives are also appropriate, such as an increase in customer repeat purchase rates or an increase in customer average order size.

Generally, direct marketers describe two basic types of objectives:

- *Quantifiable Behavioral Objectives.* Strategic marketing objectives are invariably behavioral. They are concerned with an immediate, quantifiable response such as an order for a product, a request for information, or a sales call. They should be specific about actionable results: an increase in the number of orders or the number of units sold. With these levels set, a program can be evaluated as to whether the objectives are being met.
- *Unquantifiable Nonbehavioral Objectives.* Nonbehavioral objectives include product image enhancements or attitudinal changes.

4. Alternatives

Alternatives are the strategic options or actions that appear to be viable solutions to the problem(s) a firm identifies in the strategic marketing plan. Alternatives should allow the firm to pursue opportunities while avoiding threats. Often, two or more seemingly appropriate actions are available.

The firm should prepare its list of alternatives in two stages. First, it needs to develop an initial list of potentially appropriate alternatives. After it has generated that initial list, the firm should begin refining it by combining similar actions. The firm should use information from the situation analysis to help identify which alternatives to keep and which to eliminate. Issues include whether each alternative is feasible given existing financial, productive, managerial, and marketing constraints and whether a given alternative can be expected to produce the desired results.

The descriptions of problems, opportunities, threats, and alternatives should be consistent. To help avoid any mistakes, marketing managers typically make explicit connections between the situation analysis; the problem(s), opportunities, and threats; and the final set of alternatives. The firm should also include an assessment of the advantages and limitations of the final set of alternatives, specifying each one's pros and cons.

A. Marketing Alternatives

Marketing alternatives should address as many topic areas as appropriate in terms of strategy-related marketing mix and program decisions (along with marketing objectives and target market selection). These marketing mix/program decisions should cover product line breadth and depth; positioning and branding issues; price points and discounting; and promotion mix in terms of direct mail, direct-response television, telemarketing, and other similar tools. Table 2.1 summarizes the capabilities of the major direct-response media. It shows that each has advantages and disadvantages, including differences in reach, cost, and efficiency.

The direct marketing alternatives should exemplify the result of making well-supported and well-reasoned marketing decisions. Generally, if the situation analysis is strong; if the problems, opportunities, and threats are well defined; if the objectives are well stated; and if the alternatives are logically determined and supported, the result should be a good (and defensible) decision.

B. Evaluation of Alternatives

A key to effective marketing decision making is to evaluate the financial viability of each direct marketing alternative. These calculations can be done with a computer program. Whatever way the financial analysis is done, it needs to provide sales and expense analyses and forecasts, including estimates of the profit contribution from each marketing alternative.

The first test of any marketing alternative is whether or not it is reasonable. The firm must decide if the projected outcome is likely to occur based primarily on past experience or on testing (see Chapter 17). If all the strategic, competitive, and resource assumptions look achievable, the direct marketer is ready to conduct a financial analysis that projects returns from the proposed marketing alternative.

TABLE 2.1. The Capabilities of Major Direct-Response Media

Medium	Advantages	Disadvantages
Direct mail	Reaches all households Selectivity and personalization Most suitable for testing Most flexible Maximizes customer list dollars Second highest response rates Contains all action elements	Second most expensive Long startup time Profile analysis Potential limited
Telephone	Powerful "one-on-one" capability Fastest response time Selectivity Flexibility Excellent for research and profile analysis Can increase average order size substantially Highest response rates Powerful cross- and upgrade-sell	Dangerous with prospects No visual appeal Most expensive cost per thousand persons reached (CPM) 55% household reachability
Magazines	Reach mass or class Good color reproduction Long ad life Low CPM Test inexpensively Moderate lead time	Less space to tell story Less personal Slower response Less selectivity than mail or phone
Newspapers	Shortest startup time Fast response Wide variety of formats Broad local coverage Inexpensive to test	Poor color Poor selectivity No personalization Rates vary Sometimes affected by local conditions
Television	Powerful demonstration capability Fast response Wide choice of time buys Can reach all U.S. households Strong support medium Watch for strong selectivity as cable grows	Limited copy time No permanent response device Difficult to split-test Network time scarce Limited time available in second and fourth quarters
Radio	High-frequency, inexpensive Many profiles can be isolated by choice of show and time Short startup times Powerful support medium	No response device Limited copy time No visual appeal

CPM = Cost per thousand, which is the number of dollars it costs to reach every one thousand persons by media.
Source: Dick Shaver, "Strategic Planning: An Overview," in *The Direct Marketing Handbook,* 2nd ed., ed. Ed Nash (New York: McGraw-Hill, 1992), p. 25.

The financial analysis of alternatives is a critical aspect of any strategy evaluation because the goal of all direct marketing activities is financial. Because companies need returns on the investment of their resources, all proposed marketing activities must be evaluated for their financial implications. Firms should not invest in a new $7.5 million database management system or in a $8.4

million direct-mail campaign without closely examining the financial implications of such resource allocations.

Although financial analysis can be complex, it can be simplified by focusing on a particular technique. Both Chapter 18 of this text and the accompanying computer software emphasize the discounted cash flow analysis approach to evaluating the financial viability of direct marketing plans. There are other sophisticated and complex approaches, many of which are covered in finance classes, but the discounted cash flow method is both efficacious and efficient in its ability to characterize the relative value of alternatives.

Each alternative should address the overall strategy and related marketing mix and program decisions (along with marketing objectives and target market selection) to show that the alternative was seriously considered. Because financial considerations are ultimately the most important factor in the evaluation of direct marketing alternatives, these alternatives must be reduced to a set of numbers or they are of limited value to decision makers. There are also circumstances in which the qualitative aspects of marketing objectives are relevant as well, for example, when the long-term benefits of particular sustained strategies are hard to quantify reliably.

5. Decision

The last part of developing the strategic marketing plan involves decision making based on the analysis of the firm and its products and/or services. Obviously, the quality of the decision depends on the thoroughness with which the analysis is prepared. The decision should be consistent with the situation analysis and the problems, opportunities, and threats identified. It should also follow logically from the objectives of the plan and the discussion of the merits of each direct marketing alternative.

The decision should have two parts. The first part covers recommended courses of action, and the second involves issues in the implementation and control of the decision through monitoring its progress and ensuring that adjustments are made to the strategy if unforeseen events affect the assumptions and predicted results.

A. Recommendations

The decision and associated recommendations are specific to each firm. They address what actions should be taken and why, and they include the main reasons for believing that the recommended courses of action are best, without rehashing the previous sections of the plan. It is important that the recommendations be specific and operational. Such recommendations usually include several parts; for example, one set of recommendations may include an increase in spending on direct-mail efforts and the introduction of a new product via telemarketing. The single most important factor in most recommendations is profitability. Because profits are the principal goal of all firms, nearly every marketing recommendation is influenced by monetary considerations, which ultimately affect actual or expected profits.

The marketer should avoid recommending a course of action beyond a firm's means. No organization can possibly pursue all the strategies that could potentially benefit it. The real test for a strategy decision is how reasonable the strategy appears to those who review and evaluate it. Does it appear to be based on sound assumptions? Are the expectations for results realistic? Are the resources needed for the strategy available? Is it the best option for how those resources can be used? Are the mechanisms in place to implement and monitor the strategy?

B. Implementation

This implementation section contains the marketing plan specifics, including all elements in the marketing mix, assigned tasks, and resource allocations. There may be some redundancy with the previous discussion of marketing alternatives. However, this section does need to have a self-contained description of specifically what will be done to implement the recommended marketing effort. The implementation plan shows that the decisions are both possible and practical.

C. Monitoring

The monitoring part of the decision section should address strategy and control issues. The aim is to identify what monitoring and control systems to use when implementing the strategy. Direct marketing is particularly good at strategy and program monitoring because it allows the firm to know who responded to an offer and under what circumstances.

SUMMARY

The primary purpose of a firm's marketing strategy is to allocate resources effectively, coordinate activities, and accomplish specific goals. Accordingly, managers develop strategies to articulate the desired direction for a product or service based on profit objectives and the efficient allocation of resources. Decisions are made during all phases in the planning process about what is to be accomplished, how it is to be accomplished, and how it will all occur given a firm's strengths and weaknesses; the problems, opportunities, and threats facing the firm; and its competitive advantages. Firms seek these competitive advantages through well-integrated marketing programs that coordinate the production, pricing, promotion, and distribution of their product or service offerings in an effort to satisfy the needs of their target market.

Strategic marketing planning involves achieving and sustaining a competitive advantage, where long-run, above-average performance is achieved by doing a better job than the competition in satisfying customers. The strategic marketing process involves the identification of factors that make a firm's offerings unique in the eyes of its target market on attributes that are valued by those customers in their purchase decision making.

A comprehensive strategic marketing plan includes five major areas: the situation analysis; the delineation of problems, opportunities, and threats; the setting of objectives; the description of alternative marketing strategies; and recommended courses of action or decisions, with implementation and monitoring plans. The decisions section contains marketing plans for specific products and services. These plans reflect the strategic direction of the business as outlined in the objectives and evaluation of alternatives for the firm.

REVIEW QUESTIONS

1. What is the primary purpose of a firm's marketing strategy? What steps must be taken to develop a strategy? What decisions need to be made and why?
2. What is a sustainable competitive advantage? How is such an advantage achieved? Why is having a sustainable competitive advantage important in direct marketing?
3. What is a situation analysis, and why is it important to conduct one as part of the direct marketing planning process?
4. What are the major areas included a comprehensive strategic marketing plan? What is each designed to do? How does each of the areas support and lead to the next?
5. What are problems, opportunities, and threats? How do they influence the development of direct marketing plans?
6. What are quantifiable behavioral objectives and how are they different from unquantifiable nonbehavioral objectives? What roles do these types of objectives play in a strategic marketing plan?
7. A direct marketing plan is a prediction about what will happen in the future. Given that it consists of forecasts and estimates about what will happen, how does the management of a firm know which plans are most likely to succeed?

SOURCES

BAKER, STEPHN, and GERI SMITH. "The Mexican Worker." *Business Week,* April 19, 1993, pp. 84–92.

BERNSTEIN, AARON, ET AL. "What Happened to the American Dream?" *Business Week,* August 19, 1991, pp. 80–85.

BERNHARDT, KENNETH L., and THOMAS C. KINNEAR. *Cases in Marketing Management,* 5th ed. Homewood, IL: Richard D. Irwin, 1991.

BISSELL, BRENT. "Forces for Change." *Direct Marketing,* December 1991, pp. 57–60, 70.

BLACKWELL, ROGER D.; W. WAYNE TALARZYK; and JAMES F. ENGEL. *Contemporary Cases in Consumer Behavior.* Chicago: Dryden, 1990, pp. 448–57 ("Lands' End").

"Catalog Age 100." *Catalog Age,* August 1996, pp. 1, 62–68, 72–74.

"The Computer Industry." *The Economist,* February 27, 1993, a special insert survey.

CRAVENS, DAVID. *Strategic Marketing,* 4th ed. Homewood, IL: Richard D. Irwin, 1994.

CRAVENS, DAVID, and CHARLES W. LAMB, JR. *Strategic Marketing Management Cases,* 4th ed. Homewood, IL: Richard D. Irwin, 1993.

DAVID, FRED R. *Cases in Strategic Management,* 4th ed. New York: Macmillan, 1993.

DUNCAN, TOM. "Integrated Marketing? It's Synergy." *Advertising Age,* March 8, 1993, p. 22.

FIERMAN, JACLYN. "What Happened to the Jobs?" *Fortune,* July 12, 1993, pp. 40–41.

GARLAND, SUSAN B., ET AL. "Those Aging Boomers." *Business Week,* May 20, 1991, pp. 106–12.

GOULET, PETER G., and LYNDA GOULET. "Lands' End." In *Strategic Marketing,* 4th ed., ed. David Cravens. Homewood, IL: Richard D. Irwin, 1994, pp. 638–50.

GREER, THOMAS V. *Cases in Marketing: Orientation, Analysis, and Problems,* 5th ed. New York: Macmillan, 1991, pp. 163–68 ("L. L. Bean").

HAGGIN, JEFF. "Brand Identity" *Catalog Age,* October 1994, pp. 113–18.

KOTLER, PHILIP. *Marketing Management,* 7th ed. Englewood Cliffs, NJ: Prentice Hall, 1991.
LABICH, KENNETH. "Four Possible Futures." *Fortune,* January 25, 1993, pp. 40–48.
Lands' End annual reports, catalogs, and promotional materials.
LEVITT, THEODORE. "The Globalization of Markets." *Harvard Business Review,* May/June 1983, pp. 92–102.
MOSS, GARY. "Integrated Marketing: A Client Task." *Advertising Age,* January 25, 1993, p. 19.
MULDOON, KATIE. "How Are They Doin'?" *Direct,* August 1995, pp. 59–61.
NUSSBAUM, BRUCE. "Hot Products." *Business Week,* June 7, 1993, pp. 54–57.
O'REILLY, BRIAN. "Preparing for Leaner Times." *Fortune,* January 27, 1992, pp. 40–47.
RICHMAN, LOUIS S. "The Truth about the Rich and Poor." *Fortune,* September 21, 1992, pp. 134–46.
_______. "Bringing Reason to Regulation." *Fortune,* October 19, 1992, pp. 94–96.
RIFKIN, JEREMY. *The End of Work.* New York: G. P. Putnam's Sons, 1995.
ROGERS, MICHAEL. "Brave New TV." *TV Guide,* January 23, 1993, pp. 36–40.
SCHULTZ, DON E. *Strategic Advertising Campaigns,* 3rd ed. Lincolnwood, IL: NTC Business Books, 1991.
SHAPIO, JOSEPH P. "Just Fix It." *U.S. News & World Report,* February 22, 1993, pp. 50–56.
SHAVER, DICK. "Strategic Planning: An Overview." In *The Direct Marketing Handbook,* 2nd. ed., ed. Ed Nash. New York: McGraw-Hill, 1992, pp. 3–41.
SPIERS, JOSEPH. "Let's Get Real about Taxes." *Fortune,* October 19, 1992, pp. 78–81.
STONE, BOB. *Successful Direct Marketing Methods,* 5th ed. Lincolnwood, IL: Business Books, 1995.
"Strategies for the New Mail Order." *Business Week,* December 19, 1992, pp. 82–86.
SUCHECKI, MARK. "Integrated Marketing: Making It Pay." *Direct,* October 1993, pp. 43–49.
THUROW, LESTER C. *The Future of Capitalism.* New York: William Morrow Company, 1996.
"Will New Technology Change the Marketing Rules?" *Direct Marketing,* October 1994, pp. 14–19, 40.
ZIN, LAURA, ET AL. "Home Alone—With $600 Billion." *Business Week,* July 29, 1991, pp. 76–77.
_______. "Move Over, Boomers." *Business Week,* December 14, 1992, pp. 74–82.
ZETLIN, MINDA. "Marketing by the Book." *Journal of European Business* 5, No. 4, March/April 1994, pp. 34–38.

CHAPTER 3

Segmentation and Target Marketing

OBJECTIVES

1. To explain how segmentation and target marketing are used in direct marketing.
2. To describe the differences between how segmentation is used in direct marketing versus general marketing.
3. To distinguish between the segmentation options available to direct marketers targeting individuals and those targeting businesses.
4. To list the requirements for segmentation in direct marketing and to show how each of those requirements contributes to better market segmentations.
5. To examine how the types of market segmentation are used in direct marketing efforts.

INTRODUCTION

In *market segmentation,* direct marketers focus on particular subsets of the total population that are expected to be more responsive to what the firm is selling than the whole population. By using segmentation to appeal to particular groups of consumers or businesses, direct marketers hope to reduce costs; selecting prospects who are expected to be more receptive to an offer should yield higher rates of return. Market segmentation contributes to the development of a strategy that focuses a firm's marketing mix to best fit demand in a specific product market.

Segmentation, or the idea of targeting the homogeneous components of a heterogeneous market rather than the market as a whole, was initially popularized in the 1950s. It was justified by the fact that a sophisticated economy includes highly diverse markets composed of different groups, or *segments,* each with unique patterns of income, spending, lifestyle, and product preferences. These clusters of buyers form cohesive groups that differ from one another as to their specific needs. Direct marketers exploit these differences by offering products and services fitted to individual groups' needs.

Applying market segmentation involves a three-stage process:

1. Identifying segments.
2. Selecting target segments.
3. Creating a marketing mix for each target segment.

Identifying Segments

The identification of segments involves establishing a basis for dividing consumers or businesses into groups with similar characteristics and needs. Members of each consumer or business are expected to behave similarly with respect to a particular product or service. This results in a set of segments whose members are more similar to one another than to members of other potential target market groups. Each segment is created to be as homogeneous as possible.

Selecting Target Segments

Once the segments are identified, individual target markets for a firm's products or services are selected based on the expectation of obtaining a differential response. For sound segmentation, there must be a clear difference between the responses of people who make up one group and those who compose another. If the response to a direct marketing offer is the same by all types of people, there is no need to be selective; they might as well have been treated as one group.

Although direct marketing shares with general, image-oriented marketing an interest in identifying and pursuing groups of consumers or businesses with common needs and preferences, the personal nature of direct marketing efforts makes it even more important that sales appeals are tailored to particular groups of individuals. In fact, the ability to segment markets on the basis of actual response gives direct marketing its greatest strength. There are no ambiguities about the relationship between marketing action and the buyer's response. Prospects either place an order or not.

Creating a Marketing Mix for Each Target Segment

After identifying and selecting segments, the direct marketer creates the marketing mix of product, price, promotion, and distribution to appeal to each targeted segment. This involves understanding the specific needs of the target segment with respect to what members want to buy, how much they want to pay, how they want to shop, and what will motivate them to make a purchase.

This chapter examines how direct marketing firms can identify and select segments for their marketing efforts. It begins with the idea that targeting specific individuals or businesses increases the response rate to direct marketing offers and continues by identifying the segmentation alternatives most relevant to the practice of direct marketing; it next reviews the requirements for successful segmentation and, finally, examines various types of segmentation.

TARGETING INDIVIDUALS

Unlike general advertising or sales promotion, direct marketing frequently targets specific individuals. Mailing pieces usually have names and addresses, and telephone calls are directed at specific homes or business locations. Although direct-response radio and direct-response television are still fundamentally mass-market tools, changes in communications technology may allow marketers to reach more specific segments via these media. Magazines are improving their ability to pursue individuals, including the ability to place the name of a person on a magazine or within a magazine advertisement.

This specificity in targeting significantly increases direct marketing's offer response rates. But to work properly, communications targeted at individuals must be managed by using computerized records of what is mailed or who is called and what responses are received. These capabilities are expanding as database technologies allow direct marketers to utilize lists with demographics and purchase histories to define who receives their product and service solicitations. Although there are some difficulties in using the more advanced techniques, their great potential virtually guarantees that use of these segmentation options will continue to expand.

Computer terminology refers to the smallest unit of analysis in a database as a record. When direct marketers are targeting individuals, the individual record becomes what Katzenstein and Sachs call a basic information unit (BIU), upon which direct marketing campaigns are based.[1] Because the BIU is the smallest unit for which information is kept about prospects and customers, direct marketers can customize their offerings to individuals or selected groups of individuals in targeting their marketing efforts.

TARGETING BUSINESSES

For the most part, the segmentation options available for the business-to-business direct marketer are similar to those used by direct marketers who target individuals. There are, however, some major differences. The specific variables used within particular segmentation dimensions differ between consumer and industrial segmentation analysis. In business-to-business direct marketing, demographic variables such as income and geographic location have different meanings, although they describe similar concepts. The income of a household describes how much money individuals living under one roof earn. For a business firm, income usually refers to how much money the company makes, and, in its most colloquial sense, the term *income* is used interchangeably with the term *revenue*. Regardless, the interest in business-to-business direct marketing is with the basic financial statistics of an organization, including its total sales revenues and sales by division or product line.

Although most of the bases for consumer and business-to-business direct marketing are similar, the value of those segmentation variables varies significantly. For example, while psychographics are important to firms targeting individuals, they are relatively unimportant to those targeting businesses. Similarly, while sociocultural variables such as social group membership provide a basis for segmentation in consumer direct marketing, they have no analog in business-to-business marketing. Direct marketers targeting individuals use segmentation based on cultural background, social class, and family life-cycle stage, but those targeting industries do not.

Some additional segmenting bases particularly suited for industrial markets do not have a comparable application or are seldom applied in consumer markets. These include Standard Industrial Classification (SIC) codes and end-use analysis. SIC codes are one of the simplest and potentially most valuable industrial segmentation variables. These codes are statistical government data used by business-to-business direct marketers to classify customers and/or suppliers by economic activity, including such divisions as agriculture, mining, construction, manufacturing, transportation, wholesale trade, retail trade, financial services, and public administration. (See Chapter 15 for a more detailed discussion of SIC codes.) End-use analysis focuses on segmenting based on whether and how a business-to-business marketer uses industrial products, including raw materials, work-in-process, and finished goods. This end use has an impact on the purchase decision and therefore provides a basis for segmenting industrial markets.

SEGMENTATION ALTERNATIVES

While direct marketers can segment at the individual level with media such as direct mail and telemarketing, that ability is also constrained by whether a given medium operates at the individual versus the mass level. Although direct-mail segmentations can pursue individuals with specific demographic characteristics by location and name, direct-response television relies on the same broad demographic definitions as general advertising because television is a mass-market medium. However, as the number of channels increases and more specialized channels emerge, this broadcast medium will become less mass and more individualized. With the future advent of customized programming and advertising for each home, direct marketers will have the ability to target persons through their television sets in the same way they can now use the mail.

Note that while this chapter covers various forms of segmentation, some approaches may not be very useful in defining target markets in conjunction with particular direct marketing media such as direct mail versus direct-response television. In media selection (discussed in Chapters 8 through 14), the broad range of ways in which individuals can be targeted is constrained by whether a medium has its information organized by a chosen characteristic. For example, while it is relatively easy to reach individuals or businesses based on demographic characteristics, there is a problem with psychological attributes such as timidity or aggressiveness. In contrast, as you will see in Chapter 8, almost any segmentation characteristic can form the basis for developing a direct marketing campaign creative strategy (what to say in a direct-mail piece, direct-response television ad, etc.) designed to motivate prospects to purchase products or services. Thus, the demographic, psychological, and other segmentation variables discussed below play different roles depending on whether the context is media-related prospect targeting or creative strategy development.

Some marketers argue that segmentation schemes that cannot be applied directly to the process of message delivery should not be used. However, that would significantly impact the richness of creative work and the selling potential of the appeals produced from a comprehensive understanding of target market members based on lifestyle, product or service preferences, and behavioral characteristics.

REQUIREMENTS FOR SEGMENTATION

Kotler lists four requirements for effective segmentation in general marketing: the ability to measure the segment and its characteristics; the size of the segment, which should be large enough to be serviced profitably by the firm; the accessibility of the segment via the media available to the firm; and the actionability of the segment.[2] According to Katzenstein and Sachs, the most often cited requirements for segmentation in direct marketing are substantiality, differential response, identification, stability, and accessibility.[3] Each of these is discussed in the following sections.

Substantiality

Substantiality is a matter of relative size. What may be adequate for one firm may be inadequate for another. A large firm may find a particular segment to be unattractive, while a smaller firm may have the opposite perspective.

Differential Response

As mentioned earlier, for segmentation to occur, groups of consumers or businesses must have unique and definable characteristics associated with a particular buyer behavior. This focus on correctly targeting market segments with higher propensities to buy results in higher response rates to offers and therefore to more profitable direct marketing efforts.

Identification

Market segmentation is fundamentally about quantifying the existence of target markets and using that statistical information to manage a direct marketing program. Thus, market segmentation both allocates resources and helps ensure that direct marketing efforts are productive. However, segment identification approaches that cannot also serve as a basis for reaching a target market, as opposed to just characterizing that market, are of limited usefulness. As noted previously, while it is interesting to know the psychological attributes that distinguish a firm's customers, these attributes do not form a practical basis for identifying segments for the purpose of mailing or broadcasting an offer. Nevertheless, the attributes may provide the basis for developing the creative strategy in marketing a product or service.

Stability

Marketers should target segments that are relatively stable over time. Those that lack such stability include ones formed around a fashion that changes radically in a short time. Direct marketers in particular make money by establishing long-term relationships with their customers. Few firms make a profit from the first or only purchase a customer makes from a firm. This means that direct marketing firms may consider segmentation as a long-term investment.

Accessibility

As noted previously, accessibility and identification go hand-in-hand. Accessible target market segments are efficiently reachable through one or more media that best communicate a direct marketer's offer. The efficiency of a medium and its ability to reach particular groups of customers and prospects varies by who the direct marketer is attempting to reach and how the offer is communicated. If a product is targeted at upscale consumers with an interest in foreign travel, then direct-mail offers should be sent to a list of upper-income households. If another product is for working women who have little time to shop for furniture, then a combination of direct-response television and radio ads may be the best choice.

The chapters in this book devoted to individual direct marketing media discuss the efficiencies associated with pursuing particular target markets. Each medium has its own particular costs and efficiencies that usually relate to the expense associated with reaching every 1,000 participants in that medium. For example, to run a 30-second direct-response television ad for a music collection on MTV, the cost is about $18 per 1,000 viewers; with an average audience of about 5 million, the total cost for one showing of that ad would be $90,000. Also, because direct-response ads are run many times in the course of making the offer known to the campaign's target segment, an MTV direct-response effort becomes quite expensive; if the offer is made 25 times, the total cost for the campaign would be $2,250,000.

TYPES OF SEGMENTATION

According to Schiffman and Kanuk, the criteria used to segment markets are of seven types: geographic, demographic, geodemographic, psychological, sociocultural, user behavior, and benefits sought.[4] These classifications can be broken down into innumerable subcategories; the only limitation is the imagination of the marketer. Schiffman and Kanuk's categories for segmenting markets are shown in Table 3.1. These criteria can be used independently or in combination. These single or multiple variables are then associated with estimates or data about segment offer response rates to yield target markets with unique combinations of characteristics or with ways of creating offers that motivate members of the segment to engage in buyer behavior.

Geographic Segmentation

Geographic segmentation assumes that prospects who are in the same area have similar needs that are different from those of people living in other areas. Direct marketers have found geographic differences by climate, extent of urbanization,

TABLE 3.1. Bases for Segmentation

GEOGRAPHIC SEGMENTATION	
Region	North, South, East, West
City size	Major metropolitan areas, small cities, towns
Density of area	Urban, suburban, exurban, rural
Climate	Temperate, hot, humid
DEMOGRAPHIC SEGMENTATION	
Age	Under 11, 12–17, 18–34, 35–49, 50–64, 65–74, 75+
Sex	Male, female
Marital status	Single, married, divorced, living together
Income	Under $15,000; $15,000–$24,999; $25,000–$39,999; $40,000–$64,999; over $65,000
Occupation	Professional, blue-collar, white-collar, agricultural
Education	Some high school, high school graduate, some college, college graduate, postgraduate
GEODEMOGRAPHIC SEGMENTATION	
Category	Young Suburbia, Blue-Blood Estates
PSYCHOLOGICAL SEGMENTATION	
Personality	Extroverts, introverts, aggressives, compliants
Lifestyle	Swingers, straights, conservatives, status seekers
SOCIOCULTURAL SEGMENTATION	
Culture	American, Italian, Chinese, Mexican
Subculture	
Religion	Jewish, Catholic, Protestant, other
Race	Black, Caucasian, Oriental, Hispanic
Social class	Lower, middle, upper
Family life cycle	Bachelors, young marrieds, empty nesters
USE BEHAVIOR SEGMENTATION	
Usage situation	Home, vacation, gift, weekend
Usage rate	Heavy, medium, light users, nonusers
User status	Unaware, aware, interested, enthusiastic
Brand loyalty	None, medium, strong
BENEFIT SEGMENTATION	
Benefit	Convenience, prestige, economy

Source: Leon G. Schiffman and Leslie Larzar Kanuk, *Consumer Behavior,* 4th ed. (Englewood Cliffs, NJ: Prentice Hall, 1991), p. 29.

and other such factors to be quite useful. They have also observed divergent purchasing patterns in areas that are geographically disparate.

Geography is the starting point in an industrial segmentation that divides markets by market scope factors (local/regional, national, or international) and geographic market measures. Potential customer density, standardized market areas, and census classifications are of primary importance to the business-to-business marketer. Also, such sources as *Sales and Marketing Management* magazine and U.S. government business census reports help firms target specific industries, states, or counties. Through these sources, industrial marketers can better identify market areas, define and measure sales area potential, direct promotional activities, and evaluate the success of their marketing activities.

Demographic Segmentation

Demographic characteristics are the most accessible and cost-effective means by which to identify target markets and therefore the most frequent basis for segmentation in direct marketing. Direct marketers use the age, income, and education statistics of the population to target mailings and telemarketing. For example, the Home Shopping Network (HSN) estimates that most of its customers are middle-income consumers between the ages of 45 and 55. Some 70 percent of them are women. HSN uses this information to guide what products it sells and what prices to charge.

Business demographics are similar in concept and purpose to consumer demographics but vary in their application. Businesses define market size by the number of potential customers; number of stores, locations, or plants; number of employees; years in business; technical emphasis; and so on. In contrast, consumer demographics emphasize population characteristics such as number of households, household size, income, age, and social class.

In the consumer market, many direct marketers are fighting for a share of the highly profitable mature or senior marketplace. Seniors in the United States number about 56 million and make up the fastest-growing population segment. These people have buying power, and they use it. Anyone over age 50 is a member of the "senior market" category. If a firm is selling health or insurance or investments, the senior market has some singular characteristics that demand special attention. For example, an astute direct marketer recognizes that retirement from the workforce is a major lifestyle change and that the shift into Medicare age eliminates an individual as a target for primary health insurance. However, that same individual becomes a far more receptive target for supplementary coverage, one of the most competitive of all mail-order fields.

Geodemographic Segmentation

Geodemographic segmentation is based on experience showing that consumers who live next to one another have similar incomes, needs, and lifestyles. Geodemographics describes the demographics of households in specific geographic areas by zip code and other U.S. Census designations. The availability of geodemographic information, the increasing power of computers, and the emergence of very sophisticated analytical techniques have all contributed to the growing popularity of geodemographic segmentation with direct marketers.

A number of firms specialize in producing computer-generated geodemographic market "clusters" of like consumers that are very useful to direct marketers. Those firms have clustered the 250,000 neighborhoods in the United

States into 10 to 48 lifestyle groups using information on 36,000 zip codes. Specific clusters usually include similar neighborhoods that are geographically dispersed so that neighborhoods composed of people with similar lifestyles are found scattered throughout the country. Marketers use the cluster data for direct-mail campaigns, retail site selection, and merchandise mix development.

Geodemographic clustering is not new. For example, since 1950, the White Flower Farm, a mail-order nursery of perennial flowers, shrubs, and bulbs, has been sending its 120-page catalog to homeowners living in zip codes defined by their incomes, planting conditions, and shipping distance. Similarly, the Dial-a-Dinner service in Manhattan offers home and office delivery of foods from 18 New York City restaurants. Based on their zip code, some 150,000 people are sent a 32-page catalog listing the menus of participating restaurants.

To support the targeting efforts of direct markets, Claritas/NPDC provides geodemographic data through its Potential Rating Index for Zip Markets (PRIZM) segmentation system. There are two versions. The first breaks down 500,000 U.S. neighborhoods into 40 clusters with similar demographic profiles like "Shotguns and Pick-ups" (blue-collar, lower-middle income) and "Blue-Chip Blues" (high school grads who pay their bills). The second version of PRIZM adds new clusters and subdivides old ones, increasing the number of clusters by more than 50 percent, to 62.

PRIZM is important because it looks at the United States as not just 50 states but rather 40 or more neighborhood types, each with its own distinctive boundaries, values, and buying habits. These clusters reflect the realities associated with how different consumers live. The PRIZM service is widely used by direct mailers to target consumers with specific geodemographic characteristics based on neighborhood lifestyle information. PRIZM's original 40 clusters (which also group into 12 broader social groups) are listed in Table 3.2. A comparison of two distinct PRIZM clusters, "Pools & Patios" and "Heavy Industry" is shown in Table 3.3.

A segmentation of young suburbanites helped the *Courier,* a newspaper in Evanston, Illinois, sell subscriptions more effectively. The *Courier* identified three predominant PRIZM clusters in its subscriber base: "Blue-Chip Blues," "Young Suburbia" (highly mobile thirty-somethings), and "God's Country" (white-collar baby boomers with a $50,000 median income). The *Courier* sent 1,000 prospect households a newspaper, supplements, and a letter from the company president offering a 30-day free trial. Overall, 24 percent of respondents did subscribe to the newspaper when the trial period was over.

ClusterPlus 2000, the demographic-segmentation system from Strategic Mapping Inc., has 60 neighborhood clusters. The firm's most complex system has more than seven times the level of detail compared with PRIZM, for a total of 450 so-called atomic clusters that represent specific target markets containing several hundred thousand households.

Psychological Segmentation

Psychological segmentation is based on intrinsic qualities of individuals. If available, such qualities enhance the targeting done by direct marketers primarily

TABLE 3.2. America's 40 Neighborhood Types: PRIZM

PRIZM Cluster	Thumbnail Description	Percentage of U.S. Households
Blue-Blood Estates	America's wealthiest neighborhoods, including suburban homes and 1 in 10 millionaires	1.1
Money & Brains	Posh big-city enclaves of townhouses, houses, condos, and apartments	0.9
Furs & Station Wagons	New money in metropolitan bedroom suburbs	3.8
Urban Gold Coast	Upscale urban high-rise districts	0.4
Pools & Patios	Older, upper-middle-class, suburban communities	3.3
Two More Rungs	Comfortable multiethnic suburbs	0.7
Young Influentials	Yuppie, fringe-city condo and apartment developments	3.0
Young Suburbia	Child-rearing, outlying suburbs	6.3
God's Country	Upscale frontier boomtowns	3.3
Blue-Chip Blues	The wealthiest blue-collar suburbs	6.2
Bohemian Mix	Inner-city bohemian enclaves à la Greenwich Village	1.0
Levittown, USA	Aging, post–World War II tract subdivisions	2.9
Gray Power	Upper-middle-class retirement communities	3.1
Black Enterprise	Predominantly black, middle- and upper-middle-class neighborhoods	0.7
New Beginnings	Fringe-city areas of singles complexes, garden apartments, and trim bungalows	4.1
Blue-Collar Nursery	Middle-class, child-rearing towns	2.3
New Homesteaders	Exurban boom towns of young midscale families	4.8
New Melting Pot	New immigrant neighborhoods, primarily in the nation's port cities	0.8
Towns & Gowns	America's college towns	1.6
Rank & File	Older, blue-collar industrial suburbs	1.3
Middle America	Midscale, midsize towns	3.2
Old Yankee Rows	Working-class rowhouse districts	1.4
Coalburg & Corntown	Small towns based on light industry and farming	2.0
Shotguns & Pickups	Crossroads villages serving the nation's lumber and breadbasket needs	1.9
Golden Ponds	Rustic cottage communities located near the coasts, in the mountains, or alongside lakes	5.0
Agribusiness	Small rural towns surrounded by large-scale farms and ranches	2.1
Emergent Minorities	Predominantly black, working-class city neighborhoods	1.5
Single City Blues	Downscale, urban singles districts	3.2
Mines & Mills	Struggling steel towns and mining villages	3.0
Back-Country Folks	Remote, downscale farm towns	3.4
Norma Rae-ville	Lower-middle-class milltowns and industrial suburbs, mainly in the South	2.3
Smalltown Downtown	Inner-city districts of small industrial cities	2.2
Grain Belt	The nation's most sparsely populated rural communities	1.2
Heavy Industry	Lower-working-class districts in the nation's oldest industrial cities	2.4
Share Croppers	Primarily southern hamlets devoted to farming and light industry	3.8
Downtown Dixie Style	Aging, predominantly black neighborhoods, typically in Southern cities	2.9
Hispanic Mix	America's Hispanic barrios	1.6
Tobacco Roads	Predominantly black farm communities throughout the South	1.2
Hard Scrabble	The nation's poorest rural settlements	1.5
Public Assistance	America's inner-city ghettos	2.5

Source: Art Weinstein, *Market Segmentation,* 2nd ed. (Chicago, IL: Probus, 1994), pp. 91–93.

TABLE 3.3. A Comparison of Two PRIZM Clusters

	Pools & Patios	Heavy Industry
You are	45 to 64	55 plus
You have	A college degree, grown children	Some high school education, grown children
Your home is in	Fairfield, CT, or Los Angeles, CA	Newark, NJ, or Pawtucket, RI
Your job is	White collar	Blue collar
You travel by	Cruiseship	Railroad
You like	Civic clubs, golf, mutual funds	Asthma remedies, ale, auto racing
You don't like	Roller derbies, gospel music	Compact pickup trucks, billiards
You read	*The Wall St. Journal, The New Yorker*	*The Star, Modern Bride*
You don't read	*Hot Rod, Essence, Harper's*	*Nation's Business, Grit*
You drive	Alfa Romeos, BMWs, Peugeots	Dodge Aries, Chevrolet Citations
You don't drive	Ford Fairmonts, Dodge Diplomats	Audis, Saab 9000s
You eat	Natural cereal, dry soup	Meat sticks, English muffins
You don't eat	Whole milk, meat sticks	Popcorn, frozen yogurt
You watch	*60 Minutes*	*Donahue, Nightline*
You don't watch	*Another World*	*The Today Show*

Source: Art Weinstein, *Market Segmentation,* 2nd ed. (Chicago, IL: Probus, 1994), p. 93.

when they develop the creative materials for a campaign or specific offer. However, intrinsic psychological attributes such as aggressiveness do not provide a basis for targeting individuals or groups through such media as direct mail or direct-response radio. These types of personality characteristics are probably the least used segmentation variable in direct marketing.

Psychological segmentation also includes the concept of lifestyle. This describes a consumer's orientation to life and how to live, including attitudes, opinions, and interests. Consumer segments are assigned such labels as swingers, straights, conservatives, and status seekers. The geodemographic segmentations described previously also use lifestyle concepts to identify consumer clusters.

Changing lifestyles play a major role in determining the product benefits important to consumers, providing marketers with opportunities for new products and services or the repositioning of existing offerings. Changing lifestyles also provide opportunities for modified versions of existing products.

The success of the Spiegel catalog can be traced to the firm's understanding of women's lifestyles. During the 1970s, the catalog was repositioned to target the emerging market of working women. This meant catering to their need for fashionable name brands in a way that was convenient given a busy schedule. This high-end merchandise strategy is consistent with the upscale target market of the catalog. It has been backed by an emphasis on product, service, and image that has differentiated Spiegel from its competition.

The success of Lillian Vernon is also the result of focusing on the working-women trend. Lillian Vernon is a 44-year-old specialty catalog company offering its mostly women customers gifts, household items, and gardening accessories, among other product lines. Like Spiegel, this firm recognized that catalogs gave working women a way to shop without using up their leisure time.

Lifestyle, personality, or psychographic factors are not often used in segmenting industrial markets. However, because individuals ultimately make all purchase decisions, psychographic analysis can be used for understanding purchase behavior and associated influences. As with psychographics, perceptions by individuals are not often used in business-to-business segments for direct marketing.

Sociocultural Segmentation

Sociocultural variables such as sociological (group) and anthropological (cultural) variables provide another basis for segmentation in direct marketing. Direct marketers have successfully created marketing plans based on targeting segments using cultural and subcultural group membership, social class, and family life-cycle stage.

Some direct marketers have found it useful to segment their domestic and international markets on the basis of cultural heritage, because members of the same society tend to share the values, beliefs, and customs. However, cultural segmentation is more useful when marketing internationally, where cultural differences are important factors in defining target markets. In those cases, it is important for the marketer to understand the beliefs, values, and customs of the countries into which the firm's products or services are sold.

Social class (or relative status in the community) is a popular market segmentation variable with direct marketers because it is constructed from several demographic variables, including education, occupation, and income. Consumers in different social classes vary enough in their values, product preferences, and buying habits to justify entire direct marketing plans organized around the differences between members of such groups as the working class versus the upper middle class.

Stage in the family life cycle is another basis for market segmentation in direct marketing. The family life-cycle stages are also derivable from demographic information, making them attractive to those direct marketers targeting consumers at specific stages. The stages are related to transitional periods in the lives of most individuals such as bachelorhood, marriage, parenthood, postparenthood, and dissolution, which is associated with the death of a spouse in old age.

User Behavior Segmentation

User behavior segmentation is of interest because it recognizes the importance of occasion in product choice. Direct marketers have found user behavior characteristics such as usage rate, user status, and degree of brand loyalty helpful in selecting target markets. Because direct marketers have databases on the purchase behavior of their customers, marketing plans can be built around targeting the better customers in ways not possible for general marketers. Computer technology makes it possible to pursue segments with database models that link particular response rates with special offers, seasonal promotions, and price levels. As a result, new offers can be made more relevant to buyers by being individualized according to what those buyers have historically purchased. For example,

Helzberg Diamonds, a national retailer of jewelry products with 150 stores, makes extensive use of its customer database to direct offers of gift certificates and other sales incentives designed to promote the sales of high-ticket items such as rings and watches. The firm particularly focuses on heavy buyers of jewelry items based on purchase information from its store records.

A criticism of these heavy-user strategies is that purchase data only reveal past behavior. That people were attracted to certain products by past merchandising, promotion, and pricing decisions does not necessarily make them the best potential class of future customers. The argument has some merit but little evidence to support it. Past behavior is normally the best predictor of future behavior.

Analyzing consumption patterns of existing and potential customers can be an important segmenting dimension in industrial markets, particularly in segmenting markets by users versus nonusers. There are several possibilities for workable classifications of users, including heavy versus medium versus light users (based on unit or dollar sales or number of orders); users of a firm's product or service versus the users of competitors' offerings; and loyal versus nonloyal customers.

Benefit Segmentation

Marketers have effectively segmented by clustering consumers or businesses into groups according to the *benefits* they seek. Products and services can be positioned in terms of the benefits or attributes that satisfy particular needs, regardless of whether those needs are utilitarian or emotional. The satisfaction of utilitarian needs implies an emphasis on the objective, tangible attributes of products. Emotional needs are subjective and experiential, such as the need for excitement, self-confidence, or fantasy. Of course, prospects may be motivated to purchase a product because it provides both types of benefits. The benefits a customer seeks reflect that person's lifestyle, values, and habits (past purchase behavior) and the benefits a business seeks reflect its operational priorities and needs.

By segmenting industrial markets through benefits sought, direct marketing strategies can be tailored to the needs of specific customer sectors. For business markets, utilitarian benefits tend to be more important. Businesses may purchase a fleet of cars based on such factors as price and reliability, while consumers may purchase a car for their own use based first on style and prestige and secondarily on price and reliability.

Benefit segmentation in consumer direct marketing frequently extends beyond product features to satisfying physical, emotional, or psychological needs. The Mary Kay cosmetics ad in Exhibit 3.1 explicitly lists the benefits offered by the firm's *Triple-Action*™ Eye Enhancer, which primarily includes three beauty benefits. Readers are invited to take the ad to their Mary Kay beauty consultant or to call an 800 number to locate a consultant.

EXHIBIT 3.1. Mary Kay Cosmetics

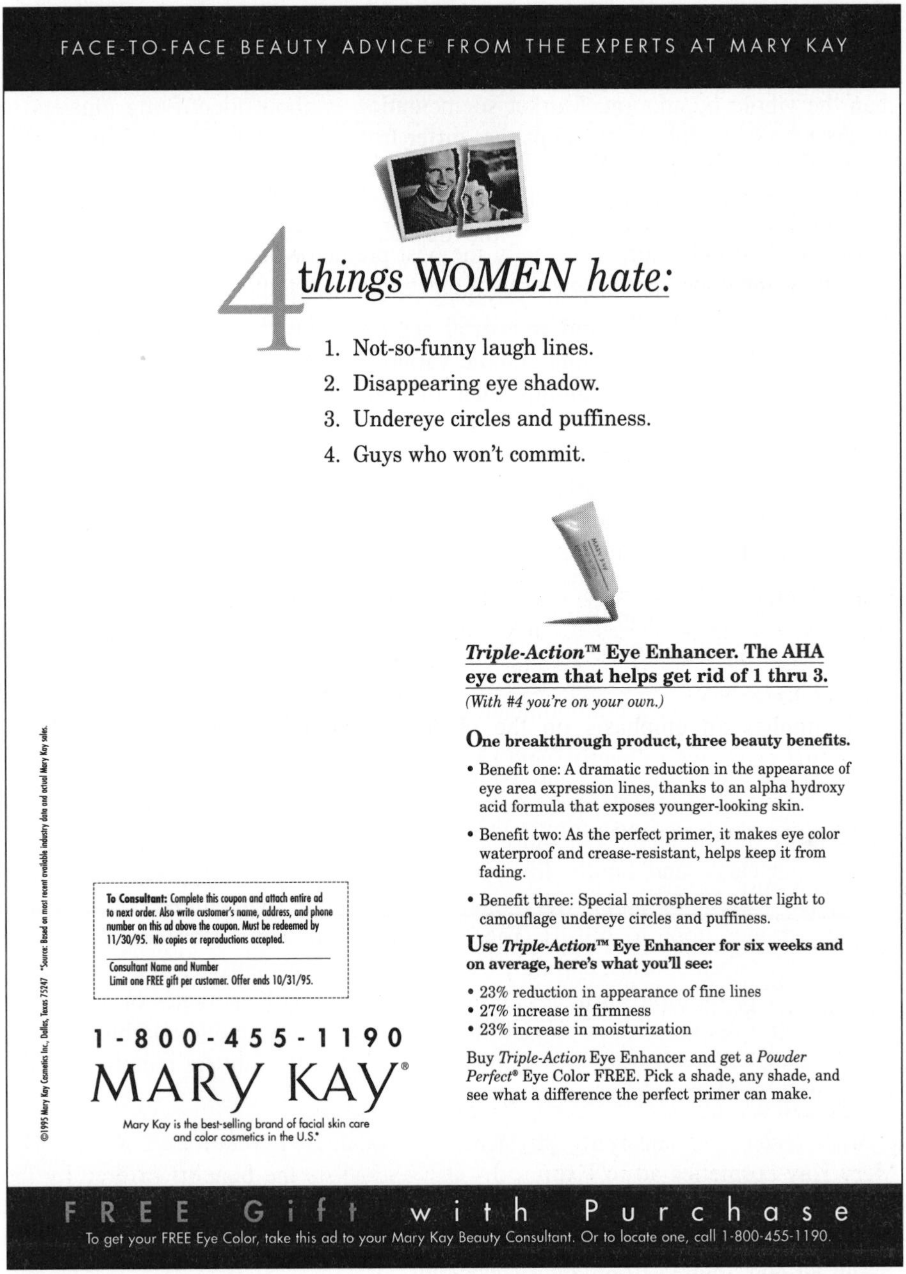

SUMMARY

Direct marketing strategies use market segmentation to focus on particular population subsets that are expected to be more responsive to what a firm is selling than the whole population. Market segmentation is about identifying clusters of buyers who form cohesive groups that differ from one another as to their specific needs. This contributes to the development of strategies with marketing mixes that best fit demand for specific products and services.

The segmentation options for the business-to-business direct marketer are similar to those for marketers that target consumers. There are, however, major differences because the specific variables used within segmentation dimensions differ between consumer and industrial segmentation analysis. In business-to-business direct marketing, demographic variables such as income and geographic location have different meanings than in consumer marketing, although they describe similar concepts.

The segmentation requirements of direct marketing are similar to those of general marketing. They include substantiality, differential response, identification, stability, and accessibility. Substantiality refers to the relative size of a particular segment. Differential response describes whether a target market has a higher propensity to buy. Identification is about being able to quantify the existence of target markets and to use that statistical information as the basis for managing a marketing program. Stability indicates whether target segments are relatively stable over time. Accessible target market segments are efficiently reachable through one or more media that best communicate a direct marketer's offer.

Direct marketers use seven types of segmentation: geographic (location), demographic (age, income, and education statistics), geodemographic (demographics of households in specific geographic areas), psychological (intrinsic qualities of individuals), sociocultural (cultural and subcultural group membership, social class, and family life-cycle stage), user behavior (usage rate, user status, and degree of brand loyalty), and benefits sought (what needs consumers or business groups hope to fulfill). These classifications can be broken down into innumerable subcategories, and they can be used independently or in combination. These single or multiple variables are then associated with estimates or data about segment offer response rates to yield target markets with unique combinations of characteristics or with ways of creating offers that will motivate members of the segment to purchase a product or service.

REVIEW QUESTIONS

1. How is market segmentation used in direct marketing? How is segmentation used differently in direct marketing versus general marketing?
2. General marketing campaigns target large groups of individuals, while direct marketing campaigns target specific individuals who are members of groups. What is meant by the observation that direct marketers target specific individuals?
3. How does computer technology contribute to the ability of direct marketers to target individuals?

4. **What is the three-stage process involved in applying market segmentation? How does that process influence a direct marketing strategy?**
5. **What are the differences and similarities in targeting individuals versus businesses with direct marketing efforts?**
6. **According to Katzenstein and Sachs, what are the requirements for segmentation in direct marketing? How does each of those requirements contribute to better market segmentations?**
7. **What are the seven market segmentation types, and how can each be used in direct marketing efforts?**

NOTES

1. Herbert Katzenstein and Williams S. Sachs, *Direct Marketing,* 2nd ed. (New York: Macmillan, 1992), pp. 117–118.
2. Philip Kotler, *Marketing Management,* 7th ed. (Englewood Cliffs, NJ: Prentice Hall, 1991), p. 278.
3. Katzenstein and Sachs, *Direct Marketing,* pp. 116–117.
4. Leon G. Schiffman and Leslie Larzar Kanuk, *Consumer Behavior,* 4th ed. (Englewood Cliffs, NJ: Prentice Hall, 1991), pp. 29–45.

SOURCES

BAUMAN, RISA. "A New Dawn for Home Shopping." *Direct,* January 1993, pp. 1, 16.

BURKA, KAREN. "Moving Targets." *Direct,* January 1994, pp. 36–40.

DEL VALLE, CHRISTINA, and JON BERRY. "They Know Where You Live—And How You Buy." *Business Week,* February 7, 1994, p. 89.

EGOL, LEN. "Mapping Goes Big Time." *Direct,* November 1994, pp. 1, 24–25.

FISHER, MANFRED M., and PETER NIJKAMP, eds. *Geographic Information Systems, Spatial Modelling, and Policy Evaluation.* New York: Springer-Verlag, 1993.

HAMILTON, RICHARD A. "Quantitative Direct Response Market Segmentation." *Readings & Cases in Direct Marketing,* ed. Herbert E. Brown and Bruce Buskirk. Lincolnwood, IL: NTC Business Books, 1989, pp. 137–47.

KATZENSTEIN, HERBERT, and WILLIAMS S. SACHS. *Direct Marketing,* 2nd ed. New York Macmillan, 1992.

KOTLER, PHILIP. *Marketing Management,* 7th ed. Englewood Cliffs, NJ: Prentice Hall, 1991.

LEWIS, HERSCHELL GORDON. "Another Look at the Senior Market." *Direct Marketing,* March 1996, pp. 20–23.

MARX, WENDY. "The New Segmentation of One," *Direct,* September 1994 pp. 45–48.

MUMMERT, HALLIE. "Reaching Out to Women." *Target Marketing* 18, no. 8 (August 1995), pp. 33–38.

ROBERTS, MARY LOU, and PAUL D. BERGER. *Direct Marketing Management.* Englewood Cliffs, NJ: Prentice Hall, 1989.

SCHIFFMAN, LEON G., and LESLIE LARZAR KANUK. *Consumer Behavior,* 4th ed. Englewood Cliffs, NJ: Prentice Hall, 1991.

STONE, BOB. *Direct Marketing Success Stories.* Lincolnwood, IL: NTC Books, 1995.

________. *Successful Direct Marketing Methods,* 5th ed. Lincolnwood, IL: NTC Books, 1995.

WEINSTEIN, ART. *Market Segmentation,* 2nd ed. Chicago: Probus, 1994.

WEISS, MICHAEL J. *The Clustering of America.* New York: Harper & Row, 1988.

CHAPTER 4

Direct Marketing and Technology

OBJECTIVES

1. To explore how changes in technology, particularly in communications and computers, are affecting the direct marketing industry.
2. To examine the opportunities and challenges that technological innovations are creating for direct marketers.
3. To describe how direct marketers are using the emerging technological innovations to better communicate with their target markets.

INTRODUCTION

Changes in technology, particularly in communications and computers, are profoundly influencing how products and services are marketed to both consumers and businesses. Media formats are proliferating, with the expansion of cable television; the growth in satellite access; the popularity of online services; and, more generally, the significant fragmentation of all media. For example, over the last 30 years, magazines have become less general and more specialized. As technological innovations are diffusing into the lives of consumers and the operation of businesses, a revolution is occurring that provides direct marketers with new opportunities and challenges.

The new technologies available to direct marketers have produced a substantial increase in the ability to divide consumer and industrial markets into target segments. The nature of competition among companies has also changed rapidly; many firms are concentrating on serving specialized niches. In today's highly competitive environment, direct marketers can no longer prosper without plans to address the needs of a multitude of market segments.

Many important technological changes have occurred in the communications and home entertainment industries. In the past decade, the number of television channels in the average home quadrupled, from 9 to 38, primarily due to the growth of cable networks, satellites, and independent stations. With digital compression and the development of electronic superhighways, many people in the home entertainment industry anticipate 500 channels in every home. Not only will this proliferation of channels change viewer habits; it also presents 500 reasons why cable and satellite television will change as direct marketing media.

Beyond the expansion of passive television to 500 channels is the emergence of two-way interactive electronic communications with the consumer. Companies now are competing with one another to establish an electronic superhighway that will bring interactive programming services to America's living rooms. Interactive programming will offer consumers personalized news, films on demand, grocery-shopping services, classes from the local university, phone-call screening, games, and much more.

In an environment exploding with communications choices, direct marketers will continue to use all forms of media to directly contact and elicit responses from their target markets. Such innovations as interactive television and online services will allow direct marketers to logically extend the strategies and tactics they employ today. Many are keenly aware of how direct-response television and print can be used as a means of interesting prospects in what is being sold. Even general marketers are recognizing that increasingly fragmented product lines, markets, and media are making it less efficient to pursue target audiences by spending ad dollars on campaigns blanketing an entire market.

While much of the discussion in this chapter revolves around what can happen and is happening, the focus is on those technologies that are expected to have the most significant impact on the nature and scope of direct marketing activities over the next 10 to 20 years. Although some of the discussion is speculative, the majority covers what is in progress now and in that sense represents a projection of current trends affecting the direct marketing industry. Also, this chapter describes innovations that satisfy the long-standing demand for greater targeting precision, it also explains how existing media options such as magazines, television, radio, and outdoor have significantly improved their ability to target advertising messages toward selective audience segments.

For example, *Newsweek* magazine was one of the first large-circulation consumer periodicals to introduce a printing technology called *selective binding.* New computerized printing techniques and databases allow advertisers to reach the subscribers they want based on a combination of demographics and purchase behavior. In addition to *Newsweek,* such diverse publications as *American Rifleman* and *PC Magazine* use the technique to customize their issues for readers by adding magazine pages related to the political district, technology interest, age, profession, and leisure activities of individual subscribers. This phenomenon is growing rapidly as more and more publishers and advertisers build databases on their subscribers and customers.

Television and radio stations also continue their movement toward a greater ability to personalize communications with their audiences. New programming formats are better meeting the needs of viewers and listeners, and are providing direct marketers with the specificity of target marketing they desire in attempting to reach particular geodemographic and psychographic groups. Cable television offers interest- and lifestyle-related programming in the form of the Golf Channel, the Sports Channel, and the Cooking Channel, among many others. In radio, musical tastes, political philosophy (in talk shows), sports interests, and religious orientation have long segmented audiences.

A 500-CHANNEL SYSTEM

For direct marketers, the emergence of a 500-channel system containing program-oriented networks, niche cable services, satellite-based channels, pay-per-view, and other offerings opens an unlimited number of advertising opportunities. It is clear that broad-based, advertiser-supported programming will be only a small part of what is available. Cable and satellite systems will experiment with more services, such as home shopping and banking. They will also use much of the new capacity for pay-per-view channels. Many cable networks and satellite-based systems will aim at small but loyal market niches, like avid golfers, and others may try to compete with existing news, sports, and music channels.

In this environment, the broadcast networks will likely continue to suffer audience erosion, and while they will still draw more viewers than cable and satellites, this may not be enough to keep them profitable. They are already being forced to take drastic measures to stay in business, including cutting employee compensation, withdrawing from broadcast time periods, specializing in news or sports shows, and merging with other programming entities. The networks are also changing their relationships with their affiliates by specializing in certain programming types and by engaging in programming practices pioneered by syndication (e.g., "multiplexing"). There is also a strong trend toward vertical integration that marries program suppliers with a network.

Like broadcasting networks, local television stations are also suffering audience losses, but they continue to gain in relative strength because of their unique ability to establish and build on a strong local identity with local news and other programming. Local stations are often asserting themselves more strongly versus the networks.

Cable is growing as an industry as it attracts more households, both to view television and to use other services. However, cable networks, as program suppliers, are increasingly challenged by competition on no-longer-scarce channel space.

As suppliers to local stations, syndicators are finding more opportunities to program new time periods as the stations become more assertive. As the networks' hold on them loosens, more producers find it advantageous to establish franchise agreements with stations, creating mini-networks in certain time periods, especially prime time. Some syndicators will establish franchise agreements with stations for certain time periods, becoming mini-networks. Many established cable networks, especially those without clear market niches, are finding their small ratings diminished further. New networks are more reliant than the older ones on scarce advertising revenues, and take longer to break even.

For direct marketers, the ability of niche networks to deliver a targeted audience in an age of viewer fragmentation leads to higher efficiencies, because those audiences contain a higher proportion of the persons the marketer actually wants to reach. Sophisticated cable and satellite technologies should let direct marketers reach consumers as they do now by direct mail and personalized mass-market magazines, with commercials targeted to individual households. The promise for advertisers is that the television will become an electronic mailbox.

The overall result of such a development will be that direct marketers will place ads not by show but by audience segment.

In television, advertisers will increasingly choose programs on the basis of reported or actual purchaser preferences rather than broad demographic profiles. In the absence of true electronic single-source data linking purchases to television viewing, new media research tools should allow media planners to link data sources that provide purchase information (scanner products, manufacturer information, or syndicated sources) to television ratings from such companies as A. C. Nielsen. This process will enable direct marketers to determine what consumers with various product usage behaviors are most likely to view.

INTERACTIVE TELEVISION

By the beginning of the 21st century, millions of people will be able to shop interactively by calling up product menus and examining specific items on their television screens via remote control. Today, when viewers see an item on the screen, they must call an operator or automated system to place an order, and they must wait for delivery. In the future, new communications and database technologies will automate this process and greatly expand the role of interactive shopping in retailing.

As mentioned earlier, the new age of television moves the medium from a passive to an interactive communications tool. The changes will be felt in two ways. Television schedules and channels will become obsolete as fully empowered consumers use menu-driven screens to decide both what and when they want to watch. The immediacy of a television commercial placed in scheduled program will disappear; advertising messages will occur at the viewer's convenience. Thus, a major revolution in the roles of program producers, distributors, and television channels is on the horizon. Moreover, of even greater consequence, television viewing will become a two-way adventure, rather than a passive experience. The records of each viewer's interactions with this medium will be a rich source of information for targeting efforts, and may replace more traditional audience measurement services entirely.

The general advertising industry is looking at developments in interactive television very closely because they offer the opportunity for demand-based advertisements, as well as new forms of advertising not currently available. These will include sponsorship of interactive menu screens, personal news and features, electronic shopping malls filled with long-form commercials and interactive sessions, electronic couponing, and two-way video conversations between home shoppers and retailers. Such advertising will become possible as the cable and telephone companies develop and install sophisticated switching technologies designed to send television programs and their commercials to specific target groups. All this creates new challenges to those who must try to deliver relevant messages to a target prospect or customer. The level of precision that will be necessary to market goods via interactive television far exceeds the geographic regional splits of broadcast television or the cable-company-level splits offered to direct marketers today. This precision, however, will allow direct marketers to offer unique versions of their product or service messages to consumers household by household.

INFOMERCIALS

As new technologies and programming concepts emerge, television infomercials are being looked at as a medium for reaching consumers with explanations and sales appeals for a variety of products and services. With the proliferation of media channels and formats and increasingly sophisticated production values, major advertising agencies and their clients are choosing infomercials as a way of expanding their businesses. Although infomercials were once the near-exclusive domain of pocket fishing poles and supersharp knives, today they are being used by several Fortune 500 companies, including Avon Products (see Case 1 at the end of this book). Infomercial programming also represents a tremendous opportunity for direct marketers to build databases of interested customers for current and future direct marketing activities.

Between 1991 and 1994, the number of infomercials increased by 119 percent. By the end of 1994, there were more than 170 infomercials on the air, driving nearly $1 billion in sales. Products sold through infomercials include self-improvement items, business opportunities, housewares, diet and weight loss products and services, automotive maintenance tools, crafts, beauty care items, entertainment, and fitness equipment.

By ignoring the traditional 30-second commercial boundaries, infomercials provide advertisers with a more conversational way of communicating detailed information, advice, and discounts on products and services. While infomercials today appear on broadcast or cable networks, and consumers must respond by telephone, tomorrow may see numerous, simultaneous showings of these messages across the predicted 500 or more channels, each of which may allow direct interaction with prospects on a highly selective basis.

HOME SHOPPING CHANNELS

Most of today's fare on home shopping television channels is the same as it has been for years: collectibles, clothing, small electronics, housewares, and jewelry. However, television shoppers of the future will be able to select from dozens of shopping channels and an extremely wide variety of goods. Major retailers such as Sears, Macy's, and Nordstroms will all have their channels. With 500 channels in every home, not only will there be a proliferation of programs from which consumers may order goods, but televised shopping will become a dominant direct marketing medium.

This technology-based expansion of home shopping channel opportunities overcomes obstacles to the growth of this form of retailing, including concerns about limited product selections and the unwillingness of consumers to sit for hours in front of their television to shop. With highly varied and selective merchandise offered across multiple channels, the shopping networks expect to increase their penetration of most consumer markets. Interactive shopping capabilities will offer consumers instant access to specific merchandise, eliminating the need to wait for products to rotate their appearance on the screen.

ONLINE SERVICES

Online services represent another way technology is affecting how people entertain themselves and shop. America Online (AOL), CompuServe, the Microsoft Network (MSN), and Prodigy Services are the leaders in providing a vehicle for direct marketers to display their products and receive customer orders online via personal computer (PC). Each offers a graphical user interface, making it easy for new computer shoppers to get started.

Prodigy offers online shopping, communications, and news service to over 2 million subscribers. It is accessible with a local call by 95 percent of the households in the United States. This "online shopping mall" provides customers with a wide range of products at prices comparable to those at retail outlets. This and other online malls are open around the clock, seven days a week. For example, Comp-u-Store Online is a shopping club available on several online services, including Prodigy, CompuServe, and America Online. Included in Comp-u-Store's product list of 250,000 items are books and magazines, home electronics, and automobile accessories.

Online Shopping

For consumers, using online shopping services can be simple and effective. Prodigy puts customers in touch with name-brand clothing at Spiegel, for instance. Sears, also available through Prodigy, offers a wide selection of items online. From their modems, business users can stock their offices with everything from paper clips to fax machines; executives can even obtain attaché cases.

Prodigy can also assist with the hassles of business travel to cities like New York. Prodigy's guide to New York includes information on nightlife, attractions, events, shopping, the weather, the lottery, dining, and lodging. Restaurants are listed in Prodigy's Mobil Travel Guide by cuisine.

About 15 banks offer home services through Prodigy, allowing customers to pay bills, receive statements, transfer funds, and open accounts. Major banks have had spotty results in encouraging customers to bank electronically, but four developments are changing that situation:

1. The automated teller machines and touch-tone telephone services provided by many banks have educated consumers.
2. As the prices of PCs have dropped, more customers have purchased one and can now link up with banks.
3. As more banks merge or fail, there will be fewer branches and longer lines.
4. New software and computer services are making electronic banking cheaper and easier than before.

In addition to regular banking services, more than 3,000 mutual funds can be researched through Prodigy. However, even though 25 percent of all U.S. households have money in mutual funds, few turn to their PCs to manage those funds.

Online Users

The main selling point for the online services is ease of use. They offer members easy access to general news, financial and business news (updated throughout the day), weather, sports, online encyclopedias, banking, stock quotes, and so on.

According to Prodigy's research, if you are a new Prodigy member, the chances are very good that you just purchased your first home computer. On an average day, Prodigy records 500,000 "sessions." (A session lasts from sign-on to sign-off on a single ID.) On that same average day, somewhere between 20 and 30 percent of Prodigy members will sign on at least once.

Some 60 percent of Prodigy users are adult males, 30 percent are adult females, and 10 percent are males and females under 18 years old. Some 10 percent of Prodigy members are over 55. Some 72 percent are married, with about 17 percent single (among which are, presumably, children) and 10 percent are divorced. These numbers seem to bear out Prodigy's orientation and initiative as a family service. Prodigy touts the attractive demographics of its audience, whose average household income is $70,000.

Consumer Needs

Several consumer needs are being satisfied by the online services:

1. *Prestige*. People gain esteem by being knowledgeable about and using the technology.
2. *Convenience*. Everything is available at consumers' fingertips; they do not have to leave the living room to shop.
3. *Instant gratification*. Formation is available when the user wants it, rather than at specified times.
4. *Novelty and excitement*. Consumers become part of the online community.
5. *Efficiency*. Consumers can engage in one-stop shopping.
6. *Ease of use*. All users have to do is just press the buttons.
7. *Timeliness*. Consumers have the advantage of "real-time" information, for example, when buying stocks.

Promotional strategies for online services focus on perceived benefits from service use such as those of convenience, value for the money, excitement, ease of use, and social interaction.

THE INTERNET

It is easy to forget how quickly the World Wide Web went from having a relatively small audience to gaining mass-market acceptance. But with consumer product companies, local television stations, and college students all boasting their own

Web pages, it is clear that the Internet is here to stay. And, despite public protestations, that fact is understood in the executive suites of the major commercial online services. Prodigy has relocated to the Web; the Microsoft Network is making a total shift to the Web; America Online debuted a separate Internet access service; and CompuServe offers its customers an Internet-only service, called Sprynet.

The commercial online networks have become, in part, victims of their own success. By stimulating the consumer appetite for easy access to information and other computer uses, companies like America Online, Prodigy, and CompuServe helped seed the market for the Web's growth. But increasingly, consumers refuse to limit themselves to a single, closed network when they can have access to the vastly greater riches of the Internet.

The Internet is made up of over 45,000 networks worldwide, and about 30 million people have some kind of Internet connectivity. Internet access providers (such as NetCom and PSI) and online services (such as America Online and CompuServe) offer consumers the ability to browse, communicate, and shop at a worldwide level. Internet servers in Europe, Asia, and South America are reached via English menus, although many international sites offer dual-language interfaces.

Demographics of Internet Users

Because the Internet operates on a worldwide scale, the development of direct marketing strategies for this new communications medium may involve tailoring efforts to discover the motivations of consumer segments that transcend national boundaries. While some information is available about users of the Internet, it emphasizes demographic characteristics and seldom motivations.

More than one-half of the Internet's computers reside in the United States; the rest are spread out among connected networks in 100 other countries. North America has the largest number of host sites, with more than 4.5 million as of July 1995, up from 2.1 million in July 1994. Western Europe has the second largest amount of Internet growth, with 1.4 million host sites in 1995. Overall, the aggregate growth outside the United States is greater than that inside.

In the United Kingdom, an estimated 500,000 people now have access to the Internet, up from 200,000 in 1994. Internet activity in France is sparse, with approximately 150,000 users. There are about 80,000 CompuServe users in Germany, and the German post office provides an expensive and slow national data network that has 600,000 users.

Current research indicates that Internet users worldwide are young (early 30s), well educated, and predominantly male (about 70 to 80 percent). While the overall size of the Internet community is 30 million, only about 3 to 4 million are consumers, with the rest from academia, corporations, and government agencies. Only 3.4 percent of U.S. households classify themselves as Internet users. They use the Internet for browsing, entertainment, and work. Shopping accounts for only 10.5 percent of Internet activity. More Europeans than Americans use the Internet for academic research (45.1 percent versus 32.6 percent, respectively).

The motivations for those who use the Internet more than 10 hours a month, excluding work activities, are exploration and discovery (browsing the Internet to explore new places and discover new things); information collection (non-work-related searching for information about personal and professional issues, including facts, opinions, reviews, and evaluations); social interaction (interacting with others through interest groups, e-mail, and forums); personal entertainment (using games, puzzles, graphics, and other forms of display that provide amusement); and interactive shopping (shopping via the Internet).

Overall, the Web consists of two major audience segments. The first is the "upstream" audience, which includes 50 percent of total users but only 10 percent of U.S. Web users. This group is 77 percent male, 23 percent female; upscale, highly educated, and professional. The second Web audience, the "other half," comprises 90 percent of U.S. Web users. They are 64 percent male and 36 percent female; most are students or recent graduates working in technical, managerial, or professional fields. They are overwhelmingly from the generation X, with some 70 percent under the age of 30.

Direct Marketing on the Internet

To establish an effective presence on the Internet, direct marketers must gain an understanding of the medium's attributes and of the segments frequenting this communications vehicle. The resultant shift in practices will change the traditional relationship between marketer and target. However, these relationships will be grounded in traditional marketing strategy, creative strategy and execution, customer service, and database management.

The key attributes for marketing on the Internet are control and dynamic communications. Control pertains to the balance of power between marketers and targets. In traditional media, the marketer initiates that relationship. The contact normally occurs during a brief period of time and is orchestrated by the marketer. Target market members decide whether they want to pay attention.

On the Internet the difference between a marketer's success and failure depends on the extent to which particular audience segments find the marketer's content appealing and relevant. A communication must have a sensory or informational appeal or users will choose not to pursue it. At the same time, it must be relevant, because what may be appealing to one segment may not be so to another segment.

Creating dynamic communications involves guiding specific audience segments to content that will address their needs. On the Internet, the relationship between marketer and target is perpetually in a state of flux, but users have ultimate control of the medium. Browsing around the Internet gives them the sense of being in total command of an infinite number of entertainment, information, and communications resources. From that point of view, a marketer must struggle to draw traffic or even get noticed, a process facilitated by creating content that appeals to specific Internet user segments.

Marketers need to link Web pages for those who have an interest in a particular product or service. In that way, an automobile manufacturer wishing to sell an economy model, for example, may offer an interested market segment a particular set of links, while that same firm will offer another set of links for selling a luxury model to a different segment. Marketers can also use the hypertext linking of the Web to create their own services, thereby making it easier for users to browse the Web. And the ability to dynamically address content to specific segments, and to help guide those segments to content that may be most relevant, works to the advantage of the direct marketer.

Exhibit 4.1 shows the home page for the Direct Marketing Association (DMA). The DMA's page has links to other parts of the association's Web site such as its research observatory, business affairs center, and lobby, which contains links to the DMA store, Research Annex, and other locations. The DMA is the largest and oldest organization dedicated solely to the evolving practice of direct marketing and the issues facing it every day. By going online, it has made its pool of information and resources instantly accessible to DMA members and nonmembers alike.

SURVIVING THE TECHNOLOGICAL REVOLUTION[1]

To survive in today's era of rapid technological change, big companies need to act smaller and small companies need to act bigger. Both need to respond quickly to events; both need vast sources of information about markets, customers, and prospects. Big companies need to create smaller units of 175 to 250 people so that workers can be entrusted with more decision-making powers. Core management teams within these units will contract out many services to reduce operating costs. Quality control will be harder to maintain but will be much more important to survival. Location will become an insignificant factor as information technology and communications improve.

Direct marketers will need to expand their customer base on a regional and global basis. Medium- and small-sized companies will need to grow smarter. Survival will become more difficult, and the need for developing strategic partnerships will become crucial. Companies that become pioneers must be able to sustain the huge risk of possible failure. If they can afford to gamble, they can grab market share and reap huge rewards. For many, following close on the tails of the pioneers will be sufficient. Ostriches who bury their heads in the sand in hopes that they may survive will soon find that they have become extinct.

The new technologies are creating victims as well as heroes of commerce. Those who are in touch with the customer and can keep up with the innovations will find an open path to new and healthy markets. The image of the superhighway and convergence technology is a poor one. A better image is a virtual marketplace where the customers pay for products and services by the microsecond. They will buy bytes or terabytes of information rather than a page or a book; they will navigate around a world of their choice. The power is in their hands. If direct marketers do not understand customers' wishes and are not quick to respond to them, the industry of direct marketing will be quickly lost in the shuffle.

Those in the direct marketing industry have to think and compete internationally. Many will not survive, and new names, many of which will be foreign to those in the United States, will become the acknowledged winners. For many, this is an exciting time. They are responding accordingly and growing with the new avenues for revenue. Some say this is a vision of the far future and they really do not have to worry for a few years—they are the ones likely to be the first victims.

EXHIBIT 4.1. Direct Marketing Association Home Page

SUMMARY

Changes in technology are making it possible to conduct direct marketing programs that divide consumer and industrial markets into even more finite target segments. These changes include advances in database and communications technologies, which are transforming how prospects and customers are targeted and marketed to. The nature of competition among companies is also changing rapidly as many concentrate on serving specialized niches. In this environment, many firms can no longer prosper without plans to address the needs of a multitude of market segments.

Media formats are proliferating, with the expansion of cable television; the growth in satellite access; the proliferation of online services; and, more generally, the significant fragmentation of all media. However, as technological innovations are diffusing into the lives of consumers and the operation of businesses, direct marketers are finding both new opportunities and new challenges as they strive for greater sales and profits.

In an environment exploding with new communications choices, direct marketers continue to use all forms of media to directly contact and elicit responses from their target markets. For these marketers, such tools as interactive television and online services are ways to extend their strategies and tactics. Even general marketers are concerned about an increasingly fragmentation of product lines, markets, and media, which makes it less efficient to reach target audiences by spending ad dollars to blanket an entire market with image-oriented campaigns.

The Internet is changing the traditional relationship between marketer and target. To establish an effective presence on the Internet, direct marketers must gain an understanding of the medium's attributes and of the segments frequenting this communications-worldwide vehicle. The key attributes for marketing on the Internet are control and dynamic communications. Control pertains to the balance of power between marketers and targets. Dynamic communications involves guiding specific audience segments to the content that addresses their needs. In this environment, the difference between success and failure depends on the extent to which particular audience segments find the marketer's Internet content appealing and relevant.

To survive in an era of rapid change, companies need to respond quickly to events by strategically using information about markets, customers, and prospects. They should focus on small operating units, where a couple of hundred workers are entrusted with more decision-making powers. These smaller core management teams will emphasize operating cost reductions, quality control, and information technology.

REVIEW QUESTIONS

1. How are changes in technology, particularly in communications and computers, affecting the direct marketing industry?
2. How is the fragmentation of all media influencing the practice of direct marketing?
3. What are the opportunities and challenges facing direct marketers from all the technological innovations occurring in the lives of consumers and the operations of businesses?
4. How can direct marketers use the emerging technological innovations to better communicate with their target markets?
5. How are innovations in interactive television and online services expanding the strategies and tactics direct marketers employ today?

NOTE

1. Adapted from Budd Margolis, "Technological Developments Delivering 500 TV Channels Are Only the Tip of the Iceberg," *Direct Marketing,* September 1995, pp. 24–26.

SOURCES

ActivMedia. "Trends in the WWW Marketplace." At http://www.activmedia.com, 1995.

Bournellis, Cynthia. "Internet '95." *Internet World,* November 1995, pp. 47–52.

"The Computer Industry." *The Economist,* February 27, 1993, a special insert survey.

Cone, Stephen A. "Back, Back to the Future: Quantum Leaps in Technology Bring Us Back to the Days of Old—Personal Service to Every Customer." In *Beyond 2000: The Future of Direct Marketing,* ed. Jerry I. Reitman. Lincolnwood, IL: NTC Business Books, 1994, pp. 57–68.

Depke, Deidre A., and Richard Brandt. "PCs: What the Future Holds." *Business Week,* August 12, 1991, pp. 58–64.

Deutschman, Alan. "Odd Man Out." *Fortune,* July 26, 1993, pp. 42–56.

"Dreamware." *The Economist,* February 13, 1993, pp. 68–69.

FIND/SVP. "U.S. Consumers on the Internet." At http://etrg.findsvp.com, 1995.

Georgia Tech. "GVU's 3rd WWW User Survey." At http://www.cc.gatech.edu/gvu/user_surveys/survey-04-1995/, 1995.

Gregston, Brent. "Power and Privilege." *Internet World,* November 1995, pp. 96–101.

"The Infomercial." *Adweek,* Special Sourcebook Issue, 1995.

Kane, Pamela. *Prodigy Made Easy,* 2nd ed. Berkeley, CA: Osborne McGraw-Hill, 1993.

Klues, Jack, and Jayne Zenaty Spittle. "A Media Planners' Guide to the Future." In *Beyond 2000: The Future of Direct Marketing,* ed. Jerry I. Reitman. Lincolnwood, IL: NTC Business Books, 1994, pp. 79–92.

Margolis, Budd. "Technological Developments Delivering 500 TV Channels Are Only the Tip of the Iceberg." *Direct Marketing,* September 1995, pp. 24–26.

"Marketing with TV by Mail." *Direct Marketing,* September 1995, pp. 48–49.

McDonald, William J. "Internet Customer Segments: An International Perspective." In *Enhancing Knowledge Development in Marketing,* ed. Roger Calantone and Cornelia Droge. Chicago: American Marketing Association 7 (Summer 1996), pp. 338–44.

Perry, Clifford. "Travelers on the Internet: A Survey of Internet Users." *Online* 19, March/April 1995, pp. 29–34.

Rebello, Kathy. "Apple's Daring Leap into the All-Digital Future." *Business Week,* May 25, 1992, pp. 120–22.

Richard, Jack. "Editor's Notes." *Boardwatch,* December 1995, pp. 8–9, 64–65.

Schlender, Breton R. "The Future of the PC." *Fortune,* August 26, 1991, pp. 40–48.

Schwartz, Evan I. "Prodigy Installs a New Program." *Business Week,* September 14, 1992, pp. 96–97.

_______. "Can GTE Outdo Prodigy?" *Business Week,* December 28, 1992, p. 42D.

Schepp, Brad, and Debra Schepp. *The Complete Guide to CompuServe.* Berkeley, CA: Osborne McGraw-Hill, 1990.

SRI International. "Exploring the Web Population's Other Half." At http://future.sri.com, 1995.

_______. "1995 Web Trends." At http://future.sri.com, 1995.

Stone, Bob. *Successful Direct Marketing Methods,* 5th ed. Lincolnwood, IL: NTC Books, 1995.

"Tuned Out and Dropping Off." *The Economist,* November 4, 1995, pp. 65–66.

Wientzen, H. Robert. "Sales Promotion and Trade Incentives: New, Electronic Horizons." In *Beyond 2000: The Future of Direct Marketing,* ed. Jerry I. Reitman. Lincolnwood, IL: NTC Business Books, 1994, pp. 149–56.

"Will New Technology Change the Marketing Rules?" *Direct Marketing,* October 1994, pp. 14–19, 40.

CHAPTER 5

Database Marketing

OBJECTIVES

1. To outline the nature and scope of database marketing activities.
2. To see how direct marketing firms use databases and database management tools in pursuing customers and prospects.
3. To examine how databases make possible sophisticated market segmentations based on a variety of consumer and business characteristics.
4. To examine the privacy issues associated with the growth in database marketing.

INTRODUCTION

When direct marketers reach a customer and/or prospect at the right time, they can communicate what their firm has to offer that exactly fits with that person's needs at that time. Today technology exists that makes possible the use of databases (collections of data) to deliver the right message to the right person at the right time. This allows companies to determine which products or services should be presented immediately, whether by fax or phone or computer, and which offers should be sent in the mail.

Consider the following three examples:

> Example 1: Imagine you live in the Near North section of Chicago and this past December you got a great bonus and bought an Armani cashmere overcoat from a major upscale retailer. On March 1 of the new year, you receive a postcard announcing a private two-week special sale on Armani spring jackets.
>
> On May 1, you get a short letter from the store manager thanking you again for the December purchase of the cashmere coat and listing three simple things you should do right away to store this coat properly over the hot summer months. The letter also states that for a small charge, the store will pick the coat up and clean and care for it until you call to have it delivered in the late fall.
>
> Example 2: You have lived in Florida for seven years and have enjoyed a sporty convertible made by one of the major full-line auto manufacturers. You accept a significant promotion with your Fortune 100 firm and put your Florida home on the market, start house-hunting in Boston, and cancel some local Florida magazines and newspapers as of November 1. Several weeks before you actually move, you receive a letter from the manufacturer of your convertible. It says if you plan to keep the car in Boston you should have it winterized at an authorized dealer immediately upon arrival. Also, the manufacturer has a number of four-wheel drive and front-wheel drive models you might want to consider at this time. A special offer is mentioned.

The letter even points out that if you buy one of these models, you can store the convertible during the winter months at one of several authorized Boston-area dealers and save it for those short but sweet Boston summers. The letter goes on to say that in the event you would rather sell your convertible before the move, the manufacturer can handle that plus delivering a new car to your new home in Boston.

Example 3: Because your advertising agency has picked up several new clients in Kansas City and you are based in Los Angeles, you have just begun traveling regularly, almost once a week, between these two cities. Suddenly, you receive a letter from your favorite credit card company detailing special hotel and restaurant highlights in Kansas City. You are told about special offers at a number of these establishments that are for you, personally, and are good for the next three months. Coupons are not necessary. The credit card company assumes you entertain clients and associates and do not wish to carry and redeem coupons, say, at a dinner with a client. Not to worry, because whenever you use your card at any of the establishments where a special offer applies, the appropriate dollar discount will be automatically credited on your next monthly statement.[1]

Massive databases with billions of pieces of information can be processed in minutes to determine which customers among thousands or millions should get particular messages in endless, unique sequences of contacts over days, weeks, or years. This is just one aspect of the extremely powerful direct marketing tool known as *database marketing.*

WHAT IS DATABASE MARKETING?

While there is no consensus about the definition of database marketing, it is widely acknowledged that computerized databases are fundamental to success in direct marketing today. As the costs associated with such databases have dropped, firms of all sizes have created customer records that include purchase and other information. They have also developed databases of noncustomers who represent prospects at whom to target direct marketing efforts. The result is a revolutionary way of doing business that includes a new definition of the relationship between a company and its customers.

According to Shaw and Stone, database marketing is an interactive approach to marketing that uses individually addressable marketing media and channels such as mail, telephone, and the sales force:

- To extend help to a firm's target audience members.
- To stimulate target audience demand.
- To stay close to a firm's target audience through database records of customers, prospects, and all communication and commercial contacts, to help improve future contacts and ensure better marketing planning.[2]

Database marketing works by creating information records about individual customers' orders and inquiries, which are used to analyze patterns for more effective targeting of product or service offerings. The information stored in the database is used to promote the benefits of brand loyalty to customers at risk from competition; to identify which customers are most likely to buy new products and services; and to support low-cost alternatives to traditional sales methods, including telemarketing or direct mail. Beyond identifying existing and prospective customers, the direct marketer can further subdivide the database into specialized segments such as recent customers, customers who have not made a purchase in the last year or two, and customers who have spent a lot of money with the firm over a certain period of time.

When a firm's database includes enough information about individual customers to determine why they are customers, the firm can tailor direct marketing appeals to individuals or businesses. Ideally, firms gather enough demographic, psychographic, or other information about known customers to be able to compare them with noncustomers. Creating a profile of typical current customers helps a firm identify the prospects most likely to become customers. This becomes the basis for a search among the prospects for those who match that profile. In this way, customers may be "cloned." The firm's subsequent marketing efforts are targeted directly at those prospects with the highest probability of responding to an offer by placing an order.

Firms that 10 years ago had barely considered how database marketing could support their activities have made major investments in the new technology. They include companies involved in breakfast foods, telecommunications, automobiles, computers, banking, insurance, and store retailing. While they may use different terminology to describe their version of database marketing, they are all using database techniques to communicate with customers and prospects. Exhibit 5.1 shows the percentage of direct marketing budgets allocated to database development and maintenance in 1993 and 1994.

EXHIBIT 5.1. Percentage of Direct Marketing Budget Allocated to Various Media

Mail spending continues to attract the highest percentage of direct-response marketing budgets.

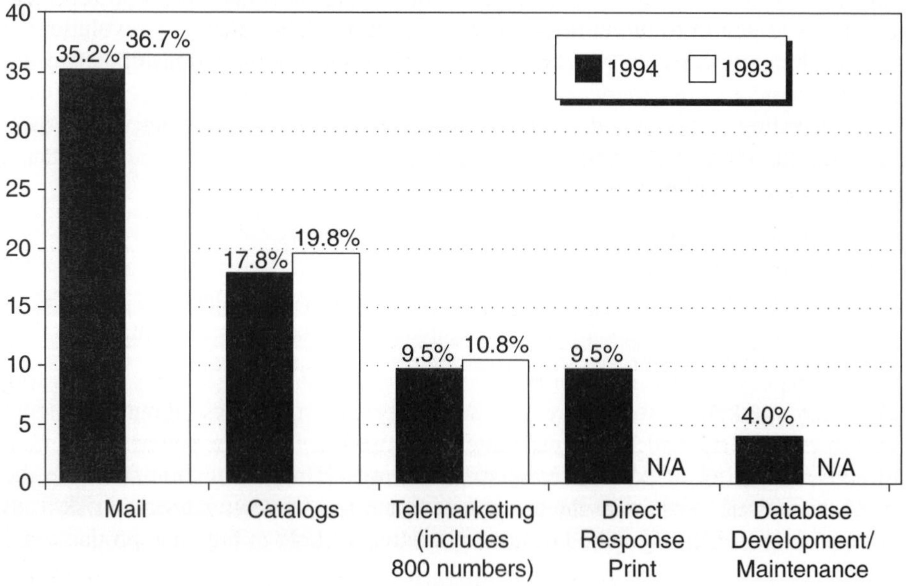

Exhibit 5.2 shows the types of data that direct marketers maintain in their databases. High on the list is purchase history information in various forms. Lower on the list are specifics about individuals and businesses. However, the lower likelihood of firms having the latter type of data is probably due more to the difficulty in obtaining that information than to firms' lack of interest in knowing more about their customers.

Database Characteristics

Although every firm approaches database marketing in its own way, databases tend to share the following common characteristics:

1. Each actual or potential customer is identified as a record on the marketing database. Markets and market segments are not identified primarily through aggregate data, which cannot be broken down into individual customers, but as agglomerations of individual customers.
2. Each customer record contains not only identification and access information (e.g., name, address, telephone number) but also a range of marketing information, including information about customer needs and characteristics (demographic and psychographic information about consumers, industry type and decision-making unit information for industrial customers). Such information is used to identify likely purchasers of particular products and how they should be approached. Each customer record also includes information about campaign communications (whether the customer has been exposed to particular marketing communications campaigns), about the customer's past responses to communications that form part of the campaigns, and about past transactions (with the company and possibly with competitors).
3. The information is available to the company during the process of each communication with the customer, to enable it to decide how to respond to the customer's needs.
4. The database is used to record responses of customers to company initiatives (e.g., marketing communications or sales campaigns).
5. The information is also available to marketing policy makers. This enables them to decide such points as which target markets or segments are appropriate for each product or service and what marketing mix (price, marketing communications, distribution channel, etc.) is appropriate for each product in each target market.
6. In large corporations selling many products to each customer, the database is used to ensure that the approach to the customer is coordinated and that a consistent approach is developed.
7. The database may eventually replace some types of market research such as usage surveys. Marketing campaigns are devised such that the response of customers to the campaign provides information that the company is looking for.
8. Concomitant with the development of the automation of customer information via the development of a large database and the tools to access it to handle transactions with customers, marketing management automation is also developed. This is needed to handle the vast volume of information generated by database marketing. It ensures that marketing opportunities and threats are

EXHIBIT 5.2. Types of Customer that Data Marketers Maintain
Most still focus on basic transactional information.

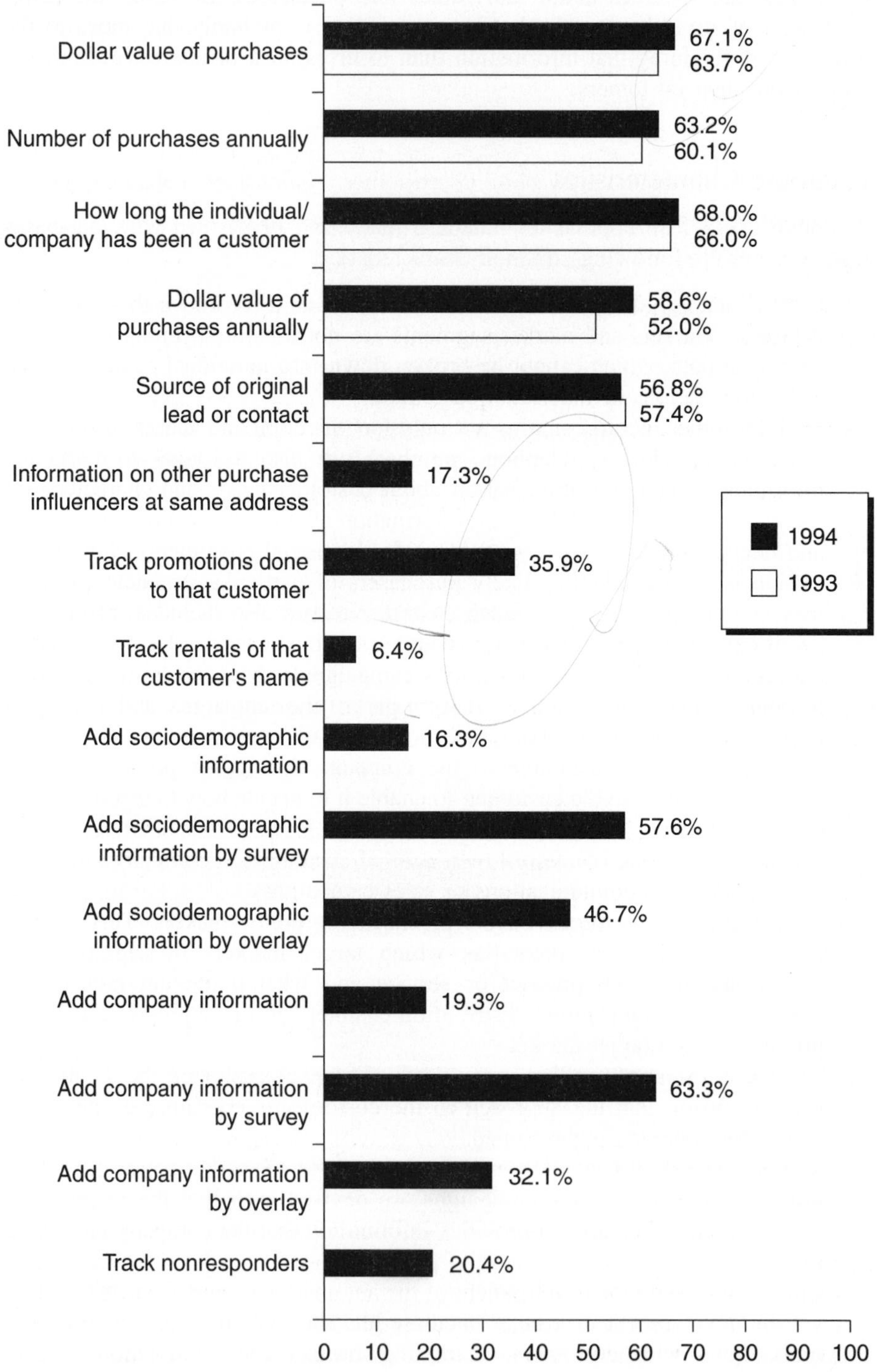

identified more or less automatically, and that ways of capturing these opportunities and neutralizing these threats are also recommended. It makes higher quality information on marketing performance available to senior management, allowing them to allocate marketing resources more effectively.[3]

Uses of Databases

A database facilitates such direct marketing tasks as selecting market segments, increasing repeat purchases by building customer relationships, enhancing cross-selling, and gaining competitive superiority.

Selection of Market Segments

Databases make possible the implementation of sophisticated market segmentations based on such characteristics as demographics, geographic location, previous purchase behavior, and likelihood of placing an order. (Refer back to Chapter 3 for more about market segmentation.) Because members of targeted segments are more responsive to a firm's direct marketing efforts than consumers or businesses that are not members, the results of database marketing include increased productivity and lower costs.

Repeat Purchases

Repeat purchases are facilitated when databases help build ongoing relationships between a firm and its customers. Sometimes repeat purchases are generated through frequent communications between the two parties, with or without a selling purpose. For example, firms selling book club memberships or magazines use continuity offers that include some form of ongoing agreement from the customer to continue receiving shipments.

Cross-selling

When a direct marketing firm owns several businesses that share a common database, it can use that database to engage in cross-selling. For example, Time Warner owns several book and magazine businesses. As a result, it has millions of names to which it can market various magazines, books, and videotapes. This synergy benefits all of the firm's businesses; each can enjoy greater sales and lower operating costs as a result of sharing information and other resources.

Competitive Superiority

A business can establish a position of competitive superiority by building and exploiting a database containing information about its existing and potential customers. Databases can even become a competitive weapon when they are used in marketing efforts directed at owners of a particular competitor's product.

Service Merchandise, a retailer with hundreds of stores nationwide, uses database technology to bolster relationships with its customers. Through a strong alliance with its internal departments and outside vendors, the firm has established a point-of-sale system that captures 100 percent of its customers' identities and transactions down to the product level—and that 100 percent includes all customers, not merely credit card and charge customers. The Service Merchandise system contains more than 20 million household records and, most important, keeps customer information in an actionable format for marketing, merchandising, and strategic decision making.

Database Management with RFM

Recency, frequency, and monetary (RFM) values define a firm's best customers, that is, those who are most likely to purchase again because they have bought most recently, bought most frequently, or spent a specified amount of money.

The RFM calculation is used to assign points to members of a firm's customer database when ranking prospects for receiving an offer such as a direct-mail piece or a catalog. This categorization provides a basis for maximizing profits because it enables a firm to use the information in its customer database to select those persons who have proved to be good sources of revenue. For example, a business-to-business marketer would assign points to customers' activities with the firm according to Table 5.1.

The recency points are computed by multiplying by 10; the inverse of the number of months since a given customer made a purchase; the frequency points are computed by multiplying by 2 the customer's number of purchases in the last 12 months; and the monetary points are computed by multiplying by .02 the customer's total dollar amount of purchases. The total score is the sum of the point scores for each of the three parts of the RFM. Customers are then ranked by the magnitude of their RFM score. In Table 5.1, customer number 00005 has the highest overall score. It is easy to see why: customer 00005 purchases frequently and spends a large amount of money each year.

Database Marketing Support Firms

Firms specializing in database marketing support services help companies interested in establishing customer databases to organize internal information and purchase outside data for the purpose of developing a database resource. Frequently, these consulting firms also help the companies analyze and segment their data to improve business performance and ensure future sales growth. The advertisement from Cahners Direct Marketing Services in Exhibit 5.3 illustrates what database management firms can do to help their clients target their offerings. Cahners's DecisionMaker Database is a multidimensional business database that contains information about more than 6 million individual decision makers in the United States and another 2 million in Europe.

The Strengths of Database Marketing

Database marketing provides benefits over other forms of marketing that make it the preferred way of doing business for a growing number of firms. According to Shaw and Stone, database marketing has the following special strengths:

- It is *measurable.* Responses to campaigns are measured, enabling firms to identify the effectiveness of different approaches.
- It is *testable.* Firms can test the effectiveness of different elements of their approach—the product, the communications medium, the offer (how the

TABLE 5.1. Recency, Frequency, and Monetary Value of Customer Purchases
(Activity in the last year)

Customer Number	Recency of Purchase (Months since Last)	Weight	Points (Recency Inverse Times Weight)	Frequency of Purchasing	Weight	Points	Total Monetary Value of Purchases	Weight	Points	Total Score
00001	4	10	2.5	3	2	6	566	0.02	11.3	19.8
00002	3	10	3.3	5	2	10	788	0.02	15.8	29.1
00003	5	10	2.0	4	2	8	332	0.02	6.6	16.6
00004	6	10	1.7	3	2	6	290	0.02	5.8	13.5
00005	1	10	10.0	6	2	12	1200	0.02	24.0	46.0
00006	2	10	5.0	7	2	14	679	0.02	13.6	32.6
00007	2	10	5.0	4	2	8	299	0.02	6.0	19.0
00008	5	10	2.0	6	2	12	890	0.02	17.8	31.8
00009	7	10	1.4	2	2	4	243	0.02	4.9	10.3
00010	11	10	0.9	1	2	2	125	0.02	2.5	5.4

EXHIBIT 5.3. Cahners Direct Marketing Services Advertisement

product is packaged to appeal to the customer), the target market, and so on. Tests can be carried out quickly, so firms can take quick action on the results. Firms can use test campaign results to forecast sales more precisely, helping them to manage inventory more effectively.

- It is *selective.* Firms can focus campaigns accurately, because they communicate with specific customers.

- Firms can *personalize* communication to each customer, by including details relevant to them and not to others. This usually raises the response rate.
- It is *flexible*. Firms can time their campaigns to have their effect exactly when they want.[4]

With database marketing, it is possible to split what have been traditionally thought of as mass markets into distinct buying segments. More niche markets also emerge as database marketers use computer resources to fragment markets into ever more finite groupings.

The Weaknesses of Database Marketing

While database marketing provides benefits over other forms of marketing, it also has some weaknesses, in particular, the expenses associated with creating and managing the database. Firms frequently need to purchase large amounts of computer equipment and hire highly trained (and expensive) new staff members. It is also difficult and time-consuming to keep the customer and prospect records up-to-date. However, on balance, the benefits far outweigh the expenses and problems associated with making direct marketing databases a fundamental part of a firm's ongoing business operations.

BEAR CREEK BUILDS A MARKETING DATABASE[5]

Bear Creek Corporation (BCC) is one of the nation's leading direct-mail marketers making extensive use of database technologies. The firm operates two businesses: Harry & David and Jackson & Perkins. This section tells the story of how BCC amassed its database and details the many uses it has.

Harry & David began selling mail-order fruit in 1934. Since then it has become America's largest direct-mail marketer of gift fruits, such as its famous Royal Rivera pears, grown at its company-owned Bear Creek Orchards. Well-known for its Fruit-of-the-Month Club, the firm has created catalogs offering a wide variety of gourmet-quality fruit, baked goods, confections, and decorative household accessories.

Jackson & Perkins, one of the world's largest suppliers of roses and foremost producers of new rose varieties, started business in 1872. In 1939, the company became the nation's first mail-order rose nursery. It also sells a variety of bulbs, ornamental plants, bushes, berries, trees, and home garden accessories.

Database Marketing at BCC

A marketing database has been in operation at BCC only since 1988. Before that, despite the fact that BCC personnel had developed and conducted extensive customer analyses and reporting, no central source of information existed. The staff had to cumulate sales and other information from several different sources, summarize the amassed information by customer, and then produce the analysis or reports without any means of permanently storing the results. The problem was not data availability but data access and organization.

BCC's marketing people did not design the reporting and analytical systems that had been developed, and it showed. Those systems produced basic response analysis by promotion, including item information, but they were inflexible and inefficient. Meanwhile, technology and marketing were advancing at a very rapid pace. Postage increases and competition also drove the need for faster and increased amounts of marketing information. Frequently, marketing management's questions could not be answered quickly, if at all. As the backlog grew, so too did the frustrations of the marketing department and its analytical staff. It was time to make a change.

In 1987, BCC began the process of developing a marketing database. The objective was threefold: (1) to implement a marketing database system to serve as a comprehensive central repository for all customer activity and demographic information; (2) to implement marketing analysis, product development, and product management systems to support the execution of targeted direct marketing strategies; and (3) to implement systems to better support the company's understanding of customer behavior and attitudes, development of strategies to ensure growth objectives, and senior management's need for information.

The Marketing Database

BCC developed a large database from customers, recipients, inquiries, and rental lists. With this new system, BCC positioned itself to pursue new marketing programs efficiently and effectively and to target customers with specific products during events, providing optimal promotional strategies for the greatest market penetration at the lowest cost. Specifically, a marketing database was justified because it would enhance the following:

Catalog circulation efficiency. Improving the efficiency of catalog circulation involved using information that was not readily available in current systems, such as refund amounts and customer service contacts. Database information was used to drive the page makeup of individual catalogs. For example, through selective binding, people more prone to buy only roses might receive a gardening catalog offering special, unique rose bushes.

Tactical information. Customer response information is particularly valuable in mail order for designing the next event. For example, product and catalog page contribution reporting, ad hoc report generation, and list and media analysis help guide what products should be in a catalog, how each product should be displayed, and to whom catalogs should be sent.

Strategic information. The database information would have a large, long-term impact on the growth of BCC. In particular, it would include lifetime customer value reporting, product affinity or preferences reporting, and profiles of customer characteristics.

Integrating Data

The marketing database at BCC integrates data associated with customer activity, marketing and merchandising activity, externally sourced data, list rental fulfillment, and system or global data maintenance. Each area of activity is comprised of multiple record types or tables of information that are related to other records by key. For example, customer activity is identified by a permanent and unique account number. Data within records can be cross-indexed and related to other records. These records are managed by a database management system.

Within the customer activity area of the database, a customer's sales history, rental history, inquiry activity, circulation history, and segmentation history are retained. The sales history includes activity as a buyer as well as a recipient or ship-to address.

The following are brief descriptions of the customer activity components of BCC's database:

Name, address, and telephone data, with source and effective dates for each customer. Additionally, carrier route and climate zone are maintained in this component.

Customer status and historical profile data with respect to catalog circulation, credit, and special handling. This includes summarized profile information on the customer such as date and amount of last activity, overall activity, type of products purchased, number and classification of merge-purge hits on rented lists, long-term and lifetime values, source of the name, SIC codes where they apply, time of conversion and source, and other demographic data.

Detailed order data, containing items such as date; financial data (e.g., gross sales, product sales, discounts, delivery charges, special shipping, taxes, remittance); number of recipients or ship-tos; and the order description information (e.g., mail vs. phone, cash vs. credit). Among the fields contained in this component is the circulation key, which contains sourcing, mailing, and testing information for a customer. Item and product category data (e.g., demand, quantity, and price) are retained as well.

Older summarized historical history, such as data on older orders for each customer and year, and summarized promotional and product information.

Order, recipient, and item adjustment data on any adjustment made to any aspect of the order. Adjustments such as returns, substitutions, cancellations, credit, refunds, and replacements are maintained in conjunction with the detailed order history.

Shipped sales order detail data for tracking on each of the items sold with respect to the detailed order record. Information in this component includes shipment type, zip code, requested arrival date, and shipment date.

Recipient gift order detail data of item, sales, and order information indicating how much activity was directed to the recipient account on the particular order.

A further breakdown of the BCC database's detailed order record gives the following:

Circulation detail data track circulation directed to the account, maintaining circulation keys, segmentation scores, postal qualifications, and processing information for every promotion for a customer within a year.

List rental history data include date and transaction information for a customer each time the customer's name is rented by a mailing list.

Inquiry detail data cover detailed inquiry information a customer or prospective customer might have, including source, date, and type of inquiry.

BCC's marketing and merchandising activity area maintains information on promotional history, circulation piece, item and product category, marketing research, and analytical model data. (See Chapter 17 for more on the importance of these models.) The following are brief descriptions of the marketing and merchandising activity components:

Promotional history data such as promotional costs, assumptions, results, projections, circulation, and testing plans.

Circulation piece data about the specific piece (e.g., catalog, digest, broadside, folder), including number of pages, space, version, and product information.

Item and product category data about relations of items and product categories, item prices, descriptions, effective dates, promotional, and circulation piece relations.

Marketing research data from internal and external research results. This component obviously requires different data structure and contents, depending on the research.

Analytical models data, which are often aggregated data outlining the parameters of analytical models such as product affinity (or preferences), lifetime value (what a customer is worth over an extended period of time), and promotional planning.

The externally sourced data area of BCC's database contains information acquired from sources outside the company. The data are indexed at the customer level or some other characteristic of a customer such as region, climate, zip code, or geodemographics (see Chapter 3).

The list rental fulfillment area (based on names of prospects from outside vendors) is the repository for data that track the financial, demographic, and physical requirements of renting house names to other companies and organizations. Chapter 6 of this text covers uses of lists in direct marketing. This area includes financial agreements, quantities requested, type of promotional piece used with the names rented, and date requested on each order for names rented. Information is also kept for each renting agency.

Use of the Database

This section contains summaries of some of the reports and processes currently produced from the database to set marketing direction at BCC.

Response analysis reports are produced showing the order, item, and sales information results of a particular mailing. The report is flexible, capable of being run based on customer segments, payment type, state, climate zone, test version, item information, and so on, on more than 25 mail-order fields (e.g., sales/circulation, response rate, average order size). This report is used by the analysts to guide the marketing direction of the company and to support planning for the next mailing. With this information, BCC does testing in its mailings such as a recent test to determine the proper size of the catalogs to send to customers versus prospects.

Product affinity is a measure of a customer's propensity to buy one item given that the customer purchased another. This is measured by cross-buying activity. This report shows the number of customers who cross-bought from one product category to another and the magnitude of that cross-buying. It has been used for the selection of merchandise and targeting. For example, it was found that a strong affinity existed between fruit and herbs. As a result, these two items were then used in the same catalog.

Media reports cover the response of media and lists across all promotional mailings, and show the performance by promotion, enabling BCC to fine-tune its use of various media (e.g., rose ads from one source worked well in a perennial promotion; the company then tried perennial ads in that source). At BCC, the cost of acquisition of a new customer, which is a result of this report, is directly compared to the customer's lifetime value in order to make a marketing decision using corporate guidelines of investment and return on investment (ROI).

Lifetime value (LTV) is a strategic planning tool used to support decisions about customer acquisition. (See Chapter 18 of this text for an in-depth discussion of the lifetime value concept.) It is an estimate of the net present value of all future contributions to profit and overhead that a firm can expect from a new customer. Using the database, BCC calculates the overall LTV of new customers by general source (list, inquiry, recipient, etc.) but also calculates it by the particular media within that segment (e.g., L. L. Bean list names or *Better Homes and Gardens* inquiries). Thus, an analyst can judge each particular source by the firm's investment criteria.

LTV information can also be used to increase new customer LTV by modifying the product mix, price points, and so on of the prospecting mailings. For example, BCC found that by adding the minirose product to the prospecting piece, it increased the conversion rate (from getting an offer to making an actual purchase) and LTV of list rental new customers. BCC also analyzes LTV by other key factors—first order characteristics (e.g., cash, credit card), product category, climate zone, and so on—to guide its prospecting strategies.

File counts are the three-year file counts for customers, recipients, and inquiries as of the end of the quarter. This shows the repurchase rates and sales and catalog circulation per name for the customer base by year of first purchase, year of last purchase (i.e., recency), frequency, and monetary level of purchase (RFM). It is used to judge the "health" of the customer base from year to year and to identify marketing opportunities or trends.

Demographic and psychographic reports are from enhancements to the database based on purchases of consumer information from outside vendors. Using LTV and file counts for 12-month buyers, these reports compare key psychographic (lifestyle) and demographic characteristics of the customers. For example, LTV by length of residence showed that list rental customers who had lived only one to two years at their home had a substantially higher LTV. Therefore, new movers were sought in list rentals.

Segmentation is operationalized through the database because it supplies all the necessary information to identify which customers should or should not receive mailings. BCC personnel extract the results from the previous mailing in order to build a regression-based segmentation model that not only ranks the names by score for selection but also predicts the proper level of mailing and resultant orders and sales from the mailing. With this database information, BCC is better able to get the right message out to the right prospects or customers at the right time. A separate model is built for each promotion targeting the appropriate names based on their sales histories.

Ad hoc studies are used when queries arise from the marketing process. They summarize the findings from a marketing effort and are used to make actionable recommendations. It is with ad hoc reporting that the true flexibility of a marketing database is tested. No two of these studies are exactly alike. Therefore, database access and reports must be adaptable to any analytical situation. These studies can supply the answers that can set the marketing direction of the company. For example, BCC has done studies to determine the impact of telemarketing on its customers and to determine how the introduction of a new product line affected sales of its core products.

Personalized mailings are created from the database. For example, using computer letter fill-ins, BCC can inform its customers of the proper time to plant in their climate zone and recommend additional plants to purchase that coordinate with their previous purchases. BCC also sends customers recipient listings that are on printed forms, showing what the customers ordered and to whom they sent gifts the previous year. These act as an order device for the customers.

Reactivation activities are conducted with the database. BCC uses it to identify "inactives" on the file. The firm then targets special pieces to these customers, reminding them that mailings will cease due to costs if they do not purchase from that piece. It is also testing a prequalifying postcard to see if customers want to continue to receive its mailings.

Other database uses include maintaining addresses (NCOA/change of address); processing customer requests to stop mailings or to receive special mailing pieces; maintaining telephone numbers for telemarketing; supplying sales information for market research; providing information for the circulation models to forecast future sales and profitability for five years out and product information to the merchants in order to integrate marketing information; developing the most efficient and profitable product mix for each catalog and the curves necessary to properly forecast orders and sales; and improving product inventory control and staffing levels in order entry.

DATABASE-RELATED PRIVACY ISSUES

While the United States has laws to protect citizens' privacy rights, the preservation of those rights has historically rested on the high costs associated with managing the volume of information necessary to significantly violate them.

However, privacy has become an issue as increasingly powerful computers have lowered costs and made possible the management of extremely large volumes of personal information. Even the smallest businesses now have the ability to collect, store, process, and disseminate significant amounts of data.

These changes are magnifying concerns about the unchecked use of data, particularly the increasing collection of personal information about individuals; the rapid and extensive exchange of data; and the use of data in ways that individuals would not know about or have any control over. In the private sector, this involves credit, banking, insurance, employment, and medical transactions and in the public sector activities such as welfare, law enforcement, taxation, and licensing programs. Private firms are building extensive computer files of individual transactions based on electronic banking and credit card transactions to create consumer activity profiles. Both state and federal governments are increasing their use of computer programs to make comparisons of welfare, employment, and tax files to identify instances of fraudulent behavior.

Information technology is also increasing the ability of firms to share and exchange data with third-party sources. This creates even more concerns about individual privacy, particularly the ethical issues associated with the collection and dissemination of personal information for direct marketing purposes.

Today, most personal information is obtained from secondary data sources, where information is accessible without the individual's knowledge. This type of data comes from database publishers who transform the data into useful marketing information. Much of the data sold or rented by the database publishers is derived from government records, public firms, and nonprofit organizations. For example, financial data providers get their information through service bureaus. Among the largest providers are Equifax Marketing Services, TRW Target Marketing Services, and TransUnion. Each has access to data about credit card purchases, installment loans, applications for credit, and payment histories for virtually every household in the United States.

Individual-specific demographic data is also available on households, including names and addresses. To develop geographically based psychographic data for their customer file, marketers can purchase data about cluster groups of customers from vendors who combine their geodemographic clusters with market research data.

While the business environment continues to provide a relatively friendly climate for accessing personal information, consumers are increasing their demands for protection. However, although more people than ever are concerned about attacks on their privacy, the courts continue to uphold the rights of commercial free speech. For example, in Oregon, the part of the Telephone Consumer Protection Act barring use of prerecorded messages to residences was found to violate the First Amendment.

Most consumers are unaware of how personal information is collected, used, and distributed, and they are unaware of how technology helps in collecting personal data. There is also widespread misunderstanding about existing privacy laws and regulations. Frustrated by their lack of control, consumers want more opportunities to determine how their personal information will be used.

In a psychological sense, privacy issues extend beyond an individual's right to select the location and timing of social contact to include the individual's right to a state of security, or a positive sense of a secure self. The evolution of information technology attacks these aspects of privacy because data gathering can be viewed as a violation of the right to choose the time and place of social interaction, and the creation and sharing of consumer data through third-party sources can be perceived as a threat to the individual's right to a psychological state of security.

SUMMARY

Database marketing is an interactive approach to marketing that uses individually addressable marketing media and channels (such as mail, telephone, and the sales force) to extend help to a firm's target audience members, to stimulate target audience demand, and to stay close to a firm's target audience through database records of customers, prospects, and all communication and commercial contacts, to help improve future contacts and ensure better marketing planning.

Database marketing works by creating information records about individual customers' orders and inquiries, which are used to analyze patterns for more effective targeting of product or service offerings. The information stored in a database is used to promote the benefits of brand loyalty to customers at risk from competition; to identify which customers are most likely to buy new products and services; and to support low-cost alternatives to traditional sales methods, including telemarketing and direct mail. Databases also make possible the implementation of sophisticated market segmentations based on such characteristics as demographics, geographic location, previous purchase behavior, and likelihood of placing an order.

In conjunction with database, recency, frequency, and monetary (RFM) calculations define a firm's best customers, who are those most likely to purchase again because they have bought most recently, bought most frequently, or spent specified amounts. The RFM calculation is used to assign points to members of a firm's customer database for ranking prospects to receive an offer such as a direct-mail piece or a catalog. This categorization approach provides a basis for maximizing profits because it enables a firm to use the information in its customer database to select those persons who have proved to be good sources of revenue.

Bear Creek Corporation (BCC) is one of the nation's leading direct mail marketers making extensive use of database technologies. Its database positions the firm to pursue new marketing programs efficiently and effectively and to target customers with specific products during events, providing optimal promotional strategies for the greatest market penetration at the lowest cost.

While information technologies provide many opportunities for better strategic and tactical marketing, there is also a growing public concern about the amount of personal data contained in those databases. While many consumers question the uses of this information, and claim an invasion of privacy in some instances, the ability to obtain detailed customer information from internal and external databases is extremely valuable to firms in marketing their products or services.

REVIEW QUESTIONS

1. What is meant by the term *database marketing?*
2. How does database marketing help direct marketers reach customers and prospects?
3. What are the strengths and weaknesses of database marketing, and how does each affect direct marketing practices?
4. How does database marketing help a company increase repeat purchases by customers, enhance cross-selling, and gain competitive superiority?
5. Describe the Bear Creek Corporation (BCC) database derived from customers, recipients, inquiries, and rental lists. How did this system enable BCC to efficiently and effectively target customers with specific products?
6. Databases make possible the implementation of sophisticated market segmentations based on a variety of consumer and business characteristics. What are some of those characteristics, and how is each used to improve the performance of a direct marketing firm?
7. What are some of the personal and business-related privacy issues associated with the growth in database marketing, and how should they be addressed?

NOTES

1. The three examples are taken from Stephen. A. Cone, "Back, Back to the Future: Quantum Leaps in Technology Bring Us Back to the Days of Old—Personal Service to Every Customer," in *Beyond 2000: The Future of Direct Marketing,* ed. Jerry I. Reitman (Lincolnwood, IL: NTC Business Books, 1994), pp. 60–61.
2. Robert Shaw and Merlin Stone, *Database Marketing and Strategy Implementation* (New York: John Wiley & Sons, 1990) pp. 3–4.
3. Ibid., pp. 4–6.
4. Ibid., p. 8.
5. Adapted from Michael Shorland and Michael Zodrow, "Bear Creek Builds In-House Gold Mine," *Direct Marketing,* January 1993, pp. 35–40.

SOURCES

AGRANOFF, MICHAEL H. "Controlling the Threat to Personal Privacy: Corporate Policies Must Be Created." *Journal of Information Systems Management* 8 (Summer 1991), pp. 48–52.

BLOOM, PAUL N.; GEORGE R. MILNE; and ROBERT ADLER. "Avoiding Misuse of New Information Technologies: Legal and Societal Considerations." *Journal of Marketing* 58 (January 1994), pp. 98–110.

BURKA, KAREN. "New Targets in Privacy Battleground." *Direct,* March 1994, p. 19.

CESPEDES, FRANK V., and H. JEFF SMITH. "Database Marketing: New Rules for Policy and Practice." *Sloan Management Review,* 34 (Summer 1993), pp. 7–22.

CONE, STEPHEN A. "Back, Back to the Future: Quantum Leaps in Technology Bring Us Back to the Days of Old—Personal Service to Every Customer." In *Beyond 2000: The Future of Direct Marketing,* ed. Jerry I. Reitman. Lincolnwood, IL: NTC Business Books, 1994, pp. 57–68.

CROSS, RICHARD. "Profiting From Database Marketing." *Direct Marketing,* September 1991, pp. 24–26.

CROSS, RICHARD H., and JANET A. SMITH. "The Coming Turnaround in Political Fund Raising." *Direct Marketing,* January 1993, pp. 16–19, 70.

________. "New Product Launches." *Direct Marketing,* August 1992, pp. 35–41.

CULNAN, MARY J. "How Did They Get My Name?: An Exploratory Investigation of Consumer Attitudes toward Secondary Information Use." *MIS Quarterly* 17 (September 1993), pp. 341–61.

DELOITTE & TOUCHE. *Profitable Retailing Using Relationship and Database Marketing.* New York: Direct Marketing Association, 1994.

Direct Marketing Association. *Statistical Fact Book 1996.* New York: Direct Marketing Association, 1996.

EGOL, LEN. "Lilliputian Solution." *Direct,* August 1995, pp. 64–65.

FOXMAN, ELLEN R., and PAULA KILCOYNE. "Information Technology, Marketing Practice, and Consumer Privacy: Ethical Issues." *Journal of Public Policy and Marketing* 12 (Spring 1993), pp. 106–119.

FOST, DAN. "Privacy Concerns Threaten Database Marketing." *American Demographics* 12 (May 1990), pp. 18–21.

GATTUSO, GREG. "Study Says Consumers Lack Control of Personal Inf." *Direct Marketing* 56 (April 1994), pp. 9–10.

GOODWIN, CATHY. "A Conceptualization of Motives to Seek Privacy for Nondeviant Consumption." *Journal of Consumer Psychology* 1, no. 3 (1992), pp. 261–84.

HOCHHAUSER, RICHARD. "The Power of Integrated Database Marketing." *Direct Marketing,* September 1992, pp. 32–35.

HOLTZ, HERMAN. *Databased Marketing.* New York: John Wiley & Sons, 1992.

HUGHES, ARTHUR M. *The Complete Database Marketer,* 2nd ed. Homewood, IL: Richard D. Irwin, 1995.

JACKSON, ROB, and PAUL WANG. *Strategic Database Marketing.* Lincolnwood, IL: NTC Business Books, 1994.

JAFFEE, LARRY. "Online List Rental Probe Launched." *DM News* 16 (October 1994), pp. 1, 118.

JONES, MARY GARDINER. "Privacy: A Significant Marketing Issue for the 1990s." *Journal of Public Policy and Marketing* 10 (Spring 1991), pp. 133–48.

KATZ, JAMES E., and ANNETTE R. TASSOE. "Public Opinion Trends: Privacy and Information Technology." *Public Opinion Quarterly* 54 (Spring 1990), pp. 125–43.

KATZENSTEIN, HERBERT, and WILLIAMS S. SACHS. *Direct Marketing,* 2nd ed. New York: Macmillan, 1992.

KING, ALAN. "Revisited: The Rise and Fall of Lotus Marketplace." *Online,* July 1991, pp. 102–4.

"Mayor of Olathe Taking Junk Out of the Mails." *Direct Marketing,* August 1993, pp. 28–30.

MCDONALD, WILLIAM J., and ELAINE SHERMAN. "Privacy Issues in Consumer Information Management: An Ethical Perspective." Working paper, Hofstra University School of Business, 1996.

METALITZ, STEVEN J. "The Proposed Data Protection Directive: At What Price Privacy?" *Journal of European Business* 2 (July/August 1991), pp. 13–17.

MILNE, GEORGE, and MARY ELLEN GORDON. "A Segmentation Study of Consumers' Attitudes toward Direct Mail." *Journal of Direct Marketing* 8 (Spring 1994), pp. 45–52.

MORRIS, LINDA, and STEVEN PHARR. "Invasion of Privacy: A Dilemma for Marketing Research and Database Technology." *Journal of System Management* 43 (October 1992), pp. 10–11, 30–31, 42–43.

NASH, EDWARD. *Database Marketing: The Ultimate Marketing Tool.* New York: McGraw-Hill, 1992.

NOWAK, GLEN J., and JOSEPH PHELPS. "Understanding Privacy Concerns: An Assessment of Consumers' Information-Related Knowledge and Beliefs." *Journal of Direct Marketing* 6 (Autumn 1992), pp. 28–39.

"The Power of Printing Technology." *Direct Marketing,* September 1994, p. 18.

"The Prescription for Success." *Direct Marketing,* November 1991, p. 28.

RAAB, DAVID M. "Shopping for a Marketing System." *Direct,* August 1996, pp. 95–96.

ROBERTS, MARY LOU, and PAUL D. BERGER. *Direct Marketing Management.* Englewood Cliffs, NJ: Prentice Hall, 1989.

ROBINSON, SUSANNE MEIER. "Privacy vs. Profit." *Journal of European Business* 4 (July/August 1993), pp. 8–10.

ROTHFEDER, JEFFREY. "Invasions of Privacy." *PC World,* November 1995, pp. 152–66.

SANTORO, ELAINE. "NBO Markets with Style." *Direct Marketing,* February 1992, pp. 28–31.

SCHWARTZ, JOE. "Databases Deliver the Goods." *American Demographics* 11 (September 1989), pp. 22–25, 68.

SHAVER, DICK. *The Next Step in Database Marketing—Consumer Guided Marketing.* New York: John Wiley & Sons, 1996.

SHAW, ROBERT, and MERLIN STONE. *Database Marketing and Strategy Implementation.* New York: John Wiley & Sons, 1990.

SHEPARD, DAVID. *The New Direct Marketing,* 2nd ed. Homewood, IL: Richard D. Irwin, 1996.

SHORLAND, MICHAEL, and MICHAEL ZODROW. "Bear Creek Builds In-House Gold Mine." *Direct Marketing,* January 1993, pp. 35–40.

"Success of Service Merchandise." *Direct Marketing,* August 1992, pp. 42–45.

STONE, BOB. *Successful Direct Marketing Methods,* 5th ed. Lincolnwood, IL: NTC Books, 1995.

VIDMAR, NEIL, and DAVID H. FLAHERTY. "Concern for Personal Privacy in an Electronic Age." *Journal of Communication,* Spring 1985, pp. 91–103.

WANG, PAUL, and LISA A. PETRISON. "Direct Marketing Activities and Personal Privacy: A Consumer Survey." *Journal of Direct Marketing* 7 (Winter 1993), pp. 7–19.

WINSTON, ARTHUR. "Where the Privacy Issue Is Now Heading." *DM News* 22 (August 1994), pp. 16, 42.

CHAPTER 6

List Selection and Management

OBJECTIVES

1. To explain what lists are and how direct marketers use them.
2. To present the types of lists, including how and when each is typically used by a direct marketing firm.
3. To describe how lists are managed to increase the effectiveness of direct marketing campaigns.
4. To define what is meant by the term *list segmentation* and to indicate how conducting a list segmentation relates to direct marketing campaign response rates.

INTRODUCTION

To direct marketers, a *list* is a collection of names and addresses of prospects and customers who could be the target of an offer to purchase a product or service. The set of lists a firm selects for its direct marketing effort is the single most important factor in determining the success or failure of any direct marketing campaign. Lists are usually stored in a computer database that contains a series of names, addresses, and other information. Databases containing lists are used in conjunction with mathematical and statistical techniques to identify individual prospects or groups of prospects based on their demographics, psychographics, and/or behavioral characteristics such as purchase histories. As explained in Chapter 5, usually the most predictive characteristic for future purchases is past purchase behavior, including when the last purchase was made, how often purchases were made, and how much was purchased on average each time a purchase was made. A firm's list of its own customers usually contains the best prospects for any offer the firm might make because those customers have shown both a propensity to buy direct and an interest in the products the firm sells.

Lists are valuable because they are structured collections of records about customers and prospects for use in both identifying market segments and ranking customers based on expectations about how responsive those individuals will be to an offer. The application of segmentation to list management is designed to uncover which list members have the most sales potential for a particular product or service. When direct marketers segment lists, they are using combinations of personal characteristics and/or buyer behavior for predicting a response to an offer for a product or service by segments consisting of potential target audience members.

Firms should develop as much geographic, demographic, and psychographic information as possible about members of their *house lists* (the list of the firm's own customers). The more information the firm has on people who have already made a purchase, the easier it will be to select prospects who may buy during the next offer the firm makes. Statistical and database sorting methods analyze data on customers and determine their areas of similarity. Many of these techniques use mathematical algorithms to determine the important similar traits exhibited by a group of customers and to predict those most likely to respond favorably to an offer, or just to define the characteristics the firm's customers have in common.

Thus, list management and segmentation allow marketers to promote only to those people from whom they expect a response rate greater than that from the population in general. List segmentation can also be used to split a list file into several smaller homogeneous files, so that a firm can send a mailing only to individuals expected to be profitable. If done well, refining a list will yield a higher response rate in any given campaign.

Technically speaking, marketers using a list first mail or telephone the names expected to be most productive and then move down the list until the incremental response rate is equal to the break-even response rate. This is what direct marketers call *list depth.* The break-even response rate is calculated by dividing the cost per piece (the marginal cost of mailing a single additional piece) or cost per call (the marginal cost of each additional telephone call) by the gross profit of a sale. These decisions should be made not on an average basis but on an incremental basis, meaning that the expected incremental value of each additional contact determines whether it is worth making.

Response rates are not the only way to calculate mailing or telemarketing list depth. In continuity programs (which offer a series of purchases rather than just one) or in markets with long-term customer loyalty objectives, the net present value (a measure of return on investment, discussed in Chapter 18) of a newly acquired customer may be a more meaningful performance criterion than the break-even point for a particular campaign. By using the net present value calculation, a firm can estimate an incremental expected value for each name or each segment in a list file. The break-even point for the program is the rate of return on investment (or how much money the firm can expect to receive for what it spends on the campaign) required from the program. A firm's break-even mailing point becomes the cost of the mail package (which is the total cost of what is sent to prospects) divided by the net present value of the new customer.

To illustrate the importance of lists, this chapter begins by looking at the list industry. Next, it examines NBO Menswear, a successful user of customer lists to expand sales. The chapter then covers the types of lists available, examines the particulars of the list rental process, and considers the economics of mailing lists, including the factors influencing the choice of lists. Finally, issues related to list segmentation and techniques for segmenting lists are discussed.

TABLE 6.1. Major List Suppliers Sales
($ millions)

Suppliers	1991	1990	1989
Business compiled:			
Dun & Bradstreet	$50–$70	$70	$70
American Business Information	42	50	42
Database America	18	18	18
Trinet	15	15	N/A
R. L. Polk	2	2	1–5
Dunhill	5	N/A	N/A
Other	15–20	1–5	1
Consumer compiled:			
Donnelley Marketing	$60–100	$60–100	$60–100
Metromail	40	60	40–60
R. L. Polk	50	50	40–60
Market Compilation Research Bureau	10	10	10
Database America	4	4	4
Harte-Hanks	3	3	3
Others	20–30	1–5	1–5
Occupant/resident addressed:			
Advo	$25–50	$25–50	$25–50
Harte-Hanks	1	8	8
Others	45–55	25–50	25–50

Source: Adapted from Arnold Fishman, "List Industry Overview," *Direct Marketing,* August 1992, p. 24.

THE LIST INDUSTRY[1]

Direct Marketing magazine's sixth annual guide to the list industry describes the major list firms and the extent of list usage volume in the United States. The report for 1991 showed for the first time an actual decline in list market usage, both in dollars and usage volume. Third-class mail volume that year was down 1.5 percent, which is significant because list rental volume is related to growth or decline in third-class unit volume. All the indications in 1991 were of substantial shifts from prospecting for new customers to customer list mailings to offset the impact of postage-rate increases. In the face of the decline in list rental volume, there were only minor increases in list rental prices. Discounting on the part of list managers was intense in this shrinking list demand environment. Overall price increases were hardly sufficient to overcome declining list rental volume to permit list revenue growth (see Table 6.1).

A smaller number of mail users in the Direct Marketing Association's (DMA) surveys reported increases in mailing volume in 1991 compared to 1990 (see Table 6.2). During the spring of 1991, the DMA reported a decline of 23 percent of mailings; in summer, a drop of 9 percent; and in the fall, a decrease of 29 percent. Further, almost as many business-to-business mailers reported a decline in 1991 mailing volume (40 percent) compared to those reporting an increase (41 percent).

TABLE 6.2. List Volume of Use: 1990 versus 1991

	Sales (Millions)		*Names (Billions)*		*Rates/Thousand*	
	1990	1991	1990	1991	1990	1991
Business compiled	$ 160	$ 156	4.5	4.3	$35	$36
Consumer compiled	220	218	8.8	8.4	25.25	36
Occupant/resident address	95	89	13.4	12.7	7	7
Response names	830	800	11.2	10.6	73.70	75
Total	1,305	$1,263	38	36	$34.32	$34.97

Source: Adapted from Arnold Fishman, "List Industry Overview," *Direct Marketing,* August 1992, p. 24.

This is an astonishing concession considering the built-in bias of mail users asked the question "How are you doing this year, compared to last year?"

However, what is more important is the quality and not the magnitude of list rental volume. Spurred by postage-rate increases, there has been an explosive growth in the pervasiveness and effectiveness of applying database enhancement technology. This trend has been reflected in the increasing value of database marketing companies compared to list processors. It is hard to imagine what the mail-order business would have been in 1991 without the advent of smart database technology.

NBO[2]

NBO Menswear has been very successful in using direct mail to build its store traffic. Based on the East Coast, this discount apparel chain for men has 39 stores in New York, Washington, D.C., and New Jersey, where it is headquartered. The combination of a dedicated president, Gene Kosack, and an aggressive management team is helping NBO sales reach nearly $100 million a year. The firm attracts and keeps customers by means of targeted prospecting, well-developed mailings, and a strong customer-service orientation. In the process, NBO built a customer file of more than 650,000 names in just over two years. Although NBO uses television, radio, and newspaper advertising, its main focus is on direct mail, including postcards, catalogs, flyers, and letters.

In 1989, NBO started in lists by obtaining some 250,000 names from running a sweepstakes to win a BMW. Customers were asked to provide their name and address in order to be eligible to win the car. Some time passed, however, before NBO figured out how best to use these customer names. The company did not send out any mailings at first because it had no way of tracking responses. The management team then found a way to begin its direct-mail campaign. In addition to the sweepstakes-generated list, NBO had records of every credit card purchase, but without the names and addresses. By having an outside service company match the credit card numbers back to name and address information, the NBO customer list was created.

It was not long after NBO's first direct-mail campaign before the management team knew they had found a powerful way to reach customers. NBO distributed its first direct-mail piece in November of 1989 to 242,000 names at a cost of $69,000. The 8½-by-11-inch double-page flyer with coupons generated $1.4 million in sales, with an average transaction per customer of $243. Prior to 1989, the average transaction for the month of November was usually between $80 to $90.

Four days into the 10-day event, NBO decided to repeat the direct-mail campaign. Although most experts would suggest waiting a bit longer to do a second distribution, NBO mailed its second 8½-by-11-inch double-page flyer only 30 days later to just over 280,000 names, at a cost of $76,000. That piece generated $2.4 million in sales and doubled the average transaction figure for that time of year.

Today, NBO primarily gathers customer names from credit card charge slips and an in-store mailing list. The point-of-sale terminal in each store captures the credit card number and what was purchased. The name and address is not captured at the terminal but soon after. Once a customer adds his name to the in-store mailing list, completes a tailoring or alteration transaction, or responds to a direct-mail piece, his name is matched against the credit card file. Once the match is made, NBO has a name to add to its customer list. Sales of that credit card number are then tracked routinely.

Not only does NBO have the customer's last date of purchase, amount of purchase, amount of purchase by year, and maximum purchase each year, it also knows that the typical customer is 30 to 64; earns generally more than $40,000; is college educated, has lived at his current residence more than three years; and, on average, has a child under 18 at home.

TYPES OF LISTS

Lists are usually classified as either *response lists* or *compiled lists.* Response lists are based on the product or service interests of the persons on the list. Names on response lists are derived from a company's files. As mentioned earlier, the list of a firm's own customers is called a house list. Regardless of which firm created it, the list contains information such as names and addresses of particular consumers or businesses that have specific product or service purchase histories based on responding to direct-response offers. Direct marketers can rent response lists from firms that rent all or part of their lists through list marketing companies and/or list brokers.

Compiled lists are put together from numerous sources and sold by list marketing companies. These compilations are derived from sources such as telephone directories, voter lists, and auto registrations or from smaller lists with a common characteristic, including gun ownership, parents with new children, and new homeowners. Because compiled lists do not necessarily include mail-order or telemarketing buyers, people on these lists are not as responsive to mail or telemarketing solicitations as those on response lists. However, compiled lists are valuable to direct marketers because they allow firms to reach large numbers of people.

Response Lists

The people on house lists have the highest responsiveness because they are already customers, while those on purchased response lists have a high likelihood of ordering by mail or during telemarketing because they have done so in the past. An in-house customer list is the most valuable list source a firm has; it will produce the highest results when used in making a direct-response offer. A response list, because it represents the customers of another firm, is also very good for prospecting and acquiring new customers.

Response lists are available from list owners, list managers, and list brokers. A *list owner* is a mail-order or telemarketing firm, a broadcast direct-response marketer, a magazine or book publisher, or other firm that makes its customer list available to the commercial list-rental marketplace. *List managers* manage and market the list owner's list for a fee, and a *list broker* is a third-party agent who rents mailing lists. Unlike the list manager, who works primarily for the list owner, the broker works primarily for the list user.

For response lists, three key factors determine usage success: recency, frequency, and monetary amount spent. This combination is sometimes referred to by the acronym RFM (see again Chapter 5). *Recency* refers to how long ago the people on the list made their last mail-order purchase. The more recent the purchase, the better. This makes sense because the people who bought within, say, the last 12 months are likely to still have an interest in the type of product purchased (or at least the benefits it offers), while people who bought, say, five years ago may no longer be interested. Recency is so important that many list owners and managers rent separately that portion of their list containing buyers who have bought very recently, that is, within the past month, three months, six months, or one year. *Frequency* refers to how often the prospect buys through the mail or via the telephone. Lists of people who have bought more than once will usually outpull lists of one-time-only buyers. Many list owners and managers rent lists of those people separately at a premium. The third key factor in evaluating response lists is *monetary amount purchased.* This refers to how much money the prospect on the list has spent on mail-order or telemarketing purchases. List brokers frequently provide an average-order dollar amount, which represents the average amount spent per purchase by people on the list. Ideally, a firm wants a response list of people who have spent an amount similar to the price it is charging for its product.

List brokers have a data card for each list they recommend. Data cards contain the basic information on each list, including price, number of names on the list, buyer behavior, selections of buyers versus inquirers, average dollar amount of sale, state counts, minimum order, and so on. Most data cards contain a few paragraphs of narrative describing the list. The cards give the marketer a good idea of who the people on the list are and whether they fit the profile of the firm's target prospect. Data cards will often suggest types of offers the list is good for, but potential list users should ask brokers whether they think the list will work for their firm. In that sense, the firm contemplating a list rental must evaluate the types of products the list members' respondents purchased, and the similarity between those products and what the firm is trying to sell. List brokers can provide valuable insight into list usage by other marketers and make recommendations based on their years of experience in the list rental business.

One of the most important facts about a response list is who else has used it. Specifically, a firm contemplating a rental needs to know whether marketers with similar offers have used or have tested a given list and, if so, whether the results were favorable or negative. Although confidentiality may prevent the broker from revealing the names of firms that have used a list, a good broker can tell a potential renter whether the list has proved successful for products and offers similar to that of the firm considering the list. If the list has been successful for other firms, then there is a good chance it will work for the firm interested in the list.

The list needs to have current names and addresses, and therefore it must be updated frequently. Some list owners, such as controlled-circulation publications with specialized readerships, update and clean their lists annually. On the other hand, many smaller mail-order firms never do so. A list that is handled by a professional list manager is likely to be well maintained. Because one out of five Americans moves every year, lists that are not updated regularly become dated quickly. At least once a year, addresses should either be updated using a change-of-residence source or removed. Many list brokers and managers guarantee their lists to be reasonably up-to-date and will refund a portion of a firm's mailing costs if the nondeliverable mailing pieces returned by the post office exceed a certain percentage. For example, a list broker may guarantee a 95 percent deliverability rate and pay the list buyer some set amount such as 25 cents for each nondeliverable piece in excess of a 5 percent return rate.

The downside to response lists is that they are generally more expensive than compiled lists, costing up to twice as much in some cases. However, because response lists contain information about direct marketing responsiveness, the higher response rates normally associated with these types of lists can more than offset the increased costs.

Compiled Lists

Compiled lists include people who may or may not be willing to buy direct but who have some identifiable characteristics that make them good prospects for becoming customers. These characteristics can include occupation, magazine subscriptions, residence location, club memberships, and product ownership. For example, a person who has a personal computer at home may be a good candidate for ordering a financial management software package such as Quicken. Intuit, which owns Quicken, would purchase a list of names, perhaps from Compaq Computer Company, and mail an offer to those persons. While these computer owners may or may not be willing to buy a copy of Quicken to manage their money, they clearly have a higher probability of doing so than people who do not own a computer.

Consumer compiled lists are also put together from public sources, including phone books, motor vehicle registrations, and census bureau data, while business compiled lists can come from the yellow pages, business directories, and other sources. Firms may even contract with a list compiler to build a list to meet their special needs. Compiled lists are typically used by marketers to fulfill a unique requirement, so compiled list owners normally append some additional information to the basic name and address information. Compiled lists are usually updated annually or biannually.

Most business lists use Standard Industrial Classification (SIC) codes as a primary segmentation tool (see Chapter 15). Frequently, these compiled lists have more than one contact per business. Some of the major list compilers have built comprehensive lists of all available businesses that include some company size and other demographic information. However, compiled lists of individuals in particular businesses tend to be outdated quickly.

Compiled lists have both advantages and disadvantages. One advantage is coverage. If a firm needs to saturate a specific demographic and/or geographical segment, compiled lists, because they encompass a majority of households in the United States, offer the requisite number of names and addresses. Compiled lists may also have demographic information such as number of children, income, and much more, although usually this information is statistically inferred from groups of households using census data, not from information on specific households. This fact highlights one of the weaknesses of compiled lists, which is that inferred information can be inaccurate, so any personalization of an offer based on compiled list data can be risky. Another weakness of compiled lists is their inability to keep names and addresses current because so many U.S. citizens change their address every year.

The biggest weakness of compiled lists, though, lies in the fact that the names they contain are not necessarily mail-order responsive. Because compiled lists include everyone, they inevitably give firms responsive people as well as nonresponsive people, and that is why response lists are so much more valuable to most firms.

Lists complied from subscriptions and memberships contain people who have demonstrated a common interest. Businesspeople who subscribe to a trade journal probably have an interest in a particular area of business activity. By advertising, mailing, or phoning the members of this group, firms are targeting that particular interest. This type of affinity is a psychographic characteristic because it implies common activities, interests, and opinions.

Membership lists, such as those of professional groups, may contain industry, business size, and other information. Most frequently, however, these lists include only names and addresses, though telephone numbers are sometimes available. Also, these lists may be out of date because groups do not always keep names and addresses of their members current. Subscription lists usually contain only names and addresses. However, this information tends to be accurate because it is the basis for periodically sending subscriber materials. Most subscription lists do not include telephone numbers, titles, or industry information.

Combining Lists

Once a firm selects the lists it wants to use, its database efforts begin. Using various computer routines, the firm needs to combine the lists and eliminate duplicate records to the best of its ability. The data-processing technique used in combining lists is called merge-purge. It refers to merging lists together then purging duplicate names and addresses. Eliminating duplicate mailings makes obvious sense, of course, from a cost standpoint. It also makes sense from a company-image perspective because duplicate mailings give the recipient a negative impression and may lead to the conclusion that the sender organization is not operating efficiently.

The merged lists can be enhanced with other information to add more data and selection factors than were available on the original lists. In an enhancement, a list is run on a computer and matched with a larger master list of people. That larger list contains fuller demographic and descriptive profiles of each person or business. Information is taken from the large master list and added to the response list. As a result, the firm knows a lot more about the people or businesses on the list and can even select portions of the list according to various demographic criteria. On a consumer list, these selection criteria can include marital status, gender, age, type of dwelling, ethnicity, number of people in a household, ages of children in a household, credit card status, income, previous direct-response buyer behavior, and many others. On a business response list, additional data include number of employees in a firm, sales volume, job function or title of prospects, industry, SIC numbers, and phone numbers.

RENTING A LIST

Nearly all of the lists a company uses outside of its own house list are rented lists. However, many of the lists a firm rents are actually the house lists of other companies, available for a fee. Other, less common ways to get lists are to purchase them or to exchange lists with another firm.

List Brokers

List brokers rent lists to firms for list owners. The vast majority of all list rentals are made through brokers. The list renter pays a fee to the list broker for the use of a list, and the list owner receives that payment less the commission the list broker takes for its services.

List brokers are list experts. They know what lists are available, how the lists tend to perform, and how they can be best used. In that sense, list brokers act as consultants to direct marketers, advising them on what response lists are available and which would most likely work for a particular offer. List brokers have broad knowledge of the many available lists and tend to be objective in their recommendations. Firms interested in offering their list for rental usually make it available to more than one list broker. Prospective list renters should get list recommendations from at least three different brokers initially, until they find a broker with whom they feel comfortable and whose advice has been proven to work. Exhibit 6.1 shows the types of services offered by list brokers by frequency.

List Compilers

As noted previously, list compilers create lists from such sources as telephone directories and census data. They then organize those lists into groups of people or businesses having some common characteristic such as households with above-average incomes or businesses with more than 1 million employees. A popular approach to list creation involves building a list by segmenting out groups of households or businesses from large master files. Instead of using many distinct sources to

EXHIBIT 6.1. List Broker Services

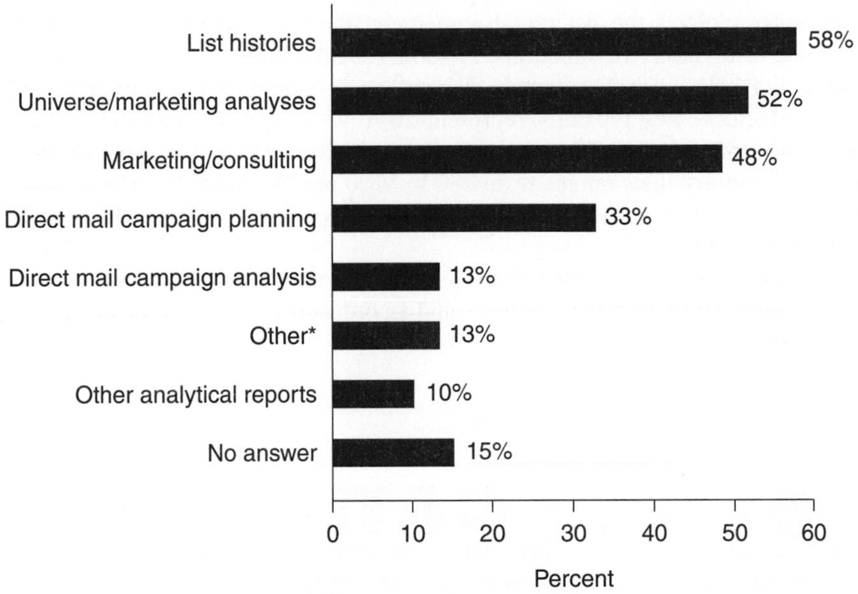

*Other—zip analysis, exchange management, predictive modeling, creative services, SCF analysis, ad hoc reports, budgets/accounting.
Note: Table does not add up to 100% due to multiplicity of response.
Source: DMA Circulation Council List Broker Quick Study, 1995.

create lists with special characteristics, large list compilers sort their master files of names and select only those names associated with certain characteristics.

List Managers

List managers represent the interests of list owners and are considered experts who understand how to get the most out of lists. They interact with the list brokers and keep track of all aspects of the process relevant to the owner. Compared to list brokers, list managers are more likely to recommend only the lists they manage.

List Rental Agreements

The most common list rental agreement is for an agreed number of uses. Beyond that, only those people on the list who respond to the firm's offer can become part of the renting firm's customer database. Generally, any firm that rents a list must get approval for what it plans to mail because the list manager may want to make sure the offer is genuine and not just a way of getting as many names as possible in response to the offer and thereby making the list a permanent part of the firm's customer file.

To ensure that a renter does not use a list more than the agreed-to number of times, list monitors insert phony names (called seed names) and addresses into their lists so that those names can be monitored. Every time the list is used, the list monitor is informed by the receipt of the offer from the firm that rented the list. If the list renter violates the list rental agreement, the list owner or manager may impose one of a variety of sanctions, including legal action.

Although prices for list rentals depend on a number of quantitative and qualitative factors, they typically represent 20 to 25 percent of the total cost per thousand of a mailing. While compiled lists typically rent for \$50 per thousand, the price of response lists ranges from \$80 to \$100 per thousand. It costs about \$5 per thousand for each portion of a list selected by specific characteristics such as gender, age, or income.

Exhibit 6.2 shows the cover of a list catalog from CompilersPlus along with types of lists available, a price schedule, and an order form. The firm has compiled

EXHIBIT 6.2. CompilersPlus Catalog

SALES LEADS & MAILING LISTS
Business Lists
• 11 Million U.S. & Canadian Businesses
• 179,000 Big Businesses
• 4.7 Million Small Business Owners
• 616,000 U.S. Manufacturers
• 1 Million Professionals
• 8 Million Presidents, Owners, Managers & Key Executives by Name & Title
• 11 Million Companies Selectable by Employee Size or Sales Volume
• Credit Rating Scores available!
• Brand New Businesses-Hot New Leads!
See page 43
Consumer Lists
(See page 44)
• 94 Million Households by Age, Income or Children
• 56 Million Home Owners
• 34 Million Mail Order Buyers
• 13.2 Million New Movers
• 28 Million Senior Citizens
• 6.2 Million Hispanics
• 6 Million Pet Owners
• 900,000 PC Owners
Market Research Service
(See inside back cover)
Compilersplus®
First in Lists —First in Service

a database of over 10 million U.S. businesses from such sources as the yellow pages. After that, the firm calls every business to verify the address and collect name of the president, owner, or manager, as well as other data. This business file can be segmented by business size, profession, or type of company. The consumer lists from CompilersPlus include 80 million residents, among whom are 2.3 million business executives, 54 million homeowners, 25 million mail-order buyers, and much more. The lists are available on cards, mailing labels, computer tape or diskette, and CD-ROM.

CompilersPlus charges different dollar amounts per name depending on which medium the list customer requests and how often the list is expected to be used. For example, a one-time use of names delivered on computer tape costs 5 cents per name. One year of unlimited use of names on computer tape costs 9 cents per name. Thus, a list of 250,000 names to be used multiple times over one year would cost $22,500.

CompilersPlus also has the ability to provide enhancements to a firm's list by adding additional prospect information such as estimates of purchase potential, census data, and SIC numbers.

LIST SEGMENTATION

When a firm decides to mail an offer to only a portion of a list rather than the whole list, that process is called *list segmentation.* List segmentation allows the direct marketer to define groups of individuals according to estimates of future offer responsiveness and profitability. It is an essential step in successfully targeting direct marketing campaigns to those most likely to buy. There are usually two distinctly different versions of the process, one for the customer list and another for list prospecting. Much of the difference has to do with the nature of the information available on the two types of lists.

The direct marketer may use its house list or a list from a list broker to sort for a particular subset of list members such as only those with a certain income or only men or only those who are known to have engaged in a particular behavior with a given frequency. With a compiled list or other list with only limited amounts of information, the firm may have difficulty choosing among list members because it does not have much data to work with.

Prospects on a rented list are presegmented to some extent because the sales potential of the list members comes from how the list was acquired. A given list may contain people who bought something from a company, or it may include subscribers to magazines or newspapers, or it may represent a collection of names gathered from phone and other directories, auto registrations, or other preexisting sources. As noted previously, these lists are frequently enhanced with demographics and other data to help create more useful segmentations. In fact, list enhancement using demographics and psychographics, credit screening, and other information-matching techniques has become commonplace.

Direct marketing strategies may vary over time, and therefore segmentation schemes should be flexible enough to handle a range of segmentation and targeting possibilities. Companies with large lists of customers have the advantage of being able to conduct segmentations of the lists to select those prospects with the highest expected responsiveness to whatever type of offer the firm intends to communicate.

Because the purpose of list segmentation is to increase the response rate to the offer a firm makes, it significantly enhances the likelihood that a given campaign will be successful. A segmented list always outperforms any random list of names, and how well a list is segmented can easily make the difference between a profitable and an unprofitable direct marketing campaign. However, achieving list segmentation's potential benefits is highly dependent on the amount of information available for each prospect on a list and the firm's ability to use sophisticated statistical routines and models (which include variables that predict direct marketing offer) to distinguish those with high sales and profit potential from the rest of the members of the list.

Characteristics on Which to Segment List Members

According to Burnett, the four main criteria in selecting consumer lists are as follows:

1. Demographics (population characteristics).
2. Psychographics (lifestyle characteristics).
3. Mail-order characteristics (relation of name to list owner).
4. Physical characteristics (mechanical characteristics).[3]

These criteria describe how list content varies from one list to another and identify how lists can be segmented to refine their potential productivity. They are the essence of list selectability and lead to the core of what makes one segment produce a differential response.

However, selecting list members by one or more of these criteria reduces the size of the list segment available for targeting. After two or three "cuts," a list may have few remaining members, perhaps so few that the firm cannot warrant using the list. Burnett provides the following illustration:

In zip code XXXXX there are	10,500 homes
Of these homes 63 percent have family incomes of over $25,000 leaving	6,600 homes
Households headed by females are 15.5 percent and are to be eliminated which leaves	5,600 homes
Those owning two or more cars are 28 percent which leaves	1,600 homes
Of these 22 percent have purchased a car in 1984 or 1985 which leaves	350 homes[4]

By using one selection criterion after another, only 350 names are left from the starting number of 10,500 homes.

Demographics

The major demographic criteria for a consumer list are such personal variables as household income; age of head of household; education of head of household; family size; age and gender of children; and residence data such as type of dwelling (single family or multifamily), length of residence, value of home, geographic location, and telephone/car registration.

Psychographics

Psychographic characteristics are also called lifestyle measures because they describe a consumer's orientation to life; they include the consumer's activities, interests, and opinions. Consumer segments resulting from a lifestyle segmentation are assigned such labels as swingers, straights, conservatives, and status seekers (see Chapter 3). Knowing consumers' lifestyles plays a major role in determining the product benefits important to them, providing marketers with opportunities to produce offers specifically designed to sell products.

Mail-Order Characteristics

The third major criterion for selecting a consumer list is mail-order characteristics, which describe the ways a given segment varies from other segments in their participation in mail-order activities. This criterion includes the popular RFM calculations (see p. 117), which are highly valued by direct marketers for determining segments in a list. It is also the most important criterion for estimating the likely profitability of mailing to an individual.

Physical Characteristics

The fourth basic list selection criterion is physical characteristics. This is included because lists can vary physically by the size, deliverability, selectability, format, means of reproduction, and accessibility. Size refers to the number of names on a given list. Deliverability describes the cleanliness of the list in terms of duplicate names and how often the list is updated. Selectability is about what variables on the list can be used to select and sort the members. Format is about the physical format of the list data file. Means of reproduction has to do with how the list is reproduced, specifically, whether it is on tape or on mailing labels. Accessibility is about when and how the list is made available as well as other time-dependent attributes such as when the list was last used and when it was last maintained.

List Segmentation Approaches

Once a firm determines which characteristics it will use to segment a list, it must decide how it will analyze the variables on the list. When only one characteristic or variable is being used, the firm can find the response behavior for different values or levels of the variable, rank-order the values, and determine a cutoff point by estimating expected sales and profit for each name on the list. Regardless of the approach the firm uses, the goal is the same: to produce one or more subsets from an overall list that are expected to exhibit a differential response to an offer. This expectation can be based on estimates of the likelihood of response, order size, or expected long-term profitability.

However, when two or more characteristics need evaluation in segmenting a list, the firm must choose from a variety of different statistical methods and list management approaches designed to identify subsets of list members who are, on average, better prospects for an offer than other members of the list. During this process, list records must be analyzed and sorted to effectively score each list record for purchase probability. This is when the different statistical techniques come into play, ranging from relatively simple methods that create a weighted average of two or three characteristics and determine the names of those in the mailing to sophisticated statistical methods that involve the analysis of several variables simultaneously. However, the latter methods can be difficult, particularly when lists are complex and there are a large number of prospect characteristics that could affect response rates and order sizes. These sophisticated techniques include many alternatives, a few of which are briefly discussed below to provide a sense of what can be done.

Multiple regression analysis (MRA) is considered by many to be the best statistical technique available for direct marketing list segmentation because it can develop a scoring formula containing many simultaneous predictors of purchase behavior. The analysis then uses the results of the scoring formula to rank-order the scores and determine a cutoff point for target segment membership. Regression-based scoring can identify segments that may appear dissimilar at first glance, although they are homogeneous in terms of such performance measures as expected offer response rates or profitability.

Like MRA, logistic regression analysis (LRA) is used in list segmentation to develop a scoring formula from many simultaneous predictors. However, a major difference lies in the fact that LRA can predict membership in rank-ordered categories rather than just a single point value. Some argue that LRA is a more appropriate approach to segmentation than MRA because the resulting formula can specifically define the variables associated with being a member of a hierarchical classification.

Multiple discriminant analysis (MDA) is similar to LRA except that it deals with situations in which what is to be predicted is categorical, meaning when the dependent variable is response or no response, although it can also be used when the outcomes of interest are classified into more than two categories such as no response, small order, or large order amount, which are not ordered or hierarchical.

The non-regression-based techniques for list segmentation do not provide a scoring equation that allows a rank ordering of an entire list of names. Rather, these techniques attempt to cluster or group list members who have similar profiles on whatever variables the analyst chooses to include. The result is a collection of prospects into clusters (or segments) that are homogeneous with respect to their demographics or some other characteristic. However, segments developed this way are not necessarily homogeneous in terms of likely performance. The performance characteristics of each cluster are defined by profiling the individual clusters on such variables as average order size or offer responsiveness. The cluster(s) with the highest scores from profiling become the best segments to mail an offer to or to call with a telemarketing script.

Cluster analysis is most often used in geodemographic work, where it identifies groups with certain aggregated neighborhood characteristics. For example, zip-code-level census demographic data is used to cluster zip codes into 20 or so categories, which are made up of demographically similar households.

It is worth noting that marketers who manage direct-response programs do not need to understand all the technical details of how the segmentation techniques operate. They only need to appreciate the power of those techniques for maximizing the profitability of a mail or phone campaign. Those marketers are not expected to be able to do the actual statistical work themselves, because statistical experts with a firm or a list process company will do the actual work and deliver the end result. Marketers need to know only the principles underlying segmentation modeling (to predict segment response rates) in order to manage the process properly.

SUMMARY

A list is a collection of names and addresses of prospects and customers who could be the target of an offer. List information is usually stored in a database.

Lists are usually classified as either response lists or compiled lists. Response lists are based on the product or service interests of the persons on the list. The names on such a list come from companies that have done business with particular customers and know something about their product or service interests. Compiled lists are put together from numerous sources and sold by list marketing companies. These compilations are derived from various sources or from smaller lists with a common characteristic. Because compiled lists do not necessarily include mail-order or telemarketing buyers, they may not be as responsive to mail or telemarketing solicitations. However, they are valuable to direct marketers in that they allow firms to reach large numbers of people.

List brokers rent lists to firms on behalf of list owners. The vast majority of all list rentals are made through brokers. The list renter pays a fee to the list broker for the use of a list and the list owner receives that payment less the commission that the list broker takes for its services. List brokers know about what lists are available, how the lists tend to perform, and how they can be best used. List compilers create lists from such sources as telephone directories, census data, and other information. They then organize those lists into groups of people or businesses having common characteristics, such as households with above average incomes or businesses with more than one million employees. *List managers* represent the interests of list owners. They interact with the list brokers and keep track of all aspects of the process relevant to the owner. Compared to list brokers, list managers are more likely to recommend only the lists they manage.

The lists are used in conjunction with mathematical and statistical techniques to identify individual prospects or groups of prospects based on their demographics, psychographics, and/or behavioral characteristics such as purchase histories. Direct marketers use list segmentation to select those people from whom they expect response rates greater than that from the population in general. List segmentation can also be used to split a list file into several smaller homogeneous files, where a firm mails only to individuals in those smaller files because they are expected to be profitable. The more a list is refined, the higher the response rate a firm will get to a given campaign. Direct marketers mail or telephone the names expected to be most productive first and move down the list until the incremental response rate is equal to the break-even response rate.

REVIEW QUESTIONS

1. What is a list? How do direct marketers use lists?
2. Describe how lists are managed through databases to increase the effectiveness of direct marketing campaigns.
3. What is meant by the phrase "past purchase behavior" and why is that information about consumers or businesses so important to direct marketers?
4. What is a *response list* and what is a *compiled list?* How and when is each typically used by a direct marketing firm?
5. What is meant by the term "list segmentation"? What are the ways of conducting a list segmentation? What is the relationship between list segmentation and direct marketing campaign response rates?
6. What are the benefits of list segmentation to direct marketers?
7. Which customer and prospect characteristics are typically used in list segmentation and why? How do those characteristics differ in consumer versus business-to-business direct marketing?

NOTES

1. Adapted from Arnold Fishman, "List Industry Overview," *Direct Marketing,* August 1992, pp. 23–24.
2. Adapted from Elaine Santoro, "NBO Markets with Style," *Direct Marketing,* February 1992, pp. 28–31.
3. Ed Burnett, *The Complete Direct Mail List Handbook* (Englewood Cliffs, NJ: Prentice Hall, 1988), p. 143.
4. Ibid., p. 145.

SOURCES

BLUMENFIELD, ARTHUR. "List Processing." In *The Direct Marketing Handbook,* 2nd ed., ed. Ed Nash. New York: McGraw-Hill, 1992, pp. 248–62.

BURKA, KAREN. "Owners Battle Back for List Control." *Direct,* January 1994, pp. 1, 26–27.

BURNETT, ED. "List Selection Criteria." In *The Direct Marketing Handbook,* 2nd ed., ed. Ed Nash. New York: McGraw-Hill, 1992, pp. 218–25.

________. *The Complete Direct Mail List Handbook.* Englewood Cliffs, NJ: Prentice Hall, 1988.

CHEVAN, HARRY. "The Changing Face of the List Industry." *Catalog Age* 10, no. 8 (August 1993), pp. 87–89.

Direct Marketing Association. *Statistical Fact Book 1996.* New York: Direct Marketing Association, 1996.

FISHMAN, ARNOLD. "List Industry Overview." *Direct Marketing,* August 1992, pp. 23–24.

GOLDBERG, BERNARD, and TRACY EMERICK. *Business to Business Direct Marketing,* 2nd ed. Yardley, PA: Direct Marketing Publishers, 1990.

HANSOTIA, BEHRAM J. "List Segmentation: How to Find Your Best Direct Marketing Prospects," In *Readings & Cases in Direct Marketing,* ed. Herbert E. Brown, and Bruce Buskirk. Lincolnwood, IL: NTC Business Books, 1989, pp. 103–12.

Hatch, Denison. "The Business of List Marketing." *Target Marketing* 18, no. 9 (September 1995), pp. 16–20.

Hauser, Barry. "List Segmentation." In *The Direct Marketing Handbook,* 2nd ed., ed. Ed Nash. New York: McGraw-Hill, 1992, pp. 233–47.

Howard, Scott. "Focus On: Expert Advice on List Selection for Telemarketers." *Telemarketing,* 14, no. 4 (October 1995), pp. 78–81.

Hughes, Arthur M. *The Complete Database Marketer,* 2nd ed. Homewood, IL: Richard D. Irwin, 1995.

Katzenstein, Herbert, and Williams S. Sachs. *Direct Marketing,* 2nd ed. New York: Macmillan, 1992.

Kendall, Dee. "Fundamentals of List Management." In *The Direct Marketing Handbook,* 2nd ed., ed. Ed Nash. New York: McGraw-Hill, 1992, pp. 193–208.

Kleinfelter, Mary Ann. "Business Lists." In *The Direct Marketing Handbook,* 2nd ed., ed. Ed Nash. New York: McGraw-Hill, 1992, pp. 209–17.

"Lists and Database." *Direct,* August 1996, pp. 77–78, 82–86.

"Mailing List Systems." *Direct Marketing,* August 1993, pp. 31–32.

Marx, Wendy. "The New Segmentation of One." *Direct,* September 1994, pp. 45–48.

McAleer, Linda. "New Heights for the List Broker: The Top Ten Challenges." In *Beyond 2000: The Future of Direct Marketing,* ed. Jerry I. Reitman. Lincolnwood, IL: NTC Business Books, 1994, pp. 69–78.

Mummert, Hallie. "Reaching Out to Women." *Target Marketing,* 18, no. 8 (August 1995), pp. 33–38.

Nash, Edward. *Database Marketing: The Ultimate Marketing Tool.* New York: McGraw-Hill, 1992.

Nykamp, Melinda. "Evaluating External Data Options." *Direct Marketing,* April 1994, pp. 33–35.

Roberts, Mary Lou, and Paul D. Berger. *Direct Marketing Management.* Englewood Cliffs, NJ: Prentice Hall, 1989.

Roberts, Steve. "Selecting and Testing Response Lists." In *The Direct Marketing Handbook,* 2nd ed., ed. Ed Nash New York: McGraw-Hill, 1992, pp. 178–92.

Rosenfield, James R. *Financial Services Direct Marketing.* Naperville, IL: Financial Source Books, 1991.

Santoro, Elaine. "NBO Markets with Style." *Direct Marketing,* February 1992, pp. 28–31.

Schultz, Ray. "Compilers Move to Capture Data Online." *Direct,* May 1995, p. 22.

———. "Let Me Handle This." *Direct,* August 1995, pp. 53–56.

Stone, Bob. *Successful Direct Marketing Methods,* 5th ed. Lincolnwood, IL: NTC Books, 1995.

Yorgey, Lisa A. "Naming Names." *Target Marketing* 18, no. 9 (September 1995), pp. 14–15.

Zukas, Tom. "List and Database Maintenance." In *The Direct Marketing Handbook,* 2nd ed., ed. Ed Nash. New York: McGraw-Hill, 1992, pp. 226–32.

MAILING LIST SOFTWARE*

With the plethora of software systems it is difficult for direct marketers to keep up-to-date. This appendix summarizes some of the software packages to help build and maintain mailing lists.

Mailing List I

Developer: Alphanetics
(Forestville, CA—707/887-7237)
Description: Features an unlimited number of entries and sorts up to 2,000 entries on a single, double-sided disk. Boilerplate entries allow you to repeat any field from the last entry entered with a single keystroke. Able to search and find any entry within six seconds, this mailing list incorporates features of programs costing four to 10 times as much, including user specified sort field for quick entry, search and edit, 10-digit zip codes, phone numbers and "attention" fields, print only newest entries and phone directories.
Operating Environment(s): PC/MSDOS
List Price: US $49.95

Mass Mailer

Developer: Alternative Software, Inc.
(West Berlin, NJ—609/435-2026)
Description: Best-rated mailing list package handles mailing lists, labels, envelopes and interfaces with most word processors including Word Perfect. Unlimited number of lists, up to 1 million names per list, so sorting required, select by field (up to 10) and/or 112 quantities.
Operating Environment(s): PC/MSDOS
Memory Requirements: 640 KB List Price: US $199.95

MailingList

Developer: Artworx Software Co., Inc.
(Penfield, NY—716/385-6120)
Description: Manage mailing list data. Address can be created, edited, added or deleted from files. Retrieve by name, key words or zip codes and sent to another disk for complete file management. Labels created in 1, 2 or 3 up format. Sorts names in alphabetical or ascending zip code number, ranges of zip codes or last initials. There is an 1,800-name capacity on single-sided disk, 4,000 on double

sided, more on hard drives. Internally documented. Help screens available.
Operating Environment(s): Macintosh
Hardware Requirements: 512K or larger Macintosh
List Price: US $24.95

Avery List & Mail Plus

Developer: Avery Label (Business Systems Division)
(Azusa, CA—818/969-3311)
Description: Stores up to 64,000 addresses. Sort, select and print on labels, cards and forms. Compatible with popular database and word processing programs.
Operating Environment(s): PC/MSDOS
List Price: C$67.99

Mail Expert

Developer: Cooperative Technologies, Inc.
(Atlanta, GA 404/452-8895)
Description: Mainframe software package that is designed to reduce postage expenses by electronically compiling multiple documents, from diverse systems, addressed to the same person into a single envelope. Envelope contents are then printed in the sequence determined to attain the best available postal discounts. Zip code barcoding is supported, as well as barcoding for variable page insertion machines. Keeps an online index of all items processed from response to inquiries regarding the status of items mailed. Reprinting of lost mail or items damaged in the mailroom is provided.
Operating Environment(s): IBM minis/mainframes, various
Software Requirements: MVS
Hardware Requirements: IBM mainframe
List Price: US $70,000

Mail List 4.0

Developer: Dynacomp, Inc.
(Webster, NY—800/828-6772) Source Language: basic
Description: Manages extensive lists of names and addresses. Options include alphabetical and zip code sorting, file merging, additions and deletions, label printing and three different printout formats and duplicate entry deletion.
Operating Environment(s): Apple II
List Price: US $34.95

MailBase

Developer: Exceiver Corp.
(Elk River, MN—612/441-8166)
Description: Maintains mailing lists in flexible form, with user-defined miscellaneous fields and up to five selection fields. User-defined fields can be given custom names that appear on entry screens. Allows use of two label formats 1–3 up.

Reports, mail merge, and label format allow sorting by name or zip, in addition to dates, SIC codes, mailers received, any portion of zip. Allows users to select first three numbers of zip for third-class mailings. Import and export of data from any program that allows it in number of formats.

OmniMailer/OmniMailer3

Developer: Janac Enterprises
(Herbron, IL—815/648-2492)
Description: A straightforward, easy-to-use mailing list manager that is limited only by the amount of disk space available. Offers a wide variety of search, select, and sorting modes, user-defined fields, and default entries. OmniMailer signals duplicate entries on input or user can search and print duplicate listings.
Operating Environment(s): Macintosh
Memory Requirements: 512 KB.
List Price: US $84.95

MailMiser

Developer: Kestrel Enterprises
(Carol Stream, IL—708/293-1910)
Description: Mailing list management program designed to reduce mailing costs. Implements zip+4 codes and corresponding barcodes with first- and third-class presorting. Also carrier route presort. Unlimited files and records; locate by last name, company or zip code; conditional print or file copy; label printing. Convert existing database files.
Operating Environment(s): PC/MSDOS
List Price: US $139

PerfectLabel

Developer: Management Information Systems (MIS)
(Watford, ON—519/876-2110)
Description: This is a versatile program designed to meet the needs of WordPerfect users. Stand-alone database manager for mail-merge info and label printing. Includes background printing, user-definable label format/contents, multiple fonts per label, nonsequential record selection, serialization and envelope printing including return address. Supplemental PerfectLabel features include the use of existing WordPerfect secondary files, new file creation, flexible sort capability, selectable case conversion and browse.
Operating Environment(s): PC/MSDOS
Memory Requirements: 640 KB
List Price: US $109.95

Pace Mailing List System

Developer: PACE Software & Systems
(Bedford, TX—817/267-1497)
Description: Mailing list development and management including removal of duplicate records, postal reports, state code standardization based on postal zip

codes, selective code printing, 1, 2, 3 and 4 up labels in either vertical or horizontal zip code sortation and more. Limited only by available disk space.
Operating Environment(s): PC/MSDOS
List Price: US $50

Client Database System

Developer: Personal Systems, Ltd.
(San Diego, CA—619/484-0347)
Description: Maintains complete database of all clients. Allows user to assign mail code which, in effect, divides the file into separate pieces for mailing purposes. Creates mailing labels and postcards which may be selected by mail code, zip code or company. Displays graph of clients by state.
Operating Environment(s): PC/MSDOS
List Price: US $49.95

Super Bulkmailer+

Developer: Software Publishers of America
(The Lakes, NV—800/233-0555)
Description: Features: virtually unlimited record storage; carrier route coding; zip+4 coding; barcoding; presorting of first-, second- or third-class mail; *N*th sampling to test the list before mailing; fully integrated word processor; custom report generator; custom label generator; Avery Label templates; standard reports built in; and instantaneous search and display.
Operating Environment(s): Macintosh

FastMail

Developer: Vertical Solutions
(Beaverton, OR—800/942-4008)
Description: List management and labeling with user-defined database that can be hot-linked so test flows to labels automatically. Includes duplicate checking, optimized data entry, sublist designation, and a report generator that produces zip code summaries for bulk mailing. Add graphics to labels with drawing, painting and importing tools.
Operating Environment(s): Macintosh
Software Requirements: System 6.0 or later
Hardware Requirements: Mac Plus or larger
Memory Requirements: 1000 KB List Price: USA $229.95

*Adapted from "Mailing List Systems," *Direct Marketing,* August, 1993, pp. 31–32. All products mentioned are trademarks or registered trademarks of their respective companies. Though Synergy Computer Consulting Ltd. endeavors to keep accurate and complete records, it cannot guarantee availability, prices, or completeness of this listing.

CHAPTER 7

Positioning and Offer Planning

OBJECTIVES

1. To define the term *positioning* and indicate why it is important in direct marketing.
2. To explain how products and services are positioned in terms of benefits or attributes that satisfy particular needs.
3. To list and describe the seven steps involved in developing a positioning strategy.
4. To explain what is meant by *offer planning* and how an offer influences a target audience.
5. To examine the elements of a direct marketing offer.

INTRODUCTION

Positioning is the act of designing a marketing mix for a particular product or service to create an image in the minds of target market members that is consistent with the needs those members are trying to satisfy. Products or services are positioned relative to those of competitors in a market in the sense that other firms have a place in the minds of target market members into which a company's offering must fit.

Offer planning is among the five decision elements of direct marketing introduced in Chapter 1 (offer, creative, media, timing/sequencing, and customer service). The offer is the complete proposition made by the direct marketer to the prospect. It positions the firm's product or service and attempts to motivate buyer behavior. Offer objectives can include attracting new customers or obtaining repeat business from existing customers.

THE SHARPER IMAGE[1]

The Sharper Image thrived as a direct marketer in the 1980s because it was an icon of that business boom decade. Its catalog offering of gimmicks and gadgets was a favorite among young white-collar professionals who tended to make expensive, self-indulgent purchases.

However, many people would not have given The Sharper Image a chance of surviving the 1980s. In fact, in 1992 the firm had to reposition itself as a retail and mail-order merchant of affordable, mostly sensible products designed for everyday use.

To illustrate how The Sharper Image has repositioned itself, consider Exhibit 7.1. The Sharper Image's Spring 1992 retail sampler catalog cover features three

EXHIBIT 7.1. The Sharper Image Catalog Cover

bathing-suit-clad young professionals. The bottom left-hand corner announces: "Thermoscan instant thermometer now in stock! Call 1-800-344-4444." The cover reflects an emphasis on practical products for upscale professionals.

Inside the catalog, the ad copy headline—"Finally, get a true temperature. Without a big struggle"—mentions not one, but two benefits that actually relate to the audience, as does the word *finally,* which captures the concerned exasperation of a parent trying to take the temperature of an ailing tot. The first two paragraphs of the body copy read:

> Want to start a fight? Try taking a sick two-year-old's temperature. The struggle can only make you both feel worse. Besides the worrisome risk of broken glass, the accuracy is no better than you'd expect from an instrument that arrived on the scene in 1867.
>
> Now, you can take anyone's temperature quickly and safely—from newborns to the elderly. Thermoscan Instant Thermometer is the affordable home version of the patented instrument physicians and hospitals use to measure body temperature via the ear.

The whole story comes through in clear, conversational expository prose. The situation: "taking a sick two-year-old's temperature." Empathy: "The struggle can only make you both feel worse." Anxiety: "worrisome risk of broken glass." Interesting little-known fact: Conventional thermometers "arrived on the scene in 1867." The benefit: "you can take anyone's temperature quickly and safely." Demographic reality vis-à-vis our aging population: "from newborns to the elderly." What it is, how it works, and why it is credible: "the affordable home version of the patented instrument physicians and hospitals use to measure body temperature via the ear."

The rest of the page, which is devoted exclusively to the Thermoscan Instant Thermometer, is equally felicitous and technically impeccable. Three subheads let the reader scan the copy quickly: "Accurate result in one second," "Safe for all ages," "Why direct readings are preferred." A large product shot occupies the lower left. The upper-right corner of the page has a photo of the product in use, with a benefit-laden caption: "Thermoscan is so quick and easy, you can take a reading while your child is sleeping." Photo captions, of course, get very high readership. There is a testimonial from a "Clinical Nurse Researcher" and a bar graph showing the differences between "Usual Home Method" and "Tympanic Thermometry"; the items charted are "Resisted or fought," "Cried but did not resist," "Ignored," and "Complied cheerfully."

Most of the other products in The Sharper Image catalog are likewise useful, sensible, and affordable. For example, there is the "Video Fitness Cycle" ($499), which lets the buyer enjoy scenery while exercising; practical footwear such as Teva Sport Sandals, whose "2,000 lb. nylon webbing strap holds the ball of your foot against the sole"; a two-time-zone travel alarm clock ($59.95); classic aviator sunglasses, at a most non-1980s $29.95; "liquid gel insoles," to soothe the buyer's no-longer-young and now-aching feet, for only $19.95; and the world's first self-closing umbrella, ($39.95). Even the Playboy "Intimate Workout" videos have been refitted for the 1990s, featuring "Secrets of MAKING LOVE . . . to the same person forever . . . Was $99.95. Now $79.95."

The catalog has well-written copy; sharp, crisp photos; intelligent design; and good organization. For example, the inside front cover, divided into unequal quadrants, is a triumph of legibility, authenticity, and sound technique. The upper-left quadrant consists of a letter from CEO Richard Thalheimer, calling attention to the eminently practical Teva Sport Sandals and the sensible Thermoscan Instant Thermometer. In his photo, Thalheimer sports a "personally selected Messico Silk Shirt ($79.95)." The lower-left quadrant is the guarantee, headed "OUR COMMITMENT TO YOU":

> Welcome to our celebration of human ingenuity . . . If one of our products doesn't meet your expectations, by all means return it . . . We make a special effort to select or create products that are energy efficient, make sensible use of resources, and assist endangered animals or ecosystems . . . We operate our business for long-term goals . . ."

The upper-right quadrant, headlined "Why Shop with Us?," follows with four subheads, which make the "no-lemon promise," highlight the availability of Federal Express shipping, and point out the advantages of visiting a Sharper Image store to get a "firsthand look" in a place where the buyer is "treated with respect." The lower-right quadrant begins with a large red 800 number and follows with two brief testimonial letters. The page, in total, focuses on brand building.

Turning to the order form, the first thing the buyer sees is an interruptive bind-in, a double card headlined "Put a friend on our mailing list." Said friends (there's room for two) get a $5 discount certificate. (The same offer appears on the order form itself, on which the buyer is instructed to mention key code number 7307. On the card, the buyer is told to mention key code number 6950.) The back of the card offers a $10 discount on orders placed before April 30. The linkage of a discount with a time limit is so routine that many direct marketers forget its power; but it remains today what it always has been, probably the most powerful way to structure an offer.

The front of the catalog order form sells the store, another example of sales channels reinforcing each other. Headline: "The benefits of shopping in a Sharper Image store." Subheads: "Try before you buy," "Walk into a showcase of the future," "Experience our friendly firsthand know-how," "Find gifts they'll never forget," "Purchase without risk." The back of the order form lists the stores' addresses and phone numbers.

The order form itself is carefully designed and enumerated step-by-step: Item 1 is the preprinted name and address, item 2 is the daytime phone, item 3 is the date of order, item 4 is the list of items ordered, item 5 is the grand total, item 6 is the method of payment, and so on. Enumeration generally leads, directs, simplifies, and soothes those who are making a purchase. The rest of the order form turns into an envelope, but not before alerting the buyer to the "1992 Frequent-Buyers Program" and giving instructions on "Ordering Made Easy." In fact, the 800 number is mentioned six times on the order form. Within reason and using judgment, a company's 800 number simply cannot be mentioned too many times.

The order form has three product illustrations, the catalog equivalent of a retail point-of-sale display, to capture last-minute impulse purchases. Below the products, a special offer appears: Fly Qantas by May 31, 1992, and receive a $300 merchandise certificate.

Overall, the new Sharper Image catalog's combination of affordable, sensible gadgets and other products in a bright, creative package is designed to appeal to consumers of the 1990s. This positioned the firm for continued sales growth and profitability, and it received much industry recognition for how well the new strategy worked.

CUSTOMER MOTIVATIONS

Customer motivations are what drive the purchasing process; they have direction and strength that stem from the customer's attempt to satisfy particular needs or achieve certain goals. Because most goals can be reached by a number of routes, a direct marketer must convince target audience members that its product or service alternative will satisfy their needs and hence attain their goals. For example, a person who decides that he needs an outdoor coat that can help him project an appropriate image and thereby be accepted by others can choose between L. L. Bean and Lands' End, both of which offer items promising to deliver those benefits.

How to satisfy a customer's need depends on the individual's unique history, learning experiences, and cultural environment. Marketing strategies are most effective when they aim to influence the direction a person will take to satisfy a need rather than when they attempt to create the need itself.

Types of Needs

Some social scientists have created universal inventories of needs that attempt to systematically explain virtually all human behavior. Henry Murray describes a set of 20 needs that alone or in combination result in specific behaviors.[2] These needs include dimensions of autonomy (being independent), defendance (defending the self against criticism), and play (engaging in pleasurable activities). In a consumer behavior sense, individuals with a high need for achievement and personal accomplishment place a premium on products and services that signify their success. Working women who are high in achievement motivation are more likely to choose businesslike clothing and less likely to be interested in apparel that accentuates their femininity.

Prior to Murray, psychologist Abraham Maslow developed a theory of motivation to help explain personal growth and the attainment of peak experiences.[3] Maslow's hierarchy of needs specifies levels of motives in which the order of development is fixed; that is, a certain level must be attained before the next higher one is activated (see Exhibit 7.2). This approach to motivation has been adapted by direct marketers because it indirectly specifies types of product or service benefits prospects might be looking for, depending on their environmental conditions. Although its use in direct marketing is somewhat simplistic, especially because the same product or activity can satisfy a number of different needs, Maslow's hierarchy of needs does provide a way to think about what motivates buyer behavior.

EXHIBIT 7.2. Levels of Needs in the Maslow Hierarchy

UPPER-LEVEL NEEDS

Self-Actualization
Self-fulfillment, enriching experiences

Ego Needs
Prestige, status/accomplishment

Belongingness
Love, friendship, acceptance by others

Safety
Security, shelter, protection

Physiological
Water, sleep, food

LOWER-LEVEL NEEDS

Source: Del I. Hawkins; Roger J. Best; and Kenneth A. Coney, *Consumer Behavior,* 5th ed. (Homewood, IL: Richard D. Irwin, 1992), p. 297.

At each level in the Maslow hierarchy, different priorities exist about desired product benefits. A person must first satisfy basic needs before progressing up the ladder from physiological concerns to an interest in status symbols, friendship, or self-fulfillment.

Direct marketers often find that multiple motives are involved in making a purchase and that motives affecting purchase behavior vary by target market. With the variety of manifest motives that may be operative in a particular purchase, the marketer needs to determine the combination influencing the behavior of his or her target market. Once the direct marketer has isolated the combination(s) of motives influencing a target market, the next task is to develop a product or service positioning and offer designed around those motives. To the extent that more than one motive is important, the positioning must convey more than one benefit and the offer must communicate those multiple benefits. The appeals to emotional motives are the most difficult to implement. If possible, any given offer should focus on only one or a few purchasing motives, while the overall campaign may cover all the important purchase motives of a target market. Thus, the overall campaign positions the product or service in the minds of the target market members in a way that corresponds with what motivates target market members to engage in buyer behavior.

Products and services can be positioned in terms of the benefits or attributes that satisfy particular needs, regardless of whether those needs are utilitarian or emotional. The satisfaction of utilitarian needs implies an emphasis on the objective, tangible attributes of products. Emotional needs are subjective and experiential; they are similar to Maslow's upper-level needs in that people expect products to meet their needs for such psychological qualities as acceptance, prestige, and self-fulfillment. Of course, target market members may be motivated to purchase a product because it provides both types of benefits simultaneously. For example, a new car gets a person from point A to point B while at the same time it indicates by its brand name and style what status in life the owner has achieved.

DEVELOPING A POSITIONING STRATEGY

According to Roberts and Berger, developing a positioning strategy involves seven distinct steps:

1. Identify the competitors.
2. Determine how the competitors are perceived and evaluated.
3. Determine the competitors' positionings.
4. Analyze the target market.
5. Select the desired segment.
6. Develop alternative positionings.
7. Implement the positioning strategy and monitor its effectiveness.[4]

Identify the Competitors

The process of developing a strategic marketing plan, as outlined in Chapter 2, includes a situation analysis of competitors. That analysis produces an evaluation of a firm's current competition and leads to an understanding about the firm's competitive situation. The identification of competitors should include a detailed analysis of how competition for customers occurs with respect to the basis on which firms compete for the attention and sales of potential target market members. Marketers should then carry out a thorough and comprehensive assessment of their competitors' marketing objectives and strategies (including product, pricing, promotion, and distribution strategies) and an analysis of each competitor's major strengths and weaknesses.

Determine How the Competitors Are Perceived and Evaluated

The strategic marketing plan development process also includes an analysis of how competitors in a market are perceived and evaluated. This information comes from subjective judgments and/or research into how members of a target market evaluate competitive products. It is important to assess the perceptions of only the actual and prospective buyers in a market, because those with little or no experience or interest can provide misleading information.

This analysis produces a description of how the competitive brands are dimensionalized in the minds of buyers for the consumer or industrial markets on key product offering attributes. Those attributes need not be specific to product design, although they frequently are. Product-design-specific attributes include features intrinsic to the product itself such as taste, size, or texture. Product design features do not include attributes related to pricing, distribution, or image. While certain characteristics are associated with a particular product, they are actually more descriptive of the entire marketing package offered by competitors.

Consumer or industrial participants in a market are frequently asked about both their perceptions of individual competitors and their ideal attribute levels. Their answers provide information about what attributes are important to them and what the levels of those attributes are for competing products or services.

Determine the Competitors' Positionings

There are two aspects to determining product- or service-related attribute information. One concerns the key attributes in a market, and the other is about which competitor's products have those attributes, and at what levels. This information is based on perceptions, but perceptions and realities need not match. Positioning is about creating an *image* in the minds of target market members and not necessarily about where a product or service actually stands on the benefits stressed in the positioning. For example, the positioning may be that a product or service is low priced and/or a good value when in reality it is not the lowest priced or the best value. Perceptions are based on a combination of promotional manipulation and experience with the product or service in question. Offerings that are not perceived as delivering what they promise do not do well in the marketplace.

There are numerous ways to represent how competitive products are positioned relative to one another. Some direct marketers create tables of product attributes and list the attribute scores for each competitive product, producing a visual representation of the attribute relationships between competing products. Another approach is to create a graph or perceptual map of the brands according to the major dimensions buyers use to determine what they want to buy.

Exhibit 7.3 shows a simplified positioning map for catalogs selling outdoor wear. The map shows how a potential target audience perceives the major marketplace competitors on the key attribute dimensions of price and quality. Each

EXHIBIT 7.3. Catalog Perceptual Map

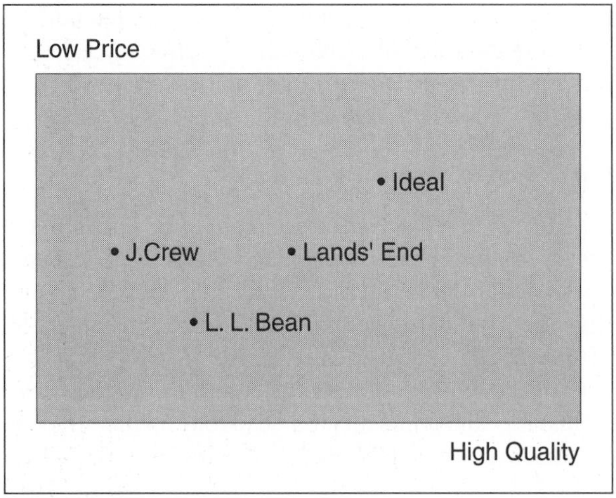

brand appears in relation to its competitors and to an ideal point. The map shows that consumers see Lands' End as closer to their ideal combination of price and quality than L. L. Bean or J. Crew.

Note that just because a particular product is strongest on one or more attributes does not mean that it gets all the customers. Members of different target markets frequently use different combinations of attributes and attribute importances to determine what to buy. Factors on an attribute list may also play different roles depending on a variety of circumstances, from situational issues to the immediacy of need for the product.

Analyze the Target Market

As indicated in Chapter 3, analyzing the target market for a product or service involves finding out which market segments, or subsets of the total population, can be expected to be most responsive to what the direct marketer is selling. Segmentation reduces costs by allowing marketers to select prospects likely to be receptive to an offer, and it helps in targeting individuals or firms with unique patterns of income or sales, spending, product preferences, and other characteristics.

Segmentation includes establishing a basis for dividing consumers or businesses into groups with similar characteristics and needs and separating them from those with different characteristics and needs. Prospects are sorted into distinct groups whose members behave similarly with respect to a particular product or service. Each segment should be as homogeneous as possible. A firm may search for product or service opportunities by looking for an unserved or underserved segment and examining whether the firm can profitably deliver attributes or benefits to prospects in that segment.

Select the Desired Segment

Once market segments are delineated, the firm should select individual targets for its products or services based on the expectation of obtaining a differential response. With direct marketing, the personal nature of promotional efforts makes it very important that appeals are tailored to the interests and perceptions of groups of individuals. The marketing mix elements of product, price, promotion, and distribution must appeal to the chosen target market.

Develop Alternative Positionings

Many direct marketers develop and test alternative positionings to maximize prospects' response to the offers they make. Chapter 17 contains a discussion about the role of testing in direct marketing. The development and testing process can be quite expensive, but it frequently results in overall higher sales and profits for a firm. Direct marketing is unique in its ability to test the market because it can establish a direct connection between the offer and the buyer's response. With the power of large databases and sophisticated decision-making tools, direct marketers can more readily achieve a profitable level of sales in a crowded marketplace.

Implement the Positioning Strategy and Monitor Its Effectiveness

The positioning selected by the direct marketer defines how the target market sees that firm's offering and how it responds, if at all. As noted previously, the direct marketer has the tools necessary to monitor how successful its positioning becomes and the extent to which it improves the overall business of the firm.

OFFER PLANNING

Roberts and Berger classify the elements of the direct marketing offer into those that are required (i.e., that must be present in every offer) and those that are optional (i.e., that may be included or not, depending on strategy and costs).[5] This classification assumes that the marketer's objective is to generate an order from the offer alone. However, if the objective is to have the prospect request information, some of the elements described by Roberts and Berger may not be necessary.

The required and optional elements for an offer are listed in Table 7.1. The listing represents a general guideline as to what may be included in an offer; keep in mind that many variations are possible. Exhibit 7.4 shows an offer summary for a dieting and weight-loss plan sold through infomercials. The Deal-A-Meal offer includes a bundle of products that support the main weight-control card system, plus some incentives.

The Required Elements

Product Positioning

As noted previously, positioning involves creating an image of the product in the minds of target audience members. The image represents how the direct marketer wants the public to perceive the benefits offered by the product and how it wants the target market to see its product versus those of its competition.

TABLE 7.1. Elements of the Offer

Required Elements	Optional Elements
Product positioning	Incentives
Price	Multiple offers
Length of commitment	Customer's obligations
Terms of payment	Purchase of additional products
Risk-reduction mechanisms	

Source: Mary Lou Roberts, and Paul D. Berger, *Direct Marketing Management* (Englewood Cliffs, NJ: Prentice Hall, 1989), p. 70.

EXHIBIT 7.4. Deal-A-Meal USA: 30-Minute Infomercial Offer Summary

Product description:

The Four-Step Deal-A-Meal Life Plan

1. The Deal-A-Meal Card System: The audiotape and instruction manual (describing the Deal-A-Meal weight-loss plan).
2. The *Golden Edition Cookbook* (low-calorie, low-fat, low-sodium recipes).
3. *Sweating to the Oldies 3* and *Stretching to the Classics* videotapes.
4. *Project Me* motivational tapes.

Price:

Three payments of $29.95 (total = $89.85).

Length of commitment:

None.

Incentives:

Two audiotapes free with order: *Take a Walk* and *Take a Hike,* plus $50 savings.

Price

The price of a product may or may not be prominently featured in the copy of the direct marketing offer. In some cases, the direct marketer wants the prospect to read about the specifics of the offer before knowing about the price. Frequently, however, the direct marketer prominently features the price because it is an important part of the product positioning: "Just look at what you can get for $25."

Whatever the price, perceptions of how high or low it is are determined by the value the prospect sees in the offer. A National Geographic Society offer, for example, might say that for only $25 the reader can become a member of the society, receive 12 monthly issues of *National Geographic* magazine, and have the opportunity to purchase other society books, videos, and similar materials. Whether or not $25 seems like a fair price for this offer depends on how the prospect perceives the listed membership benefits.

Length of Commitment

Most offers involve either a single transaction or a series of individual transactions over a period of time. The majority of offers from the Franklin Mint, a leading collectibles company, involve ordering single items such as a model of a classic car, although the company also sells whole collections through regular mailings of set items. Book-Of-The-Month Club members must purchase a fixed number of books over a specific length of time, for example, three books over two years.

FIXED-TERM OFFERS. The National Geographic Society offer mentioned above is what is called a fixed-term offer because it indicates that the prospect will receive a fixed number of magazine issues for a stated price payable at the beginning of the service. The one-year fixed term is fairly standard, although sometimes shorter terms are used in introductory offers and discounts are offered for longer-term subscriptions.

AUTOMATIC SHIPMENT PLANS. The Book-Of-The-Month Club offer mentioned above involves an automatic shipment plan. The purchase of the first book or set of books (often at a discount) indicates acceptance of the conditions of club membership and begins the automatic shipment of the remaining books, one every month. A similar automatic shipment plan is used by the Columbia House Video Library, discussed in Chapter 9.

CLUB PLANS. The Book-Of-The-Month Club adds an element of choice to the automatic shipment plan by sending the club member a bulletin offering a recommended book selection, alternative book selections, and the option of not receiving any book shipment for the current period. The bulletin contains what is called a *negative option* because the recommended selection is automatically shipped to the club member unless he or she sends in a refusal card by a fixed date.

Terms of Payment

Direct marketers provide customers payment options that include credit cards, cash on delivery (COD), and checks. Some firms allow customers to pay through installment payments. Denmark offers prospects a large catalog filled with many unique items, some of which can be paid for over several months. Included are telephone systems, VCRs, personal computers, exercise equipment, and much more.

Risk-Reduction Mechanisms

Perceived risk encompasses five areas of concern: financial risk, performance risk, social risk, time-loss risk, and source risk. This topic is discussed in depth in Chapter 10. Perceived financial risk is defined as concern over any financial loss that might occur because of the product purchase. This potential loss pertains to the initial cost of the product and the potential expense of repair, maintenance, or return. Concern over whether the product will perform as expected is known as perceived performance risk. This involves the consumer's concern about not being able to physically inspect merchandise and evaluate its characteristics such as quality, size, color, and style. With technically complex products like stereo equipment and televisions, the uncertainty is about how the product will perform. The concern about what others might think of a product purchase is known as perceived social risk. In a psychological sense, consumers purchase affiliation or social status or some other such attribute when they make their product purchases. Risks associated with these attributes are higher with the purchase of socially visible products such as clothing, clothing accessories, and household furnishings, which are likely to be seen by friends or visitors. "People often buy from catalogs in order to *save time.* That time loss might come from having to wait for a product to arrive or having to return an unsatisfactory product." Perceived time-loss risk involves concern over lost time from making a product purchase. Perceived source risk refers to a customer's concerns over whether or not he or she can trust the catalog firm and feel comfortable in doing business with the firm.

The Optional Elements

The optional elements enhance an offer by providing greater perceived value and by creating a sense of urgency. They are designed to overcome the tendency of prospects to defer a purchase decision. This is important because when a decision is postponed, a purchase is much less likely to be made.

Incentives

Incentives include a wide variety of items designed to motivate purchase behavior, including free gifts, discounts, and sweepstakes or contests. The National Geographic Society offer contains an insert about receiving a free full-color map of the world with a new membership. This type of incentive is consistent with the idea that the gift should be related to the product being sold.

Multiple Offers

Sometimes a mailing or a space advertisement will feature more than one product. Such multiple offers may be collected into a card deck that is shared by 30 or more products and services. Each prepaid postage card has a product or service description, a place to enter name and address information, and company name and mailing address.

Customer's Obligations and the Purchase of Additional Products

Some offers require the customer to purchase more items. Columbia House, a long-established direct marketer of recorded music, offers 10 CDs for a nominal fee of 99 cents, with an obligation for the customer to make six to eight additional purchases over a specified time period.

THE PLEASANT COMPANY[6]

The Pleasant Company provides a good example of how to plan offers that get results. Pleasant Company's product line of American Girls dolls and books was designed to be both educational and entertaining. The results have been significant success and a bright future.

In 1985, Pleasant Rowland launched the Pleasant Company mail-order operation in Middleton, Wisconsin. Since then, the company's main product line—the American Girls Collection of books, dolls, and related accessories—has grown into a $65 million business. While Rowland uses contemporary marketing strategies by targeting consumers, educators, and retailers, she also relies on products that memorialize the past, intertwine learning and play, and emphasize important traditional values.

Rowland calls the American Girls Collection the flagship line, "envisioned from the beginning as a multifaceted concept with long creative legs that would support the development of a wide variety of products and stimulate a broad array of marketing tactics." Relying on that line and a classic, four-color catalog, Rowland has mastered synergistic marketing strategies.

"The American Girls Collection was designed to teach young girls about American history and give them a sense of pride and self-awareness of traditions in growing up female in America," Rowland says. The basis for the line is a collection of books portraying four fictional nine-year-old heroines—Felicity, Kirsten, Samantha, and Molly—during different periods of history, beginning in 1774. Six books have been written about each girl's experiences, including friends/family, successes in school, Christmas secrets, birthday surprises, and summer and winter adventures. To bring the stories to life, Rowland created dolls, clothing, accessories, and craft projects described in the stories and designed them to be accurate for each girl's historic period.

Rowland wanted the product line to become a children's classic that would last many years and therefore decided to present it in a way compatible with the values each product stood for. In deciding the best way to market the American Girls Collection to achieve this goal, Rowland says, there were four problems:

1. Pleasant Company did not have the money to compete over shelf space with the likes of Hasbro and Mattel.
2. The "neon frenzy of discount toy stores" was not appropriate. The product had a complex story line, unlike the traditional store dolls, like Barbie and G.I. Joe, and did not lend itself to snazzy packaging.
3. The company's philosophy was opposed to television promotions, which make "parents and children victims of commercial hype."
4. The products could be licensed to manufacturers and quickly penetrate a market with broad visibility, but having the American Girls Collection appear on sleeping bags and lunch boxes would ruin the product concept and credibility of the company. Also, as a result of saturation marketing, the fad would be short-lived.

With a background in teaching and book publishing, Rowland was most comfortable communicating her message via ink on paper. According to Rowland, "Direct mail was the best way to sell a new, relatively complex product line in a softer and gentler voice to girls, mothers and grandmothers." With a catalog that reads like a storybook, Rowland hoped to lure girls to read by engaging them in the written word—a primary objective. Thus, her number one marketing decision was to sell the complete product line only in the catalog.

It was critical to the success of Pleasant Company that parents realize the educational soundness of the product line. Therefore, the catalog had to have an educational tone, promoting reading and teaching snippets of history while enticing parents to purchase the products.

Marketing of the American Girls Collection was planned around three channels of distribution: consumers, educators, and retailers. As the collection began appearing in catalogs across the country, Pleasant Company sought endorsements of its products by teachers and made its line of books available to libraries. Simultaneously, it began to sell the books to educators via direct mail and displays at educational conferences. Although most teachers are reluctant to let merchants into their classrooms, Scholastic Publishing has been able to get in the doors of academia with its products and book clubs. Making an exception to its licensing rule, Pleasant Company made a deal with Scholastic to offer the books in exchange for a royalty on sales, in order to reach children directly.

Because there are always people who will not buy a product unless they see it, Rowland began marketing her books to the retail arena. One problem Pleasant Company faced was that a few large publishing houses, wholesalers, and chains monopolize the publishing industry. The typical best-seller lasts one season, during which it is extensively marketed, and then is relegated to the sale table. Because Pleasant Company did not want to produce numerous books or see its publications' popularity wane, Rowland established a clever marketing strategy to drive retail sales. Rowland expected the dolls to be the best-selling items in the catalog and to provide a strong visual and emotional hook. She made an important early strategic decision: that no doll would be sold without a book. Rowland reasoned that kids would care more about the dolls and accessories if they became acquainted with the characters. Thus, book sales fed doll sales and vice versa. There was a synergy embedded in the product line from the very beginning. As kids flocked to stores, schools, and libraries for books, the shelves would remain stocked. The more books they read, the more dolls and accessories they would want—and the more this would fuel mail-order sales.

"The [full-color] books don't just deepen a child's interest in the product line," says Rowland; there is an important marketing tool bound in. Ninety percent of the books are sold via bookstores, but each book includes a postage-paid reply card offering a sample copy of the catalog. (Here Pleasant Company captures name, address, birth date, age, grade level, and parent's signature, as well as origination of postcard—bookstore, library, friend/relative, or catalog.)

More than 7 million American Girls books have been sold since 1986, producing about 250,000 inquiries for catalogs that convert to buyers at a rate in excess of 10 percent. Reply cards are the most profitable form of prospecting for Pleasant Company. Conversion of the Scholastic names, which reach a broad market compared to targeted catalog mailings, are almost as high. Also, the $5.95 paperbacks serve as a low entry-price point to the concept of the complete collection. It counteracts the upscale image of the products in the catalog, which can run $5 for a ribbon, increase to about $80 for a doll and book, and escalate to as high as $950 for an elaborate collection of a doll and all of the trimmings.

SUMMARY

Positioning involves designing a marketing mix for a particular product or service to create an image in the minds of target market members that is consistent with the needs those members are trying to satisfy. Products or services are positioned relative to competitors in a market because other firms have a place in the minds of target market members into which the company's offering must fit. An offer positions the firm's product or service and attempts to motivate buyer behavior. Offer objectives can include attracting new customers or obtaining repeat business from existing customers.

Customer motivations are what drive the purchasing process; they have direction and strength that stem from the customer's attempt to satisfy particular needs or achieve certain goals. Direct marketers try to convince target audience members that their product or service alternative will satisfy their needs or help them attain their goals. How to satisfy a customer's needs depends on the individual's unique history, learning experiences, and cultural environment. Marketing strategies are most effective when they aim to influence the direction a person will take to satisfy a need rather than when they attempt to create the need itself.

The process associated with developing a positioning strategy involves understanding competitors, selecting a market segment to pursue, and developing and implementing a product or service positioning. In developing a positioning strategy, direct marketers must identify the competitors, determine how the competitors are perceived and evaluated, understand the competitors' positionings, analyze the target market, select the desired segment, develop alternative positionings, implement the positioning strategy, and monitor its effectiveness.

REVIEW QUESTIONS

1. Define the term *positioning*. Why is positioning important in direct marketing? What is the result of a well-developed positioning?
2. What is an offer? What are the components of an offer, and how does an offer influence a target audience?
3. Direct marketers say that motives drive the purchasing process. What does that mean? What are those motives, and how do they influence attitudes and buyer behavior?
4. Products and services are positioned in terms of the attributes associated with satisfying particular needs. What are the types of needs? How do they influence consumer buyer behavior, and how do they influence business buyer behavior?
5. According to Roberts and Berger, what are the elements of a direct marketing offer? Which are the required elements and which are optional? *Why* are some elements of an offer required while others are optional?

NOTES

1. Adapted from James R. Rosenfield, "In the Mail: Sharper Image," *Direct Marketing,* May 1992, pp. 28–29.
2. Henry A. Murray, "Types of Human Needs," in *Studies in Motivation,* ed. David C. McClelland (New York: Appleton-Century-Crofts, 1955).
3. Abraham H. Maslow, "A Theory of Human Motivation," *Psychological Review* 50 (1943), pp. 370–96.
4. Mary Lou Roberts, and Paul D. Berger, *Direct Marketing Management* (Englewood Cliffs, NJ: Prentice Hall, 1989), pp. 84–91.
5. Ibid, pp. 69–76.
6. Adapted from Mollie Neal, "Cataloger Gets Pleasant Results," *Direct Marketing,* May 1992, pp. 33–36.

SOURCES

Bovee, Courtland L., and William Arens. *Contemporary Advertising,* 4th ed. Homewood, IL: Richard D. Irwin, 1992.

Engle, James F.; Martin R. Warshaw; and Thomas C. Kinnear. *Promotional Strategy,* 8th ed. Burr Ridge, IL: Richard D. Irwin, 1994.

HAHN, FRED E. *Do-It-YourSelf Advertising.* New York: John Wiley & Sons, 1993.

HAWKINS, DEL I.; ROGER J. BEST; AND KENNETH A. CONEY. *Consumer Behavior,* 5th ed. Homewood, IL: Richard D. Irwin, 1992.

HOLTZ, HERMAN. *Great Promo Pieces.* New York: John Wiley & Sons, 1988.

JONES, SUSAN K. *Creative Strategy in Direct Marketing.* Lincolnwood, IL: NTC Busines Books, 1991.

KATZENSTEIN, HERBERT, AND WILLIAM SACHS. *Direct Marketing,* 2nd ed. New York: Macmillan, 1992.

KOTLER, PHILIP. *Marketing Management,* 7th ed. Englewood Cliffs, NJ: Prentice Hall, 1991.

MASLOW, ABRAHAM H. *Motivation and Personality.* New York: Harper & Row, 1954.

_______. "A Theory of Human Motivation," *Psychological Review* 50 (1943), pp. 370–96.

MCCORKLE, DENNY E. "The Role of Perceived Risk in Mail Order Catalog Shopping." *Journal of Direct Marketing,* Autumn 1990, pp. 26–35.

MURRAY, HENRY A. "Types of Human Needs." In *Studies in Motivation,* ed. David C. McClelland. New York: Appleton-Century-Crofts, 1955.

NEAL, MOLLIE. "Cataloger Gets Pleasant Results." *Direct Marketing,* May 1992, pp. 33–36.

ROBERTS, MARY LOU, AND PAUL D. BERGER. *Direct Marketing Management.* Englewood Cliffs, NJ: Prentice Hall, 1989.

ROSENFIELD, JAMES R. "In the Mail: Sharper Image." *Direct Marketing,* May 1992, pp. 28–29.

SCHIFFMAN, LEON G., AND LESLIE LARZAR KANUK. *Consumer Behavior,* 4th ed. Englewood Cliffs, NJ: Prentice Hall, 1991.

SOLOMON, MICHAEL R. *Consumer Behavior,* 2nd ed. Needham Heights, MA: Allyn and Bacon, 1992.

STONE, BOB. *Successful Direct Marketing Methods,* 5th ed. Lincolnwood, IL: NTC Business Books, 1995.

CHAPTER 8

Creative Strategy and Execution

OBJECTIVES

1. To present the nature and scope of creative strategies and campaign executions in direct marketing.
2. To explain the purpose of a creative strategy statement and what each of its parts is intended to accomplish, including how the characteristics of a product or service relate to the content of a creative strategy.
3. To examine how direct-response marketers choose from among radio, television, print, telemarketing, and the mail as ways of communicating with a target audience.
4. To examine the special creative strategy and execution considerations for each direct marketing medium.

INTRODUCTION

Campaign strategies designed to accomplish specific direct marketing goals include creative strategies (the message to be directed to a target market) and media strategies (the media to be used to carry the message). The creative strategy is a formal description of the message the marketer wishes to convey and the audience intended to receive it. While creative strategies and executions for direct marketing media are considered in this chapter, Chapters 9 through 14 deal with each medium in more detail.

Chapter 7 described product or service positioning and offer planning. In relationship to the offer, positioning was defined as the act of creating an image in the minds of target members that is consistent with the needs those persons are trying to satisfy. Offer planning is the complete proposition made by the direct marketer to the prospect. Products or services are positioned relative to competitors' offerings in the sense that other firms have a place in the minds of the target market into which the firm's offering must fit.

In contrast, creative strategy and execution deal, respectively, with explicitly stating what and how a campaign will communicate about a product or service. The fundamental characteristics of that product or service determine the nature of the campaign strategy. The essence of a successful campaign strategy is finding out how to present the product in a way that promises the most utility to the greatest number of prospective customers.

A creative strategy statement defines the content of the message and specifies the positioning and objectives for the product or service. If the positioning is properly defined, the creative strategy statement specifies the market segment to be addressed and indicates the product attribute to be presented. The content serves the prospect by providing useful information about satisfying needs. Advertising content is defined in a statement about the claims and information to be communicated by the direct-response advertising. It should attract prospects for the product, present the product benefit or appeal, give evidence supporting the promised benefit, and specifically motivate purchase behavior.

After deciding on the content of the advertising and how it is to be executed, the creative team must determine how the advertising will be produced. Production of advertising refers to the process of converting creative ideas into the finished advertising materials to be used by the media. Much of this production is of a technical nature, and is therefore carried out by specialists.

CREATIVE STRATEGY DEVELOPMENT

From the direct marketer's point of view, the function of advertising content is to carry out the communications objectives of a marketing strategy. The advertising serves to translate the product features into benefits for the target market. However, the advertising content is more than a restatement of the product's attributes. The advertising copy must be written from the target market's point of view, not from that of the advertiser. The copywriter must be able to look through the prospect's eyes and translate the product features into information that is understandable, useful, and persuasive to that prospect.

Prospects are more likely to notice and act on an advertisement if they perceive it as having the ability to satisfy a need. In determining the content of the advertising, the creative specialist must first understand the needs prospects are trying to satisfy. The copywriter's task is to translate the primary product attribute into a benefit that addresses those needs. If the prospects' attention is directed to the ad and if they find that the primary benefit meets their needs, they will next seek evidence that supports the claims.

FRANKLIN MINT

Direct-response advertising from Franklin Mint represents an example of consistent creative excellence. Franklin Mint is the world's leading creator of fine-quality collectibles and personal luxury products and one of the largest direct-response marketers. The company creates originally designed, upscale home decor and luxury products and treasured collectibles. It brings works of artistic beauty and historical significance to about 10 million collectors around the globe.

Franklin Mint's consumers are primarily women aged 30 to 60 with above-average incomes, who believe that the joy of art collecting is not just possessing the object but also knowing about the object and sharing that knowledge. With Franklin Mint, art collecting has become a form of self-education and a way of socializing. All products are marketed and distributed directly and exclusively by the company. The thinking behind Franklin Mint's creative strategy development is illustrated using an example of one of its collectible offerings.

The Franklin Mint Precision Models collection includes fine-quality die-cast replicas of antique and classic automobiles and high-performance cars. This product line established a new kind of collectible model car in 1985, with the introduction of reasonably priced 1:24 and 1:43 scale model cars. Previously, collectors had to choose between inexpensive toylike cars and high-priced custom-built models. Franklin Mint models offered the quality and detail of one-of-a-kind classics at an affordable price. The company continues to bolster its automotive line with world-famous marques such as Bugatti, Packard, and Cadillac. At present, Franklin Mint offers more than 50 different model cars.

Franklin Mint is especially strong in direct-response print advertising. Its ads can be found in such publications as *TV Guide, Parade* magazine, and *McCall's.* Exhibit 8.1 shows a sample of Franklin Mint's direct-response print advertising, offering the firm's 1975 Ford Fairlane 500 Skyliner precision model.

EXHIBIT 8.1. Franklin Mint Direct-Response Print Ad

THE CREATIVE STRATEGY STATEMENT

The end product of all the effort that goes into determining what to say to the target market is a written statement that summarizes the message strategy for a product or service. It indicates to members of the creative team—which includes writers, artists, and producers, among potentially many others—exactly how they should approach the task of developing and implementing the product or service advertising. This strategy is encapsulated in what is commonly called a *creative strategy statement.* The creative strategy statement has nine parts:

1. Product description (what it is, how it works, what its unique features are).
2. The target audience description (demographically, geographically, psychographically, and behaviorally defined).
3. The audience's problem (what they miss or lack; what they need or want).
4. The advertising communications objective (what the direct-response advertiser wants to do).
5. The product's positioning (relative to the competition in the minds of the target audience members).
6. The main selling concept, which includes the primary selling benefit of the product or service.
7. An explanation of why and/or how the main selling concept should be delivered.
8. What the direct marketer wants prospects to do (place an order or ask for more information).
9. The product or service personality (expressed in terms of mood, tone, and character).

As a written statement covering the nine points listed above, the strategy is customarily no more than one page long. However, the subject of personality (point 9) is complex and may take considerably more supporting explanation. If two or more target audiences exist for a single product or service, the marketer should write a separate creative strategy statement for each.

The creative strategy statement first presents information about the product or service such as the name of the product; where it can be found; and its price, size, color(s), and style(s) (point 1). The target audience description indicates for whom the message is intended and whose attention the campaign should attempt to attract (point 2). The audience's problem describes what the audience is missing or lacking by indicating their needs or wants (point 3). Ultimately, the product must fulfill a need or solve a problem facing the target consumer or business.

For the direct-response advertising communication, the ultimate objective is to produce a response. However, the advertising communications task (point 4) involves creating or changing the prospect's state of mind, knowledge, attitudes, and/or propensity to buy. Defining this primary marketing problem involves stating the product selling issue from the perspective of the marketer by addressing the question of what the marketer is trying to do with the advertising campaign. In the Franklin Mint Skyliner ad (Exhibit 8.1), the primary marketing problem is to generate a sense of product quality and authenticity for a collectible that reflects a symbol of another decade.

The product's positioning describes the image prospects will have in their minds about the product relative to the competition based on exposure to the direct-response advertising message (point 5). The main selling concept (point 6) is the key benefit of the product, that is, the compelling aspect of the product or service or the benefit of greatest interest to the target audience. Ideally the product's key benefit is unique, compared to benefits offered by the competition. The main selling concept is directly associated with the consumer or business need to be satisfied and is stated using the language of the target audience. It is not uncommon to find direct-response ads with one main selling benefit and several secondary benefits. In that case, each of the secondary benefits should strengthen the overall ad and add to the appeal of the product or service. For the Franklin Mint Skyliner ad, the main selling concept is the availability of a quality automobile replica of another era.

Next, the marketer must explain why and/or how the main selling concept should be delivered (point 7). This is done by describing evidence to support the delivery of the promised benefit. If there are secondary benefits, those must also be supported. Prospects have a natural skepticism concerning any advertiser's product. In order to evaluate the product as an alternative, the prospect needs information that describes how this product or service is different from others that are available. This might include a special ingredient, a special manufacturing process, or the linkage of the product's efficacy to a common problem. For the Franklin Mint Skyliner ad, the reason the product delivers the main selling concept is that it is a replica of one of the most popular vintage cars, with accurate detailing and authentic features.

The action desired (point 8) is what the direct marketer wants the prospect to do, place an order or ask for more information. In the latter case, the objective is lead generation rather than immediately closing a sale. The Franklin Mint Skyliner ad urges prospects to send in an order form for the car, thereby agreeing to make five equal payments of $24.

The brand personality must conform to the desired image for the product or service (point 9). This brand personality can be expressed with words like *confident, reliable, user-friendly, forward-looking,* or *powerful.* For other types of products, such words as *intimate, sporty, romantic, adventuresome, concerned, sympathetic, caring,* or *frivolous* will help establish brand personality.

There should be a single creative strategy statement for each campaign. From that single statement, many different individual direct-response advertising executions may be created, but they all come from the campaign direction described in the creative strategy statement. This assures that all the advertising executions for the campaign deliver the same message to members of the target market.

Table 8.1 shows what a creative strategy statement for the Franklin Mint Skyliner ad might look like. It delineates each of the parts of the statement by specifying the product features, the target audience, the audience's need, the communications objective, the product positioning, the main selling concept (key benefit), the reason why that benefit is delivered, the desired action, and the personality of the product.

Managers delegate much of the creative implementation because it requires specialized skills. However, they retain responsibility for maintaining a productive relationship with the creative team, for providing information and

TABLE 8.1. Franklin Mint Skyliner Ad Creative Strategy Statement

1. Product description: High-quality model of the classic 1957 Ford Fairlane 500 Skyliner with authentic features and movable parts.
2. The target audience: Men 25–44 who have an interest in collectibles.
3. The audience's problem: A consumer needs to have a symbol of another era.
4. The advertising (communication) objective: To communicate the essence of the car, including its quality features and intrinsic value.
5. The product's positioning: A high-quality replica.
6. The main selling concept: The ability to purchase a quality replica of another era.
7. The reason why the main selling concept is delivered: The model is a replica of one of the most popular vintage cars; this version is accurately detailed and authentic.
8. Desired action: Get prospects to send in the order form for the car, thereby agreeing to make five equal payments of $24.
9. The brand personality: Upbeat and lively, with a reassuring tone.

direction to the creative team, and for evaluating the creative output in terms of specific, pre-established criteria such as those delineated in the creative strategy statement.

DETERMINING CREATIVE EXECUTIONS

Direct-response advertisers face numerous difficult choices in deciding how to approach the main selling concept and any associated benefits. In choosing between utilitarian and emotional benefits, advertisers should offer rational benefits when prospects face utilitarian needs and emotional benefits when those needs are social or psychological. The choice of how to communicate that key benefit (and other benefits) is the most critical aspect of how the creative strategy is implemented, because that decision drives the total character of the advertising execution.

The choice between promising utilitarian benefits or appealing to emotion is one almost every advertiser must face. There are various rules of thumb for deciding between those approaches. One rule, for example, suggests that certain types of products (such as jewelry and insurance) should promise emotional benefits while others (such as building materials) should use rational, utilitarian benefits. However, one of the difficulties in considering the choice between emotional and rational benefits is the wide variety of meanings given these terms. The contention that the choice between utilitarian and emotional benefits depends upon the product type is incomplete because it fails to recognize that the same product may satisfy different categories of needs. It is possible that the market for a product will contain both prospects with emotional needs and those seeking more rational benefits. These two groups represent different segments of the market and the direct-response advertiser must consider the chosen segment when selecting how the product should be positioned.

Typically, creative specialists begin by immersing themselves in information about the product, the prospect, the competition, the market, and the objectives. Next, they search for a main selling concept that will be the centerpiece or focal point in the advertisement. The creative team often seeks this not in a logical, step-by-step fashion but by ranging freely over a large number of associations.

After the main selling concept (or key benefit) has been selected, the creative team begins to construct the advertisement. With the selling concept as the centerpiece, the individual parts of the advertisement—headline, copy, illustrations—are designed so that they add to the central idea. To the creative team, then, an advertisement is not a series of individual pieces but rather a main selling concept supported and enhanced by various components.

Differences between marketers and creative people can lead to friction and conflict, which can lead to a loss in quality in the creative output. Given this potential conflict, what can the direct marketer do to establish a productive relationship? First, the best creative talent available should be selected, people in whom the marketer has confidence. Second, the marketer should be prepared to delegate the creative job to the specialists. The marketing manager should not write advertisements in competition with the creative team nor presume to rewrite their efforts, for this destroys their enthusiasm. This does not mean, however, that everything the specialists create must be accepted. A third guideline is that the direct marketer should protect the integrity of the advertisement. As explained above, an advertisement should not be seen as a series of little building blocks but rather as a central idea to which each element must contribute. Recognizing this, the marketer should act as protector of the totality of the advertisement. Many people, not creatively trained, will be tempted to add, subtract, or rearrange pieces of an advertisement according to their own standards.

Direct marketers should not make personal judgments about the creative value or ultimate effectiveness of a particular advertisement, but they should always reserve the right to conduct research on its effectiveness. Direct marketing copy research techniques are expensive, but the results can be helpful, depending on at which stage of the creative process the testing is conducted. Tests in which creative execution alternatives are shown to a sample of target market members in order to elicit their opinions often produce results that are difficult to interpret. However, tests in which different executions of a creative strategy are used in mailings or broadcasts often produce results that are quite precise.

CREATIVE STRATEGY AND EXECUTION FOR DIRECT MARKETING MEDIA

Direct-Response Television

Before entering the television market, direct marketers need to learn as much as possible about the medium. Direct marketers who specialize in telemarketing or the mail are among the savviest advertisers in the marketplace today. However, moving from telemarketing or the mail to television can be difficult.

If a company is offering a nature video with proven direct-mail appeal to wildlife enthusiasts, how should it launch that product on television? The direct-mail mentality says to target the firm's best customers and to include in the commercial the key selling and ordering information. However, if the firm focuses too closely on a single group of prospects in its target market, it may miss many potential buyers. How can the firm broaden what it has historically defined as its audience, based on its mail experience, to find an appropriate target audience for its television commercial?

The firm should not necessarily go with a strategy that has "something for everyone." Wanting to keep its audience options open does not mean that the firm should adopt a too-general creative strategy and execution that seeks to please everyone and offend no one. Whatever is worth saying in a television spot is worth saying forcefully, and this may mean alienating some potential customers even as it motivates others.

A direct-response television commercial needs to get the viewer's attention, identify the product or service being sold, make a claim for its benefits, back that claim with a guarantee, and get the viewer to pick up the phone and order or request more information. All this must occur within 120, 90, or even 60 seconds. Times for direct response advertisements tend to be longer than those for general advertising because they need to provide more information, and they are more repetitive. The average tired, hurried, distracted television viewer will simply not absorb even one benefit in so little time unless the commercial states and restates it again and again.

Direct-response television should not be subtle; it should hit the viewer with the product's main selling concept, using whatever it takes to make that point memorable. It should try to both say and show that benefit. For example, a commercial should not simply say that a knife would cut metal $\frac{1}{16}$ of an inch thick; it should show it cutting through a penny. It should not just say that a book or seminar would change the viewer's life; it should show an interview with a grateful customer.

Firms should beware of formulas in creating direct-response television advertising. If a firm discovered a winning technique on its last spot, it should by all means find a way to include that technique in its next commercial. But that does not mean that every commercial should be a clone of the last one that worked. Every new marketing challenge is different. When marketers assume they know what works, they neglect the difficult but critical job of putting themselves in the shoes of the prospect, which is key to understanding the prospect's needs and satisfying them.

Creative Strategy and Execution for Infomercials[1]

Direct marketers are enthusiastic about infomercials. If properly produced, infomercials are better than a personal demonstration for two reasons: No inadvertent mistakes can ruin the presentation, and the presentation can include many testimonials. The first reason is self-explanatory, but the advantages of testimonials deserve further attention.

Testimonials

Other than the product being sold, the single most important element in a successful infomercial is a string of testimonials from satisfied customers.

Testimonials are so important that without them the chances of producing a profitable infomercial diminish substantially. Testimonials are so crucial because prospects are frequently unsure of items with which they do not have any personal experience. This means that testimonials are especially crucial to two types of infomercials: those selling a product intended to replace an "earlier generation" product (such as a convection oven shown to perform better than a kitchen range); and those designed to overcome a natural, implicit skepticism (such as a get-rich-quick pitch where a customer claims, "I made a ton of money and so can you").

Celebrities serve a specific purpose for some infomercials: A random viewer may interrupt his or her channel hopping because of the celebrity. But, on the negative side, a celebrity can double the production cost of an infomercial.

How Long and How Strong

Most infomercials are 30 minutes long. However, they are not designed to be 30-minute dramas that peak at about 25 minutes and then go into a close. Direct marketers know that, in reality, most viewers do not watch the whole show. An infomercial is not *I Love Lucy* or *NYPD Blue.* It is a 30-minute direct-response sales pitch. Viewers watch enough to either sharpen or dull their initial mild curiosity.

If the infomercial is done correctly, it will try for a sale three times. Marketers generally think of the infomercial as a show divided into three 10-minute segments. Each segment should be self-contained, like individual pages in a catalog, and should conclude with a sales message, including a summary of the offer and an explanation of how to place an order or request more information.

What Sells and What Does Not

For infomercials, any product priced below $40 or $50 is likely to be unprofitable due to the cost of production and the cost of time on cable or broadcast stations. However, items worth less than $40 may be bundled into a group of, say, three and sold as a batch for $49.95 or some other, higher price.

Excluded from this analysis are infomercials promoting psychic or sex-related 900-number hot lines. Hot-line calls average $2.95 to $3.95 per minute, and can go on and on. These infomercials differ from others because they offer the sale of a service, which involves no overstock, no warehousing, and no shipping. And the result is often multiple calls from the same buyer, with no additional overhead.

Whether offering products or services, however, infomercials tend to fail for mechanical reasons, which include paying too much for the broadcast time, reaching the wrong viewership, and underpricing or overpricing what is being sold. They may also fail for creative strategy reasons, which include not addressing a need, not doing a good job of selling the product, and not performing one of two mandatory functions: (*a*) illustrating a previously unavailable solution to a problem or (b) illustrating easy superiority over a previous financial, social, or physical condition.

Direct-Response Radio[2]

Radio offers direct marketers a unique blend of benefits, including sales to highly segmented audiences and an opportunity to get on the air quickly. Over the years, radio stations have developed proven programming formats that appeal to listeners with similar interests and shared demographic and psychographic characteristics, thus segmenting their audiences more and more.

To use radio successfully, direct marketers need to concentrate on three basic elements. First, marketers need writers who understand radio. More than any other medium, radio demands the talent, skill, and salesmanship of a top-notch writer. The best writers are those who have both hands-on broadcast experience and a good understanding of direct response. Second, marketers must let the writers write. The best writers will listen to suggestions but will do what they believe is necessary to sell a firm's product or service. Third, direct marketers should employ production companies that can "hear" the script by just reading it and bring it to life with the right voices, music, and sound effects. Marketers should listen to this production company's demo reels to gauge their talents, but, once the production company is hired, they should stand back and let that company do its job.

After obtaining the three elements described above, marketers should heed the following 14 tips for writing direct-response radio spots:

1. Marketers should have enough time to make the sale. Some would say there is no such thing as a 30-second direct-response radio or television spot—that 30 seconds is only enough time for a general appeal. Thus, when there is a choice between 30 seconds and 60 seconds, 60 seconds is the better alternative. It provides twice as long to set up the scene, sell the product, and repeat the ordering phone number.

2. Marketers should focus on generating phone calls. There is only one reason to run a direct-response radio spot: to make the phone ring with orders or inquiries. Absolutely everything in the spot should support that goal by suggesting that listeners pick up a phone and call. Direct marketers cannot just settle for generating "awareness." The commercial must begin a meaningful relationship with potential customers by offering free information, a free consultation, a special price, or some tangible reason to *call now.*

3. Because radio spots go by quickly, they must be kept simple. They cannot be reviewed at will. Therefore, radio is no place for a long list of benefits or features. Commercials need to get the listener's attention, make a relevant offer, and generate a phone call by focusing on one selling point and emphasize that point repeatedly.

4. Direct marketers should tailor their message to the target audience. As in all forms of direct-response advertising, it is a good idea to tailor the message as specifically as possible to the intended audience. In that context, there are two basic kinds of radio programming to consider, talk radio and music radio. With talk radio, the audience has tuned in specifically to listen. Advertising within this format needs to encourage continued listening. It must either blend in to the surrounding talk or catch the listener's interest with informational content. With music radio, the music is the attraction but often as background noise. Here, a spot is an interruption. It must emerge from the surrounding clutter and generate interest before the listener touches the dial or mentally tunes out.

5. In radio, as in all other media, the main selling concept should come first. It should be the star and not get dominated by the creative execution.

6. Direct marketers should choose a creative format. There is no set way to write a radio script, but a few proven formats can help writers get started. The following six work well to convey information and lead the listener to call:

- *Straight announcer.* Nothing could be simpler than a single strong voice talking directly to the listener. The copy should be simple, direct, and clear. The announcer should speak as if addressing a single person.
- *Dialogue.* People enjoy listening to other people talk, as long as it is interesting. One of the best dialogue formats is to have one person who knows something about a product or service and another person who does not know anything about it but who could benefit from it. One person asks questions while the other relays the offer as well as any important information. The voices should match the demographics of the listeners, and the dialogue must be believable. The resulting commercial is similar to a testimonial.
- *Vignette.* This type of radio spot starts with a short slice-of-life scene illustrating a problem. It then cuts to an announcer who describes the product or service as the solution. If there is time, the commercial returns to the characters in the slice of life to show how the product or service has made things better, easier, more profitable, and so on. Of course, the commercial will close by returning to the announcer for the call to action and an 800 number.
- *Person on the street.* This type of commercial is simple to produce and highly believable. The tried-and-true person on the street is a good choice for products with wide appeal. The approach is to ask real people what they think about the product, which gets them to describe how it has benefited them. Hearing real people say good things is the best endorsement consumers or business can get for a product. It is also a good format for live product comparisons.
- *Testimonial.* This type takes the person on the street one step further and has people address listeners directly, talking about using the product and praising its benefits. Testimonials can feature experts, celebrities, or ordinary people.
- *Story.* Stories are difficult to do correctly, especially in just 60 seconds. It takes a plausible, brief plot and an announcer who understands the drama of the situation. Like a good short story, it must set up a crisis that needs resolution. Listeners must be able to relate to the situation and see themselves as part of it, and the product must be central to the resolution of the action.

7. To involve listeners, a radio commercial should appeal to the eye as well as the ear. It should use announcer copy and sound effects to help listeners picture a scene. For example, if a firm wants to sell tax-deferred mutual funds for retirement, it should not just offer a list of features. It needs to involve listeners by helping them visualize the tangible benefits of a comfortable retirement: "Picture yourself basking on a Caribbean beach, reading your favorite author, and sipping an exotic drink. And you know you can stay here for as long as you like, because for the very first time there's no work waiting for you back home. You are retired. And this vacation will last for the rest of your life." All this becomes a powerful image for anyone who has ever dreamed of retiring comfortably.

8. The commercial should identify its sound effects. It is worth remembering that on radio the listener cannot see the action and that many sounds are similar. A scene must be set up properly with narration or dialogue. If a firm is selling a new fishing lure, and the setting is in the woods near a stream, the announcer should come right out and say, "I'm standing next to a stream." Or the ad can work the location into the opening dialogue between two characters: Character 1—"There

are no fish in this stream. Not a bite in three hours!" Character 2—"Really? You should try the Bass-Snatcher 300! I've hooked eight big bass in 20 minutes!"

9. Direct marketers should use humor carefully. Some marketers would say that a radio spot is not a radio spot if it is not funny, and humor is used so often, and done so well by a select group of radio specialists, that it is tempting to think that every commercial needs to be funny. However, funny and effective are two different things. From a selling standpoint, humor is hit and miss. As often as not, listeners do not think a supposedly humorous ad is funny. And advertisers always run the risk of losing the selling message amid the humor.

10. The commercial needs to establish name identification early and often. Radio commercials should get to the point and avoid all kinds of random details. Extraneous information is deadly when the advertiser only has 30 or 60 seconds to deliver a message. The spot should give the name of the company, along with that of the product or service, early on and should repeat it several times, at least three.

11. For psychological reasons, legal copy should be located at the beginning or in the middle of a radio commercial. The most powerful position in a radio spot is the last few seconds, and that valuable time should not be wasted with legal or disclaimer copy. The absolute last words spoken in a radio spot should be the 800 number, not legal copy.

12. The ad should use a memorable and relevant 800 number. There are two schools of thought on 800 numbers. One is that the commercial should use a normal number, 800 followed by seven numbers. The other is that it should use a memorable number, such as 1-800-CALL-NOW. The "normal number people" believe that dialing a real number is easier, because the caller does not have to hunt for the letters on the phone. They also say that it is better to force prospects to write the number down or call immediately. In most media this is true, but not in radio. Until radio technology becomes fully interactive, prospects must remember the firm's number, even if there is a phone at hand. A special 800 number such as 1-800-ABCDEFG (for a reading program) or 1-800-FAX-BOOK (for a brochure on fax machines) can easily be remembered. The key is to relate the number to the firm's name or offer and to make the meaning clear. And, at a minimum, the phone number should be given early in the spot, in the middle of the spot, and one more time at the very end.

13. All direct-response radio ads need a clear call to action. Most spots never get around to telling the listener what to do, and that is a big mistake. A radio spot will only generate calls if, at the end, the prospect can answer the question "What do you want me to do right now?" The answer should always be to call the firm's 800 number. This is not the time for subtlety. For example, the announcer can simply say, "To request your free brochure on losing weight through better eating, call 1-800-LESS-FAT."

14. The ad should force a response with a time limit. Limited-time offers work in every medium, including radio. It is basic human psychology; people do not like to miss good deals.

Telemarketing

Creative strategy in telemarketing focuses on the creation of scripts that serve the same function as advertisements by communicating a sales message in a systematic fashion. However, rather than communicating in mass to members of a target audience, telemarketing makes its impression one call at a time. Most telemarketing calls are completely scripted, which means that callers deliver exactly the same message in a structured sales presentation. Script creation involves writing the parts of that presentation, which take the caller through the basic steps of introduction, qualification of the prospect, presentation of the sales message, meeting objectives, and closing. Although such a script is usually very detailed, it still requires some product knowledge on the part of the telephone representative.

The telemarketing script must introduce the target person to who is calling, describe the product or service for sale, and make the sales pitch in an organized fashion emphasizing the benefits expected to motivate the person receiving the call to place an order. The offer presentation is the most important part of the telephone message because it contains the selling proposition the firm wants to communicate and the reasons in support of that communication. The success of the call is measured by whether the prospect accepts the offer.

Unlike direct response print, radio, or television advertising, the telemarketing script must include answers to prospects' questions or objections, the majority of which can be anticipated. The caller can then use the prepared responses when questions and objections to an offer occur.

Also unlike advertising, telemarketing gets immediate results. There is feedback about whether a script is working after the first few hundred calls. This means that the script is constantly monitored and evaluated for both positive and negative prospect responses. As in the preparation process, the script may continue to evolve and improve during implementation until the firm feels the script has reached its target performance level.

Not every telemarketer uses a complete script. In fact, telemarketing presentations are unique in allowing the messenger, the phone operator, flexibility in presenting the sales message. While certain points must be covered, less structured scripts allow the caller to customize the sales message and the flow of the conversation to the prospect while at the same time communicating the selling message. This more unstructured approach, which uses relatively minimal scripting, is most commonly used for calling known customers or prospects about complicated products, including investment vehicles and insurance.

Direct Mail[3]

Direct mail should ask for the order up front and keep on asking in every element of the package, not just an order card. The package must project confidence. The direct-mail piece should try to create a "visual fascination" with the order card. It is the one piece of the package the firm wants to get into the hands of the recipient. If the offer can entice readers to want to see the order card, the firm stands a better chance of getting them involved enough to place an order. The most powerful color in direct mail is red; but firms do not want to saturate their mailing pieces to the point where readers know the firms are using a certain color as an attention-getting device. Also, the firm should always make the recipient the subject of the direct-mail efforts; for example, it should use the word *you* when enumerating the benefits of the product.

How do direct marketers pick a format for their direct-mail offers? First, they must recognize that their own beliefs do not matter; they must always consider a piece from the target market's point of view. Second, they cannot just pick formats that are easy for the printer or lettershop; however, they do need to take production costs into consideration. Finally, they should watch what the competitor is doing.

Once marketers have acknowledged these guidelines, they can move on to the core of their direct-mail offer and format: finding out what their prospects really want. If they can use research to determine the needs of their prospects, they can shape their offer to address those needs. They can make lists of those needs until they come up with a strong selling theme and then pass that theme on to the creative team to make that idea central to the direct-mail package.

To get a response, direct marketers need to tailor their offers to what matters to their prospects. The main obstacle direct mailers face in getting the response they desire is not getting the prospect's attention. There are two ways to gain attention: jolts, which attract prospects physically, and curiosity, which attracts them mentally. Some ways to jolt a prospect include using handwritten marginal notes and printing different elements of the package on different color stock. Curiosity is peaked by using teasers on the envelope or by folding a letter in half in the middle of the headline, for example.

To produce the most effective direct-mail package, it helps to hire the best copywriter possible. But even the best copywriters in the world can produce poor work if they are not given the tools they need to work their craft. It the firm wants its copywriters to do their best work, it must gather all of the available data on the product or service; the more copywriters know about the product or service, the better they are able to include its key benefits in the direct-mail package.

The firm should try not to depend on formulas for its direct-mail efforts. It is true that formulas can serve as a guideline from which to work, but straying from them every once in a while allows the firm to get a fresh perspective. Rules are good things to test. For example, even if a rule says never to use letters longer than a page, the firm should test different lengths to see which works best for its offer. If the firm finds that its customers like to skip copy, it should not try to make them read everything. Instead, the firm should use subheads and clear graphics to impart the same message; customers can choose whether to read in full or select the information that interests them. The firm should also be sure to keep the reader's eye moving; just like a song in a musical, every subhead must move the show along.

Direct-Response Print

Good direct-response ad designs attract readers' attention by making the ad stand out on a page. Once the reader's attention is captured, the design should move the eye through the copy (which includes the main selling concept) to the toll-free number or response panel. The body copy should be easy to read and quickly communicate the main selling concept. The ad must avoid any backgrounds that will make it harder for the reader to get through the copy. The ad must not be produced with a busy background, a small type size, lots of reverse type, lots of italics, or lots of words in capital letters because readability is critical. The toll-free number must not be buried, and the response device must be easily found.

Good direct-response print ad designs make intelligent use of headlines and subheads. The reader should get the entire message, particularly the main selling concept, just by reading the headlines and subheads. Subheads are essential elements for the scanning reader, which is how most readers review print ads anyway. Use underlines, bold face, bullets, indented paragraphs and numbered lists to better communicate the message of the ad. Anything that helps the scanning reader find the main points of the message will be welcomed.

The direct-response copy sells the benefits of the product or service to the prospect. It must answer the question "Why should I buy from this firm?" The ad must detail for the prospect the main selling concept and any secondary benefits of the product or service with a compelling offer to motivate action now, and then make it easy to respond. When evaluating headline concepts, direct marketers must ask themselves three questions:

- Does it talk to the audience (usually by using *you*)?
- Will it get the audience's attention?
- Does it present a strong main selling concept that is important to the audience?

If the ad headline does all of these things, the direct-mail campaign will probably meet its response rate expectations.

Catalogs[4]

Why is design so important to a catalog's success? First and foremost, more than any other type of direct mail, the catalog is a visual medium. Customers browse through catalog pages much as they would window-shop in a mall. When something catches their eye, they will stop, look and—possibly—make a purchase. Catalogs have the additional design challenge of combining all of the elements of a successful direct-mail package, a letter, brochure, order device and reply envelope, into one cohesive, user-friendly piece.

The first rule in catalog design is to know the audience. Who are they (by age, sex, motivating interests, etc.) and how they will use the catalog (reference, buying directly, etc.)? What is the positioning or niche of the catalog, and how does the writing, design, and layout reinforce that positioning? Is the catalog carefully paginated (with certain products on certain pages) to give it a flow from spread to spread and to maximize sales? What are the prospects' aesthetic expectations for the catalog (e.g., slick and upscale or price/discount oriented)? What are competitor catalogs doing, and how can the catalog differentiate itself from their design and layout? How does a catalog marketer ensure good design?

There are three major aspects of catalog design that must work together. First there is page layout. Four main layouts are grid or symmetrical, free-form or asymmetrical, single product per page, or grouping by product type. Obviously, there are numerous combinations and variations of these layouts. Second is typography. The cataloger needs to select typefaces—for headlines, footlines, captions, charts, and body copy—that complement one another. Third is color, including that used in backgrounds, heads, screens, and tints.

PAGE LAYOUTS. Should the catalog have two-page spreads or focus on individual pages? Are the layouts consistent throughout the catalog, using one or several options such as a grid or modified grid? Is the layout style—including the use of silhouettes, white space and feature photos—consistent from catalog to catalog so that customers will recognize the sponsoring firm? Does the layout effectively highlight the product and make it the true hero? Is the layout "user-friendly" with design techniques that highlight testimonials, technical tips, product education, and other copy elements that are not selling a thing except company credibility? Does the catalog have a phone number (800 or regular) and fax number on every page spread? Does it use cross-reference techniques to guide customers to other sections of the catalog to cross-sell additional products? Is each spread in the catalog designed to draw the customer's eye to key products? Does it use special symbols or icons to draw attention to values, new products, exclusive items or other unique selling features of products in the catalog? Do the layouts provide art directors and photographers with a detailed and precise blueprint from which to photograph the catalog? Do the layouts provide the copywriter with exact specifications for headline and body (product) copy length?

TYPOGRAPHY. Are the type size and font appropriate for the target audience? Is the body type a minimum of 9 points? Are the headlines readable? Is the body copy short and easy to read? Is any reverse type used in the catalog easy to read? Do any of the special typographic techniques—such as wrap-around type, centered type, reverse type, type over photos, or variegated backgrounds—hurt readability? Does any type cross the gutter between two pages?

USE OF COLOR. Is color used to add excitement, give direction, and improve customer response to the products? Does the catalog use background screens or special color tones to highlight testimonials, product specifications, and phone numbers? Does it effectively use color in page backgrounds, color bars, headlines, and so on to enhance order response and build customer acceptance of the catalog? Does selection of background and type colors take into consideration the age of the customer? For example, red type—even in headlines—is more difficult for mature audiences to read.

The Catalog Critique

Many catalogers limit the formal catalog creative review to managers and key marketing and merchandising people, but many argue that others should be involved, including merchandise or product development people; marketing circulation staff; the designer or art director; the writer(s); the photographer; the color separator and printer (for part of the meeting); and any outside marketing/merchandising consultants. The review should hit all the creative elements of the catalog. Starting with the outside and moving inward, the following seven elements should be discussed in the critique:

1. *The front cover.* This is the number one "hot spot" for grabbing customers and pulling them into the catalog. The critique team should judge the front cover on how well it attracts attention, tells who the firm is, identifies the catalog's niche/positioning, gets the reader inside, presents an offer, and sells a product.

2. *The back cover.* Like the front cover, the back cover is a major catalog hot spot. Nearly one-third of users start perusing a catalog from somewhere other than the front. Therefore, the back cover is of vital importance in getting readers' attention and getting them involved. Judge the back cover based on its functions: selling; reinforcing who the firm is and what its niche is; getting the reader inside; presenting an offer; and giving the reader vital service information, such as the terms of guarantee, which credit cards are accepted, the location of the order form, phone/fax order numbers, and so on.
3. *Other hot spots.* Hot spots in a catalog are those pages or spreads that get greater readership and attention than normal pages. The key hot spots are the inside front cover spread (p. 2–3), the inside back cover spread, the centerfold of a saddle-stitched catalog, and probably the second and third opening spreads (pp. 4–5 and 6–7). If the catalog uses these hot spots to the best advantage, each one should emphasize the product (i.e., produce sales); push best-sellers; highlight proven merchandise winners; showcase high-margin products; induce strong readership of the page; inform the reader (e.g., of company credibility, customer service information, testimonials, special product information); and involve the reader.
4. *Catalog design.* The four areas that logically fall under the design umbrella are page or spread layout, photography, typography, and use of color. Because catalogs are design-driven, no creative element is more important. The art director is king in the catalog world because he or she establishes the blueprint from which the rest of the catalog will be constructed. Layouts are to a catalog what the blueprint is to a building under construction. The photographer must work with exactness to the designer's layout. The copywriter must write to precisely the space the art director designated for headlines, body copy or special sidebar-type vignettes. Typography and color should help enhance the readability and selling power of the product, rather than detract from the selling process.
5. *Copy.* Copy is the salesperson of the catalog. Even though catalog production is not copy-driven, it is a very important component of the catalog. Copy is judged first by whether it gets the reader's attention and then by how well it informs, educates, explains, directs, entertains, assures, builds confidence, and, above all else, closes the sale.
6. *Order form.* The last physical element considered in the catalog critique is the order form. Although many business catalogs argue that an order form is superfluous for them, every catalog should include an order form or telephone organizer. Is the order form easy to use? Are there instructions? Is there sufficient room to write? Is the order form where the reader can find it?
7. *Offer.* The offer can make a major difference in the catalog's average order and response. The offer contains several parts. The basic parts are the guarantee, a toll-free number (for both ordering and customer service), a fax ordering number, the method of payment, and the method of pricing. The offer can also be more motivational and include such items as free gifts or other premiums, discounts, sweepstakes, special pricing, early bird specials, and shipping-and-handling specials. Because the key is to test offers, the creative critique should center on results of the tests and the quality of the creative execution of one offer vs. another.

SUMMARY

Creative strategy and execution deal with what and how a campaign will communicate about a product or service, including how that communication relates to the consumer or business target market's needs. Creative strategy dictates what the campaign will say, but it does not specify exactly how it will be said. That provides freedom in how campaign communications are operationalized in the campaign executions. The essence of successful campaign strategy is to find out how to do the selling task in a way that promises the most utility to the most prospects.

The function of advertising content is to carry out the communications objectives of the product or service. The advertising serves to translate the product features into benefits for the target market. However, the advertising content is more than a restatement of the product's attributes. The advertising copy must be written from the prospect's point of view, not the advertiser's. The essential skill of the copywriter is the ability to look through the target market's eyes and translate the product features into information that is understandable, useful, and persuasive to those prospects.

The choice of how to communicate the main selling concept is the most critical aspect of how the creative strategy is implemented because that decision drives the total character of an advertising execution. The direct-response advertiser faces numerous difficult choices in deciding how to approach that key benefit. In choosing between utilitarian and emotional benefits, the advertiser should offer rational benefits when prospects face utilitarian needs and emotional benefits when needs are social or psychological.

REVIEW QUESTIONS

1. What is a creative strategy statement? What are the parts, and what is each one intended to do with respect to the target audience for a product or service?
2. What is the difference between creative strategy and advertising execution?
3. How do the characteristics of a product or service relate to the content of a creative strategy?
4. What are utilitarian versus emotional advertising appeals? When should each be used and why?
5. Direct-response marketers can chose from among radio, television, print, telemarketing, and the mail as ways of communicating with a target audience. What are the special creative strategy and execution considerations for each medium? Which approaches are most appropriate for a direct seller of children's toys versus a bank interested in new customers?

NOTES

1. Adapted from Herschell Gordon Lewis, "Information on Infomercials," *Direct Marketing,* March 1995, pp. 30–32.
2. Adapted from Dean Reich, "Discovering Direct Response Radio: 14 Tips for Writing Ads That Work," *Direct Marketing,* October 1995, pp. 40–42.

3. Adapted from "The Art, Science & Arithmetic of Money-Making Direct Mail," *Target Marketing* 17, no. 6 (June 1994), pp. 51–55.
4. Adapted from Jack Schmid, "Good Catalog Design Drives Response," *Target Marketing* 16, no. 11 (November 1993), pp. 10–11.

SOURCES

"The Art, Science & Arithmetic of Money-Making Direct Mail." *Target Marketing* 17, no. 6 (June 1994), pp. 51–55.

BOVEE, COURTLAND L., AND WILLIAM ARENS. *Contemporary Advertising,* 4th ed. Homewood, IL: Richard D. Irwin, 1992.

BURGE, RANDY. "Unusual Mailings Produce Substantial and Desired Responses." *Direct Marketing,* 59, no. 4 (August 1996), pp. 30–31.

BURNSIDE, AMANDA. "Shots of Whisky." *Marketing,* August 3, 1995, pp. 30–32.

BURTON, PHILIP WARD. *Advertising Copywriting,* 6th ed. Lincolnwood, IL: NTC Business Books, 1994.

CARTER, JOAN CAMPO. "The Power of Printing Technology." *Direct Marketing* 57, no. 5 (September 1994), pp. 14–18.

"Continental Bank Unveils New Creative Print Campaign." *Bank Marketing,* 25, no. 5 (May 1993), p. 6.

DENTINO, KARL. "Approaching Direct Marketing from a Brand Orientation." *Direct Marketing,* February 1994, pp. 35–37.

ENGLE, JAMES F.; MARTIN R. WARSHAW; AND THOMAS C. KINNEAR. *Promotional Strategy,* 8th ed. Burr Ridge, IL: Richard D. Irwin, 1994.

FINLEY, TIMOTHY P. "Getting Names Off-the-Page." *Target Marketing* 18, no. 4 (April 1995), pp. 26–28.

The Franklin Mint promotional materials.

GRIFFIN, TOM. *International Marketing Communications.* Oxford, UK: Butterworth-Heinemann, 1993.

HAHN, FRED E. *Do-It-Yourself Advertising.* New York: John Wiley & Sons, 1993.

JONES, SUSAN K. *Creative Strategy in Direct Marketing.* Lincolnwood, IL: NTC Business Books, 1991.

KATZENSTEIN, HERBERT, AND WILLIAM SACHS. *Direct Marketing,* 2nd ed. New York: Macmillan, 1992.

KEDING, ANN, AND THOMAS H. BIVINS. *How to Produce Creative Advertising.* Lincolnwood, IL: NTC Business Books, 1993.

KRAKOWKA, LISA. "Oh, What a Feeling!" *American Demographics,* Marketing Tools Supplement (October 1995), pp. 29–30.

LEWIS, HERSCHELL GORDON. *Sales Letters That Sizzle.* Lincolnwood, IL: NTC Business Books, 1994.

________. "Information on Infomercials." *Direct Marketing,* March 1995, pp. 30–32.

________. "100 of the Easiest Ways to Begin an Effective Sales Letter." *Direct Marketing,* February 1994, pp. 32–34.

________. "100 of the Easiest Ways to Begin an Effective Sales Letter," *Direct Marketing,* December 1993, pp. 36–38.

________. "Why Did You Put *That* Enclosure in *This* Mailing?" *Direct Marketing,* May 1992, pp. 26–27, 36.

________. "Picking and Choosing . . . That's the Wordsmith's Job." *Catalog Age,* 10, no. 12 (December 1993), pp. 84–85.

LEWIS, HERSCHELL GORDON, AND CAROL NELSON. *World's Greatest Direct Mail Sales Letters.* Lincolnwood, IL: NTC Business Books, 1994.

MARCHETTI, KAREN J. "A Little Direct Response Know-how Can Improve Your Print Campaign Results." *Bank Marketing,* 28, no. 1, (January 1996), pp. 33–36.

———. "Building Direct-Response Advertising into Your Marketing Arsenal." *Bank Marketing,* 28 (August 1996), pp. 30–35.

MACH, RORY. "Positioning Your Product on TV." *Target Marketing* 17, no. 5 (May 1994), pp. 19–20.

MUMMERT, HALLIE. "Reaching Out to Women." *Target Marketing* 18, no. 8 (August 1995), pp. 33–38.

NEAL, MOLLIE. "Marketers Develop a New Climate." *Direct Marketing,* February 1992, pp. 26–27, 79.

PERRY, PHILLIP M. "Seven Secrets of Great Display Ads." *Cellular Business* 13, no. 5 (May 1996), pp. 68–72.

POSCH, ROBERT. "Copy Headliner Compliance More Than Mere Terms of Art." *Direct Marketing,* 57, no. 10 (February 1995), pp. 52–55.

RICCELLI, RICHARD. "Getting the Most from Your Direct Mail Copywriter." *Folio: The Magazine for Magazine Management* 23, no. 19 (source book issue), p. 174.

REICH, DEAN. "Discovering Direct Response Radio: 14 Tips for Writing Ads That Work." *Direct Marketing,* October 1995, pp. 40–42.

———. "Headline Writing Basics: What Every Headline Should Do and Nine Proven Ways to Do It." *Direct Marketing* 58, no. 12 (April 1996), pp. 44–47.

ROBERTS, MARY LOU, AND PAUL D. BERGER. *Direct Marketing Management.* Englewood Cliffs, NJ: Prentice Hall, 1989.

ROMAN, ERNAN. "The Media Mix." *Target Marketing* 18, no. 4 (April 1995), pp. 30–32+.

SANTORO, ELAINE. "Ads with a New 'View.' " *Direct Marketing,* April 1991, pp. 45–50.

SCHMID, JACK. "Good Catalog Design Drives Response." *Target Marketing* 16, no. 11 (November 1993), pp. 10–11.

———. "Don't Forget the Order Form!" *Target Marketing* 16, no. 9 (September 1993), pp. 10–11.

———. "Did You Like Your Last Catalog?" *Catalog Age* 10, no. 4 (April 1993), pp. 103–5.

SHASHO JONES. "Creative Creative." *Catalog Age,* March 1996, pp. 91–92, 94–95.

STONE, BOB. *Successful Direct Marketing Methods,* 5th ed. Lincolnwood, IL: NTC Business Books, 1995.

YORGEY, LISA A. "Cultured Creative." *Target Marketing* 18, no. 11 (November 1995), pp. 22–28.

CHAPTER 9

Direct-Mail Marketing

OBJECTIVES

1. To define the nature and scope of the direct-mail industry.
2. To define the term *direct mail* and describe what it includes.
3. To examine the advantages of direct mail that frequently make it more suitable than other alternatives.
4. To describe a "standard" direct-mail package and its common set of components.
5. To examine future trends and issues for direct-mail marketing.

INTRODUCTION

This chapter covers many types of mailing pieces, from postcards announcing specials to multipart packages with complex offers. To most people the term *direct marketing* means "direct mail" because they are accustomed to receiving daily mail pieces. However, direct-response marketing is much more than direct mail, although direct mail is a key component of the industry. Catalogs, which could be included under the heading of direct mail because they come to customers and prospects via the U.S. Postal Service, are covered in Chapter 10.

CASINOS GAMBLE ON DIRECT MAIL[1]

Atlantic City's casinos have grown to rely on direct mail to build customer loyalty and stimulate traffic in an increasingly competitive market. Today, most casinos have mailing lists with the number of names totaling six figures and more customers signing up every day.

In 1991, Atlantic City casinos gave away about $700 million worth of "complimentaries" largely by mail. These included (but were not limited to) rooms, meals, beverages, shows, and travel—including limousines to and from the customer's home or a helicopter to and from the nearest landing point to the customer's home. Complimentaries also included free gifts, free entry to special clubrooms at the casinos, and coupons redeemable for casino vouchers or cash.

Consider a mailing containing complimentaries from Harrah's that offers two free show tickets to Cole Porter's musical *Anything Goes,* $10 in credit, and a Harbour room for less than half price. Another Harrah's offer is for two free tickets to *Fiddler on the Roof,* a $10 food-and-beverage credit, and a see-how-much-you-won scratch-off card. A competitor, Merv Griffin's Resorts, offers two free tickets to its Star Struck stage show, a $10 coin bonus, an extra $10 Star Cash bonus, health and spa privileges, and a 20 percent discount on limousines.

Customers receiving particular attention are those who spend heavily each year on accommodations, entertainment, and gambling, although many "little spends" receive some complimentaries. Now, how do the casinos get their names? The high rollers are easy to track; there aren't too many of them. The casinos give these people special numbers when they see them spending big money. Every time they arrive and sit down, they must give the dealer their number, which is put on a computer. This guarantees future complimentaries for the customer, which, the casinos hope, will lead to more high rolling for them.

THE DIRECT-MAIL INDUSTRY

Direct mail is a valuable part of the marketing efforts of major companies all over the world. In 1993, the U.S. Postal Service delivered more than 200 billion pieces of mail. Organizations generated about 83 percent of that total, some two-thirds of which went to households, with the remainder going to other organizations.

Exhibit 9.1 shows the dramatic growth of U.S. mail-order sales over an 11-year period. Mail-order dollars went from about $100 billion in sales for 1983 to about $240 billion in 1993. Table 9.1 indicates that consumer product sales outnumber service-related sales in terms of dollar volume and that consumer and

EXHIBIT 9.1. U.S. Mail-Order Sales Growth

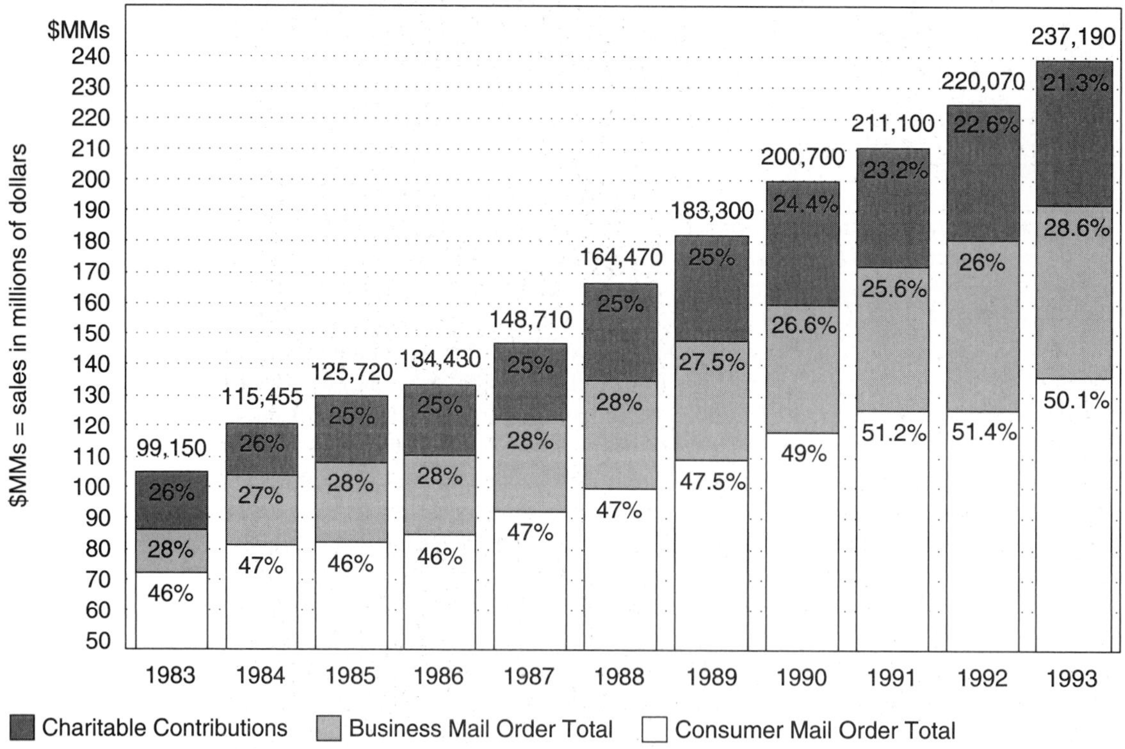

Source: Adapted from "1994 Mail Order Overview," *Direct Marketing,* August 1994, p. 28.

TABLE 9.1. Total 1993 U.S. Mail Order Sales and Contributions

	1992 Amount ($MMs)	1993 Amount ($MMs)	% Of Consumer	% Of Mail Order Total	Per Capita	% Of GNP	% Of Retail Sales	% Of General Merchandise Sales	% Of Consumer Services
Consumer:									
Products	**$ 67,510**	**$ 71,960**	**60%**	**30%**	**$279**	**1.2%**	**3.8%**	****10.3**	—
Specialty	52,860	57,760	47	24	224	0.9	3.1	8.2	—
General Merchandising	14,650	14,240	12	6	55	0.2	0.8	2.1	—
Services	**45,530**	**47,010**	**40**	**20**	**182**	**0.7**	—	—	**1.9**
Non-Financial	26,620	26,980	23	11	105	0.4	—	—	1.1
Financial	18,910	20,030	17	8	78	0.3	—	—	0.8
Consumer Total	**113,040**	**118,970**	**100**	**50**	**461**	**1.9**	—	—	—
Business:									
Products & Services	57,310	67,730	—	29	—	—	—	—	—
Charitable Contributions	49,720	50,490	—	21	—	—	—	—	—
MAIL ORDER TOTAL	220,070	237,190	—	100	—	—	—	—	—
U.S. Population	256	258	—	—	—	—	—	—	—
Gross National Product	5,950,700	6,378,000	—	—	—	—	—	—	—
Total Aggregate Sales	12,822,000	14,088,000	—	—	—	—	—	—	—
Retail Sales	1,937,390	1,888,000	—	—	—	—	—	—	—
*General Merchandising and Specialty Sales	612,201	681,900	—	—	—	—	—	—	—
Consumer Services	2,191,900	2,503,900	—	—	—	—	—	—	—

*General merchandising, apparel, drug, building materials, hardware, garden supply, mobile home furniture, home furnishings and equipment.

**Excludes mail order food (food not part of denominator)

Source: "1994 Mail Order Overview," *Direct Marketing,* August 1994, p. 27.

EXHIBIT 9.2. Average Number of Mail Pieces Received per Week

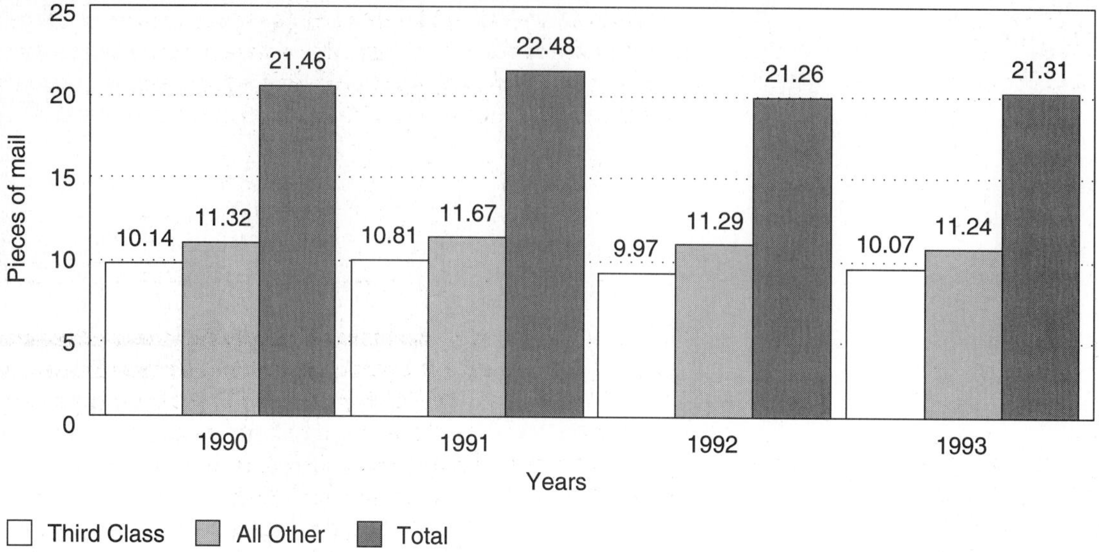

Source: USPS Household Diary Study, 1995.

business mail-order sales play an important role in the national economy. However, retail sales still far exceed those of mail order.

In 1993, the average household received over 21 pieces of mail per week (see Exhibit 9.2). Table 9.2 shows the types of products purchased by mail order and the dollar amounts spent on those products in 1990 by all consumers. Insurance is a major item, as is apparel. Even such items as prescriptions and foods are sold by mail in significant volumes.

Direct mail's customers are more likely to be women than men (see Table 9.3). The abundance of clothing catalogs aimed at women points to their influence in the catalog aspect of direct mail. Women are also the majority purchasers of a variety of other products offered through the mail.

THE ADVANTAGES OF DIRECT MAIL

The primacy of direct mail as a medium is a result of its advantages over other forms of direct marketing. When a business chooses direct marketing by mail, alone or in combination with other media, it is because it offers an advantage over alternative channels for selling that business's products. According to Katzenstein and Sachs, five important attributes of direct mail frequently make this medium more suitable than other alternatives: selectivity, personalization, flexibility, isolation, and response rates.[2]

An advantage not highlighted by Katzenstein and Sachs is the ability to test the effectiveness of different direct-mail pieces. Chapter 17 contains an extensive discussion of the role of decision support tools in direct marketing, including testing.

TABLE 9.2. Mail-Order Sales to Consumers in 1990, by Type of Product

Category	Billions of Dollars
Apparel	8.6
Auto clubs	2.0
Automotive	0.6
Books	2.0
Collectibles	2.1
Cosmetics	0.4
Crafts	1.2
Educational services	1.2
Electronic goods	2.7
Food	0.9
Gardening/horticultural	0.6
General merchandise/housewares/gifts	9.5
Health/nutrition	0.9
Insurance/financial	13.3
Jewelry	0.4
Magazines	5.8
Photofinishing	1.0
Prescriptions	0.7
Records and tapes	1.1
Sporting goods	3.6
Tools/home repair	1.1
Major catalog retailers	6.1
Department stores	11.7
Unclassified merchandise	4.2
Total consumer sales	81.7

Source: Adapted from Maxwell Sroge, *The United States Mail Order Industry* (Lincolnwood, IL: NTC Business Books, 1994), p. 19.

TABLE 9.3. 1994 Percentage of Mail Order Buyers by Gender

	Ordering Any Product	
	Relative Percent	Percent of Total Population
Men	46.9	10.3
Women	57.6	12.4
Total	100.0	

Source: Adapted from Direct Marketing Association, *Statistical Fact Book 1996* (New York: Direct Marketing Association, 1996), pp. 43, 46.

Selectivity

As noted in Chapters 3 and 4, market segmentation and the technology used to operationalize it make for a powerful combination. In no other area of direct marketing is this more evident than in direct mail. Databases of target market members provide the basis for selecting segments of consumers or businesses that have specific profiles, including geographic location (in the form of zip codes or census designations such as block groups) and numerous other demographic, socioeconomic, and buyer behavior characteristics. This permits a close matching of target markets with the product or service offerings of a firm. Mailings are sent to individuals or households or businesses with known buying habits and specific interests, no matter where they live. This eliminates large numbers of nonprospects and waste by concentrating offerings on those most likely to be receptive to offers.

With a selection process that transcends the restrictions of geographic location, direct-mail targeting is not tied to particular locations in the same way as most radio stations and newspapers, which service only a limited area. Messages communicated through these mass outlets reach an audience defined primarily by their demographics and their interest in the content being carried by the medium.

Further, mailing to a list of those who have demonstrated an interest in a product or service category or who have already made a purchase from a firm can yield a significantly lower cost per order than a mass-market commercial on television. Although the extra precision in targeting via the mails is more expensive on an individual cost per thousand basis than is a television advertisement, the response rate is likely to be much higher. The cost per thousand persons reached by direct mail averages about $300, which includes paper and printing, list rental, mailing, and postage. In comparison, the cost per thousand persons reached by television commercials can vary from only $14 to a high of $40, depending on the channel and show. The cost is relatively low because much of the audience for the television program will not be interested in the offering. In contrast, those who receive the direct mailing are much more likely to place an order because they have been predefined as having interests and/or purchasing patterns that make them better prospects.

Personalization

Direct-mail personalization is very common. Today, nearly every mailing to a firm's prospects and customers has the name of the target person, along with his or her address. The days when direct marketers sent mailings with envelopes addressed "To Resident" are nearly gone. This personalization is possible because of computing power and massive databases that contain names and addresses. Sophisticated computer programs mass-produce personalized mails by feeding names and addresses onto letters and other pages such as those in magazines. This creates the illusion of a personal contact between the seller and a target market.

Flexibility

Direct mail is flexible because of its ability to customize a message based on the audience it is appealing to and the circumstances under which that appeal is being made. As a medium, the mails have no fixed audience parameters. Unlike other media, such as television, radio, magazines, and newspapers, direct mail is not constrained in how it defines the scope and location of its target audience. Thus, the nature and size of any direct-mail effort is determined by the mailer, not the medium.

Isolation

Direct mail has no editorial environment. Its commercial message is not read incidentally as with an advertisement in a magazine. Some mailings look like offers, while others are disguised to appear to be something else. Many prospects have opened a direct-mail piece thinking it was an important notice from a bank or some urgent message from the government only to find that the envelope contained an offer for a new magazine or insurance plan.

Response Rates

Direct mail obtains higher response rates than any other medium used in direct marketing due to its ability to be personal, selective, and flexible and to deliver a custom message free of competing advertisements to a specific individual or household. Mailboxes may be clogged with many items, but the items are opened one at a time. Although many direct-mail pieces are discarded because they are seen as junk, what is read still pulls a larger response than that of any other medium.

SCOTT PAPER USES BUSINESS-TO-BUSINESS DIRECT MAIL[3]

An excellent starting point for a marketing campaign is a product that fills a clear need of a specific target group. In this example, the Scott Paper Company had a product called Scottfold, which was designed to eliminate "messy towel syndrome" in restrooms by dispensing "soft, luxurious" paper towels one at a time. Scott executives were confident that property managers at Class A office buildings would be interested in this product for a number of reasons, including increased tenant satisfaction and improved appearance in the restroom. In addition to the near-perfect dispensing of high-quality towels, the product allows for cost savings. The challenge was to market this new product effectively to the target group and encourage trial usage. Scott decided to launch a direct-mail campaign to introduce Scottfold.

It seemed that on a cost per thousand basis, telemarketing would be more efficient, but Scott felt that direct mail would leave a greater impression on prospects and customers and enhance brand recognition, further positioning Scott as a paper manufacturer. Telemarketing was used for follow-up as well as for other upcoming marketing efforts aimed at the same target audience.

The direct-mail kit was developed to encourage property managers' interest in making an appointment to see a Scott representative. The offer contained a free $50 starter kit and valuable rebate incentives to achieve a quick reply. The mailer employed personalized "grabber" headlines such as "Scottfold deals ABC Company a winning hand!"

Many aspects of the mailer were personalized, including the invitation letter and four-color brochure that featured a peel-off playing-card action device that revealed a special offer accompanied by the "winning hand" motif. Testimonials by actual customers were included to illustrate satisfaction claims and provide personal enthusiasm. All offers were guaranteed throughout the kit.

Equipping clients with three modes of contacting Scott Paper—fax, mail, and telephone—ensured easy response. Follow-up calls made by Scott START, an in-house telemarketing operation, further enhanced the effect of the direct-mail kits. Appointment-setters maximized the schedules of Scott's sales force—a technique that paid off.

Results of the program included the following:

- Scottfold sales increased 80 percent, which was attributable to both the mail campaign and increased attention to this product by the sales staff.
- A 28 percent response rate was attained with the highly personalized mailer, backed by follow-up phone calls to prospects.
- Brand identity for Scott and Scottfold had been enhanced.

The Scottfold marketing program exceeded even its own expectations. Scott believes that this success is attributed to a well-rounded program consisting of the classic aspects of direct marketing. Those aspects included clear definitions of the target audience, database development, and follow-up telephone work from the Scott START unit paired with high-impact, highly personalized direct mailers.

THE DIRECT-MAIL PACKAGE

Direct-mail packages come in so many variations that there is no such thing as a "standard" one. However, there is a format common to what most direct marketers produce. According to Roberts and Berger, that standard direct-mail package includes the following components:

- Outer envelope.
- Letter.
- Brochure.
- Response device.
- Other inserts.[4]

To illustrate the concept of a standard package, this section concentrates on a mailing from the National Audubon Society, the well known supporter of environmental causes and an active direct marketer of its memberships. It begins with the outer envelope.

The Outer Envelope

The outer envelope is the first part of the direct-mail package seen by the recipient. The envelope must be opened if the offer is to be read and acted upon, and it must be perceived as interesting enough to warrant opening by conveying the excitement or relevance of the remainder of the direct-mail package's contents. If the envelope does not provoke sufficient interest from the recipient in about 5 to 10 seconds, it will be discarded. Envelopes can be either purchased, premade, or custom designed in a nearly infinite number of sizes, colors, types, and materials. Of course, though, the envelope must conform to postal regulations.

Effective outer envelopes act as selling devices by communicating something about the contents that motivates the recipient to open it. How this motivation is best initiated depends on the product or service being sold and the nature of the target audience. The color, quality, and size of the envelope all say something to the recipient about the contents. Envelope copy and graphics testing are important so that the direct marketer can learn what works best.

The National Audubon Society's offer envelope is a good example of a well-designed, attention-getting outer package. It has color, an envelope with windows for provoking interest in the contents, and an explicit teaser about the benefits of the envelope contents.

The Letter

The letter is the most important part of the direct-mail package. It presents the offer and communicates the sales message, and it urges the reader to take action immediately.

The four-page letter shown in Exhibit 9.3 (page 180) was the one enclosed in the envelope from the National Audubon Society offering a trial membership in the society, which includes a free issue of *Audubon* magazine. Notice how the letter uses variations in formatting to create an interesting flow for the description of what the consumer will receive if he or she participates.

In general, the physical structure of the body of a letter should use short words and no jargon or complicated technical terms, unless consistent with the nature of the product being sold. It should contain short sentences, with no more than an average of about 12 words, and it should use short paragraphs of no more than about three sentences. In all, these letters should look easy to read because of short words, short sentences, short paragraphs, and appealing formatting and coloring.

In a letter, the main selling concept needs to be clearly stated and highlighted to get the prospect's attention. Once the letter has the prospect's attention, it must then build interest by telling what the benefits of the product are and why and how those benefits are delivered in a credible way. The National Audubon Society letter explains the nature of the offer and the specific things the prospect will receive.

The Brochure

While the letter is an essential part of a direct-mail package, the brochure is a significant enticement to the prospect to participate in the offer. Brochures are usually a printed piece of four or six pages that can be either folded, stapled, or bound.

There is no standard format for a brochure, but there are some useful guidelines, including the use of colorful graphics, pictures, and eye-catching headlines and text explaining the offer. The National Audubon Society brochure elaborates on the letter by providing specifics about the content of the offer, but in a very graphical way.

The cover of a brochure should consist of benefit-oriented headlines. When the brochure is opened completely, the pages should summarize all aspects of the offer with text and graphics, including narratives that explain the product concept and its major benefits. Graphics help tell the story and flow with the narrative. The text blocks should be short and broken up by illustrations. This is done irregularly to give the brochure an exciting, energetic appearance.

The Response Device

The National Audubon Society direct-mail package also contains a response device that the prospect can complete, put in the accompanying preaddressed, postage paid envelope, and send to the society. The device has affixed to it a personalized membership card and more repetition of the offer benefits.

EXHIBIT 9.3. National Audubon Society Letter

National Audubon Society

700 BROADWAY, NEW YORK, NY 10003

Dear Friend:

The members of the National Audubon Society make up only a small fraction -- less than one percent of America's population. But they are a very important fraction.

My hope is that you will want to join them.

And for this reason I have enclosed an interim membership card already inscribed in your name. I invite you to accept this free trial membership, including a free issue of AUDUBON magazine, without obligation.

As an Audubon member, you will experience the wonders of our planet in a magazine widely considered to be the most beautiful published anywhere.

At the same time, you will be helping to preserve those wonders through your support of America's most effective conservation group. There are other benefits as well, which I will outline in a moment.

<u>AUDUBON ... the beauty of a fine art book,</u>
<u>the excitement of an adventure story.</u>

In a world of throwaway publications, AUDUBON magazine is truly worth reading and worth keeping. Reading it makes you feel the same way you do after a walk in the deep woods, or a swim in a crystal-clear lake. You feel rewarded. Enriched. Uplifted.

AUDUBON radiates with magnificent color photographs, for almost 20 years it has been the premier showcase for the world's finest nature photographers...the world's most thoughtful and motivating nature writers. AUDUBON has won the prestigious National Magazine Award not once, but... four times.

Audubon will expand your world. It will bring the magnificence of nature's most breathtaking creations into your home. And, AUDUBON will alert you to progress and problems in the environmental war zone...

> <u>Starving in the wild.</u> Snowbound in a remote Minnesota cabin, you hear a thump at the window. You freeze in your tracks as your flashlight picks up the blazing yellow eyes of a wild timber wolf. He is leaning weakly against the window.

- 2 -

> Is he hurt? Would he attack?
>
> As you move outside and cautiously approach, he stares at you motionless. You pick him up, carry him inside, lay him by the fire. You wait and watch as the wolf wheezes, gasps and dies. Later you learn that the wolf was starved. His foot, mutilated in a fox trap, impeded his hunting. He died of pneumonia.

As you share this knowledge and experience with the AUDUBON writer who actually lived it, you understand why we must save our few remaining wolves. And all of wild America.

<u>Privilege Poachers!</u> The U.S. senator is decked out in his hunting togs. Toting a shotgun he heads warily toward the illegally baited Maryland duck pond. Then, sensing something amiss, he suddenly turns back to the house. How did he just barely avert a collar by agents of the U.S. Fish and Wildlife Service? Who warned the senator? None other than the director of the FWS.

AUDUBON revealed how Washington's poaching politicos -- and other fat cats -- dodge the game laws honest hunters respect.

<u>A spectacle drained of its beauty.</u> With an otherworldly shriek and clatter, an immense flock of sandhill cranes explodes into the sky over Nebraska's North Platte River. For a million years and more, this spectacle has been one of nature's most awesome.

The once mighty Platte is already 70% drained. Now new water projects threatened it dry. Merely to keep suburban lawns green.

AUDUBON detailed the devastation this could bring, not only to the cranes but to millions of other birds that need the Platte to stay alive.

<u>Why do Maine blueberry growers need rifles?</u> To kill bears. Why? Because bears raid the beehives. Why are there beehives? Because the growers have killed all the native pollinating insects with chemicals.

All our new pesticides and herbicides only bring new insects and plant diseases to the blueberry barrens. In our taming of the wild blueberry, both nature and reason seem to have gone awry. What's the point, asks AUDUBON?

Will the administration live up to its promises on clean air and wetlands protection? Can we save the last of our ancient forests from the chainsaws? Is an economy based on non-fossil energy sources an achievable dream? What can be done to prevent more catastrophic oil spills like the wreck of the Exxon Valdez?

- 3 -

AUDUBON keeps you in touch with the vital environmental issues.

<u>You cannot touch, see, or hear</u>
<u>the most important benefit of your Audubon membership.</u>

This most important benefit of membership in the National Audubon Society gives you nothing immediately tangible in return. Nothing, that is, except peace of mind. Nothing except knowing that you are doing your part to stop the senseless destruction of Earth's precious natural resources.

Your dues directly support active and vital programs to protect wildlife, promote energy conservation, and help ensure a healthier environment.

Quite simply, very few organizations do more (or more important) work to save the balance and beauty of nature plus the acquisition and maintenance of wildlife sanctuaries all over America.

<u>Free admission to Audubon Nature Centers are</u>
<u>another advantage of membership.</u>

You and your family will be awestruck by the sights and sounds along Audubon's nature trails, where birds and wildlife exist undisturbed. And where natural environments are protected from depredation by man.

The Audubon Nature Centers are among the most serene and pristine places on Earth. You can visit them in Ohio, Connecticut, California, New Mexico, and Wisconsin.

<u>Local chapter membership, exciting adventure tours,</u>
<u>special purchase opportunities, and more.</u>

Your National Audubon Society membership also gives you the opportunity to be part of the Audubon network. You can participate in enjoyable, worthwhile activities with some very interesting people in over 500 U.S. and Canada chapters. One is almost certain to be in your area.

You can also travel with fellow members to fascinating places like Africa, Antarctica, or Chilean Patagonia at reasonable costs.

And take advantage of special offers on selected Audubon products of special interest to nature lovers!

Here's all you have to do to begin receiving AUDUBON at once, your FREE BIRDFEEDER and enjoy all the other benefits of membership in the National Audubon Society.

- 4 -

Just lift the token on your enclosed invitation from the top right of the page. Press it firmly to the circle on the bottom left. Then detach the lower and return it as soon as possible in the postage-paid envelope.

You'll get a year's worth of insightful AUDUBON issues. <u>Plus</u>, a FREE BIRDFEEDER. <u>Plus</u>, all the other membership benefits. <u>Plus</u>, the satisfaction of knowing you are doing your part to preserve the Earth's precious natural resources. Later, if you wish to continue, you may do so, simply by paying our bill for only $20. Or you may cancel your membership and owe nothing.

If you decide to continue, as I hope you will, you will be joining over 500,000 of the most concerned, interesting, and informed people on the face of this struggling Earth. I look forward to welcoming you.

Sincerely,

Peter A.A. Berle
President

P.S. Act today to reserve your FREE BIRDFEEDER and become a temporary member of the National Audubon Society. You'll be joining the group doing so much to help save our threatened planet Earth. And at $20 for the year, that's more value for less money than I've heard of in a long, long time! So, please become an Audubon Society member now!

Other Inserts

A wide variety of inserts may be included in the standard direct-mail package to increase the response rate. The National Audubon Society offer has a "personal note" from Jan Beyeo, senior staff scientist, that emotionalizes the offer and encourages prospects to participate. Other types of inserts are circulars and folders.

TIMING AND SEQUENCING OF MAILINGS

The best way for a direct marketer to determine how often to send out mailings is to experiment. An experiment should measure the response rate for each mailing and the extent to which there are diminishing returns on those mailings. *Diminishing returns* means that additional mailings generate lower response rates. The direct marketer will reach a point where it is no longer profitable to mail with a certain frequency. Thus, the ideal frequency is actually the point at which the marginal cost of mailings exceeds that of the marginal revenue generated by those mailings.

Table 9.4 shows a sample working budget for one mailing sent out by a direct-mail firm. It highlights the many expenses involved in an expected mailing quantity of 100,000 pieces.

In addition to deciding how many mailings to send, the direct marketer must also determine how often to send them. A key factor in this decision is response time. For example, an offer for a magazine subscription renewal may receive a 30 percent affirmative response in 15 days and an additional 10 percent in 30 days. Offers such as a *Star Trek* video from Columbia House would be sent only once in most circumstances, but Columbia House would send other offers to the same target market within 30 days of mailing the original *Star Trek* offer. Precisely how frequently to repeat an offer or to send another offer is a question to resolve through testing. Chapter 17 discusses how testing is used to determine the sales and profit value of individual direct marketing programs. Chapter 18 examines the profitability of those programs and how the amount of money made by a direct marketing effort is related to testing.

THE MAILING LIST

As in all forms of direct marketing, the success of any direct-mail campaign is dependent on the mailing list. To the extent that offers are sent to the wrong people, the campaign will be a failure. Lists should be continuously tested for effectiveness because both customer membership and buying characteristics change constantly. Refer back to Chapter 6 for a discussion of the types of lists available to direct marketers and the relative value of each in operating direct-mail campaigns.

DIRECT MAIL AND PRIVACY[5]

Underneath consumers' mildly caustic or cynical responses to direct-mail firms (and other direct marketers such as telemarketers) are two fundamental perceptions: irritation and violation. People feel irritated when they believe they get too many direct-mail solicitations. People feel violated when they believe too much

TABLE 9.4. Direct Mail—Sample Working Budget

Great North American Widget Corporation
Consumer Solo-Mailing Campaign
Two-for-One Widget Offer
(Approx. Net Quantity, 100,000 [100M]; Scheduled Drop Date, 7/28/95)
*WORKING BUDGET**
Prepared by Frank N. Stine, Mar. 15, 1995

A. CREATIVE		
1. Preliminary roughs and dummies	$ 400	
2. Copy, including revises	3,750	
3. B&W Computer Mockup (headlines & text in place; illustrations & photos—position only)	900	
4. Contingency	500	
TOTAL	$ 5,550	(6.71%)
B. ART & PREPARATION		
1. Photography	$ 900	
1. Model fees	400	
3. Photo direction	500	
4. Line illustrations (7)	350	
5. Color Computer Mockup (final copy & art elements in position, incid. low res scans of photography)	600	
6. Color separations (2 randoms)	400	
7. Colorkeys	250	
8. Image assembly of film	600	
9. Contingency	1,000	
TOTAL	$ 5,000	(6.05%)
C. PRINTING PRODUCTION		
1. 4-pg. litho let., 8-½″ × 11″, 2 colors (105M @ $29.98/M)	$ 3,150	
2. 16-pg. booklet, 5-½″ × 8-½″, 2 colors (105M @ $108.60/M)	11,400	
3. Reply card, 3-½″ × 5-½″, 2 colors (105M @ $14.46/M)	1,500	
4. BRE, #7-¾, one color (105M @ $14.92/M)	1,550	
5. Outer env., 6″ × 9″, 2 color, cello window (105M @ $57.18/M)	6,000	
6. Contingency	2,400	
TOTAL	$26,000	(31.44%)
D. MAILING LISTS		
1. Mail order respondents (tape) 70M @ $95/M	$ 6,650	
2. Active magazine subs (tape) 45M @ $60/M	2,700	
3. Contingency	1,200	
TOTAL	$10,550	(12.76%)

(continued)

TABLE 9.4. Direct Mail—Sample Working Budget—Continued

E. COMPUTER PROCESSING		
1. Reformatting, data conversion, etc.	$ 450	
2. Merge/Purge (115M @ $11.10/M)	1,300	
3. Code and run 4-up labels (100M @ $4.20/M)	400	
4. Reports & directory printout	200	
5. Contingency	450	
TOTAL	$ 2,800	(3.39%)
F. LETTERSHOP PRODUCTION		
1. Insert, label, sort, mail, etc. (100M @ $33.90)	$ 3,400	
2. Affix bulk-rate stamps (100M @ $6/M)	600	
3. Audit & pull samples (100M @ $2.10/M)	200	
4. Contingency	300	
TOTAL	$ 4,500	(5.44%)
G. ALLOCATED FEES		
1. Ad Agency	$ 6,000	
2. Consultant	1,500	
3. Contingency	1,000	
TOTAL	$ 8,500	(10.28%)
H. POSTAGE		
1. 100M @ $198/M	$19,800	(23.93%)
BUDGETED GRAND TOTAL	**$82,700**	**(100%)**

*Rounded to the nearest $50
Budgeted Total without Cont. Reserves = $75,850
Source: Shell Alpert, CMC, Alpert O'Neil Tigre & Co., 1995.

information about their lives and personal preferences is being exchanged without their knowledge. They may believe their personal information is being rented, sold, bartered, borrowed, and perhaps even stolen by huge marketing companies with sophisticated databases and sinister motives. These two perceptions together highlight the privacy concerns of consumers. To get to the heart of the privacy issue, and to the most logical, practical solutions, we first need to understand the relationship between these two perceptions.

Consumer Perception 1: Irritation

The reason people believe they get too much direct mail and too many telemarketing phone calls is that they probably do. Some 50 percent of the billions of pieces of unsolicited direct mail delivered to mailboxes across the United States are never read. But direct-mail clutter is only half the irritation story; the other half is irrelevance. Most of the mail and phone calls that come to households are still woefully irrelevant. Combine irrelevance with clutter and what results is the perception of irritation at receiving junk.

The irritation part of the privacy issue should eventually abate, thanks to database-driven direct marketing. As more and more marketers adopt a database approach, the volume of irrelevant mail will most likely decline. Refer back to Chapter 5 for a discussion of database marketing.

Consumer Perception 2: Violation

While database marketing will help solve the first negative perception of direct mail, it can actually exacerbate the second—violation. Consider the revolutionary advancements in data-processing technology over the past 10 to 15 years that enable direct marketers to access and manipulate data better, smarter, faster, and cheaper than anyone ever dreamed imaginable. Combine these improvements in data processing with the unprecedented availability of information (the number of mailing lists on the market grows every year, as do the number of personal data selections available to mailing-list users) and add to the mix the fact that there are few restraints over how that information is used. What emerges is a prescription for privacy violation if great care is not exercised.

GOVERNMENT POSTAL RATES

Postage is one of the most expensive components of any direct-mail campaign. The rates are determined by mail class, with first-class mail being the most expensive (after Express mail and Priority mail, rarely, if ever used by direct marketers) and third-class the least expensive. As of 1995, the first ounce of a first-class letter costs 32 cents to mail, with any additional weight charged an additional amount per ounce. First-class letter mail in volumes of at least 500 pieces qualifies for a per piece reduction if presorted by zip code and another per piece reduction if presorted by carrier route and within other geographic density standards for the mailing. Third-class rates are lower because the senders do much of the work. Third-class mail pieces must be delivered to the post office in trays or bags, presorted and classified as to destination. The rates are calculated from the weight of what is mailed.

Note that postal discounts and standards can be quite complicated and can vary significantly over time. It is therefore mandatory that a marketer using direct mail closely track changes in post office pricing policies and adjust mailing approaches accordingly.

Some direct mailers are experimenting with alternatives to the regular mail such as faxes and delivery services like Federal Express. However, these vehicles are impractical for most firms mailing large numbers of catalogs or other such materials. Also, for materials that would normally be sent through the regular mail, even if a direct marketer finds an alternative to the government postal monopoly it is required by law to pay the U.S. Postal Service the value of that mailing (unless the mailing can be classified as urgent). Thus, some major U.S. firms send Washington millions of dollars each year for postal services they do not use.

WORLDWIDE MAIL-ORDER MARKETING[6]

One has only to look at the tremendous success of direct mail in the United States to realize the incredible potential of this marketing medium for the rest of the world. If what mail order has done for commerce and sales levels in the United States can be duplicated the world over, the industry is indeed headed for its brightest days ever. (See Chapter 16 for an in-depth discussion of international direct marketing.)

As technology continues to offer better, faster, and less expensive options to mail-order marketers, the prospect of worldwide direct-mail efforts seems increasingly feasible and attractive. Before these efforts can become reality, however, several major obstacles need to be overcome. These include major gaps in addressing information, lack of standards, different currencies, wide variations in national postal rates and procedures, and the need for uniformity that can ensure the smooth flow of mass mailings the world over.

These and other critical issues are being addressed by the International Direct Mail Advisory Council, which was created by the Universal Postal Union (UPU), a United Nations organization responsible for world postal affairs. The UPU has created the Direct Mail Market Development Program, designed to promote public/private partnerships in order to stimulate mail-order market growth around the world. This includes a global direct-mail marketing study and the establishment of the advisory council. The focus of the UPU effort will include determining the current state of direct marketing in each country, defining postal standards (including addressing), studying delivery mechanisms, establishing payment methods, and dealing with guarantee and return customs.

A global Direct Mail Marketing Study is currently being conducted by Arthur D. Little, Inc. This two-year study is expected to yield valuable information on marketing dynamics, best practices, address structures and standardization, list availability, automation work sharing, cross-border partnerships, product fulfillment, and a host of product management tools to address market economics and profitable direct-mail marketing.

Among the questions advisory council participants have agreed to tackle is addressing. As a primary source of information for direct-mail marketers, the council is naturally concerned about the state of names and addresses and the need for addressing standards to evolve. In many areas of the world, there are virtually no addresses. If a prospect is a well-known citizen of an underdeveloped country, his or her name alone may be enough for postal authorities to make a delivery, but failing that celebrity, delivery may be questionable. Other areas may use addresses such as "two miles down and past the well," as was the case with rural addresses in the United States many years ago. Such addresses depend heavily on the geographical knowledge of some local individuals—obviously not the most reliable way to mail. This lack of addressing, or imprecise addressing, still exists in probably more than half of the world's countries, and that creates a problem for mail-order marketers. While it is true that many citizens of developing nations are too poor to be the targets of mail-order marketers today, tomorrow will be a different story, and in even these countries now there is a huge potential among the affluent and near-affluent.

Currently, firms such as Database America have information on addressing schemes in some 140 countries. Their task is to learn about such schemes and to attempt to make them as functional as possible. This is where the UPU can be particularly helpful in its role as the clearinghouse for all international postal matters. Country-by-country analysis in the A. D. Little study will help the UPU establish standards that can remove current addressing barriers.

Although differences in postal rates and regulations from nation to nation may cause direct mailers a great deal of difficulty, economic considerations and cultural differences also present difficulties to firms seeking to mail on a global scale. For example, many countries have conflicting customs about what should be mailed. These rules may grow out of such different areas as physical packaging requirements and cultural practices or moral beliefs. A particular color may have a negative or even insulting meaning within a particular culture, and graphic images commonly seen in some countries might inflame moral sensitivities elsewhere. Such differences will inevitably affect the movement of direct mail from nation to nation. Again, the industry cries out for agreed-upon standards and regulations, and this is one of the goals the UPU effort seeks to accomplish.

ISSUES AND TRENDS[7]

At no time in the 20th century has the dynamic and changing nature of retail distribution been more in evidence than today. American retail distribution is a composite result of a high-level economy, an economy that by any comparative standards is relatively free and in which distribution is highly competitive. This section focuses on five of the critical issues and trends that will take direct-mail marketers to the year 2000 and beyond:

1. The image of direct marketing.
2. Direct mail and the environment.
3. Mergers, acquisitions, and consolidation.
4. Strategic partnerships.
5. Alternative media and an interactive marketplace.

The Image of Direct Marketing

Probably the most critical and global of all marketing issues and trends is the continual need for direct marketers to maintain and improve upon their image in the minds of consumers, businesses, and government. For the most part, regardless of the positive contributions that marketers make to society (e.g., efficient and cost-effective methods for marketing and selling goods and services), they are often looked upon as intrusive, wasteful, and even unethical.

In the minds of consumers, there are three broadly visible aspects of mail order that companies need to collectively improve upon: businesses and government privacy, environmentally sound practices, and business ethics. Only by continuing to take these issues seriously—for example, by adopting industrywide standards of conduct and developing and implementing positive public relations—will marketers be able to correct public misconceptions and avoid unnecessary government regulations.

Direct Mail and the Environment

The volume of direct mail has drawn the attention of numerous consumer and environmental groups. Although direct mail represents only 3 percent of solid waste in the United States, the issue of "junk mail" is the topic of hundreds of articles in local and national newspapers. Some marketers may believe their operational strategies for reducing waste will improve their environmental image, but it is the volume of unsolicited, poorly targeted mail that ends up in the trash that drives consumer frustration and leads to the imposition of government regulations.

Mergers, Acquisitions, and Consolidation

One of the most significant issues beginning to affect direct mail is the increasing number of mergers, acquisitions, and consolidations involving direct marketers. In 1993, there were 171 mergers, acquisitions, and buyouts that affected companies involved in direct marketing, an increase of 38 percent from 1992 (124 deals) and up 50 percent from 1990 (114 consolidations).

Several underlying factors may help explain this tremendous upsurge in consolidation activity. The principal reason is the realization by companies of all sorts that direct marketing is the most cost-effective means for targeting specific audiences and developing long-term customer relationships. Therefore, there is an increasing interest by some companies both inside and outside the industry to further penetrate the marketplace with acquisitions, alliances, and other forms of partnerships. Also, as postal, production, and operation costs increase, direct marketers and service suppliers will continue to merge and acquire other direct marketers to achieve the economies of scale that are the result of a larger, stronger firm. Both the interest in marketplace penetration and the need to achieve economies of scale will contribute to a continuing trend toward consolidation in the industry through the end of the decade.

Strategic Partnerships

Even more significant than the rate of consolidation is the proliferation of joint ventures and strategic alliances among direct marketers. In 1993 there were 86 transactions involving strategic partnerships—up 79 percent from 1992, when 48 transactions were recorded.

This strong trend represents the significant degree of change taking place. Alliances and joint ventures allow direct marketers to leverage their competitive advantages and make use of the strengths of another company. Companies selling goods and services need to constantly develop additional sources for customer names. Alliances, affinity, and relationship marketing programs with other direct marketers help these companies expand their customer base.

New, alternative forms of marketing, including electronic marketing, have given rise to a wave of alliances and joint ventures among both users and suppliers. The jury is still out on the future of most of the new media; however, direct marketers are positioning themselves now to take advantage of new media as soon as they become viable for generating new prospects and sales.

Alternative Media and an Interactive Marketplace

Many of today's partnerships focus on the development of alternative and interactive marketing technologies that will allow direct marketers to become involved in the information superhighway. These technologies run the gamut from established electronic shopping systems to yet-to-be-developed networks that provide full interactivity. CD-ROMs, online PCs, interactive television, in-flight ordering systems, PC diskettes, screen-based telephones, photo advertising, audiotex systems, infomercials, and home shopping programs are among the new formats.

SUMMARY

Direct-response marketing is much more than direct mail, although direct mail is a key component of the industry. When a business chooses direct marketing by mail, alone or in combination with other media, it is because direct mail offers an advantage over alternative channels for selling that business's products, including its selectivity, personalization, flexibility, isolation, and response rates.

While direct-mail packages come in many variations, most direct marketers produce a standard package that includes an outer envelope, a letter, a brochure, a response device, and other inserts. The outer envelope is the first part of the direct-mail package seen by the recipient. Because the envelope must be opened if the offer is to be read and acted upon, it must be perceived as interesting enough to warrant opening; therefore, it must convey the excitement or relevance of the remainder of the direct-mail package's contents. An effective outer envelope acts as a selling device by communicating something about the contents that motivates the recipient to open it. The letter is the most important part of the direct-mail package because it presents the offer and communicates the sales message, and it urges the reader to take action immediately. The brochure is a significant enticement to the prospect to participate in the offer. If the direct-mail package achieves its purpose, the prospect completes the response card, and sends it to the direct mailer. A wide variety of inserts may be included in the standard direct-mail package to increase the response rate.

REVIEW QUESTIONS

1. What is meant by the term *direct mail*? What does direct mail include?
2. What are the advantages of direct mail that frequently make this medium more suitable than other media? How does each of these advantages operate? Are they unique to direct mail as a direct marketing tool for reaching and communicating with customers and prospects? Explain.
3. What is a "standard" direct-mail package? What common set of components does a standard direct mail package include?
4. Many people feel irritated or violated by direct mail. Explain these two fundamental perceptions people have about direct mail.

NOTES

1. Adapted from Murray Raphel, "Casinos Gamble on Direct Mail," *Direct Marketing,* February 1992, pp. 32–34.
2. Herbert Katzenstein, and William Sachs, *Direct Marketing,* 2nd ed., New York: Macmillan, 1992, pp. 235–241.

3. Adapted from Edward D. Pasternack, "Scott Paper Company Achieves Growth with Innovative Marketing Campaign," *Direct Marketing,* May 1996, pp. 56–57.
4. Mary Lou Roberts, and Paul D. Berger, *Direct Marketing Management* (Englewood Cliffs, NJ: Prentice Hall, 1989), pp. 224–239.
5. Adapted from Karl Dentino, "Taking Privacy into Your Own Hands," *Direct Marketing,* September 1994, pp. 38–42, 72.
6. Adapted from Paul Goldner, "Mail Order Marketing: A World Wide View," *Direct Marketing,* May 1996, pp. 31–33.
7. Adapted from Michael Petsky, "Critical Issues and Trends for the Future of Mail Order," *Direct Marketing,* August 1994, pp. 29–32.

SOURCES

"1994 Mail Order Overview." *Direct Marketing,* August 1994, pp. 27–29.

"Coupons Maintain Redeeming Qualities." *Direct Marketing,* December 1991, pp. 25–27.

DENTINO, KARL. "Taking Privacy into Your Own Hands." *Direct Marketing,* September 1994, pp. 38–42, 72.

Direct Marketing Association. *Statistical Fact Book 1996.* New York: Direct Marketing Association, 1996.

GOLDNER, PAUL. "Mail Order Marketing: A World Wide View." *Direct Marketing,* May 1996, pp. 31–33.

GORDON, HARRIS. "Retailers Are Ready for Relationship Marketing." *Direct Marketing,* January 1994, pp. 38–44.

HACKER, BOB. "Direct Mail Arithmetic the Easy Way." *Target Marketing,* 18, no. 8 (August 1995), p. 24.

HOKE, HENRY. "The Lure of Mail Order." *Direct Marketing,* October 1994, pp. 42–44.

"International Direct Mail Trends." *Direct Marketing,* October 1993, pp. 93–98.

JONES, SUSAN K. *Creative Strategy in Direct Marketing.* Lincolnwood, IL: NTC Books, 1991.

KATZENSTEIN, HERBERT, AND WILLIAM SACHS. *Direct Marketing,* 2nd ed., New York: Macmillan, 1992.

"Mail Glut Hurts Profits." *Catalog Age,* April 1995, p. 12.

"Mail Order: Beyond Consumerism." *Direct Marketing,* August 1994, pp. 36–40.

"Mail Order Top 250+." *Direct Marketing,* July 1991, pp. 30–49.

MILNE, GEORGE, AND MARY ELLEN GORDON. "A Segmentation Study of Consumers' Attitudes toward Direct Mail." *Journal of Direct Marketing* 8 (Spring 1994), pp. 45–52.

MORRIS-LEE, JAMES. "New Technology Helps Marketers Get Personal." *Direct Marketing,* February 1992, pp. 20–23.

NEAL, MOLLIE. "Linen and Lace Graces the Mail Order Market." *Direct Marketing,* December 1992, pp. 36–38.

PASTERNACK, EDWARD D. "Scott Paper Company Achieves Growth with Innovative Marketing Campaign." *Direct Marketing,* May 1996, pp. 56–57.

PETSKY, MICHAEL. "Critical Issues and Trends for the Future of Mail Order." *Direct Marketing,* August 1994, pp. 29–32.

RAPHEL, MURRAY. "Common Direct Mail Mistakes." *Direct Marketing,* September 1994, pp. 28–29.

________. "Reviving the Dying Store." *Direct Marketing,* November 1993, pp. 20–21.

________. "Super-Markets Discover Direct Marketing . . . Works." *Direct Marketing,* June 1993, pp. 18–19.

________. "Where's the Retail Direct Mail Revolution?" *Direct Marketing,* December 1992, pp. 42–45.

———. "Casinos Gamble on Direct Mail," *Direct Marketing,* February 1992, pp. 32–34.

Roberts, Mary Lou, and Paul D. Berger. *Direct Marketing Management,* Englewood Cliffs, NJ: Prentice Hall, 1989.

Rosenfield, James R. "In the Mail." *Direct Marketing,* January 1994, pp. 24–26.

———. "In the Mail." *Direct Marketing,* November 1993, pp. 31–41.

———. "In the Mail." *Direct Marketing,* June 1993, pp. 15–17.

Rosenspan, Alan. "Is There a Future for Direct Mail? Problems and Prognosis." In *Beyond 2000: The Future of Direct Marketing,* ed. Jerry I. Reitman. Lincolnwood, IL: NTC Business Books, 1994, pp. 115–30.

Santoro, Elaine. "Here's the Scoop . . ." *Direct Marketing,* June 1991, pp. 46–47.

Schmidt, Jack. "Growth and Profit Strategies in a Maturing Industry." *Direct Marketing,* December 1992, pp. 39–41.

Sroge, Maxwell. *The United States Mail Order Industry.* Lincolnwood, IL: NTC Business Books, 1994.

Stone, Bob. *Successful Direct Marketing Methods,* 5th ed. Lincolnwood, IL: NTC Business Books, 1995.

"Strategies for the New Mail Order." *Business Week,* December 19, 1992, pp. 82–86.

APPENDIX TO CHAPTER 9: DIRECT MARKETING ASSOCIATION GUIDELINES FOR MAILING LIST PRACTICES[1]

The Direct Marketing Association's (DMA's) Guidelines for List Practices reflect the DMA's commitment to clarify and to promote high levels of business conduct. These guidelines are a part of the DMA's general philosophy that self-regulation demonstrates a sense of responsibility and a willingness to encourage sound business practices. While industry guidelines are of necessity voluntary, observance of these principles is strongly recommended. Practitioners are reminded that the best measure of protection is to deal with reputable individuals and companies. These guidelines have been produced in cooperation with the DMA List Council and DMA's Ethics Committees.

General

All involved in the transfer, rental, sale, or exchange of mailing lists—owners, managers, compilers, brokers, and users, and their suppliers and agents—should follow these guidelines.

Accuracy in Description of Lists—Article 1

All concerned should fairly, objectively, and accurately describe each list, particularly with respect to its content, age of names, selections offered, quantity, source, and owner.

Advertising Claims—Article 2

Before and at the time of distributing a list data card or promoting or advertising a list as available for rental, those who promote the list should be prepared to substantiate any claims they make and should avoid any untrue, misleading, deceptive, or fraudulent statements and any references that disparage competitors or those on the list.

Screening of Offers/List Usage—Article 3

All involved should establish and agree upon the exact nature of a list's intended usage prior to the transfer or permission to use the list. Samples of all intended mailings should be reviewed by all involved in the rental process, and only approved material should be used in the mailing, and on an agreed-upon date. Lists should not be transferred or used for an offer that is believed to be in violation of any of the DMA Guidelines for Ethical Business Practices.

Protection of Lists—Article 4

All those involved with a list transaction should be responsible for the proper use of list data and should take appropriate measures to assure against unauthorized access, alteration, or dissemination of list data. Those who have access to such data should agree in advance to use those data only in an authorized manner.

One-Time Usage—Article 5

Unless agreement to the contrary is first obtained from the list owner, a mailing list transaction permits the use of a list for one time only. Except for respondents to its own mailing, a list user and its agents may not transfer names or information to its own customer files or recontact names derived from a rented or exchanged list, or provide the names for another to make such contact, without prior authorization.

DMA Mail Preference Service/Name Removal Options—Article 6

Consumers who provide data that may be rented, sold, or exchanged for direct marketing purposes should be periodically informed of the potential for the rental, sale, or exchange of such data. Marketers should offer a means by which a consumer's name may be deleted or suppressed upon request.

List compilers should suppress names from lists when requested by the individual.

For each list that is to be rented, sold, or exchanged, the DMA Mail Preference Service name-removal list and, when applicable, the Telephone Preference Service name-removal list should be used. Names found on such suppression lists should not be transferred except for suppression purposes.

All persons involved in the rental, sale, or exchange of lists and data should take reasonable steps to ensure that industry members follow these guidelines.

Purpose of Lists/List Data—Article 7

Lists should consist only of those data that are appropriate for marketing purposes. Direct marketers should transfer, rent, sell, or exchange lists only for those purposes.

List Data/Privacy—Article 8

Direct marketers should be sensitive to the issue of consumer privacy and should limit the combination, collection, rental, sale, exchange, and use of consumer data to only those data that are appropriate for direct marketing purposes.

Information and selection criteria that may be considered to be personal and intimate in nature by all reasonable standards should not provide the basis for lists to be made available for rental, sale, or exchange when there is a reasonable expectation by the consumer that the information would be kept confidential.

Any advertising or promotion for lists being offered for rental, sale, or exchange should reflect the fact that a list is an aggregate collection of marketing data. Such promotions should also reflect a sensitivity for the consumers on those lists.

Laws, Codes, Regulations, and Guidelines—Article 9

Direct marketers should operate in accordance with all applicable laws, codes, and regulations and with DMA's various Guidelines as published from time to time.

Considerations for Mailing List Transactions

Mailing list transactions are controlled by the legal principles affecting contracts. As such, mutual understanding, good faith, clear communication, defined terms, and a meeting of the minds are imperative. To that end, a list of factors to be considered when entering into a mailing list transaction has been developed to assist contracting parties in developing a clear understanding of their respective rights and obligations as well as to help avoid the problems that typically ensue as a result of misunderstanding.

The list of factors that follows is not intended to be exhaustive, nor is it intended to dictate the terms of any agreement. Rather, it is presented to raise pertinent questions so that they may be addressed properly and adequately by the parties. The list of factors may be modified from time to time as trends develop in the industry or as technology or list usage changes.

(1) Identification of All Parties to the Transaction

Has each party to the transaction been identified by proper name and address?

Are there other parties involved besides the list owner and list user (e.g., list broker, list manager, list compiler, or service bureau)?

Have these other parties been properly identified?

Is the scope of authority of these third parties understood?

Should each of these third parties agree to be bound by the list agreement?

(2) What Is Being Transferred?

Is the agreement intended to be comprehensive?

Is any unspecified activity prohibited unless permitted?

Is any unspecified activity permitted unless prohibited?

Is the transaction an outright sale or assignment of the list?

Is the transaction an exchange or trade for the use of another list?

Is the transaction a rental or one-time permission to use?

May the list user add information to the rented list before using it (e.g., telephone numbers)?

Does adding information to the rented list change its nature?

Who owns the enhanced list after information has been added to it?

(3) What Constitutes Use?

May the user merge-purge the lists with other rented list?

Is the user permitted to add names that appear on more than one owner's list to its own list?

May the user code or tag its own file with information derived from a rented list when the rented list contains names that already appear on the user's list?

May the user impose its own "qualifications" on a list, return the names that do not "qualify," and receive a refund?

Does it matter what the qualifier is (e.g., names on more than one list, a particular carrier route, certain demographics)?

Is it all right if the list owner "qualifies" the list prior to rental?

May the user send "address corrections requested" mail and retain results?

(4) What Constitutes One-Time Use?

May the rented list be used a second time in a different medium (e.g., telephone)?

May the user mail to a name on a list one time for each rented list the name appears on?

Does it matter whether each list owner was paid for the name?

Does it matter whether multiple mailings to the same name are related (e.g., part of a series of mailings)?

Does it matter what the time period is between mailings?

May the list user or its service bureau retain names that appear on one or more rented lists for comparison with future rentals?

May the list user do so to suppress names from future mailings to the same rented list?

May the user do so for non-list-specific data?

Are there any additional purposes for which the rented list may be retained?

(5) The Method of and Basis for Payment

How many names are being rented?

What are the allowances, if any, for duplicates, undeliverables, etc?

Is there a special request or selection to be satisfied?

What is the price (e.g., dollars per thousand names)?

Has sales tax, if any, been accounted for?

Is there a broker or manager involved?

To whom is payment sent?

Are commissions spelled out?

Is there a net name agreement?

Are the terms clear?

Is there a provision for verification?

Have duplicates and multibuyers been removed or accounted for?

Is there a reuse discount?

Have the payment terms been clearly set forth and agreed upon?

(6) What Is to Be Received, Where and When?

What is the format of the rental (e.g., tapes, labels)?

How much information will physically appear on tapes or labels (e.g., name and address, address only, with Zip + 4)?

Where and when is the list to be shipped?

Who is at risk for failure to satisfy this provision?

Upon whom does loss fall if damaged in transit?

Upon whom does loss fall if mailing dates cannot be kept?

Are there any guarantees on deliverability?

(7) Approval of the Mailing and Date

Does the list owner have the right to approve the mailing?

Must each phase of a staged or sequenced mailing (e.g., catalog followed by gift certificate followed by personalized letter) be approved?

Has the mailing date been approved?

Must the list user notify the list owner if the date is to be changed?

(8) Impact on Others

Does the user have the right to prohibit the rental of a list of competitive mailing for a specific time period before and after the user's mailing date?

Do the parties employ a name-removal option, or DMA's Mail Preference Service, or, where applicable, Telephone Preference Service for the protection of those on the list?

Is the list being used only for a marketing purpose?

Has the list been seeded?

May the user refer to the source of the list in any promotion?

Is it clear that the user becomes an owner of all respondents?

When a decision is made to make your list available in the List Rental marketplace, you are accepting the responsibility for the advertising your customer will see. Most list owners who rent their list to others understand they are "licensing" their most valuable asset for monetary consideration. Protecting the value of that asset is what these Guidelines are all about.

As a list professional, the establishment of an adherence to strict ad acceptance standards not only protects your relationship with your customers, it can save your firm countless dollars. Frequently, companies that defraud consumers also defraud their suppliers.

A typical question asked by many list professionals involves the legal liabilities involved in denying a company access to a mailing list. A mailing list transaction is a matter of contract. Generally speaking, one is free to decide with whom one wants to conduct business. Thus, if one exercises his own independent judgement, he is free to deal or not to deal with whomever he chooses without incurring legal liability.

These recommendations do not deal with the legalities of advertising procedures but rather with their ethics. Nor do they deal with the do's and don'ts of technical copy writing. They do deal with DMA's desire to promote more honesty in mail order advertising, more credibility in the eyes of consumers, consequently, generate more business for direct marketing professionals.

While each advertisement must be evaluated on an individual basis, there are warning signs that may signal a fraudulent promotion. If the initial order is large, was "too easy to get," and/or was not preceded by a test, the list professional should carefully evaluate the offer by following these suggestions:

a. If the offer is unclear to you, it will be equally unclear to the recipient. If you have read the copy twice, and you still don't know the exact nature of what is being offered, insist on clarification of the copy. The mere act of requesting additional information may deter some unscrupulous advertisers.
b. Make yourself the surrogate reader. Are the copy claims outlandish or are they too strong to be believable? Be particularly wary of ads that claim to cure physical ills such as arthritis, obesity, sexual impotence, cancer, or hair loss.
c. Taste is a subjective matter, and each list professional must decide what is in good or bad taste for his audience. However, as a representative of the list owner, or as the list owner, you have a responsibility to ask for a new illustration or change of copy before you approve copy for a mailing.
d. The list professional should know the street address and telephone number of every advertiser. In many cities (such as New York) post office box numbers must be accompanied by a street address. Be aware that mail receiving agencies are sometimes used by fraudulent advertisers to appear legitimate. The list broker should become acquainted with such addresses. Finally, if the company is very small, know the address and telephone number of the principle.
e. Be extremely careful of advertisers with no address which require the use of a toll free number and charge card to order merchandise. This method of payment is often an attempt to avoid use of the mails to circumvent the jurisdiction of the United States Postal Service.

f. Another warning sign aimed directly at the list professional is payment for advertising with insufficient funds or account closed check. This disregard for ethical business practice may signal that the promoter has a similar outlook regarding responsibility to maintain truth in advertising.
g. Deceptive marketers may lull list owners into a false sense of security by placing several small orders, mailing the approved piece, and then asking for a large order for a mailing that may not meet your company's guidelines. The use of seeds or decoy names to confirm the list was mailed to the appropriate piece may be helpful in detecting such misuse.
h. When in doubt, list professionals should ask for a sample of the merchandise. Be careful that the sample is an actual production sample and not a handmade mock-up. If the advertiser cannot submit the sample before the closing date, you should consider declining the order.

If you have any suspicions regarding the offer, you may want to verify past performance of the company with such agencies as the Better Business Bureau, local consumer agencies and the United States Postal Inspection Service. These agencies can be a source of information and may aid in the decision of whether to accept a list order. These agencies may also be helpful if your company has been defrauded by a deceptive advertiser.

In addition to the consumer agencies which can provide list professionals with information on the history, business practices and general reputation of a firm submitting questionable advertising, DMA may be able to provide assistance in evaluating ad copy by providing you with a copy of DMA *Guidelines for Ethical Business Practice.*

NOTE

1. Ethics Department; Direct Marketing Association, Inc.; 1111 19th Street, N.W., Suite 1100; Washington, DC 20036-3603.

CHAPTER 10

Catalog Marketing

OBJECTIVES

1. To define the role of catalogs in direct marketing.
2. To compare and contrast consumer and business-to-business catalogs.
3. To differentiate catalog merchandise buyers from traditional retail shoppers by their demographics, lifestyles, shopping attitudes, and other factors.
4. To examine the key factors that determine the success or failure of a catalog and how those factors differ by consumer versus business target markets.
5. To explain the role of catalog attributes in catalog selection and merchandise purchases.
6. To examine how computer technologies, especially databases, help catalog marketers more efficiently market their merchandise.
7. To describe the role of perceived risk in catalog merchandise buyer behavior.

INTRODUCTION

Today, catalog firms in the United States mail between 12 and 13 billion catalogs a year (see Exhibit 10.1). The largest firms in the catalog marketing field are listed by their sales in Table 10.1. J. C. Penney has the most dollar sales among the top 10. One-time leader Sears has fallen below the top 10, while relative newcomers such as J. Crew and Victoria's Secret are growing rapidly.

While many catalog firms have experienced dramatic growth in recent years, some of the largest have not fared so well. Alden's (1981 sales of $320 million) went out of business in 1982. Montgomery Ward (with 1984 catalog sales approaching $1 billion) ended its catalog operation in 1985. Sears discontinued its large, mass-market catalog in the early 1990s to concentrate on speciality catalogs. Smaller but long successful firms such as Sunset House have also disappeared from the marketplace. These firms failed because they no longer had sufficient appeal to their customers or to prospects to maintain a profitable enterprise. Frequently such loss of appeal is related to the company's poor understanding of customer needs and less-than-adequate customer service.

As the consumer marketplace changed in the 1960s, 1970s, and 1980s, large general merchandise catalogers such as Montgomery Ward and Sears found that their offerings were no longer competitive or profitable. That signaled the end of the time when poorly targeted and unfocused catalogs could achieve any success. Because consumer mailboxes are crowded with catalogs from the many vendors interested in displaying of their wares, a catalog must stand out with a specific image, a distinctive line of products, and an eye-catching way of presenting its merchandise.

EXHIBIT 10.1. Catalogs Mailed per Year: 1985–94
(data in thousands)

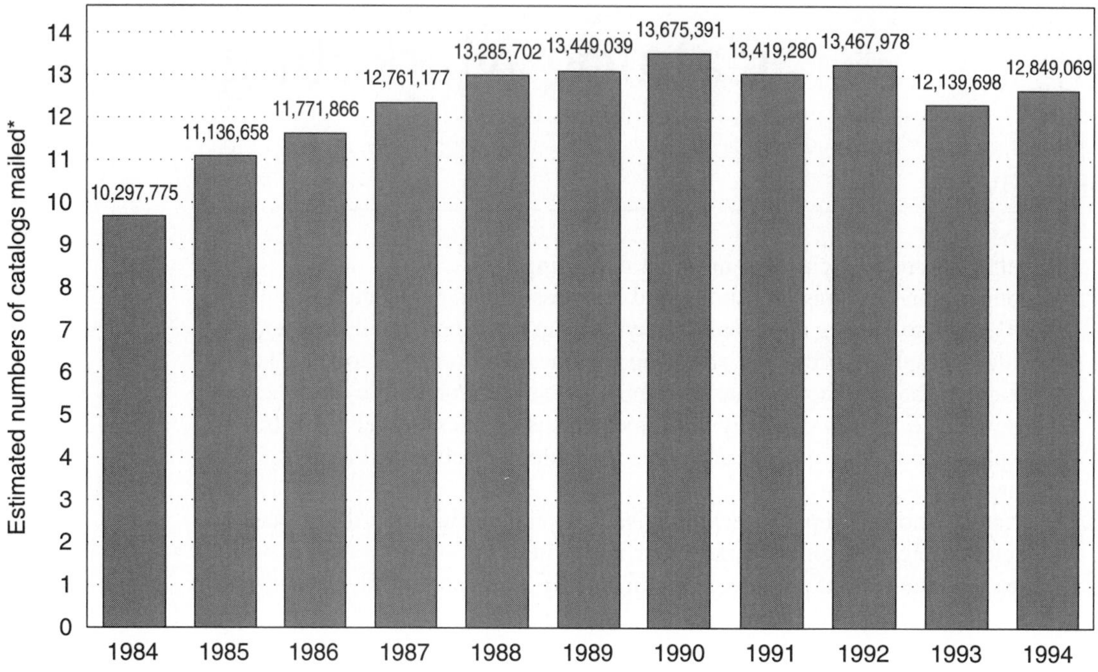

TABLE 10.1. The 10 Largest General Merchandise and Apparel Catalog Retailers
Companies are ranked by 1995 total catalog sales in millions of dollars.

1. J. C. Penney	$3,738
2. Fingerhut	1,826
3. Spiegel	1,751
4. Lands' End	1,030
5. L. L. Bean	945
6. Hanover Direct	750
7. Victoria's Secret	661
8. J. Crew	640
9. Brylane	601
10. Blair Corp.	561

Source: Adapted from "Catalog Age 100," *Catalog Age,* August 1996, pp. 1, 62–68, 72–74.

The current trend is to offer specialized merchandise such as shoes, jewelry, specific foods, computer supplies, and auto parts in catalogs by themselves. Then, by refining the selection of mailing-list members to those who are interested in purchasing that specific category of product, the catalogs produce more orders and are more profitable.

THE HISTORY OF CATALOGS[1]

The word *catalog* was derived from the Greek *katalogos,* meaning "to list." The use of the word *list* may seem rudimentary, but even today catalogs are most often both visual and verbal listings of products for sale. Products are pictured with informational copy designed and worded to entice the reader to buy. Sophistication of design, photographs, art, ink, and glossy paper have transformed the original unadorned "list" into one that is fully costumed and ready to entertain, educate, and sell with the flip of a page.

The first catalog, a listing of books, was produced in Europe in the 15th century. Here in America, Ben Franklin, the first postmaster of the United States, produced the first version of a mail-order catalog in 1744. It was a listing of several hundred books. That catalog was a natural outcome of Mr. Franklin's profession as a postmaster and publisher. In those days, postmasters could send any type of printed matter through the mail, at no charge.

But the individual most publicly recognized for starting the first mail-order catalog is Montgomery Ward. In 1872 Ward put out a small flyer listing such items as handkerchiefs, coats, and tablecloths at below-retail prices. Quantity purchasing and the elimination of the middleman helped Ward to achieve low prices. This first flyer was only a single page, but in a few years it grew to eight pages. The 1985 Spring–Summer Montgomery Ward catalog had 376 four-color pages, with professional photographs of each product complete with information and pricing.

Since the first mail-order catalog, enormous strides have been made in the type of merchandise offered and the manner in which it is presented. Today the mail-order catalog is most often a glossy, four-color jewel with page after page of enticing pictures and informative copy. Through catalogs, small towns like Big Sandy, Texas (the home of Annie's Attic); Millstone, West Virginia (the home of Alice in Wonderland Creations); and Freeport, Maine (the home of L. L. Bean) can all sparkle as brightly as New York City to the customer. Fifth Avenue, with its plethora of merchandise, is transported into the customer's or prospect's home. The general consumer is educated, entertained, and pampered by thousands of wonderful catalogs containing millions of products to be purchased at will. And what could be more convenient than shopping from one's own home, from the kitchen table or favorite easy chair?

The business-to-business world is also realizing how mail-order catalogs can lead to success. Costs for sales calls are rising quickly. One sales call costs in excess of $200 for large corporations and as much as $291 for companies with fewer than 10 salespeople. Because of these costs, many small customers or prospects would have to be ignored if it were not for catalogs. With catalogs, a company can easily service accounts and inform customers about its products or services. Time delay is kept to a minimum through toll-free numbers and warehouse fulfillment centers across the United States, or even around the world. In fact, an individual can now select the product to be purchased from a catalog, call the order in, and receive the merchandise the next day.

Customers want convenience shopping and look to mail-order catalogs for it. Indeed, convenience is just below "merchandise not available elsewhere" as the most important factor for shopping by mail. Why? One of the most significant factors influencing how consumers shop is the changing role of women in society. Women now make up over half of the labor force, and 30 percent of all households have two incomes, allowing for more discretionary income. More women have less time outside of their work and family obligations. Shopping in retail stores can be exhausting and time-consuming, sapping energy and taking away time that could be used for job, family, and recreation. Shopping by mail-order catalog has become a pleasurable, no-hassle experience.

Catalogs have become a relied-on source of accurate and detailed product information. How many times has a consumer walked into a retail store and asked a clerk a question about a product only to receive a blank stare, mumbled words, or a bland "I don't know"? A catalog that presents products well, both visually and verbally, informs the customer or prospect thoroughly about each product listed. It enthusiastically presents products in such a way as to build confidence and encourage a purchase. This is why catalog design is so important.

TYPES OF CATALOGS

Catalogs are first classified according to whether they are for consumers or business organizations. Consumer catalogs have mass circulations, while business catalogs have much lower circulations. Consumer catalogs are distinguishable by the types of items they carry, the target markets they want to reach, and the quality of their appearance and design. While some consumer catalogs are designed to generate retail store traffic, the majority are from firms that concentrate almost exclusively on catalog sales. Specialty catalogs dominate today's consumer catalog landscape. They are the fastest growing part of the catalog market and far outnumber the few remaining general merchandise catalogs. The specialty catalogs, which carry items ranging from clothing to food, are designed to cater to specific tastes associated with lifestyle preferences, including differences in interests, activities, attitudes, and values.

Business-to-business catalogs sell such items as office supplies and computer accessories. They usually carry specific types of items such as paper products or electronics as opposed to a general selection. Customers place orders through an 800 number, by mail, or by fax. These catalogs are mailed often to a select list of prospects or to those buyers who have placed an order during a fixed period of time. Over the last decade, business-to-business catalogs have come to look more and more like consumer catalogs with their emphasis on colorful, well-designed merchandise displays and motivational sales copy.

Table 10.2 shows the 10 largest business-to-business catalogers. The list is dominated by Dell Computer, which specializes in IBM-compatible personal computers for home and business use. Most of the other firms on the list are also involved in the computer industry. Viking Office Products is a good example of an office supply firm that uses well-designed and well-produced catalogs and low prices to motivate its customers to make a purchase. Once a business is on Viking's mailing list, it receives the firm's general catalog and as many as 10

TABLE 10.2. The 10 Largest Business-to-Business Catalogers
Companies are ranked by 1995 total catalog sales in millions of dollars.

1. Dell Computer	$5,296
2. Gateway 2000	3,676
3. Digital	3,000
4. Micro Warehouse	1,308
5. IBM Direct	1,070
6. Viking Office Products	921
7. Deluxe Direct	679
8. Global DirectMail Corp.	635
9. Computer Discount Warehouse	601
10. Henry Schein Inc.	616

Source: Adapted from "Catalog Age 100," *Catalog Age,* August 1996, pp. 1, 62–68, 72–74.

speciality catalogs a year, depending on which items the customer has ordered in the past. These speciality catalogs include ones focused on office furniture, paper, or copier supplies.

THREE INNOVATIVE CATALOG MARKETERS

Bland Farms, Southern Touch Foods, and Linen and Lace are examples of modern, innovative catalog marketers that offer consumers niche products. All three have achieved considerable success.

Bland Farms[2]

Travel on I-75 in Georgia and you will see huge four-color billboards promoting the sweet flavor of Georgia-grown Vidalia onions. The outdoor posters invite travelers to send for a Bland Farms mail-order catalog. Just call 1-800-VIDALIA, or visit the Bland Farms store in front of its packing plant in Glennville, Georgia.

The posters work well in producing calls to Sandra Bland's 25-station telemarketing center. This and the firm's other direct-response advertising generates more than 27,000 catalog requests per year. These new names are coded by source and added to an ever growing database of some 480,000 customers, inquirers, and people who shop in the firm's farm store. This forms the core of lists used to mail some 5 million catalogs annually. See Exhibit 10.2 for a sample catalog cover.

Sandra, Delbert Bland's wife, supervises the mail-order operation. She works closely with Fred Allen of Mt. Pleasant, Texas, who is on the phone nearly every day advising her on innovative database-building ideas, new lists to test, how to interpret results, and how to reshape the mail-order program to increase profits and improve customer service.

How else does Bland Farms find new customers? From half-inch labels, or decals, put on each onion as they are packed in 50-pound containers and shipped to supermarkets around the country. CALL 1-800-vidalia is printed on each decal.

EXHIBIT 10.2. Bland Farms Catalog

During 1993, 64 million such decals were stuck on onions packaged in 800,000 netted sacks.

Then there are countless half-column space ads in consumer publications that ask the reader to call 1-800-VIDALIA for a catalog. Publications have been a major factor in generating new names ever since the firm's first experience with *Southern Living* magazine. The first Bland Farms ad in that magazine resulted in more than 1,000 inquiries, and a modest follow-up produced profitable orders and the beginning of a mail-order business that today generates 30 percent of Bland Farms' $15 million annual sales. Interestingly, those catalog sales represent only 1 percent of the annual crop of all onions sold; 90 percent are sold through supermarkets.

Delbert Bland oversees marketing and administration for the 4,000-acre family enterprise, 2,800 acres of which are devoted to the Vidalia business. He is restless, ambitious, and determined to make the family's fortune. His father, Raymond, prefers to work in the fields with his hands. Mama Jean, Raymond's wife and Delbert's mother, is often seen on the phone in Sandra's mail-order division, taking calls and updating computer records for name and address changes. She has also developed recipes for relishes, sauces, and the like, jars of which are offered in the catalog and store. The Vidalia catalog today displays Mama Jean's many relishes in 10.5-ounce jars, as well as onion-based salad dressings, mustard, tartar sauce, pickles, tomatoes in June, quiches, sweet onion breads, cookbooks, cold cuts, hams, turkeys, jams, pies, cakes, nuts, candy, and even a Vidalia sweet onion storage cabinet for the home.

Southern Touch Foods[3]

Although muscadines have long been a traditional favorite of Southern families, their popularity never extended much beyond that region, largely because they can only be grown in vineyards in the fertile, well-irrigated soil of the Southeast. The largest of these vineyards covers 770 acres of Clarke County, Mississippi, and is owned by Paui Broadhead, founder of Southern Touch Foods Corporation. This unusual retail and mail-order operation is reaping the rewards of a down-home philosophy shared with its customers and neighboring farmers.

However, unless you grew up in the southeastern United States, you have probably never heard of muscadines, much less tasted one. The relatively unknown fruit, sometimes referred to as the "scuppernong" or "Southern grape," is a grape berry of 200 different varieties. Its taste has been described as similar to a cross between a strawberry and a grape. Southern Touch currently harvests a total of 2,500 acres of muscadine vines.

Products made from muscadines seem to be as numerous as the varieties of the fruit. Jam, jelly, preserves, syrup, and juice predominate, but barbecue sauce, dessert toppings, and a sparkling beverage are also gaining popularity. In the beginning, Southern Touch offered these products only through a one-page brochure; by the second year, their popularity and supply had grown enough to consider grocery-store placement a viable option. Ron Kahrer, executive vice president of Southern Touch, recalls that many stores expected steep payments to place the products, but such arrangements were impossible for the fledgling company.

As sales continued to grow, Southern Touch sought ways to widen its audience without incurring huge marketing costs. In 1989, it distributed its first catalog, a 24-page issue that brought in $750,000 in sales from a mailing to 500,000 people. Although this first effort only broke even, Southern Touch decided catalogs were the way to go and continued with a holiday edition that year. In 1990, six issues of the catalog were mailed, with a total sales response reaching approximately $3 million.

The catalogs themselves are enough to make the reader's mouth water for Southern food—especially dessert. The holiday 1990 edition displayed a full array of muscadine products, as well as a selection of other traditional Southern foods, in 48 pages of full color. A two-page editorial introduction personalized the catalog, explaining the background of both the company and muscadines themselves, with photographs of berries on the vine as well as of the company's state-of-the-art processing facility. A note from Broadhead recalled his "golden memories" of muscadine seasons of his childhood, and invited non-Southern readers to add "the Southern Touch" to their menus.

The firm's catalog offers all the conveniences recipients have come to expect from more established mail-order companies, including a choice between a mail-in order form, an 800 number, or a fax number for ordering; free standard shipping or overnight shipping at a charge; and a full refund guarantee.

Southern Touch's catalogs also feature an expanding range of products particular to the Southeast. Because the company's mission in developing the muscadine crop was to improve the economy of the South, it has formed alliances with other producers to market their products in the catalog. Featured in the holiday 1990 catalog were blackberry, peach, blueberry, and honey products with the Southern Touch label, as well as jams and peanut butter from other small area manufacturers. But the items were not limited to spreads and juices. More than 20 pages featured such diverse products as smoked meats, South Carolina–grown tea, peanuts and pecans, and Southern cakes and cookies along with a selection of Cajun items, including spices, recipes, and how-to videos from world-famous New Orleans chef Paul Prudhomme.

Nonfood items were also in the 1990 catalog. Three pages offered flowers commonly found in the South, such as the amaryllis, crocus, and paperwhite. A new introduction in 1990 was a limited-edition collector's plate, featuring a painting of a well-known Mississippi antebellum mansion.

Linen and Lace[4]

Linen and Lace is new to the mail-order scene but has already found its niche. By using unique marketing and merchandising strategies, it has developed a sound business platform in today's tough catalog marketplace. In just two years, the company outgrew its kitchen-table operation in a bed-and-breakfast inn and now resides in a pre–Civil War home and various warehouses.

The firm boasts a 200,000-name list of customers and prospects. It does not go for expensive prospecting, because it receives well-qualified leads from space ads in magazines like *Good Housekeeping* and *Better Homes and Gardens.* The remaining 15 percent of its sales come from referrals.

The firm's first ad was simple yet effective. A black-and-white photograph was taken from a lace sample, with copy and an 800 number (800-332-LACE). The ad in *Country Home* magazine initially pulled in 5,000 requests, which was more than the firm had catalogs. By charging $2 for each catalog, Linen and Lace was able to pay for more printing. In total, the first ad pulled in 10,000 requests in just a few months. Exhibit 10.3 shows a sample catalog cover.

A customer list is maintained in-house, and an average 10,000 of the newer, 16-page catalogs are mailed each week, except for preholiday mailings, which increase. Catalogs are dropped in waves to protect Linen and Lace's cash flow. Only three full-time employees are needed on the phones to take orders. When the phones are quiet, the workers are busy cutting lace.

Because the firm mails only to customers and well-qualified prospects, it boasts response rates ranging from 3 percent to 8 percent, depending on the

EXHIBIT 10.3. Linen and Lace Catalog

season. Names are kept on the list for two years, as the first, second, or third mailing may not evoke a reaction, but the fourth time might do the job.

Each catalog features an introduction in which one of the joint owners in Linen and Lace's husband-and-wife team, Sunny Drewel, reminisces about childhood memories of lace curtains in her grandmother Lizzie's house in Indiana and talks of the ribbons and lace her grandfather Van Nice peddled from store to store in the 1900s. Sunny stresses the importance of being personal in her catalog, noting the many catalogers that have gotten away from that because of their concern for the number of items they can put on each page.

The catalog has grown to a four-color glossy but maintains its Old World charm with photographs of windows adorned with different lace and linen products. The romantic appearance of the lace is carried through with the copy. For example, the Chelsea curtain is explained with the following copy: "Let a garden, lush with English roses, bloom in your window. A dusting of point d'esprit, fragile as snowflakes, embellishes this antique design. We traveled to Scotland and pored through archives to find you this ravishing pattern of delicate ten-point lace." Other lace patterns have romantic, homey names like Trellis Rose, Victoria, and Cottage Garden.

The catalog is sprinkled with customer testimonials and copy detailing product care and history. The typical order size is about $105, but orders can run as high as $300+ for some of the Scottish laces.

THE CATALOG SHOPPER OF THE 1990s[5]

Catalog shoppers are different from traditional retail shoppers in their demographics, lifestyles, shopping attitudes, and other factors (see Exhibits 10.4 and 10.5). They are better educated, work in professional and managerial capacities, earn

EXHIBIT 10.4. Catalog Shopper Demographics

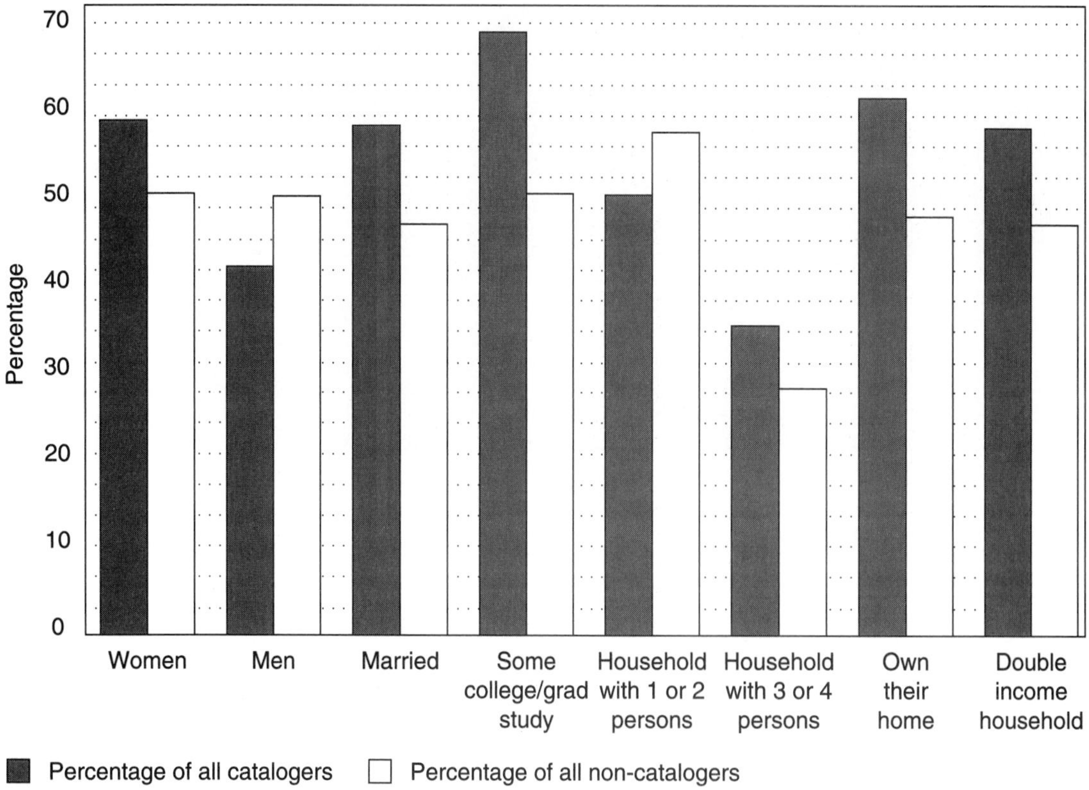

more money, are more comfortable with modern technology, and own stocks and bonds. They like familiar brands and prefer traditional clothing. Catalog shoppers are also do-it-yourselfers who make repairs on their homes and cars.

Demographics

Women outnumber men among catalog shoppers, 58 percent to 42 percent. In contrast, among those who never buy through catalogs, there are just as many men as there are women. The percentage of married consumers is higher among the catalog shoppers; some 57 percent of them are married, compared with only 45 percent of non–catalog shoppers. Breaking down the two groups by age, larger percentages of catalog shoppers are in the midrange age brackets: 25–34, 35–44, and 45–54.

Twenty-five percent of catalog shoppers are in the critical and populous 35-to-44-year-old group, while only 17 percent of non–catalog shoppers fall in that age group. But the larger percentages of non–catalog shoppers, who are on average three years older, are in the 55–64 and 65-and-over brackets.

One-person households are more common among non–catalog shoppers, while a larger percentage of catalog shoppers belong to three- and four-person households and households with children. More catalog shoppers own homes than

EXHIBIT 10.5. Catalog Shopper Age

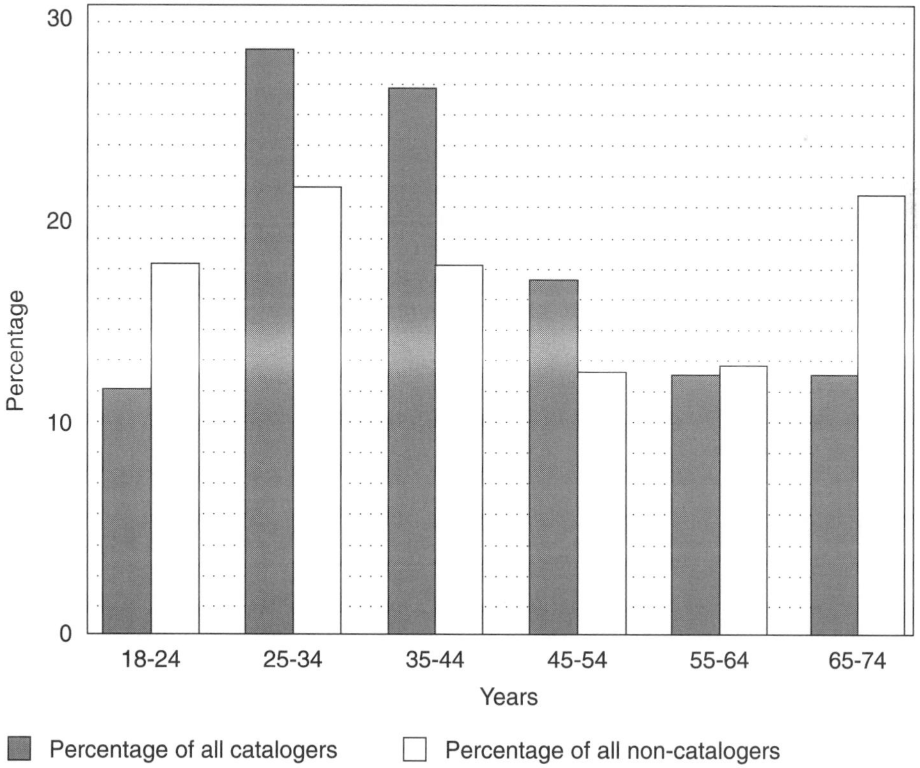

rent. And a larger percentage of catalog shoppers (66 percent) live in houses rather than in apartments or condos.

The catalog shoppers are better educated, with more than two-thirds having attended college. On the other hand, only a little more than half of those who never buy through catalogs have attended college. Education may explain why much higher percentages of catalog shoppers are professionals, business managers, and secretaries, while higher percentages of non–catalog shoppers are factory workers, laborers, drivers, and salespersons.

More than half of those who regularly buy through catalogs earn between $30,000 and $99,000 annually. By contrast, only about 38 percent of those who never buy through catalogs earn in that range. The income difference is particularly obvious in the $50,000 to $74,999 range, into which almost 18 percent of the catalog shoppers fall, as opposed to just over 11 percent of the non–catalog shoppers. One reason for the differences in income may be the difference in dual-income households; while more than 54 percent of the catalog shoppers have two incomes, only about 44 percent of the non–catalog shoppers have two incomes.

Lifestyles

Catalog shoppers seem more in tune with the modern world. Larger percentages of catalog shoppers use every type of home technology, including VCRs, home computers, and answering machines. Those who regularly shop catalogs take more airline flights and are more likely to use the yellow pages. They also use automated teller machines and bank and store credit cards in greater percentages; are much more likely to purchase stocks, bonds, IRAs, and other financial instruments; and are even more likely to own a pet.

In leisure activities the pattern continues, with catalog shoppers being more active. They read more; eat at full-service restaurants more often; and go to movies, concerts, and live theater more frequently. They shop more too. Despite all this activity, catalogers also watch more television.

Media Reach

Catalog shoppers spend a few minutes more each day than do non–catalog shoppers with television, radio, and newspapers. They are more likely to listen to phone solicitations and to read mail advertisements, billboards, and transit ads.

CATALOG ATTRIBUTE PREFERENCES

Success in catalog marketing depends on an understanding of patterns in consumer or business choice behavior. Because consumers or businesses must deal with a multiplicity of alternatives, the choices they make represent preferences for particular catalog attributes. A direct marketer's ability to define how consumers and businesses make these distinctions is essential to capturing and maintaining a strong market position.

Many factors contribute to the success of a catalog. Vital ingredients include merchandising, list selection, customer service, toll-free numbers, fulfillment, print production, mailing, research, computer support, order forms, creativity, and, particularly, positioning or image. Consumers define catalogs through both functional qualities and psychological attributes symptomatic of the needs they can expect to satisfy through their buyer behavior.

Tucker defined eight key factors in the perceived appeal of mail-order catalogs (in order of importance):

1. Convenience.
2. Desirability of merchandise.
3. Credibility of catalog name.
4. Catalog presentation (graphics and quality reproduction).
5. Succinct, informative copy.
6. Psychological use of color.
7. Timing of mailing (seasonality).
8. Previous mail-order fulfillment experience.[6]

McDonald found that eight attributes define catalog preferences in the women's apparel catalog market:

1. Ease of catalog use.
2. Convenience.
3. Reputation.
4. Merchandise variety.
5. Good value.
6. Catalog attractiveness.
7. Low financial risk.
8. Merchandise uniqueness.[7]

Customer Preference Structures

McDonald observed that alternative consumer or business preferences suggest different catalog marketing strategies.[8] The purpose of examining those preferences is to develop strategies that are appropriate to market conditions, particularly the nature of consumer or business needs and competition to satisfy those needs.

The Psychological Meaning of Customer Preference Structures

As noted in Chapter 6, the motivation to satisfy needs is the reason for customer buyer behavior. Motives are the unseen, inner forces that stimulate and compel a behavioral response, providing a specific direction to that response. For example, the purchase of apparel illustrates the nature of consumer motivation and goal-directed behavior. At a basic level, apparel purchases are motivated by a physical need for clothing. At a psychological level, the consumer motivation is to purchase apparel that fulfills a need for status, self-esteem, or social acceptance.

A catalog's image communicates to customers and prospects its distinctive positioning, encouraging them to believe that the catalog contains items that will satisfy their needs. These needs define a customer segment membership. For example, although both groups need clothing, young adults have different apparel needs than the elderly.

Over time, customers show preferences for sets of catalogs based on the desirability of the attributes those catalogs possess. The idea that one set of catalogs can better satisfy the needs of a customer segment than another is the psychological basis for a customer preference structure analysis.

Customer Purchase Decisions

An application of customer preference structure analysis demonstrates the strategic importance of understanding competitive market structures and customer preferences. Exhibit 10.6 shows a customer preference structure for the women's apparel catalog market. In this market, consumers first make a choice based on reputation. Some catalogs are excluded, while others are included. Next, they make a choice based on merchandise variety and ease of use. Again, some catalogs are included and others are out. Finally, they make a value-based choice.

The premise of this analysis is that consumers travel down the branches in the structure based on their needs, which are expressed as catalog preferences. This is a market segmentation issue. For example, some consumers are Neiman-Marcus shoppers; others are more likely to purchase from Sears. A woman who normally shops in a Sears catalog is much more likely to look in a J. C. Penney catalog than in a Neiman-Marcus catalog if Sears does not have the item she wants. If neither Sears nor J. C. Penney has the item, she is much more likely to look at a Lands' End or Avon Fashions catalog than at other women's apparel catalogs.

Thus, catalog customers have distinct perceptions of those offerings and definite notions about which competitors carry comparable items. Customer need segments have these strong tendencies, unless special occasions or circumstances arise, and they shop most often within a given catalog set for what they want to buy.

EXHIBIT 10.6. Customer Preference Structure

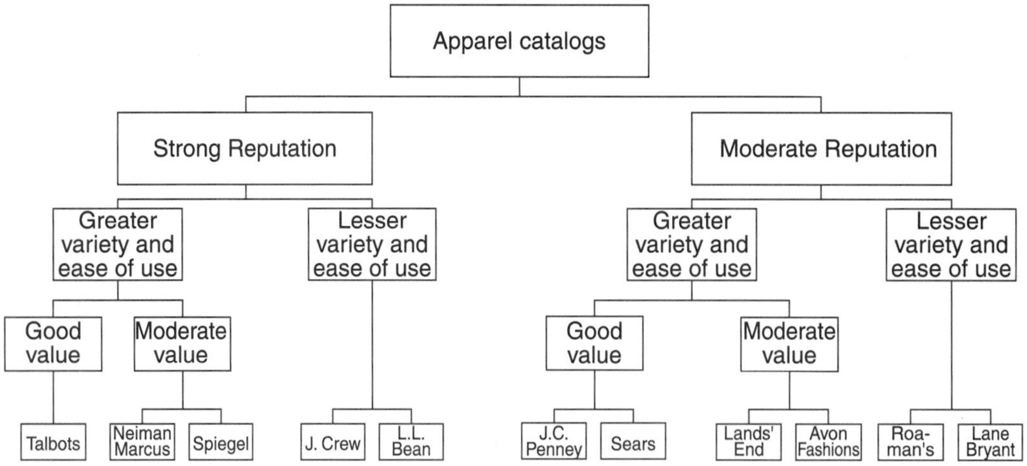

Today, successful catalogs have a concept that appeals to a specific segment of the market. That segment may include those who like outdoor clothing (L. L. Bean), those who enjoy unusual gadgets (The Sharper Image), or those who purchase intimate apparel (Victoria's Secret). The most popular catalogs organize their merchandise offer around a specific concept and ensure that all aspects of catalog design are guided by that basic theme, with the catalog's overall look and its way of presenting merchandise creating an image in the eyes of the customer or prospect.

According to Roberts and Berger, the basic catalog design decisions are the size of the catalog, the catalog layout, how the merchandise is arranged, the visual presentation of the goods and copy, and the order form.[9]

Size of the Catalog

Catalog size is determined by the number of items and the space each requires for effective display as well as the theme of the offering. The most common size is 8½ by 11 inches, but there are many exceptions. Catalogs vary in length from the 60-page variety by Lands' End to the over-100-page versions used by Victoria's Secret (see Exhibits 10.7 and 10.8 although they are not reproduced to scale) and Avon Products. The typical Lands' End or Victoria's Secret catalog is 8½ by 11 inches, as are the offerings from L. L. Bean and J. Crew. While Avon's catalogs have many pages, they are only 5½ by 7½ inches. USA Flex, which has produced computer catalogs, has had unusual sizes for its covers compared to its competition. USA Flex Catalogs have been 6 by 11 inches, averaging about 70 pages.

Catalog Format

The typical Lands' End catalog has cover and end pages that enclose many instances of two facing pages or spreads. The front and back covers establish the theme of the catalog and stimulate interest in its contents. The covers need to be distinctive and recognizable, prominently featuring the firm's name and colors, textures, and seasonal merchandise to indicate any special aspects of the catalog's contents.

Inside a catalog, pairs of pages are laid out as units rather than as individual pages, with their basic designs varied throughout the catalog to add interest value. Each set of facing pages is usually designed using a *grid layout* or a *free-flowing design.* Grid layouts divide the pages into boxes that present individual products, while free-flowing designs allow for more flexibility and can give catalogs a distinctive look. Page layout is an integral part of a catalog's image.

While the number of possible spread designs is immense, there are some guidelines about how they should be formatted. For example, too many items on a page is not effective; the design of the pages should allow for smooth eye movement; and variety in page layout from pair to pair stimulates reader interest and buyer behavior. Ideally, catalog firms should test various combinations of page designs and page flows to determine what works best.

EXHIBIT 10.7. Victoria's Secret Catalog Cover

Merchandise Arrangement

Merchandise placement within a catalog is usually by merchandise category and/or user type. For example, the 1995 Lands' End Christmas holiday catalog in Exhibit 10.8 grouped its items by separate types such as knit shirts, sweaters, and sleepwear. The major sections of the catalog were separated by user, with men's

EXHIBIT 10.8. Lands' End Catalog Cover

and women's sections, a women's-only section, and a men's-only section. Additionally, the catalog had gift, children's, luggage, and sheets and towels sections. The center of the catalog had an order form and information about how to place an order.

Victoria's Secret catalogs are organized around wearing occasions and by type, with the undergarments on separate pages from the outergarments. The pages for outergarments offer outfits such as jacket and trouser combinations, along with dresses. Some pages mix wardrobe items with accessories such as watches and bags.

Avon Products organizes its large catalogs around biweekly themes. Every two weeks, Avon issues a new catalog to its hundreds of thousands of sellers in the United States who use that catalog as a basis for obtaining customer orders. Depending on the time of year, a catalog may focus on seasonal events. Christmas catalogs feature gift items in the front, with Avon's standard product offering of cosmetics, jewelry, skin care, and fragrances, followed by non-Christmas items.

Visual Presentation

Photographs are the focal point of most catalogs. They provide a visual representation of the merchandise that is designed to inform and motivate the reader. Well-designed photographs are fundamental to the selling process; they put the item in the best possible light by using attractive models, special lighting and camera angles, and background situations that enhance the appeal of the merchandise. Photographs also show the details of the merchandise, provide an indication of how certain items might be worn or used, and indicate whether the company's product line is consistent with the lifestyle of the target audience. They add credibility to the offer by showing what the merchandise will look like when it is received. This reduces the risk the reader associates with purchasing the item and reassures him or her that the merchandise will look and function as expected.

Catalog Copy

Catalog copy must be complete yet concise. Its main function is to sell; for each item in the catalog, the picture and the copy must work together to motivate the reader to make a purchase. The picture reinforces the copy and vice versa. The copy describes a product's benefits and explains why a purchase should be made. After the selling points, the copy must give order-related specifics such as the product unit number, size options, color, price, and any other facts the customer needs in placing an order. Exhibit 10.9 shows a preliminary catalog production creative budget. See Chapter 7 for more on catalog creative strategy.

The Order Form

Typically, order forms are bound into the center of a catalog. The Lands' End order form in Exhibit 10.10 is designed to be folded and put in an envelope that has the firm's address printed on it. The customer can also order by calling a 24-hour toll-free phone number or by sending a fax. All the shipping terms and options are described in the same area as the order form.

While there are many possible variations in how order forms are designed, they all have one purpose: to make it as easy as possible for the customer to place the order. The instructions must be clear and easy to follow. The order form must have places for such key data as name and address, items ordered, color and size, and credit card information.

EXHIBIT 10.9. Preliminary Catalog Production Creative Budget
The budget outline shown below is a typical summary of the detail that a cataloger might expect to receive from an outside creative resource that's producing or redesigning a catalog.

Components: Catalog—32 pages, 4-color, 8 3/8″ × 10 7/8″, 2-color order form.
Assumptions: 140–150 photos (15–20 with models).

Creative concepting
Conceptual development including pagination, positioning, offers, and niche development. $3,000

Conference and travel time
Time spent with the copywriter, artist, and others defining the project and target audience 2,000

Layout & design
Design concept 3,000
Cover design and color comp 900
Page spread design and color comp 900
Page formatting and computer layout 6,925

Copy
Copy, editing, and headlines 4,500

Production art
Copy fitting and page production to disk 995
Stats, prints, and art materials. 750
Alterations allowance. 1,500

Project supervision
Supervision of project up to color separations. 3,000

Miscellaneous
Federal Express, messenger, FAX, etc. 700
Total creative without photography $28,170*

Photography / Illustration

Photography, including film and processing
Color shots with model. . . . .$150/per shot
Color shots—tabletop . . . .$100/per shot
Cover photo. . . . .$600/per shot
Model fees. . . . . .Direct billing to client
Photo art direction $660/day
Stylist. $250/day
Sets, props, and accessories. . . . . .To be determined

*Not included: Sales tax, travel expenses, out-of-pocket expenses.
Please note: All client alterations are additional.
Source: Catalog Age, J. Schmid & Associates, Inc., 1994.

EXHIBIT 10.10. Lands' End Order Form

LANDS' END
DIRECT MERCHANTS

Lands' End, Inc., 1 Lands' End Lane
Dodgeville, WI USA 53595

Call us toll-free 24 hours a day, 7 days a week to charge your order: 1-800-356-4444
FAX: 1-800-332-0103

Ho Ho Ho

Ordered by: IMPORTANT: If this is not your own name and address, please cross out and correct below

Ship to: (Only if different from "Ordered by".)

Name ____________________

Address ____________________

City __________ State/Prov. __________ Zip/Postal Code __________

Country ____________________

Gift card message ____________________

From ____________________

Daytime phone ( ) __________ Evenings ( ) __________ Ask for __________

Item Number	Page No.	Description	Size	Dress shirt sleeve length	Pants Inseam length	Pants Cuffs Yes	Pants Cuffs No	Color (write complete name)	Alternate color (if first choice is not available)	*Monogramming-see page 3 of order form ($5 each or $10 for towel sets) First initial	Middle initial	Last initial	Word/Name w/punctuation	Style No.	*Gift Box $5 each	Qty.	Price Total

For additional orders, use a separate sheet of paper.

Method of Payment:
All prices stated in US dollars.

Please include credit card number and expiration date with charge orders!

☐ Charge to my *(circle one)*: Discover Visa MasterCard American Express

Expiration Date ___/___ Month Year

X ____________________
Signature (as shown on credit card)

☐ Check or Money Order Enclosed (US funds only)

Thank You!
©1996, Lands' End, Inc.

*** WI residents of Iowa, Dane and Sauk Counties-5½%, Milwaukee County-5.6%, remaining counties-5%.

Page 1

Charges below are for first "Ship to" address.(USA)

Total Price of Items	Shipping, Packing and Handling
$0-30.00	$4.25
$30.01-70.00	$5.75
$70.01+	$6.95

Shipping to each additional address add $4.25.

We ship USA orders by UPS (AK and HI by Airmail). If you'd prefer parcel post or next day service, please check below.

☐ Parcel Post ☐ UPS Next Day Air (additional cost)

**Applicable to non-apparel items.

Total price of items	
*Monogram ($5 each, $10 set) or Gift Box ($5 each)	
Delivery in IL add 6¼%, IA 5%, MN** 6½% sales tax	
USA Shipping, Packing and Handling (see left)	
UPS Next Day Air ($6 additional; AK & HI, $16)	
Shipping to each additional address ($4.25 each)	
Canadian/International Shipping (see reverse side)	
Total	
Delivery in NY and WI***, add all applicable sales taxes	
Total New York and Wisconsin deliveries	

IJ Holiday Prospector Remail

CATALOGS AND DATABASE TECHNOLOGY[10]

Companies involved in the catalog industry have traditionally made more of an effort to target their customers effectively than have other industries. The catalog industry, by its nature, requires the collection of a vast amount of data from customers in order to process orders. Nevertheless, the data have not always been used in the most effective manner for marketing purposes. Some catalogers, for example, have used summarized data to mass-market to entire segments of potential customers.

Recent increases in postal and paper costs have dramatically increased the cost of producing and mailing catalogs. Catalog companies are now finding that traditional cost models are not working anymore. While the cost per catalog is increasing, response rates have not risen. Therefore, companies are finding that profits are decreasing quickly, even to the point of crisis for some.

A growing number of firms have begun exploring alternative sources for revenue, such as Web sites, online ordering, or CD-ROM catalogs, but these are long-term efforts still in the embryonic stage. As mentioned earlier, alternative media look very promising for the future, but they have yet to return a profit for most catalog marketers.

Therefore, companies are seeking ways to reduce expenses while increasing response rates from the typical 2 percent in the catalog industry. With 98 percent of catalogs going to recipients who do not buy, the most obvious way to reduce expenses is to eliminate those mailings. But how can a company go about doing so?

One of the easiest ways to begin is quite simple—send catalogs only to those customers or prospects most likely to be profitable. While that may seem obvious, many companies do not consider this aspect of profitability. Even companies using traditional recency, frequency, and monetary (RFM) models (see Chapter 5) find that they do not provide the level of detail needed. For example, one cataloger looked at the profitability of its best customers as defined by RFM and found that 8 percent of those "best customers" were actually unprofitable due to a high rate of merchandise returns that were not being tracked. Catalogers using RFM also tend to overpromote to their best customers, bringing response rates down over time.

If they wish to optimize their return on internal promotion budgets over time, catalog companies must think about long-term marketing goals rather than just the next mailing. To do this, catalogers must fine-tune their ability to segment customers by lifestyle, life-cycle stage, and historical buying patterns.

The key to cutting mailing expenses without cutting profits is contact management. The cataloger must also understand whom to contact and how often. This will help the company avoid overpromoting to its best customers and underpromoting to other potentially profitable customers. Oversaturating a company's best customers with 12 mailings when 6 would generate the same amount of revenue is not good business. Tracking the revenue generated with reduced mailings helps the company pinpoint the optimal number of catalog mailings necessary to maintain its revenue base. The idea is to make the optimum number of the right contacts. A marketing database can monitor and facilitate this process.

A marketing database focuses specifically on sales and customers, making it possible to analyze all available customer data at the individual transaction level detail. Some of the vast range of available criteria include product usage and purchase history, promotion response, media usage and characteristics, demographics, psychographics, geography, organization, time, and seasonality, as well as RFM. This level of detail allows catalog companies to allocate limited resources most effectively, manage customer relationships, track which customers are performing well, and track which products they are purchasing.

The information contained in a marketing database improves market segmentation, allowing more selective market penetration to maximize marketing program impact. Catalogers can focus on loyal, profitable customers to ensure that those customers are retained and to identify possibilities for cross-selling or upgrading these existing customers. In addition, the database helps identify those prospects most likely to be receptive to the company's messages.

It is just as important to identify bad customers as it is to identify the best customers. A marketing database can help a cataloger with all aspects of customer development, including leads qualification, reactivation, and retention.

Qualified leads can be obtained through many avenues, including list rentals and space ads. Catalogers with a marketing database can screen out undesirable leads, suppress certain zip codes, and even identify characteristics of those potential customers. The database allows the company to track which methods achieve the most profitable customers for the least amount of money. Tracking of lead acquisition methods helps companies manage promotional expenses and avoid unprofitable methods of lead acquisition in the future.

Reactivation is another method for customer development. The marketing database permits the identification of those customers who have been inactive for over a year. It can then test offers with these prospects, for example, offering a percentage discount on a catalog or adding a "last catalog unless you order" sticker (see Exhibit 10.11). The marketing database then tracks these customers and recommends deletion if necessary. Without a marketing database, it is virtually impossible to pinpoint inactive customers.

The last aspect of customer development is retention, which reduces customer turnover and increases loyalty. First, it is important to determine which customers qualify as "best customers" by tracking net revenue. That information helps the company exclude chronic returners and debt customers. Once the best customers are identified, a menu of benefits can be activated to achieve greater loyalty, including discounts, overnight delivery, and guaranteed in-stock merchandise.

The marketing database also allows the identification of a second tier of still profitable but lower performing customers. These customers can be sent a smaller,

EXHIBIT 10.11. Catalog with Last Order Cover

lower-cost catalog than that sent to the top tier. This continues addressing these potentially profitable customers while reducing the expense of repeated catalog mailings.

The tracking ability provided by a marketing database allows for cross-selling, upselling, and price testing. For example, customers who buy children's items are good prospects for home fashions. With a marketing database, customers can be tracked and sent additional appropriate catalogs when certain criteria are met.

In addition to reducing customer turnover, increasing customer loyalty, cross-selling or upgrading existing customers, and lowering the cost of customer acquisition, marketing databases can be used for many other business applications, including channel analysis, market penetration, pricing, market research, new product development, and promotional campaign tracking.

PERCEIVED RISK IN CATALOG SHOPPING[11]

McCorkle notes that mail-order catalog shopping involves five specific types of perceived risk: financial risk, performance risk, social risk, time-loss risk, and source risk.

Perceived Financial Risk

Perceived financial risk is defined as the customer's concern over any financial loss that might be incurred because of a product purchase. This potential loss pertains to the initial cost of the product and the potential expense of repair, maintenance, or return. As a result of perceived financial risk, a prospective catalog shopper may ask the following questions: Is the product worth its total price? Does the addition of shipping and handling charges and sales tax make the product too expensive? What is the likelihood of additional postpurchase expense?

The degree of financial risk depends on the total price of the product and the socioeconomic status of the buyer. Even though higher-priced items are likely to create a greater concern for financial loss, the individual with a higher income would most likely perceive less financial risk. This may explain why in-home shoppers have higher-than-average household incomes.

A catalog firm can reduce the amount of perceived financial risk by offering competitive prices relative to retail stores. This can be accomplished by offering special prices, special discounts, or reduced shipping and handling charges. Lands' End's monthly catalogs always include several pages of "Clear the Deck Clearance." These items are usually overstocks and close-outs. Victoria's Secret offers a free gift or cash discount only to catalog clients, based on the total amount of the order. The Sharper Image catalog offers a Frequent Buyers Program in which customers earn gift certificates based on their total annual purchases.

A cataloger can also reduce the level of perceived financial risk through non-price-competition by increasing the perceived value of the product. A cataloger might offer unconditional guarantees, special gifts, or convenient payment options. For example, the L. L. Bean catalog provides a 100 percent satisfaction guarantee with no time limit and no questions asked. Other methods of reducing perceived financial risk focus on the different options for payment. These may include acceptance of national credit cards, in-house credit, or special handling of credit charges.

Perceived Performance Risk

Concern over whether a product will perform as expected is known as perceived performance risk. The customer's greatest concern is about not being able to physically inspect merchandise and evaluate product characteristics such as quality, size, color, and style. In the case of technically complex products like stereo equipment, televisions, or computers, the uncertainty is about how the product will perform.

One method by which a customer might address perceived performance risk is to rely on prior experience in making a purchase decision. For example, the purchase of a familiar brand of clothing that is known to offer a satisfactory fit, color, and style may influence the customer to repeat this experience with more confidence. However, in the absence of prior brand experience, the shopper is left to rely on risk-reduction information provided by the catalog, including guarantees or warranties, samples or trial use of the product, and testimonials or expert endorsements. Additionally, the manner in which the size or color of the product is portrayed in the catalog may help to alleviate perceived performance risk.

Perceived Social Risk

Concern about what others might think of a product purchase is known as perceived social risk. In a psychological sense, consumers purchase affiliation or social status or some other such attribute when they make their product purchases. Risks associated with these attributes are higher with the purchase of socially visible products such as clothing, clothing accessories, and household furnishings, which are likely to be seen by friends or visitors. The question consumers are most likely to ask is, Will others think less of me for making this product purchase?

One way for consumers to reduce perceived social risk is to purchase brands that are well known as socially acceptable. They may reduce their own perceived social risk by soliciting product or brand recommendations from family, friends, or associates. Realizing this, many catalogers invite their customers to recommend a friend to whom a catalog might be sent. If clearly recognized as such, a prospective customer might be much more receptive to purchasing from a catalog that was recommended by a respected friend or acquaintance.

Perceived social risk can also be reduced through an association with a socially accepted company or retail store. For example, upscale brands sold through mail-order catalogs are seen as less socially risky if the catalogs come from prestigious retail stores. Examples include the Bloomingdale's by Mail, Neiman-Marcus, and Saks Fifth Avenue catalogs.

Perceived Time-Loss Risk

Perceived time-loss risk involves concern over lost time from making an incorrect product purchase. There are two types of perceived time-loss risk: front-end and back-end. Front-end perceived time-loss risk involves concern for the lost time between the order of merchandise and receipt of the merchandise. Back-end perceived time-loss risk involves concern over time lost in trying to return unsatisfactory merchandise.

With front-end perceived time-loss risk the prospective customer is likely to ask, How long will I have to wait for delivery of my mail-order purchase? When an individual first addresses the concern of time-loss risk, the convenience offered by mail-order shopping immediately comes to mind. Techniques used by mail-order catalogers to offer more convenience on the front end include toll-free phone ordering and acceptance of major national credit cards. To address waiting-time concerns, many catalogers offer rush shipping services through Federal Express or UPS. However, while express delivery may properly address the concern of front-end perceived time-loss risk, the added expense could easily increase the degree of perceived financial risk.

In the situation where performance or financial risk is high, the customer may also experience concern over perceived time-loss risk on the back end. Before finalizing a purchase decision, the shopper may ask the following questions: How difficult will it be to return an unsatisfactory purchase, and how much time might be lost in attempting to do so? Too often the instructions for returning unsatisfactory merchandise are included only with delivery of the product. Back-end perceived time-loss risk should be addressed prior to the actual purchase for the benefit of the customer's preresponse evaluation.

Perceived Source Risk

Perceived source risk refers to concerns over whether or not the prospective customer can trust the catalog firm and feel comfortable in doing business with the firm. The source of a message exerts a strong persuasive influence on receivers. Source credibility involves the set of perceptions that receivers of communication hold toward a source. This credibility is associated with believability, trustworthiness, and expertise. If perceptions of the source are positive, then the extent of perceived source risk is reduced.

Perceived risk associated with a product is transferable to the store that sells the product. For this reason, addressing perceived source risk could be crucial when catalogers are seeking new customers. A money-back guarantee is only as good as the credibility of the source offering it. Attempts to reduce other types of perceived risk may be successful only after the source risk has been reduced. If the perceived source risk is high, then other types of risk are also very likely to be high. Conversely, a customer may have negligible perceived source risk yet be very reluctant to purchase a particular product due to high levels of product-related types of perceived risk such as financial, performance, or social factors.

To reduce perceived source risk, the cataloger needs to establish a credible identity in the mind of the potential buyer. One of the first questions that the prospective customer may ask is, Can I trust this company? Among inexperienced or less-experienced catalog shoppers a more serious question may also be asked: Does the company actually exist?

Catalogers that do not operate retail stores or that have a limited number of locations must rely upon methods other than store reputation to obtain a credible identity. The Lands' End catalog, for example, runs full-page stories about interesting employees.

Perceived source risk can also be reduced through education. A potential buyer is likely to harbor greater feelings of trust toward a cataloger that does more than just attempt to sell them products. Catalogers should make a concerted effort to teach their customers how to be better mail-order shoppers and how to make more efficient purchase decisions. The mail-order shopper may not have adequate skills to judge quality from a distance. If the cataloger teaches a prospect how to identify and buy quality, then the prospect may assume that the cataloger is a quality business, therefore reducing perceived source risk and possibly performance risk simultaneously. The L. L. Bean catalog provides, free of charge, extensive information about buying sleeping bags, hunting apparel, knives, and many other of their own product categories. The Lands' End catalog recently dedicated a full page to offering helpful packing tips from Lands' End customers.

Many catalogers display the Direct Marketing Association (DMA) logo and other references on their order forms. To a knowledgeable mail-order shopper, membership in the DMA may indicate that the cataloger adheres to a special set of ethical guidelines. For the unknowing and, more likely, the infrequent or non–catalog shopper, the firm should provide information about DMA membership, in-home shopping laws, and their rights as mail-order customers.

SUMMARY

Catalogs are sent to either consumers or business organizations. Consumer catalogs are distinguishable by the types of items they carry, the target markets they want to reach, and the quality of their appearance and design. Business-to-business catalogs sell specific types of items such as office supplies and computer accessories rather than a large variety of products. For either type of catalog, customers place orders through an 800 number, by mail, or by fax.

Consumer specialty catalogs are the fastest growing part of the catalog market and far outnumber the few remaining general merchandise catalogs. The specialty catalogs carry items ranging from clothing to food, and they are designed to cater to specific tastes associated with lifestyle preferences, including differences in interests, activities, attitudes, and values.

Catalog buyers are different from traditional retail shoppers in their demographics, lifestyles, shopping attitudes, and other factors. Women outnumber men among catalog shoppers, 58 percent to 42 percent. Among those who never buy through catalogs, there are just as many men as women. Larger percentages of catalog shoppers are in the middle age ranges of 25–34, 35–44, and 45–54. Catalog shoppers are better educated, work in professional and managerial capacities, and earn more money than non–catalog shoppers.

Success in catalog marketing depends on an understanding of patterns in consumer or business choice behavior. Because consumers or businesses must deal with a multiplicity of alternatives, the choices they make represent preferences for particular catalog attributes. A direct marketer's ability to define how they make these distinctions is essential to capturing and maintaining a strong market position.

The vital ingredients in the success of a catalog include merchandising, list selection, customer service, toll-free numbers, fulfillment, print production, mailing, research, computer support, order forms, creativity, and, particularly, positioning or image. Consumers define catalogs through both functional qualities and psychological attributes symptomatic of the needs that they can expect to satisfy through their buyer behavior. Perceptions of risk in catalog shopping are associated with financial risk, performance risk, social risk, time-loss risk, and source risk.

REVIEW QUESTIONS

1. Why have large general merchandise catalogs significantly declined in number while speciality catalogs have flourished?
2. In what ways are consumer and business-to-business catalogs similar, and in what ways are they different?
3. Describe catalog merchandise buyers versus traditional retail shoppers by their demographics, lifestyles, shopping attitudes, and other factors.
4. What are the key factors that determine the success or failure of a catalog? Do those factors differ by consumer versus business target markets?
5. What role do catalog attributes play in consumer catalog selection and merchandise purchases?
6. What roles do perceived financial risk, performance risk, social risk, time-loss risk, and source risk play in catalog merchandise buyer behavior? How can the catalog marketer design and position a catalog to address these perceptions of risk?
7. In what ways do computer technologies, especially databases, help catalog marketers more efficiently market their merchandise?

NOTES

1. Adapted from Maxwell Sroge, *How to Create Successful Catalogs* (Lincolnwood, IL: NTC Business Books, 1988) pp. 1–3.
2. Adapted from Henry R. Hoke, "Family Tastes Sweet Success with Onions," *Direct Marketing,* January 1994, pp. 32–33.
3. Adapted from Lori A. DiBella, "The Southern Touch," *Direct Marketing,* March 1991, pp. 45–46.
4. Adapted from Mollie Neal, "Linen and Lace Graces the Mail Order Market," *Direct Marketing,* December 1992, pp. 36–38.
5. Adapted from Harvey Braun, "The Catalog Shoppers of the '90s," *Direct Marketing,* March 1993, pp. 15–18.
6. Jo-Von Tucker, "Catalog Sales," in *The Direct Marketing Handbook,* ed. Edward L. Nash (New York: McGraw-Hill, 1984) pp. 715–43.
7. William J. McDonald, "Consumer Preference Structure Analysis," *Journal of Direct Marketing,* Winter 1993, pp. 20–30.
8. Ibid.
9. Mary Lou Roberts, and Paul D. Berger, *Direct Marketing Management,* Englewood Cliffs, NJ: Prentice Hall, 1989, p. 262.
10. Adapted from Cary Stronach, "Effective Use of Marketing Databases for Catalog Companies," *Direct Marketing,* April 1996, pp. 48–50.
11. Adapted from Denny E. McCorkle, "The Role of Perceived Risk in Mail Order Catalog Shopping," *Journal of Direct Marketing,* Autumn 1990, pp. 26–35.

"Catalog Age 100." *Catalog Age,* August 1996, pp. 1, 62–68, 72–74.

Braun, Harvey. "The Catalog Shoppers of the '90s." *Direct Marketing,* March 1993, pp. 15–18.

DiBella, Lori A. "The Southern Touch." *Direct Marketing,* March 1991, pp. 45–46.

Direct Marketing Association. *Statistical Fact Book 1996.* New York: Direct Marketing Association, 1996.

Hoke, Henry R. "Family Tastes Sweet Success with Onions." *Direct Marketing,* January 1994, pp. 32–33.

Jones, Susan K. *Creative Strategy in Direct Marketing.* Lincolnwood, IL: NTC Business Books, 1991.

Katzenstein, Herbert, and William Sachs. *Direct Marketing,* 2nd ed. New York: Macmillan, 1992.

McCorkle, Denny E. "The Role of Perceived Risk in Mail Order Catalog Shopping." *Journal of Direct Marketing,* Autumn, 1990, pp. 26–35.

McDonald, William J. "Consumer Preference Structure Analysis." *Journal of Direct Marketing,* Winter 1993, pp. 20–30.

Miller, Jack. "Someone Changed the Rules. Why Wasn't It Me?" *Direct Marketing,* January 1994, pp. 16–20.

Morris-Lee, James. "Push-Pull Marketing with Maglogs." *Direct Marketing,* June 1993, pp. 23–26, 47.

Neal, Mollie. "Linen and Lace Graces the Mail Order Market." *Direct Marketing,* December 1992, pp. 36–38.

_______. "Catalogia: C'est Bien." *Direct Marketing,* February 1992, pp. 18–19.

Raphel, Murray. "Where's the Retail Direct Mail Revolution?" *Direct Marketing,* December 1992, pp. 42–45.

Roberts, Mary Lou, and Paul D. Berger. *Direct Marketing Management.* Englewood Cliffs, NJ: Prentice Hall, 1989.

Schmidt, Jack. "Growth and Profit Strategies in a Maturing Industry." *Direct Marketing,* December 1992, pp. 39–41.

Sroge, Maxwell. *How to Create Successful Catalogs.* Lincolnwood, IL: NTC Business Books, 1988.

_______. *The United States Mail Order Industry.* Lincolnwood, IL: NTC Business Books, 1994.

Stone, Bob. *Successful Direct Marketing Methods,* 5th ed. Lincolnwood, IL: NTC Business Books, 1995.

"Strategies for the New Mail Order." *Business Week,* December 19, 1992, pp. 82–86.

Stronach, Cary. "Effective Use of Marketing Databases for Catalog Companies." *Direct Marketing,* April 1996, pp. 48–50.

Tucker, Jo-Von. "Catalog Sales." In *The Direct Marketing Handbook,* ed. Edward L. Nash. New York: McGraw-Hill, 1984.

CHAPTER 11

Telemarketing

OBJECTIVES

1. To define the nature and scope of telemarketing activities.
2. To examine the different types of telemarketing and the functions they serve.
3. To look at how telemarketing is integrated with other forms of direct marketing.
4. To present the major issues and considerations associated with executing a telemarketing program in-house versus using a telemarketing service bureau.
5. To examine how a telemarketing operation operates at peak efficiency and effectiveness.
6. To explain the roles and functions of telemarketing scripts.

INTRODUCTION

Telemarketing, the application of the telephone to direct marketing efforts, is the largest direct advertising medium in the United States today. An estimated $385.6 billion was spent on outgoing and incoming calls in 1995—and the amount spent on telemarketing is expected to grow to $599 billion by the year 2000. Telemarketing has been in common use for many years in insurance sales, contribution solicitation, credit card promotions, and many other businesses. Today, telephone marketing extends to international programs, including calls terminating and originating in the United States and foreign countries.

Telemarketing can be an important part of an integrated marketing communications program. The telemarketing objective is to reach customers in a personalized, cost-effective interaction that meets customer needs. A well-planned telephone marketing program is a carefully thought-out and controlled activity in which the persons called have been identified as actual or potential members of a firm's target market; thus, telemarketing helps build and maintain satisfactory customer relationships.The most effective telemarketing programs make use of the latest technologies, including communications hardware and software, particularly database technologies.

Telemarketing methods are categorized as *inbound,* where customers are calling a firm to place an order or to request more information or customer service, and *outbound,* where the firm is calling customers and prospects to make a sale or to offer information which it hopes will lead to a sale. Table 11.1 shows the types of telemarketing calls consumers received in December 1994. Many firms are involved in both inbound and outbound telemarketing. For an average company,

TABLE 11.1. Types of Telemarketing Calls Consumers Receive*

	All Respondents	Listed Only	Unlisted Only
Credit card offers	45%	50%	29%
Household items	49	55	33
Household services	27	30	17
National charity	48	51	36
Local charity	62	69	38
Long-distance telephone	63	65	54
Financial services (investments)	21	23	15
Sweepstakes	23	23	22
Free vacations	29	30	22
Tickets with charity	33	37	19
Magazines	46	49	36
Magazines with charity	17	16	11

*Reese Brothers conducted a national telephone survey with a random sample of adults in December 1994 to determine the types of calls consumers receive and how they feel about telemarketing calls. A total of 400 interviews were conducted.

Source: *Consumers Talk About Telemarketing,* Reese Brothers, 1995.

how much emphasis should be placed on one or the other type depends on that company's products or services.

A well-managed telemarketing operation monitors every calling station to ensure quality customer and prospect service, uses full-time supervisors for all its calling operations, develops a professional telemarketing staff, and uses professionally prepared scripts to guarantee that the firm's sales message is delivered to its customers and prospects with consistency and with the correct emphasis on what the firm wants to communicate.

Although there have been failures, telemarketing generally works for most companies and should be a part of an overall marketing strategy for many firms. Sometimes telemarketing is supportive of direct mail, catalogs, print advertising, commercial broadcasting, and/or field selling, and sometimes it is used to replace sales representatives as a way of handling marginal accounts.

Telemarketing is a powerful tool because it has the ability to create a positive image through a personal interaction with a customer or prospect. Therefore, marketers need to think carefully about what the objectives of their telemarketing strategy should be and how to achieve those objectives. As with any other marketing effort, telemarketers need to define an audience, formulate a budget, implement the plan, and measure the results.

THE SCOPE OF TELEMARKETING

The scope of telemarketing is limited only by the imagination of the direct marketer. Although no other direct marketing tool can match the cost-effectiveness, flexibility, control, and speed of the telephone, it takes more than just telephones to get good results. A telemarketing firm must have qualified telephone operators who have been well trained in the use of the telephone as a marketing tool. This includes training in proper voice inflections, listening skills, persistence, and patience.

According to Fidel, the seven most significant uses of telemarketing are the following:

1. Selling, including outgoing and incoming calling.
2. Setting qualified appointments.
3. Generating leads.
4. Surveying.
5. Providing customer service.
6. Advertising (public relations).
7. Pursuing collections.[1]

Selling

Telemarketing-based selling involves outgoing (or outbound) solicitations for a firm's products or services. Selling by telephone is the most profitable telemarketing application. With existing customers, it can be used to elicit reorders, sell additional products or services, or increase the volume of products purchased. It can also resell inactive customers, sell new prospects, and handle smaller customers that are not profitable to sell in person. Incoming (or inbound) telemarketing must be used in conjunction with some other method of promotion such as direct-response television advertising, print placements, or direct mail. In this role, telemarketing primarily involves order taking because the buyer sees an offer and calls to place an order.

Inbound telemarketing calls that result in sales are primarily associated with 800 numbers. The 800 number (and now also 888 numbers, added because of the volume of demand for 800 numbers) is a nationwide or statewide service for which the caller is not charged. It is used mainly as a channel of communication for responding to advertising and direct-mail campaigns. Both business-to-business and consumer programs use toll-free numbers heavily. Inbound telemarketing is rapidly increasing as more and more direct marketing firms provide toll-free access to their businesses. The availability of an 800 number entices those who want to place an order or just get more information to call. The importance of inbound telephone calls and the competitive imperative of offering an 800 number have changed the direct marketing industry forever. Exhibit 11.1 shows an ad with an 800 number. The product is QuickSite, an Internet tool for creating and operating a Web site.

The use of 900 numbers has also increased in popularity in the last several years. The 900 "area code," however, indicates that the caller will be billed for the service. Some companies use 900 numbers to generate leads when selling to businesses because this saves them money and provides a better indication of how interested the caller is in what the firm is selling. Many companies that want to have a way of charging consumers for the time they spend in sales or customer service use 900 numbers. Included are a wide array of companies, from those that operate sex talk lines to such firms as Microsoft, which established a 900 number to reduce the cost of providing customer support.

EXHIBIT 11.1. QuickSite Ad with 800 Number

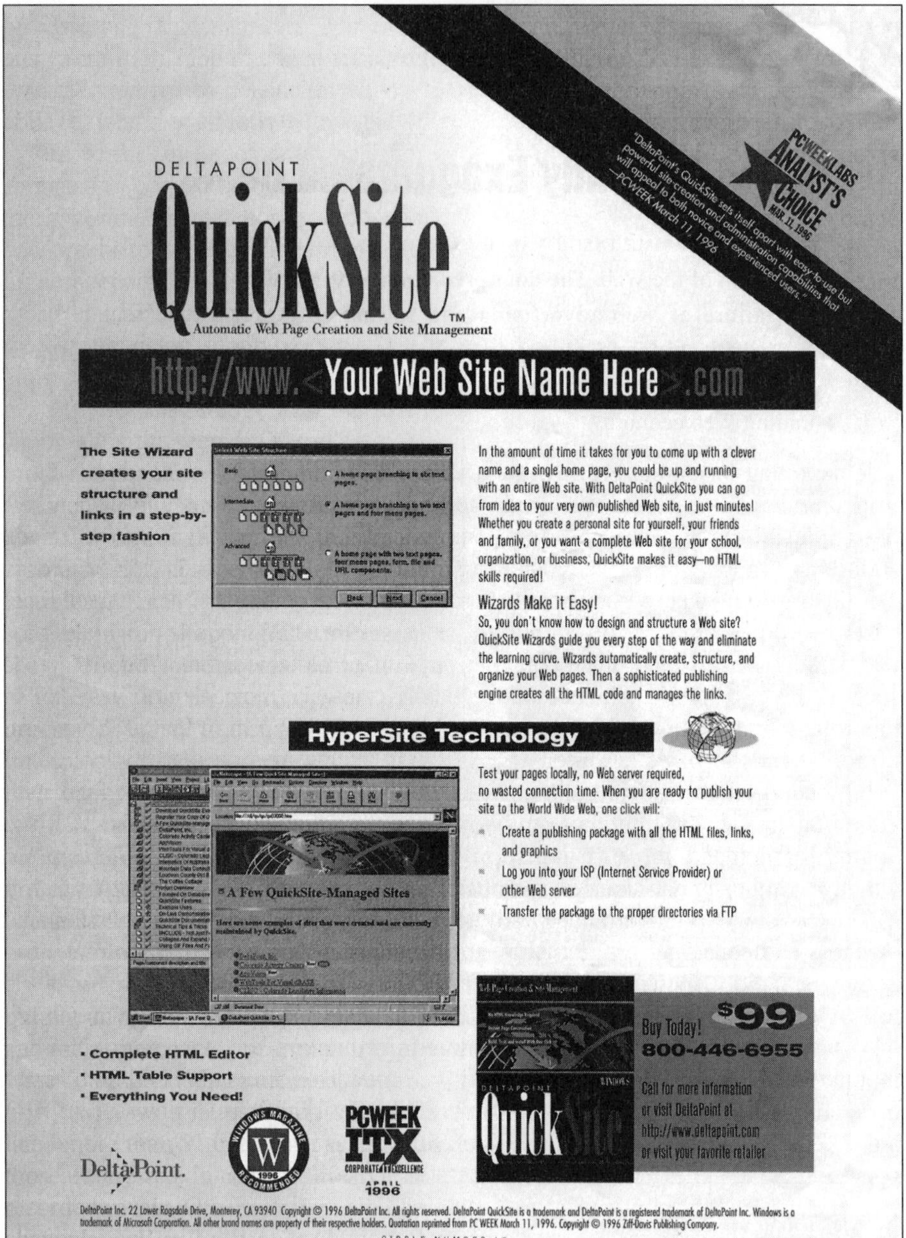

Setting Qualified Appointments

Setting qualified appointments involves calling prospects, qualifying them, and setting appointments for salespeople. Salespeople have a variety of duties they must perform as part of their jobs, including preparing and giving face-to-face presentations, writing proposals, and completing paperwork. As a result, they may have relatively little time to prospect actively for new customers. A trained telemarketer who does little else besides set appointments for salespeople usually becomes more and more proficient and can often outperform salespeople in this role. Even though salespeople may have much more knowledge about the firm's product line, telemarketers can do better because of their concentrated focus on prospecting. Without the burden of prospecting, salespeople are free to spend more time selling, which sharpens their selling skills and improves their closing ratios.

Generating Leads

A lead-generating program provides a source of information about prospects who have expressed an interest in the product or service offered by a firm. As a result, the prospect is contacted by a sales representative or is sent more information to stimulate a sale. To ensure the success of lead-generating programs, the firm needs to manage a database of every lead. Sales representatives should fill out a contact form after each appointment and each follow-up call. Data from these forms become part of the database.

Outbound telemarketing is only as effective as the prospect list it uses. A firm can have the best product or service in the marketplace, but only a list of target market members who are good prospects to make a purchase will result in a successful campaign. Therefore, it is imperative that the names of those to telephone are carefully selected. These leads may be either customers with whom the firm already has a relationship or people who fit the profile of the firm's existing customers and therefore should have a high propensity to buy.

Surveying

Some firms use telemarketing surveys to gather market data about customers and prospects, including information about who makes the decisions in the household or business, what the customer(s) product needs are, and any product purchasing plans. This activity generates leads by identifying potential candidates for future selling. The information collected through surveys is entered in a database for future reference. Note, however, that the Direct Marketing Association (DMA) does not consider it appropriate to attempt to disguise the purpose of a sales call by representing it as a survey. It considers such a misrepresentation an unethical practice and actively tries to discourage it. The DMA's guidelines for acceptable telephone practices are given in Appendix 11C at the end of this chapter.

Providing Customer Service

When telemarketing is used in connection with a customer service function, customers call, for example, to inquire about where their order is, to complain that they have received the wrong products, or to report that their shipment has been damaged. After solving the customer's problem, the customer service representative may take the opportunity to announce new products or product modifications, along with price information.

Advertising (Public Relations)

Advertising that serves a public relations function involves calling companies or individuals that could benefit from a firm's products or services and describing the opportunity to them. Such calls are scripted in much the same way as general advertising copy. The caller communicates information about a new product or service or a modification to an existing product or service. No sales attempt is made on this kind of call because it just informs the other party of something he or she should find of interest.

Pursuing Collections

Credit department telemarketing does not sell a company's products or services. Rather, it pursues receiving payment. Collections are an often overlooked aspect of telemarketing. The credit department's phone-related activities also include credit verifications.

TELEMARKETING AT AMOCO[2]

Amoco's service stations throughout 28 states can easily supply gasoline to the thousands of cars that pass through daily, but a service station does not live by selling gasoline alone. Additional revenue can be made from offering mechanical services. For example, the average full-facility service station should sell between $10,000 and $20,000 per bay each month in service revenue. Out of the 12,000 Amoco stations in the United States, 6,000 offer mechanic services. As a way of supporting these services, Amoco sells tires, batteries, and accessories with telemarketing.

Amoco knows that its dealers need to be fully stocked with tires, batteries, and accessories if promotional support is to have a meaningful impact. The objective of Amoco's Tires, Batteries, and Accessories (TBA) division is to support the dealerships that sell at Amoco facilities that have service bays. In the early 1980s, all Amoco sales representatives were responsible not only for the sale of gasoline but also for TBA products. However, without much structure in the TBA area, selling such products was mostly a side function for the sales representatives, who concentrated on selling gasoline to dealers. Therefore, Amoco decided to make the job of its sales representatives, who visit the dealerships regularly, more efficient.

It became clear that the establishment of a freestanding TBA business unit—with its own revenue and profit-and-loss responsibilities, dedicated sales force, and management staff—could be instrumental in Amoco's goal: to add more value to its dealers. The TBA's independence was important because it not only allowed Amoco to systematically provide service to its dealers but also was intended to create customer loyalty at each dealership location. The support offered by a strong TBA division would allow the individual dealerships to have the option to bring in additional business.

Amoco's TBA unit does approximately $50 million in business yearly. Although that amount is only a small part of the $20 billion a year Amoco brings in overall, the TBA unit is nonetheless clearly focused under the Amoco corporate umbrella. Its success is due in part to the establishment of a well-cared-for relationship with a Milwaukee-based agency, Hunter Business Direct (HBD). HBD was chosen to create a telemarketing and back-end operation whose goal would be to fully support the Amoco sales representatives out in the field.

Originally, the TBA unit's telemarketing role was as both a basic outbound operation that called dealerships about product specials and an inbound customer service center for order taking. Now there is an entire new dimension to the telemarketing operation. The telemarketers, with the guidance of HBD, have developed a strong relationship with the field sales representatives. The 37 sales representatives, who cover the entire marketing area, work hand in hand with the telemarketing staff to take a proactive role in servicing the dealerships with Amoco's thousands of product alternatives.

The result is a team of sales representatives who can now take on more of a business-consulting role when working with the dealers, while leaving the order taking to the telemarketers. However, the telemarketers are trained to be much more than order takers. They know each dealer in their territory just as well as the sales representative. They routinely check with the dealers to see if they can be of any assistance in selling tires, batteries, and accessories. Call schedules are established so as to reach busy dealers at the same time each week or month so that they can expect the call.

Amoco's telemarketing staff also works with the field representative to establish sales objectives for each dealer, so both are working to the same end. By having a field representative as well as a telemarketer to call on, the dealership is provided with two contacts to keep business up to speed. The field representatives and their telemarketing counterparts talk every day on the phone, and the telemarketers even visit the dealerships with the field representative to become familiar with the client.

While on the phone, the telemarketer works from a database that provides a complete profile of the dealership's activities. This up-to-date information enables the caller to foresee any problems that may arise during the scheduled conversation. The field representatives, in turn, are provided with weekly and monthly updates on all activity that may have occurred. In some instances, the telemarketer can act as a reinforcement to the field representative who may not, for example, have been able to close a tire sale at one of his dealerships. The field representative will ask the telemarketer to try to close the tire sale the next time she makes her periodic calls to the dealer. The telemarketer, as well, may remind the field representative to follow up on the sale of a particular product that did not sell well on the phone but may be more successful in person. One of the reasons this relationship works so well is that both the field sales representative and the telemarketer are paid on a commission basis. Both share in the sale to a dealer no matter who closes the sale, and their salaries are based on total territory sales.

In 1987, the telemarketers generated 45 percent of the TBA unit's revenue; in 1990, that number was 71 percent. At the same time, expenses as a percentage of telemarketing revenue declined from 5.1 percent to 2.8 percent, while the length of a telemarketer's call more than doubled, from just over two minutes to almost four and a half minutes. And, with the full support of dedicated field sales representatives and the staff of HBD—who not only supply telemarketing support but assist in customer service, accounting, data entry, and mailing operations—Amoco dealerships have the best of both worlds.

TELEMARKETING AT RYDER SYSTEM[3]

The use of predictive dialers, which use database information to sort and prioritize prospects for outbound telemarketing, is not new in the direct marketing field. But the creative integration of the latest telecommunications, database, and predictive dialing technology is noteworthy. As mentioned earlier, the best new leads for a product or service are the ones that are prequalified, that is, people or businesses who are already in the market and have demonstrated some interest or need to buy a firm's product or use its service. The company that can reach those prospects who already have been identified as having a readiness to buy is certainly a step ahead. The challenge for national marketers has been to figure out a way to apply the new predictive dialing technology to those targets who both are ready to buy and represent the highest dollar value or profit potential to a company.

Ryder System, the international transportation and logistics company, which is best known for its familiar fleet of yellow rental vans and trucks, uses a variety of criteria when analyzing sales prospects for its short- and long-distance "do-it-yourself" moving business. Some 16 million Americans move during the peak summer moving season. Do-it-yourself moving continues to gain in popularity as many of those customers discover the benefits of moving themselves. In fact, self-movers can save as much as 80 percent compared with the cost of using a moving company.

In 1995, Ryder stepped up its efforts to identify and win over more "high-ticket" self-movers, through a combined inbound and outbound marketing program enhanced by the use of a high-speed predictive dialing software program that helped the firm go after the best new leads faster and more efficiently.

Ryder had laid the groundwork for such a program over several years by using advertising and promotional tools to establish its brand identity and to make consumers familiar with its 1-800-GO-RYDER national reservations line. As a result, in three years, the company's once unprofitable do-it-yourself moving business grew substantially, with Ryder holding some one-third of the overall market.

Working with Precision Response Corporation, a direct marketing support firm that already handled several Ryder service programs, the company's strategy was to capitalize on some of the 5 million phone calls a year that come in to the company's national toll-free reservations line and other sources.

The program got under way when Precision Response offered its integrated Predictive Dialer Software and Marketing Database Systems to provide clients with advanced technology. Precision Response had worked with Ryder's management on a number of comprehensive direct response and customer-service support programs and knew that its marketing database capability would meet Ryder's needs when coupled with the existing inbound program and its new high-speed predictive dialing systems. Now, instead of reaching four or five prospects an hour, a well-trained agent can talk to as many as 15 to 18 customers, people who have indicated a readiness to use the service.

Ryder knew from its research and the existing inbound calls that people planning a move often call several rental van companies from three days to three weeks before their moving date to compare services, features, and rates. These prospects are prime candidates for do-it-yourself moves using Ryder rental vehicles.

To help build a database of these prospect names, addresses, and telephone numbers, the inbound telemarketers at Precision Response were trained to ask for specific information that helped Ryder determine the sales-readiness of each caller. They also offered to send the caller a Ryder brochure, "The Movers Advantage," in order to obtain this information. The goal of this approach is to learn the prospect's planned moving date, the distance to be traveled, the size of the home, and whether the customer will be towing a car, all of which helps to indicate how large a vehicle is needed to accommodate the family's belongings.

With the new software and systems in place, Precision Response was able to launch the national outbound effort for Ryder System in a very short time, one that almost immediately began generating a higher number of reservations per hour than either company had anticipated. With millions of call inquiries a year, even a small improvement in conversion rates means a substantial increase in business for Ryder.

An advantage of the proprietary software Precision Response uses is that it can be programmed to update the calling queue constantly to put the very best leads first, based on rapidly changing criteria. This means Precision Response can alter calling patterns as truck inventory levels or rates move up or down to more accurately address the inventories of each of the 4,800 Ryder dealer locations coast-to-coast.

The new program allows Ryder to target callers in locations where the company wants to boost sales as well as to facilitate the movement of inventory from a location that is overstocked to another that is short of trucks. Ryder also can prioritize calls to help smooth out the customary self-move "peaks and valleys" by selecting prospects who are planning to move on slower days, for example, midweek rather than over the weekend. And the system can be programmed to take best advantage of promotional rates to help motivate fence-sitters to make a reservation commitment.

When it began using the predictive dialing technology to identify the most likely prospects, Ryder saw an immediate increase in confirmed reservations. The targeted follow-up process is helping the company provide better customer service, as well as increasing the number of quality reservations it delivers to its dealers. Getting a second chance to describe the many benefits of doing business with Ryder really gives its sales effort a tremendous boost. Now, Ryder is looking at expanding the integrated program to the commercial market, and it expects its business-to-business communications to be tailored to its needs as successfully as the consumer program has been.

SCRIPTS AND TELEPHONE MARKETING

Roberts and Berger note that the basic decision variables for telephone marketing are the same as those for any other direct marketing program: the offer, creative, timing/sequencing, customer service, and implementation.[4] However, a major uniqueness of telemarketing is its use of scripts that serve the same function that advertising serves, but on a call-by-call basis.

Despite their drawbacks, completely scripted telephone contacts are frequently necessary. There are many situations in which good scripts delivered by callers with appropriate training are the correct approach. Script development is usually necessary because, in the professional telephone selling process, each call is a sales presentation. These calls should include the basics: introduction, qualification of the prospect, presentation of the sales message, responses to objections, and closure.

Telemarketing scripts introduce the person at the other end of the line to who is calling, describe the product or service, and make the sales pitch in an organized fashion. That sales pitch functions like any other advertisement in that it describes a product and its benefits and attempts to get the person receiving the call to place an order.

For business-to-business telemarketing calls, the caller may also need to question the person on the other end of the line about what role he or she plays in the product or service purchase decision-making process. Is the decision made by more than one person? That is, is joint decision making involved? In industrial markets, many purchase decisions are made by several people. Even when there is a primary decision maker, that person may not act independently. When phone calls are intended to generate sales leads, they serve a different function than do sales calls, but the same questions about qualifying the prospect still apply.

The offer presentation is the most important part of the telephone message because it contains the selling proposition the firm wants to communicate and the reasons in support of that communication. The scripted message explains the product or service and indicates the benefits the prospect can expect to gain from making a purchase. If the prospect accepts the offer, the call is a success. However, the prospect may have questions or raise objections. The majority of these questions and objections can be anticipated so that answers and responses can be prepared in advance and included in the script. This enables the caller to use the prepared responses when the prospect raises questions or objections to an offer.

With a script, all telephone solicitors conduct identical presentations, almost word for word. In mass cold calling, this approach makes sense because it stops telephone solicitors from using their own words, which can result in a poorly communicated sales message. Strict adherence to the script is also important when the caller has limited product knowledge or when such knowledge is not really required.

For some telemarketing presentations, phone operators are allowed flexibility in presenting the sales message as long as certain points are covered. Callers can customize the sales message and the flow of the conversation to the prospect while at the same time communicating the message. This more unstructured approach, which uses relatively minimal scripting, is most commonly used for calling known customers or prospects about complicated products, including investment vehicles and insurance. While this approach may sound more personable and may be more customer oriented, it also necessitates significantly more operator training.

Appendix 11B at the end of this chapter contains a sample script. It illustrates how a firm offering training supplies sells its products through business-to-business telemarketing. Although this script is detailed, it does require some product knowledge on the part of the telephone representative. Good scripting does not seem "canned" to the person who is called.

Telemarketing offers immediate results. A firm can know whether a script is working after the first few hundred calls and can therefore adjust it as needed. This means that it is constantly monitored and evaluated for both positive and negative prospect responses. As in the preparation process, the script may continue to evolve and improve during implementation until the firm feels the script has reached its peak level of performance.

INTEGRATING TELEMARKETING WITH OTHER MEDIA

An important aspect of telephone marketing is understanding how it can best be integrated with other media. Both inbound and outbound telemarketing enjoy a synergy with other media because responses to a media combination will be greater than responses to only one medium. One reason for this is that people do not respond in the same way to messages in different media. A printed ad does not convey the same set of images as a person's voice elicits on a telephone. These differences argue for the use of a media mix to create varied yet mutually reinforcing impressions.

Telemarketing and Print Advertising

Many newspaper and magazine ads feature either a local number or an 800 number for getting information or placing an order. Also, such space advertising usually contains a coupon the prospect can fill out and mail in. However, telephone inquiries and orders are increasingly more popular than mail-in options.

Telemarketing and the Yellow Pages

According to Stone and Wyman, there are over 6,400 yellow pages directories published in the United States, and 16,000 headings under which advertising can appear, 4,000 of which are national.[5] Also, some $8.3 billion is spent in yellow pages advertising each year. National advertisers buy space in the yellow pages just as they do in magazines or newspapers. With a single space order, they can get either national coverage in many directories or regional coverage in just a few.

Firms put their 800 numbers in their yellow pages advertising to encourage inbound calls. This type of advertising is widely used by airlines. Most businesses, large and small, list their local phone numbers in their yellow pages ad to encourage potential customers to call and get more information about the products or services they sell.

Telemarketing and Catalogs

Telephone ordering, especially the 24-hours-a-day, seven-days-a-week variety, has been a boon to the catalog business. Catalogs have enjoyed considerable success with 800 numbers because they offer callers toll-free ordering privileges. The average phone order is 20 percent larger than the average mail order. Part of that difference in average order size may well be attributable to the use of credit cards, but some of it is clearly the result of personal interactions between the customer and a well-trained telemarketer.

Telemarketing and Direct Mail

Telemarketers have learned that providing direct-mail recipients with the choice of either making a toll-free call or returning a reply card increases the total response to an offer. Compared to a mail solicitation, a phone call can evoke a more immediate action and a shorter response time to an offer. Telephone follow-ups can also clarify mailings that deal with complicated or complex products.

Telemarketing and Television Advertising

Television offers exciting opportunities for selling goods and services directly to the consumer by linking the television ad with the telephone. Many direct-response marketers sell directly to the consumer through television, particularly when their products lend themselves well to demonstrations and/or testimonials.

Telemarketing and Radio

Radio does well as a medium for promoting phone-in information requests and orders. Radio has the advantages of specific program formats, which lend themselves to market segmentation, and low costs for its time periods. The key to success in radio is selecting the correct station format based on the audience the firm has decided to target.

SERVICE BUREAUS VERSUS IN-HOUSE TELEPHONE OPERATIONS

Once a firm has chosen to institute a telemarketing program, it must decide if it should execute its own telemarketing program in-house or use a telemarketing service bureau. The firm may also begin the program at a service bureau and then transfer the effort in-house. Every situation is unique and requires a review of the needs and requirements of the firm to determine the advantages and disadvantages.

Advantages of Service Bureaus

Service bureaus provide production-oriented operations that specialize in handling high call volumes, whether incoming or outgoing. Because these firms focus on telemarketing, they tend to utilize the most advanced technology available to stay efficient. They are useful if a firm does not have the resources to handle the business of a telemarketing campaign, as when the firm is planning for a large number of phone calls over a short period of time.

Another application for a service bureau is in handling incoming telemarketing in response to a new television campaign or other direct-response program. This is especially true if a firm does not have an accurate forecast of the number of calls it will receive as a result of its marketing effort.

According to Fidel, there are four main advantages to using an outside service bureau to conduct a firm's telemarketing program:

1. Low initial investment.
2. Fixed operating costs.
3. Quick start.
4. Time flexibility.[6]

Low Initial Investment

If a firm elects to use a service bureau, it pays for the program only on a short-term or limited basis. There is no large investment for creating a telemarketing unit, which includes the need for more employees, telephones and lines, and other additional equipment. If the firm is starting from scratch, such costs can be considerable, thus making the service bureau an attractive alternative.

Fixed Operating Costs

A service bureau offers a defined rate schedule, allowing a company to project exactly what the operation will cost. There normally is a setup charge, but the amount of that charge depends on whether the firm's program is inbound or outbound and the nature of its complexity. Firms may be charged on a per-call or per-hour basis. Per-call charges are usually applied to inbound activity, while outbound calls are charged at an hourly rate. The per-call charges are computed from the amount of information required and the projected length of call. This is added to a minimum guaranteed fee.

Quick Start

Telephone service bureaus can quickly implement a telemarketing program. But how long implementation takes is highly dependent on program complexity and the service bureau's existing projects.

Time Flexibility

Service bureaus generally offer 24-hour, seven-day-a-week service for inbound programs and, as required by law, restricted hours for outbound calling. This means that outbound activity tends to occur during the day and in the early evening, while customers may call to place orders at any time of the day or night.

Disadvantages of Service Bureaus

The potential disadvantages of using an outside service center include the following:

1. Lack of direct control.
2. Lack of direct security.

3. Lack of employee loyalty.
4. Mass-market approach.
5. Caliber of personnel.[7]

Lack of Direct Control

A firm does not have direct control of the operation of a service bureau. This may lead to problems in precisely implementing some aspects of a telemarketing plan, including specifics about operator training and monitoring.

Lack of Direct Security

Because a service bureau is at an external location, a firm does not have its customer information in its exclusive possession. Nevertheless, because these bureaus do take elaborate security measures to protect confidential information, there are seldom any real grounds for confidentiality concerns.

Lack of Employee Loyalty

Service bureau employees work first for the bureau that employs them and second for the firm that pays for the bureau's services.

Mass-Market Approach

Because bureaus are volume businesses, the quality of work for any one firm paying for their services can suffer.

Caliber of Personnel

Service bureaus are businesses that operate based on the difference between their hourly fees or their per-call fees and the wages they must pay. Some control this cost by paying the lowest possible wages to their telemarketing staff. As a result, they do not always attract the most motivated or qualified people.

In-House Operations

Fidel sees a relatively narrow role for in-house operations versus that of service bureaus.[8] He recommends that only if a firm is selling a product or service that is extremely technical in nature and requires detailed product knowledge to answer complex questions should it establish an in-house telemarketing program for both incoming and outgoing calls. He also sees a role for in-house operations for firms selling products or services where highly confidential or proprietary information is involved.

In-house telemarketing operations also work well for firms selling specialized products or services that have low volume and high prices. This type of selling frequently involves repetitive contacts with the same customers and prospects and the need to build a relationship with those persons to further the firm's sales objectives. An in-house program is also a better option for firms with offerings that demand a high level of professionalism with respect to firm and product knowledge.

MANAGING AND MOTIVATING TELEMARKETING REPRESENTATIVES[9]

How does a telemarketing operation reach and maintain peak efficiency and effectiveness? Effective telemarketing operations are based on four primary elements: planning, people, processes, and tools. How well a telemarketing operation fares in each of these areas may well determine its success.

Most telemarketing operations tend to do well with planning, processes, and tools. They spend a great deal of time and resources planning for their telemarketing operations, developing appropriate processes, and selecting and implementing various phone and information systems to support their telemarketing activities. The most common problem of telemarketing operations is how to use the people they employ more effectively and efficiently.

Management

Most telemarketing operations can benefit from improvements in how they manage their phone representatives. This management involves directing and guiding those phone reps to achieve maximum results. Without proper day-to-day management, phone reps individually, and the telemarketing program as a whole, will perform at less than optimal levels.

Managing phone reps is simple in concept yet sometimes difficult in practice, because it deals with the least controllable aspect of a telemarketing operation, namely, people. However, by carefully following a few tried-and-true steps, managers can make their jobs both easier and more rewarding:

- Determine exactly what the phone reps are to do, that is, determine their job responsibilities and operating procedures.
- Establish performance measurements and expected performance levels.
- Prepare a job description.
- Provide phone reps with feedback based on the performance measurements.

Determining Job Responsibilities

Determining what phone reps should be doing while on the job includes spelling out everything from the scope of their overall responsibilities to the step-by-step procedures they must follow when taking or making a phone call and recording information gathered during that phone call. The operating procedures should be so detailed that anyone not familiar with the job could sit down next to a phone rep making a call and follow along in the procedure manual.

Establishing Performance Measurements and Expected Performance Levels

After determining job responsibilities, the next step for telemarketing managers is to establish measurements that indicate how well a phone rep is performing the job as defined by the operating procedures. These measurements should be based on the most important aspects of the phone rep's position. For example, if the phone rep is making outbound calls to sell a product and there is a definite correlation between the number of outbound calls completed and ultimate sales made, one option is to select "completed calls per hour" and "total sales volume per hour" as important performance measurements. If the quality of the call is important and low-quality calls tend to result in returned goods because some aspect of the product was not explained well enough by the phone rep, the manager might want to add "rate of returned sales" as a performance measurement.

Once the performance measurements are determined, the manager needs to establish the level of each measurement that phone reps are expected to achieve. For different positions, there will probably be a different set of performance expectations. For example, three sales per hour may be required from an entry-level phone rep, but five from a rep with considerable tenure and additional training.

The performance expectations should be as objective as possible so that the firm can impartially gauge whether or not phone reps are performing at acceptable levels. In addition to being objective, performance expectations must be consistent with the overall goals of the telemarketing group. For example, the performance expectations for each phone rep in an incoming call group might include the following:

1. Answer all calls within three rings.
2. Maintain an average call time of less than three minutes.
3. Sell an average of at least $3,000 worth of products each day.

Obviously, the performance expectations must be reasonable and attainable, but they should require some effort to keep reps from becoming too complacent. The expectations must also make sense financially, from a labor cost standpoint.

Preparing the Job Description

Once the manager has determined the performance expectations, he or she must prepare a detailed job description for each phone rep position in the telemarketing group. The job description should include an itemized listing of the major elements of phone reps' duties and responsibilities, as well as performance expectations. The entire job description, and especially the performance expectations, should be carefully explained to phone reps so they fully understand them. Some managers even give their new phone reps a written quiz to make sure they understand how their performance will be evaluated and exactly what level of performance is expected of them. Others require that each phone rep sign a statement attesting to the fact that he or she fully understands the performance expectations.

Providing Feedback

As important as job knowledge and performance are to a phone rep's success, by themselves they are not enough to guarantee achieving the highest level of efficiency from a telemarketing operation. As the final step in this process, managers need to provide phone reps with frequent performance feedback, both formal and informal, so that they maintain a positive attitude on a continuing basis. Some phone reps may need feedback more frequently than others, either because their performance needs to improve or because they tend to work better with more consistent reinforcement. Formal feedback should be provided at least semiannually and preferably quarterly. Informal feedback, both positive and negative (if needed), should be provided for phone reps at least weekly by their immediate supervisor or manager.

Newly hired phone reps require particular attention with respect to performance feedback. To help assure that they are learning their new positions correctly and are becoming proficient as quickly as possible, the training program should include daily performance feedback for two to six weeks, depending on the degree of difficulty of an operation, followed by weekly feedback for up to six months. In order for this process to be effective, the manager must have completed the necessary research to determine as precisely as possible what level of performance the reps should be attaining at various tenures; meaningful feedback must be based on those levels.

A requisite characteristic of performance expectations is consistency. Phone reps tend to accept performance requirements if they know the expectations are objective and fair, and are being consistently applied to all phone reps in the group. This requires carefully designed performance measurement and reporting systems.

Hiring the right type of phone reps, and managing them by establishing performance expectations and providing feedback, will generally result in good overall performance in a telemarketing group. However, to get the most of those valuable human resources, a firm must also motivate them to achieve higher performance levels.

Motivation

The two most proven motivators for phone reps are recognition and compensation. These may be supplemented or combined with other types of motivation.

Recognition

Surprisingly, many job satisfaction surveys conducted in the telemarketing industry have found that recognition for a job well done and a sense of achievement on the job tend to rate higher than financial compensation in determining employee satisfaction. This assumes, of course, that wages are at least adequate and competitive for the position in the local area. But the main lesson for direct marketers is that they can provide a significant amount of job satisfaction and motivation for relatively little cost.

Recognition programs abound. They can be as simple as listing high achievers in a company or department newsletter, displaying "high performer of the month" plaques, or merely mentioning the names of high performers in employee meetings. The idea is that the firm should take every opportunity to recognize both high performance and substantial improvements in performance by the lower performing phone reps.

Recognition not only provides phone reps with the type of positive reinforcement that most of us seek but also motivates other phone reps to perform well in order to receive that same recognition. For newer or lower performing phone reps, recognition often provides them with the confidence they need to continue believing that attaining higher performance levels is possible.

Compensation

Most phone reps are paid with a combination of a base wage and a variable payment in the form of commission, bonus, or incentive. Generally, wage rates should be based on the type of telemarketing work the phone rep is performing and on competitive wage rates available locally. The adage "You get what you pay for" holds true for phone reps. If a firm offers low wage rates, it tends to attract people with little ambition or ability to perform well or advance in an organization. A higher wage rate will likely attract people who will learn, produce, and earn more quickly. Phone reps who receive higher wages will tend to be more mature, experienced, and stable. In the long run, paying higher wages to attract better phone reps is usually more than justified by lower costs of hiring and training, and avoiding high turnover helps to avoid a tendency toward diluting overall group productivity.

Although recognition can, and does, provide an essential form of motivation, seasoned phone reps may still be profoundly motivated by the ability to earn additional compensation based on their performance. As a starting point, most telemarketing firms offer their phone reps annual or semiannual merit pay increases based on performance evaluations. While this form of compensation increase is generally regarded as necessary for recognition of long-term performance achievement, it does not provide the recognition and reward that tend to motivate phone reps on a more immediate basis.

Pay-for-performance programs that provide extra compensation for performance on a monthly or weekly basis have been found to produce the most sustained impact on phone rep motivation. The pay-for-performance compensation comes typically in the form of incentive bonuses or commissions. If the primary determinant of the compensation is the amount of goods or services sold, the compensation is usually a commission; if the primary determinant is based on other performance criteria, such as productivity and quality measurements, the compensation is usually an incentive bonus.

To be effective, incentive programs must be fair, easy for the phone reps to understand, and easy for the company to administer. They also must provide benefits for both the phone rep and the employer. All factors used to determine the amount of the commission or bonus must be objective and measurable. Phone reps typically dislike pay-for-performance programs with "subjective" elements because they believe such factors may lead to inequities in determining distribution of incentive rewards.

Other Types of Motivation

In addition to ongoing incentive and bonus programs, periodic contests, if well thought-out and organized, can often increase motivation in the short run. Contests in a telemarketing group can be especially effective in building team spirit within the group. Contests can provide prizes for best performance (e.g., most calls completed or highest sales volume) or for most improvement from an existing baseline measurement. They can be designed to recognize and pay individuals, as well as groups or teams, within a telemarketing group. Contests can effectively increase short-term motivation; however, certain rules must be followed to ensure success.

First, prizes must be meaningful in light of the effort required to win. Second, the duration of the contest must be relatively short to ensure high and continued interest. Third, the contest must be fun and fair. Failing to observe these three fundamental rules will usually result in employee apathy and/or burnout. Some of the most effective contests are run for only a single day, with no prior announcement. Contests should never last longer than one month, the rule of thumb being that once the "fun" of the contest subsides, it loses its effectiveness.

Despite their individual effectiveness, none of the recognition and compensation methods for motivating phone reps, addressed singularly, can raise an organization to the level where it wishes to compete. The truly effective and efficient telemarketing operation uses a multifaceted compensation and recognition program to recruit, manage, retain, and motivate its phone reps. For example, the compensation program may consist of a competitive base wage rate (hourly or salaried) monthly commissions based on specific sales amount targets (with increasing commission percentages at higher sales levels), a monthly incentive program based on individual productivity and quality performance, periodic contests, and frequent recognition of the better performers.

To be most effective, a compensation plan should find ways to pay and recognize, not ways not to pay or not to recognize. Motivational efforts that "aim too high" may not only fail but backfire as well, creating an attitude among phone reps that the firm is only trying to take advantage of them. The goals need to be realistic and attainable for most of the phone reps involved.

FTC TELEMARKETING RULES[10]

In 1995 the Federal Trade Commission issued a comprehensive set of rules that will significantly affect all telemarketers. These rules are aimed at curbing telemarketing fraud and abuse by prohibiting certain types of conduct, imposing various oral and written disclosures, prohibiting certain types of misrepresentations, and stopping credit card laundering and other forms of assistance to deceptive telemarketers.

Coverage

The FTC rules adopt an extremely broad definition of telemarketing. For example, they cover the sale of goods or services by telephone as well as by computer modem or any other telephonic medium. As a result, online interactive services as well as traditional telephone sales are covered.

All outbound calls are covered. The rules also cover inbound calls from consumers responding to any direct-mail or other targeted solicitations, with the exception of catalogs. In addition, all inbound calls in the following categories are covered: business ventures, investment opportunities, prize promotions, and credit-related programs.

There is an exemption for inbound calls generated to place an order from a catalog, but only if the person taking the order does not engage in any further solicitation on the phone. Because it is commonly part of any telemarketing script for the operator to inquire as to whether the customer would like to order anything else, there is a severe limitation on the exemption.

Disclosure Requirements

The FTC rules also impose mandatory oral and/or written disclosures. The nature and type of disclosures required depend in part on the type of program being conducted. For example, the sale of business ventures, investment opportunities, and sweepstakes chances are subject to extremely rigorous disclosure requirements.

At the beginning of the call, the caller's first and last name and the fact that it is a sales call must be disclosed. If the solicitation is for a charitable donation, the telemarketer's status as a paid professional fund-raiser and the purpose of the call must be disclosed. In addition, before any request for payment is made, all material information about the offer, including total costs and any material restrictions; the quantity of goods or services offered; and the seller's refund, exchange, or cancellation policies must be disclosed.

Telemarketing programs that include any offer of a prize are affected the most. In addition to the general disclosures, the fact that no purchase is necessary, the retail value of the prize or prizes, and the odds must be disclosed. In addition, before requesting or accepting any payment the marketer must mail a written document to the consumer containing detailed disclosure about the prize offer and must obtain a signed acknowledgment of receipt of this written disclosure from the consumer before seeking or accepting payment. The written disclosures must be printed on one page in no less than 10-point type and must be sent in an envelope containing no other enclosures. This written requirement, which also applies to investment opportunities, will effectively prevent telemarketers from using sweepstakes in connection with their offer.

Prohibited Misrepresentation

The FTC rules contain a prohibition on misrepresenting any information required to be disclosed by the rule and any material aspects about the solicitation or the offered goods or services.

Prohibited Conduct

The FTC rules also prohibit certain types of business practices and conduct, which would severely alter many common business practices. For example, the rules prohibit obtaining any money or debiting a customer's account without express authorization, directing a courier to pick up payment from a customer, resoliciting customers before the initial transaction is complete and fulfilled, calling consumers more than once every three months to sell the same thing, failing to distribute all prizes offered in a prize promotion within 18 months of the offer, and calling consumers who have indicated they do not want to be called. The rules also restrict the time of day during which calls can be made to between 8:00 AM and 9:00 PM.

Assisting Telemarketing Fraud

In keeping with its stated commitment of expanding the net of liability to include those who provide support services to a telemarketer, the FTC has ruled that anyone who provides substantial assistance to telemarketers may be potentially liable if the program is ultimately found to be unlawful. Examples of what constitutes "substantial assistance" include receiving consideration for delivering a testimonial or endorsement, or for providing customer lists or other fulfillment materials. The rule also contains provisions relating to credit card laundering, programs for investment opportunities and business ventures, and programs relating to credit and credit repair and loan services.

SUMMARY

Telemarketing represents the integrated and systematic application of telecommunications and information processing technologies and management systems. The objective is to reach customers in a personalized interaction that better meets customer needs and improves cost effectiveness. A well-planned telephone marketing program makes use of the latest technologies, including communications hardware and software, particularly database technologies.

Telemarketing methods are categorized as inbound, where customers are calling a firm to place an order or to request more information or for customer service, and outbound, where the firm is calling customers and prospects to make a sale or to offer information which it hopes will lead to a sale. Many firms are involved in both types of telemarketing. For any company, how much emphasis it should place on one or the other type of telemarketing depends on its products or services.

The basic decision variables for telephone marketing are the same as those for any other direct marketing programs: the offer, creative, timing/sequencing, customer service, and implementation. However, a major uniqueness of telemarketing is its use of scripts that serve the same function that advertising serves, but on a call-by-call basis. Despite their drawbacks, completely scripted telephone contacts are frequently necessary because there are many situations in which good scripts delivered by callers with appropriate training are the correct approach. Script development is usually necessary because, in the professional telephone selling process, each call is a sales presentation. These calls should include the basics: introduction, qualification of the prospect, presentation of the sales message, response to questions or objections, and closure.

An important aspect of telephone marketing is understanding how it can best be integrated with other media. Both inbound and outbound telemarketing enjoy a synergy with other media because responses to a media combination will be greater than responses to only one medium. One reason for this is that people do not respond in the same way to messages in different media. A printed ad does not convey the same set of images as a person's voice elicits on a telephone. These differences argue for the use of a media mix to create varied yet mutually reinforcing impressions.

After a firm has chosen to institute a telemarketing program, it must decide if it should execute its own telemarketing program in-house or use a telemarketing service bureau or begin it at a service bureau and then transfer the effort in-house. Service Bureaus are useful if a firm does not have the resources to handle a telemarketing campaign; they provide production-oriented operations that specialize in handling high call volumes, whether incoming or outgoing. However, every situation is unique and requires a review of the needs and requirements of the firm to determine the advantages and disadvantages.

Effective telemarketing operations are based on four primary elements: planning, people, process, and tools. How well a telemarketing operation fares in each of these areas may well determine its telemarketing success. Most telemarketing operations tend to do well with planning, processes, and tools because they spend time and resources planning their telemarketing operations and developing appropriate processes and selecting and implementing various phone and information systems to support those activities.

The most common problem of telemarketing operations is to more effectively and efficiently use the people they employ. In that sense, improvements in a telemarketing operation involves directing and guiding phone representatives to achieve maximum results by creating a drive or desire on the part of the reps which improves their performance.

The Federal Trade Commission has issued a set of rules aimed at curbing telemarketing fraud and abuse by prohibiting certain types of conduct, imposing various oral and written disclosures, prohibiting certain types of misrepresentations, and stopping credit card laundering and other forms of assistance to deceptive telemarketers. The rules adopt a broad definition of telemarketing. As a result, online interactive services as well as traditional telephone sales are covered.

REVIEW QUESTIONS

1. What is telemarketing? What is it designed to do? In what ways do direct marketers use telemarketing? How is telemarketing integrated with other forms of direct marketing?
2. What is outbound telemarketing? What is inbound telemarketing? How do telemarketers use them to sell products or services?
3. What is a telemarketing script? What is it designed to do? How do the scripts used to market to consumers differ from those used to market to businesses? What are the major differences between a structured and an unstructured script?
4. What are the major issues and considerations involved in choosing to execute a telemarketing program in-house versus using a telemarketing service bureau? What are the advantages and disadvantages of each choice?
5. How does a telemarketing operation operate at peak efficiency and effectiveness? In particular, what are the issues associated with managing and motivating people to achieve telemarketing success? How can managers ensure that phone representatives are used effectively?

NOTES

1. Stanley Leo Fidel, *Startup Telemarketing* (New York: John Wiley & Sons, 1987), pp. 12–21.
2. Adapted from Elaine Santoro, "Beyond the Gas Pump," *Direct Marketing,* March 1991, pp. 28–29.
3. Adapted from "Inbound, Outbound Telemarketing Keeps Ryder Sales in Fast Lane," *Direct Marketing,* July 1995, pp. 34–36.
4. Mary Lou Roberts and Paul D. Berger, *Direct Marketing Management* (Englewood Cliffs, NJ: Prentice Hall, 1989), pp. 5–8.
5. Bob Stone, and John Wyman, *Successful Telemarketing,* 2nd ed. (Lincolnwood, IL: NTC Business Books, 1992), p. 5.
6. Fidel, *Startup Telemarketing,* pp. 35–38.
7. Ibid, pp. 39–40.
8. Ibid, pp. 33–35.
9. Adapted from Kevin Reichley, "World Class Telemarketing," *Direct Marketing,* May 1996, pp. 44–47.
10. Adapted from Linda Goldstein, "FTC Telemarketing Rules Issued," *Telemarketing* 13 no. 11 (May 1995), pp. 38–39.

SOURCES

"Advanced Call Center Technology Helps Bell Canada Regain Market Share." *Direct Marketing,* March 1996, pp. 62–65.

BENCIN, RICHARD L. *Encyclopedia of Telemarketing.* Englewood Cliffs, N.J.: Prentice Hall, 1989.

________. "When to Use Telemarketing . . . and When Not To!" In *Readings & Cases in Direct Marketing,* ed. Herbert E. Brown and Bruce Buskirk. Lincolnwood, IL: NTC Business Books, 1989, pp. 165–168.

BRADBURY, GEORGE T., AND JUDY SHAPIRO. "Outbound Telemarketing." In *The Direct Marketing Handbook,* 2nd ed., ed. Ed Nash. New York: McGraw-Hill, 1992, pp. 319–29.

BURSEY, DONNA. "Targeting Small Businesses for Telemarketing and Mail Order Sales." *Direct Marketing,* September 1995, pp. 18–20.

CAIN, RITA MARIE. "The State of Telemarketing Regulation in the States." *Journal of Direct Marketing* 9 (Autumn 1995), pp. 76–83.

CHESTERS, SARA. "Defusing the Demographic Bomb." *Direct Marketing,* May 1991, pp. 35–38.

Direct Marketing Association. *Statistical Fact Book 1996.* New York: Direct Marketing Association, 1996.

FIDEL, STANLEY LEO. *Startup Telemarketing.* New York: John Wiley & Sons, 1987.

GOLDSTEIN, LINDA. "FTC Telemarketing Rules Issued." *Telemarketing,* 13 no. 11 (May 1995), pp. 38–39.

GOTTLIEB, MAG. "Telemarketing and the Law." *Direct Marketing,* February 1994, pp. 22–23.

HAWTHORNE, TIMOTHY R. "Infomercial Telemarketing: 14 Keys to Success." *Telemarketing Magazine,* 11 no. 10 (April 1993), pp. 83–85.

"Inbound, Outbound Telemarketing Keeps Ryder Sales in Fast Lane." *Direct Marketing,* July 1995, pp. 34–36.

Jones, Lynn. "This Is Getting Complicated." *Direct,* January 1996, pp. 53–54.

Katzenstein, Herbert, and Williams Sachs. *Direct Marketing,* 2nd ed. New York: Macmillan, 1992.

Kordahl, Eugene B. "Inbound Telemarketing." In *The Direct Marketing Handbook,* 2nd ed., ed. Ed Nash. New York: McGraw-Hill, 1992, pp. 330–40.

Lewis, Robert. "Tempting Telecommunications Technologies." *Direct Marketing,* February 1991, pp. 55–57.

Morrall, Katherine. "Smart Strategies in Telemarketing," *Bank Marketing,* 27, no. 10 (October 1995), pp. 15–20.

Reichley, Kevin. "World Class Telemarketing." *Direct Marketing,* May 1996, pp. 44–47.

________. "Telemarketing Programs Require Periodic Evaluation." *Direct Marketing,* September 1995, pp. 14–15.

Roberts, Mary Lou, and Paul D. Berger. *Direct Marketing Management.* Englewood Cliffs, NJ: Prentice Hall, 1989.

Roman, Ernan. "Integrated Telemarketing: Sheathing the Double-Edged Sword." In *Beyond 2000: The Future of Direct Marketing,* ed. Jerry I. Reitman. Lincolnwood, IL: NTC Business Books, 1994, pp. 139–147.

Rubel, Chad. "Striffer Rules for Telemarketing as U.S. Cracks Down on Fraud." *Advertising Age,* February 26, 1996, pp. 1, 8.

Santoro, Elaine. "Beyond the Gas Pump." *Direct Marketing,* March 1991, pp. 28–29.

Stone, Bob. "How to Get More Orders." In *Readings & Cases in Direct Marketing,* ed. Herbert E. Brown and Bruce Buskirk. Lincolnwood, IL: NTC Business Books, 1989, pp. 168–71.

________. *Successful Direct Marketing Methods,* 5th ed. Lincolnwood, IL: NTC Books, 1995.

Stone, Bob, and John Wyman. "The Mathematics of Telemarketing." In *Readings & Cases in Direct Marketing,* ed. Herbert E. Brown and Bruce Buskirk. Lincolnwood, IL: NTC Business Books, 1989, pp. 172–180.

________. *Successful Telemarketing,* 2nd ed. Lincolnwood, IL: NTC Business Books, 1992.

Symon, Jeff. "The Blossoming of Telemarketing." *Direct Marketing,* May 1991, pp. 47–48.

Wetzler, Andrew. "Telemarketing Tactics." *Direct Marketing,* January 1992, pp. 17–18.

APPENDIX 11A: TELEMARKETING AND THE LAW[1]

Forty-nine states met in legislative session in 1993 (Kentucky's legislature does not meet in odd-numbered years). Telephone marketing was the subject of a variety of bills in several states, as shown on the accompanying chart (see Table A.1). An *x* indicates that legislation on that topic was introduced in a state; an asterisk (*) indicates that a bill was enacted into law. Telephone legislation in the states generally falls into the following broad categories.

Asterisk versus In-House Suppression

An "asterisk" bill is legislation that would typically require a telephone company or the state government to maintain a list of persons who object to receiving unsolicited telephone solicitation calls. Marketers would then be responsible for obtaining the list, often at a cost, and purging those names from their calling lists. These laws can be difficult to enforce, given the interstate nature of marketing, and can expose sellers to the risk of litigation if the lists are not kept up-to-date and consumers are inadvertently contacted against their wishes.

In the wake of enactment of the federal Telephone Consumer Protection Act, the introduction of asterisk legislation is falling off in favor of legislation conforming to the federal law, which mandates in-house suppression. In-house suppression means that marketers may contact consumers on their calling lists. However, if the caller requests that the marketer not contact him or her again, the marketer must remove that name from company calling lists and ensure that the consumer's name is not rented or otherwise disseminated to other marketers. In-house suppression is supported by the Direct Marketing Association (DMA) as a voluntary alternative to the asterisk system. As mentioned previously, in-house suppression is mandated by federal law and is widely accepted by state legislatures as preferable to a state-by-state patchwork of "do-not-call" laws.

Registration

"Registration" legislation is a law that seeks to require the registration of telephone solicitors in a state, generally with the attorney general or secretary of state. These registration provisions often include bonding requirements, submission of scripts and/or names of employees, and other administrative devices designed to help the states create a "paper trail" to track fraudulent marketers.

The DMA works with state legislators and law enforcement officials to ensure that legitimate marketers operating in good faith are not unduly penalized in the states' laudable efforts to crack down on fraud.

TABLE A.1. Telephone Legislation Introduced as of December 1, 1993

	Asterisk	In-House System	Registration	Hours	Contracts/Cancel	Record/Monitor
Alabama			x		x	
Alaska	x		*		*	*
Arizona			x			x
Arkansas			*			*
California			*			*
Colorado			*		x	
Connecticut	x	x	x		x	
Delaware		x				
Florida			*			
Georgia						
Hawaii						x
Idaho			*			
Illinois				x		x
Indiana						
Iowa						
Kansas						
Kentucky						
Louisiana			*			
Maine						
Maryland	x			x		
Massachusetts					x	x
Michigan		x		x		
Minnesota	x					
Mississippi			*	*	x	
Missouri					x	
Montana			x			
Nebraska		*	x			
Nevada			*			x
New Hampshire	x					
New Jersey						
New Mexico						
New York	x	x	x	x	x	x
North Carolina				x		
North Dakota			x		x	
Ohio						
Oklahoma						
Oregon	x		x			
Pennsylvania						
Rhode Island						x
South Carolina						
South Dakota						
Tennesee						
Texas			*			x
Utah			*			
Vermont					x	
Virginia						
Washington	x		x			
West Virginia						
Wisconsin						
Wyoming						

Hours

Hours legislation seeks to restrict the hours during which telephone-marketing calls may be made. The laws generally seek to limit the hours to no later than 9 PM local time. These provisions are supported by the DMA.

Contracts/Cancellation

Contracts and cancellation bills seek to prohibit the completion of some types of telephone sales unless a written contract is signed and returned by the consumer. The DMA works with state legislatures to ensure that marketers who offer consumers a right of examination and return in exchange for a refund are exempt from contract provisions.

Recording/Monitoring

In response to labor complaints, many state legislators introduce legislation that would prohibit or restrict the practice of service observation of customer service employees who work via the telephone. The DMA urges legislators to enact laws that protect employees from illegal or abusive use of information collected during service observation while at the same time protecting employers' rights to monitor their employees' contact with the public. This is best achieved by notifying employees in advance that they may be monitored and specifying why and how the information will be used.

APPENDIX 11B: TELEMARKETING SAMPLE SCRIPT[2]

This section contains a sample telemarketing script. In order to understand its context, a brief introduction to the company using the script is provided.

The Company

VIDEX/VIDEOTRAIN, INC., is a leader in the field of audiovisual (AV) corporate education. It offers the broadest spectrum of film strips, slides, cartridges, videocassettes (both stop-action and full-motion), and allied materials available to train business professionals in corporations across the United States and worldwide.

VIDEOTRAIN, the original product line, is a name synonymous with good but elementary training programs, one recognized by most executives from their basic business education. Primary emphasis is on establishing VIDEX as the innovative producer of consistently superior advanced AV products, without losing the positive association of the VIDEOTRAIN reputation. To that end, VIDEX continues its commitment (1) to create a high-quality, creatively produced AV product, a "no-frills" didactic approach packing a great deal of technical information and complex skills-teaching without sacrificing professionalism, and (2) to present state-of-the-art information by utilizing the nation's top experts in each field as consultants. Business specialists are on hand as in-house consultants for any technical questions or comments from executives.

Of the thousands of companies in the United States, 3,500 are already VIDEX customers. The remaining companies represent a vast, largely untapped market; many of them may have heard of VIDEX or purchased products previously, but some of the latter have gone two or three years without follow-up. Some regular customers may buy one to four times a year, while others have not bought for several years.

Sales are currently engendered through inbound calls; outbound calls are made when time allows, and not according to any fully adhered-to system.

VIDEX wants to expand exposure to its products with an aggressive telemarketing program directed to the target company's president or director of training or other title variation, such as director of marketing or human resources. The goal is to reach the decision maker(s) involved in the selection, purchase, and use of AV training materials.

Because corporations vary greatly in size, the number of decision makers may also vary greatly: A small company may have a single decision maker in complete charge of the budget, while a large company may have a substantial budget but many decision makers. The firm is targeting those companies with 25 to 500 employees.

The usual approach to a sale is through a 14-day preview of an AV film or videocassette for a $25 fee, with follow-up in two weeks. This fee is being waived, in hopes that more previews will be converted to sales and that the current preview-to-sale rate, now at 25 percent, will be increased by 10 percent.

VIDEX has produced over 1,000 AV education and training materials used in basic business education, retraining, upgrading skills, and continuing education. Each year the company brings to market 50 to 70 new programs, introduced by way of catalogs, direct mail announcements, and public relations news releases. A selection of seven motion video packages, consisting of 2 to 12 individual titles, forms the nucleus of this telemarketing effort. The basic cost of each film or video is $395.

The objectives of the telemarketing effort are sevenfold:

1. To expand VIDEX's active customer base by 3,500 (doubling the current base).
2. To increase revenue by $2.5 million over the next 12 months.
3. To improve preview-to-purchase rate: for films, from 10 percent to 20 percent; for videos, from 25 percent to 35 percent.
4. To develop a consistently successful tracking system.
5. To integrate optimally the telemarketing arm with existing departments.
6. To gather research data for future product development and marketing strategy.
7. To build awareness of VIDEX's highly professional products and services.

Call Flowchart

The call flowchart is actually a road map that shows how an ideal telemarketing call should progress from initial contact to close. Every stage performs a certain role in taking the caller to a successful conclusion.

The key points in each stage are identified for reference. In essence, the call flowchart contains the skeleton of the telemarketing script and should not be expected to contain specific phrases, buzzwords, and dialogue that is more fully developed in the script (see Exhibit A.1).

EXHIBIT A.1. VIDEX Call Flowchart

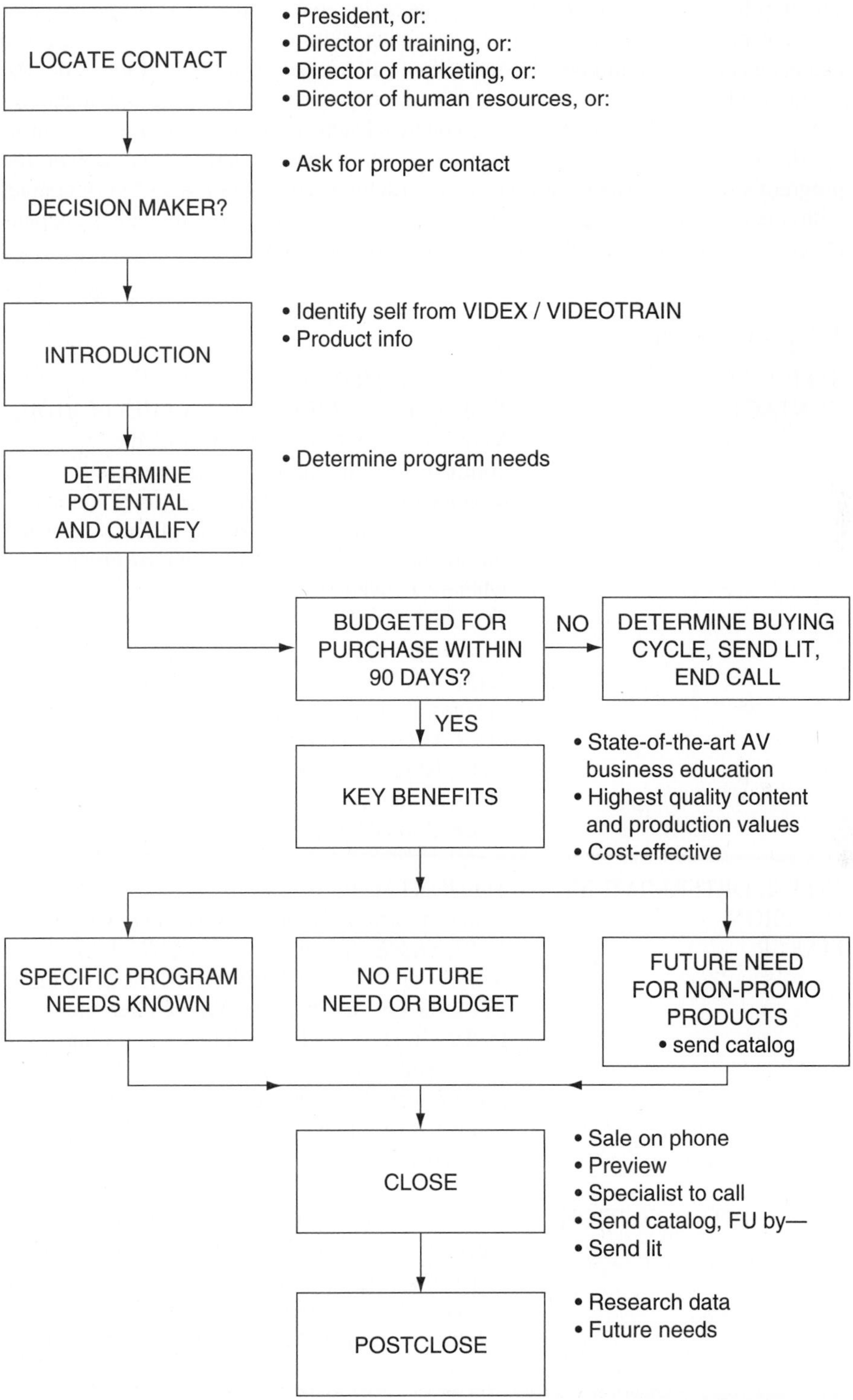
LOCATE CONTACT
• President, or:
• Director of training, or:
• Director of marketing, or:
• Director of human resources, or:
DECISION MAKER?
• Ask for proper contact
INTRODUCTION
• Identify self from VIDEX / VIDEOTRAIN
• Product info
DETERMINE POTENTIAL AND QUALIFY
• Determine program needs
BUDGETED FOR PURCHASE WITHIN 90 DAYS?
NO
DETERMINE BUYING CYCLE, SEND LIT, END CALL
YES
KEY BENEFITS
• State-of-the-art AV business education
• Highest quality content and production values
• Cost-effective
SPECIFIC PROGRAM NEEDS KNOWN
NO FUTURE NEED OR BUDGET
FUTURE NEED FOR NON-PROMO PRODUCTS
• send catalog
CLOSE
• Sale on phone
• Preview
• Specialist to call
• Send catalog, FU by—
• Send lit
POSTCLOSE
• Research data
• Future needs

Telephone Script Introduction

The step-by-step structure of the telephone script enables almost any type of caller to adapt his or her technique to the established flow of the script. The specific language can and should be adjusted to fit a caller's personal comfort level, but the integrity of the steps as outlined should be preserved. They assure a natural progression from start to finish. The sequenced steps protect against loss of control by the caller and prevent conversations of excessive length that defeat the program's purpose. Most important, the structured approach makes every contact with a lead as compelling as it can possibly be, no matter how the caller happens to feel. It guarantees an effective presentation consistently.

Telephone Script

STEP 1: LOCATE CONTACT.	TO RECEPTIONIST: "Hello, this is (*FIRST, LAST NAME*) of VIDEX. May I speak with the president of the company?" (*OR:* director of training; *OR:* director of marketing; *OR:* director of human resources; or other appropriate office as indicated on prospect's card; use full name of prospect whenever given.) TO OFFICE SECRETARY: "Good morning (afternoon), this is (*FIRST, LAST NAME*) of VIDEX, the AV specialists in business training. I'd like to speak to (*NAME ON CARD*). Is he (she) in for a minute? (IF NOT, NOTE change on contact form—not included here.) Proceed to STEP 2.
STEP 2: DETERMINE IF DECISION MAKER.	TO CONTACT: "Good morning (afternoon), (*FIRST NAME, LAST NAME*) this is (*FIRST NAME, LAST NAME)* of VIDEX/VIDEOTRAIN, a division of SPRING ENTERPRISES. We've been the leaders in state-of-the-art business training for 10 years. You're the person responsible for selecting AV products for training, right?" (Note on contact form other decision makers in this area.) Proceed to STEP 3.
STEP 3: INTRODUCTION.	"We're very excited about our new live-action videos that teach skills in actual business situations. These cassettes were developed using the nation's top experts—so you're safe in knowing you're getting the best in specialized training.

"We have some excellent opportunities to offer you today—but first, let me update my records."
Proceed to STEP 4.

STEP 4: DETERMINE POTENTIAL.

"Tell me a little about your training programs. Overall, what do you like about them?" _______
"What would you like to improve?" _________
____
"What do you have coming up in terms of specific training?"
____
____
"Orientation?"__________________________
"Retraining?" __________________________
NOTE responses to all of above on contact form. "Do you keep records?" _____________
"What kind of budget do you have?" ________
____
NOTE responses to all of above on contact form.
"If you got really excited about our videos, and saw that they really suited your needs, would you have the budget available within the next 90 days?"_____________________________
____
IF NO:
"When would the money open up?"
NOTE on contact form.
"If we could demonstrate that it was more cost-effective to use our videos in your training program, would that free up the budget?"
NOTE on contact form.

STEP 5: SUMMARY.

"Let's see . . ." (Read back information and qualifications you have recorded on contact form; e.g., "You will be covering nonverbal communication skills next fall, your budget is open," etc.)
"I know something about you. Now let me tell you a little more about us. Here's what makes us the innovative leaders in AV training programs:

"*STATE-OF-THE-ART HEALTH CARE INFORMATION USING THE BEST CONSULTANTS IN THE COUNTRY.* All our programs are developed with top experts recommended by specialty organizations and professional associations. Is expert training important to you?

"*HIGHEST QUALITY CONTENT AND PRODUCTION VALUES.* We spend thousands and thousands of dollars to assure the highest caliber result. How does that sound?

"In fact . . . over $2 million per year is spent on new programming.

"COST-EFFECTIVE; consider the dramatic savings possible with AV programs: You can play them again and again so they can be used to train your whole staff at very little cost, right?

"Your people can view them at their convenience, so it doesn't interfere with their work schedules. That's a plus, too, isn't it?

"Your staff can stop and start the tape so they learn at their own individual rate. Isn't that effective?

"Also, they can supplement your training staff and increase learning effectiveness. Doesn't that make sense?"

Proceed to STEP 6.

STEP 6: CLOSE.

A. IF SPECIFIC PROGRAM NEEDS HAVE BEEN MENTIONED:

"Since you say that you have need for one nonverbal communication, I suggest you use our NVC series. It's a package of three cassettes. You can choose the whole package, or individual titles such as 'USING BODY LANGUAGE TO SELL.' The package sells for $750, or you can choose individual videos at $295 each." (Note: Refer to comments on each package on page 00.)

"Or, if you choose five videos, we will give you three free. Which do you prefer? VIDEX has a 30-day return policy—the most liberal preview/return policy in the industry. So you can feel safe, right?

"Which do you use—Beta or VHS or ¾? . . . Fine. I'll ship your cassettes out today."

B. IF NO SPECIFIC PROGRAM IS MENTIONED:

"Let me tell you about our new releases." (Note: refer to comments on package description sheet, p. 00.)

"Which one of these would you be most interested in reviewing?"

NOTE on contact form.

"The package sells for $750, or you can select individual titles for $295. Or, if you buy five, we'll give you three free. What's better for you—the whole program, or individual videos?

"VIDEX has a 30-day return policy—the most liberal preview policy in the industry. Do you use Beta, VHS, or ¾? . . . Fine. I'll ship your cassettes out today."

C. IF DON'T PURCHASE OVER THE PHONE:
"I can understand that; still I'd really like to get the video cassette(s) out today for you to preview. By the way, there's no charge for this, and you have 14 days to look at them. Fair enough?

"If you preview a video and like it, is there any reason you wouldn't decide to keep it? I'll be calling you in a couple of weeks."

D. IF NEEDS MORE TECHNICAL INFORMATION:
"I'll be happy to have one of our specialists get back to you by (*date*) to answer your questions."

E. WANTS TO SEE CATALOG:
"I'll send the catalog out today and see that you're called by (*date*)."

F. LAST RESORT:
Thank politely, send literature.

STEP 7: POSTCLOSE—RESEARCH AND FUTURE NEEDS.

"Briefly, would you tell me who else is involved in making decisions about AV material?"
(NOTE on contact form; ask to be transferred, *IF FEASIBLE*.)
"Who is your supplier of AV materials, if you don't purchase from VIDEX? Is there any particular reason you HAVEN'T chosen VIDEX products?"
(NOTE on contact form.)
"When you see our catalog, you're going to find many programs that will be perfect for future needs. We'll be checking back soon to talk about them. I know you'll feel good about VIDEX products."
BACK UP DATA.

Objection— "We don't have the money."

Answers— "I can certainly understand that, and still your people could use the training, right? If money were no object, which videos would you want?" (Write names down.)
"Good. You send your people to seminars don't you? What about finding some money in your seminar and travel budget? You know, we're only talking about $295 for training you can use again and again and again, right?"
"I'll get that out to you and you'll have 30 days to find the money—fair enough?"

Objection— "Still too expensive."

Answers— "Here are some other ways we can help you save money."
"If you trade in your old films with similar titles for the new videos, we'll arrange a $75 discount on each video. Do you have any old films that you don't use very much?"
"Also, every five programs you buy, we'll give you three more programs free. That's a savings of $885, isn't it?"

Objection— "What if it's not what I need?"

Answers— "Seeing is believing—that's the beauty of the preview program. If what you see doesn't suit your needs, simply send the videos back to us within 14 days, and don't pay for them. What could be fairer than that?"

Objection— "What about outdated material?"

Answers— "Our state-of-the-art information is produced using top consultants in every area, with programs geared to today's business environment and the latest technology."
"If a video is revised within a year after purchase, we'll give you an equal trade. Does that make you feel better?"

Questions and Responses

Question— "What about service? And delivery?"

Responses— "We have 800 number phone lines to serve you, with representatives who'll respond immediately to your needs."
"We have a 30-day return policy, and a superior shipping record. We ship UPS for delivery within two weeks. If you request it, we can ship UPS BLUE for emergencies (at your expense, of course)."

APPENDIX 11C: DIRECT MARKETING ASSOCIATION GUIDELINES FOR TELEMARKETING[3]

The Direct Marketing Association's *Guidelines for Marketing by Telephone* are intended to provide individuals and organizations involved in direct telephone marketing with accepted principles of conduct that are consistent with the ethical guidelines recommended for other marketing media and with all federal and state laws and regulations. These specific Guidelines reflect the responsibility of DMA and telephone marketers to consumers, the community, and the industry.

Telephone marketers should be aware of DMA's *Guidelines for Ethical Business Practice,* the more comprehensive guidelines for all direct marketing. The guidelines are self-regulatory. Telephone marketers are urged to honor them in spirit and in letter. In addition, all telephone marketers should be familiar with the business compliance guides involving telephone marketing practices, for instance, "Complying with the Telemarketing Sales Rule" and "A Business Guide to the FTC's Mail or Telephone Order Merchandise Rule."

These guidelines do not cover all of the regulatory requirements that apply to marketing by telephone. Persons who engage in marketing by telephone should take appropriate steps to ensure that their practices comply with all relevant federal, state, and local laws and regulations, including the Telephone Consumer Protection Act (TCPA), the Telephone Disclosure and Dispute Resolution Act (TDDRA), and the Telemarketing Sales Rule.

These guidelines are part of DMA's general philosophy that self-regulatory measures are preferable to governmental mandates whenever possible. Self-regulatory actions are more readily adaptable to changing technologies and economic and social conditions. Further, self-regulation encourages widespread use of sound business practices.

Prompt Disclosure: Identity of Seller/Purpose of Call

Article 1

When calling a consumer, telephone marketers should promptly disclose the name of the seller, the name of the individual caller, and the primary purpose of the contact. Additional information to allow contact with the seller should also be provided.

All documents relating to the telephone marketing offer and shipment should sufficiently identify the full name, street address, or telephone number of the seller so that the consumer may contact the seller by mail or by telephone.

If a telephone marketer is placing or receiving calls on behalf of a seller, and the consumer inquires about the telephone marketer's identity or affiliation to the seller, the telephone marketer should disclose its own name, address, and telephone number as well.

Honesty

Article 2

All offers should be clear, honest, and complete so that the consumer may know the exact nature of what is being offered and the commitment involved in the placing of an order or donating to a charity. Before making an offer, telephone marketers should be prepared to substantiate any claims or offers made. Advertisements or specific claims which are untrue, misleading, deceptive, fraudulent, or unjustly disparaging of competitors should not be used.

No one should make offers or solicitations in the guise of research or a survey when the real intent is to sell products or services or to raise funds.

Disclosure of Terms of the Offer/Tactics

Article 3

Prior to asking consumers for payment authorization, telephone marketers should disclose the cost of the merchandise or service and all terms and conditions, including payment plans, the availability of refund and cancellation policies, limitations on use, and the amount or existence of any extra charges such as shipping and handling and insurance. At no time should high-pressure tactics be utilized.

Reasonable Hours

Article 4

Telephone contacts must be made during reasonable hours, as specified by federal and state laws and regulations.

Use of Automated Dialing Equipment

Article 5

When using automated dialing equipment for any reason, telephone marketers should only use equipment which allows the telephone to immediately release the line when the called party terminates the connection.

ADRMPS (Automatic Dialers and Recorded Message Players) and prerecorded messages should be used only in accordance with tariffs, federal, state, and local laws, FCC regulations, and these Guidelines. Telephone marketers should use a live operator to obtain a consumer's permission before delivering a recorded solicitation message.

When using any automated dialing equipment to reach a multi-line location, the equipment should release each line used before connecting to another.

Taping of Conversations

Article 6

Taping of telephone conversations made by telephone marketers should only be conducted with notice to or consent of all parties, or the use of a beeping device, as required by applicable federal and state laws and regulations.

Monitoring

Article 7

Monitoring of telephone marketing and customer relations conversations should be conducted for purposes of training, quality assurance, and to ensure compliance with consumer protection laws and regulations. All employees should be informed of call monitoring, should be made fully aware of why and how call monitoring is done, and should be informed of the results of any monitoring.

Name Removal/Restricted Contacts

Article 8

Marketers should remove consumers' names from telephone marketing lists upon consumer request and at no charge. Marketers should maintain and suppress names of consumers who do not want to be called as part of their in-house suppression practices and in accordance with applicable federal and state laws and regulations. Prior to the use of any outbound calling list of consumers, marketers should use the DMA Telephone Preference Service and, when applicable, the DMA Mail Preference Service name-removal lists. Names found on such suppression lists should not be rented, sold, or exchanged.

A telephone marketer should not knowingly call anyone who has an unlisted or unpublished telephone number, or a telephone number for which the called party must pay the charges except in instances where the number was provided by the consumer to that marketer.

Random dialing techniques, whether manual or automated, in which identification of those parties to be called is left to chance should not be used in sales and marketing solicitations.

Sequential dialing techniques, whether a manual or automated process, in which selection of those parties to be called is based on the location of their telephone numbers in a sequence of telephone numbers should not be used.

Collection and Transfer of Data

Article 9

Consumers who provide data that may be rented, sold, or exchanged for marketing purposes should be informed promptly and periodically thereafter of the potential for the rental, sale, or exchange of such data and of the opportunity to opt-out of the marketing process.

Consumer requests regarding restrictions of the collection, rental, sale, or exchange of data relating to them should be honored.

Telephone marketers using Automatic Number Identification (ANI) should not re-use or sell, without customer consent, telephone numbers gained from ANI except where a prior business relationship exists for the sale of directly related goods or services.

Promotions for Response by 800, 888, and 900 Numbers

Article 10

Promotions for response by 800 and 888 numbers should be used only when there is no charge to the consumer for the call itself and when there is no transfer from a toll-free number to a pay call.

Promotions for response by 900 numbers or any other type of pay-per-call program should clearly and conspicuously disclose all charges for the call. A preamble at the beginning of a 900 or other pay-per-call should include the nature of the service or program, charge per minute and the estimated total charge for the call, as well as the name, address, and telephone number of the sponsor. The caller should also be given the option to disconnect the call at any time during the preamble without incurring any charge.

The 900 number or other pay-per-call should only use equipment that ceases accumulating time and charges immediately upon disconnection by the caller.

Children

Article 11

Because children are generally less experienced in their rights as consumers, telephone marketers should be especially sensitive to the obligations and responsibilities involved when dealing with them. Offers suitable only for adults should not be made to children.

Pay-per-call services should not be directed to children under 12, unless the service is a "bona fide educational service." For promotions directed to consumers between the ages of 12 and 18, the advertising and the call preamble should clearly disclose that parental or guardian permission should be obtained.

Prompt Delivery

Article 12

Telephone marketers should abide by the FTC regulation regarding the prompt shipment of prepaid merchandise, the Mail or Telephone Order Merchandise (Thirty-Day) Rule. As a normal business procedure, telephone marketers are urged to ship all orders as soon as practical.

Laws, Codes, and Regulations

Article 13

Telephone marketers should operate in accordance with the laws and regulations of the United States Postal Service, the Federal Communications Commission, the Federal Trade Commission, the Federal Reserve Board, and other applicable federal, state, and local laws governing advertising, marketing practices, and the transaction of business by mail, telephone, print and broadcast media, or any other media.

NOTES

1. Adapted from Mag Gottleib, "Telemarketing and the Law," *Direct Marketing,* February 1994, pp. 22–23.
2. Adapted from Stanley Leo Fidel, *Startup Telemarketing* (New York: John Wiley & Sons, 1987), pp. 227–43.
3. Source: Ethics Department, Direct Marketing Association, Inc.; 1111 19th Street, N.W., Suite 1100; Washington, DC 20036-3603.

CHAPTER 12

Direct-Response Television

OBJECTIVES

1. To describe how direct marketers use television in selling their products and services.
2. To examine what direct-response television advertisements are designed to do and why that is important to direct marketers.
3. To present the different types of direct-response television tools and explain how they operate.
4. To define and explain the terms *ratings, reach, frequency, continuity*, and *gross rating points* and to explain their role in television media planning.

INTRODUCTION

In the 1970s and 1980s, marketers discovered that direct-response television advertising was a useful if not innovative medium. This type of advertising has several features that make it particularly attractive. First, it is accountable; firms know exactly how many sales result from the dollars spent. Second, firms can fine-tune a direct-response campaign by monitoring daily response rates when the advertising is airing. This type of direct marketing can also use one commercial to make more than one sale because a club or continuity approach, with or without membership commitments, encourages customers to accept regular monthly product shipments.

The direct marketing uses of television include direct response and support, infomercials, and home shopping channels. Like any other direct-response medium, television can be used for sales or lead generation. When it is used to generate sales, those who respond to the programming place an order, but when they ask for more information, they provide a lead for the firm in its pursuit of sales. Once someone requests information because of a televised program, that person can be further marketed to via telemarketing and direct mail. Direct-response television can also be used to support other forms of direct marketing.

Exhibit 12.1 shows a lead-generation ad for Volkswagen. This ad, which ran on British television, encourages viewers to call a phone number and obtain more information about a car deal. The viewer is not expected to purchase the car based only on what is said in the ad. Rather, he or she is expected to be intrigued enough about the car to have an interest in more information.

EXHIBIT 12.1. Lead-Generation Ad for Volkswagen

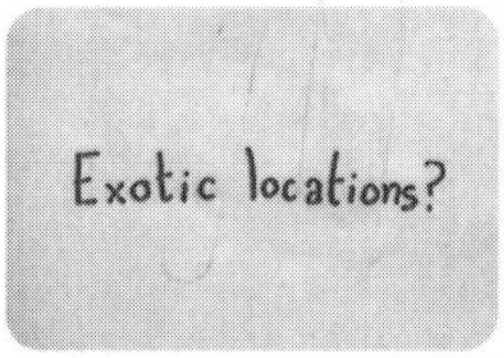

1. *Video:* A spot resembling a home video. Super: "Exotic locations?" *Audio:* Spirited music throughout the film.

2. *Video:* Behind a toy car, a Golf, a number of picture postcards sliding past.

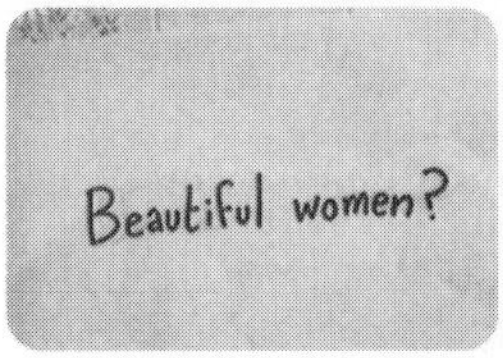

3. Cut to handwritten super: "Beautiful women?"

4. Cut to a Barbie doll rather unceremoniously placed on top of the toy car. A few soap bubble float by, apparently to enhance the atmosphere.

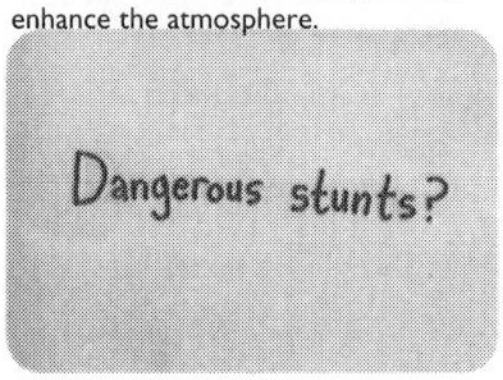

5. Super: "Dangerous stunts?"

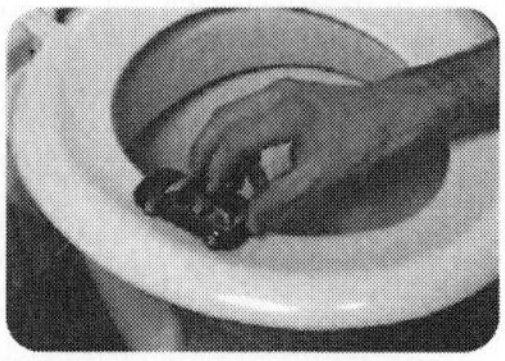

6. (Cut) A hand pushing the toy car along a toilet seat.

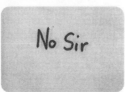

7. Cut to super: "No Sir."

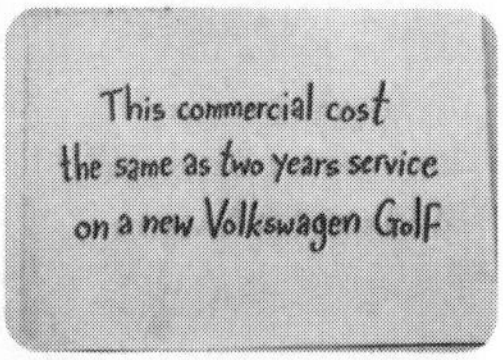

8. Super: "This commercial cost the same as two years service on a new Volkswagen Golf."

9. Cut to a cheque. It has the word "Nothing" written on it.

10. Then a phone number to call to get more information on the deal.

11. Super: "(That's free too.)"

12. Super: "And now the big stunt!"

13. Cut.

14. (Cut) With a ruler, the "Golf" gets catapulted through the air and disappears inside ...

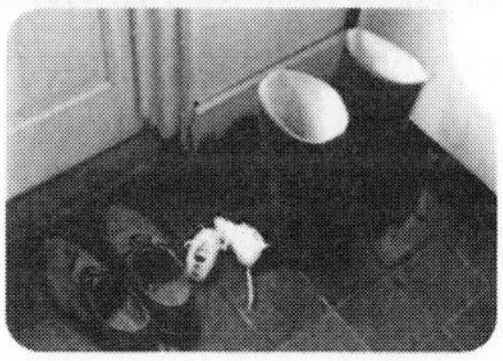

15. (Cut) ... a pair of rubber boots.

VW Dealers "Exotic" : 40 : BMP DDB Needham, London : Tony Davidson, Nick Gill : Mike Rudman

EXHIBIT 12.2. AT&T Direct-Response Ad

(MUSIC)
AVO: If your business is saving less than you'd hoped
since leaving AT&T
if you miss AT&T quality,
We want you back.
And now every business in America can afford to come back.
AT&T PRO WATS
with AT&T PRO® WATS.
A discount plan that gives you very competitive prices.
ONE MONTH FREE
UP TO $2,000
Switch now and get one month of long distance free.
From Miami to Minneapolis,
WE WANT YOU BACK
1 800 222-0400
WE WANT YOU BACK.
Call 1 800 222-0400.
AT&T
The right choice.
1 800 222-0400

The AT&T ad in Exhibit 12.2 is from the firm's "We want you back" campaign, designed to get former AT&T business customers to return. The ad reminds the viewer of AT&T's service quality, describes its PRO WATS discount plan, and offers one month of free long distance. The ad shows an 800 number that businesses can call to switch back to AT&T.

DIRECT-RESPONSE TELEVISION COMMERCIALS

Witek says that today's revolution in direct marketing is most evident in the way direct-response commercials look, implying that the audiences react primarily to the creative approach of what they see.[1] However, like any other form of advertising, direct-response commercials seek to communicate to members of the target market a primary product benefit, along with any secondary benefits. As the benefits are described, a set of supporting reasons for why the product delivers those benefits is explained. These reasons establish the credibility of the product and the offer and may be linked to tangible attributes of the product such as how it works or how it is made or designed. Credibility is often derived from demonstrations and testimonials.

Direct-response advertisements are designed to provoke a specific action from the prospects. The object may be to get the viewer to place an order by calling an 800 number or, less frequently, to write for more information.

Most direct-response television advertisements are 60 seconds long, but some are only 30 seconds. The former gives the advertiser enough time to grab the viewer's attention, explain the product, and provide ordering information. Those commercials must be shown repeatedly because one 60-second exposure seldom reaches many members of the firm's target audience or convinces the ones it does reach to place an order.

The most successful commercials offer a bargain, guarantee satisfaction, and make the product easy to order. Each of these reduces the risk the consumer may perceive in placing the order by making the shopping experience easy, convenient, safe, and economical.

Direct-response television offers produce 60 to 80 percent of their orders via toll-free phone, with the rest coming in by mail. Toll-free numbers (800 numbers) connect the caller with phone centers that handle incoming calls. They operate seven days a week and are staffed to handle the anticipated phone volume.

DIAL-A-MATTRESS[2]

Dial-A-Mattress is a direct marketer of mattresses and other home furnishings that built its $65 million business primarily from direct-response television. (See Case 5 at the end of this book.) The firm was founded by Napoleon Barragan, who started as a store-based retailer and evolved into a highly successful direct marketer. He sells mattresses on television and invites interested prospects to phone him at 1-800-MATTRES ("Leave off the last S for Savings").

Barragan was a regular print advertiser until he became curious about television. He had someone produce an inexpensive commercial, which ran in late-night slots. Sales soared as he moved the commercial around to different time slots on cable stations that delivered his customer's demographics. Sales continued to climb as he offered name brands like Sealy, Simmons, and Serta; two-hour delivery; free placement in the home and removal of the old mattress; guaranteed satisfaction on delivery or no obligation; and prices well below those of department stores. The firm advertises that its merchandise can be bought for 60 percent less than at department stores, but its biggest selling point is its hassle-free delivery.

As the direct-response commercial airs, interested buyers pick up the phone and dial 1-800-MATTRES. They reach one of 50 telemarketers manning the booths in the utility's warehouse and headquarters. The representative asks for the size mattress wanted (twin, regular, queen, or king); tells the caller the price; and determines when delivery can be made within a two-hour time frame. If the caller wants immediate delivery, the order is phoned to a roving driver. If delivery is requested for a later, specific two-hour time slot, orders are accumulated and given to the appropriate driver attending the delivery area during the slot requested. Some 30 percent of new orders come from referrals of satisfied customers.

WHY DIRECT-RESPONSE TV COMMERCIALS?

According to Witek, a direct-response television commercial is more like a direct-mail package than it is like an ordinary television commercial.[3] Both direct-response television and direct mail ask for an immediate decision from the viewer or reader. In that sense, this type of advertising is classic direct marketing.

A direct-mail letter speaks to a single customer. Direct mail can do this because it is specific and can make reasonable assumptions about the people on mailing lists. In direct-response television, the sex, age, education, and income of many prospects are known in advance, as are the time of day or night they watch television and the seasonality of their buying habits. Direct-response advertisers also know the approximate number of viewers for a show and which programs will encourage or discourage responsiveness to an offer.

In addition to their attempt to target logical prospects, direct-response commercials have other elements similar to those of direct mail. The commercial informs and shows just as the direct-mail letter provides information and the brochure shows the product. A direct-mail response card and direct-response TV commercial's telephone number both serve as ways for prospects to place an order.

Planning and executing direct-response and support television commercials require all the detailed knowledge of the medium needed by a general advertiser plus a thorough understanding of the special requirements of direct-response or support advertising. Television is a mass-audience advertising medium that reaches nearly 100 percent of all U.S. households. Direct marketers can address specific target audiences, but the level of selectivity is well below that of list-based tools such as direct mail and telemarketing, where specific individuals can be identified and targeted. Television advertising is also expensive, both in terms of producing commercials and purchasing airtime. Because it seldom makes sense to run a direct-response advertisement just once, direct marketers think in terms of campaigns, which consist of multiple showings of an ad to build reach (the number of target market members exposed to the ad) and frequency (the average number of times each target market member sees the ad).

Offers that work on direct-response television must appeal to general audiences or to audiences segmented by the demographics by which television programming is sold, particularly by age and gender, or by the programming content in which they are shown. The *Sports Illustrated* subscription ads that run just prior to Christmas offer the viewer an opportunity to order a year's worth of the magazine and a bonus videotape, usually with a football theme. These ads run during sporting events and on the Lifetime cable channel, which has a predominantly female audience.

The most successful direct-response television ads focus on one product or service and detail the benefits associated with making a purchase. The abundance of 60-second ads by legal offices illustrates this point. While some offer a variety of services, the more successful ones emphasize such specifics as divorce law or personal injury law. Most 30-second lead-generation ads for the online services are also singular in their focus on the benefits of signing on. Although Prodigy has many kinds of entertaining features, its ads tend to emphasize one or two of those features in depth.

Infomercials (discussed in detail on pp. 273–275) usually focus on the details of one product over a 30-minute period. This provides ample time for testimonials and demonstrations. The Psychic Friends Network, for example, airs half-hour infomercials about the benefits of calling an 800 number for psychic predictions. The infomercial itself is replete with stories of how the network's trained psychics have successfully predicted future events for individual callers. Predictions also occur during the show for members of the studio audience. Table 12.1 shows that the Psychic Friends Network was the top-ranked infomercial in 1994.

TABLE 12.1. Top-Ranking Infomercials, 1994

Only 9 infomercials out of nearly 500 that aired in 1994 achieved a number one ranking on the Jordan Whitney Weekly Top Thirty Infomercial chart during the year, according to the Tustin, CA–based firm's "Greensheet" Direct Response Television Monitoring Report. The rankings are based on a formula comprising media budgets, frequency of airing, and longevity.

Name of Infomercial	No. of #1 Rankings	Product	Price	Distributor	Host
Psychic Friends	14	900-number psychic phone line	$ 3.99/min.	Inphomation	Dionne Warwick
Passion, Profit and Power	9	Self-hypnosis tapes	$ 89.85	Positive Response Television	Marshall Sylver
Memory Power	8	Memory program	$ 89.85	Positive Response Television	Dick Cavett
Gravity Edge	6	Exerciser	$399.95	SLM Fitness	Lorenzo Lamas
Dura Lube	4	Auto oil additive	$ 29.95	The Media Group	Jim Caldwell
Hip & Thigh Machine	3	Exerciser	$199.90	USA Direct	Jake Steinfeld
Power Walk Plus	3	Exerciser	$319.80	National Media	Bruce & Kris Jenner
Perfect Hair	3	Hair extensions	$89.85	Positive Response Television	Mike Levy
Secret Hair	2	Hair extensions	$149.85	Guthy-Renker	José Eber

Source: Jordan Whitney Greensheet Direct Response Television Monitoring Report, as reported in *DM News,* March 1995.

RYDER TRUCKS[4]

It does not seem logical to be sentimental about a used truck, but that is exactly how Ryder has approached the subject. It combined sentimentality with humor in a 1991 direct-response television ad about the relationship between Ryder trucks and the mechanics who care for them. Ryder teamed up with comedian Steve Landesberg to target small businesses that might be in the market for a used truck.

Through 60-second and 120-second television spots, the viewer heard Landesberg explain how well maintained the trucks are and that Ryder also sells used vans, tractors, and trailers. Enter several weepy mechanics who beg Landesberg not to offer the viewer the Ryder toll-free number for fear that "their trucks" will be taken from them. "We've been caring for them since they were new," one mechanic sobs. The television campaign was developed in response to several marketing problems Ryder was experiencing. Besides an increasingly depressed market for used vehicles and aggressive sales objectives within a more competitive environment, there was inconsistent awareness that Ryder also sold trucks. (The success of Ryder's telemarketing campaign for its truck *rental* services was described in Chapter 11.)

The campaign not only offered a continuous presence in the marketplace but presented two specific ideas to generate response. The first was the establishment of "Road Ready" as a symbol of reliability, safety, and value. In addition, viewers were told they could receive a free "How to Buy a Used Truck" booklet by calling the ad's toll-free number.

After running the spots in local markets for five months, the commercial generated over 35,000 responses, at a cost of $18.29 per response.

MEDIA PLANNING FOR DIRECT-RESPONSE TELEVISION COMMERCIALS

Establishing media objectives is the first step in the process of formulating a direct-response media plan. However, before establishing media objectives and general guidelines, it is necessary to understand the key concepts upon which media objectives are built.

Concepts indispensable to the direct-response media planner in formulating objectives include ratings, reach, frequency, continuity, and gross rating points (GRPs). These media variables are manipulated to achieve a firm's direct-response marketing media objectives.

Media Ratings

The rating of a given program describes the proportion of target audience members reached by one broadcast of that program. If 20 percent of an audience is reached by one showing of a television program, that program has a rating of 20.

Media Reach

In contrast to ratings, reach is a measurement of audience accumulation because it tells direct marketers how many different prospects are in a commercial's audience over a period of time. The term *different* indicates that no prospect is counted more than once in any assessment of campaign reach. In contrast, frequency is the average number of times in a given period an advertisement is exposed. This exposure describes the average number of commercials seen in a specific period.

Reach is usually expressed as the percentage of a target market with whom a direct response advertiser is communicating, for example, the percentage of women 18 to 34. Reach is unduplicated because it indicates what percentage of the target audience was exposed at least once to the campaign. To find this percentage, the audience of a television or radio program is measured over a four-week period. Four weeks is a standard measuring unit in broadcasting because there are 13 four-week periods in a year, making annual planning easier to accomplish.

To clarify the concept of reach, think of 10 persons. In week 1, let's say, 4 of the 10 see a direct-response advertisement, resulting in a reach of 40 percent. In week 2, an additional person sees the ad, while two of the first four persons see the ad again; the reach is now 50 percent, because viewers are counted only once. In week 3, one new viewer is added and four of those who saw the ad before see it again, so the net reach is up to 60 percent. In week 4, five of those who saw the ad before see it again, but no new person sees the ad, so the reach is still at 60 percent.

Individual audience members are counted only once during the four-week period no matter how many times they see the ad. In situations where five television programs are part of one advertising campaign, some audience members may be exposed four or five times to only one television program, while other audience members may be exposed to all five television programs a different number of times. But if they see any one of the five advertisement showings at least once, they are counted as having been reached in that four-week period.

Reach for television commercials accumulates, or builds, in a fairly consistent pattern over time. The first time a commercial is telecast, it accumulates the largest number of viewers. The second time it is telecast, most of the viewers are repeat viewers, although some new viewers are added. The third and subsequent telecasts accumulate even fewer new viewers. If viewing over a four-week period were plotted on a graph, the curve drawn for the same commercial telecast over a long period of time would eventually flatten out and become almost horizontal, though it would never become perfectly horizontal because there would still be some people, somewhere, seeing the ad for the first time.

Media Frequency

Frequency describes the average number of times target audience members were exposed to a broadcast commercial within a four-week period. While reach is a measure of message dispersion, indicating how widely the message is received by the target audience, frequency is a measure of repetition, indicating to what extent audience members are exposed to the same commercial or group of commercials.

Frequency is usually calculated from data about media performance, which are available for many media from audience tracking services or from the medium itself. The formula for computing frequency is as follows:

Frequency = Reach / Rating

If a broadcast program telecast once each week has an average rating of 20 and a four-week reach of 50, the frequency is 2.5:

Frequency = 50 / 20 = 2.5

Remember that frequency is an average and not an absolute number. A distribution of the frequency statistic indicates whether some segments are getting disproportionately more frequency than others. These frequency distributions provide direct marketers with a way to determine the pattern of repetition that a media plan provides.

Media Continuity

Continuity refers to how direct-response advertisements are scheduled over the time of a campaign. This encompasses the entire dimension of timing, that is, whether media are scheduled continuously or in separated periods of media usage. This ranges from continuous advertising, in which the media effort remains relatively constant throughout the entire campaign period, to "flighting" (or "pulsing"), in which the media effort goes from media use to nonuse and then vice versa.

Flighting may be used to concentrate a firm's budget to specific times of the year because of limited funds. It can also be used to focus the budget on peak buyer-behavior periods, including, for example, Valentine's Day, Mother's Day, and Christmas. Usually, flighting parallels expected sales and is largely determined by the expected relative volume of business during the year.

Media Gross Rating Points

Gross rating points (GRPs) are an essential part of media decision making. They are used to characterize the gross weight of a given media effort against a defined target market, usually stated in terms of demographics. The effort may be anything from a single media buy for only one commercial showing to a combination of many media buys for many commercial showings over an entire campaign. GRPs are computed by multiplying reach times frequency, describing the gross weight of advertising during a designated period in a media schedule.

Note that media objectives calling for maximization of both reach and frequency are impractical because budget constraints usually result in trade-offs between reach and frequency. Any move toward maximizing reach sacrifices frequency, and vice versa. If a direct-response advertiser is willing to take a periodic hiatus during a campaign period, the budget will allow both reach and frequency to be enhanced during each flight of the direct response advertising. If a steady flow of media dollars is needed to support continuous advertising, there are automatic limits on the opportunity to maximize reach or frequency during any portion of a campaign.

Reach and frequency occur at the same time, but at different rates and in an inverse relationship. Within a given number of gross rating points, as one goes up, the other goes down. The formula is as follows:

Gross rating points = Reach × Frequency

A direct-response advertising schedule composed of a 50 reach with a 4.2 frequency yields 210 GRPs. If these same 210 GRPs were obtained in a different mixture of media, the reach might increase, but the frequency would decline. In contrast, a 210 GRP schedule in still another media mixture might produce higher frequency but less reach.

Up to a certain point, it is relatively easy to build reach. By selecting different programs in which to place commercials, it is possible to reach more target audience members. However, there is a point of diminishing returns where each attempt to build more reach by selecting more and different kinds of programs results in reaching the same persons again and again, increasing frequency rather than reach.

INFOMERCIALS[5]

Many firms have shunned infomercials in the past, but they can no longer ignore the medium; it is estimated that $750 million per year is spent on infomercials and that figure is growing. Exhibits 12.3 and 12.4 show how sales of products through infomercials and expenditures on infomercials changed between 1990 and 1994. While the annual sales generated by infomercials have declined overall, the number of dollars spent on them has increased significantly.

EXHIBIT 12.3. Total Sales Generated by Infomercials

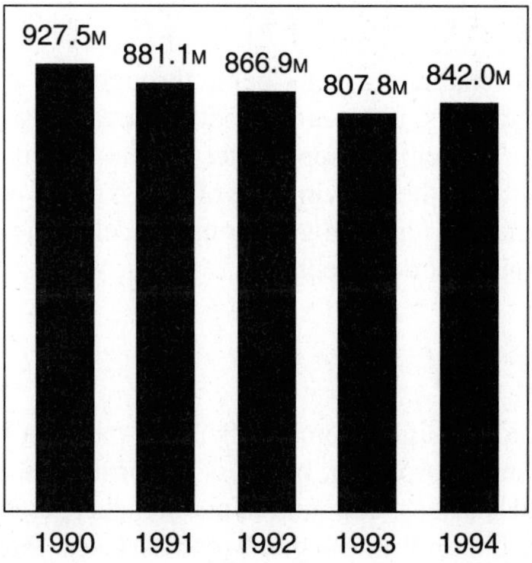

EXHIBIT 12.4. Amount Spent on Infomercials

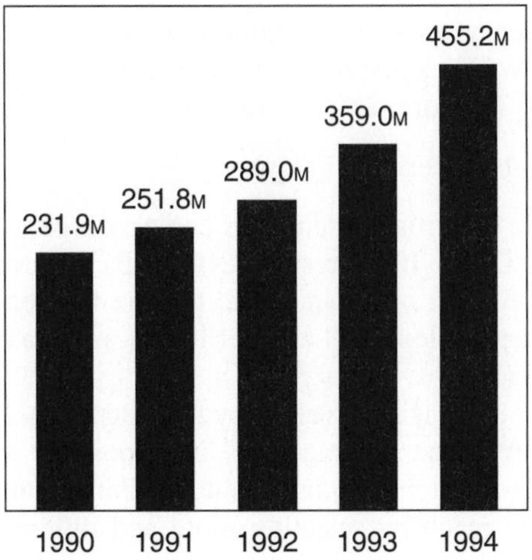

As a medium, infomercials are emblematic of an approaching explosion in media alternatives. Infomercials are currently a major subject of discussion in the *Wall Street Journal,* the *New York Times,* the *Financial Times of London,* and *The Economist* magazine. Even ABC television is now experimenting with "Nitecap," a new late-night infomercial concept hosted by Robin Leach from "Lifestyles of the Rich and Famous."

"Nitecap" is a new concept in marketing programming that exemplifies the redefinition of infomercials. In "Nitecap" Leach presides over a kind of transactional salon in which celebrities and personalities promote their products during visits with him at what looks like a chic soiree, while attractive extras mill about in the background. The viewing audience attends a trendy late-night party where products are for sale. The 800 numbers are flashed on the screen, and couponing helps drive sales.

The Growing Use of Personalities

For infomercials, the challenge is to burst through the clutter. This involves constantly seeking new tools, increasing production values, and expanding the use of celebrities. Victoria Principal's appearance on the "Secrets to Beautiful Skin" infomercial is indicative of the growing use of well-known personalities. Look for infomercials to become shorter, with greater use of celebrities, as they move in the direction of stand-alone entertainment.

Types of Products Sold

Products that have sold through infomercials in the past can be roughly divided as follows: self-improvement products, business opportunities, housewares, diet and weight loss goods and services, automotive maintenance, crafts, beauty care items, entertainment, and health and fitness goods and services. Pain remedies may be a promising field for the near future, as are "self-originated knockoffs," which are copies of a product marketed by the producer of the original product to undercut competition. The trend has been for product knockoffs to become available shortly after it is discovered that there has been a success in a product category. The self-originated knockoff is also meant to counter the copycat competition.

Many people believe that the product categories for infomercials will remain fairly stable while the marketing approach will change. Others look for higher involvement and higher priced items to come through infomercials as the format becomes more credible to customers and clients. Already, Microsoft and Eastman Kodak are producing infomercials to explain the technical subtleties of their products in a way that 30-second impulse spots are incapable of doing.

In 1992, a 30-minute infomercial campaign by NordicTrack, the marketer of cross-country ski exercisers, led to a significant increase in sales of cross-country ski simulators—sales jumped 19 percent. However, as of 1994, the infomercial competition for home fitness equipment dollars had become so pervasive that the product area accounted for 40 percent of infomercial sales. NordicTrack also places numerous 30- and 60-second commercials on cable channels to keep consumer awareness of its product line high. These ads stress the benefits of using a NordicTrack machine and encourage viewers to call an 800 number to place an order or to get more information. Just by calling a phone number, prospects can order a brochure and/or videotape. NordicTrack uses free videotape and brochure inquiries to generate leads for its telemarketing and direct-mail efforts, following each prospect through three or more outbound telemarketing and direct-mail efforts.

HOME SHOPPING CHANNELS

Home shopping channels are the result of creative programming in conventional television, which makes use of a combination of selling and entertainment to hold the attention of its viewers. Home shopping viewers use their telephones and credit cards to place orders.

The Home Shopping Network (HSN) is the largest competitor in the home shopping arena. The firm broadcasts several channels, each with its own target audience and product offerings. HSN's main facilities can handle 20,000 phone calls per minute. HSN's main channel was able to sell more than $1.2 million in Diane von Furstenberg dresses and silk separates in less than two hours.

If televised-shopping shows can make these kinds of sales, should traditional retailers and catalogers wonder how their businesses would be affected? Will television draw shoppers away from their stores and catalogs? Part of the answer, of course, lies in recognizing the types of people who buy via television.

Television shoppers are younger and more active than many observers of the retail industry might think. Almost half of this group is 25 to 44 years old. Furthermore, the television shopper is more likely to enjoy amusement parks, night clubs, snow skiing, gambling resorts, photography, and eating out, while the market average consumer is more likely to enjoy sedentary activities such as reading, listening to music, and watching television.

Forty-three percent of television shoppers are married, and 8 percent are widowed. By occupation, the largest television shopper group is made up of professionals and managers. More than 34 percent of television shoppers graduated from high school, compared to 31 percent of the market average. And more than 27 percent of television shoppers have completed one to three years of college, which is slightly below the 30 percent of the market average.

In terms of income levels, the average household income of television shoppers is $34,900, compared to $38,000 of the market average. Consumers in the lower income categories, below $30,000, are more likely than market average consumers to be television shoppers. But the percentages are very close at the highest income levels. While 9 percent of consumers in the market average earn more than $75,000 a year, 8 percent of television shoppers earn that much. In other words, television shopping appeals to consumers at the upper as well as lower ends of the income scale.

For viewers tuning in for the first time, what is most striking about television shopping is the seemingly endless parade of jewelry. Jewelry makes up about half of all merchandise sold on home shopping channels. One reason is that it is often an impulse buy, and another is that it shows up well on the television screen. It also can yield higher profits than many other types of goods. Aside from jewelry, currently hot products include clothing, small appliances, bedding, and collectibles.

Television shopping also offers an element of entertainment, supplied by the shows' friendly and accessible hosts. They point out all the details of a product and solicit testimonials from viewers. Throughout this process there is a sense of urgency designed to turn the watcher into a buyer. Sometimes, the networks show time clocks on the screen, which suggest to viewers that time is running out on their opportunity to buy.

The basic television-shopping experience is similar to buying from a mail-order catalog. When customers call a toll-free number they are connected with an order taker or with an automated order-taking system. Most home shopping channels accept personal checks, money orders, and major credit cards. After the order is placed, the customer gets an estimated delivery date and an order number.

Until recently, most major retailers resolutely shunned television shopping, but not anymore. Now department store chains, specialty outlets, catalog retailers, and mass merchants are reexamining home shopping. Some now plan to sell their wares on the existing channels, such as QVC or HSN. Saks Fifth Avenue went on QVC twice with items from its Real Clothes private-label collection and accumulated more than $1 million in sales. Many others will follow Saks's lead, including those interested in selling lifestyle-related items, health products, videos, and recorded music. Other retailers are hoping to launch their own television shopping channels, and still others are laying plans for interactive television services.

SUMMARY

Direct marketers use television for direct response and support, infomercials, and home shopping channels. Like any other direct-response medium, television can be used for sales or lead generation. When it is used to generate sales, those responding to the ad place an order or ask for more information. Once someone requests information because of a televised program, they can be further marketed to via telemarketing and direct mail. Direct response television can also be used to support other forms of direct marketing.

Like any other form of advertising, direct-response commercials seek to communicate to members of the target market a primary product benefit, along with any secondary benefits. As the benefits are described, a set of supporting reasons for why the product delivers those benefits are explained. These reasons establish the credibility of the product and the offer. They may be linked to tangible attributes of the product such as how it works or how it is made or designed. Credibility is often derived from demonstrations and testimonials. Direct-response advertisements are designed to provoke a specific action from the prospects. Most often, the object is to get the viewer to place an order by calling an 800 number or, less frequently, to write for more information.

Concepts indispensable to direct response media planning include: ratings, reach, frequency, continuity, and gross rating points (GRPs). These media variables are manipulated to achieve a firm's direct-response marketing media objectives. The rating of a program is the proportion of target audience members reached by one broadcast. When broad message dispersion patterns are needed, high levels of reach are planned. But when a great deal of repetition is needed, high frequency levels are planned. Continuity refers to how the advertising is scheduled over a time that represents when the direct response campaign is on the air (for television or radio). Gross rating points describe the relationship between reach and frequency because the multiplication of reach times frequency results in the GRP number.

Many firms that have ignored infomercials in the past now see them as a way to sell their products and services. As a medium, infomercials are part of an explosion in media alternatives. Home shopping channels are also the result of creative programming in conventional television which makes use of a combination of selling and entertainment to hold the attention of its viewers.

REVIEW QUESTIONS

1. In what ways do direct marketers use television in selling their products and services?
2. What are direct-response television advertisements designed to do, and why is that important to direct marketers?
3. According to Witek, a direct-response commercial is more like a direct-mail package than it is like an ordinary television commercial. What does that statement mean? In what ways are direct mail and direct-response television alike?
4. What is an infomercial, and what is it designed to do? What makes for a successful infomercial? What are the different types of infomercials, and in what ways are they different?
5. What is a home shopping channel and what is it designed to do? What makes for a successful home shopping channel?
6. What do the terms *ratings, reach, frequency, continuity,* and *gross rating points* mean? Why are they important to a direct marketer? How does the manipulation of the different variables influence the ability of a direct-response plan to achieve its objectives?

NOTES

1. John Witek, *Response Television* (Lincolnwood, IL: NTC Business Books, 1992), pp. 21–28.
2. Adapted from "Barragan Family Sleeps Well at Night," *Direct Marketing*, October 1993, pp. 52–57.
3. Witek, *Response Television*, (Lincolnwood, IL: NTC Business Books, 1992) pp. 13–16.
4. Adapted from "The Crying Mechanics," *Direct Marketing*, November 1991, p. 29.
5. Adapted from Andrew Susman, "Switching the Channel," *Direct Marketing*, January 1993, pp. 44–46, 70.

SOURCES

BARBAN, ARNOLD M.; STEPHEN M. CRISTOL; AND FRANK J. KOPEC. *Essentials of Media Planning*, 3rd ed. Lincolnwood, IL: NTC Business Books, 1995.

"Barragan Family Sleeps Well at Night," *Direct Marketing*, October 1993, pp. 52–57.

BRADY, FRANK R., AND J. ANGEL VASQUEZ. *Direct Response Television.* Lincolnwood, IL: NTC Business Books, 1995.

BRAUN, HARVEY. "Guess Who's Watching?" *Direct Marketing*, July 1993, pp. 21–23.

"The Crying Mechanics." *Direct Marketing*, November 1991, p. 29.

Direct Marketing Association. *Statistical Fact Book 1996.* New York: Direct Marketing Association, 1996.

DOYLE, MARE. *The Future of Television.* Lincolnwood, IL: NTC Business Books, 1992.

EICOFF, AL. *Direct Marketing through Broadcast Media.* Lincolnwood, IL: NTC Business Books, 1995.

________. *Eicoff on Broadcast Direct Marketing*. Lincolnwood, IL: NTC Business Books, 1988.

"The Infomercial." *Adweek*, Special Sourcebook Issue, 1995.

JONES, SUSAN K. *Creative Strategy in Direct Marketing.* Lincolnwood, IL: NTC Business Books, 1991.

KATZ, HELEN. *The Media Handbook.* Lincolnwood, IL: NTC Business Books, 1995.

KATZENSTEIN, HERBERT, AND WILLIAMS S. SACHS. *Direct Marketing*, 2nd ed. New York: Macmillan, 1992.

LEWIS, HERSCHELL GORDON. "A Fast Once-Over of Direct Response Television." *Direct Marketing*, October 1994, pp. 41, 72.

MARGOLIS, BUDD. "Technological Developments Delivering 500 TV Channels Are Only the Tip of the Iceberg." *Direct Marketing*, September 1995, pp. 24–26.

"Marketing with TV by Mail." *Direct Marketing*, September 1995, pp. 48–49.

MCDONALD, WILLIAM J. "Home Shopping Channel Customer Segments: A Cross-Cultural Perspective." *Journal of Direct Marketing* 9 (Autumn 1995), pp. 57–67.

ROBERTS, MARY LOU, AND PAUL D. BERGER. *Direct Marketing Management.* Englewood Cliffs, NJ: Prentice Hall, 1989.

SILVERMAN, GENE. "Planning and Using Infomercial Campaigns Effectively." *Direct Marketing*, September 1995, pp. 18–20.

SISSORS, JACK Z., AND LINCOLN BUMBA. *Advertising Media Planning*, 4th ed. Lincolnwood, IL: NTC Business Books, 1993.

STONE, BOB. *Successful Direct Marketing Methods*, 5th ed. Lincolnwood, IL: NTC Business Books, 1995.

SURMANEK, JIM. *Introduction to Advertising Media.* Lincolnwood, IL: NTC Business Books, 1993.

________. *Media Planning.* Lincolnwood, IL: NTC Business Books, 1992.

SUSMAN, ANDREW. "Switching the Channel." *Direct Marketing*, January 1993, pp. 44–46, 70.

"Tuned Out and Dropping Off." *The Economist*, November 4 1995, pp. 65–66.

WITEK, JOHN. *Response Television.* Lincolnwood, IL: NTC Business Books, 1992.

DIRECT MARKETING ASSOCIATION GUIDELINES FOR THE ACCEPTANCE OF DIRECT-RESPONSE BROADCAST ADVERTISING[1]

The Direct Marketing Association and television and radio stations share the goal of consumer protection. By maintaining the consumer's trust, business is generated for television and radio stations as well as advertisers. Most direct-response advertisers follow ethical and responsible business practices. These guidelines suggest some steps that can be taken to identify potentially troublesome advertising.

A Word about These Guidelines

The Direct Marketing Association is eager to help stations foster ethical practices on the part of the companies whose direct-response advertising they carry. Advertising credibility generates business for television and radio stations as well as for advertisers. These guidelines do not attempt to deal with legal questions relating to advertising. Practically all major group broadcasters and most individual stations have in place their own code of good practices for commercial acceptance. In the case of network commercials, the three major networks have their own Program Practices activities. By adhering to those codes, stations will in most cases minimize ethical and legal problems as well as complaints. When consumer complaints do occur, they tend to be in two principal categories:

1. Nondelivery of merchandise.
2. Misrepresentation of an offer.

Late delivery of merchandise is often caused by honest miscalculation of the success of an offer or by a production mishap. Such occurrences are often inadvertent and can be dealt with by a straightforward explanation from the advertisers.

You should be aware that the Federal Trade Commission regulations require that an item be shipped within 30 days after payment unless otherwise stated in the advertisement or solicitation. There are also specific regulations on what a company must do in regard to refunds or replacements should merchandise not be shipped within the time frame promised or required by law.

Other serious problems, such as product misrepresentation, should be dealt with, if possible, before the commercial is aired, since they can be especially harmful to the consumer, the station, and the image of direct marketing.

Suggestions for the Station

Samples of the Offer

Ask to see a sample of the merchandise being sold, particularly if the offer seems "too good to be true." Samples should be from regular production, not handmade mock-ups. If the advertiser does not submit the requested sample before the commercial's air date, a station should delay airing the commercial pending sample receipt. You also should request samples of any printed material which advertises the product or service, for further information.

Screening Procedures

Although most stations have their own procedures for checking advertiser credit and reliability, the following points should be emphasized:

1. A broadcast station should be familiar with or inquire into the advertiser or the principals behind the company. Addresses and telephone numbers as well as personal references are useful, and in some cities (such as New York) post office box numbers must be accompanied by a street address. Often the mere act of requesting information will deter unscrupulous advertisers.
2. If the advertiser is unknown to a station, you should investigate beyond credit worthiness and references from other stations which have run the commercial. It is wise to check also with the Better Business Bureau, local consumer agencies and the U.S. Postal Service. If you air a commercial that generates complaints, let these agencies know.
3. Station personnel sometimes place an order during an ongoing direct response advertising campaign to verify that the product is actually being delivered as advertised. If the seller is using a telephone number to take orders, calling that number can spot a variety of problems, including "bait and switch" tactics.

Additional Suggestions

Here are some further steps that should be taken by stations:

1. Questionable copy/visuals: Most advertising messages are presented with good taste. However, if you think the commercial may be deceptive or offensive, request changes in the relevant copy and/or visual.
2. Follow your instincts: If you have reason to question an offer, you should do so.
3. Vague offers: If the offer made in the commercial is unclear to you, it will be equally unclear to the viewer or listener. Ask the advertiser for a clarification.
4. Audio-visual consistency: Insure that the commercial accurately specifies both offer and merchandise. TV screen crawls should be readable and move slowly

enough to be read by the average viewer. Visual and audio claims should be consistent.

5. Credibility: Does the copy and/or visual seem exaggerated? A visual presentation should accurately simulate a real-life situation in order not to mislead the viewer. Are the claims so strong as to be unbelievable? If the consumer is disappointed in the offer or receives unsatisfactory treatment from the advertiser, he or she may blame the station that aired the commercial.

After the Commercial Has Aired

1. Most direct response commercials are welcomed by the viewer or listener and are profitable to the station. As a rule they do not generate complaints. However, if you do receive complaints, keep a tally. If they occur frequently, discuss them with the advertiser, and satisfy yourself that effective corrective action is being taken.
2. As an initial step, rely on your own experience with a problem advertiser before accepting a commercial.

Suggestions for Your Viewers/Listeners

Although most direct marketers make every effort to deliver merchandise promptly, consumers should be aware that delays may take place from order to delivery. In addition, when responding by mail to the commercial, consumers should be sure to:

1. Print clearly the name and address to which the order is to be shipped.
2. Include their own zip code on the order, as well as the company's zip code on the mailing envelope.
3. Send check or money order only, not cash.
4. Keep a written record of your order.

NOTE

1. Source: Ethics Department, Direct Marketing Association, Inc.; 1111 19th Street, N.W., Suite 1100; Washington, DC 20036-3603.

CHAPTER 13

Direct-Response Radio

OBJECTIVES

1. To examine the structure of direct-response radio commercials.
2. To explore the relationship between radio programming and station demographics, and the implications for direct-response radio advertising.
3. To describe the roles for radio as a support medium when used with other forms of direct marketing media.

SIGNET BANK

A 60-second direct-response radio spot for Signet Bank that features a fast-talking man explaining his busy day was judged *Advertising Age*'s best radio commercial of 1993. Martin Agency, of Richmond, Virginia, created the commercial, titled "Wake Up Male" (and a companion spot featuring a fast-talking female), for Signet, which has about 240 branches in Maryland, Virginia, and Washington, DC. The man, portrayed by Andrew Anthony, crammed 182 words into 45 seconds of the humorous spot, taking the listener from his wake-up call through the busy day and back to dreamland. That left just 15 seconds for the announcer to explain that since "you do a lot in a day," Signet's telephone banking center is open 24 hours a day, seven days a week.

Advertising Age's judges liked the way the commercial's rapid-fire delivery kept listeners' attention, while the closing message was on target, playing off the humorous scenario with a sensible solution to finding time to do banking. A transcript of the "Wake Up Male" radio commercial follows.

> Man: "Wake up, hit the snooze, attempt to kiss wife. Get out of bed, step on the dog, brush teeth, gargle, kiss wife again. Shower, dry hair, put on boxers, shirt, pants, socks, shoes, tie, jacket. Pour a cup of coffee, trip over toy truck, spill coffee, change tie. Kiss wife, baby, wave at neighbor Ernie. Start car, drive to work. Notice woman staring at me at stoplight. Turn on defrost. Park. Walk to work. Sit at desk, work, work, work. Meet with boss. Promise to kill boss. Eat lunch, work, work, work. Meet with boss again. Boss gives you bonus, promotion. Put plans to kill boss on hold. Drive home, run over toy truck. Park. Kiss wife, baby, step on dog. Eat dinner, play with baby, feed baby, burp baby, change baby, put baby to bed. Talk to wife; celebrate promotion, bonus. Pick up remote, turn on TV, read paper, fall asleep on sofa, wake up to national anthem. Get up, step on dog, take off pants, shirt, socks. Brush teeth, gargle, climb in bed, kiss wife, sleep. Dream of stepping on dog."
>
> Announcer: "You have a lot to do in a day, so we make it easy for you to talk to a Signet banker. Call our telephone banking center anytime, 24 hours a day,

seven days a week. It's as easy as 1-800-2-SIGNET. All Signet banks are equal opportunity lenders. Members FDIC."[1]

The Signet radio commercial is a good example of strong direct-response radio advertising. It has a clear main selling concept, an entertaining message, and a clear call to action.

INTRODUCTION

The use of radio as a direct-response medium predates similar uses of television by many decades. Long before people sat before the television to watch their favorite shows, they gathered around the radio to listen to the most popular programs of that time. Today, however, the role of radio in the American entertainment spectrum has changed dramatically. Radio has not traditionally been considered a strong medium for direct-response marketing because people usually listen to the radio while they are doing something else, such as working or driving. Thus, it is usually not convenient for them to write down a telephone number or mailing address. Besides, by the time they find the pencil and paper, the ad is over and their memory has faded. Nevertheless, radio is a useful direct-response medium if properly situated as either the heart of a direct marketing campaign or as a supplement to a campaign whose primary emphasis is some other medium such as television.

Radio offers direct marketers a unique blend of benefits, including sales to targeted, highly segmented audiences and an opportunity to get on the air fast. Radio stations with proven programming formats appeal to listeners with similar interests and shared demographic and psychographic characteristics.

A direct marketing radio commercial must accomplish a great deal in the short period of time it has to communicate its message. It must get its audience's attention, define a relevant problem, characterize the solution, and address any fears the audience may have by offering a money-back guarantee. In between all that, the advertisement needs to repeat a phone number and mailing address so that the target can respond. The length of the commercial should be determined by how long it takes to sell the product.

A major attraction of radio is its ability to reach highly segmented audiences. In that sense, the current emphasis on the regionalization of marketing strategies by national marketers makes the local nature of the radio audience attractive. Furthermore, direct-response radio is cheaper than television and has the potential for being more personal with its listeners. As a result, national marketers are becoming important local tactical partners with advertisers. New consumer formats can meet the needs of listeners and advertisers for a variety of geodemographic and lifestyle groups in any number of markets. Some stations are moving away from one exclusive format to multiple formats, depending on the time of day and demographics they are trying to appeal to.

Radio can help direct-response advertisers strengthen retail business alliances with specially designed promotions and events through their local expertise. Radio is among the most portable of all the media; it can be used to deliver important brand-reminder messages close to the point of purchase, which is known as proximity advertising.

THE ESSENCE OF DIRECT-RESPONSE RADIO ADVERTISING

Experienced direct marketers know that radio needs special attention in order to produce sales. The commercials must be memorable, particularly the phone number setup. Because a large number of radio listeners are in a car, it is especially important that they be able to remember what they heard without having to write anything down. The phone number (and/or mailing address) must be announced several times in the course of a commercial. Because radio programming focuses on narrow audiences, the direct marketer should confine product or service messages to specific stations with the correct demographics.

The starting point for developing a radio script is the product or service being sold. Research information about the needs, interests, and activities of the target audience members is an extremely important source for ideas about what to put in a radio script. Done properly, radio integrates the description of product or service benefits with an attention-getting, interest-keeping script that will prevent the potential buyer from turning the dial or pressing the radio channel button.

Radio Station Formats

In using radio commercials, it is important to consider a station's format because each station tends to have a different listening audience. Some people listen to country-and-western music, while another audience listens to an all-news station. There are also different people listening to rock versus rap versus disco music. Regardless of station format, the radio commercial needs to be consistent with the environment in which it will play. However, it should avoid the kind of sameness that makes it get lost in the station's normal programming. It needs to deliver its message in a way that is tailored to the format of the station but at the same time be distinctive enough to break through the clutter and deliver its message.

Most radio commercials use music, but many use a nonmusical script that is read either by the radio station show host live or by a recorded commercial that features a spokesperson. Radio is an emotional medium; many people listen to it to change their mood. This means that the better radio advertising makes an emotional pitch to its target audience by way of music and words designed to deliver the selling message.

Creating Radio Commercials

The main selling concept must be the star of the commercial; it must not be dominated by a creative concept. However, this does not mean that selling needs to be boring. The product, the phone number, the offer, or some relevant selling idea must be the main thrust of the radio spot, and it helps to use a standard format, but this still leaves room for creativity. The spot can focus on a straight announcer; it can emphasize dialogue with people talking to each other; it can use a vignette in which the radio spot starts with a short slice-of-life scene illustrating a problem and end with telling the listener to call an 800 number for the solution; it can focus on a person on the street who tells the listeners about the benefits of the product; it can use testimonials in which experts, celebrities, or ordinary people attest to the product; or it can tell a story that describes a situation in which the product is central. The ad should use a memorable and relevant 800 number along with a clear call to action with a time limit.

From a creative standpoint, radio might be the simplest advertising medium there is. With a straight-forward radio spot, marketers can literally be on the air in days, if not hours. Radio spots are powerful, cheap, and easy to produce.

A radio commercial needs enough time to make the sale, so when there is a choice between 30 seconds and 60 seconds, 60 seconds is the better alternative. It provides twice as long to set up the scene, sell the product, and repeat the ordering phone number. Marketers should focus on generating phone calls with orders or inquiries. Everything in the spot should focus on motivating the listener to pick up a phone and call. The direct marketer cannot just settle for generating "aware-

EXHIBIT 13.1. "The Gunfighters" Radio Script

SFX: GUNSHOTS, BULLETS RICOCHETING.

ANNOUNCER: October 26, 1881: THREE DEAD, THREE WOUNDED AS THE EARPS BATTLE THE CLANTONS AT THE O.K. CORRAL!

SFX: BANJO OR DANCEHALL MUSIC.

ANNOUNCER: Now follow the "blazing gun battles" that splashed across the Old West's headlines in *The Gunfighters*—your introductory volume in a rip-roaring series from TIME-LIFE BOOKS called The Old West. You'll meet the meanest desperadoes ever to shoot their way across the West: Billy the Kid, Clay Allison, John Wesley Hardin, who was so mean he once shot a man for snoring. You'll see the towns they fought in, the actual saloons where they gambled, the outlaw girls like Belle Starr who rode beside them. And you'll meet the lawmen who brought them down: Pat Garrett, Bat Masterson, Judge Roy Bean—who once fined a dead man forty dollars for carrying a concealed weapon. Each of the big books in The Old West is packed with 235 pages of rare photographs, authentic Western paintings and eyewitness accounts . . . and the gold-stamped covers have the look and feel of hand-tooled leather.

SFX: FADE BANJO MUSIC.

ANNOUNCER: Begin with *The Gunfighters,* yours for a free 10-day examination as a guest of TIME-LIFE BOOKS. If you aren't satisfied, simply return it. If you decide to keep it, the cost is only $7.95 plus shipping and handling. Then, once every other month, you'll receive future volumes like *The Cowboys, The Indians, The Pioneers,* and more—always for a 10-day free examination. Keep only the books you want—and you can cancel your subscription at any time. Start by sending for *The Gunfighters* today!

SFX: DOUBLE GUNSHOT (2 beats).

ANNOUNCER: To order, here's all you have to do . . .

Source: Al Eicoff, *Eicoff on Broadcast Direct Marketing* (Lincolnwood, IL: NTC Business Books, 1988), pp. 96–97.

ness." The commercial must begin a meaningful relationship with potential customers by offering free information, a free consultation, a special price, or some tangible reason to call right away.

Highly creative and attention-getting radio commercials tend to use words like *exciting, new, revolutionary,* and *only.* And, of course, they always include "satisfaction guaranteed or your money back!" To bridge the credibility gap, radio commercials frequently use celebrities and professional endorsements. User testimonials are probably among the strongest selling techniques available. In radio commercials, words, sounds, music, and even silence are woven together to produce a moving tapestry of thought, image, and persuasion. Connection with the listener is direct, personal, and emotional.

Most radio commercials include an opening that summarizes the offer; a middle that sets forth the problem, presents the solution, and gives the phone and mailing instructions for obtaining the offer; and a close that repeats the offer and the mailing address and phone number. Because radio does not have the advantage of visual presentation, it is essential that the phone number or mailing address be repeated several times in the commercial.

Exhibit 13.1 contains a script for a highly successful direct-response radio commercial. It is a Time-Life Books offer for books about the Old West. The ad establishes the premise for the product, followed quickly by benefits associated with placing an order for a free 10-day examination of the first book in the series, *The Gunfighters*. It ends with a clear call to action that tells the listener to call an 800 number (not shown in the exhibit).

DIAL-A-MATTRESS

Dial-A-Mattress Corporation built its $65 million business by using television direct-response marketing supported by direct response radio. For details about the company's offering, see again Chapter 12, page 267, and see Case 5 at the end of the book.

In 1994, Dial-A-Mattress spent $10 million on direct marketing, 80 percent of which was on direct-response television, 15 percent on direct-response radio, and 5 percent on direct mail. Sales are directly proportionate to the amount of advertising the company does. The company can increase sales at any time of the year, month, or day simply by increasing its advertising expenditures.

The typical 60-second radio commercial provides enough time to communicate most commercial messages. Most Dial-A-Mattress radio commercials include about 200 to 250 words of copy, about half of which detail the terms of the offer. That leaves only 100 to 125 words to use in describing the product or service benefits and for motivating the listener to take immediate action. The ad must attract attention with its headline and move the listener on from interest to action.

Exhibit 13.2 contains a sample Dial-A-Mattress radio commercial. Like the firm's television advertising, the spot emphasizes availability of product, price savings, and customer service, particularly convenience and speed.

EXHIBIT 13.2. Dial-A-Mattress Radio Transcript

When you want to buy a new mattress, you want three things: you want it easy, convenient, and fast. By calling Dial-A-Mattress, that's as simple as 1-2-3.

It's easy: just dial 1-800-MATTRES. We'll deliver a name-brand mattress, a Sealy Posturepedic, Serta Perfect Sleeper, or a Simmons Beautyrest right to your home at the right price.

It's convenient: Just call 1-800-MATTRES any time 24 hours a day, seven days a week. We carry all the styles and sizes you need. Even folding king-size mattress that fit through the tightest hallways and doorways.

It's fast. Just dial 1-800-MATTRES and sleep on your new mattress tonight. Our express delivery gets it where you want it and when you want it.

Source: Dial-A-Mattress, 1995.

MAKING GOOD USE OF RADIO

According to Stone, radio differs from other direct marketing media in that it is more personal.[2] Because radio usually serves as background for some other activity, it is more casual and less intrusive than media such as television, which can demand both attention and concentration. Stone also points to another unique feature of radio: it is the medium of the imagination. Listeners supply important elements in a message as they use their own imagination to think about and visualize the radio broadcast. This helps listeners remember what they heard and reinforces the advertiser's commercial message with both auditory and mental images of what is on the radio.

Which Products Are Best for Radio?

Radio does best with products and services that do not need a demonstration. The Time-Life Books ad in Exhibit 13.1 is rich in imagery even though the listener never actually sees anything about the Old West. The Dial-A-Mattress ad in Exhibit 13.2 works well in part because the listener can obtain all the necessary facts without seeing the product in action. Other products that sell well on radio include insurance policies and professional services such as those offered by lawyers.

Radio as a Support Medium

The general principles that apply to using support programs in print media or television also apply to radio. Support media must address the same target audience and follow the same timing as the primary media. For example, television could serve as the primary medium, while radio would be a secondary medium. Radio, alone or combined with television, can be a highly effective support medium. Because most radio stations have such low ratings, stations should be chosen based on programming that reaches the target audience.

Eicoff uses the example of a record club to describe how radio can provide support:

> Where the demographics of the target audience are men and women between the ages of 14 and 30, the best rock stations should be selected, and the support should incorporate 40 to 50 30-second spots on each selected station. When supporting a Sunday newspaper insert, the campaign should run Thursday, Friday, Saturday, and Sunday morning. When a radio commercial supports an insurance mailing, news, talk, and middle-of-the-road music stations with audiences over 35 should set the pattern for the support buy. In the case of an insert, the Thursday, Friday, Saturday, and Sunday pattern should be followed. In the case of a mailing, in which the date of delivery is uncertain, the campaign should begin two days prior to the expected first day of delivery and should continue until the estimated next-to-last day of delivery.[3]

Network Radio for Direct Marketing

There are literally dozens of radio network combinations, ranging from music to news, but the most effective network formats are the news formats of CBS and NBC and the talk format of the Mutual Network. Because people listen intently to Larry King on the Mutual Network and because of the availability of time, Mutual offers one of the best opportunities for direct-marketing offers. Because of the number of radio network combinations, a direct marketer should stay in constant contact with the various radio networks, particularly for distressed availabilities that either can be purchased at extremely low rates or are available on a price-per-placement basis.

Direct-Response Radio as a Mass Medium

Radio is a mass medium, but it is possible to buy radio on a more selective basis than broadcast television. There are many more radio stations than television stations, and each has its own personality, which is reflected in its programming. Some stations feature rock-and-roll music, some classical; some are "talk" or "all news" stations. Each selects its audience (or vice versa) by its programming format. And, of course, radio costs less to use—both in media charges and production—than television.

According to Roberts and Berger, the size and geographical distribution of radio offers a number of advantages to all advertisers, including direct marketers:

1. *It is ubiquitous.* Radio is available to most people at any place at any time.
2. *It is selective.* The limited geographical reach of most stations and their specialized programming formats attract audiences that tend to be quite homogeneous in terms of demographics and lifestyles.
3. *It is economical.* Radio's cost per thousand audience members (CPM) is relatively low and has increased more slowly than that of other advertising media for the last decade. Despite a noticeable increase in the demand for radio advertising time in recent years, that trend is expected to continue through the 1990s. Also, production costs for radio commercials tend to be low compared to those for other media.

4. *It offers rapid access.* An advertiser who has an urgent need to communicate information can get a live radio commercial on the air within a few hours. Recorded commercials can be completed within a few days. Contrast this to the weeks, or even months, required for production and publication in some other media.
5. *It is involving.* Radio is a personal medium and listeners develop strong loyalties to specific stations. They may engage in participatory behavior such as calling the station to express their opinions or to request musical selections. Radio tends to involve listeners by encouraging them to use their imaginations to supplement the communication being received through the auditory sense.
6. *It is flexible.* When the situation demands it, a new radio commercial can be written and aired live within a few hours. Existing commercials can be revised quickly without incurring substantial cost. The relatively low cost and flexibility of radio make it a useful test medium for offers that may eventually be run in any medium. Commercials can be developed and refined easily and the results are available almost immediately. Experience indicates that 90 percent of the responses will be received within five minutes of the airing of the commercial.[4]

Radio audience selection is based almost solely on demographic characteristics. When a direct marketer wishes to place advertising on a particular station or group of stations, he or she must match the demographics of the target audience for a product or service with the radio audience. People differ sharply according to what they like to listen to on the radio; these differences relate to such demographics as gender and age.

Table 13.1 shows gender differences in preferences radio listeners have for certain station formats. Men prefer album-oriented rock, all news, classical, golden

TABLE 13.1. Radio Listening by Gender and Station Format
(Average daily Monday through Friday, morning to midnight)

Format	Men	Women
Adult contemporary	86*	113
Album-oriented rock	133	70
All news	111	90
Classical	118	83
Classical rock	125	77
Rock	92	107
Country	99	101
Golden oldies	110	90
Lite/soft contemporary	91	108
Nostalgia	93	107
News talk/business talk	116	86
Religious	78	121
Urban contemporary	97	103

*Note: An index value of more than 100 means greater-than-average listening levels, and a value of less than 100 means below-average listening levels.

Source: Simmons Market Research Bureau, Inc., 1994.

oldies, and news talk/business talk, while women tend to prefer adult urban contemporary and religious programming.

In addition to audience selection decisions, radio advertisers, like television advertisers, must determine which parts of the day they wish to have their radio commercials on the air. The largest audiences are available during the times when the most people are in their cars. These so-called drive times are from 6 to 10 AM and 3 to 7 PM. With these larger audiences also comes a higher cost for advertisers; drive times have the most expensive advertising slots. The drive times are also the most tricky to do direct-response advertising in because when much of the audience is in their cars, it is difficult for them to physically record any information contained in an ad. That highlights the importance of memorable 800 numbers, although with the increasing popularity of cellular telephones, there are now millions of people who can call while driving. This does not totally solve the problem, however, because many ordering situations require that a credit card number be read to the seller to finalize the sale.

Radio, like all media, exists primarily to deliver entertainment, information, and advertisements to a vast audience throughout the country. Radio delivers individuals who buy products and services from advertisers. These listeners choose media first on the basis of the kind and quality of entertainment and information it delivers and a far second for the kinds of advertisements they carry. Consumers have specialized needs that each specific medium can meet in its own way.

No matter which kind of audience direct-response advertisers want to reach, they must plan the purchase of that medium in a way that is consistent with the deadlines associated with prepublication and prebroadcast dates established by the media. Media planning consists of a series of decisions about what the best means are of delivering advertisements to prospects; how many prospects need to be reached; how often the ads should be delivered; and how much money should be spent.

Mass media such as radio, newspapers, magazines, and television are especially well suited for delivering advertisements along with news and entertainment. They appeal to a widespread audience. They deliver large audiences at relatively low costs, and they can deliver advertisements to special kinds of audiences who are attracted to each medium's editorial or programming content.

Broadcast media are seldom sought out by people for the advertisements alone. Commercials are seen as intrusive; they break into the play or action of a program and attempt to grab and hold the attention of listeners. Whether any given listener or viewer will listen to or watch a particular commercial is determined by the needs of the consumer and the interest and entertainment value of the commercial itself. The effectiveness of the commercial to communicate thus affects the degree of influence it will have on the target and the number of those who will read, see, or hear it.

As mentioned earlier, radio is able to reach certain kinds of specialized audiences very well. Radio is also a high-frequency medium where a great deal of repetition is necessary. There are usually many stations with time available for building a high-frequency media plan.

Radio's limitations are associated with the large number of stations in any one market and its ability therefore to only reach a limited number of persons via any one station. If an advertiser wants to build a large reach with radio, it must buy more than one station and, in some areas, many stations. Another consequence of the large number of stations available is the fragmentation of audiences caused by specialized programming. While specialized programs reduce any waste in terms of types of persons reached, it may be too fragmented for some advertisers. Like television ads, radio messages are usually forgotten as quickly as they are heard.

For local radio, coverage means the number (or percentage) of homes or other locations with radios within the signal area of a given station that can tune in to that station because they can pick up the station's signal. Whether or not they choose to tune in depends on a number of factors such as whether the programming of the station is interesting enough to attract them; and the power of the station, because stronger stations can cover a greater area than weaker stations.

SUMMARY

Radio commercials must be memorable, particularly the phone number for receiving calls. Because a large number of radio listeners are in a car, it is especially important that they be able to remember what they heard without having to write anything down. The phone number (and/or mailing address) must be announced several times in the course of a commercial.

Radio programming focuses on narrow audiences with particular demographics. Radio stations have developed proven programming formats that appeal to listeners with similar interests and shared demographic and psychographic characteristics. These listeners have specific needs, interests, and activities that may be directly incorporated into a radio script. Done properly, radio integrates the description of product or service benefits with an attention-getting, interest-keeping script that will prevent the potential buyer from turning the dial or pressing the radio channel button.

A direct marketing radio commercial must get its audience's attention, define a relevant problem, characterize its solution, and address any risk-related fears the target audience may have. In between, the advertisement needs to repeat a phone number and/or mailing address so that the target can respond. The length of the commercial should be determined by how long it takes to sell the product. However, most radio commercials are either 30 or 60 seconds long.

REVIEW QUESTIONS

1. What is the relationship between radio programming and station demographics, and what are the implications for direct-response radio advertising?
2. What are the benefits of direct-response radio advertising, and how do radio's benefits compare to those of television?
3. What can direct-response marketers do about the fact that radio listeners are frequently doing something else and thus may not pay full attention to an ad message?
4. Why is the length of a direct-response radio commercial important to communicating a direct marketer's selling message?
5. What are the possible roles for radio as a support medium with other forms of direct marketing media?

NOTES

1. "Radio," *Advertising Age,* May 9, 1994, p. 41.
2. Bob Stone, *Successful Direct Marketing Methods,* 5th ed. (Lincolnwood, IL: NTC Business Books, 1995), pp. 288–90.
3. Al Eicoff, *Direct Marketing through Broadcast Media* (Lincolnwood, IL: NTC Business Books, 1995), p. 114.
4. Mary Lou Roberts and Paul D. Berger, *Direct Marketing Management* (Englewood Cliffs, NJ: Prentice Hall, 1989), pp. 376–77.

SOURCES

Barban, Arnold M., Stephen M. Cristol, and Frank J. Kopec. *Essentials of Media Planning*, 3rd ed. Lincolnwood, IL: NTC Business Books, 1993.

"Barragan Family Sleeps Well at Night," *Direct Marketing*, October 1993, pp. 52–57.

Book, Albert C., Norman D. Cary, and Frank R. Brady. *The Radio & Television Commercial*, 3rd ed. Lincolnwood, IL: NTC Business Books, 1994.

Direct Marketing Association. *Statistical Fact Book 1996*. New York: Direct Marketing Association, 1996.

Eicoff, Al. *Direct Marketing through Broadcast Media*. Lincolnwood, IL: NTC Business Books, 1995.

_______. *Eicoff on Broadcast Direct Marketing*. Lincolnwood, IL: NTC Business Books, 1988.

Goldblum, Risa. "Springing to the Top." *Direct*, October 1993, pp. 51–54.

Katz, Helen. *The Media Handbook.* Lincolnwood, IL: NTC Business Books, 1995.

Klues, Jacj M., and Jayne Zenalt Spittler. "A Media Planner's Guide to the Future." In *Beyond 2000: The Future of Direct Marketing*, ed. Jerry I. Reitman. Lincolnwood, IL: NTC Business Books, 1994, pp. 79–95.

"Radio." *Advertising Age*, May 9, 1994, p. 41.

Reich, Dean. "Discovering Direct Response Radio: 14 Tips for Writing Ads That Work." *Direct Marketing*, October 1995, pp. 40–42.

Roberts, Mary Lou, and Paul D. Berger. *Direct Marketing Management.* Englewood Cliffs, NJ: Prentice Hall, 1989.

Robinson, Julia. "Dial-A-Mattress Uncovered." *Bedtimes*, September 1994, pp. 8, 31–33, 37–44, 47.

Schulberg, Pete. *Radio Advertising*, Lincolnwood, IL: NTC Business Books, 1995.

Sissors, Jack Z., and Lincoln Bumba. *Advertising Media Planning*, 4th ed. Lincolnwood, IL: NTC Business Books, 1993.

Stone, Bob. *Successful Direct Marketing Methods*, 5th ed. Lincolnwood, IL: NTC Business Books, 1995.

Surmanek, Jim. *Introduction to Advertising Media*. Lincolnwood, IL: NTC Business Books, 1993.

_______. *Media Planning*. Lincolnwood, IL: NTC Business Books, 1992.

CHAPTER 14

Direct Response in Print Media

OBJECTIVES

1. To define the principal types of magazines used by direct marketers and the audiences they reach.
2. To examine the factors that influence the success or failure of direct-response print advertising.
3. To explain the primary differences between consumer and business magazines.
4. To describe the main reasons for using magazine space advertising and the advantages and disadvantages associated with it.
5. To describe the main reasons for using newspaper space advertising and the advantages and disadvantages associated with it.

INTRODUCTION

Magazines and newspapers convey messages on printed pages to mass audiences or highly segmented audiences, depending on which specific publication is selected. Direct marketers benefit from print's (1) longer shelf life compared to direct mail, (2) pass-along readership potential, and (3) regional and demographic segmentation. Print also allows direct marketers to widen their customer base to non-mail-order buyers.

As an advertising medium, magazines differ from newspapers in many important ways. A number of newspapers circulate in small or regional geographic areas. However, most magazines have national distribution, though in many instances circulation is targeted to specific reader interests. Compared with newspapers, consumer magazines cover a wider area, but they do so with less intensity. The large-circulation magazines offer regional editions, but their coverage of local markets remains relatively weak.

In 1996, these two print media together accounted for about $21.8 billion in advertising: $7.3 billion for magazines ($3.2 billion in consumer magazines and $4 billion in business-to-business magazines) and $14.5 billion in newspapers ($8.4 billion in consumer newspapers and $6.2 billion in business-to-business newspapers). Table 14.1 shows print advertising expenditures for 15 industry categories. However, direct-response advertising represents only a small percentage

TABLE 14.1. Print Space Advertising Expenditures: 1994 versus 1993
(Ranked by 15 industry categories)
The *LNA/Media Watch Service* is published quarterly by Competitive Media Reporting and reports advertising expenditures in 10 major media. For magazines, LNA measures and compiles all paid advertising space and expenditures in PIB member publications, currently 180+ consumer magazines, and four Sunday magazines. For newspapers, LNA measures space in 180 newspapers in the top 30 ADIs.

Industry Class	Magazines	Sunday Magazines	Newspapers
Retail	209,165	109,416	4,764,509
	216,628	125,902	4,925,714
Automotive, auto	1,210,849	39,471	2,492,945
access/equipment	1,055,159	31,342	2,409,186
Business and consumer	651,801	45,158	1,637,293
services	615,890	45,321	1,578,487
Entertainment and	76,202	3,647	608,562
amusement	82,640	3,908	634,314
Food and food products	511,077	49,566	21,991
	467,523	46,285	21,857
Toiletries and cosmetics	854,019	27,543	11,894
	811,785	34,307	10,527
Drugs and remedies	432,734	72,496	107,827
	365,979	38,606	118,480
Travel, hotels, and resorts	436,725	45,417	889,779
	369,081	44,306	852,696
Direct-response	822,837	404,286	67,806
companies*	708,754	369,919	67,546
Confectionery, snacks	80,143	4,892	5,666
and soft drinks	63,569	1,820	12,763
Insurance and real estate	160,299	18,237	610,154
	120,272	16,681	625,561
Apparel, footwear, and	538,979	46,563	19,905
accessories	509,981	41,078	15,005
Sporting goods,	173,284	848	6,427
toys and games	170,146	1,546	4,005
Publishing and media	256,952	8,978	194,911
	214,175	9,246	165,562
Beer and wine	38,868	4,056	6,426
	38,382	2,751	7,335

*LNA's definition of a direct-response ad is one in which the end product for which a customer is writing or calling is received in the mail.
Source: Leading National Advertisers, Competitive Media Reporting, 1995.

of the total of all magazine and newspaper advertising done in the United States because both are primarily vehicles for general advertising.

Magazine and newspaper advertising coverage is determined by circulation patterns. Direct marketers reach their prospects by matching the audience characteristics of either media with their target markets. For some direct marketers, magazines or newspapers are a primary way of reaching potential buyers, but for others these media supplement activities in television or radio. Direct-response print ads can also extend the reach of a mailing list by exposing a firm's offer to a broader audience than what is possible with lists alone.

Preparation for advertising in magazines and newspapers starts with a systematic look at why a firm wants to advertise and what it expects to get out of the effort. The firm's goals must be quantifiable, such as a definite sales increase at a specific point in a campaign. A firm may seek help on setting its goals from the publications in which it plans to advertise, but a better source for the estimate of campaign responsiveness may be the firm's own results from similar previous campaigns. Regardless, the firm needs to have kept good records of past marketing efforts and have stored that information in a database so it can be reviewed. Ideally, the firm's overall goal determines the amount of money the firm should spend on the campaign.

Exhibit 14.1 contains a Fingerhut direct-response print offer for a 10-karat gold cubic zirconia solitaire ring. The ad comes from a 1994 issue of *TV Guide.* It is typical of the firm's ongoing effort to get new customers through mass-market publications.

Fingerhut's success in the 1990s has been due in part to a heavy reliance on direct-response print advertising. Fingerhut's revenue growth exceeded 17 percent in 1993, a 15th consecutive record year. Fingerhut has used general merchandise catalogs since the early 1970s to reach consumers in approximately 31 million households across the United States. Catalogs and other promotions mailed expanded to 476 million during 1993.

MAKING MAGAZINE AND NEWSPAPER ADVERTISING WORK

Direct-response magazine and newspaper space advertising must ask the reader to do something. To make a sale, the ad must present enough information to stimulate a purchase decision or generate an inquiry, which will be followed up by mail or a personal sales call. Magazines and newspapers that contain a heavy volume of direct-response ads usually outperform those that do not have many such ads. This is probably true because particular magazines or newspapers have readers with a positive attitude toward direct marketing activities.

Direct marketers have learned that success or failure with direct-response print is influenced by audience characteristics; the cost per thousand readers delivered; the editorial climate of the publication and editorial adjacency (which means what materials the ad is near); the physical position of the ad in the publication and the position of the ad on a page; the advertising copy itself; and the scheduling, timing, and testing of the ad.

EXHIBIT 14.1. Fingerhut Direct-Response Print Offer

Audience Characteristics

For general-population newspapers, audience characteristics are not overly significant because the sheer size of their circulations makes the compilation of detailed audience profiles difficult. The best results come from newspapers that deliver the most readers per dollar spent, meaning the cost per thousand readers. Magazine audiences are more specialized, and therefore audience characteristics are extremely important, making cost per thousand of lesser significance than with newspapers except for relative magazine comparisons when two magazines serve the same audience.

Times Mirror, a major publisher of magazines and newspapers, offers advertisers not only reader demographic and lifestyle information but also reader product preferences based on consumer transactional data supplied by Marketing Information Technologies (MIT). Though MIT keeps consumer purchase data in its own database, it can match its files to Times Mirror's files to come up with a picture of Times Mirror subscribers and prospects that meet targeting specifications requested by its advertisers. This gives magazine advertising an entirely new way to meet the marketing needs of the firms that place ads in its magazines and newspapers.

Times Mirror's magazine group consists of 10 men's special-interest titles, including *Field & Stream, Popular Science, Outdoor Life, Golf Magazine, The Sporting News,* and *Salt Water Sportsman.* Times Mirror newspapers include the

Los Angeles Times and the *Baltimore Sun.* The firm uses its database of all subscribers to identify people who subscribe to any of its newspapers as well as to any of its magazines. While most of the magazine subscribers are outdoors-oriented men, most of the newspaper subscribers are women. One advantage of this combined database is the ability to offer advertisers joint newspaper-magazine promotions. Because of their local character, newspapers also offer magazine advertisers the opportunity to target heavy concentrations of people geographically.

Exhibit 14.2 shows an NRI Schools direct-response print ad that appeared in the Times Mirror publication *Popular Science.* NRI Schools offers training in such areas as electronic equipment servicing, automotive repair, and air conditioning. The training is positioned as a way to become your own boss by learning a trade.

Over and above telling more about readers, present and past, the Times Mirror database is a valuable asset to help its more sophisticated advertisers reach highly segmented prospects. Consumer magazines are under pressure from their advertisers to become more efficient sales tools. To that end, all of Times Mirror's 10 magazines offer selective binding, which enables printers to version each copy of a magazine to a specific reader.

Cost for Readers

Knowing in which publications to advertise, when to advertise in them, and where to go to pay the lowest prices is crucial to the success of a firm's sales or lead-generation program. The companies that succeed and those that fail are separated by how they answer the following key question: What is the lowest cost per thousand readers (CPM) I can pay for my media plan?

EXHIBIT 14.2. NRI Schools Direct-Response Print Ad

Before venturing into print media, a firm should do a quick profit-and-loss (P&L) analysis of what numbers it needs to achieve for its direct marketing program to be a success. (See Chapter 18 for a discussion of P&L statements.) A P&L analysis shows the firm how much circulation its print media budget should buy, how much it must sell or how many leads it might generate, and how many orders it will need to make a profit.

Editorial Climate and Adjacency

Editorial climate is the mental or psychological atmosphere in which people find themselves when reading a publication. These climates range from sports to business magazines and from conservative to liberal newspapers. Editorial adjacency refers to the content of the article or articles next to which the ad will appear. Advertisers have very little control over the flow of editorial material in a publication.

Physical Position

Physical position in publications is about where in a magazine or newspaper a direct marketer's ad gets placed. There is much debate over this subject, but if a publication charges more for a particular location, it is likely that it expects that location to get more traffic and a higher chance of being read. Physical position on the page is where an ad is placed. There is also much debate about this issue. The key is to stand out on the page. Color helps, as does some device to outline the ad, such as a box. Testing can determine how differences in page location and page attributes affect the audience's response to an ad.

Advertising Copy

The advertising copy positions a firm's product or service. It communicates a message to the reader about the reasons for making a purchase or an inquiry and tries to get the reader to pick up a telephone or send in a postcard. In general, the most successful direct-response ads feature a headline that communicates a benefit to the reader. As stressed throughout this book, unless an ad appeals to a particular need, it will not achieve maximum results. (Refer back to Chapter 8 for more on creative strategies for direct-response print advertising.)

Scheduling, Timing, and Testing

Scheduling and timing issues are associated with when and how often a direct-response ad appears in a given publication. Testing involves using variations in the ad or in the print media to evaluate alternative campaign approaches. (See Chapter 17 for more on testing.) If a firm places direct-response ads in several publications, it needs to have a means of tracking the responses to each ad version. To make its campaigns work, the firm needs to determine exactly which publications are the best vehicles for its ads. And, the firm should test its creative plan and offer with key codes on ad coupons or with 800 numbers that have unique extensions.

TYPES OF MAGAZINES

On the basis of the audience served, direct marketers use two principal types of magazines:

1. *Consumer magazines.* Consumer publications are read by people who buy products for their own consumption or for household consumption.
2. *Business magazines.* Business publications include three types: (a) trade papers, which appeal to retailers, wholesalers, and other distributors; (b) industrial magazines, which appeal to those involved with manufacturing; and (c) professional magazines, which appeal to specialized audiences in medicine, law, and other areas.

Consumer Magazines

Consumer magazines can be divided into a large number of subclassifications, from airline magazines to youth magazines. Publications such as *Reader's Digest* are considered general-interest magazines. Consumer magazines are also distinguished on the basis of their distribution. Women's service magazines include both circulation-distributed magazines such as *Ladies' Home Journal* and store-distributed magazines such as *Woman's Day.*

The magazines most familiar to the general population are those sold directly to consumers for their entertainment and/or education. There are hundreds of such magazines for sale in the United States, and the trend is for more to be developed. The primary reason behind this growth is increasing magazine specialization.

Specialized magazines allow for more refined market segmentations because good information is available about their audiences. Many magazines that sell throughout the United States also publish regional editions, which advertisers can use to reach only parts of the country or to change the advertising messages from one region to another. There are even metropolitan editions in which advertisers can run ads only in the magazine copies that will be sold and distributed in and near selected cities.

One advantage of consumer magazine advertising is that readers take longer with the content than in other media, so there are more opportunities to sell or generate leads with the ads. Another advantage is that more than one person may read a copy of a magazine. These extra readers are important to advertisers because they represent a larger audience for their advertising message. The readers who buy the magazine or subscribe to it are the primary audience, and the "pass-along" readers are the secondary audience. Also, magazines come out at varying times, so there is flexibility in scheduling, and magazine formats permit different sizes of advertisements, as well as foldouts, inserts, color, and even smell. On the negative side, general consumer magazines may have wasted circulation (that is, many readers may not be attracted to a given ad) and advertisements can easily be ignored.

TV Guide is a highly successful general consumer magazine. Aside from the strength of its articles and features, its mass-market appeal results from the popularity of television. Exhibit 14.3 shows part of a Franklin Mint direct-response ad for a white polar bear sculpture that appeared in *TV Guide.* The advertising copy describes how the offering was inspired by art commissioned by

EXHIBIT 14.3. Franklin Mint Direct-Response Ad

The power of porcelain. The sparkling brilliance of crystal.

Alaska. Home to the most majestic wildlife on earth. Among those magnificent creatures, the mighty Polar Bear. Living embodiment of nature's grandeur. And the inspiration for this original work of art commissioned by The Alaskan Wildlife Conservation Trust. The creation of world-renowned wildlife artist Chris Denbigh, this extraordinary sculpture is crafted in fine Tesori® porcelain, a specially prepared sculptor's blend of powdered porcelain and resins. The sculpture comes to life on its own display base, custom designed in fine crystal art glass, specially contoured to suggest the animal's natural environment.

Just $37.50. From The Franklin Mint, Franklin Center, PA 19091-0001.

SATISFACTION GUARANTEED

If you wish to return any Franklin Mint purchase, you may do so within 30 days of your receipt of that purchase for replacement, credit or refund.

The polar bear is captured in all its awesome power in a sculptured portrait of astonishing realism.

The Polar Bear

The Alaskan Wildlife Conservation Trust
c/o The Franklin Mint
Franklin Center, PA 19091-0001

Please mail by November 10, 1996.

Please enter my order for The Polar Bear.

I need SEND NO MONEY NOW. I will be billed $37.50* when my sculpture is ready to be shipped to me.

*Plus my state sales tax and $3.95 for shipping and handling.

SIGNATURE ____________
ALL ORDERS ARE SUBJECT TO ACCEPTANCE.

MR/MRS/MISS/MS ____________
PLEASE PRINT CLEARLY.

ADDRESS ____________ APT. # ______

CITY/STATE ____________ ZIP ______

TELEPHONE # (______) ____________

16883-45-001

the Alaskan Wildlife Conservation Trust. The polar bear sells for $37.50. Ordering is as easy as filling out the removable card and putting it in the mail.

Compared to *TV Guide,* several of the other large consumer magazines are much more specialized. They include *Better Homes & Gardens, Family Circle,* and *Woman's Day,* which are oriented toward family service and homemakers, and *National Geographic,* which features stories and pictures from different parts of the world. As mentioned earlier, the growth in magazines has been among specialized publications like these, which appeal to certain interests or hobbies.

Color printing is very good in most magazines. On average, a four-color advertisement will get 50 percent more readership than a black-and-white advertisement. Thus a four-color advertisement will generally cost about half as much as a black-and-white advertisement of the same size in terms of cost per thousand readers (CPM).

When marketers want to compare two magazines to see which one is more economical, they use the CPM measurement. Both magazines and newspapers have rate cards that contain CPM figures. Rates are also published in a source called *Standard Rate and Data Service (SRDS).* Marketers can look up the advertising rates for most consumer magazines in the appropriate volume of *SRDS. SRDS* contains more than just advertising rates: marketers can find out how often a publication comes out, when they should get their advertisement to a publication for a certain issue, the sizes of the pages and of the advertisements available, an estimate of the circulation, and other information.

Exhibit 14.4 shows advertising rate information for *Sports Illustrated,* the popular sports entertainment magazine. *Sports Illustrated*'s advertising space rates differ by whether the ad is black-and-white or color, as well as size and location. A full-page color ad on the back cover is the most expensive.

Business Magazines

While there are hundreds of consumer magazines, there are thousands of magazines directed to certain kinds of business and industrial purposes. These business publications have many of the same characteristics as consumer magazines, and they operate in much the same way, except that their articles and advertising are usually oriented toward specific business interests.

General business publications such as *Fortune* and *Business Week* serve a relatively broad audience of businesspeople. In contrast, trade magazines or papers are read mostly by retailers, wholesalers, and original equipment manufacturers; examples are *Direct Marketing* magazine and *ComputerWorld.* Industrial magazines may cover the field in either of two ways: horizontally or vertically. The horizontal publication is aimed at a specific function or activity within many industries, while the vertical one attempts to do a complete job of covering one

EXHIBIT 14.4. *SRDS* Information for *Sports Illustrated*

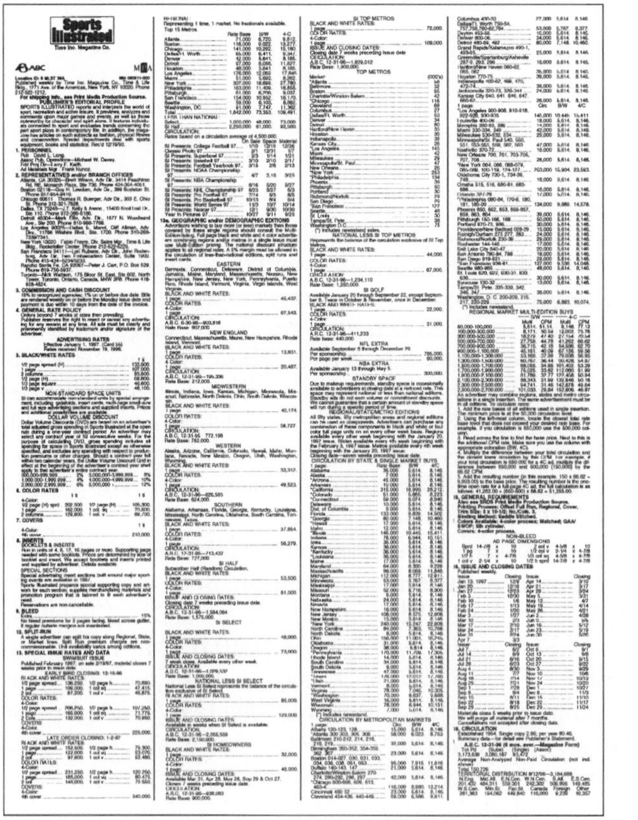

industry. *Sales & Marketing Management*'s coverage is horizontal because it is edited for sales managers and their staffs. By contrast, *Progressive Grocer,* a vertical publication, covers the grocery industry.

Business publications are often read during working hours, so the readers' minds are on business, with few distractions. They also reach directly the persons who have responsibility for the items being promoted. The disadvantage is that there may be a lot of competing advertising.

It is also important to distinguish between controlled and paid circulation for business magazines. The publisher of a controlled-circulation magazine concentrates on a specialized business audience, limits coverage to that one group, and tailors its editorial material to the needs of that group. The publisher usually sends the magazine free to this select group in order to obtain high coverage because the magazine depends entirely on audience-related advertising revenue for support. If just anyone may receive a publication, it is uncontrolled circulation. Most business publications, however, are supported by paid circulation just as most consumer magazines have mostly paid circulation. Also, business publications are less likely than consumer magazines to be sold at newsstands.

Fortune magazine, however, is sold by subscription and at newsstands. It reaches a wide audience of business professionals in managerial positions. Exhibit 14.5 shows a *Fortune* magazine direct-response ad for Hyperion Software. The ad invites readers to contact Hyperion via telephone or the Internet, about its new Spider-Man Intranet application.

EXHIBIT 14.5. Hyperion Software Ad as Seen in *Fortune*

EXHIBIT 14.6. Learning International Ad that Appeared in *Sales & Marketing Management*

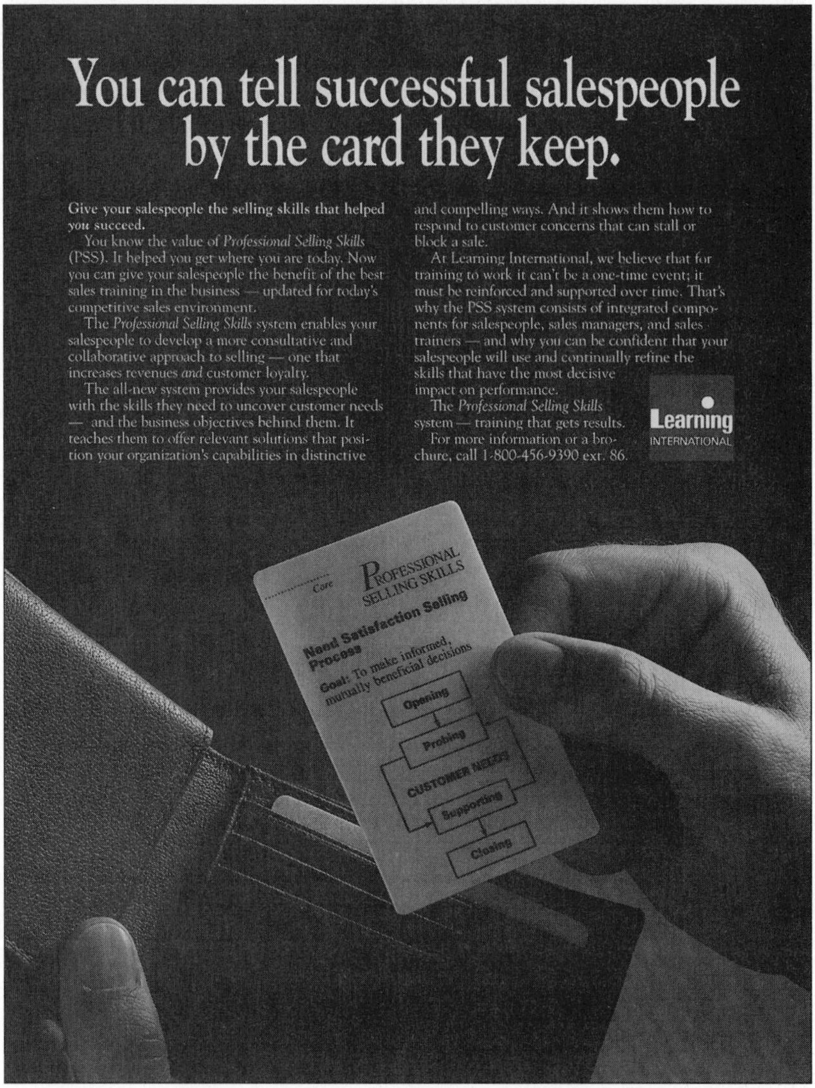

Ads in *Sales & Marketing Management* are more focused than those found in *Fortune*. Exhibit 14.6 shows a fourth-cover direct-response ad for Learning International offering the Professional Selling Skills system, which enables a firm's salespeople to develop a more consultative and collaborative approach to selling. Readers are invited to call an 800 number to get more information or a brochure.

Exhibit 14.7 shows advertising rate information for *Sales & Marketing Management*. In determining its rates, the magazine differentiates by black-and-white or color, size, and location. It also has geographic and demographic editions representing four regions.

EXHIBIT 14.7. ***SRDS*** **Rate Information for** ***Sales & Marketing Management***

Sales & Marketing Management

A Bill Communications, Inc. Publication

BPA

Location ID: 7 BLST 131A **Mid 004812-000**
Published 13 times a year by Bill Communications, Inc., 355 Park Ave., South, New York, NY 10010. Phone 212-592-6300. Fax 212-592-6309.
E-Mail sales@smmmag.comedit@smmmag.com
URL http://www.salesandmarketing.com
For shipping info., see Print Media Production Source.

PUBLISHER'S EDITORIAL PROFILE

SALES & MARKETING MANAGEMENT is a business magazine published for executives who manage the sales and marketing functions in their companies. Rec'd 10/16/91.

1. PERSONNEL
Grp Pub-Richard O'Connor.
Assoc Pub—Tom Larranaga.
Editor—Charlie Butler.
Prod Mgr—JoAnn DePalma.

2. REPRESENTATIVES and/or BRANCH OFFICES
New York, NY 10010— 355 Park Ave. South. Phone 212-592-6200.
Huntington Beach, CA 92647-3072—7711 Center Ave., Suite 340. Phone 714-379-2240. Fax 714-379-2295.
Chicago, IL 60601—180 North Michigan Ave. Phone 312-782-1266. Fax 312-782-5282.
Atlanta, GA 30329—1482 Druid Valley Dr. Phone 404-321-4654. Fax 404-325-1991.

3. COMMISSION AND CASH DISCOUNT
15% on gross billing to recognized agencies on space, color, bleed and position, provided account is paid by 10th of month following invoice date. Commission is not allowed on other charges, such as engraving, statistical or art services, reprints, merchandising service, back-up or folding charges. Net 30 days.

4. GENERAL RATE POLICY
No cancellations accepted after closing date.

ADVERTISING RATES
Effective January 1, 1997. (Issue/Card)
Rates received November 6, 1996.

5. BLACK/WHITE RATES

	1 ti	3 ti	6 ti	12 ti	15 ti	24 ti
1 page	10,110.	10,000.	9,860.	9,550.	9,330.	9,040.
2/3 page	7,810.	7,450.	7,220.	7,130.	6,950.	6,780.
1/2 pg isl	6,770.	6,540.	6,280.	6,170.	6,010.	5,830.
1/2 page	6,210.	6,010.	5,790.	5,590.	5,420.	5,270.
1/3 page	4,140.	3,990.	3,900.	3,760.	3,650.	3,530.
1/4 page	3,360.	3,260.	3,170.	3,060.	2,980.	2,900.
1/6 page	2,360.	2,270.	2,220.	2,130.	2,070.	1,990.

1/6 page not accepted for Statistical Section of Survey of Buying Power and Survey of Media Markets.
Frequency discount based on 12-month period.

6. COLOR RATES

	1 ti	3 ti	6 ti	12 ti	15 ti	24 ti
4-Color:						
1 page	13,140.	13,030.	12,890.	12,580.	12,360.	12,070.

Standard color, extra .... 805.
Matched, extra .... 1010.
4-color, extra .... 3030.

7. COVERS
2nd cover .... 13,876. 4th cover .... 14,369.
3rd cover .... 13,876.

8. INSERTS
Supplied multiple page inserts available.
Non-commissionable.
Bind-in charge .... 550. Tip in charge, extra.... 2195.

9. BLEED
No charge.

10. SPECIAL POSITION
Inside book, extra 5%

11. CLASSIFIED/MAIL ORDER
See Business Publication Advertising Source Classified section.

13a. GEOGRAPHIC and/or DEMOGRAPHIC EDITIONS
REGIONAL EDITIONS
Regional ROP editions are available in all issues of Sales Management except Survey issues.
Full page units only.

NORTHEAST
ME, NH, VT, MA, RI, CT, NY, NJ, PA, DE, MD, DC, VA, WV.
SOUTHEAST
NC, SC, GA, FL, TN, AL, MS.
MIDWEST
OH, KY, MI, MO, WI, KS, IA, NE, SD, ND, MN, IN, IL
SOUTH CENTRAL
OK, TX, AR, LA
WEST
NM, CO, AZ, CA, OR, NV, ID, WY, WA, UT, MT, AK, HI

	NE	SE	MW	SC	W
Black/white	5395.	3210.	5395.	3210.	4335.

Color:
Standard, black/white space rate, extra .... 645.
Matched, black/white space rate, extra .... 870.
4-color, black/white rate, extra .... 1620.

14. CONTRACT AND COPY REGULATIONS
See Contents page for location—items 1, 2, 3, 5, 7, 12, 13, 15, 16, 17, 18, 23, 28, 30.

15. GENERAL REQUIREMENTS
Also see SRDS Print Media Production Source.
Printing Process: Offset Full Run.
Trim Size: 8 x 10-3/4; No./Cols. 3.
Binding Method: Perfect.
Colors Available: 4-color process; Matched.

NON-BLEED
AD PAGE DIMENSIONS

1 pg	7 x 10		1/3 h	7 x 3-1/4
2/3 v	4-1/2 x 10		1/3 sq	4-1/2 x 4-3/4
2/3 h	7 x 6-1/2		1/4 v	3-3/8 x 4-3/4
1/2 isl	4-1/4 x 7-1/4		1/4 h	7 x 2-1/4
1/2 h	7 x 4-3/4		1/6 v	2-1/8 x 4-3/4
1/3 v	2-1/8 x 10			

(*) 2/3 horizontal, 1/3 horizontal and 1/4 horizontal are only available in section C of Survey Issue.

16. ISSUE AND CLOSING DATES
Published 13 times a year.

Issue:	Closing	Issue:	Closing
Jan	11/18	Aug	6/18
Feb	12/18	Mid-Aug	7/18
Mar	1/18	Sep	7/18
Apr	2/18	Oct	8/18
May	3/18	Nov	9/26
Jun	4/18	Dec	10/24
Jul	5/18		

18. CIRCULATION
Established 1918. Single copy 4.95; per year 48.00.
Summary data—for detail see Publisher's Statement.

B.P.A. 12-31-96 (6 mos. aver. qualified)

Total	Non-Pd	Paid
61,053	...	61,053

Non-qualified paid subscriptions and or non-paid requests 3,321
Single Copy Sales 3,118
Average Non-Qualified (not incl. elsewhere):
Total 8,512

TERRITORIAL DISTRIBUTION 11/96—61,678

N.Eng.	Mid.Atl.	E.N.Cen.	W.N.Cen.	S.Atl.	E.S.Cen.
4,035	8,358	11,975	4,540	9,245	2,003
W.S.Cen.	Mtn.St.	Pac.St.	Canada	Foreign	Other
4,330	2,667	8,647	4,507	1,291	80

Non-qualified paid subscriptions and or non-paid requests 2,860
Single Copy Sales 3,738

BUSINESS ANALYSIS OF CIRCULATION
1 —Manufacturers.
2 —Service Organizations.
3 —Wholesale or Distribution.
4 —Retail.
5 —Others Allied to the Field, incl. Schools, Universities, Libraries, Gov't and Libraies.
TL Qual —Total Qualified
6 —Non-qualified paid subscriptions and or non-paid requests
7 —Single Copy Sales
TL —Total

TL. Total. A. Pres., Owners, Partners & Gen. Mgrs. B. Vice Presidents. C. Sls; Mktg Dirs. Mgrs. Assts or Product; Brand Mgmt., individual Assts D. Reg'l Sales; Mktg. or Dir or Mgr. E. Adv; Mktg. Service Dir or Mgr. F. Company Copies. G. Other Titled & Non-Titled Pers. incl. Co. Copies.

	TL	A	B	C	D	E
1—	22,579	2,654	3,704	9,461	3,252	1,552
2—	23,856	6,125	3,633	7,182	2,012	1,753
3—	7,759	2,025	1,226	2,684	946	359
4—	2,325	629	291	754	205	171
5—	5,159	364	174	435	135	180
TL Qual—	61,676	11,797	9,028	20,516	6,550	4,015
6—	2,860	...	...	...	...	...
7—	3,738	...	...	...	...	...
TL—	68,276	...	...	...	...	...

	F	G
1—	319	1,637
2—	772	2,379
3—	93	426
4—	52	223
5—	2,506	1,365
TL Qual—	3,742	6,030
6—	...	...
7—	...	...
TL—	...	...

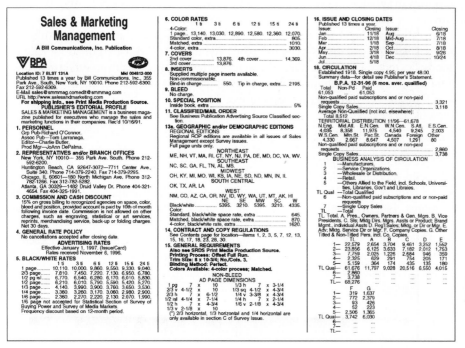

DIRECT MARKETING IN MAGAZINES

Direct-response advertising in consumer magazines is dominated by ads for collectibles, books, music, and self-help products and services such as weight-loss plans. Aside from ads in general business magazines such as *Fortune* or *Business Week,* direct-response ads in business publications tend to focus on the products and services of most interest to the specific magazine's readership. Similarly for consumer publications, the more specialized magazines contain ads for products and services that are very specific to the editorial content of the magazine. Fishing magazines such as *Field & Stream* contain ads for fishing equipment, and personal computer game magazines such as *PC Gamer* contain ads for the latest games.

Ads in consumer or business publications benefit direct marketers by playing a particular role in a firm's overall marketing strategy. Direct-response magazine space ads are used to generate sales, acquire customers, and test offers.

Sales Generation

Magazine space advertising has the potential to generate considerable sales for direct marketing firms. Franklin Mint (which was discussed in Chapter 8) and Bradford Exchange, competitors in the marketing of consumer collectibles, both make extensive use of direct-response ads in *TV Guide.*

Avon Products has long produced and marketed a wide variety of cosmetics, toiletries, fragrances, jewelry, gifts, and decorative items; more recently, Avon has introduced new entries such as lingerie, preschool educational toys, and videotapes. Most products are for women; some are for men and children. Although Avon is well known for its sales force of "Avon ladies" who are famed for ringing doorbells, today about one-third of its worldwide sales comes from direct-response print ads that tout the options for ordering from the Avon catalog: phone, fax, mail, or a traditional Avon sales representative.

Customer Acquisition

New-customer acquisition is another major reason for using space advertising. Financial services such as Fidelity Investments, the largest mutual fund company in the United States, find receptive audiences for direct-response offers of their literature. Fidelity's ads can be found in such publications as *Business Week, Forbes, Fortune,* and *U.S. News & World Report.*

Fidelity also makes heavy use of direct mail to solicit business and to keep in contact with its customers. Prospects who call the telephone number in one of Fidelity's print ads are sent a packet of information about the fund described in the ad.

Offer Testing

Magazine space advertising is a good medium in which to test alternative offers and creative approaches. Because many magazines offer split runs and regional editions, a firm can test several versions of its offer copy.

DIRECT RESPONSE IN NEWSPAPERS

Newspapers are the major advertising medium for direct-response retailers that operate store locations, banks, and other similar retail locations. It is easy to understand the attraction newspapers have for these marketers: newspapers have large circulation; they have distribution in specific trading areas; they make day-after-day appearances; and they are used as shopping guides.

Newspapers are usually classified according to their frequency of publication, with some published daily and others only weekly. In addition, a number of dailies publish a Sunday edition. Daily newspapers are often categorized on the basis of the size of their market area. Thus, advertisers may decide to take the "first 10 markets," "first 50 markets," and so on. Usually, the weekly or community newspaper is published in a small, homogeneous community. This may be a small town in the Midwest or a suburb of a major city on the East or West Coast.

Like magazines, newspapers can be classified according to paid circulation or controlled circulation. Shopping newspapers, or "shoppers," for example, are normally distributed free and therefore have controlled circulation. The majority of newspapers, however, are not distributed free.

Newspapers may also be distinguished on the basis of the audience they attract. Thus, in contrast to the general-interest newspapers, many newspapers cater to special groups; foreign-language papers and trade papers are two examples. These papers are like magazines in many ways, although their format is similar to that of other newspapers. Size is another criterion for classifying newspapers. Some newspapers are tabloids and others come in a standard size. Run-of-paper (ROP) color (see p. 310) offers advertisers still more flexibility in their use of newspapers.

Newspapers offer direct-response advertisers special techniques that improve the impact of their advertising, including zone editions, color preprints, inserts, and other such services. Through the use of zone editions, newspapers can break out their circulation according to the geographic area they serve and thus offer an advertiser only a portion of their total circulation. For example, the *New York Times* offers zone editions, allowing an advertiser to place ads in one or more of those territories. This service has special appeal for a retailer with a limited trading area, but national advertisers seeking to develop segmented targets can also use it. Color preprints and inserts involve high-quality color advertisements produced by a specialized printer and shipped to the newspaper for insertion into a particular issue. This technique allows magazine-quality color ads that are superior to run-of-paper color. Advertising in newspapers can run up, down, or across the page, or it can be positioned in the middle of the page.

As with magazines, direct marketers can use the rates published in the *Standard Rate and Data Service (SRDS)* to compare newspapers. Marketers can look up the advertising rates of daily and weekly newspapers. Newspapers have rate cards that contain cost-per-thousand (CPM) figures and indicate how often the publication comes out, advertising submission deadlines, the sizes of the pages for advertisements, circulation estimates, and other information. Exhibit 14.8 lists the

EXHIBIT 14.8. *New York Times* Advertising Rates

The New York Times

229 W. 43rd St., New York, NY 10036.
Phone 212-556-7777. TWX710-581-6599. Fax 212-556-7787.

ABC

Location ID: 1 NSNL NY **Mid 017018-000**
Member: NAA; ABC Coupon Distribution Verification Service; ACB, Inc.
MORNING, SATURDAY AND SUNDAY.

1. PERSONNEL
Pub—Arthur Ochs Sulzberger Jr.
Senior VP Adv—Daniel H. Cohen.
VP/Adv Sales—Alexis Ruryk, Jyll Holzman.

2. REPRESENTATIVES and/or BRANCH OFFICES
Atlanta 30350-8300—Dunwoody Place. Phone 770-643-0053. FAX 770-643-9345.
Bloomfield (NJ) 07003—1515 Broad Street. Phone 201-338-8303. FAX 201-338-8706.
Boston 02109—2 Faneuil Hall Marketplace. Phone 617-227-7820. FAX 617-742-0379.
Chicago 60601—233 N. Michigan Ave. Phone 312-565-0969.
Dallas 75219—3500 Maple Ave., Ste. 1360. Phone 214-526-1983. FAX 214-526-1984.
Detroit (Troy) 48084—755 W. Big Beaver Rd., Suite 1622. Phone 810-244-8989.
Garden City (NY) 11530—1325 Franklin Ave. Retail Phone 516-747-0511. Classif. Phone 516-747-1005. FAX 516-747-1159.
Houston 77055—9143 Bronco. Phone 713-464-0082. FAX 713-464-0378.
Los Angeles 90064—11835 W. Olympic, Suite 1065E. Phone 310-312-8650.
Miami 33132—100 N. Biscayne Blvd. Phone 305-379-1601.
Philadelphia 19106—740 The Bourse, Independence Mall East. Phone 215-925-8414.
San Francisco 94111—655 Montgomery, Suite 510. Phone 415-421-9700.
Washington 20006—1627 I Street, N.W. Phone 202-862-0414. FAX 202-862-0323.
White Plains (NY) 10604—701 Westchester Ave. Phone 914-428-2699. FAX 914-428-2428.
Dusseldorf, Germany—J.A.R. Communications.
London—SW1E 6AU, Basil Bicknell, London Bureau, 66 Buckingham Gate. Phone (44-171) 799-2981, FAX (44-171) 799-2982.
London—Powers Oversees LTD.
Paris, Publicitas LTD.
Mexico, Publications Representatives International, Inc.
Toronto-M4K1M7, JHD Media Group, Inc., 86 Dearbourne Ave. Phone 416-465-6444, FAX 416-465-7885.

3. COMMISSION AND CASH DISCOUNT
15% commission to recognized agencies only when invoices are paid by the 15th of the month following insertion. No cash discount. Insertion orders containing disclaimers are not accepted and agencies re responsible for payment of invoices for advertising placed by them on their own behalf or on behalf of their clients.
Insertion orders containing disclaimers are not accepted and agencies are responsible for payment of invoices for advertising placed by them on their own behalf or on behalf of their clients.

4. POLICY-ALL CLASSIFICATIONS
Minimum five days notice given of any rate revision.
Advertising is accepted by the Times subject to all terms and conditions contained herein.
Alcoholic beverage and cigarette advertising accepted.
When requested to insert a box number in a full run ad and to remail the box number replies, the service charge is 192.00 full run, 44.00 for zoned ads. Charges are not commissionable. Only bona fide box number replies will be forewarded to an advertiser.

ADVERTISING RATES
Effective January 1, 1997.
Received January 17, 1997.

5. BLACK/WHITE RATES
MISCELLANEOUS ADVERTISING RATES:
Apply to all other display advertising categories not listed here. For details, call your sales representative.

	Weekday	Sunday
SAU open, per inch	650.00	741.00

Inches charged full depth: col. 21; pg. 126.

Within 1 year:	Weekday	Sunday
1 pg/126"	632.00	720.00
5 pgs/630"	619.00	706.00
10 pgs/1,260"	605.00	690.00
20 pgs/2,520"	582.00	663.00
40 pgs/5,040"	571.00	651.00

Non-Standard Units: Inch rates, plus 5%.

ANNUAL BLANKET CONTRACT
Full run general contract advertisers may apply magazine linage, color and monotone, to fulfillment of their black and white contracts. The rate for such linage is same as though amount of space used were equivalent to the specified in black and white space contract.

11. SPECIAL DAYS/PAGES/FEATURES
Best Food Day: Wednesday.
Main News, Metropolitan News, Business Day & Theme Section, Daily; Sports Monday, Monday; Science Times, Tuesday; Living Section, Wednesday; Home Section, Thursday; Weekend, Friday.

12. R.O.P. DEPTH REQUIREMENTS
One col. 1"; 2 cols. 2"; 3 & 4 cols. 5.25"; 5 & 6 cols. 7". Ads over 18 inches deep charged full col.

13. CONTRACT AND COPY REGULATIONS
See Contents page for location of regulations—items 6, 15, 18, 25.

14. CLOSING TIME
Published Morning, Saturday and Sunday.

Day:	Time	Closes	Day:	Time	Closes
Mon	4:30pm	Fri	Thu	4:30pm	Tue
Tue	4:30pm	Fri	Fri	4:30pm	Wed
Wed	4:30pm	Mon	Sat	4:30pm	Thu

SPECIAL SECTIONS

Day:	Time	Closes
Sports	4:30pm	Thu
Science Times	4:30pm	Fri
Living Section	12n	Fri
Home Section	2pm	Tue
Weekend	5pm	Wed

Insert proofs not delivered to advertiser until after publication.

15. MECHANICAL MEASUREMENTS
PRINTING PROCESS: Offset.
6 col; ea 2-1/16"; 1/8" betw col.
Inches charged full depth: col. 21; pg. 126.

16. SPECIAL CLASSIFICATIONS/RATES
These rates are for ads ordered and accepted under designated classifications. Ads ordered elsewhere are charged general advertising rates, unless classification is higher. Position charges extra.
Display ads of bonafide agencies promoting service of own agency, 20% from card rates, less contract discounts. No agency commission.

ENTERTAINMENT

	Weekday (Per inch)	Sunday (Per inch)
Open	505.00	605.00
Within 1 year:		
1 pg/126"	503.00	603.00
3 pgs/378"	501.00	601.00
5 pgs/630"	499.00	597.00
10 pgs/1,260"	497.00	595.00
20 pgs/2,520"	495.00	593.00
40 pgs/5,040"	486.00	581.00
60 pgs/7,560"	480.00	574.00

NEIGHBORHOOD ENTERTAINMENT

Within 1 year:	Weekday (Per inch)	Sunday (Per inch)
Open	401.00	473.00
1/2 pg/63"	392.00	463.00
1 pg/126"	383.00	449.00
5 pgs/630"	372.00	437.00
10 pgs/1,260"	360.00	425.00

MOTION PICTURES

Within 1 year:	Weekday (Per inch)	Sunday (Per inch)
Open	511.00	614.00
2 pgs/252"	504.00	606.00
5 pgs/630"	499.00	597.00
10 pgs/1,260"	488.00	587.00
20 pgs/2,520"	481.00	577.00
40 pgs/5,040"	470.00	564.00
60 pgs/7,560"	457.00	550.00
100 pgs/12,600"	445.00	536.00
150 pgs/18,900"	439.00	532.00
200 pgs/25,200"	435.00	528.00
250 pgs/31,500"	432.00	525.00
300 pgs/37,800"	430.00	522.00
350 pgs/44,100"	427.00	519.00
400 pgs/50,400"	424.00	516.00

Ads repeated on Saturday within 3 weeks, 345.00.

FINE ARTS/ANTIQUES

	Weekday (Per inch)	Sunday (Per inch)
Open	440.00	567.00
1/2 pg/63"	420.00	537.00
1 pg/126"	402.00	526.00
2 pgs/252"	394.00	513.00
3 pgs/378"	388.00	499.00
5 pgs/630"	382.00	491.00
7 pgs/882"	374.00	485.00
10 pgs/1,260"	366.00	477.00

Weekday ads repeated on Sunday within 9 days, 308.00, (identical ad must run).
3 Consecutive Sundays 540.00.

BUSINESS DAY/SUNDAY BUSINESS

	Weekday	Sunday
Open	650.00	729.00
1 pg/126"	632.00	685.00
5 pgs/630"	619.00	674.00
10 pgs/1,260"	605.00	667.00
20 pgs/2,520"	582.00	660.00
40 pgs/5,040"	571.00	653.00
60 pgs/7,560"	552.00	641.00
75 pgs/9,450"	540.00	631.00
100 pgs/12,600"	519.00	610.00
150 pgs/18,900"	488.00	554.00
200 pgs/25,200"	471.00	529.00
250 pgs/31,500"	455.00	502.00

Applies to weekday combination 375.00 ads repeated from Sunday Business section within 3 weeks, (identical ad must run); weekday/Sunday charges will be billed separately on a pro-rata basis. Daily/Sunday and Northeast/National charges are billed separately.

FINANCIAL NOTICES/SECURITIES OFFERINGS/ REDEMPTION NOTICES

	Weekday (Per inch)	Sunday (Per inch)
Open	525.00	583.00
1 pg/126"	497.00	553.00
5 pg/630"	460.00	512.00
10 pg/1,260"	445.00	496.00
20 pg/2,520"	435.00	484.00

RESTAURANTS (Going Out in New York/Catering/Night Clubs/Caberets)

	Weekday (Per inch)	Sunday (Per inch)
Open	394.00	481.00
1/2pg/63"	368.00	449.00
1pg/126"	347.00	434.00
2pgs/252"	331.00	413.00
4pgs/504"	316.00	394.00
6pgs/756"	296.00	371.00
8pgs/1,008"	278.00	347.00

Ads repeated within 7 days (identical ad must run), 262.00; 3 consecutive Fridays, same size ad must run and must be submitted on one insertion order, 326.00.

RESORTS, HOTELS AND DOMESTIC DESTINATIONS

	Weekday	Sunday
Open	531.00	597.00
1 pg/126"	500.00	562.00
5 pgs/630"	492.00	552.00
10 pgs/1,260"	484.00	544.00
20 pgs/2,520"	476.00	534.00
40 pgs/5,040"	465.00	523.00

Sunday Travel Section pg 2 & back pg position charges, 28.00.

TRANSPORTATION/TOUR OPERATORS/TRAVEL AGENTS/FOREIGN GOVERNMENT TOURISM

	Weekday (Per inch)	Sunday (Per inch)
Open	576.00	597.00
1/2 pg/63"	561.00	579.00
1 pg/126"	559.00	571.00
3 pgs/378"	557.00	563.00
5 pgs/630"	554.00	560.00
10 pgs/1,260"	551.00	557.00
20 pgs/2,520"	549.00	554.00
40 pgs/5,040"	540.00	550.00
60 pgs/7,560"	534.00	540.00
75 pgs/9,450"	529.00	536.00
100 pgs/12,600"	524.00	532.00

Sunday ads repeated on a weekday (same size within 7 days), 370.00. Sunday Travel Section pg 2 & back pg postion charges, 28.00.

SHOPPING WORLD

Within 1 year:	Weekday (Per inch)	Sunday (Per inch)
Open	373.00	447.00
1/2 pg/63"	354.00	425.00
1 pg/126"	336.00	403.00
2 pgs/252"	317.00	380.00
4 pgs/504"	298.00	358.00
10 pgs/1,260"	279.00	335.00
20 pgs/2,520"	223.00	268.00

Sunday ads repeated in weekday theme sections within 3 weeks, (identical ad must run) 285.00.

NATIONAL GROCERY PRODUCTS

	Weekday (Per Col. Inch)	Sunday (Per Col. Inch)
Open	488.00	558.00
1 pg/126"	420.00	479.00
5 pgs/630"	390.00	445.00
10 pgs/1,260"	366.00	417.00
20 pgs/2,520"	342.00	383.00

Full-run advertising earns credit toward part-run contracts; however, part-run advertising cannot be credited toward completion of full-run contracts.

BOOK PAGE

	Weekday	Sunday
Open	564.00	651.00
1 pg/126"	553.00	638.00
5 pgs/630"	542.00	626.00
10 pgs/1,260"	531.00	613.00
20 pgs/2,520"	517.00	595.00
40 pgs/5,040"	502.00	579.00

Saturday ad repeated from any weekday within 3 weeks, 375.00.

17. CLASSIFIED RATES
For complete data refer to classified rate section.

19. MAGAZINES

Book Review Section

SUNDAY.

Effective January 1, 1997.
Received January 17, 1997.

BLACK/WHITE RATES

	Open	126"	630"	1,260"
Full	23,900.	23,425.	22,950.	22,590.
4/5 pg	21,030.	20,615.	20,195.	19,880.
3/4 pg	20,245.	19,840.	19,440.	19,135.
3/5 pg	16,205.	15,880.	15,560.	15,315.
1/2 pg	13,790.	13,515.	13,240.	13,035.
9/20 pg	12,550.	12,300.	12,050.	11,860.
2/5 pg	11,160.	10,940.	10,720.	10,550.
3/10 pg	8,555.	8,385.	8,215.	8,085.
1/5 pg	5,905.	5,785.	5,670.	5,580.
3/20 pg	4,420.	4,335.	4,245.	4,180.
1/10 pg	3,010.	2,950.	2,890.	2,845.
1/20 pg	1,600.	1,570.	1,540.	1,515.

	2,520"	5,040"	*
1 pg	22,110.	21,390.	65.00
4/5 pg	19,455.	18,825.	52.00
3/4 pg	18,725.	18,115.	48.75
3/5 pg	14,990.	14,500.	39.00
1/2 pg	12,755.	12,340.	32.50
9/20 pg	11,610.	11,230.	29.25
2/5 pg	10,325.	9,990.	26.00
3/10 pg	7,915.	7,660.	19.50
1/5 pg	5,460.	5,285.	13.00
3/20 pg	4,090.	3,955.	9.75
1/10 pg	2,785.	2,695.	6.50
1/20 pg	1,480.	1,435.	3.25

Non-SAU per column inch 597.00.
Combination rate for book page and ROP, must be submitted on one insertion order, 395.00.
Discount for multiple pages in one issue of Book Review: 5% off earned rates for 2 facing pages in same issue or more, 10% for 6 pages or more.

POSITION CHARGES

Page 2, First lefthanded page	620.00
Page 3, Table of Contents, pg 1/5 V	200.00
Page 4, Letters, 3/5 V	440.00
Page 5, First righthand page facing Letters	620.00
Page 6, Full pg facing review page	440.00
Page 8, Full pg facing first editorial	440.00
Page 10, Full pg facing second editorial	440.00
Righthand page facing Best Sellers	620.00
1/5 V on Best Sellers page	200.00
Righthand page facing Paperback Best Sellers	620.00
Back cover	1,400.00
Opposite "Bookend" feature (2 options):	
Facing full page	440.00
Facing 2/5 V	300.00

Gutter bleed, 2 facing pages with use of gutter charged 10% extra. For center spread gutter bleed, submit one velox measuring 22-3/8" wide.
Reproduction material submitted deeper than 10-1/2" will occupy and be charged full col. depth. Minimum depth for preparing reproduction material for broken columns: 1 inch for 1 col., 2 inches for 2 cols., 5.25 inches for 3 cols, 5.25 inches for 4 cols., 7 inches for 5 cols.
Split runs available. Minimum size 3/5's page or larger. 500.00 (net).

SPECIAL CLASSIFICATION/RATES

	Per agate line Sunday
Open	27.50
26 Sundays in 1 year	26.00
52 Sundays in 1 year	25.00

Minimum space 4 lines. Word count: 6 to line.

CLOSING TIMES
Friday, 16 days before Sunday publication date.

MECHANICAL MEASUREMENTS
PRINTING PROCESS: Offset.
Page size 14" x 5 cols.

Magazine Section

SUNDAY.

Effective January 1, 1997.
Received January 17, 1997.

BLACK/WHITE RATES

	Open	3 pages	6 pages	12 pages
1pg	40,400.	38,380.	37,170.	35,955.
4/5pg	35,395.	33,625.	32,565.	31,500.
Jr.pg*	34,700.	32,965.	31,925.	30,885.
3/5pg	25,455.	24,180.	23,420.	22,655.
1/2pg	24,010.	22,810.	22,090.	21,370.
1/2pg (facing)**	45,975.	43,675.	42,295.	40,920.
2/5pg	15,940.	15,145.	14,665.	14,185.
Sq.Third	14,110.	13,405.	12,980.	12,560.
1/5pg	10,405.	9,885.	9,575.	9,260.
1/10pg	5,445.	5,175.	5,010.	4,845.

	18 pages	30 pages	60 pages
1pg	34,745.	33,530.	32,320.
4/5pg	30,440.	29,380.	28,315.
Jr.pg	29,840.	28,800.	27,760.
3/5pg	21,890.	21,130.	20,365.
1/2pg	20,650.	19,930.	19,210.
1/2pg (facing)	39,540.	38,160.	36,780.
2/5pg	13,710.	13,230.	12,750.
Sq.Third	12,135.	11,710.	11,290.
1/5pg	8,950.	8,635.	8,325.
1/10pg	4,685.	4,520.	4,355.

(**) For two facing, 1/2 page horizontal ads.
Volume discounts may only be earned on advertising inserted within a 12 month period.

MULITIPLE PAGES DISCOUNT

In 1 issue:		In 1 issue:	
4 - 7 pages	5%	12 or more pages	15%
8 - 11 pages	10%		

INCREMENTAL SPACE DISCOUNTS (GEN'L & RETAIL)
Contract advertisers with 1 or more pages during previous contract period, discounts apply to incremental pages or page equivalents.

New York Times' advertising rates. These rates are quite complex and detailed because the newspaper has many paper, magazine, and insert locations in which it carries ads.

Exhibit 14.9 shows a Mystery Guild book club ad that appeared in the Sunday *New York Times Book Review* section as the back page. The ad is well placed in the part of the newspaper of most interest to people who enjoy books. The reader of the ad is invited to complete the area in the lower left corner with a name, address,

EXHIBIT 14.9. Mystery Guild Ad Placed in Sunday *New York Times* Book Section

and introductory book selection. The customer next mails the coupon to the "mail-to" address and later receives his or her shipment of books.

Circulation patterns vary somewhat by type of paper. In general, a morning paper will be dispersed over a larger geographical area than will an evening paper in the same city. More morning newspapers will be mailed out on rural routes, and more evening papers will be picked off the newsstand. People who read the paper usually comprise a cross section of the people who live in the trading area served by each newspaper. In itself, newspaper is not a selective medium; men and women at all educational and income levels read newspapers.

A direct marketer who purchases newspaper space must do so with the knowledge that reaching target market members in several geographic areas simultaneously can be expensive. Because of this cost factor, all newspapers or even all the newspapers in any classification are rarely purchased. Sometimes an extensive newspaper list will be used for a single advertisement, such as a special book club offer. But when a sustained effort is to be made, newspaper advertising is usually planned in "flights" and often in selected areas and selected markets. For example, a book club company may run three flights, each of eight weeks' duration, during a given calendar year. These flights might be spaced uniformly throughout the year, or they might appear during periods when a particular type of club offer has gotten the highest response rate.

ADVANTAGES AND DISADVANTAGES OF NEWSPAPERS

Roberts and Berger see newspapers as offering a number of special advantages to any advertiser, including the direct marketer:

- *Frequency.* Most newspapers, with the exception of small suburban and rural papers, publish six or seven times per week, and some large urban papers offer both morning and evening editions.
- *Immediacy.* For black-and-white advertising, the close (the time by which the ad must be submitted for inclusion in a particular edition) is often only 48 hours prior to publication for camera-ready copy.
- *Reach.* Newspapers offer high penetration of households in their primary geographical area. A 50 percent penetration of households in the locality is not uncommon, and some newspapers have a penetration of 70 percent or more.
- *Local shopping reference.* No other medium has been able to supplant the newspaper as the primary reference to local shopping opportunities. Readers expect to learn of merchandise availability, sales, and special events in the pages of their newspapers. Special sections, like the midweek food sections, provide a focused environment for the advertiser of related product categories.
- *Fast response.* Since most newspapers are a daily medium, the direct marketer knows quickly whether a particular offer is producing a satisfactory response.[1]

Newspapers offer direct-response advertisers more territorial flexibility than do other media. Whether they use them for basic coverage or to fill in gaps left by television, they are able to advertise heavily in one area and lightly in another. In many areas, advertisers can reach more than 90 percent of the homes through a single newspaper. In most areas, all except a few homes (mostly those low on the economic scale) read some paper. Almost every newspaper includes news of interest to all groups of the population, including sports fans, homemakers, and businesspeople. Advertisers can select customers of a particular group by placing their advertisement in a special-interest section such as the sports or entertainment pages.

Despite their advantages, newspapers have limitations. They are usually discarded the day after publication and have little chance of having any impact beyond their first day. The chances that a direct-response ad will be read more than once are therefore very low. This also means that the direct marketer's offers should appear fresh and timely. The average reader spends about 30 minutes on the paper. This means the ad must make its impression quickly or it will fail to deliver its message. Finally, newspaper reproduction quality is well below magazines in appearance and quality, including generally poor color reproduction (with the exception of the more expensive color inserts).

ROP Advertising

Because newspapers reach a large, heterogeneous market, they do not provide the precise targeting that most direct marketers require. For example, run-of-paper (ROP) advertising can appear on any page, in any position in a column, or even buried among other ads; the choice of where the ad will appear is left to the editor. If the advertiser wants to make sure an ad is next to reading matter, he or she can usually order specific pages or positions at an extra charge. ROP color space will, of course, cost more than black-and-white space of the same size.

Display and Classified Advertising

Display and classified advertising account for most of a newspaper's total dollar volume. Retailers selling dresses or manufacturers selling air conditioners are interested mainly in display advertising. In fact, display advertising accounts for the majority of the advertising revenue for most newspapers. Display advertising has strong attention value because of illustrations, the arrangement of headlines and body text, the white space, color, or other visual devices. In contrast, classified ads are published without conspicuous display. As the name implies, classified advertisements are arranged under subheads according to what product or service is advertised. Direct-response classified advertising is used to sell houses, cars, and other similar items. Classified display advertising allows more flexibility or arrangement than regular classified in that borders, larger type, white space, photos, and occasionally color may be used. Some newspapers have the advertising of real estate agents and builders handled under classified display, others under retail.

Freestanding Inserts

Freestanding inserts (FSIs) are a major part of newspaper advertising. Placed in the Sunday editions of major American newspapers, they allow publishers to reach myriad zones and geographic segments. The entire medium is responsible for some 54 million copies in circulation per week. An advertiser has the FSI produced by a printer, who in turn ships the material to the newspaper, which becomes the distributor of the insert material. FSIs are particularly popular with direct-response retailers. They offer a great deal of flexibility because virtually any kind of print promotional format (reply cards or envelopes, single sheets, tabloids, catalogs, brochures, etc.) can be adapted to the FSI. Geographic and demographic options also offer flexibility in the size and type of market reached.

Some FSIs are collections of offers from more than one manufacturer, such as one Nabisco cereal offer that appeared in the Sunday edition of the *New York Times.* To participate, the consumer had to mail in an order form. As a result, he or she would save $1.50 with the purchase of any two Post or Nabisco cereals; also, with the purchase of any Post or Nabisco cereal and $5.95 plus postage and handling, the person could use the mail-in offer in the lower left hand of the page to get a collection of Dream Team gear.

FSIs reach the loyal readership of a particular newspaper and confer the credibility of that publication on the advertisement. Large and sophisticated advertisers—including retailers, travel and financial services firms, nonprofit organizations, and manufacturers of consumer packaged goods—have consistently used FSIs successfully.

Newspaper Supplements

Newspaper supplements include what are often called Sunday magazines. Like FSIs, they are produced at a central facility and distributed to newspapers for insertion in Sunday editions. They combine the frequency, reach, and rapid response of newspapers with the high-quality graphics reproduction of magazines. Because their content is feature articles as opposed to news, they are retained longer than newspapers by consumers, giving advertisers more opportunity for exposure. However, such supplements lack the immediacy of the newspaper itself because closing dates can be as long as 90 days prior to publication.

There are two types of supplements: the syndicated national supplement and the locally edited supplement. Each syndicated supplement is compiled, edited, and printed by a central organization. It is then sold to newspapers at a fixed cost per thousand. Newspaper supplements often compare favorably with leading national magazines in the quality of editorial matter. Group rates are frequently available for supplements that are part of newspapers in multiple markets. Sunday newspapers distribute *Parade* all over the United States; the cost of advertising space in it is a group rate for all these newspapers.

The paper on which newspaper supplements are printed is heavier and better finished than newsprint. Therefore, reproduction, both in black-and-white and in color, is superior to anything that can be offered in the regular newspaper columns. The same mechanical advantages are found in the locally edited supplements. Advertising can be bought separately in each of them, but for greater convenience to marketers and to compete successfully with the syndicated supplements, a number of the local supplements are produced by cooperative selling groups.

SUMMARY

Magazines and newspapers convey messages on printed pages to mass audiences or highly segmented audiences, depending on which specific publication is selected. For some direct marketers, magazines or newspapers are their main way of reaching potential buyers, but for others these media supplement activities in television or radio. Direct-response print ads can also extend the reach of a mailing list by exposing a firm's offer to a broader audience than what is possible with lists alone.

Direct-response magazine and newspaper space advertising must ask the reader to do something. To make a sale, the ad must motivate the prospect to make a purchase decision or an inquiry, which will be followed up by mail or a personal sales call. Magazines and newspapers that contain a heavy volume of direct-response ads usually outperform those that do not have many such ads.

The success or failure of direct-response print advertising in magazines and newspapers is influenced by audience characteristics; cost per thousand readers delivered; the editorial climate of the publication and editorial adjacency; the physical position of the ad in the publication and the position of the ad on a page; the advertising copy itself; and the scheduling, timing, and testing of the ad.

The two principal types of magazines used by direct marketers are consumer magazines and business magazines. Consumer magazines are read by people who buy products for their own consumption or for household consumption. Business magazines include trade papers that appeal to retailers, wholesalers, and other distributors; industrial magazines that are focused on those involved with manufacturing; and professional magazines that appeal to specialized audiences in medicine, law, and other areas.

The main reasons for using magazine space are sales generation, customer acquisition, and offer testing. Magazine space advertising has the potential to generate considerable sales for direct marketing firms. New-customer acquisition is another major reason for using space advertising. Magazine space advertising is a good medium to use in testing alternative offers and creative approaches. Because many magazines offer split runs and regional editions, a firm can test several versions of its offer copy.

Newspapers are the major advertising medium for direct-response retailers that operate store locations, banks, and other similar retail locations. Newspapers fit retail communication well because of their circulation distribution in specific trading areas, they make day-after-day appearances, and they are used as shopping guides. Newspapers are usually classified according to their frequency of publication with some published daily and others only weekly. In addition, a number of dailies publish a Sunday edition. Daily newspapers are often categorized on the basis of the size of their market area. Newspapers can be classified according to paid circulation or controlled circulation. Shopper newspapers are normally distributed free and therefore have circulation that is controlled, while the majority of newspapers are not distributed free.

Newspapers may also be distinguished on the basis of the audience they attract. Thus, in addition to the general-interest newspapers, there are many newspapers that cater to special groups such as foreign language papers and trade papers. These papers are like magazines in many ways, although their format is similar to that of other newspapers. Size is another criterion for classifying newspapers. Some newspapers are tabloids and others come in a standard size. ROP (run-of-paper) color offers advertisers still more flexibility in their use of newspapers.

REVIEW QUESTIONS

1. What are the two principal types of magazines used by direct marketers and what audiences do they reach?
2. What factors influence the success or failure of direct-response print advertising?
3. What are the primary differences between consumer and business magazines?
4. What are the main reasons for using magazine space advertising?
5. What are the advantages and disadvantages of magazine advertising for direct-response marketers?
6. What are the main reasons for using newspaper space advertising?
7. What special advantages do newspapers offer direct marketers? What are the limitations of newspapers in direct-response print advertising?
8. What are the different types of newspaper advertising, and how can they be used by direct-response advertisers?

NOTE

1. Mary Lou Roberts and Paul D. Berger, *Direct Marketing Management* (Englewood Cliffs, NJ: Prentice Hall, 1989), pp. 349–50.

SOURCES

Barban, Arnold M.; Stephen M. Cristol; and Frank J. Kopec. *Essentials of Media Planning,* 3rd ed. Lincolnwood, IL: NTC Business Books, 1995.

Bovee, Courtland L., and William Arens. *Contemporary Advertising,* 4th ed. Homewood, IL: Richard D. Irwin, 1992.

Direct Marketing Association. *Statistical Fact Book* 1996. New York: Direct Marketing Association, 1996.

Egol, Len. "Work in Progress at Times Mirror." *Direct,* January 1995, pp. 29–30.

Engle, James F.; Martin R. Warshaw; and Thomas C. Kinnear. *Promotional Strategy,* 8th ed. Burr Ridge, IL: Richard D. Irwin, 1994.

Endicott, R. Craig. "Direct Ads Spur 12% of Consumer Sales." *Advertising Age,* October 9, 1995, p. 34.

"Fidelity Changes Tack." *Economist,* August 8, 1992, pp. 67–68.

Finley, Timothy P. "Getting Names Off-the-Page." *Target Marketing* 18, no. 4 (April 1995), pp. 26–28.

Hahn, Fred E. *Do-It-Yourself Advertising.* New York: John Wiley & Sons, 1993.

Katz, Arnie. "Nothing Is Constant Except Change . . ." *Computer Game Review,* March 1994, p. 60.

Katz, Helen. *The Media Handbook.* Lincolnwood, IL: NTC Business Books, 1995.

Katzenstein, Herbert, and William Sachs. *Direct Marketing,* 2nd ed. New York: Macmillan, 1992.

King, Elliot. "Charting a New Course." *Target Marketing* 15, no. 8 (August 1992), pp. 12–13.

Marchetti, Karen J. "A Little Direct Response Know-How Can Improve Your Print Campaign Results." *Bank Marketing* 28, no. 1 (January 1996), pp. 33–36.

______. "Some Print Campaigns Need Direct Help." *Marketing News* 29, no. 22 (October 23, 1995), pp. 4, 8.

Mummert, Hallie, and Lisa A. Horget. "Printing for a Market of One." *Target Marketing* 18, no. 6 (June 1995), pp. 20–31.

Neal, Mollie. "Fingerhut Movin' Ahead." *Direct Marketing,* September 1994, pp. 30–32, 72.

Roberts, Mary Lou, and Paul D. Berger. *Direct Marketing Management.* Englewood Cliffs, NJ: Prentice Hall, 1989.

Roman, Ernan. "The Media Mix." *Target Marketing* 18, no. 4 (April 1995), pp. 30–32+.

Ross, Maxwell C. "Newspapers and Magazines." In *The Direct Marketing Handbook,* 2nd ed., ed. Ed Nash. New York: McGraw-Hill, 1992, pp. 278–289.

Schein, Eliot. "Outstanding, Freestanding Inserts." *Folio: The Magazine for Magazine Management* 23, no. 10 (June 1, 1994), pp. 41–42.

Sissors, Jack Z., and Lincoln Bumba. *Advertising Media Planning,* 4th ed. Lincolnwood, IL: NTC Business Books, 1993.

Smith, Geoffrey. "Fidelity Jumps Feet First into the Fray." *Business Week,* May 25, 1992, pp. 104–6.

Stone, Bob. *Successful Direct Marketing Methods,* 5th ed. Lincolnwood, IL: NTC Business Books, 1995.

Surmanek, Jim. *Introduction to Advertising Media.* Lincolnwood, IL: NTC Business Books, 1993.

______. *Media Planning.* Lincolnwood, IL: NTC Business Books, 1992.

DIRECT MARKETING ASSOCIATION GUIDELINES FOR THE ACCEPTANCE OF PRINT MAIL-ORDER ADVERTISING[1]

This set of guidelines does not attempt to deal with the legalities of advertising procedures, but rather the ethics. Nor does it deal with the dos and don'ts of technical copywriting. It does deal with the DMA's desire to promote more honesty in mail-order advertising, more credibility in the eyes of the consumer, and thereby more business for publishers and their advertisers.

There are basically two types of complaints:

1. Nondelivery of merchandise.
2. Misrepresentation of offer.

The non-delivery of merchandise—whether caused by an honest miscalculation of the success of an offer, a strike, a production mishap—can be dealt with by simple procedures. These are after-the-fact problems, or after the ad has appeared.

The complaints of a far worse nature deal with misrepresentation of advertised merchandise. These should be dealt with before the ad appears.

Helpful Consumer Advice

Publishers and consumers should be aware that it may take three or four weeks for normal delivery of merchandise. Although it may serve as a sales deterrent, publishers may wish to include this information on their mail-order pages—along with other helpful advice such as:

a. Be sure to print your order clearly.
b. Print the name and address to which the order is to be shipped.
c. Be sure to include your zip code on your order, as well as the company's zip code on the envelope.
d. Send check or money order only, no cash.

Publishers should ask for a sample of the merchandise when the ad is in the least bit suspicious. For example, if the offer seems too good to be true, be sure to get a sample—a production sample, not a handmade mock-up. If the advertiser cannot submit the sample before the closing date, pass and wait until the next closing date. When you get the sample and you feel certain copy changes should be made to make the offer more representative, ask for them. You'll be surprised how many advertisers are glad to comply with your requests.

Warning Signals

If the advertiser is new to your publication and plans to run a large ad, check to verify integrity, stability, and performance of the advertiser. The Better Business Bureau, the local consumer agencies, and the United States Postal Inspection Service in the advertiser's area are good sources to check. Better yet, when you have bad experiences let these agencies know that as well.

Here are some warning signals:

1. Experience trains your intuition. If some intuitive reaction tells you to check an ad out very thoroughly, do so. Don't let it slip by.
2. If the business was "too easy to get," or if a large order came in "over the transom" be suspicious. Check out the credit. Check out the offer. Check out the source.
3. When the "buy" isn't smart—wrong season, wrong regions, wrong product for your publication—check it out. Some advertisers flood the market with impressive-looking contracts, hoping some will get by.
4. When an advertiser breaks all the rules in setting up an ad, be suspicious. He may indeed be the new creative genius on the scene, but more often than not, something is awry.
5. If the offer is vague, don't approve it. If you have read the copy through twice, and you still don't know what you're getting, ask the advertiser for a clarification of the copy. Don't accept an offer unless it is spelled out.
6. Make yourself the surrogate reader. Is the copy outlandish? Are the claims so strong as to be unbelievable? Be particularly wary of ads that claim to cure physical ills such as arthritis, psoriasis, gout.
7. Taste is a subjective matter, and each publisher must decide what is in good or bad taste for his audience. However, don't be afraid to ask for a new illustration or a copy change if you feel the ad has gone too far. You will probably get it.
8. The publisher should know the street address and telephone number of every advertiser. In many cities (such as New York) post office box numbers must be accompanied by a street address. If the company is very small, know the home address and telephone number of the principal.

Complaints: How to Appraise Them and What to Do with Them

Keep a tally of the complaints you receive. It can be a simple sheet like a "scorecard" or a sophisticated computer printout week by week. However you do it, keep score.

When the number gets out of proportion to the size of the ad or the amount of circulation covered, give the first warning to the advertiser by phone. Note the date. If complaints persist, issue a second and third warning—preferably in writing. After such warnings, it is suggested that the publisher consider dropping this advertiser from the publication. Bear in mind that for each complaint you get, there are probably many more with similar unhappy experiences.

Establish a procedure for handling reader complaints.

Recommended Policy

The publisher should stand behind his advertising pages if one of his advertisers defaults on shipment or defrauds his readers. If all attempts fail to obtain replacement of merchandise or refunds for the reader directly from the advertiser, the publisher should consider—in the interests of good business—offering a refund to the reader himself. He should then continue to try to be reimbursed by the advertiser.

Keep the lines of communication open within your own organization. When complaints start mounting, advise your own credit department. Frequently, nondelivery problems go hand-in-hand with credit problems.

Reinstatement of an Advertiser

Once you have resolved an old complaint situation, it is entirely possible this advertiser will want to come back into your publication. At the time you reinstate an advertiser who has had a bad complaint record, it is a good idea to require a "performance bond." This is an amount of money to be held in escrow (by the publisher) equal to at least two times the value of the complaints received the last time the ad ran. If the complaint situation repeats itself, you should then consider dropping the offending advertiser indefinitely.

NOTE

1. Source: Ethics Department, Direct Marketing Association, Inc.; 1111 19th Street, N.W., Suite 1100; Washington, DC 20036-3603.

CHAPTER 15

Business-to-Business Direct Marketing

OBJECTIVES

1. To define the nature and scope of business-to-business marketing.
2. To examine the objectives of business-to-business marketing.
3. To show how business-to-business marketing differs from consumer direct marketing.
4. To examine the media of business-to-business direct marketing.

INTRODUCTION

Business-to-business direct marketing is difficult to define because it can mean so many things to so many individual marketing professionals. This form of direct marketing spans a wide range of strategies and techniques, and it includes advertising for such diverse products as office supplies, books, and computers. Business-to-business activities encompass the full range of direct marketing approaches, including direct mail, telemarketing, direct-response print, and catalogs. They can either supplement sales-force activities or reduce the size of the sales force by providing another avenue for communicating with customers and prospects. Direct marketing can both sell products and services and generate qualified sales leads for firms selling to other businesses.

Business-to-business direct marketers need to understand all of the important strategic issues of direct marketing planning and implementation. These include list selection and management, offer planning and positioning, creative strategy and execution, and media strategies. Business-to-business direct marketers face the same kinds of planning issues as those in the consumer end of the business. However, there are critical differences associated with how business customers operate, particularly with respect to what and how they buy, that distinguish them from consumer customers.

This chapter shows how all firms involved in business-to-business selling, from the largest to the smallest, can benefit from using direct marketing methods. In fact, selling direct, without any other distribution channels, is commonplace today in business-to-business marketing. Direct marketing allows firms to free themselves from the high cost of face-to-face selling and the difficult task of developing and managing a dealer and/or distributor organization. What is more, they can contact prospects and customers as often as they wish while minimizing the expenses associated with producing those interactions and sales.

THE SCOPE OF BUSINESS-TO-BUSINESS DIRECT MARKETING

Business-to-business direct marketing involves promoting goods and services that are used in the production of further goods and services. These goods can either become part of an end product or be used in the manufacturing process. The buying decision-making process, and the direct marketing used to facilitate buying, vary according to the type of business product or service being sold. In selling personal computer systems to businesses, firms such as Dell Computer face a situation very different from that faced by companies selling janitorial services to school systems. Another type of business-to-business direct marketing to wholesalers and retailers involves selling goods and services that are then resold. Direct marketing to professionals such as doctors and dentists is used to generate leads for selling medical equipment and health care industry supplies.

Selling to organizations versus consumers requires a different orientation, although essentially the same direct marketing techniques apply to both types of markets. While some will argue that buyers are buyers no matter what they buy, the more common perspective is that consumers and businesspeople not only buy different things but also buy in different ways because of unique motives and decision-making processes. While it is true that both consumers and businesspeople are responsive to special offers and other forms of promotion, they are dissimilar in other fundamental ways that have significant implications for how each group should be approached and what each group will respond to in terms of particular products and services.

Business-to-business direct marketing is the fastest growing segment of the direct marketing industry. The underlying reason for its dramatic growth is the accelerating cost of sales calls, which have passed the $300-per-call mark and continue to increase. And, with five sales calls needed to produce a sale, that means an average cost of about $1,500 per consummated selling effort. Direct marketing works against this rising expense by significantly reducing the cost per sale. Few business-to-business marketers have sales forces or dealer/distributor organizations of sufficient size to contact all likely prospects. Indeed, even if they could, the potential of those prospects dictates that a sales organization cannot afford to call on all of them in person because they are considered marginal in terms of their potential sales contribution.

With the high and steadily increasing cost of field selling, a productive way to reduce sales-force-related expenses is necessary. Direct-response methods do that by providing qualified leads for salespeople and thereby virtually eliminating the need for unproductive personal cold calls. Direct marketing also allows a firm to actually sell a product or service when the sales potential does not warrant the expense of a personal sales call. Thus, direct response business-to-business marketing helps firms deal with relatively small customers. Industries as diverse as telecommunications, parcel delivery services, office supplies, and personal computers need to communicate with a multitude of customers in many organizational units and physical locations. This is an ideal setting for direct-response marketing because customers and prospects are identifiable, and they are purchasing items that do not require any special handling. Direct marketing can also be used in territories temporarily without a sales representative.

THE OBJECTIVES OF BUSINESS-TO-BUSINESS DIRECT MARKETING

The objectives of business-to-business direct marketing are essentially the same as those of consumer direct marketing. As explained in Chapter 1, those generic objectives are as follows:

1. Product or service sales.
2. Lead generation.
3. Lead qualification.
4. Customer relationship building and maintenance.

Product or Service Sales

The most common objective of business-to-business direct marketing plans is to sell products or services. The second most important activity is to generate qualified leads of prospective customers for a sales force. Members of the sales force pursue those qualified leads in an effort to close a sale primarily through traditional personal sales calls and/or through telemarketing.

Lead Generation

No company can conduct business by dealing only with its current customers. New customers are needed for a firm to survive and grow. These prospects can be found in a firm's existing markets or in new ones. A lead-generation program develops new customers through a multistep sales approach that assumes that information gained by prospects in the first stage results in a certain conversion rate to actual purchase activity in the second stage. Leads can be generated in many ways, including by telephone, mail, and direct-response print ads. Lead follow-up consists of lead qualification, which determines the value of the lead; lead fulfillment, which involves providing the prospect with more information such as a brochure; and lead tracking, which requires that a firm keep a database of information on leads.

Lead Qualification

Leads usually come from requests for more information. This may involve a request for literature based on the prospect having seen a direct-response print ad or having received a direct-mail piece. Lead qualification screens out bad leads or nonserious prospects. The screening process covers a wide range of options but ultimately results in a grading of leads according to some sales-potential-related criteria. The way those leads are qualified depends on how a firm sells its products or services. A firm that makes all its sales by mail is much less concerned about strictly qualifying its leads than is a firm that uses person-to-person contacts, because the latter is so much more expensive than the former.

Lead qualification is mostly done by telephone, although mail-in cards with questions also play an important role. In calling the prospect, the objective is to get enough information to determine whether the lead is worth pursuing, not to sell anything. When the lead responds to an 800 number, the answering operator can qualify the prospect with a few simple questions. Leads generated from direct-mail campaigns must be qualified by outgoing telephone calls.

Customer Relationship Building and Maintenance

Ongoing communications between a firm and its customers build relationships and, as a result, promote the long-term fortunes of a firm. In business-to-business direct marketing, the maintenance of relationships with customers frequently involves managing a database of customer information, including both historical purchasing behavior and some details about the business the customer operates.

BUSINESS-TO-BUSINESS VERSUS CONSUMER MARKETS

One way to understand business-to-business marketing is to contrast it with consumer marketing. The major differences between the forms of direct marketing concern characteristics inherent to each of the two types of selling situations. The market for a particular business good typically consists of a relatively small number of customers. Although there are fewer customers, their purchases can involve large sums of money. Some of this situation results from the high cost of the goods themselves and some from the quantity of purchases and repeat purchasing. Many products are classified as raw or semifinished goods; however, such goods are rarely sold in the consumer market. Products sold in the business market usually are more technical in nature than consumer products, and many are purchased on the basis of specifications. Pricing for business goods is often less important than quality and uniformity of products, delivery schedules, servicing, technical assistance, and the ability to extend credit to customers.

The business and consumer markets are also different because of the characteristics of their buyers. The industrial market is normally characterized by technically qualified, professional buyers. Their motives are usually considered more rational than those found in the consumer market. Buying decisions are often made on the basis of such factors as specifications, vendor analysis, and cost effectiveness as opposed to the emotional or impulse-purchasing factors that influence consumers. Multiple buying influences are involved in almost all industrial purchases, and this means that decisions to buy are not made by one person but rather by groups of individuals. Committee buying is where a group of people in various positions in the purchasing firm have the responsibility for choosing a vendor and for making the buying decisions. Industrial purchasing people may select two or more suppliers from which to buy the same product just to protect themselves against the possibility of a single supplier's not being able to meet their requirements.

Direct marketers need to be concerned with the many people who contribute to the process of decision making in companies. Their various roles include those of users, who actually make use of the product but may or may not have any influence at all in the actual purchase decision; influencers, who can affect a decision in a variety of different ways by providing information or criteria for purchases; and gatekeepers, who screen information and control the flow of it to decision makers. These roles may be shared to some extent so that a gatekeeper may also serve as an influencer and a user may also serve as a gatekeeper.

The decision-making processes within a household are considered very different from the decision-making processes within an organization because one falls into the domain of consumer behavior and the other into the domain of organizational behavior. For the consumer market, a marketer needs to be concerned with how its product fits into the decision-making spectrum. Is the decision making highly routinized and habitual, or does it involve extensive problem solving? Or does it fall somewhere in the middle? For the business market, there is a similar spectrum, in which routine decisions about what paper clips to buy or where to purchase copier paper are approached much differently from decisions about what computer system to buy or what material to use in product development.

In the area of advertising, many marketers treat business-to-business ads as if they were entirely different from consumer ads. Some argue, however, that business-to-business advertising is very similar to consumer advertising in many respects. In reality there are both similarities and differences. Although the basic communications principles are the same, business ads should follow certain guidelines that do not necessarily apply to consumer ads. For example, business advertisements are aimed at people who are experts in their field, and the copy should therefore be technically correct and should avoid exaggeration. Because business-to-business direct marketing involves communicating with industrial marketers, middlemen, and professionals such as doctors and lawyers, the copy must be specific, provide news and information, and be easily understood. Communications strategy differences between business and consumer advertising appear most often in how products and services are characterized and in what emphasis is placed on price.

As in every other area of direct marketing, the offer can make or break the success of a campaign. Creating the correct offer is the key to generating sales and/or leads. Although firms make different kinds of offers to businesspeople versus consumers, both involve the same principle, which is that offers control response rates. But for lead generation, high response rates mean nothing if commitment levels are low and there is little chance for conversion or follow-up purchases. Conversely, low response rates may be excellent if the conversion rate is high. However, this is the same math whether it is applied to consumer or business-to-business direct marketing situations.

Many marketers assume that communicating with businesses is the essence of business-to-business direct marketing. However, the process is always a communication with people who play roles in their work lives just as they do in their home lives. The difference is only the setting in which those roles occur. In that sense, they are the same people; they do not leave behind their needs, hopes, fears, or motives when they enter the office door. Therefore, because people are people, business-to-business direct marketers need to follow some of the same principles that hold for all forms of direct marketing, especially in terms of creative strategy and execution.

In industrial markets, complex decision making occurs on a regular basis because, as mentioned earlier, purchase decisions often involve many people. Business-to-business direct marketers face more deliberate and rational buyers than do those marketing to consumers. Like consumer marketers, business-to-business direct marketers have the opportunity to build close relationships with their customers, although they frequently deal with a smaller number of buyers than consumer marketers and therefore may be able to develop strong ties with customers based on an intimate understanding of each customer's business operations and product or service needs. While the segmentation options for the business marketer are similar to those of the consumer marketer, there are major differences. There are also some additional segmenting bases particularly suited for industrial markets.

The next several sections summarize how geography, demographics, usage rates, benefit segmentation, industrial classifications (particularly Standard Industrial Classification [SIC] codes), and end use are options in segmenting markets for business-to-business direct marketing.

Geography

Segmentation based on geography is very common in business-to-business direct marketing. This approach divides prospects and customers by such geographic designations as country, region, county, zip code, or census classification. Marketers also look for differences in prospect or customer density and proximity to distribution points. With information from *Sales & Marketing Management* magazine and government business census reports, direct marketing firms can target specific industries by state or county. In conjunction with that information, marketers can formulate elaborate segmentation schemes that identify geographic areas and the firms in those areas by their sales potential.

Demographics

Demographics are important to segmenting both industrial and consumer markets, although the specifics of those demographics are quite different. For consumer markets, age and gender are major ways to characterize prospects and customers, while for business-to-business marketing, firm size according to sales volume and/or number of employees is important. Demographics on both individuals and businesses are collected by the federal government as part of its census and survey activities. Demographics can also play a role in industrial market segmentation by allowing the marketer to characterize decision makers.

Usage Rates

Differences in product or service consumption patterns by customers and prospects are important segmentation dimensions in industrial markets. Category users are distinct from nonusers, and users are further differentiated by their level of usage. Most usage-based segmentation schemes compare heavy versus medium versus light users (based on unit or dollar sales or number of orders). Another possibility is to differentiate between users of a firm's product or service and users of competitor offerings. Usage is also understood by the degree of loyalty a customer shows to the offerings of any one firm. Some customers purchase from only one seller and are therefore very loyal, while others may exhibit little loyalty by purchasing from several sellers. For example, some purchasing departments at large firms concentrate their PC purchases with one vendor while others shop around for the best value each time they need to obtain more machines.

Benefit Segmentation

Benefits are important to both consumers and businesses, but the nature of those benefits varies significantly. For consumers, emotional benefits play a major role in purchase decisions, while for businesses, rational benefits dominate emotional ones. A business that is considering the purchase of a personal computer may look for such benefits as high processing speed, network compatibility, and reliability. These benefits may be differently weighted by segments in the business-to-business market. Differences in emphasis coupled with perceptions associated with alternative offerings by such business-to-business direct marketers as Dell Computer, IBM, and Compaq strongly influence the choice of vendor. Personal computer firms traditionally have competed on the bases of price and quality.

Industrial Classifications

Standard Industrial Classification (SIC) codes are based on government data collections designed to monitor business activities in the United States. They also serve as a valuable tool for segmenting industrial markets. The *Standard Industrial Classification Manual* contains SIC information on U.S. economic activities including, but not limited to, the divisions of agriculture, mining, construction, manufacturing, transportation, wholesale trade, retail trade, financial services, and public administration. There are two-, six- and eight-digit codes. Table 15.1 lists all of the two-digit SIC codes.

The SIC system is a widely accepted reference that helps marketers organize and link multiple sources, because much business-oriented information has direct links to SIC codes. Although the SIC codes can be helpful in analyzing markets, most direct marketers use SIC information in conjunction with proprietary data in their industrial segmentation efforts. Nevertheless, the SIC codes do have some limitations. The basic manual for the codes is infrequently updated and is therefore somewhat unresponsive to the service-based, high-tech global economy. The classifications do not always correspond to those of most interest to business-to-business direct marketers, and some of the codes are too broad while others are too narrow.

End Use

The end-use approach to segmentation emphasizes the final application of a product by a particular industry. Industrial products can take many forms, including raw materials, work-in-process, and finished goods. For example, in the

TABLE 15.1. SIC Code Numbers and Industry Descriptions

Code Number	Industry Description	Code Number	Industry Description
01	Agricultural production—crops	49	Electric, gas, and sanitary services
02	Agricultural production—livestock	50	Wholesale trade—durable goods
07	Agricultural services	51	Wholesale trade—nondurable goods
08	Forestry	52	Retail building materials, hardware, garden supply
09	Fishing, hunting, and trapping	53	Retail general merchandise stores
10	Metal mining	54	Retail—food stores
12	Coal mining	55	Retail—automotive dealers and gas stations
13	Oil and gas extraction	56	Retail—apparel and accessory stores
14	Mining and quarrying of minerals	57	Retail—furniture/home furnishings
15	Building—general contractors	58	Retail—eating and drinking places
16	Heavy construction	59	Miscellaneous retail
17	Special trade contractors	60	Banking institutions
20	Manufacturing—food and kindred products	61	Credit institutions
21	Manufacturing—tobacco products	62	Security and commodity brokers
22	Manufacturing—textile mill products	63	Insurance carriers
23	Manufacturing—apparel and fabric products	64	Insurance agents, brokers, and service
24	Manufacturing—lumber and wood products	65	Real estate
25	Manufacturing—furniture and fixtures	67	Holding and other investment offices
26	Manufacturing—paper and allied products	70	Hotels and lodging places
27	Manufacturing—printing and publishing	72	Personnel services
28	Manufacturing—chemicals	73	Business services
29	Manufacturing—petroleum refining	75	Automotive services
30	Manufacturing—rubber and plastics	76	Miscellaneous repair services
31	Manufacturing—leather and leather products	78	Motion pictures
32	Manufacturing—stone, gloss, clay, and concrete	79	Amusement and recreation services
33	Manufacturing—primary metal industries	80	Health services
34	Manufacturing—fabricated metal products	81	Legal services
35	Manufacturing—machinery and computer equipment	82	Educational services
36	Manufacturing—electronic/electrical equipment and components	83	Social services
37	Manufacturing—transportation equipment	84	Museums, art galleries, botanical, and zoological
38	Manufacturing—measuring/controlling instruments	86	Membership organizations
39	Miscellaneous manufacturing industries	87	Engineering, accounting, research, and management
40	Railroad transportation	88	Private households
41	Highway passenger transportation	89	Miscellaneous services
42	Motor freight transportation	91	Government
43	U.S. Postal Service	92	Justice, public order, and safety
44	Water transportation	93	Public finance, taxation, and monetary policy
45	Air transportation	94	Human resources programs
46	Pipelines, except natural gas	95	Environmental quality and housing programs
47	Transportation services	96	Administration of economic programs
48	Communications	97	National security and international affairs
		98	Nonclassifiable establishments

Source: *American Statistics Index, 1995* (Bethesda, MD: Congressional Information Service, 1995), pp. 1054–61.

personal computer industry, there are components and parts manufacturers, original equipment manufacturers, and aftermarkets that specialize in maintenance and repair. Each of these segments of the industry represents a distinct grouping for direct marketers interested in promoting the sale of their products and services based on end use.

THE MEDIA OF BUSINESS-TO-BUSINESS DIRECT MARKETING

This section examines the role of specific media in business-to-business direct marketing. Probably the most important function of direct marketing in business promotions is to create a favorable climate for personal selling. As already indicated, personal selling is generally the major promotional tool in the business-to-business marketing mix. Direct marketing primarily serves to back up and support this sales-force function by paving the way for a sales call in situations where the expense is justified by the expected value of the sale. However, there are many circumstances in which businesses sell products of such small dollar value to so many customers that no sales force is involved.

Direct marketing can reach prospective buyers that are either unknown or inaccessible to salespeople. In many companies, salespeople may call only on certain individuals, usually purchasing agents. However, several other individuals may influence the purchase decision. Direct-response advertising in trade magazines may be the only way of reaching such inaccessible decision makers. In other cases, the salesperson simply does not know all of the decision influences in a company, and to rely solely on personal selling would be risky. In that case, direct-response advertising serves to broaden the reach of a firm's promotions.

Although the types of media available to business marketers are exactly the same as those available to marketers of consumer goods and services, the emphasis placed on each option is significantly different. For example, while television is a popular medium for reaching consumers, it is much less likely to be used by business marketers. Also, how businesses use media differs sharply from how consumer marketers use media. The major differences are clarified in the following sections about how business-to-business direct marketing uses direct mail, catalogs, telemarketing, and magazines and newspapers.

Direct Mail

Business-to-business direct-mail marketing sales have grown rapidly in recent years. In 1990, mail-order sales to businesses grew by 15 percent over the previous year (see Table 15.2). Computer supplies and accessories sales grew the most, at 31.8 percent, followed by general office supply equipment at 20.3 percent. Business-to-business mail-order sales in the 1980s showed strong growth throughout that decade. Since 1985, the industry has grown at an average of 17 percent per year, going from $53.2 billion in 1988 to $145.9 billion in 1994.

Direct marketers have found that mail order is a profitable way to sell a wide array of business products, from custom-designed consumable products to sophis-

TABLE 15.2. The 1990 Business-to-Business Mail-Order Market

	$ Billion	% Change (1989 vs. 1990)
General office supply equipment	4.371	20.3
Special office: medical, dental supplies	0.743	14.5
Educational services	0.676	6.5
Subscription products	1.650	15.6
Industrial products	1.584	12.1
Computer supplies and accessories	7.014	31.8
General business-to-business products	58.592	13.1
Business-to-business total	74.63	15.0

Source: Adapted from Maxwell Sroge, *The United States Mail Order Industry* (Lincolnwood, IL: NTC Business Books, 1994), p. 30.

TABLE 15.3. Business-to-Business Direct Marketing Advertising Trends
(Billions of dollars)

Medium	1990	1996	2000
Direct mail	8.9	13.5	18.3
Telephone marketing	26.0	38.7	53.7
Newspapers	4.3	6.2	8.5
Magazines	2.7	4.0	5.5
Television	4.6	7.7	11.8
Radio	1.6	2.4	3.3
Other	3.5	5.0	6.6
Total	51.6	77.5	107.7

Source: Direct Marketing Association, *Statistical Fact Book 1996* (New York: Direct Marketing Association, 1996), p. 321.

ticated, high-tech equipment. The penetration of computers and network systems in offices has given rise to the fast growth of computer supplies, accessories, and software. Many merchandisers and marketers view mail order as a synergistic adjunct to distribution through wholesalers, dealers, and distributors. As mail order approaches the 21st century, expectations are for continuing high growth rates in excess of those for consumer mail-order sales. Business-to-business advertising grew from $51.6 billion in 1990 to $77.5 billion in 1996 and is expected to reach $107.7 billion in the year 2000 (see Table 15.3).

Direct mail offers the business marketer several advantages. It is a highly personal medium in which a message can be tailored to specific individuals. Because many business markets are very narrow, with a relatively small number of decision makers, such personalization is all the more important. Direct-mail respondents tend to be of high quality because the message they receive is targeted to their particular interests.

Direct mail is an effective supplement to sales-force activities. It provides an economical way of regularly communicating with customers and prospects. Business-to-business direct mailings do an efficient job of either selling products or generating qualified sales leads. Because a salesperson usually explains a product or service to a prospective customer, direct mail can also effectively be used as a follow-up to a sales call.

The fact that many business-to-business promotions are technical and detailed also accounts for the popularity of direct mail. An ad in a business publication may be able to highlight only the specifications of a product, but a direct-mail piece can tell a much longer story with a letter, a brochure, and other supportive materials. In fact, the variety of direct-mail pieces ranges from simple postcards to full-color catalogs. This allows great flexibility in the amount and type of information that can be communicated.

Today, it is fairly common to find business-to-business direct-mail pieces with handsome illustrations, clever copy, elaborate designs, and bright colors. Although the items being promoted are described in language common to the trade, the way they are presented represents the ability of business-to-business direct marketing firms to use the latest in production and printing technology at a relatively low cost.

Although marketers develop and maintain their own mailing lists, they also rely on companies that are in the business of selling or renting lists of business prospects. (Refer back to Chapter 6 for the specifics of mailing lists.) Publishers of specialized business magazines and newspapers develop many mailing lists of individuals in a particular industry. Regardless of their source, lists account for the majority of a firm's success with direct mail in producing a lead or an order.

Chapter 9 examined the standard direct-mail package primarily in terms of consumer marketing. However, the same considerations and rules that apply to marketing to consumers generally apply to marketing to businesses. And, as with consumer-targeted direct marketing efforts, there are a wide variety of approaches to soliciting a response. Some business direct-mail packages are very elaborate; others may include all the elements of a standard direct-mail package but utilize a unique format. These efforts usually represent a combination of a specialized message and attention-getting considerations related to projecting an image and detailing a complex offer.

Exhibit 15.1 contains the cover page from a good example of a business-to-business direct-mail package. The offer was for a 1996 conference on how to market products on the World Wide Web, which is a user-friendly interface for the Internet. In some 16 pages, this oversized mailing described the four conference topics: intracorporate communications, customer service on the Internet, sales and marketing opportunities on the Internet, and the development of business applications on the World Wide Web. The conference presenters were persons active in providing Internet services, from such well-known firms as Microsoft, Federal Express, and NETCOM. The conference solicitation was aimed at senior managers, strategic planners, and technological architects in charge of implementing Internet technology for a firm. Those interested in attending the conference could choose from two major packages, with the option of adding additional seminars. The cost of package 1 covered the full three-day conference, while package 2 added the pre- and post conference management/technical seminars. At the heart of this mailing was a series of two-page spreads devoted to describing each of the four conference topics and listing what would be covered by time of day and individual session focus.

A more typical business-to-business mailer can be found in Exhibit 15.2. This is a letter-size solicitation from Dun & Bradstreet Information Services offering

EXHIBIT 15.1. Business-to-Business Direct Mail: Conference Offer

Dun's Regional Business Directory. This directory provides listings of up to 10 executive names for each of the 20,000 top-performing businesses in a region for $250. The letter promoting the directory offering provides an 800 number for respondents who wish to place an order. The recipient can also fill out a card (for placement into the included envelope) requesting that he or she be called about purchasing a directory. The mailing from Dun & Bradstreet Information Services also includes a fold-open, two-sided promotional piece for the regional directories (see Exhibit 15.3).

Direct marketers often use something less than a complete package, especially when the nature of the product does not warrant it or when they are exploring new markets or segments. Self-mailers (a single folded sheet without an outside envelope to a complex package) are frequently employed by both manufacturers and distributors. They are particularly useful for updates including announcements of promotional activities or new product introductions.

Card decks contain a collection of product and service offerings on postcards. They tend to pull large numbers of inquiries at a low cost. Careful tracking of responses can provide useful information for product positioning and media planning. Newsletters are another good way of maintaining relationships with customers and prospects. They are relatively inexpensive, and their soft-sell approach tends to make them especially well-received.

Mailing list usage is a major success factor in this business-to-business direct marketing. Compiled lists—those put together from numerous sources and sold by

EXHIBIT 15.2. Business-to-Business Direct Mail: Dun & Bradstreet Directory Offer

GET A DETAILED DIRECTORY OF THE 20,000 HIGHEST POTENTIAL PROSPECTS IN YOUR REGION.

Dun's Regional Business Directory℠ isolates the top companies in your area, and gives you the information you need to get in touch with their key decision makers.

Select any one of 54 separate regional areas, and we'll provide you with a detailed listing of the top 20,000 companies in that region. Each listing gives you:

- Up to 10 executive names per company
- Industries
- Address/phone
- Sales ranking and more!

Reach thousands of key decision makers!

Call 1-800-665-5115, or fill out the enclosed coupon today to order your own Dun's Regional Business Directory from D&B – just $250. Order two Directories and get the second for half price! (If you choose to call, please have your customer number ready – it's located on the enclosed coupon.)

Order or call for more information before July 31, 1995, and get an added bonus – a free "How To Target Your Best Prospects" guide.

Dun & Bradstreet
Information Services
a company of
The Dun & Bradstreet Corporation

list marketing companies—can be selected by sales volume, number of employees, Standard Industrial Classifications (SICs), and geographic area. When a business-to-business firm has a profile of its customer base, mailings can be targeted to the most likely prospects, even by names and titles. However, these marketers are not restricted to compiled lists. Many have found direct-response lists, those from inquiries and buyers of other business marketers, to be highly productive. What makes direct-response lists so productive is that they contain the names of businesspeople who have proved their propensity to inquire or buy by mail or telephone.

Catalogs

Business-to-business mail-order sales via catalogs has significant comparative cost advantages over other forms of selling. The average cost of a personal sales call is significantly greater than the cost of a catalog and its mailing. This reality encourages direct marketers to include both low-end and high-ticket merchandise

EXHIBIT 15.3. Business-to-Business Direct Mail: Dun & Bradstreet Information Services Offering

Dun & Bradstreet
Information Services

DB a company of The Dun & Bradstreet Corporation

Mr. William J. McDonald
Gen. Mgr
Winston Associates
200 Winston Dr. #3111
Cliffside Pk, NJ 07010

Dun's Regional Business Directory℠ helps you spend your prospecting time wisely.

Dear Mr. McDonald:

Have you ever wasted valuable time giving your sales pitch to the wrong person? Or the wrong company? Well, I'd like to tell you about a way to isolate the <u>best</u> companies in your region, and get in touch with their <u>key</u> decision makers.

Dun's Regional Business Directory gives you <u>up to 10 executive names</u> for each of the 20,000 top performing businesses in your region for $250.

The detailed listings in this directory are arranged three ways -- by company name, geography, and industry. And there are <u>54 separate regional areas to choose from</u>. Each directory listing provides:

- Up to 10 executive names per company
- Industries
- Address/phone
- Sales ranking and more!

Get in touch with prospects worth pursuing. Order your Dun's Regional Business Directory today for just $250. Order two Directories and get the second for half price! Just call 1-800-665-5115 <u>or</u> complete and mail the coupon below, and a D&B representative will call when it's convenient for you. (If you choose to call, please have your customer number ready -- it's located on the coupon below.) Our representative will take your order and promptly ship your Directory.

Order or call for more information before July 31, 1995, and receive a free "How To Target Your Best Prospects" booklet. It's filled with valuable tips for successful prospecting.

We're looking forward to hearing from you soon to discuss improving your prospecting efforts with the Dun's Regional Business Directory. Thank you.

Sincerely,

Deborah Richman

Deborah Richman
Vice President

P.S. Don't wait! Call 1-800-665-5115 <u>or</u> send in the coupon below before July 31, 1995, to order your Dun's Regional Business Directory and get your free "How To Target Your Best Prospects" booklet.

in catalogs. Time is also a factor for busy businesspeople who may prefer to purchase through a catalog rather than spend time with a salesperson.

As with consumer catalogs, business-to-business catalogs play a major role in the success of firms selling products and services. The simplest business catalogs are merely listings for referencing and ordering. Slightly more sophisticated business catalogs contain technical information about a product line and ordering specifics such as quantity and price. When products cannot be differentiated because they are essentially commodities, there is little need for fancy or elaborate catalogs. Thus, many business catalogs are designed to be reference documents. They are well indexed so that the purchaser does not have to browse to find items.

As business catalogs grow more numerous, competitive, and specialized, they are becoming more attractive and compelling to entice potential buyers. Specialty products, no matter what their price, are more likely to be promoted via a consumerlike catalog. These catalogs, which have high-quality glossy paper and make extensive use of color, are often used in such product categories as personal computers, office supplies, and even telephone accessories.

Viking Office Products is a leading direct marketer of basic business supplies such as paper products, computer diskettes, chairs, and cabinets. Viking prints major catalogs that contain the vast majority of items it offers for sale. In addition, it sends targeted mailings to customers based on their purchase behavior records. Exhibit 15.4 contains a sample catalog cover for one of Viking's special mailings to a customer who has purchased mostly paper products from the firm. This cover reflects Viking's expertise at targeted mailings to the business customer who has purchased from the firm in the past.

Viking has a positioning that emphasizes low prices, free delivery, and a one-year guarantee on all items sold. Its catalog pages show colorful pictures of items along with descriptions and pricing. The printing in Viking's catalogs is attractive and gives a clear impression of what is offered. Because Viking delivers all the items it sells, it also addresses the needs of businesspeople who do not want to take substantial time away from other activities to manage office supplies.

The 1994 *Catalog Age* ranking of 100 catalogs includes 45 business-to-business marketers, up from 38 in 1993; those business mailers accounted for sales of $17.6 billion, nearly 47 percent more than the $37.6 billion represented in the 1993 *Catalog Age* 100. What is more, business catalogers grew 25 percent on average in 1994, while consumer marketers showed only a 5 percent growth.

Catalog Age believes that the rising prominence of business marketers partly reflects the fact that more and more businesses are using catalogs and telemarketing to service small- and midsize accounts instead of members of their sales forces. Also, the rapid rate of growth in the number of business-to-business catalogs is due to the rise of the computer mail-order business, which now represents a major part of catalog marketing. Business-supplies mailers such as Viking have also experienced significant growth. In fact, the leading business direct marketers sell either business and office supplies or computer hardware and software.

Telemarketing

The increasing cost of making a sales call in person has led to greater use of telemarketing to handle smaller customers and set up appointments for sales-

EXHIBIT 15.4. Viking Office Products Catalog Cover

people. Some firms use telephone salespeople who specialize in making calls as opposed to going to sales meetings. Some salespeople make sales calls using the telephone and are paid commissions on what they are able to accomplish. As in consumer telemarketing, business telemarketing usually uses a script to control the message delivered to a prospect over the telephone. (Refer back to Chapter 11 for a detailed discussion of telemarketing.)

Inbound business-to-business telemarketing involves handling calls coming to the firm from customers and prospects. They may be responding to a direct-mail piece, a catalog offering, or a direct-response print ad. The volume of inbound calling is difficult to predict because it is determined by how responsive customers and prospects are to a firm's business-to-business marketing efforts. However, history on inbound calling volume is a firm's best indicator of what its future telemarketing load will involve.

Outbound telemarketing is driven by a firm's business-to-business marketing efforts. The firm determines when, to whom, and how often calls are made; the purpose of those calls; and what the results should be. However, outbound business-to-business telemarketing is subject to some constraints that do not affect firms selling to consumer markets. While consumers can be reached by telephone from 9:00 AM to 9:00 PM, and on weekends, businesspeople can normally be reached only from 9:00 AM to 5:00 PM and not on weekends. It is also more difficult to reach a decision maker in a business setting than to reach one in a household. People at work also tend to be busier than those at home and therefore have less time to spend listening to an offer.

In spite of these obstacles, business-to-business telemarketing, both inbound and outbound, is enjoying explosive growth. Why? According to Roberts and Berger, the following reasons seem to be the most important:

1. Telemarketing allows personal contact with customers and prospects at the optimum frequency and at an affordable cost.
2. A wide variety of goods and services, covering a wide range of price points, can be sold over the telephone.
3. Telemarketing can, and usually should, be used in conjunction with other promotional media.
4. Telephone marketing can provide a cost-effective alternative to a field sales force for small businesses.
5. Telemarketing is completely measurable.[1]

In general, telemarketing works because it helps sell products and services, helps generate and qualify leads, and saves firms money by selling to small accounts where face-to-face selling is not profitable.

Magazines and Newspapers

Magazines and newspapers that specialize in business audiences provide an effective platform for business-to-business direct-response advertising. Direct-response print ads are efficient at communicating with businesspeople in particular occupational roles. Most business publications have small circulations, averaging 50,000 to 100,000 readers. However, this is adequate to cover most specialized industry, trade, or professional groups.

As described in Chapter 14, for direct marketers, the business-to-business press has the important role of delivering both general business audiences and highly segmented groups with narrowly defined occupational roles. Broad-based business publications include such well-known titles as *Business Week, Forbes,* and *Fortune*. Magazines edited for more particular occupations and industries include three main types of business publications: trade, vertical, and horizontal (or professional). Trade publications are merchandising vehicles that go mainly to distributors and other intermediaries. Vertical magazines seek audiences affiliated with a given industry, irrespective of position. They allow direct marketers to cover an industry by advertising in one or two publications. Horizontal or professional magazines cover a large number of occupations, but each one specializes in just one of those occupations. The audiences available range from computer programmers to lawyers to all sorts of other professionals.

Sales & Marketing Management is a leading business magazine (see Exhibit 15.5) for those involved in sales, salesforce management, trade shows, and other selling and marketing activities. The magazine contains numerous business-to-business direct-response print ads such as the one in Exhibit 15.6 for the Proxima multimedia projector, which allows computer images to be shown on a large screen or wall with a high degree of sharpness and clarity.

Which type of copy approach to use in a business-to-business direct-response print ad depends on the ad's target audience. General-interest business magazines and newspapers contain ads that resemble those found in consumer magazines. They tend to have prominent illustrations and simple language. Ads in more specialized magazines use copy specific to an industry or occupation. They may contain technical details and industry-specific terminology.

Many business magazines offer advertisers reader services such as "bingo cards," which are postage-paid cards containing numbers matching those on the individual ads in the magazine. Readers can circle the number of one or more ads on the bingo card and receive further information from the companies that ran those ads in the magazine. Exhibit 15.7 contains a bingo card from an issue of *Sales & Marketing Management.*

EXHIBIT 15.5. ***Sales & Marketing Management*** **Magazine Cover**

EXHIBIT 15.6. Direct-Response Business Ad in *Sales & Marketing Management*

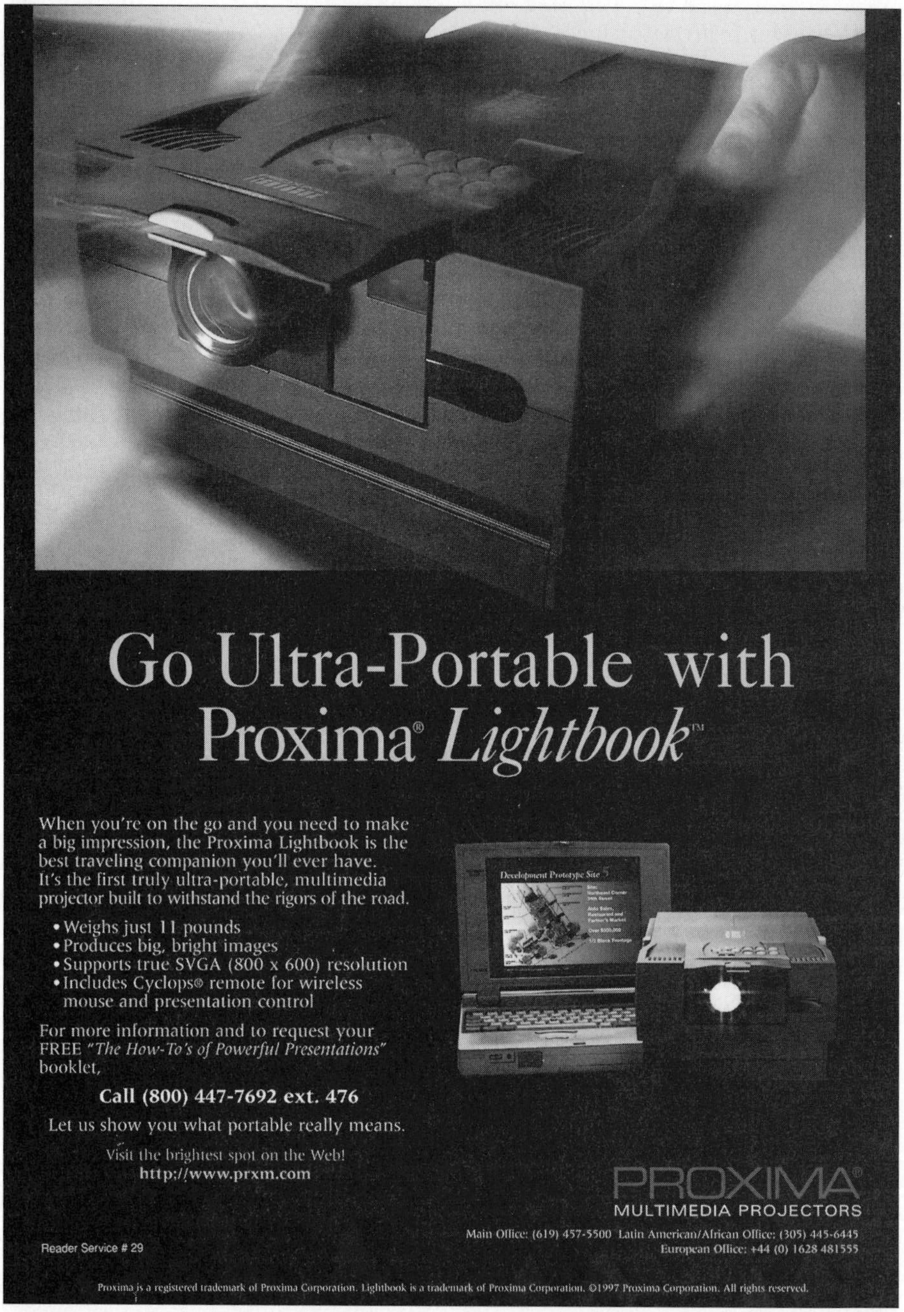

Go Ultra-Portable with
Proxima® Lightbook™
When you're on the go and you need to make a big impression, the Proxima Lightbook is the best traveling companion you'll ever have. It's the first truly ultra-portable, multimedia projector built to withstand the rigors of the road.
• Weighs just 11 pounds
• Produces big, bright images
• Supports true SVGA (800 x 600) resolution
• Includes Cyclops® remote for wireless mouse and presentation control
For more information and to request your FREE *"The How-To's of Powerful Presentations"* booklet,
Call (800) 447-7692 ext. 476
Let us show you what portable really means.
Visit the brightest spot on the Web!
http://www.prxm.com
PROXIMA®
MULTIMEDIA PROJECTORS
Main Office: (619) 457-5500 Latin American/African Office: (305) 445-6445
European Office: +44 (0) 1628 481555
Reader Service # 29
Proxima is a registered trademark of Proxima Corporation. Lightbook is a trademark of Proxima Corporation. ©1997 Proxima Corporation. All rights reserved.

EXHIBIT 15.7. Sales & Marketing Management Bingo Card

Sales & Marketing MANAGEMENT Free Product Information

Use this postage paid reply card to find out more about the products featured and advertised in ***Sales & Marketing Management.***

Or FAX to (413) 637-4343.

For faster service, please complete these questions:

1. Approximate annual sales volume of your company or division:

01 ☐ Under $10,000,000
02 ☐ $10,000,000 – $24,999,999
03 ☐ $25,000,000 - $99,999,999
04 ☐ $100,000,000 – $249,999,999
05 ☐ $250,000,000 – $499,999,999
06 ☐ $500,000,000 – $999,999,999
07 ☐ $1 billion or more

2. Number of salespeople working in your company or division?

08 ☐ 1 – 10
09 ☐ 11 – 20
10 ☐ 21 – 30
11 ☐ 41 or more

To start your subscription to Sales & Marketing Management circle #1.

1	2	3	4	5	6	7	8	9	10	11	12	13	14	15	16	17	18	19	20
21	22	23	24	25	26	27	28	29	30	31	32	33	34	35	36	37	38	39	40
41	42	43	44	45	46	47	48	49	50	51	52	53	54	55	56	57	58	59	60
61	62	63	64	65	66	67	68	69	70	71	72	73	74	75	76	77	78	79	80
81	82	83	84	85	86	87	88	89	90	91	92	93	94	95	96	97	98	99	100
101	102	103	104	105	106	107	108	109	110	111	112	113	114	115	116	117	118	119	120
121	122	123	124	125	126	127	128	129	130	131	132	133	134	135	136	137	138	139	140
141	142	143	144	145	146	147	148	149	150	151	152	153	154	155	156	157	158	159	160
161	162	163	164	165	166	167	168	169	170	171	172	173	174	175	176	177	178	179	180
181	182	183	184	185	186	187	188	189	190	191	192	193	194	195	196	197	198	199	200
201	202	203	204	205	206	207	208	209	210	211	212	213	214	215	216	217	218	219	220
221	222	223	224	225	226	227	228	229	230	231	232	233	234	235	236	237	238	239	240
241	242	243	244	245	246	247	248	249	250	251	252	253	254	255	256	257	258	259	260

NAME .... TITLE ....

BUSINESS ....

( ) ....
BUSINESS PHONE

BUSINESS ADDRESS ....

CITY .... STATE .... ZIP ....

S&MM -2

SUCCESSFUL BUSINESS-TO-BUSINESS DIRECT MARKETERS

Allen-Edmonds and Catalogia are examples of two highly successful business-to-business direct marketers. Both use catalogs and other direct selling techniques to market their high-quality goods. The firms exemplify the importance of combining a strong product line with sophisticated direct marketing approaches.

Allen-Edmonds Shoes[2]

Allen-Edmonds Shoes maintains high standards in the manufacturing and marketing of its upscale products. These high standards are the very thing that makes the company's products so popular in 3,000 retail locations in 33 countries. Allen-Edmonds's prices match the elegant names of its products—the average pair of Allen-Edmonds shoes costs $230, but a pair of alligator shoes can run as high as $1,500.

Allen-Edmonds was established in 1922 as a high-quality shoe manufacturer. Its manufacturing techniques are based on the belief that nothing of quality can be hurried. Today, Allen-Edmonds is becoming well known as the Rolls Royce of shoes, with its highly successful manufacturing, wholesaling, retailing, and catalog operations doing more than $44 million in sales each year.

The company's main thrust is in the wholesaling of its products to upscale specialty retail stores like Nordstrom, family shoe stores, and men's clothing shops. It aligns itself with not only quality retailers but also financially strong retailers. The products are also found in some catalogs like Jos. A. Banks.

Allen-Edmonds sends hundreds of thousands of its catalogs each year to the stores that carry its products to help with marketing because these business customers usually do not have the staff or marketing know-how to do it themselves. Retailers can order an entire line or just some of the products; they can also place individiual orders for specific sizes and styles that are not in stock. In this case, Allen-Edmonds ships the shoes quickly to the customer on behalf of the store.

Allen-Edmonds understands the importance of promoting store traffic. It maintains the retailer's customer lists on a computer. Allen-Edmonds will compile a list selected by zip code for a retailer and send a promotion to drive customers and prospects into that store. Simultaneously, the company will run ads in two to three types of media for expanded exposure. For example, if a Philadelphia store is interested in a special promotion, Allen-Edmonds will send a mailing and run ads in a local business magazine and in a newspaper, such as the *Philadelphia Enquirer.*

Catalogia: C'Est Bien[3]

French mail-order marketer Catalogia has developed a special niche among top management with its eclectic offering of upscale office furniture and accessories. While this company is very young in age, it is mature in marketing strategies—and those are paying off.

Catalogia was established in Strasbourg, France, in 1987. Although the premier catalog was sent to only 150,000 people and the second one went to 200,000, the first year's sales were $3 million. Catalogia attributes its early success to more than the slick 32-page catalog. In Neiman-Marcus-like style, the premier catalog featured a $2 million helicopter to attract attention to the unknown company. This move created much media publicity. Both the general and trade press in France ran numerous articles spotlighting the catalog and its offering of products, which ranges from a reasonably priced pen set to the helicopter.

While the manufacturer had sold only two such helicopters in France the previous year, Catalogia surprisingly generated 10 qualified leads for the company. More important to Catalogia's bottom line was the attention it received. More than 10,000 people wrote letters, called, or faxed the new company for a catalog.

Catalogia learned two things from its first two issues: (1) how to reach a target audience and (2) that there is no limit to the things that can be sold through the mail. The company continued attracting attention by offering Harley Davidsons, $50,000 1950-model Rolls Royces, and $2 million luxury boats in a few of the following issues of the catalog, but these types of items were phased out so that Catalogia could focus on the marketing of its core products—upscale office design furniture and accessories.

While Catalogia's core target audience is made up of male professionals in upper management, the company quickly found that its intention to be solely a business-to-business cataloger was diverted. After professionals began taking the catalogs home to show friends and family in order to get interior design advice for their offices, many consumers began requesting the catalog and ordering from it, contributing some 10 to 15 percent of annual sales. As a result, the company has evolved into both a business-to-business and a consumer catalog marketer.

The most recent issue of Catalogia ran 168 pages and was sent to 250,000 businesspeople. The "big book" now mails two times each year and brings in an average order size of $500, which is three to four times the average order size of competitors. The products range in price from $10 to $10,000. In order to get responses, the firm must offer style, design, and an image, and it must combat those who are selling clones of its products at a lower price.

Catalogia makes it clear that it does not often mail catalogs to nonbuying customers. Those who wish to continue receiving the catalog are offered a subscription. Catalogia can also be purchased at kiosks and newsstands.

The firm sees its big catalog as a real "working tool, a work horse" that people purchase from long after it has been mailed. In turn, Catalogia selected the best customers from its house file and tested a smaller mail-order book, Catalogia Design Office. This catalog runs 70 to 90 pages and features goods that may not necessarily complement the products offered in the big book. Catalogia also uses the smaller catalog to test products. If successful, the products are then placed in the next issues of the large catalog. This smaller catalog mails every two months in order to maintain ongoing communications with Catalogia's best customers. The price range runs from $10 to $2,000, much less than the big book.

SUMMARY

Business-to-business direct marketing spans a wide range of strategies and techniques and includes such diverse firms as those that sell office supplies, publish books, and sell computers. Business-to-business activities encompass the full range of direct marketing approaches, including direct mail, telemarketing, direct-response print, and catalogs. They can either supplement sales-force activities or just reduce the size of the sales force by providing another avenue for communicating with customers and prospects. Direct marketing can both sell products and services and generate qualified sales leads for firms selling to other businesses.

Business-to-business direct marketing involves promoting goods and services that are used in the production of further goods and services. These goods can either become part of an end product or be used in the manufacturing process. The buying decision-making process and the direct marketing used to facilitate buying vary according to the type of business product or service being sold. Business-to-business direct marketing to wholesalers and retailers involves selling goods and services that are then resold. Direct marketing to professionals such as doctors and dentists is used to generate leads for selling medical equipment and health care industry supplies.

Business-to-business direct marketing is the fastest growing segment of the direct marketing industry. The underlying reason for that dramatic growth is the accelerating cost of sales calls. Direct marketing works against this rising expense by significantly reducing the cost per sale. Few business-to-business marketers have sales forces or dealer/distributor organizations of sufficient size to contact all likely prospects. Indeed, even if the sales force were large enough, the organization could not afford to call on all prospects in person because many are considered marginal in terms of their potential sales contribution.

The objectives of business-to-business direct marketing are essentially the same as those of consumer direct marketing: product or service sales, lead generation, lead qualification, and customer relationship building and maintenance. The most common objective of business-to-business direct marketing plans is to sell products or services. The second most important activity is to generate qualified leads of prospective customers for a sales force. Members of the sales force pursue those qualified leads in an effort to close a sale primarily through traditional personal sales calls and/or through telemarketing. Leads usually come from requests for more information. This may involve a request for literature based on the prospect having seen a direct-response print ad or having received a direct-mail piece. Lead qualification screens out bad leads or nonserious prospects. Ongoing communications between a firm and its customers build relationships and, as a result, promote the long-term fortunes of a firm. In business-to-business direct marketing, the maintenance of relationships with customers frequently involves managing a database of customer information, including both historical purchasing behavior and some details about the business the customer operates.

Although the types of media available to business marketers are exactly the same as those available to marketers of consumer goods and services, the emphasis placed on each option is significantly different. Also, how businesses use media differs sharply from how consumer marketers use media. The major differences involve how business-to-business direct marketing uses direct mail, catalogs, telemarketing, and magazines and newspapers to generate sales and profits.

REVIEW QUESTIONS

1. What is meant by the phrase *business-to-business direct marketing?*
2. Why is business-to-business direct marketing growing so rapidly?
3. What are the advantages and disadvantages of business-to-business direct marketing?
4. The objectives of business-to-business direct marketing include product or service sales, lead generation, lead qualification, and customer relationship building and maintenance. How does each objective relate to the sales and profits of a firm marketing to businesses?
5. How does business-to-business direct marketing differ from consumer direct marketing?
6. What are the media of business-to-business direct marketing? How are they the same or different from those used in consumer marketing?
7. How are each of the media of business-to-business direct marketing used to sell products and services?

NOTES

1. Mary Lou Roberts and Paul D. Berger, *Direct Marketing Management* (Englewood Cliffs, NJ: Prentice Hall, 1989), pp. 398–403.
2. Adapted from Mollie Neal, "If the Shoe Fits . . . Market It," *Direct Marketing,* January 1992, pp. 19–22.
3. Adapted from Paul Neal, "Catalogia: C'est Bien," *Direct Marketing,* February 1992, pp. 18–19, 34.

American Statistics Index, 1995. Bethesda, MD: Congressional Information Service, 1995.

BLOCH, RICHARD. "Business-to-Business Marketing." In *The Direct Marketing Handbook,* 2nd ed., ed. Ed Nash. New York: McGraw-Hill, 1992, pp. 744–56.

BLY, ROBERT W. *Business to Business Direct Marketing.* Lincolnwood, IL: NTC Business Books, 1994.

BOVEE, COURTLAND L., AND WILLIAM ARENS. *Contemporary Advertising,* 4th ed. Homewood, IL: Richard D. Irwin, 1992.

BURSEY, DONNA. "Targeting Small Businesses for Telemarketing and Mail Order Sales." *Direct Marketing,* September 1995, pp. 18–20.

"Catalog Age 100." *Catalog Age,* August 1996, pp. 1, 62–68, 72–74.

CHEVAN, HARRY. "Make Room at the Top." *Catalog Age,* August 1995, pp. 1, 64–72.

Direct Marketing Association. *Statistical Fact Book 1996.* New York: Direct Marketing Association, 1996.

EMERICK, TRACY, AND BERNARD GOLDBERG. *Business-to-Business Direct Marketing,* 2nd ed. Yardley, PA: Direct Marketing Publishers, 1990.

ENGLE, JAMES F.; MARTIN R. WARSHAW; AND THOMAS C. KINNEAR. *Promotional Strategy,* 8th ed. Burr Ridge, IL: Richard D. Irwin, 1994.

HAHN, FRED E. *Do-It-Yourself Advertising.* New York: John Wiley & Sons, 1993.

KATZENSTEIN, HERBERT, AND WILLIAM SACHS. *Direct Marketing,* 2nd ed. New York: Macmillan, 1992.

KLEINFELTER, MARY ANN. "Business Lists." In *The Direct Marketing Handbook,* 2nd ed., ed. Ed Nash. New York: McGraw-Hill, 1992, pp. 209–17.

MESSNER, FRED. *Business to Business Communications Handbook.* Lincolnwood, IL: NTC Business Books, 1994.

MORRIS-LEE, JAMES. "Marketer Handles SICs with Care." *Direct Marketing.* April 1992, pp. 38–41.

NEAL, MOLLIE. "If the Shoe Fits . . . Market It." *Direct Marketing,* January 1992, pp. 19–22.

______. "Polaroid's New Focus." *Direct Marketing,* February 1991, pp. 32–34.

NEAL, PAUL. "Catalogia: C'est Bien." *Direct Marketing,* February 1992, pp. 18–19, 34.

PATTI, CHARLES; STEVEN HARTLLEY; AND SUSAN KENNEDY. *Business to Business Advertising.* Lincolnwood, IL: NTC Business Books, 1994.

PRZYBYLSKI, TOM. "The B-to-B Bible." *American Demographics,* Marketing Tools Supplement, May 1995, pp. 80–86.

ROBERTS, MARY LOU, AND PAUL D. BERGER. *Direct Marketing Management.* Englewood Cliffs, NJ: Prentice Hall, 1989.

SROGE, MAXWELL. *The United States Mail Order Industry.* Lincolnwood, IL: NTC Business Books, 1994.

STONE, BOB. *Successful Direct Marketing Methods,* 5th ed. Lincolnwood, IL: NTC Business Books, 1995.

WEINSTEIN, ART. *Market Segmentation,* 2nd ed. Chicago, IL: Probus, 1994.

WOJTAS, GARY W. "Exploring New Response Avenues." *Direct Marketing,* February 1991, pp. 44–46.

CHAPTER 16

International Direct Marketing

OBJECTIVES

1. To define the nature and scope of international direct marketing activities.
2. To examine why American direct marketing firms go overseas in terms of the benefits they hope to gain.
3. To show how uncontrollable elements can affect the profitability of direct marketing practices overseas.
4. To examine the benefits direct marketers derive from both the globalization and standardization of their activities.
5. To review the advantages and disadvantages of alternative entry modes for foreign markets.
6. To look at examples of international direct marketing activities undertaken by a variety of firms.

INTRODUCTION

International direct marketing involves the performance of business activities that channel a firm's goods and services to consumers or businesses in more than one nation. Direct marketers' interest in international markets can be explained by changing competitive structures coupled with shifts in demand throughout the world. Although the vast U.S. domestic market continues to provide opportunities for growth, it must now be shared with a variety of foreign companies and products. With the American market becoming increasingly competitive, direct marketing firms pursuing opportunities with customers in foreign markets are still able to significantly improve their year-to-year sales and earnings. Direct marketers with foreign operations find that earnings from those operations make an important overall contribution to total firm profits. For some companies, the profits from foreign sales are better than those from U.S sales.

While companies that never ventured abroad until recently are now seeking receptive foreign markets, those with existing foreign operations realize they must work harder to succeed against global competitors. They have also found it necessary to spend more money and time improving their marketing positions abroad because competition is intensifying. For firms venturing into international direct marketing for the first time and for those already experienced, the requirement is a thorough and complete commitment.

The movement beyond a firm's domestic borders accounts for the complexity and diversity found in international direct marketing operations. However, direct marketing concepts, processes, and principles are universally applicable, with the goal, as always, to make a profit by promoting, pricing, and distributing products or services for which there is a demand. The problems direct marketers face in reaching their profit goals lie in the differences between domestic and international markets, but the issue is not different concepts of marketing in the environments within which marketing plans must be implemented. Rather, the uniqueness of foreign marketing comes from a range of problems and opportunities and the variety of strategies and tactics necessary to cope with those differences.

Differences in infrastructure and technology, competitive dynamics, legal and government restrictions, customer preferences and culture, and any number of other uncontrollable elements can, and frequently do, affect the profit outcome of all direct marketers, even those with a successful history in the United States. The marketer cannot control or influence these elements but instead must adapt to achieve business success. Operating abroad becomes a challenge because the controllable elements of marketing decisions—such as product, pricing, promotion, and distribution—must be accommodated to the frequently unique, uncontrollable elements of the foreign marketplace.

According to Cateora, the more significant elements in the uncontrollable international environment include (1) political/legal forces, (2) economic factors, (3) competitive dynamics, (4) levels of technology, (5) structure of distribution, (6) geography and infrastructure, and (7) cultural forces.[1] These elements create uncertainty for international marketers and must be considered in designing any marketing program.

Marketers attuned to one environment may not easily recognize the potential dangers within another environment. The uncertainty of different foreign business environments creates the need for a close study of the operating environment within each new country. Different solutions to fundamentally identical marketing tasks are often necessary because of unique environmental conditions. A strategy that is successful in one country can be rendered worthless in another by differences in political climate, stages of economic development, or cultural variations.

For example, adding the new elements of long distance, language, customs, and duties to the normal complexities of fulfillment can seem forbidding for many direct marketers. Among the traditional fulfillment steps that are most likely to be affected by offshore marketing are response mechanisms, order entry, data processing, payment processing, and shipping. When designing the order form, the marketer must view the ordering process from the vantage point of a foreign national. Data entry, with its inherent problems, is a critical factor often overlooked by marketers new to the international scene. Finding economical ways to ship printed matter is of particular importance in international direct marketing because the industry relies heavily on the distribution of catalogs and other promotional material.

The world's largest international direct marketers are consumer-goods companies, and, as Table 16.1 shows, Americans are at the forefront of this activity. This is probably so because many of the same trends experienced in the United States are driving the development and growth of direct marketing in industrialized nations around the world. Many countries have the technological infrastructure necessary to support direct-response activities, including sophisticated postal

TABLE 16.1. World's 10 Largest Mail-Order Companies

Rank	Company Name	Country	Year of Data	Sales ($ Millions)	Type of Merchandise
1	Otto Versand	Germany	1991	10,890	General
2	Quelle	Germany	1991	7,040	General
3	Sears, Roebuck & Company	United States	1991	5,580	General/insurance
4	United Automobile Association Services	United States	1991	4,868	Insurance
5	Time Warner	United States	1991	3,471	Cable
6	J. C. Penney	United States	1991	3,170	General/insurance
7	Great Universal Stores	United Kingdom	1991	2,910	General
8	American Association of Retired Persons	United States	1991	2,768	Health/insurance
9	Tele-Communications	United States	1991	2,645	Cable
10	Reader's Digest Association	United States	1991	2,032	Publishing

Source: Arnold Fishman, "International Mail Order Overview," *Direct Marketing,* October 1992, p. 30.

systems, computerized databases, credit cards, toll-free telephone numbers, and electronic communications networks. At the same time, these countries are experiencing demographic changes, especially the entry of women into their labor forces, and resulting lifestyle changes similar to those in the United States.

There are also major differences in the nature and development stage of direct marketing activities in countries around the world. These differences usually involve the size of the direct-response industry, customer acceptance of direct marketing activities, the availability of mailing lists and sophisticated databases, service levels provided by postal and telephone systems, and the extent of government regulation. Thus, it is important for firms to understand both differences and similarities in direct marketing activities in countries where such activities have become established.

SUCCESSFUL INTERNATIONAL DIRECT MARKETING

Many direct marketers do not need to be told that there are markets worth exploring overseas; they are already operating in foreign markets and are enjoying significant successes. To illustrate, the following sections describe what several companies are doing to apply direct marketing strategies in international markets by emphasizing customer retention versus customer acquisition, building customer loyalty and customer databases, finding additional customers, and tailoring communications to customers' needs.

British Airways

British Airways (BA) has gone beyond its core business customers to find a new leisure market in Japan. The recession in Japan fueled a steep decline in overseas travel by Japanese tourists. That decline particularly hurt foreign airlines. It was the worst downturn in several decades of service between Europe and Japan.

So BA and its agency, Kobs & Draft/YOMIKO, a joint venture between Tokyo's YOMIKO Advertising and Chicago-based direct marketing specialists Kobs & Draft, elected to bypass the company's traditional target market, Japanese businessmen, and instead focus on housewives and older marrieds or retired couples who maintain considerable savings specifically for travel.

Because mailing lists for such prospects are rare in Japan, BA chose to build its own database using sweepstakes. Entry forms were made available in newspapers and travel agencies; the prizes consisted of European vacations on BA. Of the 100,000 names solicited by the draw, BA qualified roughly half on the basis of having taken two or more leisure trips.

BA offered these roughly 50,000 prospects who had traveled outside of Japan a free subscription to its *Speedbird* catalog of international package tours, which includes detailed descriptions of eight tours offered through four representative Japanese travel agencies, as well as listings of schedules and prices. The presence of feature articles and photography of British and European destinations make the booklet seem more like a magazine than a catalog. That is not to say that BA did not include concrete incentives. There were also Visa gift certificates worth $300 to $500 offered to those subscribers who purchased any tour featured in the spring/summer edition. The response rate was 20 percent, in line with BA's target of building a base of 20,000 subscribers.

Hearst Corporation

The Hearst Corporation, the well-known magazine publisher, thought Russian women were ready to read *Cosmopolitan.* The first Russian edition of *Cosmopolitan* hit Russian newsstands in 1993. However, Hearst is no stranger to international publishing ventures. Either alone or with joint venture partners, the company publishes titles in Mexico, France, Germany, Australia, and elsewhere. But Russia is different. *Cosmo* was the first women's magazine ever published in Russia. As a result, Hearst tried to minimize its risks, launching the magazine as a joint venture with Independent Media, the publisher of the *Moscow Times.*

In the United States, magazine launches are usually accompanied by mail drops to potential subscribers, often from lists of existing subscribers to other magazines. That approach was not feasible in a country where the mails are notoriously unreliable and where, until recently, ordinary Russians subscribed to publications by filling out a form at their local post office. Often, Russian publications had no idea who their subscribers were and went by post office numbers when measuring circulation.

Because mailing lists in Russia are so unreliable, Hearst decided to forgo direct mail in the launch of the magazine altogether. Instead, it counted on newsstand sales to distribute the first issues to potential readers, hoping for large pass-along rates, and for readers to return one of almost a dozen reply cards bound or blown in to every issue.

General Motors and Ford

The General Motors MasterCard introduced in America in 1992 helped the automaker sell more cars and was one of the biggest direct marketing success stories of recent years. Six million GM credit cards are now held in the United States, and some 60,000 cars have been sold with rebates given to those cardholders. In 1993, GM and rival automaker Ford, which followed GM with its own card, together spent $30 million on direct-response advertising and other direct marketing to launch competing European versions, first in Britain with a later rollout on the Continent. The car makers hoped to match their American success, although their purposes in Europe were different from what they were in the United States. Unlike the American car market, which had started to bounce back from the recession by the time Ford launched its card in 1992, the European market remained stagnant. Auto sales fell to about 10.7 million in the first 11 months of 1993, down from 12.5 million for the same period in 1992.

GM fired the opening shot in the auto credit card battle with full-page newspaper ads. It announced the card and provided a toll-free number and coupon to entice prospects to preregister for a card. The company received over 3 million applications. Ford offered a Visa-MasterCard-Optima partnership with the United Kingdom's largest credit issuer, Barclaycard. Ford plugged into an ongoing Barclay program serving 3 million of Barclaycard's existing U.K. cardholders by mail.

In the United Kingdom, auto executives of both companies are optimistic about their programs' prospects for boosting sales. Ford U.K. estimated that its program was involved in about 20 percent of its U.K. sales in 1993, with that number rising to 50 percent of sales over the next several years. Ford expected its incentive programs, such as credit cards, to help the U.K. market recover to an estimated 5 percent growth rate in 1994 and projected annual sales of 2 million Ford cars by 1997.

Neiman-Marcus Direct

Neiman-Marcus Direct hopes to skim the cream of Mexico's consumers by mail. The fact that the average Mexican household receives only 10.1 pieces of mail a year should leave plenty of Mexican mailboxes open for an American mailing or two—if only there were enough mailboxes. A dearth of mailboxes, however, is just one of the problems Neiman-Marcus Direct faced in mailing its international catalog to Mexico. Among the others: a scarcity of Mexican lists, a postal service infamous for corruption and slow delivery speed, long address lengths, no demonstrated consumer propensity to shop through the mail, and no established Mexican catalog industry.

Despite those obstacles, Neiman-Marcus Direct sent south 100,000 copies of an abridged Spanish version of its American catalog. Prices were listed in pesos and included all tariffs and duties. Orders went into a bilingual telemarketing center in Dallas. The results were good enough for Neiman-Marcus Direct to keep the program progressing. Catalogs are now mailed out four to six times a year.

BENEFITS OF INTERNATIONAL BUSINESS

When competing internationally, firms derive many benefits from both the globalization and standardization of their activities, including incremental profits from economies of scale in production and marketing, growth opportunities greater than those available in the domestic market, survival because of more demand and less competition, and a way to diversify business operations through obtaining new markets and customers.

Economies of Scale in Production and Marketing

The proponents of global, standardized marketing strategies maintain that selling the same things in the same way everywhere is justified by cost considerations, superficial regional and national differences, and the homogenization of market segments due to the influences of technology. In contrast, those who believe in localization advocate the differentiation of marketing programs depending on the idiosyncrasies of major identifiable markets. The argument is that individual country markets are unique and that successful marketing overseas requires specialized plans for each geographic area a direct marketing firm wishes to enter. A compromise position calls for firms to design products and sell them according to the needs of specific international markets. Under the latter scenario, firms achieve success by being global and acting local, starting with a good understanding of buyer behavior.

This long-standing controversy about the standardization versus the specialization of strategies for reaching specific markets also concerns how customers and prospects should be segmented. Some marketers advocate the identification of target market segments across countries that have homogeneous product and service interests. With this approach, international segmentations are based on target market member characteristics and not on countries. This *intermarket segment concept* provides a basis for plans that address needs and buyer segments at a worldwide or global level.

Growth Opportunities

Many U.S. firms are finding that they can expand faster overseas than at home. The most attractive markets have a growing middle class accompanied by an expansion in purchasing power. However, countries with large populations do not necessarily have the consumer or business base needed to support the sales objectives of these firms. Companies need to be cautious in assessing what the actual growth opportunities may be and how realistic it is that they can benefit from expanding into a country.

Survival Motives

Given the highly competitive nature of the U.S. marketplace, some firms expand overseas to survive. While other countries may not have a similar level of discretionary income, population size, or market size, they can represent a safe environment for firms that have poor prospects in America. In fact, many firms enjoy a higher degree of competitive advantage in foreign markets.

Operational Diversification

Some companies expand overseas to diversify their sales and thus stabilize risk and revenue fluctuations associated with being tied to the economic and other cyclical factors of one country. These other markets may also be at different technological or economic stages and can therefore counterbalance the ups and downs experienced in the United States.

INTERNATIONAL STRATEGIES

This section is concerned with international strategies and the two closely related topics of entry modes and strategic alliances. According to Hill, entry modes for foreign markets include exporting, licensing, franchising, joint ventures, and setting up wholly owned subsidiaries.[2] Each of these options has its advantages and disadvantages, with the magnitude of those advantages and disadvantages determined by such factors as transport costs, trade barriers, political risks, economic risks, and firm strategy. The optimal entry mode varies from situation to situation. While some firms should enter a given market by exporting, other firms should set up a wholly owned subsidiary or enter into a licensing agreement.

Strategic alliances are agreements between actual or potential competitors that allow firms to operate cooperatively in a market. Hill notes that the term is often used to describe a wide range of arrangements between firms, including cross-shareholding deals, licensing arrangements, formal joint ventures, and informal cooperative arrangements.[3] The motives for entering strategic alliances vary, but often they include market access agreements that provide an entry mode. In fact, entry modes such as licensing, franchising, and joint ventures are strategic alliances, although strategic alliances tend to involve much more than just market access.

Entry Modes

When a firm is considering entering a foreign market, questions arise as to the best means of achieving that goal. Hill defines six different ways to enter a foreign market: exporting, developing a turnkey project, licensing, franchising, entering a joint venture, and establishing a wholly owned subsidiary.[4]

Exporting

Most manufacturing firms begin their global expansion as exporters and only later switch to another mode for serving a foreign market. Exporting has the advantage of avoiding the costs of establishing manufacturing operations in a host country, which are often substantial. By manufacturing the product in a centralized location and exporting it to overseas national markets, a firm may be able to realize economies of scale. On the other hand, exporting has drawbacks. For example, shipping from a firm's home base may not be appropriate if the firm can realize location economies by moving production elsewhere. Exporting may result in high transport costs that make it uneconomical, particularly for bulk products. And problems sometimes arise when an export firm delegates its marketing to a local agent who does less than an adequate job.

L. L. Bean and Lands' End, two of the largest U.S. catalogers operating in Japan, follow very different strategies: one operates from offshore; the other has set up shop in Japan. L. L. Bean's strategy to develop the market completely from offshore has been very successful. The company mails into Japan from the United States, receives orders in the United States, and fulfills orders from the United States. Its only concession to a local presence is several customer service desks in Tokyo, which it contracts to a third party. Full-page advertisements are placed in local newspapers (in the Japanese language) offering a free catalog. English-language catalogs contain Japanese-language instructions and order forms. Customer service staff take incoming telephone calls and help customers fill out the order forms correctly.

By managing its business in Japan from offshore, L. L. Bean is enjoying a significant reduction in its mailing costs. Shipping out of the United States costs 38 cents per 50-gram item, whereas local postal rates in Japan are 90 yen per 50-gram item less a 30 percent discount for volume and sorting (which comes to about 63 cents per item). If L. L. Bean had any corporate presence in Japan, the Japanese post office would require it to mail domestically within Japan, paying full local postal rates. For this reason, even the company's retail outlets in Japan are franchised. By using an offshore strategy, L. L. Bean also avoids a 55 percent corporation tax in Japan, which is the highest in the developed world. Currently, L. L. Bean has an arrangement with Federal Express for parcel fulfillment, enabling it to cut delivery time to Japan from two weeks (using air parcel) to three or four days. It has been averaging deliveries of 9,000 parcels a day to Japanese customers. A couple of years ago, its customer file was around 200,000 names; it is now at least 600,000, although the company keeps the exact figure secret.

The cataloger Lands' End has taken a completely different route by establishing itself onshore as a Japanese company. It offers both an English-language catalog with U.S. dollar pricing and a Japanese-language catalog with prices in yen.

Although mail-order industry sales are increasing in Japan, there are few support services such as labeling, fulfillment, or mailing. Half the companies do it themselves. The services that are available deal with the back end of the business, including inbound telemarketing for order processing and customer service, and warehousing and distribution. What is still lacking is a service infrastructure to help with the front end, particularly with regard to lists. Although many compiled lists and credit card lists are available, most owners of mail-order response lists are still reluctant to release their names for rental. Rather than release names on tape, many list owners require that catalogs be sent to their own lettershop for addressing, and there are still no major third-party merge-purge service bureaus that have earned the trust of list owners. Particularly important is the careful handling of consumer data because of privacy concerns. Many list owners are apt to decline to rent out their lists for that reason. Thus, it is not easy for list brokers to locate consumer lists in Japan. The best lists to use are international publication and merchandise buyer lists containing Japanese addresses. These individuals have previously responded to an international offer from offshore and therefore are predisposed to respond again. In addition, businessmen are also consumers and will respond from their offices as well as their home addresses.

Turnkey Projects

Firms that specialize in the design, construction, and start-up of turnkey plants are common in some industries, but not in direct marketing. In a turnkey transaction, a contractor agrees to handle every detail for a foreign client, including the training of operating personnel, which results in a full operational plant and/or business. This approach is useful when foreign direct investment is limited by host-government regulations or when the political and economic environment of the country exposes firms to unacceptable political and/or economic risks. The drawbacks of a turnkey strategy are associated with firms not having a long-term interest in the foreign country and the fact that firms may inadvertently create competition—by selling their technology, firms may also be selling competitive advantages to potential or actual competitors.

Licensing

With licensing, a foreign licensee buys the rights to manufacture a firm's product in its country for a negotiated fee. Fees normally consist of royalty payments on the number of units sold. The licensee then supplies the capital necessary for the overseas operation. The advantages of licensing are that a firm does not have to incur the development costs associated with opening up a foreign market and that it avoids risking any commitment of financial resources to an unfamiliar market. However, licensing has drawbacks: the licensing firm does not have the tight control over manufacturing, marketing, and strategy that is required for realizing experience benefits and location economies; the firm receives limited royalties to use in expanding into other countries; and the firm risks losing control of its business and technological know-how to foreign companies.

Avon Products runs the best-known direct marketing operation in China, but many copycat companies are emerging. Avon first focused on Guang-dong, investing considerable time and effort in training its sales force there. It recently expanded to the greater Shanghai market. In direct marketing operations in most countries, the company delivers its products through the mail; in China, however, trucks do the physical distribution of products.

After 17 years of economic reforms in China, almost all foreign-invested enterprises (FIEs) still confront obstacles to the seamless distribution of goods. Although Beijing has loosened control over distribution, differences in the speed of development among regions continue to hinder nationwide distribution efforts. FIEs cope with these difficulties by developing various ways to get their goods into Chinese consumers' hands. Some rely completely on outside companies to handle all aspects of product distribution; others handle distribution concerns in-house. Since different goods and geographic locations demand different distribution approaches, the best method for a particular company depends on the volume and type of goods sold and the enterprise's size, resources, and level of local involvement.

Franchising

Franchising is similar to licensing, except that franchising involves much longer-term commitments. Also, whereas licensing is pursued primarily by manufacturing firms, franchising is employed primarily by service firms. In a franchising agreement, a franchisor sells limited rights to the use of its brand name to a franchisee in return for a lump-sum payment and a share of the franchisee's profits. The franchisee agrees to abide by strict rules as to how it does business. As a result, the franchisor is relieved of the costs and risks of opening up a foreign market on its own because the franchisee typically assumes those costs and risks.

Franchising has fewer disadvantages than licensing. Because service companies use franchising, there is less reason for concern about sharing experience or technology. A more significant disadvantage of franchising is quality control. Franchising arrangements have value because of the brand name involved and the expectations customers have about the quality of the product or service. However, the geographical distance of the firm from its foreign franchisees can result in poor quality management.

Joint Ventures

Joint ventures are a popular mode for entering a new market by non–direct marketing firms. Usually the arrangement is a 50/50 venture, in which each party holds 50 percent ownership and contributes a team of managers who share operating control. Some firms seek a majority share and thus tighter control. Joint ventures enable firms to benefit from a local partner's knowledge of the host country's competitive conditions, culture, language, and politics. There is frequently also some technology knowledge transfer. Firms can reduce their development costs and risks of opening a foreign market, and, in many countries, political considerations make joint ventures the only feasible entry mode. On the negative side, joint ventures are associated with potentially losing control over subsidiaries and/or technology.

Asia is one of the three most profitable markets for American Express. In a joint venture with Northwest Airlines, AmEx was looking to attract the airline's Worldperks frequent flier members to the AmEx card, and Northwest wanted AmEx members to sign up for its frequent flier program. A mailing of 200,000 letters, which offered to fly a friend free with the purchase of one airplane ticket with the AmEx card, brought in $14 million in sales.

Eddie Bauer Japan was formed in 1993 as a joint venture with Otto-Sumisho, Inc., to develop Eddie Bauer stores and distribute catalogs in Japan. The company also has the licensing rights for the use of Eddie Bauer trademarks in Japan. Eddie Bauer Japan's first major effort was a 16-page Eddie Bauer sportswear insert in the For You catalog in summer 1994. The following year, the company mailed four Japanese-language catalogs. For 1996, plans called for the mailing of five Japanese-language catalogs: two in spring, one in summer, and two in fall. The catalog business has fueled marketing efforts by reaching potential Eddie Bauer customers well beyond the traffic at its store locations. Important synergies have been created through these dual-channel marketing efforts.

Eddie Bauer Germany was announced in 1995 as part of a joint venture between Eddie Bauer Inc., Heinrich Heine GmbH, and Sport Scheck, the latter two part of the Otto Versand Group. The new venture, which is headquartered in Munich, allows Eddie Bauer Germany to develop Eddie Bauer stores and catalogs in Germany and certain other European markets. The firm entered the German market in 1994 with inserts in the spring/summer and fall/winter editions of Sport Scheck, one of the country's largest catalogs. Eddie Bauer currently mails two catalogs a year in Germany for the spring/summer and fall/winter seasons. To date, the retailer's catalogs in Germany have obtained almost twice the demand originally projected.

Wholly Owned Subsidiaries

In a wholly owned subsidiary, a firm owns 100 percent of the new subsidiary in a foreign market. The firm can either set up a completely new operation in that country or acquire an established firm and use it as a springboard for promoting its products. With a wholly owned subsidiary, a firm's competitive advantage is still under its control; it can maintain tight supervision over operations in the country, and it benefits directly from the experience gained from operating in the market. On the other hand, establishing a wholly owned subsidiary is generally the most costly method of serving a foreign market, because the firm must bear the full costs and risks of setting up overseas operations. It must also bear all the risks associated with learning to do business in a new culture.

Bertelsmann AG, Europe's largest media company, with $22 billion in annual revenues, recently decided to put its one-year-old Book Club India on hold following an intensive six-month review of the club's profitability. This means that it would not spend another single deutsche mark on a business that already had the equivalent of $10 million invested, and that it might put the business up for sale. This experience is relevant for direct marketers looking to expand into emerging markets, particularly because the U.S. Department of Commerce is touting India as one of the world's top 10 growth markets. India has a population approaching 1 billion; the largest concentration of English-speaking people outside the United States; and well-educated, although small, middle and upper classes.

The problem Bertelsmann discovered was that after segmenting for affluent prospects in the nation's 23 largest cities, those people who would pay more than a dollar or two for a book were a relatively small number of consumers. Of the 15.5 million households in those major cities, only 5 million had income levels worth targeting, and only a million of those households were English speaking. In the end, research showed that the market potential was really no more than 297,000 club members. Bertelsmann was making some money on its initial effort but not enough to warrant a major push. As long as the market of potential members does not grow significantly, and middle-class purchasing power does not rise, India will remain a market of low priority for Bertelsmann.

Strategic Alliances

As defined earlier, strategic alliances are agreements between potential or actual competitors that allow firms to operate cooperatively in a market. Firms ally themselves with competitors for various strategic purposes. Such alliances facilitate entry into a foreign market; allow the firms to share the fixed costs and associated risks of developing new products or processes; bring together complementary skills and assets that neither company could easily develop on its own; and help the firms establish technological standards for the industry that benefit both firms overall. Disadvantages include giving competitors a low-cost route to new technology and markets and giving away more than the firm receives.

Strategic alliances include everything from formal joint ventures, in which two or more firms have equity stakes, to short-term contractual agreements in which two companies agree to cooperate on a particular task, such as developing a new product. A key part of making a strategic alliance work is selecting the right kind of ally. A good partner helps the firm achieve its strategic goals, shares the firm's vision for the purpose of the alliance; and is unlikely to try to exploit the alliance for its own ends by expropriating the firm's technological know-how.

DIRECT MARKETING AND THE GLOBAL ECONOMY

Tremendous global opportunities exist today for direct-response marketers. For example, many marketers see the recent European unity measures as a way to exclude outside competition, but that view ignores the benefits that will result when the 12 nations of the European Economic Community drop barriers that once impeded the flow of goods, services, money, and people. Goods shipped to Europe will require just one document, instead of up to 70 separate customs forms, and shipments between countries will take far less time than they do now.

Then there is the added boost from the collapse of communism in the former satellite countries of Central and Eastern Europe. This brings into the market economy 140 million more people. The events in the Soviet Union are even more dramatic because they add some 290 million people to the world market economy, opening up vast new opportunities for direct marketing.

For more opportunities, direct marketers need only to look at the booming economies of Asia, where growth has been three times faster than in much of the rest of the world. In the next decade, we can expect world economic output to come from four roughly equal quarters: the Pacific Rim, Europe, the United States, and the rest of the world.

Mail Order

Internationally, mail-order offerings, including catalogs, are growing in use, especially in business-to-business sales, but they are limited by postal constraints and by the shortage of useful mailing lists. Where the postal systems do work well, they can be too expensive for mass marketing. For example, Japan has an excellent postal service, with reliable and fast deliveries, but the costs can be prohibitive. The lone exception to the usually inadequate national postal systems in Third World countries is Brazil, where there is overnight delivery of first-class letters 86 percent of the time. In Europe, where direct-mail is in general use, amounting to about half the frequency of America, direct- mail lists are hampered by the tendency of list owners to keep them to themselves. Readers generally buy magazines at newsstands, not by mail subscriptions; hence there are few lists that are obtainable from publishers. Moreover, government privacy regulations often limit the use of mailing lists by businesses. Table 16.2 contains a listing of mail-order sales for selected countries.

An increased competition among postal services and others seeking to carry bulk mail from the United States to Europe and elsewhere is founded on the economic reality that there is significant growth to be had for North American direct mailers who want to serve other countries. Not only is the European market not saturated, it is not yet even particularly well served. The average U.S. household receives 977 items of direct mail a year versus an average of only 52 items a year in Europe. While some observers suggest that Americans get too

TABLE 16.2. International Mail-Order Sales

	1992 Mail-Order Sales (Millions)	1992 Annual Growth Rate	1992 Share of Retail Sales	1992 per Capita Direct Marketing Sales (Millions)
Europe				
Austria	$ 1,356	5.70%	3.80%	$178
France	$ 8,520	5.40	2.60	$151
Germany	$ 23,306	2.00	4.80	$290
Italy	$ 1,412	3.40	5.40	$ 30
Switzerland	$ 1,422	N/A	2.80	$294
United Kingdom	$ 6,253	1.10	2.50	$133
Non-Europe				
Canada	$ 6,707	10.0	N/A	$250
Japan	$ 14,435	8.0	1.20	$117
United States	$168,050	5.0	3.50	$656

Source: David Evans and Jefferey M. O'Brien, "Americans Abroad," *Direct,* June 1994, p. 40. Evans and O'Brien cite from *Portable Mail Order Industry Statistics,* 1993 ed.

much mail, it is incontrovertible that U.S. direct mailers can achieve very profitable growth without wearing out their welcome in Europe.

The challenge in direct marketing to Europe is to take advantage of growth opportunities while controlling the quality of the direct mail dispatched so that as volume grows recipients continue to find it useful. Technology is available to track customers individually without violating any of the privacy laws in the various European countries. Direct marketers can access databases that tell them not only whether or not a prospective customer has the income level to afford their products or services but also whether, based on past purchases, that consumer or business might be interested in what a firm wants to sell them now.

Face-to-face business transactions have long been considered an essential ingredient for success in the Japanese market. When SunExpress, the aftermarketing division of Sun Microsystems, Inc., decided to service the Japanese market in 1992, it focused on direct marketing rather than on personal relationships. Business-to-business direct marketing was new to Japanese customers, especially in the complex area of high-tech products. However, with a large, installed base of Sun customers in Japan, SunExpress viewed real potential in pioneering the Japanese aftermarket.

SunExpress is dedicated to building relationships with Sun customers by ensuring that they have easy, convenient access to the information and products needed to enhance and expand their SPARC and Solaris enterprise solutions and heterogeneous computer networking environments. After Sun customers make their initial investments in the company's products, SunExpress provides the attention, services, information, and further products needed to address their ongoing use of the product.

The initial challenge for SunExpress was in contacting Sun customers. Japan's complex, multilayered distribution made it difficult for SunExpress to identify and communicate with Sun end users. SunExpress Japan learned quickly that customers were fascinated with the promise of fast, quality mail-order sales but were skeptical that a direct marketing company could live up to its promises. SunExpress also discovered that customers demanded a higher level of service for business purchases than for consumer goods. The same Japanese customers who were willing to order consumer catalog items and risk returning them for the right size or color had little tolerance for inaccurate or late high-tech purchases. As SunExpress delivered on its promises, it found that it earned trust and loyalty. Japanese customers desired the same product availability, quick delivery, and knowledgeable sales representatives that SunExpress provided in North America and Europe.

Though the Japanese market presented many obstacles, the opportunities in direct mail can be good. The $14 billion Japanese direct mail market has been growing at an annual rate of about 12 percent for 5 years, but it remains relatively undeveloped. As noted previously, one of the biggest obstacles for U.S. companies attempting mail order in Japan is postage, which costs two to three times more there than in the United States, and further limitations include payment options for Japanese consumers and difficulties surrounding the acquisition of good mailing lists. The traditional source of direct-mail lists—magazine and newspaper subscribers—is not plentiful because nearly all publications in Japan are sold on newsstands. Instead of paying by personal check, Japanese consumers and business executives use bank transfers or credit cards. To get paid, foreign companies frequently must set up an arrangement with a Japanese bank. In addition, Japanese consumers are unlikely to respond to mailing solicitations from foreign companies if those firms are unfamiliar.

Unlike Americans, Japanese consumers do not yet suffer from direct-mail overexposure. More than one-third claim to welcome solicitations. In addition, 62 percent of Japanese consumers read almost every piece of direct mail advertising they receive, and an additional 35 percent read anything that looks interesting. Items that are currently selling well include recession-buster products that help businesses cut costs or improve service, such as automation devices or computer software. Branded consumer goods and services also are strong sellers.

American mailers should be aware, however, that opening a Japanese fulfillment center may lock a company in to mailing from Japan. Trade regulations require most Japanese companies to mail from within their home country's borders, and an office in Japan technically qualifies a foreign firm as being Japanese.

Catalogs

European mail-order marketers have been operating under handicaps relative to their U.S. counterparts because of higher postal rates, limited list media, low credit card penetration, fragmented markets, and stricter regulations. However, expansion into European markets is well established for many U.S.-based mail-order companies, and the pace of expansion of European-based mail-order companies into the United States is startling. The former has come by virtue of market growth in Europe, as well as increased efforts in the United States by companies like Time Warner, Grolier, and Reader's Digest.

Catalogs in Europe are big business, particularly in the consumer sector. One German catalog company has a database of 8 million names available for rent. A catalog company in France has a database of 15 million names, which is a lot considering that there are only 18 million names in the French telephone book. U.K. catalog companies also have massive databases, although not as big as the German or the French ones. However, there are more catalog companies in the United Kingdom, so they are cumulatively important. The top five U.K. catalog companies accounted for most of the $7.5 billion sales in the United Kingdom in 1991. And out of a population of 57 million, 20 percent of all U.K. inhabitants purchased goods from catalogs that year. The total catalog sales figure for Germany is $26.2 billion. France, at $8.3 billion, is a little above the United Kingdom but still way below Germany. The total catalog market across the 12 member countries of the European Community is now worth $49 billion.

Worldwide, Europe accounts for 40 percent of catalog sales, and 80 percent of that figure is accounted for by just Germany, France, and the United Kingdom. No fewer than nine European countries have catalog sales in excess of $130 for every man, woman, child, and infant in that country. There is big money being spent in Europe, though not really comparable to the amount spent by Americans.

Catalog marketers have grappled with the Asian market for close to a decade. Hampered by a dearth of reliable mailing lists, a scarcity of local talent, inadequate phone systems, and the inability to fulfill orders through traditional retailers, they have fought an uphill battle in their attempts to reach Asia's 500 million or more consumers and its millions of businesses. Some 60 U.S. catalogs have tested Japan over the last few years, but only 15 remain. However, those that survive—such as L. L. Bean, The Sharper Image, Lands' End, and Patagonia—are very successful. They have made it by offering high-quality products that have a unique appeal supported by money-back guarantees.

Direct-Response Ads

Direct-response advertising through newspapers and magazines is still the most popular medium for direct sales in Europe. Britain leads the way with newspapers filled with mail-order ads for everything from financial services to housewares. Direct marketers are not mailing to the Mexican market yet, but it is only a matter of time before Mexico's under-25 population (59 percent of the total) becomes a prime direct marketing target.

Exhibit 16.1 shows a direct-response ad for IBM's ThinkPad computer. This German-language print ad appeared in *Der Spiegel* as the last page of the magazine. Readers of the ad are invited to call a phone number for more information about the notebook computer.

Telemarketing

Telemarketing is another medium for direct marketing overseas, but it too is more limited than in the United States and varies from country to country. One reason door-to-door selling is popular in Asia is that customers there tend to put as much importance on who they are buying from as what they are buying. For the same reason, telemarketing is not widespread in Asia, although it is growing. Japanese consumers thus far consider sales by telemarketing as too aggressive. There are important cultural differences to consider in selecting telemarketing in addition to choosing what to sell. High on that list of differences are language problems, which must be considered in how product or service offers are made to prospects.

EXHIBIT 16.1. IBM Direct-Response Act from *Der Spiegel*

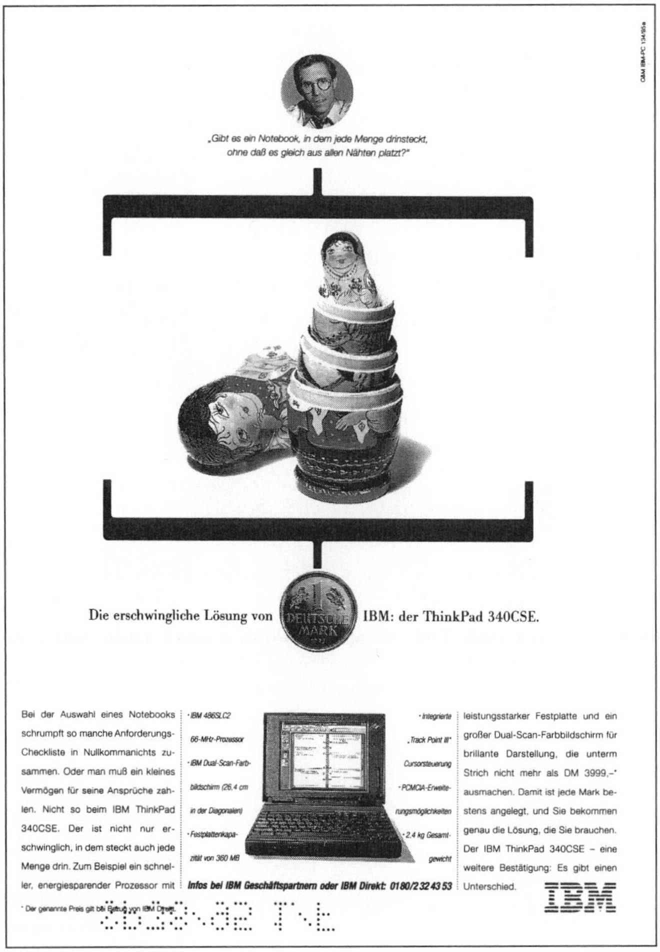

Television

Television is evolving rapidly as a sales medium in many foreign markets. In most European countries, television has historically been government-owned and strictly controlled. That changed rapidly in the 1980s and will accelerate with European unity. Seventeen new national television channels started up in Europe in the last decade. All but one of them accept advertising. The growth of cable and satellite channels has been explosive since the first one began in 1984 and, along with that, opportunities for advertisers. There were about 50 million cable homes in Europe in 1995, and observers expect substantial growth well into the next century.

Exhibit 16.2 contains a storyboard for a British Airways ad. The subject of the direct-response commercial is the many places the airline flies at specific prices. The last frame of the ad invites watchers to call a phone number for more information.

EXHIBIT 16.2. British Airways Direct-Response Television Ad

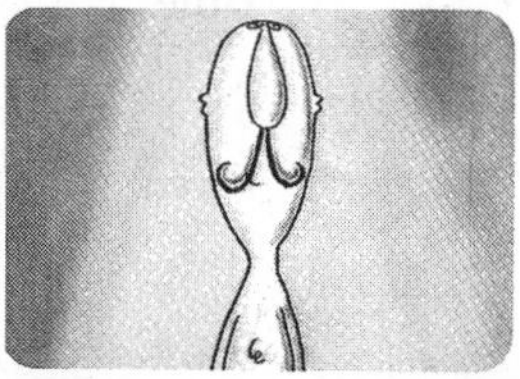

1. ***Video:*** An acrobat swings to the front,

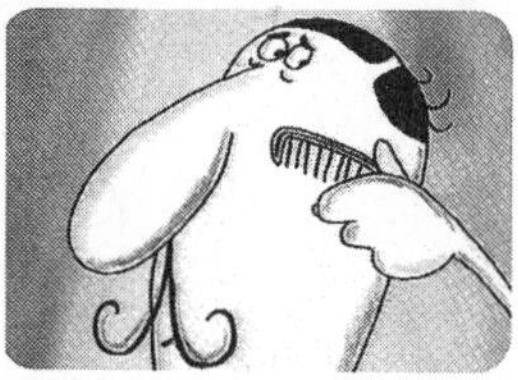

2. ... combs his black hair, ...

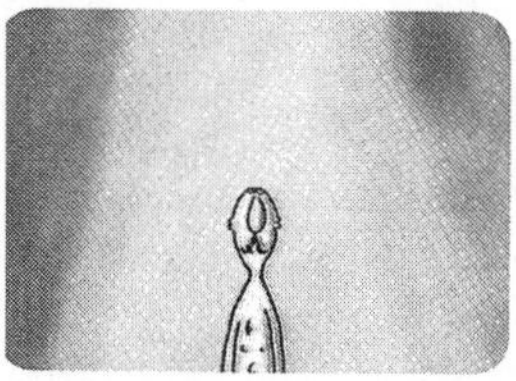

3. ... and swings back again.

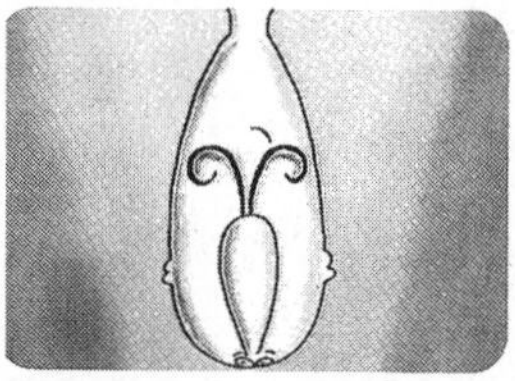

4. More of the same, now upside down.

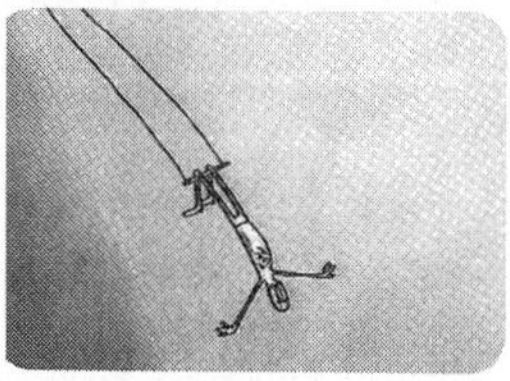

5. We now see that he is hanging from a trapeze.
Audio: Drum roll.

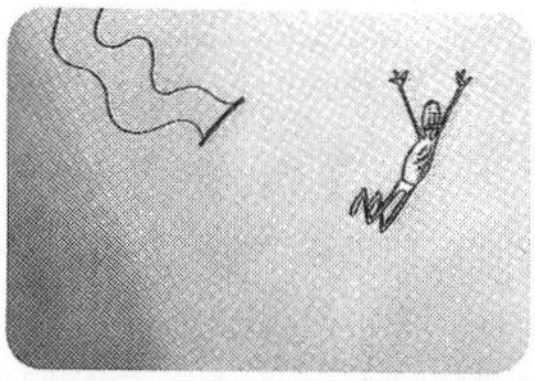

6. ***Video:*** He lets go of the trapeze ...

7. ... and waits to be caught by his partner - in vain.

8. He worriedly glances down in mid-air.

9. ***Audio*** (acrobat, with a French accent): "Where is everybody?"

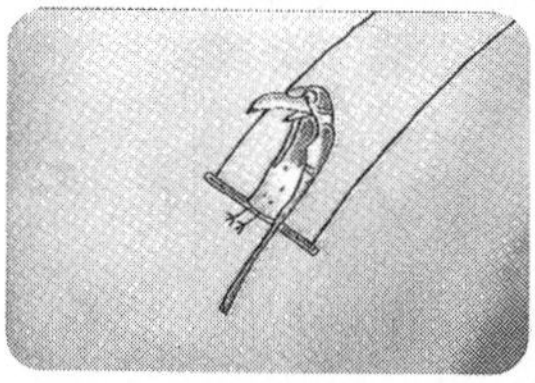

10. ***Video:*** On the other trapeze a lonely parrot.
Audio (parrot, croaks): "Where is everybody? Where is everybody?"

11. ***Video:*** Cut to super: "Nice, from £99 return."
Audio: "La Cucaracha" starts playing.

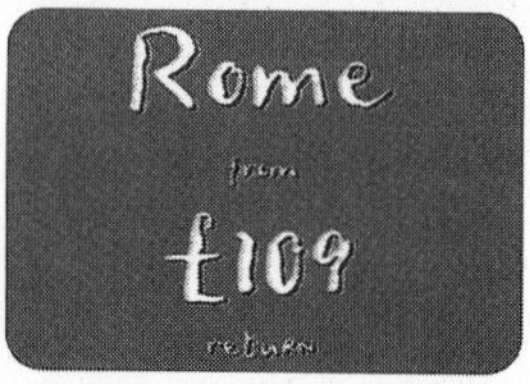

12. ***Video:*** Super: "Rome, from £109 return."

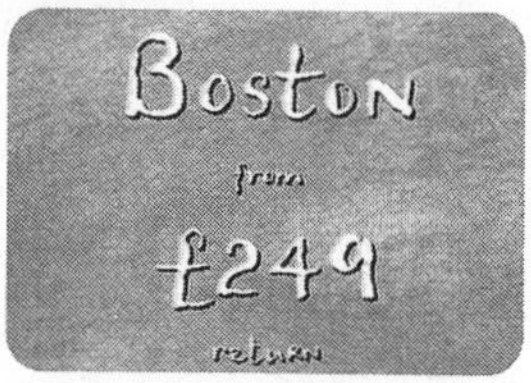

13. Super: "Boston, from £249 return."

14. Super: "World offers."

15. Cut to the British Airways logo and a phone number for more information.

British Airways "Acrobat" : 20 : M & C Saatchi, London : Carlos : Keith Bickel : Picasso Pictures

Direct-response television ads are used even less in Asia than in Europe, and their numbers pale in comparison to those of sales by door-to-door salespersons or direct mail, even in Japan. Japanese broadcasters are too inflexible in rate structures now to make television an attractive medium.

SUMMARY

The interest by direct marketers in international markets can be explained by changing competitive dynamics coupled with shifts in demand throughout the world. Today, the U.S. domestic market must be shared with a variety of foreign companies and products. As a result, firms with only domestic markets have found it increasingly difficult to sustain their historical sales and profit growth rates. However, companies that have never ventured abroad soon come to realize that they must work harder to succeed against global competitors.

The movement beyond a firm's domestic borders accounts for the complexity and diversity found in international direct marketing operations. However, direct marketing concepts, processes, and principles are universally applicable. The problems direct marketers face in reaching their profit goals lie in the differences between domestic and international markets, but the issue is not different concepts of marketing in the environments within which the marketing plans must be implemented. Rather, the uniqueness of foreign marketing comes from a range of specific problems and opportunities and the variety of strategies and tactics necessary to cope with those differences.

Differences in infrastructure and technology, competitive dynamics, legal and government restrictions, customer preferences, and any number of other uncontrollable elements affect the profit outcome of direct marketing firms operating overseas. Marketers cannot control or influence these elements but instead must adapt to achieve any business successes. Operating abroad becomes a challenge because the controllable elements of marketing decisions—such as product, pricing, promotion, and distribution—must be accommodated to the frequently unique uncontrollable elements of the foreign marketplace.

When competing internationally, firms derive many benefits from both the globalization and standardization of their activities, including incremental profits from economies of scale in production and marketing, growth opportunities greater than those available in the domestic market, survival because of more demand and less competition, and a way to diversify business operations through obtaining new markets and customers.

REVIEW QUESTIONS

1. Why are more and more American direct marketing companies interested in expanding overseas?
2. What problems, opportunities, and threats exist for American companies interested in expanding in Asia versus Europe versus South America?

3. What are the entry modes and strategic alliances available to direct marketing firms? Which ones are more commonly used and why? What are the reasons for choosing one approach over another?
4. What are the catalog, telemarketing, direct-mail, direct-response television, direct-response radio, and direct-response print opportunities in the various regions of the world? Why are they different, and what factors influence the likely success of each one by country?
5. How do differences in infrastructure and technology, competitive dynamics, legal and government restrictions, customer preferences and culture, and any number of other uncontrollable elements influence the direct marketing activities possible in various countries?
6. How does the long-standing controversy about the standardization versus specialization of strategies for reaching specific markets relate to the direct marketing of products or services in various countries?
7. How is the segmentation of customers and prospects influenced by whether a direct marketer is operating internationally or just in the American market?
8. What do the examples of international direct marketing in this chapter tell you about the challenges facing firms interested in expanding to other countries?

NOTES

1. Philip R. Cateora, *International Marketing,* 8th ed. (Homewood, IL: Richard D. Irwin, 1993), pp. 11–12.
2. Charles W. L. Hill, *International Business* (Homewood, IL: Richard D. Irwin, 1994), pp. 402–409.
3. Ibid, p. 411.
4. Ibid, pp. 402–409.

SOURCES

Baalbaki, Imad B., and Karesh K. Malhotra. "Marketing Management Bases for International Market Segmentation: An Alternate Look at the Standardization/Customization Debate." *International Marketing Review* 10 (1993), pp. 19–44.

Bachman, Katy. "Infomercials Go Global, Carefully." *Direct,* July 1994, pp. 12–13.

Baines, Adam. *The Handbook of International Direct Marketing,* 2nd ed. The European Direct Marketing Association, 1995.

Bird, Drayton. "The Future Is International." In *Beyond 2000: The Future of Direct Marketing,* ed. Jerry I. Reitman. Lincolnwood, IL: NTC Business Books, 1994, pp. 21–31.

Bruner, Richard. "Consuming Passions." *International Management* 49, no. 4 (Europe Edition, May 1994), pp. 40–41.

Campbell, Cary E. "Mexico's Young Market." *Target Marketing* 17, no. 11 (November 1994), pp. 20–21.

Cateora, Philip R. *International Marketing,* 8th ed. Homewood, IL: Richard D. Irwin, 1993.

Di Talamo, Nicholas. "Getting U.S. Catalogs into Europe." *Direct Marketing,* December 1992, pp. 21–24.

Dowling, Melissa. "Crumpets & Catalogs." *Catalog Age* 12, no. 6 (June 1995), pp. 173–80.

______. "Translating from German." *Catalog Age,* February 1995, pp. 53–55.

EDER, PETER. "Direct Marketing in Europe: Understanding Differences in Language, Culture, and Regulations." *Direct Marketing,* March 1996, pp. 49–51.

EGOL, LEN. "Endnote on Book Club India." *Direct,* January 1996, p. 67.

______. "TV Shopping Grows in Japan." *Direct,* March 1995, pp. 45–50.

EVANS, DAVID, AND JEFFEREY M. O'BRIEN. "Americans Abroad." *Direct,* June 1994, pp. 35–46.

FISHMAN, ARNOLD. "International Mail Order Overview." *Direct Marketing,* October 1992, p. 28–32.

GARRITY, ROBERT E. "Marketers with a Yen." *Direct Marketing,* November 1991, pp. 46–51.

GOLDNER, PAUL "Mail Order Marketing: A World Wide View." *Direct Marketing,* May 1996, pp. 31–33.

GREAVES, JANE. "From Factory to Consumer." *China Business Review* 22, no. 5 (September/October 1995), pp. 14–15.

GUSTTAVSON, JOHN. "Direct Marketing in Canada: Discovering Opportunities within Challenges." *Direct Marketing,* March 1996, pp. 57–60.

HILL, CHARLES W. L. *International Business,* Homewood, IL: Richard D. Irwin, 1994.

"International Mail Order Trends." *Direct Marketing,* October 1993, pp. 93–98.

JAIN, SUBHASH C. "Standardizations of International Market Strategy: Some Research Hypotheses." *Journal of Marketing* 53 (January 1989), pp. 70–79.

JEANNET, JEAN-PIERE, AND HUBERT D. HENNESSEY. *Global Marketing Strategies.* Boston: Houghton Mifflin, 1992.

KATZENSTEIN, HERBERT, AND WILLIAMS S. SACHS. *Direct Marketing,* 2nd ed. New York: Macmillan, 1992.

KREUTZER, R. T. "Marketing Mix Standardization: An Integrated Approach in Global Marketing." *European Journal of Marketing* 22, no. 10 (1988), pp. 19–30.

LANDIS, ANITA. "Direct Mail Programs Overseas Are Taking Hold, But the Rules Are Complex." *Direct Marketing,* March 1996, pp. 44–47.

LEVITT, THEODORE. "The Globalization of Markets." *Harvard Business Review,* May/June 1983, pp. 92–102.

LINEN, CHRISTOPHER. "Marketing and the Global Economy." *Direct Marketing,* January 1991, pp. 54–56.

MARGOLIS, BUDD. "Direct Marketing: A Worldwide Perspective." *Direct Marketing,* March 1996, pp. 33–35.

MARISKA, MARK D. "Direct Marketing in Russia." *Direct Marketing,* January 1995, pp. 38–41.

MCCRACKEN, GRANT. "Culture and Consumption: A Theoretical Account of the Structure and Movement of the Cultural Meaning of Consumer Goods." *Journal of Consumer Research* 13 (June 1981), pp. 71–81.

MILLER, DICK. "Getting the Goods There!" *Target Marketing* 17, no. 3 (March 1994), pp. 36–40.

MILLER, RICHARD N. "Cultural Barriers in Cross-Border Marketing." *Direct Marketing,* March 1996, pp. 66–69.

______. *Multinational Direct Marketing,* New York: McGraw-Hill, 1995.

"Multinational Direct Marketing." *Direct Marketing,* May 1995, pp. 44–51.

NEAL, MOLLIE. "Catalogia: C'est Bien." *Direct Marketing,* February 1992, pp. 18–19.

ORR, ALICIA. "Why Japan Is Hot for Catalogers." *Target Marketing* 18, no. 11 (November 1995), pp. 64–67.

PASTERNACK, EDWARD D. "Eddie Bauer Expanding in Japan and Germany." *Direct Marketing,* March 1996, pp. 36–39.

POWELL, CHRIS. "International Direct Mail Comes of Age." *Direct Marketing,* December 1995, pp. 42–43.

ROBERTS, MARY LOU, AND PAUL D. BERGER. *Direct Marketing Management.* Englewood Cliffs, NJ: Prentice Hall, 1989.

SORICILLO, STEVEN. "Going Direct into Overseas Markets." *Direct Marketing,* March 1996, pp. 53–54.

SROGE, MAXWELL. *The United States Mail Order Industry.* Lincolnwood, IL: NTC Business Books, 1994.

STERN, AIMEE. "Land of the Rising Mail." *International Business* 6, no. 11 (November 1993), pp. 28–30.

______. "Spanning the Bridge to the Pacific." *Direct,* April 1992, pp. 1, 31–33.

"SunExpress Bucks Convention: Pioneering Business-to-Business Direct Marketing in Japan." *Direct Marketing,* March 1996, pp. 40–43.

"Understanding the Japanese Market." *Direct Marketing,* April 1993, pp. 39–42.

UPDIKE, EDITH HILL, AND MARY KUNTZ. "Japan Is Dialing 1 800 Buy America." *Business Week,* June 12, 1995, pp. 61, 64.

CHAPTER 17

Direct Marketing Decision Support Tools

OBJECTIVES

1. To define the roles and importance of marketing research, testing, experimentation, and statistical models in the management decision-making process.
2. To appreciate the complexities associated with determining which of several direct marketing plan alternatives will produce the greatest business result.
3. To examine examples of how firms involved in direct marketing activities have used sophisticated decision support tools to understand the relationships between elements of their plans and responses from customers and prospects.

INTRODUCTION

In 1994, Publishers Clearing House, one of the nation's leading direct-mail marketers selling magazines through million-dollar contests, placed the following employment ad in the American Statistical Association newsletter, *Amstat News*:

> Marketing Statistician
>
> We are a leader in the direct marketing field with an available position for a highly motivated statistician reporting to the Director of Statistical Development. As a contributing member in our Marketing Department, you will analyze marketing data and provide additional statistical support. Successful candidate will have a minimum of 3 years statistical analysis experience in marketing applications, excellent writing skills, the ability to program in PC and mainframe languages and working knowledge of marketing databases and statistical analysis software (SAS). An MBA or MS is strongly preferred; however, individuals with a BA and significant experience using statistical methodologies in direct mail operations will be considered.
>
> Please send your resume and cover letter including salary history to:
>
> L. Baumann, Personnel Department:
> PUBLISHERS CLEARING HOUSE
> 382 Channel Drive
> Port Washington, New York 11050
>
> An Equal Opportunity Employer M/F

The advertisement is for a person who is able to analyze information from marketing tests and experiments and who can build models or statistical formulas that predict the sales and profits of direct marketing efforts. This is a high-skill and high-tech position; the person who fills it is expected to make a significant contribution to the marketing operations of Publishers Clearing House.

The ad content highlights the importance of testing, experiments, and modeling in the operations of a direct marketing firm. Data and databases are the engines of direct marketing. The people who manipulate and manage those data and databases make the difference between success and failure at many companies. This is possible because direct marketing is the most data-driven and measurable element of any marketing plan.

This chapter covers how direct marketing efforts are measured, evaluated, and forecast through marketing research, tests, experiments, and modeling. In general, direct marketers are positive toward these techniques; they are an important part of how marketers think about conducting their business and making decisions. The premise is that there is no reason to invest a large amount of resources in a marketing program unless there is a high probability of success. Because direct marketers have a significant amount of control over their contacts with customers and prospects, they have the opportunity to estimate or forecast the probability of success with a relatively high degree of accuracy. As a result, marketing efforts can be allocated to programs with the highest expected value in terms of sales, profits, and/or potential for building a customer base for future operations.

Concepts from courses in basic and advanced statistics, research, testing, experimental design, and statistical model building are important in direct marketing plan measurement, evaluation, and forecasting. Research uses surveys of consumers or businesses to provide information on *why* things happen. In contrast, testing and experiments tell the direct marketer *what* happened in terms of sales and profit effects from direct marketing campaigns. Testing involves conducting comparisons between alternative ways of proceeding with a campaign without structuring those comparisons in such a way as to isolate exactly why a difference in performance by one or more of the alternatives may have occurred. Thus, a simple *field test* involves some direct marketing variables that usually concern the nature of an offer. In contrast, an *experiment* is a carefully designed study in which there are controls and manipulated conditions that isolate how one or more offer variables affect the behavior of a target market, and ultimately a sales and profit outcome.

Experimentation has a different focus from that of testing because experiments try to isolate why differences between campaigns occur to ensure that the assessment of differences between offers measures only a small number of changes, which are controlled. Direct marketers may test or experiment with several mailing packages before deciding which one to use. During that process, they can compare a variety of customer or prospect lists to see how well each does before using a particular list or some portion of that list. They can also test or experiment with different offers and campaign themes to determine which one generates the greatest response. Statistical modeling involves applying forecasting methods to historical purchase data and/or experiments to predict future sales levels.

Direct Marketing Research

There are whole books and courses devoted just to the topic of marketing research. It is a complex professional field requiring an understanding of sampling, questionnaire design, statistical analysis, and reporting. Direct marketing research involves studies conducted among consumers or businesses. Much of this research is done before any testing or experimentation occurs. Generally, marketing research provides information on attitudinal questions.

Research can involve person-to-person individual interviews or discussion sessions with groups of customers and/or prospects. These individual interviews or discussion sessions are conducted with small numbers of people. They produce transcripts of what was said, but not numbers. This is called *qualitative research.* In contrast, surveys involve contacting relatively large numbers of customers and/or prospects by mail or telephone to ask structured questions using a questionnaire (such as an attitude scale). Surveys produce statistics that show the number of persons who hold particular opinions. This is called *quantitative research.*

Both qualitative and quantitative research can be used to evaluate ideas for direct marketing campaigns. Surveys are considered more reliable than interviews, because surveys systematically collect opinions from large groups of people, whereas personal interviews and discussion groups contact relatively small numbers of people.

A company's research activity level may depend on what the company can afford. It is worth noting that the typical direct marketing firm has little money with which to conduct expensive surveys. Although qualitative research is much cheaper than quantitative research, it may be misleading because of the smaller numbers of people who usually end up participating in the research and because of potential interviewer biases that may influence the research findings.

Research cannot replace direct-response testing or experiments, but is useful in tandem with those methods to help a company produce a more effective direct-response campaign. Research can contribute to successful campaigns in four main areas: (1) identifying the target market, (2) determining what to say in the campaign or offer, (3) determining what image to project, and (4) developing new products and services.

Direct marketers are more likely to reach their goals if they determine which consumers or businesses represent their best opportunity. Therefore, an important function of research is to provide a clear picture of a target market and its product or service preferences. The data can be gathered by sending surveys to current customers and/or prospects. From such surveys, the direct marketer can define a target demographically, by product or service usage, and, for the purposes of developing good offer strategies, psychologically. (Refer back to Chapter 8 for a discussion about how demographics, usage rates, and psychological characteristics contribute different types of information to use in developing direct marketing campaigns or offers.)

Direct marketing campaign or offer research aids the creative process by showing which of the campaign or offer alternatives is likely to produce the best response from target market members. The results can be quite precise and thus often help a company pick a winner as opposed to just providing guidance about how to make improvements in the alternative campaigns or offers.

In the same sense that research results can help create better campaigns or offers, they represent a sound basis on which to determine what image to project. One type of research involves asking customers and/or prospects about their perceptions of a firm's product or service offering versus that of direct competitors. The results can give a firm a solid understanding of where its offering stands versus that of its competition on the key product or service attributes that matter most to target market members.

Research tools are also available for determining new product and service opportunities. These opportunities usually represent gaps in a consumer or business market that define unmet needs. A savvy direct marketer will use this information to develop new products and services. However, once new offers are created, further testing is needed to ensure that marketplace need is addressed.

DIRECT MARKETING TESTING AND EXPERIMENTATION

Direct marketers generally agree about the importance of testing and experiments. Nevertheless, how and when to do that testing and experimentation is the subject of much debate. This is true because there are a variety of testing and experimental procedures from which to select and because there is more than one possible decision criterion upon which to determine whether a test or an experiment is a success or a failure.

However, there is a consensus among the more sophisticated direct marketers that using the statistical methods and experiential designs employed in the social sciences, and in business in general, is the most appropriate way to analyze direct marketing alternatives. There is also consensus that financial outcomes are the most important decision criteria; these outcomes may include the acquisition of customers with a lifetime value (see Chapter 18) rather than just making money from one particular campaign or offer.

Often a marketer is faced with alternatives that are seemingly equal, and there might be differences of opinion about which alternative is the best one. A way to resolve these differences is through testing or experimentation. Another reason for testing or experimenting is to avoid making costly errors. Direct marketing offers are expensive to develop and execute. Firms want more and better proof that they are getting their money's worth from their direct marketing efforts.

As noted previously, however, a test does not isolate exactly why a difference in performance exists between alternatives. In contrast, an experiment controls and manipulates conditions of a campaign to see how one or more experimental variables affects buyer behavior, but experiments are usually significantly more expensive than tests. Experimentation ensures that the assessment of the differences between campaigns provides the information direct marketers need to control the performance of their business efforts through understanding what works or does not work.

In theory, the results of a test or experiment can be projected to a large universe of prospects or customers. However, results may be inadequate because they do not take competitive action or reaction into consideration. The experimental process implies that marketers can draw conclusions about what will have applications in the larger world, but marketers must remember that even if an experiment points to an optimum offer, it usually does not anticipate competitive plans or other unforeseeable marketplace changes.

There are many books that describe statistical methods, testing, and experiments. Most of the subject of statistics is well beyond the scope of this book. However, this chapter will examine examples of what might be done to evaluate some direct marketing offers at their various stages of development.

A BASIC DIRECT MARKETING TEST

Some of the factors involved in testing print advertisements are editorial fit; audience composition; magazine circulation; ad placement cost; position of the ad in the magazine; timing of the ad placement; frequency, or how often the ad is placed; and the color rendering of the ad. One way to gain information about which ad performs better is to use an A/B split, in which different versions of a direct marketing campaign are placed in alternating copies of the same magazine. However, the A/B split does not eliminate all other influences because it indicates only which execution is better suited for the environment in which the test occurred. It is a test, not an experiment, because there are still myriad factors that could explain the specifics of why one or the other ad did better. In particular, the content of the two ads is not varied systematically to determine exactly which of the executional elements (such as positioning, theme, or visual content) produced the sales differences. Nevertheless, this type of test provides useful information in that it shows the relative performance of one execution versus another in roughly the same environment during the same time period.

Companies with long-term space advertising campaigns frequently start with small tests and trial and error before they arrive at a suitable level of response to their ads. Some campaigns that have worked well in direct mail or television have failed in direct-response print advertising. The explanations for this phenomenon sometimes have to do with how the campaigns are converted to the print media, whether the firm tested the correct print media, whether the firm paid too much for the ad space, or some combination of factors.

To limit risk, direct marketers want to spend as little money as possible, without compromising their ability to understand the information from a test. How much copy is needed to make a convincing offer? If a firm uses a four- to eight-page direct-mail letter, it probably needs a full-page magazine ad to convey the same information. Product offerings with price tags of $200 and beyond are sometimes tested in a two-step approach, where the ad offers readers both a phone number and an address. This type of test is realistic for more expensive items because they are seldom sold without a two-step process anyway.

Experimental designs have two basic purposes: (1) to provide answers to specific questions and (2) to control variance, thereby eliminating alternative explanations for results. A well-designed experiment will enable the direct marketer to answer questions with validity, objectivity, and accuracy—and to do so as economically as possible. The questions should be stated in the form of hypotheses, such as "A 10 percent average reduction in the prices of items in a catalog will increase overall sales by 20 percent." This is a proposition that can be numerically evaluated. There are, however, as many designs for experiments as there are questions. Whatever design is chosen should be carefully worked out to yield dependable and valid answers to the marketing questions framed as hypotheses.

An experimental design sets up the framework for comparing relations among variables. Experimenters manipulate specific variables in a direct marketing plan and look for changes in the business results. The design can indicate what alterations to make, how to make them, and how to analyze the observations. An experimental design suggests how many observations to make, which variables to manipulate, and how to represent the results. It also suggests which statistical techniques are appropriate and what possible conclusions can be drawn from the analysis.

Consider the following question posed by a catalog marketer of men's and women's apparel: What impact will a 20 percent increase in the page length of a catalog have on overall catalog sales? The page count should be increased by adding more of the same types of items, not by including additional lines of merchandise (thus holding that variable constant). However, if additional lines of merchandise were added, those items would become another variable in the experimental design. In that case, the cataloger could systematically vary the types of additional lines to see if adding one line or another has a differential impact on catalog sales.

For this experimental example, the cataloger is also concerned about whether adding more pages will have a differential impact on the buying behavior of those who have historically purchased often from the firm in any one year. Thus, in this experiment, the independent variables (the ones being examined) are catalog size and historical buyer behavior, while the dependent variable (the result of interest) is the size of each order. The number of orders and the average order size are important to understanding how the total sales amount for each catalog version was produced, because the multiplication of the number of orders by the average size of the orders produces the total sales for a catalog. If the larger catalog sells more than the smaller one, the firm will conduct a financial analysis of that difference (assuming a certain measurement error range) to determine if the additional sales are profitable.

Note that this illustration is simplified because the firm may find an initial increase in sales but later find that those who purchase more than their historical average when sent the larger catalog purchase less than average from subsequent catalogs they receive. In reality, direct marketers are wise to conduct their experiments for more than one purchase cycle. This allows them to determine whether the results from an offer really add incremental sales or just cannibalize (take away from) future sales.

However, it is also easy to argue that extended experimentation is neither practical nor possible in a competitive environment. Certainly, when a direct marketing firm begins experimenting with alternative marketing approaches, it is possible that competitors will find out what is going on and respond. If the experiment lasts as long as a year, a firm's competitors will have an opportunity to prepare for the new approach long before it is widely introduced.

Therefore, what many firms do is conduct experiments to determine the short-term impact of whatever change they make and use the results to build scenarios about the long-term consequences of the change as it might affect future sales. In that sense, they use the findings from the experiment to help forecast a long-term business result.

Returning to the catalog experiment, the experimental hypothesis is that a 20 percent increase in the number of catalog pages will have a significant impact on the firm's average sales. To evaluate the hypothesis, the catalog firm selects at random 25,000 customers from its database who will receive the larger catalog and another 25,000 to receive the normal catalog. Because many catalog firms mail millions of catalogs a year, an experiment that compares two groups of 25,000 is practical. (Note, however, that the per-catalog cost of producing small runs of 25,000 is much higher than the per-catalog cost of 100,000 or more, which makes conducting an experiment just that much more expensive.) If the firm obtains a 2 percent response rate to the mailings, it will have approximately 500 respondents in each group to analyze. The firm will, of course, keep a record of which customers received what catalog. This allows it to analyze how much each group orders in relation to the size of the catalog it receives.

In the analysis phase, the catalog firm will compare the average order size from each of the two catalog versions overall and by previous level of purchase behavior. This involves evaluating differences by catalog size, previous buyer level, and interactions between the two variables as they affect sales. The interaction would indicate whether catalog size affects how much a customer normally purchases.

THE *TV GUIDE ONLINE* EXPERIMENT [1]

TV Guide Online was slated to be launched by the end of 1994. The service, to be available for IBM-compatible and Apple Macintosh personal computer users who have a modem, was to share a similar graphical look with the magazine itself. In that sense, this service was intended to have a personality very much like a print product in that it would contain text to read and pictures to view. In the interest of maintaining the feel of the magazine, *TV Guide*'s designers were put in charge of *TV Guide Online*'s format.

Users were expected to interact in real time with the editors, look at current program listings, access historical television information, and read articles about topical subjects concerning entertainment and television. Crossword puzzles and horoscopes in an interactive format were also scheduled to be a part of the online service mix. There would be no charge for the software or monthly subscriptions because per-hour charges were to be payable by credit card. And, unlike magazines already carried on services such as CompuServe and America Online, *TV Guide Online* was to be a discrete service.

Before the service's introduction, *TV Guide* management was unsure about how much to charge and whether or not the service should include advertisements like those in the printed edition. Although the ads would be like those in the print version of *TV Guide,* they would be smaller and imbedded in the online pages users would see as they went from page to page while in the online service.

TV Guide decided to conduct an experiment to determine which approach to take in introducing the new online service. The experiment had four cells, or conditions: (1) a low price and no ads; (2) a high price and no ads; (3) a low price and ads; and (4) a high price and ads. All other aspects of the online service were the same from cell to cell.

To conduct the experiment, *TV Guide Online* randomly selected 40,000 names from its list of Delphi subscribers (an Internet service provider) and sent them free software to use in accessing *TV Guide Online* with a description of what the service provided and an offer of 10 free hours. These persons were randomly assigned to the four cells of the experiment so that each cell was sent 10,000 offers.

A summary of the experimental design is as follows:

	Condition I	Condition II	Condition III	Condition IV
Participants (those offered the service)	10,000	10,000	10,000	10,000
Cost per hour	$6.00	$8.00	$6.00	$8.00
Presence of ads	No ads	No ads	Ads	Ads

The experiment ran for six months, after which time the results were analyzed to determine (1) whether any of the conditions produced a significant usage rate and (2) which of the conditions produced the most revenue. For question 1, the hypotheses were that 20 percent of those offered any one of the four versions of the service would enroll and that after the initial enrollment, half of the enrollees, or at least 10 percent of the original sample, would still be using the service.

The hypotheses for question 2 were that the condition with the greatest proportion of users after six months and the highest number of hours per user would be the low-price-and-no-ads condition, but that the high-price-and-ads condition would produce the most revenue and therefore should likely be the final structure of the new online service. If the hypotheses of either question were not confirmed (at the traditional 5 percent significance level), the service would not be introduced. Specifying a decision rule before the test was conducted ensured that the decision would be made objectively. Ultimately, a financial analysis of the experimental results would determine the most profitable alternative.

Note that the sample size for an experiment is determined by applying a formula that associates the required level of measurement accuracy with the likely variation to be found in the variables being measured. Controlling the sample size is important in most circumstances because it has a significant impact on the cost of conducting an experiment. For this example, the sample size for each condition is more a matter of administrative convenience because the cost of having more service users in each condition is minimal. Also note that the very large samples used in this experiment guarantee that any measurement taken will have very little error associated with it. For example, if an opinion poll of only 1,000 persons has an accuracy rate of +/– 2.5 percentage points, the range of measurement error around several thousand persons is quite low.

Analyzing the Results

Table 17.1 shows the number of mailings sent, the response rate, the number and proportion of those still with the service after six months, and their average monthly service usage in month 6 for each of the four conditions in the *TV Guide Online* experiment. The analyses for hypotheses 1 and 2 are simple tests of proportions. For each of the conditions, the actual initial enrollment is beyond 20 percent and the sixth-month enrollment is beyond 10 percent.

To evaluate the differences in hourly usage, the appropriate statistical analysis technique is an analysis of variance (ANOVA). ANOVA is a complex statistical technique used to evaluate differences between mean or average values of the various conditions of an experiment. As noted previously, the *TV Guide Online* experiment has four cells or conditions, each with mean values. Those mean experiment values come from the data in Table 17.1. The hypotheses for this experiment define the ordering of differences in magnitude expected for the mean values. The ANOVA tells us if the mean differences in Table 17.1 are statistically significant. However, it does not tell us which of the means are different. It tells us only that at least two of them are statistically different from one another.

The ANOVA produces a table, like Table 17.2, indicating which of the experimental manipulations (price or presence of ads or the interaction between the two) in the experiment is significant. For the *TV Guide Online* experiment, Table 17.2 shows that price (or cost per hour) and the presence of ads significantly influence how many hours per week a customer uses the service. It also shows that there is no interaction between price and the presence of ads. Thus, judging by the data values in Table 17.1, the lower price without the presence of ads gets the most usage hours.

However, the story is not over. Assuming that the differences in Table 17.1 are point values (they actually have ranges around them due to the fact that they represent samples), the next step is to conduct a financial analysis for each of the experimental conditions. In other words, while the customers in the experiment

TABLE 17.1. Average Monthly Service Usage Hours by Experimental Variable

Experimental Condition	Code	Mailings	Participants	Percent	Participants in Month 6	Percent	Month 6 Usage Hours
Low price, no ads	LPNA	10,000	3,135	31%	1,456	15%	6.33
High price, no ads	HPNA	10,000	2,896	29	1,235	12	6.01
High price, ads	HPAS	10,000	2,788	28	1,134	11	5.77
Low price, ads	LPAS	10,000	3,008	30	1,345	13	6.23
Total		40,000	11,827	30	5,170	13	6.09

TABLE 17.2. ANOVA for *TV Guide Online* Experiment

Source	Sum of Squares	Degrees of Freedom	Mean Square	F-Value
Cost per hour	4,247.32	2	2,123.66	75.58
Presence of ads	1,223.33	2	611.67	45.33
Cost by presence	13.84	4	3.46	0.29
Error	4,063.43	11,819	0.34	

TABLE 17.3. *TV Guide Online* Experiment Financial Analysis
(Month 6 analysis)

	LPNA	HPNA	HPAS	LPAS
Revenue				
Expected mailings	20,000,000	20,000,000	20,000,000	20,000,000
Participation rate	15%	12%	11%	13%
Active service users	2,912,000	2,470,000	2,268,000	2,690,000
Average usage hours	6.33	6.01	5.77	6.23
Hourly charge	6.00	8.00	6.00	8.00
Total user revenue	110,597,760	118,757,600	78,518,160	134,069,600
Ad revenue per user	0.00	0.00	1.75	1.75
Total ad revenue	0	0	3,969,000	4,707,500
Total service revenue	110,597,760	118,757,600	82,487,160	138,777,100
Expenses				
Mailings (list & average of 3 mailings per name, etc.)	11,440,000	11,440,000	11,440,000	11,440,000
Magazine advertising	5,000,000	5,000,000	5,000,000	5,000,000
TV advertising	15,000,000	15,000,000	15,000,000	15,000,000
Sales force for ads	0	0	1,200,000	1,200,000
Customer service	14,560,000	12,350,000	11,340,000	13,450,000
Service operations	43,680,000	37,050,000	34,020,000	40,350,000
Other expenses	5,000,000	5,000,000	5,000,000	5,000,000
Overhead	5,500,000	5,500,000	5,500,000	5,500,000
Total expenses	100,180,000	91,340,000	88,500,000	96,940,000
Income				
Income before taxes	10,417,760	27,417,600	(6,012,840)	41,837,100
Taxes (at 38%)	3,958,749	10,418,688	(2,284,879)	15,898,098
After-tax profit	6,459,011	16,998,912	(3,727,961)	25,939,002
Profit % to revenue	6%	14%	–5%	19%

used the service more in the low-price-and-no-ads condition, that is also the condition where the revenues per hour are lowest because the hourly fee is the lowest and there are no ad revenues. In contrast, the high-price-and-ads condition could bring in the most revenue.

Table 17.3 contains an abbreviated version of the financial analysis comparing the revenues, expenses, and profits for each of the four experimental conditions. The low-price-and-ads condition brings in the most revenue and has the highest ratio of after-tax profit to revenue. It does not, however, result in the largest number of user hours. The low-price-and-no-ads condition results in the most usage of the service.

Interpreting the Results and Making a Decision

The *TV Guide Online* experiment represents a complex and expensive undertaking, with massive initial investments, including the hiring of hundreds of people, the purchase of significant amounts of equipment, and the use of the creative and managerial talents of many specialists in computers, marketing, and management. Highly trained specialists should analyze the experiment; people with years of experience in evaluating investment opportunities should do the financial analysis. When the results of the experiment are completely analyzed, both statistically and financially, executive management must make a decision about which alternative, if any, to use as the basis for a national introduction of the service.

Most people in managerial positions know virtually nothing about the mechanics of experiments and statistical analysis. They do not know what an ANOVA is, nor do they understand the issues associated with projecting the results of experiments to large-scale business operations. The average finance person has some understanding of statistics and perhaps a little exposure to the mechanics of experimental designs. However, he or she relies on those who designed and conducted the experiment to produce the numbers for the financial analysis.

In the process of making the decision about which alternative to go with, the *TV Guide* executive management group would listen to presentations of results from those who conducted the experiment and from those who did the financial analysis to produce the figures in Table 17.3. Based on that information, management must make an investment decision. If management makes a decision based only on the numbers from the experiment, the choice would be a low-price service with advertising. If the managers do not decide to use the numbers, or if they have other considerations beyond the numbers, they might pick another alternative. But how is that possible?

Well, imagine that management did not think the service would get advertisers to sign on and that part of the effort would not succeed. They might then choose the high-price-and-no-ads alternative as more likely to actually meet the forecast in Table 17.3. They might also decide that although the low-price-and-no-ads alternative is the third most productive alternative, it has a better chance for success because they expect more competition than what occurred during the experiment.

If the managers decide not to pick the highest money-making alternative in the experiment, they would be making the selection based on the idea that the results of the experiment could not take into account other factors. That is, they may be uncertain about whether or not the experiment can actually forecast results of the national introduction of the service. In fact, the rise in popularity of the World Wide Web and the growth of free television listings offered by the cable services ultimately did lead *TV Guide* management to offer the service for free under the name *iGUIDE,* while leaving the question of making a profit for sometime in the future. You can see the *iGUIDE* Web site at http://www.iguide.com.

Direct marketing offers an especially rich environment in which to develop and implement various marketing models. There are a number of well-defined variables under management's control—including price, promotion, and merchandising—and a well-defined set of decision criteria, particularly sales and profit. The models normally include marketing variables that relate to recurring decisions that are ongoing concerns of management. For nonrecurring decisions, models have a limited role, if any; in that case, both managerial judgment and current practice tend to dominate the decision-making process.

Every model designed to support management decision making must incorporate some representation of the marketplace and a sales response function. That representation is a description of expected marketplace behavior based on historical relationships between market variables and various marketing results, including firm sales. These ideas about marketplace behavior must be developed and evaluated before the sales response function component of a direct marketing decision model is useful. The creation of such a practical aid depends heavily on specifying variable relationships and on the interplay between technical and managerial considerations in determining the structure of a model. The result should be a model that characterizes or predicts the likely result of a firm's direct marketing efforts.

These models are mathematical and statistical representations of how markets work and how customers respond to campaigns or individual offers. They perform both an analytical and a simulation role because they are used to understand past patterns and to predict future responses. Ideally, a sales response function model is based on historical data from ongoing business operations and/or experiments. The ideal sales response function model includes explicit consideration of marketing mix effects, carryover or lag effects from past efforts, competitive influences, and as many other dimensions of a firm's marketing activities as possible.

Direct marketing models are used extensively in market segmentation and list management where the personal, business, and buyer-behavior characteristics of customers become the basis for developing predictions of who should get a firm's offers (see again Chapters 3 and 6). Models can also be used to formulate new campaigns by relating the attributes of previously sent offers to their success rates. For example, how a catalog is physically designed influences how much merchandise is sold. A model of past relationships between catalog attributes and the amount sold can guide management about what catalog design should be used to maximize sales.

Thus, when direct marketing firms model offer attributes and customer responses, they have a strong basis for maximizing the performance of their business. In the process, they also create a knowledge base that provides a potential competitive advantage. However, this wealth of information is of little use if it is not an integral part of the firm's management decision-making process. It provides a formal way of supporting new and recurring management decisions. This contrasts with informal methods of making decisions, such as ad hoc procedures based solely on intuition or personal experience. Two fundamental aspects of the validity of a firm's decision support system are the system's ability to predict sales responses in actual market situations and its compatibility with how the firm makes decisions.

Building Direct Marketing Models

The process of model building involves going from a relatively simple representation of the marketplace in which a firm competes to a more complex model of that marketplace based on refinement and further experimentation. The process begins with a statement of the objectives for the model. For instance, the purpose of the model might be to recommend the combination of catalog attributes such as merchandise mix and page sequencing that should generate maximum profits. If the initial version of the model provides a rudimentary solution to achieving the objective, then the next version can be made more complex to increase the firm's ability to accurately predict profits. Also, each successive version of the model should be examined by processing new data in order to evaluate whether they are a reasonable representation of the underlying marketplace dynamics. The results of this process may suggest appropriate modifications. However, the process involves more than just creating a formula, because the variables in the model must have some intrinsic meaning and be meaningful to the direct marketers in management positions who must use the output of the model in their decision making.

Model development is a combination of art and science. This is true because there are different solutions depending on how the model is constructed with respect to which variables are included and the decision rules used to arrive at the final model. And while there is wide latitude in formulating a model, in the end the model must make intuitive sense. For example, while there may be an association between the number of priests in the United States and a firm's sales, that relationship is both managerially irrelevant and intuitively unlikely because there is no reason to believe that the association is anything more than a statistical anomaly or coincidence.

In model building, it is important to start with a logical structure that permits an evolutionary development of the model. This means that the model-building process should start with a list of possible variables that are managerially relevant, make intuitive sense, and have data points consistent with those of the proposed dependent (or outcome) variable of the model. For example, it may include historical sales by direct marketing campaign (the dependent variable) as they relate to the number of pages in a catalog, the average price of items in that catalog, the season of the year the catalog is distributed, and many other possibilities. Confidence in the model is influenced by the degree to which it relates to previously known results and by its sensitivity to changes in assumptions as much as by its intuitive plausibility.

Applying Direct Marketing Models

Direct marketing models thrive on historical data in the sense that they are created from relationships in past data, which are analyzed and then summarized. In list management, models are based on relevant information about individuals listed in a database. That information becomes the basis for predictions about which customer characteristics are associated with the best direct marketing campaign outcomes. Thus, direct marketing models are key to finding the best targets and to selecting the right marketing strategies and tactics to maximize sales.

Frequently, the modeling objective is to segment a firm's list of customers in order to identify the best ones. Some direct marketing managers argue that the top 20 percent of customers produce 80 of a firm's sales and therefore the firms that market to those 20 percent, or to prospects with the characteristics of that 20 percent, are likely to increase their chances for success.

However, this effort may require the development of more than one model of the firm's best customers. Even a simple classification of those customers based on purchase frequency may not be complete, because purchase frequency is merchandise-dependent. That is, the best customers for jewelry may be poor customers for coats. Thus, the firm should also look for opportunities to segment its customers and prospects according to what they are good customers for and organize its marketing efforts around models of those subgroups.

Models are also often used to determine what merchandise mix a firm should carry. Given a range of ways a firm can offer its merchandise—for example, in terms of catalog item arrangement—it is possible to use models of historical and experimental data to determine what merchandise offering format is most likely to maximize sales and profits under a number of different marketing scenarios.

Models also predict the sales response to individual direct marketing campaigns based on the historical performance of previous campaigns with similar attributes. However, models cannot predict events without some form of historical data. This means that models must be constructed from information that includes a range of merchandise manipulations and sales outcomes. Of course, this is true because these models can predict the future only from patterns in the past. Experiments are a good source of data for model construction because they can produce a range of data for estimating the likely result of a range of direct marketing alternatives.

THE AMEX MAIL-ORDER CATALOG CAMPAIGN MODEL [2]

American Express (AmEx) spends millions of dollars each year on direct-mail campaigns to promote its green, gold, platinum, and Optima cards; its merchandise catalog; and other services. The AmEx merchandise catalog offers cardholders watches, luggage, and other travel-related items. When AmEx wanted to mail copies of the catalog to noncardholders, it needed an efficient and profitable way to focus on a list of those persons who represented the best prospects.

AmEx decided to use what it knew about those in its cardholder database—which contains information on who ordered from the merchandise catalog, along with information on non-AmEx customers—to predict who among those noncardholders would place catalog orders. This meant building a model of AmEx customer responsiveness to catalog mailings from its in-house customer list and applying that model to a rented list containing both good and poor prospects. Once AmEx ranked its own customers on their likelihood of purchasing from the catalog, it was in a position to apply that model to a rented list and rank persons in that file so as to target only those with the highest potential for placing catalog merchandise orders.

While AmEx purchased millions of names from a list vendor, it was interested in mailing only 500,000 catalogs each quarter (or four times per year) to those with the highest order potential. To arrive at that list of 500,000 prime prospects, the firm needed to process all of the records from the rented list and then rank them; the 500,000 names with the highest scores would receive AmEx catalog mailings.

The following information (in the order in which it appeared) was available in the AmEx database for modeling the responsiveness of cardholders to catalog mailings:

1. Proportion of mailings in which there were catalog merchandise purchases in last two years.
2. Consecutive nonresponses to catalog mailings in last two years.
3. Amount of last catalog order.
4. Time since last catalog order.
5. Time since first catalog order.
6. Total amount purchased from the catalog in last two years.
7. Years since becoming an American Express cardholder.
8. Years since becoming an Optima cardholder.
9. Average yearly American Express card charges.
10. Average yearly Optima card charges.
11. Annual income of cardholder household.
12. Age of cardholder.
13. Gender of cardholder.
14. Street address.
15. Town.
16. State of residence.
17. Zip code.

While all 17 characteristics could have been used to build a model, only some of them were important because the rented list contained only some of the information, specifically items 11, 12, 13, 14, 15, 16, and 17. The other information is unique to the AmEx database.

AmEx also realized that there were other possibilities, such as census data and/or PRIZM classifications (refer back to Chapter 3 for more about this classification), which, when added to the AmEx database and a rented list, would produce a better picture of both the AmEx cardholders and list member prospects. Therefore, AmEx added the census and PRIZM data to its own cardholder file and to the rented file.

AmEx was most interested in predicting the total dollar amount value of catalog merchandise purchased in the last two years by those in its customer database, so that was the variable it chose as the one its model would predict. That model used variables 11 through 17 in the AmEx customer and census data and PRIZM classifications to predict the dollar value per year. Once the model was created with the AmEx database, it was applied to the rented list to produce an estimate of how much each of the members of that file would purchase if mailed an AmEx catalog quarterly for two years.

The first step in model development involved categorizing the variables in the AmEx database to match those of the rented list with its census data and PRIZM enhancements. That is, AmEx classified its income and age numbers into the same interval categories as those found in the census data. Next, the AmEx customer address information was used to put cardholders into a census classification and into a PRIZM group. With these steps completed, the AmEx customer database model included the following variables from which the prediction of the two-year purchase amount would be made:

1. Annual household income.
2. Age of household head.
3. Gender of household head.
4. PRIZM classification.

Next, AmEx conducted a regression analysis with income, age, gender, and PRIZM classification as the predictors and the two-year purchase amount as the dependent variable or outcome to predict using the variables. The resulting model showed how much weight should be given to each of those predictors in estimating the two-year purchase amount likely to result from mailing catalogs to each of the persons on the rented list. Applying the model of catalog responsiveness developed on the AmEx data file to the list vendor data file produced an estimate of the dollar amount that each person would spend over a two-year period. After ranking the members of that list on that dollar amount, the 500,000 with the highest dollar-amount estimates were sent merchandise catalogs for the next two years.

SUMMARY

This chapter covers how direct marketing efforts are measured, evaluated, and forecast through marketing research, tests, experiments, and modeling. Those techniques make important contributions to how direct marketers conduct their businesses and make decisions. Because direct marketers have a significant amount of control over their contacts with customers and prospects, they have the opportunity to estimate or forecast their probability of success with a relatively high degree of accuracy. As a result, marketing efforts can be allocated to programs with the highest expected value in terms of sales, profits, and/or building a customer base.

Marketing research in support of direct marketing efforts involves studies conducted among consumers or businesses. Much of this research is done before any testing or experimentation occurs. Generally, the research provides information on why things happen because it focuses on getting the answers to questions. In contrast, testing and experiments help direct marketers understand what happens in terms of sales effects when direct marketing campaigns are varied. However, testing or experimentation does directly not tell marketers anything about the customer attitudes or preferences that drive sales.

Testing or experimentation is frequently necessary when direct marketers need to make specific decisions. They are faced with alternatives that are seemingly equal, and there might be differences of opinion about whether to use a given alternative. A way to resolve these differences is through testing or experimentation, both of which help marketers avoid making costly errors.

However, testing does not isolate exactly why a difference in performance exists between alternatives. In contrast, an experiment controls selected conditions of a campaign to see how one or more experimental variables affects buyer behavior. Thus, experimentation ensures that the assessment of the differences between campaigns focuses on information direct marketers can use to control the performance of their business efforts. With experiments, special efforts are taken to exclude from a study any uncontrolled variables that could seriously bias the findings.

Statistical models support management decision making because they incorporate some representation of the marketplace and a sales response function that describes expected marketplace behavior based on historical relationships between direct marketing variables and various marketing results, particularly firm sales. These ideas about market behavior must be developed and evaluated before the sales response function component of a direct marketing decision model is useful. The creation of such a decision aid depends heavy on specifying variable relationships and on the interplay between technical and managerial considerations in determining the structure of a model. The result should be a model that characterizes or predicts the likely result of a firm's direct marketing efforts.

REVIEW QUESTIONS

1. Why are direct marketers positive about measuring, evaluating, and forecasting through tests, experiments, and modeling?
2. How do direct marketers use research in developing marketing plans? What are the types of research, and what contributions do they make to the management decision-making process?
3. How do direct marketers use testing in developing marketing plans?
4. How do direct marketers use experimentation in developing marketing plans?
5. In what ways is statistical modeling used in direct marketing? How does such modeling contribute to management decision making?
6. What are the major differences between tests and experiments? Under what circumstances is one or the other preferred?
7. Why is it said that surveys of consumers or businesses provide information on *why* things happen and testing and experiments tell the direct marketer *what* happened in direct marketing campaigns?

NOTES

1. This example is offered for illustrative purposes only. The data are not actual numbers from a *TV Guide* study.
2. This example is offered for illustrative purposes only and does not contain actual data from AmEx's direct-mail campaign database.

SOURCES

ADAMS, MARK. "Growing 'TV Guide.' " *Mediaweek* 5, no. 27 (July 10, 1995), p. 5.
ASBURY, EVE. "Give Your Readers What They Want." *Folio: The Magazine for Magazine Management* 24, no. 21 (December 15, 1995), pp. 57–59+.

Berniker, Mark. "*TV Guide* Going Online." *Broadcasting & Cable* 124, no. 24 (June 13, 1994), p. 49.

Burnett, Ed. *The Complete Direct Mail List Handbook.* Englewood Cliffs, NJ: Prentice Hall, 1988.

Boyd, Malia. "A Case for Incentives." *Incentive* 167, no. 12 (December 1993), pp. 96–97.

Castelli, Joseph. "Research Methods." In *Readings & Cases in Direct Marketing,* ed. Herbert E. Brown and Bruce Buskirk. Lincolnwood, IL: NTC Business Books, 1989, pp. 132–37.

Chakravarty, Subrata N. "A Credit Card Is Not a Commodity." *Forbes*, October 16, 1989, pp. 128–30.

Churchill, Gilbert A., Jr. *Marketing Research,* 5th ed. Chicago: The Dryden Press, 1991.

Davis, Duane, and Robert M. Cosenza. *Business Research for Decision Making.* Boston: PWS-Kent, 1988.

Egol, Len. "Modeling's Mutts: The Hybrid Debate." *Direct,* February 1995, pp. 53–54.

Fisher, Manfred M., and Peter Nijkamp, eds. *Geographic Information Systems, Spatial Modeling, and Policy Evaluation.* New York: Springer-Verlag, 1993.

Friedman, Jon, et al. "Can AMEX Win the Masses—and Keep Its Class?" *Business Week*, October 9, 1989, pp. 134–37.

Green, Paul E.; Donald S. Tull; and Gerald Albaum. *Research for Marketing Decisions,* 5th ed. Englewood Cliffs, NJ: Prentice Hall, 1988.

Hacker, Bob. "Direct Mail Arithmetic the Easy Way." *Target Marketing* 18, no. 8 (August 1995), p. 24.

Hamilton, Richard A. "Quantitative Direct Response Market Segmentation." In *Readings & Cases in Direct Marketing,* ed. Herbert E. Brown and Bruce Buskirk. Lincolnwood, IL: NTC Business Books, 1989, pp. 137–47.

Katzenstein, Herbert, and Williams S. Sachs. *Direct Marketing,* 2nd ed. New York: Macmillan, 1992.

Knowles, Thomas W. *Management Science.* Homewood, IL: Richard D. Irwin, 1989.

Manly, Lorne. "*TV Guide* Tunes In to Online Service." *Folio: The Magazine for Magazine Management* 23, no. 11 (June 15, 1994), p. 62.

———. "*TV Guide Online* Revs Up with Delphi Deal." *Folio: The Magazine for Magazine Management* 22, no. 18 (October 15, 1993), p. 17.

Meehan, John, et al. "Pushing Plastic Is Still One Juicy Game." *Business Week*, September 21, 1992, pp. 76–78.

Parsons, Leonard J., and Randall L. *Marketing Models and Econometric Research.* New York: North-Holland, 1976.

Reese, Shelly M. "Suitcase Savvy." *American Demographics Marketing Tools,* June 1995, pp. 56–63.

Roberts, Margaret Rose. "The Mechanics of the A/B Split." *Target Marketing* 18, no. 5 (May 1995), pp. 22–25.

Roberts, Mary Lou, and Paul D. Berger. *Direct Marketing Management.* Englewood Cliffs, NJ: Prentice Hall, 1989.

Saporito, Bill. "Who's Winning the Credit Card War?" *Fortune,* July 2, 1990, pp. 66–71.

———. "Melting Point in the Plastic War?" *Fortune,* May 20, 1991, pp. 74–77.

Sissors, Jack Z., and Lincoln Bumba. *Advertising Media Planning,* 4th ed. Lincolnwood, IL: NTC Business Books, 1993.

Stone, Bob. *Successful Direct Marketing Methods,* 5th ed. Lincolnwood, IL: NTC Business Books, 1995.

Weinstein, Art. *Market Segmentation,* 2nd ed. Chicago: Probus, 1994.

CHAPTER 18

Direct Marketing Profitability

OBJECTIVES

1. To define the role of profit calculations in developing direct marketing plans.
2. To examine the nature and scope of the profit-and-loss (P&L) statement.
3. To look at the various calculations that are done to determine the financial performance expectations for direct marketing plans.

INTRODUCTION

In any business, the primary objective is to make a *profit.* To pursue that objective, a firm must develop one or more business plans that indicate how and when that profit will be achieved. This chapter examines the issue of profitability and how companies develop direct marketing plans that describe how much sales revenue and profit to expect in the future. These budgets or profit-and-loss (P&L) statements are essential components of a firm's overall marketing plan and operating programs. The numbers in the P&L statement are a translation of individual direct marketing programs into financial terms, and of the proposed actions and expected benefits into income.

As part of the profit-planning process, estimates of sales, expenses as uses of firm resources, and income are consolidated into P&L statements designed to predict what will happen as a result of the firm's direct marketing activities. Profit planning enables management to judge the financial consequences of any proposed actions and to make decisions about how to proceed. The operating plan should answer questions about how much revenue a marketing activity will bring in; how much it will cost; and how much income will result. This income, or more specifically the after-tax profit, is the overriding concern of any marketing budget.

Sales-related expenses and profits are described in plans that project one or more years into the future. Such plans are short-term, tactical descriptions of direct marketing programs or campaigns and their likely business impact. These plans also become the standard against which management evaluates the performance of a business effort. Most businesses have an overall operating plan derived from the plans for individual product lines. However, not all of the plans that are proposed obtain approval by top management. Sometimes there are rival plans or plans that request different allocations of a firm's limited resources. To be approved, a plan must purport to make money and must appear likely to make that money; that is, the results described in the plan must have a good chance of being achieved.

Determining whether or not a firm is or will be profitable is basic to the budgeting process. Firms attempt to be profitable in the aggregate; in other words, overall profitability results from the accumulation of the profits from each individual product or service. The objective is to have total expenses be less than sales revenue. In any given marketing plan, the projected difference between sales revenue and expenses must be great enough to justify the risk of the expenses. For example, a totally risk-free return is obtainable from investing in insured certificates of deposit. In contrast, investments made in direct marketing activities are highly risky, although that risk can be systematically reduced through testing. Many new direct marketing activities are failures, as are many business activities in general. However, the ones that do succeed must do so in such a way as to provide an incentive for firms to take the risks associated with normal business operations and the introduction of new products and services.

The majority of firms in the direct marketing business are relatively small. They are operated by one or two persons, who may employ several helpers if they are successful enough to have that level of sales revenue. These entrepreneurs face customer demand that is difficult to predict, significant financial consequences for failure, and a multilevel governmental structure (federal, state, and local) that taxes away nearly half of any success that occurs. And they know that, even with a lot of enthusiasm and effort, some 90 percent of new entrepreneurial efforts will fail. So why do entrepreneurs take risks with their money? Why do as many as 40 percent mortgage their home to begin their own businesses? There are many reasons, but the more popular ones include freedom from having to work for someone else and the lure of the high incomes associated with being successful.

Note that although the discussion in this chapter emphasizes the quantitative nature of evaluating direct marketing plans, the first test of any proposed plan is whether or not it seems reasonable. The marketer must ask himself or herself if the projected outcome is likely to occur based on historical precedent or on testing (see again Chapter 17). If all the strategic, competitive, and resource assumptions look reasonable, the marketer should then conduct a financial analysis of the projected returns.

WAYS TO MAKE MONEY

While there are many ways for a direct marketing firm to increase its profits, the alternatives can be grouped into four categories. A firm can (1) attempt to get more business from its current customers; (2) invest in new-customer acquisition, which involves pursuing prospects who probably have the same characteristics as the firm's current customers; (3) invest in new direct marketing tools; or (4) add new products or services to its business.

These initiatives may have as their goal any one of many specific financial outcomes. They may be designed to increase sales and/or profits, or they may have the objective of maximizing return on investment. Some marketers argue that sales growth is not a good goal unless it is profitable, which is also a statement about the importance of a firm's return on investment. It says that firms need to achieve a profit level consistent with the risk associated with operating its business. In other words, overall profitability is more important than having a business that sells a lot but does not make enough money to justify the time and effort involved in running the operation. If a firm can achieve a risk-free rate of return of 8 percent from financial instruments, why would that same firm invest its money in a proposed new product line that promises the same rate of return at a substantially higher level of risk?

BASIC CATALOG START-UP NUMBERS[1]

Before beginning more detailed discussions of how firms quantify and evaluate sales and profit opportunities, this chapter examines some simple direct marketing plan numbers using examples related to catalog firms. Staying with the theme of providing simple examples of profit calculations before beginning more difficult illustrations, the following sections describe some of the math associated with calculating catalog profits.

Pricing and Markup

Importers and resellers often work with a 50 percent gross margin or net sales (price minus the cost of goods) and a $75 average order size. Manufacturers often work with a 70 percent gross margin and a somewhat lower average order size. Either way can be profitable. But a 20 percent gross margin will not accomplish that goal, because the gross margin must cover all the marketing and operational costs and 20 percent is not enough to do so. And, if a firm's average order size is low, even 50 percent may not be enough. For example, food catalogers often have an average order size of $40, and for them a 50 percent gross margin leaves only $20 to cover all operational, marketing, and overhead costs. That is not enough. By contrast, upscale gift and decor catalogers commonly have a much higher average order size; $120 is typical, and thus the same 50 percent gross margin yields $60 per order, which should cover all costs and leave some profits.

Inventory Issues

How much inventory should a firm buy? After a firm has gained some actual sales experience with a product, it is able to predict sales (and hence appropriate inventory levels), but a firm just starting out should be cautious. It is true that buying smaller quantities increases the firm's cost of goods and number of back orders, but that is better than being stuck with a warehouse full of unsellable merchandise.

What level of customer returns (due to some dissatisfaction) should a firm expect? Food returns are usually less than 1 percent; hard goods such as gifts frequently have a 3 to 6 percent return rate; and apparel is the worst, with returns as high as 25 to 40 percent. Some products are restockable (that is, they can be put back in inventory for resale), but some are not.

How many inventory items should a firm have? More merchandise in a firm's catalog means more opportunities for each customer to find something to buy. However, doubling the number of items will not double response rates, sales, or profits. Some experts say that, to be profitable, catalog firms need 150 products (each available in a range of sizes and colors), but highly targeted niche catalogs can make profits from just 25 products, representing 75 individual items in terms of size and color variations.

Higher product density per page lets firms offer more products without increasing their printing or mailing costs. That is why so many catalogs these days are looking packed with merchandise. Catalog design is a specialized field, and firms are better off using designers and copywriters who have catalog experience.

Printing and Mailing

Printing and mailing are potential problems for new catalogers. Ideally, start-up catalog firms print and mail in small quantities, with many versions, to test various design concepts, merchandise selections, and pricing levels. The winning combinations can then be rolled out in higher volumes. (Refer back to Chapter 17 for a discussion about the benefits of this kind of testing.) But the economics of printing and mailing often will not permit this. The price penalty for printing quantities below 100,000 catalogs becomes severe. So new catalogers generally must choose between accepting the high per-catalog costs associated with small test quantities or risking substantial sums of money on large-volume printing.

Normally, firms should opt for lower volume printing to limit total financial exposure until a new catalog has proved itself. The alternative is simply too risky. Of course, this means that new ventures will not likely be profitable at first. But it is certainly better for a firm not to go broke while it is learning about its audience and merchandise. After it has fine-tuned its catalog operation, it can graduate to higher volume production and thereby dramatically lower its printing and mailing costs.

Lists

New catalogers are always surprised to learn that rental lists and ads are expensive and that they usually absorb all the profit generated by the first sale to each customer. In other words, a firm's first sale to a customer usually generates a loss, and only repeat sales earn profits. Therefore, the key to long-term catalog profitability is to build a large house list of repeat customers.

The fast, expensive way to build a house list is to rent lists and take out ads that will produce names of respondents. The slower, more economical way to build the house list is to use a variety of nonstandard list-building techniques. A firm can generate "free" names via techniques like building public relations; using other lists it may already own; piggybacking its prospecting message with other vehicles that it is already sending out (packages, inserts, warranty cards, labels, general ads); using in-store guest books; and so on. Except for building public relations, these techniques mostly apply to established firms, but public relations can work particularly well for entrepreneurs.

Response Rates

The vast majority of new catalog firms will not get even a 5 percent response rate from any rented list. If the firm mails a well-constructed catalog to a well-qualified response list of proven mail-order buyers who have bought something similar to the firm's product by mail, it will get a 1 percent response, if it is fortunate. If it mails to a compiled list containing people identified only by their demographic characteristics, it will get even less of a response rate. A little arithmetic shows that with any reasonable set of costs, a firm will lose money on the first sale to customers gathered via mailing lists. However, as noted previously, a firm should rent lists in order to build its house list, not to earn money on the first sale.

Can a firm do better than 1 percent on a cold mailing to a rented list? Probably not. Many beginning catalogers inflate their projections by applying 3 percent or 4 percent response rates to their rented lists, but this is unrealistic. It is better to use reasonable response rates and think of the loss on the first sale as a cost of adding new customers to the newly developed house list.

What response rates can a firm earn from its house list? Catalogers commonly earn house list response rates of 3 to 10 percent, and sometimes more from certain subgroups. And, because the firm owns its house list, its costs are lower too. Repeat sales to house list customers will be the firm's main source of profits.

Order Processing and Fulfillment

Each firm incurs order-related costs from the moment an order arrives until after the product is shipped. This cost is from order processing and fulfillment. Some firms have total costs as low as $7 per order, and others as high as $30 per order. However, there is no necessary relationship between cost and customer benefits. A $7-per-order operation can be fast, responsive, and efficient, while a $30-per-order operation can be slow and irritating to its customers.

Firms should try to keep total costs below $15 per order, preferably below $10. Some proven ways to hold down operation costs without sacrificing customer service include keeping the return rate (and hence customer service costs) low. One good way is to show each product in the catalog realistically so that customers will not be disappointed. Another is to pick and pack accurately in assembling and sending orders. The catalog should answer as many questions as possible. When customers call with questions, that means the catalog is not doing its job. Firms should keep a question log and pack the answers in their next catalog.

A SAMPLE INFOMERCIAL CAMPAIGN

Table 18.1 shows a detailed P&L statement for an infomercial campaign designed to sell a home exercise equipment item. The product is a stomach machine, such as those often seen on television. The business effort is to last for five weeks. During that time, the firm conducting the campaign plans to run its infomercial 50 times. It will not use a direct-response agency to produce the infomercial or to manage the media associated with the campaign. Rather, the firm plans to conduct both media production and management itself. It will, however, employ a telephone service to accept order calls generated by the infomercial product offer. While the firm already markets several different exercise equipment items in the $150 to $650 price range, this new venture sells for just $89.95. Customers must make three installment payments of $33.33 each when making a purchase.

Table 18.1 includes the following items:

1. The *selling price* is the price to customers if they were to pay for the item with one payment. However, this item is to be paid for in three installments only.
2. The *deferred payment price* is the amount of the installment payment which customers make each of three times. These payments are automatically

TABLE 18.1. Profit and Loss Estimates for a Home Exercise Machine Infomercial Campaign

	Unit Value	Number of Units	Total Dollars
Sales			
1. Selling price	89.95	55,000	4,947,250
2. Deferred payment price (three payments)	33.33	55,000	1,833,150
3. Shipping and handling	11.56	55,000	635,800
4. Average gross order value	111.55	55,000	6,135,250
5. Less returns (15%)	111.55	8,250	920,288
6. Average gross sales	111.55	46,750	5,214,963
7. Cost of goods per sale	49.43	46,750	2,310,853
8. Net sales	62.12		2,904,110
Expenses			
9. Telephone fulfillment	1.13	55,000	62,150
10. Order receipt and processing	1.22	55,000	67,100
11. Credit card fee ($3\frac{1}{2}$%)	3.50	46,750	163,609
12. Installment billing	1.50	46,750	70,125
13. Customer service	0.43	55,000	23,650
14. Shipping and handling	11.56	55,000	635,800
15. Bad debt (3%)	3.35	46,750	156,449
16. Returns postage	9.44	8,250	77,880
17. Returns handling	1.34	8,250	11,055
18. Returns reconditioning	8.78	8,250	72,435
19. Infomercial production (one)			125,000
20. TV time for infomercial (50 exposures)			650,000
21. Traffic for placement			10,000
22. Overhead			150,000
23. Total expenses			2,275,253
Income			
24. Income before taxes			628,857
25. Taxes (at 44%)			276,697
26. After-tax profit			352,160
27. Profit % to net sales			12.13%

deducted from the customer's credit card, which is the only form of payment the firm will accept for this offer.

3. *Shipping and handling* represents the amount each customer pays for having the item shipped.
4. *Average gross order value* is the sum of three times the deferred payment price plus the shipping and handling. The shipping and handling is subtracted back out under expenses because it is not actually permanent revenue to the firm.
5. *Less returns* describes the percentage of items that are expected to be returned by customers. The item carries a 30-day, no-questions-asked return policy to stimulate sales. This is expected to result in a high number of returns because the exercise machine is of relatively low quality and not especially durable. Also, most people who buy home exercise equipment seldom actually use it,

which means that a percentage of those who purchase this item will realize that fact within the 30-day window and return it.

6. *Average gross sale* is the deferred payment (and shipping and handling) less the returns.
7. *Cost of goods per sale* is the cost of goods delivered to this firm's shipping point. In this example, the firm running the infomercial purchases the item it is selling from a manufacturer. If the seller were also the manufacturer, the cost of goods per sale would be the unit production cost.
8. *Net sales* (or gross margin) is the difference between average gross sales and cost of goods.
9. *Telephone fulfillment* is the cost associated with the telephone operations necessary to accept orders for the item during the infomercial showings.
10. *Order receipt and processing* is what it costs the firm to process each order after it is phoned in by the customer.
11. The *credit card fee* applies to all orders because only the payment plan for sales is used and no mail-in or COD orders are accepted.
12. *Installment billing* is the expense associated with processing the second and third payments when sending in a charge slip to the credit card companies.
13. *Customer service* describes the expense associated with servicing customer calls about product assembly, operations, and returns. This number is an average amount that applies to all item sales, but clearly not all customers will call with service needs.
14. *Shipping and handling* represents the amount each customer paid for having the item shipped. This is expended in sending the item to the buyer and is thus an expense.
15. *Bad debt* includes the money lost due to such causes as customers receiving the item and refusing to allow charges for the remaining installments or customers committing fraud (for example, when the credit card used is not the property of the person who placed the order).
16. *Returns postage* is the amount paid to have the returned items sent back to the firm. The 30-day, no-questions-asked return policy includes a statement that the firm will return the customer's money if the customer is not satisfied and will pay to have the item shipped back.
17. *Returns handling* describes the expense associated with handling the customer returns.
18. *Returns reconditioning* is the expense involved in repackaging the returned item so that the manufacturer will accept it back. Returned items are not repackaged and sold again to another customer.
19. *Infomercial production* is the cost of writing and producing the infomercial. By most standards, the total of $125,000 for creating an infomercial is quite cheap. This is possible if the production does not include any star spokesperson and is very simple, meaning it does not have any special sets or expensive props.
20. The *TV time for infomercial* is the total amount of money spent on infomercial broadcast time. With 50 showings, that works out to about $13,000 per broadcast (30 minutes each). This relatively low price per showing assumes that the infomercial is run late at night and on cable. The infomercial is on 10 times per week for five weeks to build campaign exposure.

21. *Traffic for placement* is the expense associated with reproducing the infomercial and sending it to the stations that run it. It also includes the labor involved in planning and monitoring the placement of the infomercial broadcasts.
22. *Overhead* describes the fixed costs of the firm that are allocated to this campaign, including a portion of the office and warehouse operations. This line in the P&L statement is controversial because there is debate about how to allocate the general costs of a firm to a new business venture. The practice of assigning overhead costs to operations is called *absorption* or *full costing.* The idea is that all parts of a business should share its overall operating costs. These costs include charges directly traceable to the new plan and those associated with resources shared with other company activities such as the salaries of executive management.
23. *Total expenses* is the sum of all the expenses associated with this infomercial campaign.
24. *Income before taxes* is the difference between the net sales and the total expenses.
25. *Taxes (at 44%)* is the combined federal and state government tax on business income. This tax has a substantial impact on the ability of the firm to make a profit on this or any other new business venture. If you assume that the firm has a target profit for any new business effort, say a 10 to 12 percent ratio of profit to net sales, then the taxes are in effect built in to the price of the item being sold and it is the customer, not the firm, who pays them. However, because these taxes increase the cost of the item, they reduce demand for the product and may significantly inhibit the ability of the firm to conduct a successful new business venture.
26. *After-tax profit* is the amount of money the firm gets to keep after subtracting the tax payment to all levels of government.
27. *Profit % to net sales* is the ratio of net sales to income after taxes. If this firm has a target of at least 12 percent, this plan exceeds that criterion.

The P&L statement represents an estimate of what will happen when the actual campaign is conducted. It is likely that the expense estimate is much more stable than the estimate for sales because those numbers represent what the firm thinks it can accomplish. If it sells less than the forecast, it may in fact lose money on this new business venture. The minimum number of items it needs to sell is called the break-even amount.

The break-even point can be figured by a formula:

$$BE = F/(1 - V/R)$$

where

BE = Break-even point
F = Total fixed cost
V = Total variable cost
R = Total revenue

The total fixed cost for this plan is $935,000, which represents those expenses that do not vary with the number of responses obtained from showing the infomercial. They include the infomercial production cost, the cost of 50 television exposures, the expense associated with commercial placement, and the firm overhead attached to the plan (items 19 through 22 in Table 18.1). The total variable cost is the sum of the telephone fulfillment, order receipt and processing, credit card fee, installment billing, customer service, shipping and handling, bad debt, returns postage, returns handling, and returns reconditioning (items 9 through 18). This amount is expected to be $1,340,253. Total revenue is the net sales dollar value forecast of $2,904,110, which is a function of the expected response to the infomercial plan.

In this infomercial example, the difference between revenue per unit (which is the net sales divided by the number of units sold, or $2,904,110/46,750) and variable cost per unit (the sum of the variable costs divided by the number of units sold, or $1,340,253/46,750) is $62.12 – $28.67 = $33.45. This difference is known as the *marginal contribution per unit.* This means that $33.45 of every sale goes toward meeting all nonvariable costs and profit goals. Every unit sale has the same variable cost and marginal contribution. When the marginal contribution equals fixed costs, the break-even point is reached, but profits are zero then because revenue exactly only covers variable and fixed costs.

Using the break-even formula with the values from Table 18.1 results in the following break-even point:

$$BE = \$935{,}000 / [1 - (\$1{,}340{,}523 / \$2{,}904{,}110)] = \$1{,}736{,}311$$

At a net sales contribution of $62.12 per item, the firm would have to sell approximately 27,951 units to cover all costs ($1,736,311 / $62.12 = 27,951). This break-even unit volume can also be calculated by the formula $BE = F/MC$, where MC is the marginal contribution per unit. Substituting in the equation, the break-even volume is again $935,000 / $33.45 = 27,951.

Break-even analysis is a fast, relatively uncomplicated way of assessing risk because it shows how much must be sold in order not to lose money on a new venture. However, the break-even volume is just an estimate, as are the rest of the numbers in the P&L statement. Also, break-even analysis becomes complex for direct marketing activities involving multiple products. For example, with catalogs each item may have a different variable cost and profit-to-volume ratio. The analysis can be conducted at the catalog item level or at the entire catalog level, where the numbers would represent average figures.

AN AMERICAN EXPRESS TRAVEL SERVICES CARD MEMBER CAMPAIGN [2]

American Express (AmEx) spends millions of dollars a year to promote its green card as well as the more recent gold, platinum, and Optima additions. Because AmEx's green, gold, and platinum cards (collectively known as "The Card") require customers to pay their entire balance every month, the company makes money on them in only two ways: annual fees charged to cardholders and the so-called discounts collected from merchants, a charge that has historically been 2.5 to 4.5 percent of each transaction. AmEx's green, gold, and platinum cards are known as charge cards because no credit is offered. Credit cards, including

AmEx's Optima card, make money in three ways: annual fees, interest on balances, and collections from merchants on each transaction.

Because AmEx makes money from membership fees and discounts collected from merchants, the revenue from a new member is the annual fee plus the discount percentage received from the merchant where the customer does business. Therefore, both of these revenue sources need to be considered in computing the benefit from campaigns designed to get new cardholders.

Thus, this simplified example assumes that each new member will pay an average annual fee of $76.37 dollars (across all types of AmEx debit cards) and that the average amount the member will charge with the new card in its first year of use will be $3,500.

However, that revenue is not perpetual. AmEx must assume some attrition rate for the new cardholders. This leads to an estimate of the total value of a new customer or the revenue on average the firm obtains from each new cardholder it signs up. This lifetime value is discussed in relation to the AmEx example in the section beginning on p. 391.

The P&L statement in Table 18.2 is for a direct-mail campaign to increase the number of AmEx cardholders by 250,000 per year for each of five years. The statement shows only the incremental impact of the plan on AmEx's business and not all the sales, expenses, and profits for the firm, which are not part of this new cardholder effort. This display of only those financials directly related to the plan is the normal way these types of business initiatives are analyzed.

According to the plan, some 4 million persons are sent from one to three mailings annually, depending on whether they respond to any one mailing during a year. The yearly response rate for the campaign is 6.3 percent. The P&L statement also includes attrition rates for the new cardholders. Some leave during the first year they become members, while others leave during their subsequent years of membership. At the end of five years, AmEx has 3,750,000 – 375,000, or 3,375,000, net new cardholders. Total revenue has increased by a total of $848,070,724 and net cash flow or profits after taxes are up by $353,149,005. To get this result, AmEx did some 10.2 million mailings per year. It also spent $10 million on support television advertising to remind people to look for the mailings.

THE NET PRESENT VALUE OF A NEW VENTURE

The net present value concept is used to evaluate the cash flow from a direct marketing proposal by calculating the net present value of the future cash from the investment. This is the discounted cash-flow approach to investment analysis. With it, the value of a proposal is the sum of all future cash flows discounted to their present value (using a required rate of return) minus the initial investments. A proposal is either accepted or rejected based on the result of this calculation (sometimes versus the calculated values from other marketing proposals). The net present value approach is a preferred way of evaluating the overall financial viability of a proposed direct marketing plan.

The net present value computation for the entire new cardholder acquisition plan is at the bottom of Table 18.2. That value is $53,164,498, which far exceeds AmEx's criteria of a 10 percent rate of return on its investments.

The minimal acceptance criterion is that a plan must have a discounted present value of cash inflows that exceeds the present value of cash outflows (with the value of the initial investment removed). The rationale behind this acceptance criterion is that the firm expects to earn a positive, adjusted return on a marketing proposal, and thus it expects the proposal to have a net present value greater than zero.

Many firms go by the saying "a safe dollar is worth more than a risky one." That is, they will avoid risk when they can, even if that means sacrificing small increments in return. The concepts of present value and the opportunity cost of capital still make sense for risky investments. But it is proper to discount the payoff by the rate of return offered by a comparable investment. Firms need to think of *expected* payoffs and the *expected* rates of return on alternative investments. In reality, not all investments are equally risky, nor are their outcomes equally likely.

Once a firm has developed the necessary net present value estimate, it has quantified the attractiveness of a marketing proposal. Generally, it should assume that the risk or quality of all the proposed marketing alternatives under consideration do not differ on their risk of investment or on the certainty of their expected outcomes. In financial terms, the decision is either to accept or to reject each marketing alternative based on projected returns to the firm.

Unfortunately, adjusting rates of return for uncertainty is often more complicated than the AmEx example suggests. Therefore, the firm will need to ignore the problem of risk by either treating all marketing proposal payoffs as if they were known with certainty or thinking about expected cash flows and rates of return without worrying how risk is defined or measured.

THE LIFETIME VALUE OF CUSTOMERS

The AmEx example highlights the value of new cardholders over the entire period that each person is with the company. Rather than just figuring the value of each new cardholder for one year, the P&L statement shows the value of a plan that lasts five years. In fact, the returns for new customers are even greater than the five-year total in Table 18.3 because the contributions of those who enter in year 1 and stay beyond five years are not included. Likewise, the contributions of those who enter in year 2 and stay beyond five years are not included. This progression applies to those who join in years 3, 4, and 5 too.

The true value of each new cardholder to AmEx is computed using a formula. That longer term perspective takes into consideration what is called the *lifetime value (LTV)* of a new customer, which is defined as the net present value of all future contributions to overhead and profit. It depends on a variety of considerations, but the four most important factors contributing to a customer's lifetime value are future forecast revenues, expenses, profits, and the cost of capital.

TABLE 18.2. American Express Strategy (*for all cards*)

Cash flow analysis for new cardholders AmEx strategy; all currency amounts are in real dollars.

		19×1	19×2	19×3	19×4	19×5	Total
Revenue (per unit)							
1. Number of mailings		10,200,000	10,200,000	10,200,000	10,200,000	10,200,000	51,000,000
2. New cardholders		250,000	500,000	750,000	1,000,000	1,250,000	3,750,000
3. Average charges per year		3,500	3,500	3,500	3,500	3,500	
4. Merchant fees revenue (at 4.5%)		39,375,000	78,750,00	118,125,000	157,500,000	196,875,000	590,625,000
5. Lost cardholders		25,000	50,000	75,000	100,000	125,000	375,000
6. Average charges per year		1,750	1,750	1,750	1,750	1,750	
7. Merchant fees revenue (at 4.5%)		1,968,750	1,968,750	1,968,750	1,968,750	1,968,750	9,843,750
8. Annual fee per cardholder (weighted)		76.37	76.37	76.37	76.37	76.37	
9. Total annual fee yearly revenue		19,092,105	36,275,000	53,457,895	70,640,789	87,823,684	267,289,474
10. Total merchant fees revenues		37,406,250	76,781,250	116,156,250	155,531,250	194,906,250	580,781,250
11. Total revenue		56,498,355	113,056,250	169,614,145	226,172,039	282,729,934	848,070,724
Expenses							
12. Number of names purchased		4,000,000	4,000,000	4,000,000	4,000,000	4,000,000	20,000,000
13. Mailing list (at 16 cents per name)	0.16	640,000	640,000	640,000	640,000	640,000	3,200,000
14. Postage per mailing	0.16	1,632,000	1,632,000	1,632,000	1,632,000	1,632,000	8,160,000
15. Production of mailer	0.15	1,530,000	1,530,000	1,530,000	1,530,000	1,530,000	7,650,000
16. Fulfillment of offer	3.15	787,500	787,500	787,500	787,500	787,500	3,937,500
17. Supporting TV ads		10,000,000	10,000,000	10,000,000	10,000,000	10,000,000	50,000,000
18. Total marketing		14,589,500	14,589,500	14,589,500	14,589,500	14,589,500	72,947,500
19. Other expenses		2,500,000	2,500,000	2,500,000	2,500,000	2,500,000	12,500,000
20. Overhead		10,000,000	19,000,000	27,000,000	35,000,000	41,000,000	132,000,000
21. Total expenses		27,089,500	36,089,500	44,089,500	52,089,500	58,089,500	217,447,500
Income							
22. Net income before taxes		29,408,855	76,966,750	125,524,645	174,082,539	224,640,434	630,623,224
23. Taxes at 44%		12,939,896	33,865,370	55,230,844	76,596,317	98,841,791	277,474,218
24. After-tax profit (operations cash flow)		16,468,959	43,101,380	70,293,801	97,486,222	125,798,643	353,149,005
Net Cash Flow		3,529,063	9,236,010	15,062,957	20,889,905	26,956,852	75,674,787
Net Present Value							
25. (at 10% cost of capital)							53,164,498
26. After tax profit/total revenue		29.1%	38.1%	41.4%	43.1%	44.5%	41.6%
27. Campaign response rate		6.3%	6.3%	6.3%	6.3%	6.3%	

TABLE 18.2. (Continued)

Line	Comment
1.	Number of direct mailings per year (one to three depending on if and when they respond).
2.	Number of new card members.
3.	Average charges per new cardholder.
4.	Cardholders charges times average to AmEx of 0.045.
5.	Attrition of new cardholders.
6.	Average charges per lost new cardholder.
7.	Lost cardholders charges times average to AmEx of 0.045.
8.	Membership fees per year weighted for green, gold, and platinum ratios.
9.	Total annual fee revenue.
10.	Total dollars obtained from merchant sale.
11.	Total revenue is increase in merchant revenue minus loss of annual fee revenue and merchant fee revenue.
12.	Number of names purchased to mailings.
13.	Cost of each name on the mailing list.
14.	Postage for each time a mailing is done.
15.	Cost of design and production of mailer.
16.	Fulfillment per offer includes setting up the account and issuing the card.
17.	TV ads (two) run in support of the mailings, which asks prospects to look for letters.
18.	Total marketing expense for mail campaign.
19.	Other expenses directly related to the campaign.
20.	Overhead for AmEx in general applied to this campaign.
21.	Total campaign expenses.
22.	Net income before taxes.
23.	Federal and state taxes on business activities.
24.	Profit after removing taxes.
25.	Net present value positive.
26.	This ratio is line 24 divided by line 11.
27.	This ratio is line 2 divided by line 12.

TABLE 18.3. Rate of Return Calculations for the Value of a Customer in the AmEx Example

Year	Revenue	Expense	Net	Taxes	Cash Flow
1	56,498,355	27,089,500	29,408,855	12,939,896	16,468,959
2	44,804,934	9,000,000	35,804,934	15,754,171	20,050,763
3	33,111,513	8,000,000	25,111,513	11,049,066	14,062,447
4	21,418,092	7,000,000	14,418,092	6,343,961	8,074,132
5	9,724,671	6,000,000	3,724,671	1,638,855	2,085,816
Total	165,557,566	57,089,500	108,468,066	47,725,949	60,742,117
Five-year average	33,111,513	11,417,900	21,693,613	9,545,190	12,148,423
Net present value					48,917,852

The most important use of customer LTV information is for decision making in the areas of customer reactivation and customer acquisition. How much is it worth to get an additional customer? This is the most important calculation a direct marketer makes. A conservative rule of thumb is that a firm should invest no more than 40 percent of lifetime value in customer acquisition.

In the past, direct marketers would mistakenly consider only the initial profits from an offering to represent the potential value of a customer. However, to the majority of direct marketing firms, repeat customers are the foundation of their business. In direct marketing, repeat business is usually a major consideration and the primary source of the profitability of a firm. Many companies do not even attempt to acquire any customers if they do not expect to obtain more than one sale.

The LTV calculations refer to an "expected" or "average" value of a customer. This is because firms usually cannot be certain about whether a new customer will be profitable. Financial analysis addresses the issue of predicting overall profitability, but it is still an average because two customers with exactly the same profile will not exhibit the same purchase behavior. And, because of the need to average to arrive at an assessment of lifetime value, historical data on customer buying patterns is required to do the calculations. Some of the formulas for computing the lifetime value of a customer require at least two or three years of data.

The lifetime value of a new customer comes from computing the expected value of that customer's purchases multiplied by the number of times the customer is expected to make purchases. Or, stated in another way, the computation is the average amount of total dollars per customer for each sale multiplied by the number of repeats. The firm uses its historical database to estimate those two quantities.

Exhibit 18.1 shows average LTV values for 1995 versus 1993 across a large number of industries and firms. The most common number is for customers, subscribers, donors, and so on with a value of $200 or more.

In the case of the preceding AmEx illustration, for every 100 cardholders who join, 10 percent are gone by the end of the first year, an additional 10 percent are gone by the second year, and another 10 percent are lost for each year after that

EXHIBIT 18.1. Lifetime Value of a Customer

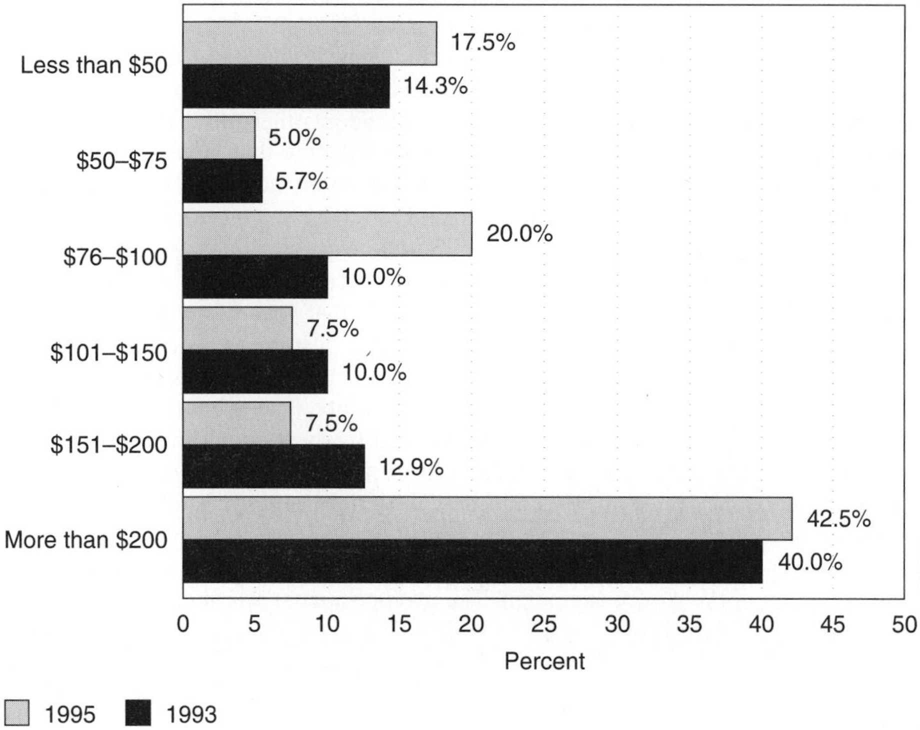

until about the fifth year of membership, when all who make it that far tend to remain for many years with AmEx. The attrition rate means that for every 100 persons who join AmEx in any one year, only 50 percent are left after five years.

The most common way to calculate the lifetime value of a customer involves a two-step procedure that includes examining historical records to understand what happened in the past, and then using that data to extrapolate those events into the future. This assumes that predictions about future events are reliable.

New customers are regarded as an asset in which a firm invests. That investment is the difference between the sales revenue associated with the purchase behavior of a new customer less the total cost of acquiring that new customer. The firm's return on that investment is the net of the sales, the initial acquisition, and all costs associated with those sales.

In the AmEx example, in the first year of the plan the company spends $27,089,500 to acquire 250,000 new cardholders, who in turn contribute $56,498,355 in revenue in the first year they are with the firm. The acquisition rate per customer averages $88.30 (excluding overhead expenses allocated to the campaign), and the customer who stays a full year contributes an average of $233.87 ($157.50 from transactions with merchants and $76.37 in membership fees) a year. With a time horizon of five years, a customer who stays with AmEx adds 5 × $233.87, or $1,169.34, to the firm's revenues.

In this illustration, the value of an AmEx customer is calculated using three common techniques businesses apply to assess the value of investments in customers: *payback, rate of return,* and *net present value.*

The payback method is widely used, but it is not actually a technique for assessing return on investment. Rather, it concerns itself with the length of time it takes to recoup the initial investment. Payback adopts the rule that, other things being equal, revenue coming in earlier is more valuable than revenue coming in later, placing an implicit but vague time value on money. The method favors proposals with high short-term returns and discourages those with long-term potential even though the impact of the latter may eventually be greater. The AmEx investment pays back in the first year because the cost of acquiring a customer is less than what each one contributes in that year. Many plans take two or three years before the money spent to acquire a customer is recouped.

The rate of return method relates net earnings from a business activity to the cost of investing in that activity over its effective life. The average rate of return is defined as average net annual income divided by average net investment. This calculation is illustrated for the AmEx information as follows: The total investment in year 1 new customers is $57,089,500 (including allocated overhead for each of five years). The average investment is $57,089,500 divided by 5, or $11,417,900. The year 1 customers contribute a total of $60,742,117 in income for the five years of the AmEx campaign. The average annual return can be computed as $60,742,117 divided by 5, or $12,148,423. Therefore, the average rate of return is then $12,148,423 / $11,417,900 = 1.06 (or 106 percent). This computation does not take account of the timing in monetary inflows, and therefore it fails to consider the advantages of money coming in by a certain date.

The net present value approach emphasizes calculating the discounted expected future income adjusted by the rate of return offered by comparable investment alternatives. This rate of return is often referred to as the discount rate, hurdle rate, or opportunity cost of capital. It is called the opportunity cost because it is the return forgone by investing in the new marketing alternative rather than investing in some other business venture.

To see how the method works for the value of a customer in the AmEx example, refer back to the profit projections of Table 18.3. Assuming a 10 percent cost of capital, the present value of all customers acquired in year 1 is $48,917,852, and the average value of one of those customers is $48,917,852 / 250,000, or $195.67. Because the present value of earnings is larger than the present value of investment, the cost of acquiring new customers met the firm's capital cost requirement.

J. C. PENNEY LIFE INSURANCE COMPANY'S DISCOVERY OF THE LONG-TERM VALUE OF A CUSTOMER [3]

The J. C. Penney Life Insurance Company has become one of the most successful insurance marketing organizations in the nation. The key to success has been a focus on the customer. However, in 1986, J. C. Penney Life was a traditional, conservatively underwritten product company targeting J. C. Penney credit card customers and enjoying an average growth of about 7 percent each year.

There was a sudden, increased competition for insurance dollars in the late 1980s, when the insurance industry faced a variety of regulatory, legal, and economic concerns. These forces shaped the need for change; the company had to increase its marketing opportunities. In 1987, it decided to refocus itself and approach the business from the customer's point of view: every new product, every form, every telephone call, every employee, every process, and every procedure had to focus on the customer. With this new marketing focus, the company saw customers as a valuable corporate asset in the long term.

Consequently, J. C. Penney Life began to apply the calculations of customer lifetime value to its marketing efforts. Leveraging information from the J. C. Penney database, it quickly realized that J. C. Penney Life's market was fragmented. Its cardholders could no longer be addressed as a homogeneous group, because within the large group were many different lifestyles and buying preferences. Some members preferred to react to specific media, such as direct mail/billing inserts and telemarketing, and others preferred to buy directly from an agent.

As the second half of the 1980s progressed, so did the information the company was accumulating. It became clear that product configurations needed to address the differences as opposed to the similarities among consumers in its market. For example, in place of generic hospital indemnity offers, there was a much greater impact by having six or seven benefit and feature variations, which also had within them copy variations that appealed to specific segments. This was combined with information about the type of media to which individual segments preferred to respond. The results were very positive.

In 1985, J. C. Penney Life was writing about 250,000 new policies a year. Today, the company writes 250,000 policies a month. In 1990, the company had $222 million of premium in force; that number increased to $286 million in 1991, a 29 percent increase, far exceeding the 7 percent growth rate experienced in previous years. In 1988 the company had 1 million policyholders; by 1991 that number had increased to 3.9 million, counting 1.5 million credit insurance customers. And new business? In 1988, J. C. Penney Life wrote $45 million in new premiums. In 1992, the company wrote $143 million. And, the numbers have continued to increase every year since.

SUMMARY

The financial analysis of alternatives is a critical aspect of any direct marketing plan evaluation. Because the ultimate goal of all marketing activities is financial, and because companies need returns on the investment of their resources, all proposed marketing activities must be evaluated for their financial implications. Firms should not invest in a new $5 million marketing information system or in a $35 million new catalog venture without closely examining the financial implications of such resource allocations.

To pursue a profit, a direct marketing firm must develop one or more business plans that show how and when that profit will be achieved. This involves budgets or profit-and-loss (P&L) statements in those plans to indicate what will be achieved and how it will be achieved. As part of this process, estimates of sales, expenses as uses of firm resources, and income are consolidated into the P&L statement. This enables management to judge the financial consequences of any proposed action and to make decisions about how to proceed. The operating plans answer questions about how much revenue a plan will bring in; how much will it cost; and how much income will result.

The net present value approach emphasizes calculating the discounted expected future income adjusted by the rate of return offered by comparable investment alternatives. This rate of return is often referred to as the discount rate, hurdle rate, or opportunity cost of capital. It is called the opportunity cost because it is the return forgone by investing in the new marketing alternative rather than investing in some other business venture.

The lifetime value of a customer describes the contribution of that person to a firm for the entire period that he or she does business with a company. The most important use of customer lifetime value information is for decision making in the areas of customer reactivation and customer acquisition. The lifetime value calculations refer to an expected or average value of a customer.

REVIEW QUESTIONS

1. Why do firms develop one or more direct marketing plans to indicate how and when sales and profit will be achieved?
2. What is a profit-and-loss (P&L) statement, and what contribution does it make to understanding direct marketing plans?
3. What is break-even volume, and how is it computed? What is the importance of break-even volume?
4. What is the net present value approach to financial analysis? How is the new present value computed? What does it mean in assessing a direct marketing plan?
5. What is the lifetime value of a customer, and why is it important in direct marketing?

NOTES

1. Adapted from Susan McIntyre, "Everything You Ever Wanted to Know about Starting a Catalog," *Target Marketing* 17, no. 6 (June 1994), pp. 22–29.
2. This example is offered for illustrative purposes only. The data do not represent the actual numbers from an AmEx promotional campaign.
3. Adapted from Donald R. Jackson, " 'Penney's' Is Heavenly," *Direct Marketing,* October 1994, pp. 36–39.

SOURCES

"The Art, Science & Arithmetic of Money-Making Direct Mail." *Target Marketing* 17, no. 6 (June 1994), pp. 51–55.

BLUMENFIELD, ARTHUR. "How to Figure Your Fulfillment Costs." *Target Marketing* 16, no. 10 (October 1993), pp. 30–31.

Brigham, Eugene F. *Fundamentals of Financial Management,* 6th ed. Forth Worth, TX: Dryden Press, 1992.

Chakravarty, Subrata N. "A Credit Card Is Not a Commodity." *Forbes,* October 16, 1989, pp. 128–30.

Direct Marketing Association. *Statistical Fact Book 1996.* New York: Direct Marketing Association, 1996.

Friedman, Jon, et al. "Can AMEX Win the Masses—and Keep Its Class?" *Business Week,* October 9, 1989, pp. 134–37.

Hacker, Bob. "Direct Mail Arithmetic the Easy Way." *Target Marketing* 18, no. 8 (August 1995), p. 24.

Jackson, Donald R. " 'Penney's' Is Heavenly." *Direct Marketing,* October 1994, pp. 36–39.

Katzenstein, Herbert, and Williams S. Sachs. *Direct Marketing,* 2nd ed. New York: Macmillan, 1992.

Kolb, Robert W., and Ricard J. Rodriguez. *Principles of Finance,* 2nd ed. Lexington, MA: D. C. Heath, 1992.

McIntyre, Susan. "Everything You Ever Wanted to Know about Starting a Catalog." *Target Marketing* 17, no. 6 (June 1994), pp. 22–29.

Meehan, John, et al. "Pushing Plastic Is Still One Juicy Game." *Business Week,* September 21, 1992, pp. 76–78.

Passavant, Piere A. "The Dollars and Sense of Direct Mail: Practical Concepts of Math and Finance." In *Readings & Cases in Direct Marketing,* ed. Herbert E. Brown and Bruce Buskirk. Lincolnwood, IL: NTC Business Books, 1989, pp. 155–64.

Roberts, Mary Lou, and Paul D. Berger. *Direct Marketing Management.* Englewood Cliffs, NJ: Prentice Hall, 1989.

Saporito, Bill. "Who's Winning the Credit Card War?" *Fortune,* July 2, 1990, pp. 66–71.

———. "Melting Point in the Plastic War?" *Fortune,* May 20, 1991, pp. 74–77.

Spiro, Leah Nathans, et al. "AMEX Fights to Discourage Defectors." *Business Week,* July 1, 1991, pp. 56–58.

Stone, Bob. *Successful Direct Marketing Methods,* 5th ed. Lincolnwood, IL: NTC Business Books, 1995.

CHAPTER 19

The Fulfillment Process

OBJECTIVES

1. To define the term *fulfillment.*
2. To examine what fulfillment activities involve and why those activities are important to direct marketers.
3. To explore the considerations involved in choosing to do fulfillment in-house versus with an outside fulfillment service.

INTRODUCTION

When Apple Computer, Inc., wrote the direct marketing plan for Performa (one of Apple's leading brands), it included an infomercial among its strategies and tactics. Apple wondered about how many inquiries it could generate and how many it could convert from an inquiry to a sale. Apple also had to decide how it would determine whether its venture into the world of infomercials was a success. It decided to look at the level of inquiries.

When prospects called the infomercial's 800 number, they received product and software information. Apple also personalized the fulfillment kit with the prospect's name. Using the zip code from the caller, Apple printed the fulfillment kit cover letter with three retailers where that prospect could find an Apple Performa.

Apple used its database firm, Epsilon, and another company called Marketers to do the actual fulfillment. These two firms were needed to meet the huge demand for the fulfillment kits. They used a zip code file and software that checked Apple's dealer referral database to do the retailer personalization. West Telemarketing captured the caller's name and address, and the information was sent electronically the same day. At one point, Apple was getting 30,000 to 40,000 names a weekend. In the end, Apple found three to four times the level of inquiries that it expected.

What did Apple's fulfillment package cost? With roughly 90 cents going to fulfillment, plus the cost of the materials themselves, the total came to about $1.50 per package.

WHAT IS FULFILLMENT?

The term *fulfillment* is used in a variety of ways, because it constitutes a range of activities and because of the differences in how direct marketers operate their businesses. However, the core activity of fulfillment is filling a customer's order after it has been received; thus, fulfillment encompasses order forms, receiving orders, processing orders, inventory management, warehousing, customer service, and planning and control.

Order Forms

Order processing requires that products offered for sale must be numbered with identifications that distinguish variations in size, color, and other attributes, and that buyer-related information such as address, payment type, and shipping method be indicated. Therefore, consideration must be given to the design of the order form involved in this activity to ensure that the customer understands all aspects of placing an order and to manage any order-processing errors once the order is received by the seller. Clarity of the order form helps ensure timely order processing and prompt receipt of the order by the customer.

Customers need to know precisely what it is they are purchasing, and the order form can help in providing that knowledge. Such devices as separated checkoff boxes (or their equivalent) for different sizes and colors and other variations, and a specific place with sufficient space for recording the buyer's name and address are essential. A great many order-processing errors result from incorrect entries on the order form. Preaddressed labels are one answer to the problem, but that pertains only to mail orders. For telephone orders, the problems involve verbal communication issues related to how clearly and accurately an order is enunciated and understood.

Receiving Orders

Most solicitations give customers a choice between mailing and phoning in orders. In recent years, the percentage of orders made by phone has been increasing, particularly for large mail-order firms. The ideal is to have order-taking telephone lines answered 24 hours per day. If this is not feasible, a decision has to be made about whether to have an answering machine in use during off-hours. A good telephone-order approach retains the best aspects of ordering by mail: a written record of the buyer's name, address, and choice of product, payment method (with credit card information, if applicable), and other supporting information. The person who takes the call records all this information directly onto a regular order form or, preferably, a computer screen order form to avoid handwriting errors. A phone contact also provides an opportunity to upgrade and cross-sell (sell other products or services to the customer). Answering machines present a problem because they do not permit the resolution of ambiguity, which would presumably be revealed through the two-way communication process of live order taking.

Direct marketing firms receive a lot of mail, only some of which is for orders. The incoming mail must be sorted into categories such as payments, orders, and other correspondence. Payments are subdivided based on the type of payment, separating cash, credit card, and check submissions. Cash payment handling must conform to laws about when product delivery takes place and options the customer has to cancel the order. Credit card payments need validation, particularly for transactions exceeding an amount determined by the firm. This transaction validation is directed at credit-related fraud. Personal-check handling includes policies for clearing the check.

Processing Orders

Order processing procedures are similar regardless of whether that order is received by mail or over the phone. Orders received by mail are logged into a computer when the firm initially receives the order. Telephone order information is usually entered into a computer while the customer is still on the phone.

Subsequent processing involves checking the firm's customer files to see if that person or firm made previous purchases or is for some other reason (e.g., made an inquiry) already in the database. The computer also performs a credit check (if past data are available) and updates the customer's record if that customer's name is already in the database, or enters the name with accompanying purchase information in the database if the name is new. If the dollar size of the order is sufficiently large, an outside credit check is conducted. If payment is via personal check, the name and order are placed in a holding file until the check clears.

Once the customer's credit is approved or the check clears, product inventory files record decrements for the items ordered and any stockouts noted (plus any action taken with respect to customer notification). The computer generates a warehouse hard copy of order items, an invoice, and a shipping label for the order. Notification of other offerings is also usually included with the order.

If the firm extends credit or takes credit cards, it should use a credit service that can support its needs. The major business catalogers have as much as a 15 percent credit rejection rate and still have a 2 percent average of bad debt. Each firm must decide its acceptable credit risk and the cost of the services, and weigh them against its cost per order. Offering credit in some form is definitely to a firm's advantage. This is true because the easier a firm makes the ordering process, the more orders it will receive. If it requires cash with an order, or even a purchase order, it will receive fewer orders. The problem of getting a check or purchase order from the business's accounting department can easily stop someone from doing business with a firm.

Firms may be tempted to use low-paid clerical people for order processing. However, this is not the best place to economize because it is usually the point at which most customers have contact with a company. Customers will perceive either good or poor customer service from their contact with a firm's order processors. Information incorrectly handled at this point can have far-reaching and expensive repercussions. And, while all companies make mistakes, how well a firm deals with those errors and satisfies a customer's concerns is a major determinant of a firm's future success or failure. Firms need to establish meaningful quality control measures to evaluate how well they deal with customer service calls.

Order processing also involves billing so that a firm gets paid for its merchandise. This is necessary regardless of how the payment is made. Direct marketers have three billing approaches available to them: prebilling, postbilling, and a combination of the two. Most firms employ the prebilling system, in which an invoice is prepared before the merchandise is assembled. This approach works best when shipping and handling charges are predetermined and the information on inventories is up-to-date. In this situation, the firm sends invoices along with order selection and shipping instructions. At the warehouse, invoices are adjusted for out-of-stock items when an assessment is made about merchandise availability.

Firms should always include a bill with each shipment. If they cannot, they should bill as quickly as possible after shipping the order. This will help the firm's cash flow and it will be easier for business customers to get an invoice approved when the memory of the product is still fresh in their mind. Firms should not bill prior to the product being shipped because that can cause irritation and result in a dissatisfied customer.

No matter how hard firms try, they will have some complaints and returned goods. Customer service departments generally expect contact with 2 to 8 percent of a firm's customers. Problems should be handled as quickly as possible. Refunds or credits should also be processed promptly. If a firm is responsive, it will keep its customers; if it holds refunds for an extended period of time, it will lose those customers.

Inventory Management

Inventory management is primarily concerned with determining, for each item, the answer to questions about how much to order and how often to replenish an item. The mechanics of good inventory management are beyond the scope of this book. However, it is worth noting that many of the available business management software packages offer several methods to use in managing inventory. Each approach has certain advantages and disadvantages; trade-offs must be made between carrying costs and potentially lost sales. Demand forecasting also plays an important role in inventory management.

Firms should be frugal in their inventory management but not at the expense of customer satisfaction. Firms cannot ship what they do not have. The opportunity cost of a lost customer who does not get the products ordered can be higher than all of the cost savings combined and multiplied by 10. And, whenever a firm back-orders an item, it increases its cost through increased handling and shipping. This also will affect its cash flow.

For in-stock conditions, firms should monitor their inventory by keeping a percentage calculation of their back-ordered items. This calculation should be tracked by product manager or category, by vendor, and overall. The firm should also know the total number of orders with a back order. For order turnaround time, the firm should monitor the number of days from receipt to shipment of all orders. Slow order fulfillment could indicate too many items due in; inadequate staffing in the warehouse; a backlog in order processing; or some combination of all of the above. Firms should set a target number of days to fulfill an order. All orders falling outside the target should be reviewed to correct the cause of the holdup. The faster the order is fulfilled, the higher the customer reorder rate. In general, orders should be fulfilled one or two days after receipt.

Warehousing

Warehousing encompasses everything done with goods from the time they are acquired for inventory to the time they are shipped out to customers. In the majority of cases, this aspect of fulfillment begins with orders for items in the warehouse, continues with order processing, and ends with the order being sent to the customer. In some cases, the process continues with the unpacking and refurbishing of returned goods.

A firm doing direct marketing can fill orders in-house or out-of-house. Fulfillment from in-house warehouses provides greater control and lower costs, but the marketer must have the sales volume and financial resources to support its own warehouse. The outside fulfillment houses build a profit margin into their operations, which becomes an extra cost for firms choosing them. Large direct marketing operations are much more likely than small firms to own fulfillment operations.

Customer Service

Customer service operations are important because fulfillment is very difficult to carry out perfectly. In addition, customers may change their mind about a purchase or may be dissatisfied in some way with the quality of the product itself, the condition in which it arrived, or some other aspect of the order. As a result, customers need to make returns, complain about lost and damaged shipments, point to missing and incorrect items, and so on. The firm needs to have a mechanism in place where customers can make additional contacts with the company and request that product-related issues be addressed.

What customer service does varies from firm to firm, but there is much consensus that whatever those duties are they are critical to the survival of a firm. According to Roberts and Berger, there is general agreement that customer service consists of (1) the availability of the product, (2) the timing of the delivery, and (3) the quality of the delivery.[1] If products are not available when ordered, this stockout causes delays in delivery. Some extra costs related to a separate delivery and additional paperwork result when items are not in stock. If deliveries are not timely, customers cancel orders and profits are lost. If the items in the correct colors, size, and type are not in good condition upon arrival, there are problems with customer satisfaction.

Planning and Control

Any direct marketing operation involves a significant amount of planning and control. Controlling the fulfillment process requires data collection, analysis, and reporting to evaluate sales levels, inventory levels, returns, customer service, credit, billing, and quality control. These operational statistics provide information about orders received and inventory levels by product type, including the turnover rates of individual items and customer service activities such as returns and billing issues.

FULFILLMENT IN-HOUSE OR OUTSIDE?[2]

The American Management Association handles fulfillment in-house for 12 of its 15 publications, and has Neodata Services, Inc., do the rest. This subscription fulfillment firm works with more than 400 magazines. The myriad functions of magazine fulfillment—generating labels, mailing back issues, handling account reconciliation, preparing publisher's statements, and storing and maintaining data—can be overwhelming for magazines with less than 20,000 circulation. Thus, managers of these smaller magazine titles may have no choice but to delegate fulfillment tasks to an employee. One major advantage of that decision is that in-house fulfillment gives the publisher full control over the subscriber list. Small-circulation magazines that opt for outside fulfillment run the risk of rejection by fulfillment houses that deem their circulations (say as little as 6,000) too small or their financial credibility too sketchy.

Whether a firm should use in-house fulfillment or choose an outside fulfillment service depends on a number of considerations. Outside fulfillment services contribute a lot of expertise. They have usually invested in the newest technology and they already have an idea of what works, from the size of the envelope to the types of offers that sell. They also have postal expertise and responsive customer service. Large fulfillment services can offer invaluable help for start-ups or businesses that want to expand. Fulfillment houses can help design order forms, invoices, and promotions, as well as ensure that the postal information is correct and properly placed. A fulfillment service can do personalized renewal notices, deal with credit card orders, and analyze what comes back from mailings. They generally set prices on a per-transaction basis.

Financial constraints tend to force small firms to think carefully about how to handle their fulfillment. Whether or not to stay in-house also depends on the level of knowledge a firm starts with. If the firm stays in-house, it usually has to hire additional personnel to manage the fulfillment activities, which is a difficult choice given that most small direct marketers are already stretched thin in their merchandising and marketing activities. Equipment also has to be purchased, and it can take as long as five years to make the initial expenditure pay for itself. Many firms that are new to fulfillment do not realize how long it takes to process order forms and invoices.

Some firms divide their fulfillment tasks between in-house order taking and outside fulfillment houses for delivery and postpurchase transactions management. Firms also have the option of taking orders in-house and then telecommunicating them to a fulfillment house, which generates mailings and maintains a customer database.

PICKING A FULFILLMENT SERVICE [3]

If the choice is to go with an outside fulfillment service, it is important to plan carefully. There should be a good fit with a fulfillment vendor. That vendor should have experience with the firm's type of product and have a management philosophy compatible with the firm's and, of course, a reputable track record.

One big error companies make in searching for outside services is to assume that they will find a vendor who is as close to perfect as possible and then put their fate in that vendor's hands. Such companies abdicate responsibility rather than sharing it. A service bureau can only be as good as the planning that goes into using the service. It is the hiring firm's responsibility to determine and define the objectives for the service contract, its scope, and the activities the vendor should undertake. Reputable vendors will have standard operating procedures that can be useful in helping firms plan the actual details, but they still need to stay involved through the implementation of the fulfillment activities. Agreements between firms and fulfillment services should address critical quality issues, including a list of scheduled activities, activity levels, and forecasts of expected demand levels.

Thus, the success of the outsourcing relationship depends directly on how well the venture is planned. For instance, consider the product-receipt phase, which is a critical element near the front end of the fulfillment process. What quality control or inspection procedures does the firm want the vendor to employ: full inspection, *n*th selection, random spot-checking? What types of things does it want inspected: condition of product, packaging, color lots, labeling, sizing, expiration dates, brand names? If problems are discovered, should there be a higher level of inspection? What kinds of quality control reports does it want? How does it want to track quality back to merchandise returns? What types of fulfillment-related reports does it want? The firm must be able to monitor what the fulfillment service is doing, including what is happening with inventory, order volumes, and customer service.

The direct marketing firm looking for a fulfillment service needs to estimate activity levels and what factors might cause a deviation from expectations. These projected activity levels cover such things as forecasts of order volume by medium (mail, phone, or fax), by day, by average line items, by average dollars, and others. It also includes anticipated daily order volumes by shipping method and by new customers versus current customers. And it includes new requests and inventory returns. Obviously, forecasts are only estimates, but they should be made with the best data available, and they should cover every conceivable activity.

The final concept to keep in mind in selecting a fulfillment service has to do with shared responsibilities. Each activity needs to be assigned a responsible party from both the vendor's staff and the firm's own staff. One executes and the other monitors, and some of these activities will actually be shared. For instance, the fulfillment vendor will take responsibility for training telephone service representatives on acceptable telephone procedures, but the hiring firm might take responsibility for training the representatives on merchandise (which the fulfillment vendor will monitor). Both might share the monitoring of ongoing order entry and customer service through on-site or remote listening link to the fulfillment vendor's telephone system. Exhibit 19.1 shows the results of a study on how customer service is handled by in-house versus a service bureau, or both.

FULFILLMENT IN ACTION

QVC, a major home shopping channel, is on live 24 hours a day, seven days a week. Viewers can order items anytime so long as the items are still in stock. QVC does not take back orders. Its goal is to get products in its warehouse, sell those products, and ship them right away. However, recently the company established a "wait list." QVC now offers either to call customers who request an out-of-stock item when the item comes in again or to just ship them the item automatically. QVC offers liberal return policies, including up to 30 days after the buyer receives the item, and money-back guarantees; accepts most major credit cards and its own card; and offers installment plans on more expensive purchases.

The key to success is keeping customers happy. That includes not overselling, no easy task with such a large operation. In addition to tracking orders instanta-

EXHIBIT 19.1. Customer Service by Service Bureau versus In-House

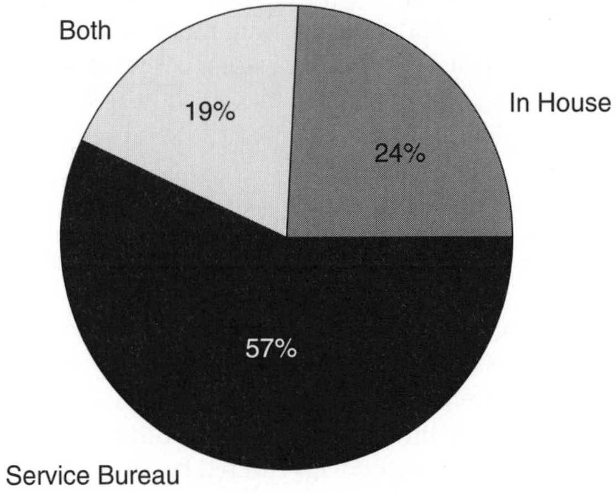

neously and knowing when the stock is gone, QVC has a monitor that shows it the starting quantity of an item, the remaining quantity, the number of people on the phones, and gives running calculations so that QVC knows where it stands. Computers are at the heart of QVC's business.

Every month, about 100,000 television viewers place their first order, and almost 60 percent of those viewers become repeat buyers. The company produces its own programs, selects all the products, fulfills the orders from its own distribution centers, and does its own direct mail. QVC's proprietary computer system tracks orders instantaneously and, as soon as the stock is gone, the terminals will not accept any more orders for that item. QVC's telephone system gives it the flexibility to redirect calls among its three order sites in West Chester, Pennsylvania; San Antonio, Texas; and Chesapeake, Virginia. QVC also has 100 percent redundancy in its phone system at each site. If the phone lines at one site were cut, QVC could immediately switch over to lines at another location. The network uses AT&T's 800 service as well as its software that allows the rapid line switching. While it is QVC's policy not to rent its customer lists, order histories are kept in support of QVC's customer service activities.

QVC's philosophy is that when customers call in, if at all possible they should get a person. But, during peak periods, it gives callers the option of using an automated system. An announcement comes on the line saying "All operators are busy. If you want to try our automated system, call this 800 number . . ." Call volume varies tremendously. QVC might get as few as 1,000 orders coming in at an hour like 4 AM but may receive as many as 200,000 calls an hour in a prime-time period. It is for those times that it adds the automated voice response units; QVC has 1,825 such units available.

When callers place orders, they are given an expected delivery date, and the order is moved to one of QVC's three warehouses. Orders ship within 24 hours for credit card purchases; QVC does not accept checks by phone, but customer orders can be mailed in and the shipment made then. Delivery is quoted as 7 to 10 days; Federal Express delivery is offered for an additional fee. Returns are not a problem, although QVC gets as many as any mail-order operation. These returns vary by category, with apparel having high returns because of size variations, and jewelry (except for rings) having low returns. QVC tries to work with vendors who use standardized sizes, and it sends out measuring guides to customers. QVC's easy return policy is used to make customers feel at home while shopping from their television. The company has a fourth warehouse, in Centerville, Pennsylvania, devoted solely to handling returns.

SUMMARY

Fulfillment involves filling a customer's order after it has been received. It encompasses order forms, receiving orders, processing of orders, inventory management, warehousing, customer service, and planning and control. Fulfillment can be done in-house or through an outside fulfillment service.

Order processing requires that products offered for sale must be numbered with identifications which distinguish variations in size, color, and other attributes, and that buyer-related information such as address, payment type, and shipping method be indicated. Customers need to know precisely what it is they are purchasing. Most solicitations give customers a choice between mailing and phoning in orders. Order-processing procedures are similar regardless of whether that order is received by mail or over the phone. Orders received by mail are logged in to a computer when a firm initially receives an order. Telephone order information is usually entered into a computer while the customer is still on the phone. Inventory management is primarily concerned with determining how much to order and how often to replenish an item. Warehousing involves everything done with goods from the time they are acquired for inventory to the time they are shipped out to customers. Customer service operations focus on customer problems and complaints.

Whether a firm chooses to do its own fulfillment in-house or to use an outside fulfillment service depends on a number of considerations. Staying in-house also depends on the level of knowledge a firm starts with. Outside fulfillment services have a lot of expertise, the newest technology, and experience with what works. If a firm stays in-house, it usually has to hire additional personnel to manage the fulfillment activities and spend funds on computers and other fulfillment-related equipment.

REVIEW QUESTIONS

1. What is meant by the term *fulfillment?* What activities does it encompass, and why are those activities important to direct marketers?

2. What are the considerations involved in choosing to do fulfillment in-house versus going with an outside fulfillment service?

NOTES

1. Mary Lou Roberts, and Paul D. Berger, *Direct Marketing Management* (Englewood Cliffs, NJ: Prentice Hall, 1989), p. 179.

2. Adapted from Lambeth Hochwald, "Fulfillment: In-House or Outside?" *Folio: The Magazine for Magazine Management* 24, no. 9 (Source Book Supplement, 1996), pp. 174–75.
3. Adapted from Ernie Schell, "How to Pick a Fulfillment Service," *Target Marketing* 17, no. 2 (February 1994), pp. 44–46.

SOURCES

BLUMENFIELD, ARTHUR. "How to Figure Your Fulfillment Costs." *Target Marketing* 16, no. 10 (October 1993), pp. 30–31.

COBB, ROBIN. "Facing the Fulfillment Factor." *Marketing,* August 12, 1993, pp. 24–25.

COHEN, WARREN. "Purchasing Power." *U.S. News & World Report,* January 31, 1994, pp. 56–59.

DAVIS, RICCARDO A. "Home Shopping Moves to Radio." *Advertising Age,* January 17, 1994, p. 27.

Direct Marketing Association. *Statistical Fact Book 1996.* New York: Direct Marketing Association, 1996.

DRUCKER, MINDY. "At the Top of Its Game." *Target Marketing* 17, no. 3 (March 1994), pp. 17–22.

DWORMAN, STEVE. "Apple Computer Blazes an Impressive Trail for Fortune 500 Companies." *Mediaweek Infomercial 95,* (1995), pp. 12–15.

FITZGERALD, KATE. "Home Shopping Comes Up Short." *Advertising Age,* March 21, 1994, p. MI-14.

"Fulfillment Centers." *Mediaweek Infomercial 95* (1995), pp. 43–47.

GOLDBERG, BERNARD A., AND TRACY EMERICK. *Business to Business Direct Marketing,* 2nd ed. Yardley, PA: Direct Marketing Publishers, 1990.

HERTZOG, LEO. "Taking Control of Information Fulfillment." *Direct Marketing,* February 1992, pp. 52–54, 79.

HOCHWALD, LAMBETH. "The Small-Magazine Fulfillment Scramble." *Folio: The Magazine for Magazine Management* 24, no. 3 (February 15, 1995), pp. 56–57+.

_______. "Fulfillment: In-House or Outside?" *Folio: The Magazine for Magazine Management* 24, no. 19 (1996), pp. 174–75.

KALAMON, CHRIS. "Your Fulfillment Service: Resource Central." *Folio: The Magazine for Magazine Management* 23, no. 16 (October 1, 1994), p. 39–40.

KATZENSTEIN, HERBERT, AND WILLIAMS S. SACHS. *Direct Marketing,* 2nd ed. New York: Macmillan, 1992.

"Luxury Fulfillment." *Distribution* 94, no. 5 (May 1995), p. 12.

"Mail Order Fulfillment (Part I)." *Direct Marketing* 56, no. 2 (June 1993), pp. 27–28.

MILLER, DICK. "Getting the Goods There!" *Target Marketing* 17, no. 3 March 1994, pp. 36–40.

PATZ, DEBBY. "Publishers Step Up Billing Efforts." *Folio: The Magazine for Magazine Management* 23, no. 7 (April 15, 1994), p. 18.

ROBERTS, MARY LOU, AND PAUL D. BERGER. *Direct Marketing Management.* Englewood Cliffs, NJ: Prentice Hall, 1989.

SCHELL, ERNIE. "How to Pick a Fulfillment Service." *Target Marketing* 17, no. 2 (February 1994), pp. 44–46.

YORGEY, LISA A. "The Directory of Fulfillment Services." *Target Marketing* 18, no. 4 (April 1995), pp. 38–52.

APPENDICES TO CHAPTER 19

APPENDIX A: FULFILLMENT CENTERS[1]

Some fulfillment centers are briefly profiled here, with contact information.

ARROW PRODUCTS, INC.
P.O. Box 410
Elkhorn, WI 53121
414-741-6200
Fax: 414-723-6750

Tom Landeraf, President; Carl Mancini, CEO;
William Wolf, Executive Vice President.

Arrow Products will receive product; manage inventory; and pick, pack, and ship. EDI-based and computer-driven, Arrow offers accepting order key-strokes, same-day shipping by electronic system, immediate invoicing, and movement verification.

COMAR ACQUISITIONS, INC.
25060 Ave. Tibbitts
Valencia, CA 91355
805-294-2700
Fax: 805-294-2717

Jack Gersh, President; Bruce Gersh, Vice President; Janet Beckerman, Director of Sales; Ingryd Janson, Executive Assistant.

For more than a decade, Comar Acquisitions has been providing fulfillment services for companies around the world. Whether you need assistance with warehousing, credit card processing, telemarketing, packaging, customer service, or continuity programs, they can do it all.

ELECTRONIC DIRECT MARKETING
39 Casebridge Court
Scarborough, Ontario, M9W 6X3 Canada
416-282-1201
Fax: 416-282-1897

Ken Crema, President; Don Cochrane, John Fisher, Hema Sikand, Beth Walpole.

Electronic Direct Marketing offers complete fulfillment management services for North America including product fulfillment, payment processing, accounts receivable, management, customer service, data entry, outbound telemarketing, and database management.

FOSDICK CORP.
10 Alexander Drive
Wallingford, CT 06492
800-759-5558
203-269-0211
Fax: 203-265-1697

Steven Konstantino, Vice President, Sales and Marketing; George Fanolis.

Fosdick has provided full-service fulfillment since 1965 with a "Dedicated to Quality in Fulfillment" client commitment. That's more than 30 years of varied direct-response programs with a specialty in consumer television and infomercial order processing. Fosdick uses the fastest, most up-to-date packaging methods and machinery. Clients can take advantage of Fosdick's multipay installment billing and reporting systems, mail-order processing, bounce-back processing, and computerized inventory control and reporting, interfacing with credit card processors and telemarketing companies. The company has 500,000 square feet of warehouse space in addition to a state-of-the-art call center.

M5 PROCESSING
7847 E. Florence Ave., Suite 105
Downey, CA 90240
800-824-9333
Fax: 310-927-3178

Janet Myers, President/Partner; Dieter Ammann, Partner.

M5 Processing is uniquely positioned among order processing and fulfillment companies because it assumes the overall responsibility to ensure that telemarketing, order processing, and fulfillment are successfully completed and coordinated. Using its custom software and what it calls the "hub" approach, M5 integrates all aspects of direct-response marketing to ensure that its clients and their customers are completely satisfied.

NATIONAL MEDIA CORP.
1700 Walnut Street
Philadelphia, PA 19103
215-772-5000
Fax: 215-772-5018

Mark P. Hershhorn, President; David Carman, Executive Vice President, President of Quantum Int'l; James Jernigan, Executive Vice President, North American Operations; Dolores Dinyon, Senior Vice President, Global Production Development and Marketing.

National Media Corp. is the world's largest publicly held infomercial programmer and has built a strong integrated global marketing company through direct-response television.

NIGHTINGALE-CONANT
7300 N. Lehigh Avenue
Niles, IL 60714
800-572-2770
Fax: 708-647-7145

Vic Conant, President; Kevin McEneely, Vice President.

The premier creator and manufacturer of educational, inspirational, and motivational audio and video programs in the world is now making available its complete back-end facility to a limited number of companies involved in television marketing. Nightingale-Conant's capabilities include state-of-the-art credit card processing fulfillment, customer service, and database marketing.

PACKAGE FULFILLMENT CENTER, INC.
1401 Lakeland Avenue
Bohemia, NY 11716
516-567-7000
Fax: 516-567-7801
1680 Timocuan Way
Longwood, FL 32750
407-260-5700
Fax: 407-260-5752

Jim Valenti, NY Contact; June Forsythe, NY Contact; Bob Parcow, FL Contact; John Craig, FL Contact.

Package Fulfillment Center offers complete support services all under one roof. Housed in 70,000 square feet, with 225 employees, PFC specializes in full-service, timely product fulfillment, collating and package assembly, full-scale caging operation (Visa, AmEx, MC), data entry, order and data processing, group I merge-purge, and postal presorts; customer service, polybagging, shrinkwrapping, and layout and design; and laser, inkjet, and impact printing, full mailing services, video jet inserting, metering, and sorting. PFC has an in-house postal facility and complete warehousing facilities, including secured storages and distribution. Call for a free customized quote.

PROFESSIONAL MARKETING ASSOCIATES, INC.
903 S. Hohokam Drive
Tempe, AZ 85281
602-829-0131
Fax: 602-829-9202

Vicki Karl, Lou Hagen, Nelda Rodriguez.

Professional Marketing Associates was founded seven years ago by two veterans with over 50 years of combined experience in direct response. Specializing in long and short forms, PMA is proud of its unblemished reputation for providing fulfillment for top infomercials. PMA is committed to protecting and processing customers' credit cards with a fanatical belief about customer service becoming customer satisfaction. The most vital ingredients PMA cares about in your successful promotion are your product, your customers, and your money!

PROMOTIONAL PRODUCTS FULFILLMENT & DISTRIBUTION
89 Mills Road
Ajax, Ontario, L1S 7L3 Canada
800-263-4678
Fax: 800-993-0543

Wayne Perna, Vice President; Gilbert Kee, Director of Operations; Owen Officer, Sales Manager.

Promotional Products provides direct access to the Canadian marketplace with complete fulfillment and distribution services. Services include: 1-800 direct response, live order processing, on-line inventory access, pick-pack and kit assembly, audited cast management, and a national delivery network, complete with full cross-border, hassle-free connections. From concept design to implementation of customized programs, they put it all together.

PROMOTIONS DISTRIBUTOR SERVICES
10303 Norris Avenue
Pacoima, CA 91331
818-834-8800
Fax: 818-834-8840

Bernie Gainey, President; Gary Radniecki, Vice President.

Promotions Distributor Services provides state-of-the-art fulfillment services.

TYLIE JONES FULFILLMENT GROUP
3519 W. Pacific Avenue
Burbank, CA 91505
800-922-0662
Fax: 818-955-8542

Tylie Jones, CEO; Sandra Lokman, Vice President; Don Goglia.

Tylie Jones offers direct-response fulfillment; superior customer service; bicoastal shipping and savings; detailed and flexible reporting; multipay and continuity programs; and fast, accurate assembly and shipping.

UNIVERSAL DISTRIBUTION SERVICES
1395 Greg Street, Suite 111
Sparks, NV 89431
702-352-2300
Fax: 702-352-2315

Patrick J. West, President; John L. West, CEO.

UDS is a full-service fulfillment center located in Nevada, where there are no inventory or corporate income taxes. Setup fees are nominal, and there are no monthly minimums. Their computer systems are state-of-the-art for direct response.

VTM FULFILLMENT
10847 Sherman Way
Sun Valley, CA 91352

818-503-2711
800-598-8827
Fax: 818-503-9413

David Kluge, President.

VTM offers fulfillment services and merchant accounts. They are very flexible, with no minimums. Zone skipping.

APPENDIX B: FULFILLMENT SOFTWARE[2]

With the plethora of software systems available today, it can be difficult to find the right one or to keep up with what is new. The following is a sampling of mail-order fulfillment programs.

Controller+

Developer: Sigma/Micro Corp. (Indianapolis, IN—317-631-0907)

Source language: ANSI 85 COBOL

Description: Mail order management system. Includes OE and customer service, order fulfillment, IC and purchasing, marketing analysis, mail list management and financials modules. Provides hot key access to customer database, ad hoc report writer, and customer profiling. Optional GL and AR modules and entry-level version available. Customer support: support agreement available.

Operating environment(s): IBM minis/mainframes

Hardware requirements: IBM/AIX

List price: USA $25,000 (8-users) UNIX

Software requirements: SCO UNIX

List price: USA $25,000 (8-users)

Direct Marketing System

Developer: Rigden (Boulder, CO—303-442-8190)

Description: Mail order accounting system. Includes financials, IC, OE and list management modules. Performs order processing, order fulfillment, accounting, customer service and inventory management.

Operating environment(s): PICK Hardware Requirements: Advanced PICK

Easy Order

Developer: The MicroTyme Network, Inc. (Garland, TX—214-840-9313)

Description: Order fulfillment system with duplicate list flagging, up to 32 items per order, product cost averaging, credit card number entry verification, invoice printing, sales tax calculation, database searching, sales report printouts, database I/O utilities and more.

Operating environment(s): PC/MS-DOS

Hardware requirements: Hard disk

Memory requirements: 640 KB.

List price: CDN $99

Integrated Marketing Software

Developer: Ruf Corp. (Olathe, KS—913-782-8544)

Source language: IMPRS

Description: Includes multi-user telemarketing, database marketing, marketing research, mapping, sales and customer service system, fulfillment and direct mail system. Ties to integrated OE system for validation and targeting purposes. Customer support: Maintenance fee 15 percent of purchase price per year.

Operating environment(s): DEC mainframes

Hardware requirements: DEC VAXNMS, Disk storage required: 20 MB

Memory requirements: 1000 KB.

Mail Order Merchandising System (MOMS)

Developer: Computer Solutions, Inc. (Miami, FL—305-558-7000)

Source language: RPG II, 400

Description: Order fulfillment and information system. Includes media statistics, profitability analysis, product analysis, credit card authorization, invoice/pick tickets, order inquiry, POs and receivings and drop shipments. Maintains advertising schedules. Forecasts sales. Customer support: 90-day free phone support.

Operating environment(s): IBM minis/mainframes

Hardware requirements: IBM S/36 or 36 PC or AS/400

Memory requirements: 256 KB.

List price: USA $29,500 and up (source code included)

MIRACLE Warehouse Management System

Developer: Calidus Systems, Inc. (Waltham, MA—617-684-1200)

Description: Supports all aspects of stock management from receipt to order fulfillment and shipping. Provides both single and two-stage receiving and cross docking option. Stands alone or integrates with other MIRACLE systems.

Customer support: Maintenance fee 15 percent of purchase price per year.

Operating environment(s): DEC mainframes

Hardware requirements: DEC/VMS

List price: USA $40,000 and up

OASIS

Developer: CommercialWare, Inc. (Norwood, MA—617-551-0650)

Source language: RPG II, III, RPG/400

Description: Catalog and mail order fulfillment and accounting management system for retail or business catalogers, direct marketers, and distributors. Supports all daily operations and marketing analysis. Customer support: Maintenance fee 12 percent of license fee per year.

Operating environment(s): IBM minis/mainframes

Hardware requirements: IBM AS/400 or S/36 or 38/SSP or CPF

Memory requirements: 512 KB.

List price: USA $30,000 to $140,000 (Source code included)

OFS

Developer: Quality Data Processing, Inc. (Baltimore, MD—301-377-0013)

Source language: RPG III; COBOL

Release date: 1978

Description: Order fulfillment system for retail trade. Includes OE, credit card clearing, picking, packing and shipping documents including truck manifests and UPS tickets. Includes advertising analysis and results tracking. Provides follow-up system for catalogs including nursery products.

Operating environment(s): IBM minis/mainframes

Hardware requirements: IBM S/38 or AS/400

Memory requirements: 128 KB.

Order House

Developer: Elefunt Software (Berkeley, CA—510-343-7725)

Description: Multi-user integrated business environment for distributors, wholesalers and mail order businesses. Provides lead management, mail labels and envelopes, mail merged business letters, UPS shipping, OE, invoicing, back-order fulfillment, inventory, purchasing, bookkeeping, check management, statements, and reporting capabilities. Includes GL with trial balances, aged receivables and payables, P&L, balance sheet, and audit trail. Provides notes and reminder lists.

Operating environment(s): Macintosh

Version: 3.0

Hardware requirements: Apple Macintosh LC or SE/30 or II

Disk storage required: 3-7 MB, mouse required/recommended

Memory requirements: 2500 KB.

List price: USA $2,995 to $3,995 DEC mainframes

Version: 3.0

Hardware requirements: DEC VAX.

Disk storage required: 3-7 MB, mouse required/recommended

Memory requirements: 2500 KB.

List price: USA $2,995 to $3,995

Order Power!

Developer: Computer Solutions, Inc. (Miami, FL—305-558-7000)

Source language: RPG 400

Description: Catalog/mail order system. IBM/SAA compliant. Includes OE and fulfillment, customer service, purchasing, inventory management, mail list management, credit card processing, AR, AP, GL, barcode and electronic credit card support modules available.

Customer support: tech support via on-line access.

Operating environment(s): IBM minis/mainframes

Hardware requirements: IBM AS/400

Disk storage required: 600 MB

Memory requirements: 8000 KB.

List price: USA $22,000 to $70,000 (Source code included)

Response Ltd.

Developer: Colinear Systems, Inc. (Marietta, GA—404-578-0000)

Description: Provides total management of the mail order or catalog fulfillment and reporting functions. Order entry, shipping, inventory control, backorder processing, credit card charges, etc., are all supported. Single-use only version.

Operating environment(s): PC/MS-DOS

Version: 3.3+

Hardware requirements: IBM compatible; 40 MB hard drive

List price: USA $975.

NOTES

1. Adapted from "Fulfillment Centers." *Mediaweek Infomercial 95* (1995), pp. 43–47.
2. Adapted from "Mail Order Fulfillment (Part I)." *Direct Marketing* 56, no. 2 (June 1993), pp. 27–28.

CHAPTER 20

The Future of Direct Marketing

OBJECTIVES

1. To obtain an overview of the changes expected in the nature of direct marketing in the future.
2. To describe the types of new media that will dominate in the future and what roles they will have in direct marketing.
3. To examine the struggle between cable and satellite television information and entertainment providers and implications for the future of direct marketing.
4. To examine the nature of hybrid channels and why they are an important new way of offering products and services.

INTRODUCTION

The business world today stands on the threshold of an integrated marketing system that will unify all areas of marketing specialization in a simultaneous, cohesive, and powerful way. The traditional differences between general image-oriented advertising, direct-response advertising, sales promotion, packaging, event marketing, point-of-sale materials, and database marketing are blurring as marketers focus on building product and service equity under cohesive company images. They are creating businesses with multiple means to establish and build customer loyalty and future purchases.

Imagine the following scenario:

> The time is September 1999. Let's say that you work in a satellite office for a major law firm. However, your office is fully equipped, and instead of working out of a high-rise, you are at home with your computer notebook, built-in fax/modem, and miniature copier. You keep all your client records and specialty law abstracts on a miniature disk that fits into what looks like a Walkman CD player. Because you work at home, you create your own time schedule. You take a couple of hours to relax before catching a flight to a teleconferencing center with your other colleagues to learn about a new federal tax regulation scheduled for next year.
>
> During one of your favorite TV shows, "60 Minutes," which you called up through your on-demand communications center, you are asked to provide instant feedback to the network about your level of satisfaction with the program. Immediately following, a commercial introduces Armani's new men's fashion collection and offers you a free coordinating shirt when you make a purchase. Using an interactive device, you order the brown wool sports coat, size 44 long,

> and you confirm the rest of your measurements to finish the order. During the middle of the show, there is a promotional offer for a magazine. *Forbes* is offering first-time subscribers two free season tickets to Dodger Stadium. You order the magazine and mark the dates on your electronic calendar. At the end of the program you watch an ad for the Lexus sport model XJS 2000, which you have been eyeing. The 30-second commercial has ended, but you want to know more. So you use your channel changer to find another ad. A three-minute infomercial gives you much more information about the XJS 2000. You know you cannot afford it right now, but you are about due for a performance review. You have been leading the region in productivity and know that you will get a reward. So you ask for the dealer nearest you and say you will be in the market for it in six months.[1]

Does that sound improbable? How did they know that you are a partner in a law firm and that you played on the college baseball team? The fact is that consumer promotion and technology are inextricably bound together. The preceding scenario is possible as the result of a sophisticated database containing information about every customer or prospect. Combined with media technology, such as interactive cable television, this marketing network allows companies to present more relevant, targeted promotions to individuals.

FORCES OF CHANGE[2]

Mail and telemarketing have traditionally been the workhorses of direct marketing. However, recent technological advancements in computers, satellite dishes, cable television, WATS lines, online services, and fax machines—and in media of the foreseeable future, including interactive television and voice-activated telecommunications—promise to vastly enrich the arsenal available to direct marketers.

Heavy reliance on single-digit response rates mined from large-scale mailings is giving way to more tightly monitored, purchase-timed, database-marketing-driven efforts that target small groups of consumers or businesses. These efforts are producing marketing strategies that are powerful multidimensional selling thrusts.

It is practical now for direct marketers to cultivate multidimensional relationships with their customers and prospects. The development of these relationships depends on the introduction and continuation of dialogues in which buyers, free to act on their own initiative, can lead sellers in real marketplace movement. The sellers then have direct and timely access to experiential data that paves the way for truly market-trend communications and products.

In the era of the individual, it is only through the participation of the consumer or businesses that relationships between sellers and buyers will occur. This participation is best exemplified by the purchase dynamics of information obtained from customers and prospects as they voluntarily respond to radio, television, newspaper, magazine, or other media communications.

There are a number of factors to examine before direct marketers can begin to understand what is behind these forces of change. Once marketers recognize the underlying dynamics, however, they can better accept the inherent challenges and put them to work in their marketing efforts.

No Longer Business as Usual

Four imperatives will cause direct marketers to make adjustments in their business practices as they approach the next century: information overload, marketplace congestion, globalization, and the targeting of individuals.

The dynamics of the marketplace have combined to form new marketing challenges at a pace never before experienced in such a short span of time. The challenges are equaled only by the opportunities and rewards to be gained. Clearly, it is not even more information that is desired but rather relevant information, edited to meet marketing needs and dispensed at the appropriate time to gain a marketer's attention and action. When faced with volumes of material to sort through, it is no wonder that individuals struggle to discern what is most relevant, noteworthy, and beneficial. For the most part, direct marketers do realize this problem and are working to simplify and unify messages to ease consumers' burdens.

Information Overload

In today's information-rich business and personal environment, everyone is inundated with all types of data. Daily people receive letters, memos, computer-screen and voice-mail messages, and spoken presentations from co-workers and associates. Welcome and unwelcome information accosts the senses through radio, television, telephone, fax, books, video and audiotapes, newspapers, and magazines. Direct marketers are perceived as contributing to this overload—a perception that they must work to change.

Marketplace Congestion

Competition in the marketplace for a share of the consumer's mind is intensifying. From 1977 to 1984, before the more intense escalation of recent years, 40 percent of the 175 new products introduced in supermarkets were extensions of established brands. Today the key to breaking through marketplace congestion is to reach individuals. The importance more and more companies now place on customer data acquisition is evident in their increasing use of packaged-goods discount coupons with sweepstakes. This combination allows consumers to feel they are getting a deal while allowing companies to acquire name, address, and other information for later marketing efforts.

Globalization

As the world evolves toward becoming open and unified, the tools of direct marketing are more widely available country by country. Technology now allows one-on-one selling across the nation and around the globe. No single medium can be depended on to deliver prospects and customers alike. The diversification of target and product markets across national borders broadens the scope of direct marketing.

Targeting the Individual

The trend toward greater segmentation is precisely why marketers must use an array of media in combination to seek out special tastes and address them with tailored goods and services. Consumers cannot be standardized in terms of either products or styles. The success of a program depends on properly addressing the right person with the right offer. Knowledge of current and potential customers then allows effective strategy planning and media selection.

It is this vision of tomorrow's society that is driving technology innovation to speed the delivery of what consumers or businesses want, with an absolute minimum amount of inconvenience. Therefore, direct marketers must keep an open mind about adapting today's technological innovations to selling and servicing. Creativity, boldness, and decisiveness will be rewarded by increased market share.

NEW MEDIA[3]

It is almost impossible to ignore the constant stream of press stories about *new media,* defined as any electronic, interactive communications media that allow the user to request or receive delivery of information, entertainment, marketing materials, products, and/or services. In 1995 alone, more than 20,600 articles were written about the Internet, the World Wide Web, commercial online services, and CD-ROMs. However, a topic that has received far less attention is the strategic use of new media that are already a reality for consumer and business-to-business direct marketers. Products and services are currently being sold online, via the Internet, and through CD-ROM catalogs. While such a fact might appear intimidating, it is important to realize that new-media revenues and, more important, profits, are still extremely small in comparison with those derived from traditional channels of distribution. New-media-related revenues are less than 2 percent of total revenues for most direct marketers. However, the probability is very high that new-media revenues will increase substantially in the next few years.

Although new media are not dramatically affecting revenues and profits today, it is imperative that direct marketers begin now to explore the application of new-media technology for their future potential. To help marketers understand this potential, the best analogy is the development of television in the 1950s. When first introduced, television was expensive, offered a relatively crude picture quality, and was available to very few people. Marketers of the day scoffed at the importance of the new technology. But within a decade, television had become pervasive in society and gained wide acceptance, not only as a vehicle for providing entertainment and information but also, and more importantly, as a new marketing channel. New-media technologies are currently in the early stages of trial and acceptance. Direct marketers who begin to experiment with new media and learn more about them today will be better positioned to exploit their potential as they are utilized by more and more people in the future.

Key Characteristics and Challenges

Major marketers, both direct and general, are experimenting with and using new-media technologies such as CD-ROM, the World Wide Web, and commercial online services. Nearly 80 percent of direct marketers—including companies of all sizes and across many industries—use some form of new media for sales and marketing applications.

Moreover, the reality of new media today is that they offer future large-scale revenue and profit-generating capabilities that remain largely untapped. Business-to-business marketers have led the way in the development and implementation of many new-media applications because of greater technology penetration and concentration of customers in the business-to-business marketplace. New media have the potential to fundamentally change critical market dynamics due to the increased availability of customer information. However, these technologies can be thought of as discontinuous because they create opportunities that are dramatically different from those that existed 24, 12, or even 6 months earlier.

Enhanced information availability leads to potential changes in (1) the customer's ability to find out more about goods and services, (2) the time required for marketers to notice and react to market changes, and (3) the relationship between corporate size and marketing clout. In this dynamic, a company's new-media application is akin to a magnet, where the objective is to attract customers. New media can also accelerate the time frames of direct marketing activities. Processes that required weeks to months can be collapsed to days and hours. This has implications for the staffing and management of critical functions, including product sourcing, order processing, customer service, and promotion analysis. New media direct selling applications require robust back-end capabilities such as fulfillment, customer service, database marketing, response analysis, and customer segmentation. The instant gratification afforded by new media will stress the timely delivery of products (both informational and physical).

Through new media, companies are able to communicate with and sell directly to customers. The technology can allow manufacturers to disintermediate—that is, to bypass intermediaries in the supply chain, such as wholesalers, retailers, and, most important, direct marketers. The management of the new media's disintermediation effects is one of the most challenging issues that companies will face. Disintermediation marks a 180-degree shift from target marketing. Now the customer will come to the company. As a result, companies need to learn how to respond.

New media can level the playing fields between competitors of different sizes. Because new media are not the same as broadcast media, where clout is driven by advertising spending, relatively small companies can have the same technological presence as larger ones. While traditional direct marketing involves significant variable costs in the paper, printing, and postage for a mailing, new forms of marketing using electronic media may involve insignificant variable costs.

The importance of building strong brand-name recognition is heightened with new media. Having strong brand names enhances the marketer's ability to draw consumers into their new media "stores." More important, leveraging the corporate brand name can be an effective mechanism to counteract the disintermediation effects of manufacturers trying to sell directly to consumers—as well as the effects of small competitors being able to enter the market easily.

New media also eliminate geographic constraints. They can provide companies with a marketing and sales presence in areas where they currently do not have stores, salespeople, or distributors. In addition, marketing offers posted through a commercial online service or on the Internet are immediately available overseas.

This borderless environment has implications for companies that are not ready to accept, or fulfill, international orders. For companies with international reach, new media open up additional revenue channels.

Strategic and Planning Issues

Linking new media strategy with the overall business strategy is an important first step in developing a firm's capabilities. While this step is easily overlooked, establishing this link helps marketers prioritize new-media initiatives, ensure the consistency of marketing messages across channels, and eliminate the potential for duplication of development efforts. Strong support from senior management is also needed to ensure that new-media efforts complement and reinforce the corporate marketing strategy. The Internet is nothing but direct marketing in reverse. Direct marketers are in a superior position to gain from new media, but they must remember that customers will come to them only if they create an offer that is valuable and relevant. Fortunately, that is what direct marketers are good at.

Because new media rely on electronic transmission of data, customer privacy and security issues are an intrinsic part of any new-media strategy. Privacy and security policies should be planned in advance so that the company can educate customers about how data are protected and used, and give customers some control of how their information will be applied in future marketing efforts. Leading new-media marketers develop these policies early in the strategic planning process to ensure that the infrastructure exists to manage these issues.

New media's fit with existing sales channels must be planned in advance. The two most common approaches to integrating new media with existing channels consist of using new media as complements to existing sales channels and using new media as additional sales channels. While both approaches focus on new media's marketing potential, the second approach uses new media only for purchase transactions.

Following a formalized tactical planning process is the best practice for new-media implementation. After establishing a strong link between the business strategy and the new-media strategy, implementation efforts should address the functional application, the requisite technology, criteria and measurements of success, and change-management issues.

Unlike direct marketing measurement, new-media measurement (particularly for interactive media) is challenging. With new media, there is no mailing, so traditional response rates cannot be calculated. In addition, control groups are difficult to establish with new media. Hits on a Web page are common new-media measurements; however, this measure can be misleading because the number of hits does not correspond directly with the number of people who have viewed a Web site because some persons will visit a site several times.

Leveraging New Media

While the challenges of new media are formidable and growing, direct marketers are better positioned to leverage new media than are traditional marketing or retail organizations. This conclusion is based on the fact that the standard direct marketing operating model contains many of the required new-media functions and skills necessary to properly exploit the technology (e.g., database marketing, response analysis, order fulfillment, and customer service). In addition, direct marketers already have experience communicating product concepts and ideas in dialogue format, which is a fundamental skill in the information-intensive new-media era.

Some of the most critical implications of new media for direct marketers include the importance of *relationship marketing skills.* As direct marketers know, relationship marketing skills are necessary to reach and communicate with customers in any medium. New media build on relationship marketing because they are customer-driven and dialogue-oriented. Direct marketers must therefore integrate the additional data generated by new media into their response analysis to better target their offers.

Database marketing will play an increasingly important role in conjunction with new media. Direct marketers, long known for their database marketing expertise, will have to perform this critical task in near real-time speed. Analyses of what marketing promotions are effective (and to which customer segments) will need to be performed online as sales are occurring. Therefore, the ability to rapidly recognize and respond to marketing trends will be critical to new-media direct marketing success.

THE INTERNET [4]

The Internet has the potential to fill a major gap in the direct marketing media mix. But direct marketers who approach it expecting to find a commercially ready service for selling goods will be disappointed. Doing business on the Internet requires a whole new approach to customer and prospect communications. Commercial activity on this vast, global network of scientific, military, and research computer networks has been increasing rapidly ever since the early 1990s, when the National Science Foundation relaxed its "acceptable use policy" to permit limited commercial activity. Drawn by this more business-friendly environment, large and small pioneers have been exploring the medium's potential for selling everything from consulting services to software, and from flowers to online magazines.

Early "Inter-preneurs" had to contend with technical and cultural obstacles. Some transgressed the unwritten rules of this shared community resource, and died in a volley of bitter "flaming," which is the Internet term for publicly ridiculing the person or organization whose online behavior arouses disdain. Others have prospered, forming a whole new class of online businesses that understand the Internet's secret: The Internet is more about people than about technology. Any direct marketer contemplating its use needs to be very clear about this. The Internet is a relationship medium uniquely suited to providing low-cost, near-instant dialogue. Marketers should approach it as a vehicle for listening to the marketplace and for developing one-to-one relationships with people who ask for what the marketers are offering. If they try to use it as a way to send unwanted commercial messages, they will not only fail but also make the way more difficult for other would-be cybermarketers.

Opening the Paths to Cyberspace

The Internet community consists of tens of millions of worldwide users. It has doubled in size annually for a decade and now spans 150 nations and countless consumers and businesses. Internauts, as users are sometimes called, are justifiably proud of the shared virtual community they have created on "the Net." Owned and operated by no single body, the Internet is filled with an unimaginable range of information resources, many of them posted and maintained by dedicated volunteers, while others are funded by universities or government agencies.

Since the early 1970s, this collection of gateways and connections has linked networks run by universities, school systems, libraries, federal and state governments, and the military. The Internet has evolved into an elaborate communication system comprising electronic mail, thousands of specialized discussion forums called newsgroups, bulletin boards, and World Wide Web sites offering everything from weather reports and census counts to arcane dissertations and free software.

Until the 1990s, commercial enterprises could generally gain entry to this private world only if they had some needed technology or information resources they were willing to share. This fact, combined with the technical savvy required to navigate the network's thousands of computer nodes, tended to limit the Net's use to engineers, computer programmers, and scientists.

Broader business use of the Net became possible in the early 1990s, when the efforts of a private consortium called the Commercial Internet Exchange Association (CIX) secured agreement from the Internet community that commercialization was essential to its further development. Now, thanks to that effort, anyone willing to pay a monthly access charge can get an Internet address and take full advantage of its resources. Even commercial online services such as Prodigy, America Online, and CompuServe have added Internet access.

Technical barriers are coming down, too, thanks to other private-sector initiatives. The front-end searching environment called the World Wide Web has added hypertext capability to the public domain indexing tools already available on the Internet, spawning the development of a whole software industry to help casual users browse among the Net's resources or add their own postings or advertisements.

All of this has led to a rush of new users, including individuals, nonprofit organizations, and businesses of all sizes. This new population is growing by double-digit percentages each month. And commercial trade on the Net has grown dramatically.

Power Shifts to Prospects

Simply transposing traditional advertising and selling paradigms onto this new medium will not work. The Internet is not a place for broadcasting image-building messages or for sending out prospecting mail in a hunt for new business leads. But the medium is uniquely suited to developing higher levels of relationships, to establishing dynamic customer communities, and to allowing satisfied customers to become a firm's champions by telling others in the Internet community about them.

This points to an important characteristic of interactive marketing. When everybody is connected to everybody else, the balance of power shifts. The

Internet as a commercial environment is highly democratic; prospects can and do exercise more power here than in other marketing situations. They can give instant feedback to marketers. And they can expand beyond two-way dialogue to draw others into the interaction (in what is called a multilogue). They can use this power to encourage marketing activities they approve of and to squelch those they find intrusive or unwanted.

Various writers have made attempts to define what works for companies wanting to advertise on the Net. Their advice is illuminating. Some urge marketers to find out what is acceptable, to post messages only to the specific discussion groups to which they apply, to keep messages short, and to avoid sensationalism. The business world is going to have to learn a new language when it communicates to the Internet community—that is, a language of content-based, interactive, community-oriented dialogue. Some writers urge companies to tend carefully to audience identification before they start any advertising program. There is no need to guess. Using the network's search tools and then following the discussions in likely groups will quickly reveal which groups are a good match for a particular company. Even without posting a message, companies will learn a lot about the norms and culture of the network by monitoring a number of groups. Also essential is the quality of the information posted on the Internet and the ease with which customers can respond and conduct a dialogue with the company.

Some marketers propose a set of guidelines for anyone interested in advertising on the Internet:

1. Do not send intrusive messages.
2. Do not sell customer data without the express permission of the user.
3. Post advertising only in designated newsgroups and list servers.
4. Conduct promotions and direct selling only under full disclosure.
5. Conduct research only with a person's informed consent.
6. Never use Internet communications software to conceal functions.

After reading all these rules and guidelines, direct marketers might conclude that they will do everything but sell when marketing on the Internet. To be sure, this will be true if they fail to observe "netiquette." Perhaps the most famous example is that of a Scottsdale, Arizona, couple, Laurence Cantor and Martha Siegel, who advertised their immigration law services on the network by inserting their ad into every available discussion group. This procedure, known as "Spamming" (to evoke the effect of a can of Spam thrown into a fan), earned them hundreds of thousands of hate-mail responses and got them thrown off the network—although Cantor and Siegel claim that they gained $100,000 in new business.

Adding Value to the Shared Community Resource

Offsetting horror stories such as that of the two Arizona lawyers are numerous success stories, from those involving large technology companies such as Apple Computer to those of small entrepreneurial firms like Grants Flowers and Greenhouses in Ann Arbor, Michigan. In various ways, businesses are using the Internet to let people know about their products and services, to get feedback on what customers like or do not like, to solve customer problems, and to understand their markets.

Electronic malls and catalogs are popping up all over the Internet, offering the business wares and services of Internet-savvy programming, hardware, software, design, and consulting firms; of publishers; and even of consumer goods companies. A slew of online magazines and newsletters is available on every conceivable topic, with some accepting advertising from selected vendors. An online radio station, Internet Talk Radio, sends selected news features by sound across the community. And new encryption technology is available in commercial software packages, permitting secure credit card transactions to be conducted over the Internet.

This period of transition is rich with opportunity. Entrepreneurial opportunities abound for organizations willing to add new resources or to add value by organizing, analyzing, and explaining resources that already exist. CARL Systems of Denver, Colorado, enjoyed unexpected success by doing just that in the early 1990s. It launched a paid database service called UnCover, which features a table of contents pointing to thousands of journal titles. Payments were handled using deposit accounts that have now been augmented by a credit card transaction service and a document retrieval service.

What technologies can direct marketers use to reach customers on the Internet? There are essentially five:

- *Electronic mail.* E-mail is a one-to-one medium, exceptionally good for communicating and building relationships with prospects and customers. One major database marketer believes that some preferred customers have completely given up phone and fax in favor of electronic mail. For mass outbound messages, customers can be added to subscriber lists for important news, in some cases even eliminating the need for newsletters. E-mail, of course, provides a handy way to get replies from those outbound messages.
- *Forums (also known as newsgroups).* Forums are a one-to-many medium. With 6,000 to 7,000 USENET newsgroups in existence on the Internet, those dialing the Net can find discussions going on about virtually any topic they can imagine.
- *Newsgroups.* Newsgroups do not take well to advertising, but marketers can certainly approach appropriate groups to ask for focus group volunteers or to set up an on-line discussion forum where users of a firm's products or services could get help, suggest new ideas, or voice complaints. Nonprofit organizations such as Public Citizen are exploring the creation of their own newsgroups to strengthen their communities of donors and supporters and to build activist networks. And anyone, from CEOs to journalists, can monitor newsgroups quietly to gain ideas about the interests and trends of a particular interest group.
- *Bulletin boards.* All it takes to start a bulletin board system (BBS) is the software, a computer, and someone to operate it (known as a SYSOP). Or marketers can work with another organization to post an Internet resource, that is, software, a catalog listing, an advertisement, a publication, or some sort of information service, on their bulletin board. Bulletin boards are passive

communication devices that enable firms to add value to the Net. They may be able to identify users of the bulletin board and what they choose to read, but there is no real dialogue involved. Most bulletin-board postings offer the owner's e-mail address for users to respond to.

- *World Wide Web sites.* Web sites are just computer locations on the Internet where anyone with the address (and sometimes a password) can go to read pages of information and/or to download files. These sites are easily created with a computer and the appropriate software. As of the end of 1995, there were thousands of such sites on the Internet run by firms such as Microsoft, ABC television, and *TV Guide* magazine. Through the World Wide Web, people can also access various agencies of government, including the White House and many colleges and universities. The World Wide Web is the fastest growing part of the Internet and promises to lead the way in its expansion to millions more users worldwide.

Winning the Prize

The Internet, along with subsequent generations of this interactive network, offers the ideal medium for creating and sustaining true customer dialogues. Through it, direct marketers have the opportunity to achieve new levels of customer relationships.

Every opportunity comes with obstacles and challenges, and the Internet is fraught with them. Every element of the Internet infrastructure is constantly changing, from the tools and methods used to access it to the nature of its ability to handle financial transactions. Copyright and ownership questions abound. Security is still an issue. And even though a company can reach audiences all over the world through a computer and a modem, it is still often easier to use the telephone or fax (particularly to communicate with someone in Africa or France).

But firms should weigh the obstacles against the advantages of an exploding universe of information-hungry audiences, the lower cost of building and maintaining customer relationships, the immediacy of customer feedback, and the potential to bring new product ideas to customers faster than ever before.

As the information superhighway and direct marketers become closer partners, working together with many similar goals, marketing and promotion in general can benefit both from the advances in technology and the lessons learned through years of direct marketing.

MARKETING IN CYBERSPACE

While businesses and entrepreneurs are rushing into cyberspace, a question nags: Is there a market for this commercial zeal? The attraction for business is obvious: For an investment of as little as $30 a month, almost anybody with a personal computer and a modem can set up a base of operations on the World Wide Web. To many, the Internet marks the dawn of a radical new commercial era in which a single medium combines elements that used to be conveyed separately: text, voice, video, and graphics. Countless firms will be transformed in the process, including publishers; bankers; retailers; and deliverers of health care, insurance, and legal services.

However, as already mentioned, there are major obstacles for firms trying to sell on the Web. First, most information on the Internet is already free, as is much software. Experienced Internauts, not used to paying for things they download, may be reluctant to pay as they go. Second, as spectacular as the Web technology is, it still has a considerable way to go to become attractive to the great numbers of consumers who are used to the amenities of mall and catalog culture.

Commerce will begin in earnest on the Web when the computer becomes as easy to use as a telephone or a microwave oven. It can be daunting to turn on a computer, phone a help-line consultant to learn how to use the software, and seek help often while figuring out how to negotiate cyberspace. The computer is evolving into an information appliance, but that day will not truly arrive until computers are easy for everyone to use and conveyors, telephone companies, and cable television companies hook up homes with high-speed data lines that end those annoying delays that so often occur when users try to download a picture or a sound bite from a Web site.

Consumers have to feel a lot safer transacting business on the Web than they do now. The Internet was never built to be highly secure, yet it is already as secure as many of the services people use daily and probably more secure than telephones and faxes. Even if transactions become more secure, however, there are many other unresolved privacy implications of the Web that might bother many consumers. Companies can already track trails over the Internet, finding out which Web sites individuals go to and for how long.

Still, overcoming these concerns is only the beginning of the challenge to entice consumers. Conducting business on the Web, a phenomenon with no parallel in communications history, will demand new strategies in advertising and marketing. Unlike broadcasting and print, which are one-to-many entities with a passive audience, the Internet is a many-to-many medium in which everyone with a computer and modem is a potential publisher. Web surfers, for example, tend to be self-directed. They typically have little patience for "brochureware," advertisements that are thrown up like so many billboards.

The Web gives commerce a unique opportunity to communicate directly with employees and customers around the world. The Web can be a powerful tool for fostering connections, building associations, delivering information, and creating online communities. These activities are much more subtle than home shopping. As mentioned earlier in the discussion of new media, the Web levels the playing field, so that small businesses and entrepreneurs can battle bigger foes on a more evenhanded basis. Advertising on major media like television involves major cash. But establishing a Web site is inexpensive, and a site is relatively easy to update daily and can thus become a cheap, effective marketing mechanism.

Eventually, the Internet could replace or supplement everything from television to telephones. Recently, Intel Corp. announced the development of Intercast, which will link the Internet and television to personal computers. PC sales are exploding, and sooner or later, just about all those users are going to wind up on the Internet. What other marketing medium offers that kind of potential growth? The message for businesspeople contemplating their place in cyberspace is simple and direct: Get linked or get lost.

The Cable Industry

The cable television industry is still chasing the interactive dream. It was not that long ago that the TV cable was destined to be the most important wire in the home. The cable industry, after years of borrowing heavily to string the country with coaxial cable, predicted it would do more than just deliver television programs. The promise of cable was that customers could interact with the network to order a nearly endless supply of movies, the latest fashions, or even books from digital libraries. However, testing for consumer demand has shown disappointing results and the medium has been anything but the dazzling showcase that was promised. At this point, the cable industry is not really sure when true interactive television will come.

Now the cable industry has a new way to become interactive. It is betting on high-speed modems that can be used with personal computers. These devices are capable of pulling pages off the World Wide Web at 1,000 times the speed of conventional modems. However, the industry still has to work out some problems, including the $500 price tag for each modem. Also, a lack of nationwide cable-network standards severely complicates efforts to come up with a universal device. Cable operators are hoping the pure speed of the modems will turn couch potatoes into information ad dieters. But the real payoff will come if cable operators can sell the modems as part of a package of services, along with television shows and voice services.

Satellite Television

Anyone interested in a satellite dish for television reception rather than a cable connection can arrange for a professional installer right away. After the new DSS® system is installed and activated, the customer is provided with hands-on instruction on how to use it. Some companies also offer a self-installation kit that comes complete with clear, concise instructions. With whichever option customers choose, they receive the DSS system equipment: the 18-inch DSS satellite dish, the digital receiver, and the remote control that allows them to get started in enjoying all the exciting entertainment.

The 18-inch DSS satellite dish (about the size of a large pizza) receives digitally compressed signals from a satellite. The digital receiver (about the size of a VCR) sits on top of the television to unscramble the signals from the dish. The remote control allows viewers to select programs, lock out certain types of programs, order pay-per-view movies, and more. The dish can be placed in almost any outdoor location, as long as it has an unobstructed view to the southern sky. The digital receiver hooks up to the television to unscramble the signals received by the dish.

Because of the ease with which consumers can obtain satellite television, some observers wonder about the future of cable television. The public is snapping up satellite, but the cable companies are not. In fact, in some parts of the country they are actively fighting it. Why? What does the DSS system offer that cable does not? And will DSS make cable obsolete? Only the future will tell, but the opening salvos in the war are definitely creating more options for consumers.

First, understand what DSS does. GM/Hughes Electronics sent two satellites into space that receive from broadcasters and send to homes as many as 150 different television channels. RCA is the only maker of the small, 18-inch satellite dish and set-top decoder that are required to receive the signals; and two companies, DirecTV and USSB, are providing the programming. After buying the dish and set-top box at a retailer, installing it or having it installed, consumers can subscribe to some channels from one or both broadcasters. They pay the up-front purchase price for the hardware and a monthly fee for the programming, the amount of which varies depending on the number of channels to which they subscribe. At any point, consumers can add or drop channels, or buy individual pay-per-view events.

So far that sounds pretty much like cable. So why buy hardware? What is the attraction? Well, first of all there is a choice of programming packages. The ones from USSB and DirecTV offer some special programming that up to now only owners of the large satellite dishes have been able to access. For example, suppose your household really enjoys movies. Instead of simply paying an extra $10 a month to your cable system for HBO, you can get five different HBO choices as part of your package. That means that at any one time you can choose among five different movies on HBO. Showtime and Cinemax also have multiple offerings—and you can structure your packages the way you want to include the channels you want, or you can take the prepackaged offerings that the programmers have put together at a discount.

The same kind of choice is available to sports fans. You might be a Pittsburgh Steelers fan, but have no chance of seeing Steelers games on local TV because you live in Tampa. Of course if you had one of those giant satellite dishes you might be able to pick up Steelers games. But with the DSS system, you can buy a special NFL package and get access to any NFL game you want on any weekend, as long as it is not being shown on local television. There is a similar plan for the NBA, and lots of college football and basketball games are available on regional broadcasts that you can pick up no matter where you live.

A second advantage for satellites is the digital signals, which means that much greater picture quality is possible. Depending on the program being sent, the picture on a good TV coming from the DSS system can have up to 400 or more lines of horizontal resolution. That is the same picture quality as video laserdiscs and the high-quality Super VHS and Hi8 millimeter camcorder formats. In other words, satellite offers a 65 percent sharper picture than VCR tapes and a 30 percent better picture than current television broadcasts, whether from antenna or cable. Third, using digital signals also means consumers can get compact disc–quality sound. Imagine watching a live sporting event with a laserdisc-quality picture and sound as good as your audio CD player, not to mention all the possible surround-sound effects.

That is why the cable industry is scared. But cable systems are fighting back. One way they are doing so is to run commercials pointing out the drawbacks of the DSS system. And of course, like anything else in this world, DSS does have drawbacks. For example, it does not carry local TV stations, so anyone who wants local news and weather has got to either use an antenna or subscribe to what is commonly called cable lifeline service. Most cable companies now offer local channels (network and PBS) at a minimal fee, usually less than $10 a month. So some DSS customers stay linked to cable for the local channels. Others invest in one of the newer indoor antennas that can be hidden in a closet. But it is a fact—customers do need to make special arrangements to get local stations when they buy a DSS system.

More than 3 million small satellite dishes have been sold since 1994—the most successful electronic-product introduction ever. Pushed by the success of the dish, other promised forms of home television service are finally beginning to hit the market. Up to now, there has been more talk than action when it comes to changing television service. For years, cable operators, phone companies (which can now send out television signals over special lines), and others have been promising a flood of new and improved services. But they have generally been slow to deliver on their promises, unsure whether they can recoup the investment.

Direct-Response Television Marketing Opportunities

A shift in the nature of retailing is putting mass marketers in a decidedly weaker competitive position. As rapid communications and convenience become more important to everyone in an increasingly fast-paced society, new scenarios about how to live, work, and buy are emerging.

As these new communication devices are introduced, they are changing every service from transportation to marketing to merchandising so drastically that it appears they are permanently altering the way business is done. At the forefront is the marketer's need to develop a personal relationship with customers or prospects. The engine driving this is the database of not just household or business characteristics but other, more specific characteristics as well.

Savvy marketers who have been developing and nurturing their databases will be the first to capitalize on the communications developments. They will already have established relationships with customers and can continue to make buying from them more convenient and simpler. They will be able to use their databases to define those customers who present the best lifetime value, maximizing their investments. Innovative direct marketers will have been prepared for the mega-change by developing dynamic and sophisticated databases with the customer at the center.

THE EMERGENCE OF HYBRID CHANNELS [5]

As another glimpse into the changing nature of direct marketing, consider the activities of Avon, Mary Kay, Uni-Vite, and others that are creating hybrid channels for reaching American consumers. These firms are sounding the first volley of a major new competitive threat to single-channel sellers, particularly packaged-goods manufacturers who rely heavily on retail and/or catalog sales. It is part of a revolution born in a largely unnoticed corner of the marketing establishment, where it has been quietly gaining momentum for years. Add database marketing, and this revolution could rapidly restructure the traditional boundaries between direct marketing, personal selling, and retailing.

Multichannel marketing is not new, but multichannel marketing built around a core channel of independent sales representatives is. For example, Avon Products, Inc., the nation's oldest and largest direct selling organization, now allows its independent sales representatives to sell without ever seeing the customer or sending them literature directly. (See Case 1 at the end of the book.) Avon, like Encyclopedia Britannica and Mary Kay before it, has discovered the benefits of combining innovations in direct marketing with direct selling. Other old-guard direct sellers, such as Tupperware, Shaklee, and Princess House, are also developing direct marketing programs. And newcomers like Uni-Vite, the manufacturer of the Amazing Micro Diet Program, are going even further, integrating direct response, direct sales, and retail into a channel mix.

Double-Digit Responses

Multichannel marketing using database marketing technology gives direct sellers several important benefits:

1. *Response rates of 3 percent, 10 percent, and more.* This phenomenal performance may be due to the fact that the current generation of direct support programs takes advantage of the affinity between the representative and the customer while also reinforcing it. All try not to cannibalize sales by competing directly with sales representatives; usually the representative receives a percentage of the sale in commissions.
2. *Sales representative recruitment and retention.* Direct sellers, like retailers, are plagued with sales-force turnover rates of 100 percent and more a year. The classic 80/20 rule applies: 20 percent of a company's sales force usually accounts for 80 percent of its sales. The remaining 80 percent of representatives may give up after only a few weeks or months, or remain on the books without being active for long periods of time. Because of this high turnover, most firms position their direct support programs as perquisites and then provide tools that boost the salesperson's earning power.
3. *Customer retention.* Because direct selling companies never had direct access to their end customers, they often lost touch with them when a sales representative became inactive. Building customer databases is therefore important for continuity.
4. *More opportunities to sell.* Because direct selling companies are frequently competing against packaged goods in a grocery store or pharmacy, they have to give customers a benefit and make it easy for them to order. Using the mail medium, direct sellers get more opportunities to put their products in front of customers than they could politely get by having reps pick up the phone or knock on the door.
5. *Greater depth and breadth of sales.* Sales representatives tend to find some part of the product line they are comfortable selling and then ignore the rest. Companies with diverse product lines have a real vested interest in getting those products in front of customers. With database marketing, they can do that through direct mail. Some programs give customers the option of ordering directly via an 800 number, by mail, or even, in Avon's case, by fax. Uni-Vite starts off selling directly and then gives the customer's name to a distributor for follow-on sales.

6. *Low-cost or no-cost medium.* Most direct support programs are self-liquidating. Sales representatives pay the manufacturer for the service of having a catalog or some other selling device presented to customers of their choice. Often, each mailer is personalized with the sales representative's name, address, and phone number, and the representative is encouraged to follow up with telemarketing.

Although many direct sellers offer low-priced, relatively low-margin products, selling costs are much lower than in competing channels. Direct sellers have an advantage when it comes to database marketing. They have a built-in and largely free advertising and promotional medium in their sales force. The marketing and distribution costs are borne by that sales force. So, if a direct seller targets the market well, it can really boost sales much more effectively than a freestanding direct or retail sales effort.

Managing Customer Contact

Current direct support programs work best for the representatives who are generally the most active anyway. The challenge is to design a program to support the lowest level of salespeople, where turnover is the greatest. A database can also help companies reassign customers to new representatives and support prospecting programs targeted to specific market niches.

Databases can help companies design differentiated programs that meet their marketing needs. There are four types:

1. *Event mailing.* In event mailing, which is done by Mary Kay, Shaklee, and Princess House, every mailing is an individual promotion.
2. *Subscription program.* Avon offers a subscription program, in which customers sign up for repeated mailings. The advantage is efficiency.
3. *Trigger mail.* Trigger mail programs can be tied to actionable data, such as a reorder point. No direct seller is doing this today.
4. *Discovery selling.* In discovery selling, databases help direct sellers move excess inventory and spike off-season sales.

What Is Next?

Companies that use direct selling are rapidly embracing direct marketing, and those that do not will be left behind. If a firm marries a marketing database with the reach of its direct sellers, it has a powerful advantage that no retail store can match. Supported by a database that is the core of their marketing strategy, such firms can develop an optimal channel mix for each target market.

SUMMARY

In the future, integrated marketing will unify all areas of marketing specialization in a simultaneous, cohesive, and powerful way. The traditional differences between general image-oriented advertising, direct-response advertising, sales promotion, packaging, event marketing, point-of-sale materials, and database marketing are blurring as marketers focus on building product and service equity under cohesive company images. Mail and telemarketing have traditionally been the workhorses of direct marketing. However, recent technological advancements from computers, satellite dishes, cable television, WATS lines, online services, and fax machines—along with media of the foreseeable future, including interactive television and voice-activated telecommunications—promise to vastly enrich the arsenal available to direct marketers.

Heavy reliance on single-digit response rates mined from large-scale mailings is giving way to more tightly monitored, purchase-timed, database-marketing-driven efforts that target small groups of consumers or businesses. All these efforts are producing marketing strategies that are powerful multidimensional selling thrusts. The development of these relationships depends on the introduction and continuation of dialogues in which buyers, free to act on their own initiative, can lead sellers in the direction of real marketplace movement. The sellers then have direct and timely access to experiential data that paves the way for truly market-trend communications and products.

The use of new media by direct marketers continues to grow. New media include any electronic, interactive communications media that allow the user to request or receive delivery of information, entertainment, marketing materials, products, and services. Products and services are currently being sold online, via the Internet, and through CD-ROM catalogs. However, new-media revenues and, more important, profits, are still extremely small in comparison with the profits derived from traditional channels of distribution. Nevertheless, the probability is very high that new-media revenues will increase substantially in the next few years.

As rapid communications and as convenience become more important to everyone in an increasingly fast-paced society, new scenarios about how to live, work, and buy are emerging. As new communications devices are introduced, they change every service—from transportation to marketing to merchandising—so drastically that the way business is done is permanently altered. At the forefront will be the marketer's need to develop personal relationships with customers or prospects. The engine to drive this is the database of not just household or business characteristics but other, more specific characteristics as well.

Hybrid channels provide another way for reaching American consumers. Add a database and an integrated marketing orientation, and direct marketing companies have a strong formula for outperforming traditional marketers. This multichannel marketing is not new, but multichannel marketing built around a core channel of independent sales representatives is a new approach to reaching more prospects and customers more often.

REVIEW QUESTIONS

1. What changes do you expect for direct marketing in the future?
2. What is meant by the term *new media,* and what roles will those media play in the future of direct marketing?

3. What are the direct marketing implications of the struggle between cable TV and satellite television information and entertainment providers?
4. Some direct marketers think that hybrid channels are an important new way of offering products and services. What do you think? What role do you see for hybrid channels in the future?

NOTES

1. Adapted from Robert McKim, "The New Interactive Marketing Opportunities," *Direct Marketing,* September 1993, pp. 30–31, 67.
2. Adapted from Brent Bissell, "Forces for Change," *Direct Marketing,* December 1991, pp. 57–60, 70.
3. Adapted from A. T. Kearney, *Marketing in the Interactive Age* (New York: Direct Marketing Association, 1996).
4. Adapted from Richard Cross, "Internet: The Missing Marketing Medium," *Direct Marketing*, October 1994, pp. 20–23.
5. Adapted from Janet A. Smith, "Channel Wars," *Direct Marketing*, April 1992, pp. 33–36.

SOURCES

BISSELL, BRENT. "Forces for Change." *Direct Marketing*, December 1991, pp. 57–60, 70.

BOROUGHS, DON L. "New Age Advertising." *U.S. News & World Report*, July 10, 1995, pp. 38–39.

BOURNELLIS, CYNTHIA. "Internet '95." *Internet World.* November 1995, pp. 47–52.

CONRAD, PAUL. "The 3 Rs." *Direct Marketing,* February 1991, pp. 35–36.

COY, PETER. "I-Way or No Way Cable." *Business Week,* April 8, 1996, pp. 75–81.

CROSS, RICHARD. "Internet: The Missing Marketing Medium." *Direct Marketing,* October 1994, pp. 20–23.

DIBELLA, LORI A. "Not Just for the Little Guys." *Direct Marketing,* May 1991, pp. 20–22.

DOYLE, MARC. *The Future of Television.* Lincolnwood, IL: NTC Business Books, 1992.

EMERICK, TRACY. "The Multimedia Mix." *Direct Marketing,* June 1993, pp. 20–22.

FORREST, EDWARD, AND RICHARD MIZERSKI. *Interactive Marketing ó The Future Present.* Lincolnwood, IL: NTC Business Books, 1996.

FOSKETT, SALLY. "Online Technology Ushers in One-to-One Marketing." *Direct Marketing,* November 1996, pp. 38–40.

GATTUSO, GREG. "Lillian Vernon Looks to the Future." *Direct Marketing,* August 1994, pp. 33–35.

_______. "Taking Care of Business." *Direct Marketing,* February 1993, pp. 20–21.

GREGSTON, BRENT. "Power and Privilege." *Internet World,* November 1995, pp. 96–101.

HODGDON, PAUL N. "The Role of Intelligent Agent Software in the Future of Direct Response." *Direct Marketing,* January, 1997, pp. 10–17.

KEARNEY, A. T. *Marketing in the Interactive Age.* New York: Direct Marketing Association, 1996.

LEWIS, HERSCHELL GORDON, AND ROBERT D. LEWIS. *Selling on the Net.* NTC Business Books, 1996.

LEWIS, ROBERT. "Tempting Telecommunications Technologies." *Direct Marketing,* February 1991, pp. 55–57.

MARGOLIS, BUDD. "Technological Developments Delivering 500 TV Channels Are Only the Tip of the Iceberg." *Direct Marketing,* September 1995, pp. 24–26.

"Marketing with TV by Mail." *Direct Marketing,* September 1995, pp. 48–49.

MCKIM, ROBERT. "The New Interactive Marketing Opportunities." *Direct Marketing,* September 1993, pp. 30–31, 67.

MORRIS-LEE, JAMES, AND DAVID ERICKSON. "Advertising Production Connects to Database Marketing." *Direct Marketing,* February 1991, pp. 24–27.

NEAL, MOLLIE. "Marketers Develop a New Climate." *Direct Marketing,* February 1992, pp. 26–27.

O'MALLEY, CHRIS. "The Wireless World." *Popular Science,* November 1995, pp. 55, 57–62.

PERRY, CLIFFORD. "Travelers on the Internet: A Survey of Internet Users." *Online,* 19 (March/April 1995), pp. 29–34.

ROSENBLOOM, BERT. *Direct Selling Channels.* New York: Haworth Press, 1992.

ROSENSPAN, ALAN. "Is There a Future for Direct Mail? Problems and Prognosis." In *Beyond 2000: The Future of Direct Marketing,* ed. Jerry I. Reitman. Lincolnwood, IL: NTC Business Books, 1994, pp. 115–30.

RUST, ROLAND T., AND RICHARD W. OLIVER. "The Death of Advertising." *Journal of Advertising* 23, no. 4 (December 1994), pp. 71–77.

SCHULTZ, DON E. "The Natural Evolution of Direct Marketing: Integrated Marketing and Integrated Communications." In *Beyond 2000: The Future of Direct Marketing,* ed. Jerry I. Reitman. Lincolnwood, IL: NTC Business Books, 1994, pp. 3–13.

SEGAL, JOSEPH. "The Information Superhighway—Separating Hype from Reality." *Direct Marketing,* February 1994, pp. 18–22.

SMITH, JANET A. "Channel Wars." *Direct Marketing,* April 1992, pp. 33–36.

________. "The New Frontier." *Direct Marketing,* May 1991, pp. 25–27.

________. "The New Frontier." *Direct Marketing,* August 1991, pp. 20–22.

SROGE, MAXWELL. "Catalogs: New Technology, New Markets, New Horizons." In *Beyond 2000: The Future of Direct Marketing,* ed. Jerry I. Reitman. Lincolnwood, IL: NTC Business Books, 1994, pp. 131–37.

"Technology Projections: 2001." *Direct Marketing,* May 1992, pp. 23–25.

TRUMFIO, GINGER. "The Future Is Now." *Sales & Marketing Management,* November 1994, pp. 74–80.

TURKLE, SHERRY. *Life on the Screen: Identity in the Age of the Internet.* New York: Simon & Schuster, 1995.

VOS, GRUPPO & CAPELL, INC. *Interactive Direct Marketing: A Planning Guide to New Media Opportunities.* New York: The Direct Marketing Association, Inc., 1995.

"Will New Technology Change the Marketing Rules?" *Direct Marketing,* October 1994, pp. 14–19, 40.

WOJTAS, GARY W. "Exploring New Response Avenues." *Direct Marketing,* February 1991, pp. 44–46.

________. "Consumer Fantasies Fulfill Marketer's Dream." *Direct Marketing,* August 1991, pp. 40–49.

Case 1: Avon Products, Inc.

INTRODUCTION

Direct selling is a way to distribute products and services to consumers through face-to-face interactions that occur outside of fixed business locations. Direct selling is defined by the Direct Selling Association (DSA) as "personal contact between a salesperson and a consumer away from a fixed business location such as a retail store." Major modes of direct selling include one-on-one selling in a home or a workplace and sales parties in homes, places of business, or other locations such as churches. This form of selling is an important marketing channel both in the United States and around the world.

In 1991, direct selling revenues totaled approximately $13 billion in the United States. These sales were produced by more than 5 million sales representatives. In 1991, sales of direct selling companies in 16 countries of Europe were about $6.6 billion, based on the activities of some 1.3 million salespeople. The industry includes both relatively small, little-known firms and those that are household names, such as Avon, Amway, Tupperware, Mary Kay, Fuller Brush, and Herbalife. The products sold encompass cosmetics, vitamins, reference books, cutlery, vacuum cleaners, clothing, cleaning products, kitchenware, and much more.

Direct selling companies provide job opportunities for people with a wide range of backgrounds and personal characteristics. People in direct sales represent many education levels, occupational groups, and income levels. Thus, these jobs are accessible to a broad spectrum of people regardless of prior business experience or specific qualifications.

The direct selling salespeople are usually independent agents, many of whom work only part-time so they can coordinate their direct sales efforts with family and other responsibilities. Many also work either part-time or full-time for a regular employer in addition to maintaining their direct selling activities. They come to direct selling with a variety of work motivations. Some want to earn extra income, and others do it for psychological or social reasons such as building self-esteem or making friends. Still others want to improve their entrepreneurial skills or learn more about the business world.

The two major areas of managerial concern in direct sales are the customer side and the selling side. The customer side is about who purchases from direct selling representatives, what they want, and how satisfied they are with the sales experience and the products and services they receive. The selling side has to do with sales-force management issues, such as sales representative turnover, and with the efficiency of the direct channel in delivering a firm's goods or services to its target market.

Avon Products, Inc., is the world's largest manufacturer and direct seller of cosmetics, fragrances, and toiletries. It also sells costume jewelry; gift and decorative items; and, more recently, new entries such as lingerie, preschool educational toys, and videotapes (see Case Exhibit 1.1). Most of Avon's products are for women; some are for men and children. To illustrate Avon's consumer franchise, six product lines are profiled in Case Table 1.1: perfume and cologne, face creams and lotions, foundation makeup, mascara, eyeshadow, and eye liner. The table shows Avon products ranking among the top five competitors in each of the six categories.

Among the company's best-known offerings is the Avon Color line, which includes more than 350 shades of lip, eye, face, and nail colors. This line is intricately organized to present exactly the right shades for each customer so that a total "look" is coordinated.

Selling for Avon in the United States is done mostly direct by door-to-door or workplace sales representatives who, armed with a new brochure of products (80 to 100 pages) every two weeks, make money from an approximately 40 percent commission on sales. These representatives are independent agents, not employees of Avon. After taking orders from their customers, the representatives buy products on credit from a regional distribution center. Avon ships each order, which includes all the items for the representative's individual customers, within 72 hours.

Although Avon is best known for its sales force of "Avon ladies" who ring doorbells, these sales representatives no longer just call on suburban homes. Only about one-third of Avon's worldwide sales comes from traditional door-to-door selling, which represents a reduced but still substantial market. Another one-third is produced by selling in the workplace. In the past, Avon discouraged representatives from selling where they were employed or from making calls on offices and plants. However, Avon's studies show that managers and owners of businesses often encourage such selling because it keeps employees on the premises rather than running out to do shopping. Selling is generally done only during lunch or coffee breaks. The final one-third of Avon's sales comes from telemarketing and other direct marketing sales efforts.

Avon's employment opportunity appeals more to the middle-aged than to the young. The job attracts a typically middle-American, working-class crowd of those who are short on money. Avon's attraction to blue-collar, working-class people is probably based on the company's image and its moderate-income fashion connotations, combined with low-end prices and quality. Realistically, the image is not high fashion or chic but rather suburban, working-class frumpy. A regional sales meeting for Avon representatives will host a collection of women in their late 30s and 40s, almost all of whom are not glamorous by Madison Avenue standards. Nevertheless, those who buy cosmetics, fragrances, toiletries, clothing, and fashion accessories at Sears or Kmart are likely to be happy with the offerings in the Avon brochure.

CASE EXHIBIT 1.1. Avon U.S. Category Sales Distribution
(1991 estimated)

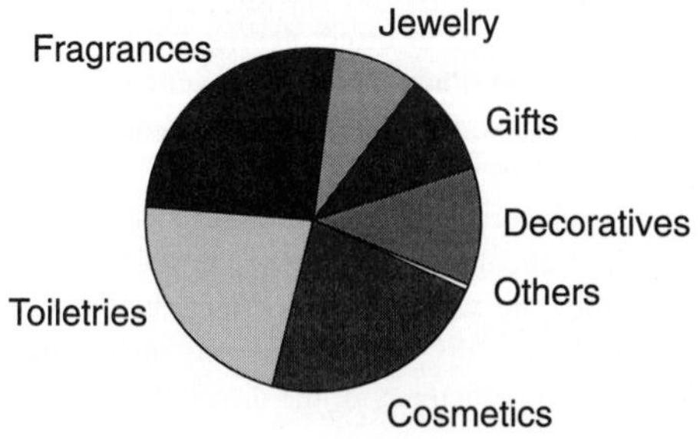

Source: Estimated from various sources.

Avon's ability to recruit sales representatives is directly related to the economic situation in the United States. Typically, women become Avon representatives to earn some money for Christmas or another special event. However, the income potential is low; the average representative earns only about $3,000 per year. The number of representatives depending on Avon for their primary income increases during poor economic times. However, long-term sellers represent only about 20 percent of the total sales force. Many sales representatives leave Avon when better, higher paying jobs become available.

Avon's main business expansion took place after World War II with the growth of disposable income, the spread of suburbanization, the increase in large families, and the tendency for women to stay at home. Prior to that, Avon was just getting by. In 1946, the company sales were only $17 million, which was small progress for a company already 60 years old. Although the economic and sociological trends in the late 1940s, 1950s, and 1960s were consistent with the way Avon does business, recent changes in lifestyles, the emergence of the career-oriented woman, consumerism, competitive threats, and so on all have posed challenges to Avon's vitality and its growth potential.

During the 1980s, Avon's sales representatives received increased training, enhanced materials, and the opportunity to earn more by participating in a tiered sales system. These programs, available to approximately 20 percent of the United States sales force in 1991, were rolled out nationally during 1992. Supporting both sets of strategies are image-enhancement programs, including a redesigned brochure and a return to television and magazine advertising.

The 1980s was a turbulent decade for Avon. Its net sales from all operations declined from 1981 to 1985 before they increased again (see Case Exhibit 1.2). Net income from all operations bottomed out in 1988 (see Case Exhibit 1.3). Nevertheless, Avon has come a long way since its founding. Its 1991 annual report showed that it had 1,120,000 active representatives that year, operating in Avon's four geographic divisions—Europe, the Pacific, the Americas, and the United States.

Historically, Avon's marketing costs have been lower than those of its competitors. And, through the use of direct sales representatives and modest advertising, Avon has been able to obtain high gross margins. But, with changing times and costs, Avon realizes that it must consider new alternatives.

CHANGING THE SALES SYSTEM

In 1991, Avon U.S. began implementation of its twin sets of strategies to establish the company as the "best place" for consumers to buy and the "best place" for representatives to sell. Consumers were offered alternative ways to buy and a variety of new products.

To increase U.S. sales, Avon has also been adding retail outlets, testing ads, and running infomercials with 800 numbers. By using 800 numbers in advertising and exploring retail

CASE TABLE 1.1. Top Five Brand Market Share Rankings

Rank	Perfume and Cologne	Face Creams and Lotions	Foundation Makeup	Mascara	Eye Shadow	Eye Liner
1	Avon	Oil of Olay	Cover Girl	Maybelline	Maybelline	Maybelline
2	Estée Lauder	Avon	Mary Kay	Cover Girl	Cover Girl	Cover Girl
3	Charlie	Mary Kay	Avon	Avon	Avon	Avon
4	Giorgio	Pond's	Clinique	Mary Kay	Mary Kay	Mary Kay
5	Chanel	Clinique	Estée Lauder	Estée Lauder	Estée Lauder	Revlon

Source: Simmons Market Research Bureau, 1991.

CASE EXHIBIT 1.2. Avon Products Worldwide Net Sales

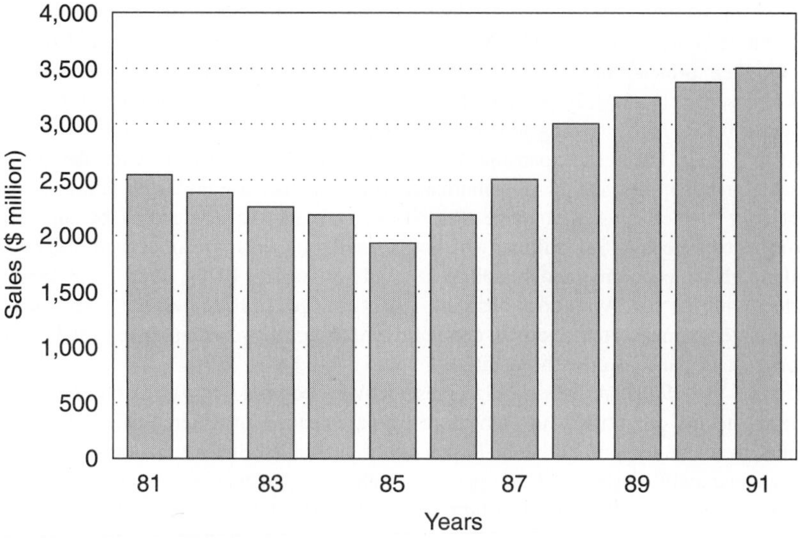

Source: Avon Products 1991 annual report.

CASE EXHIBIT 1.3. Avon Products Worldwide Net Income

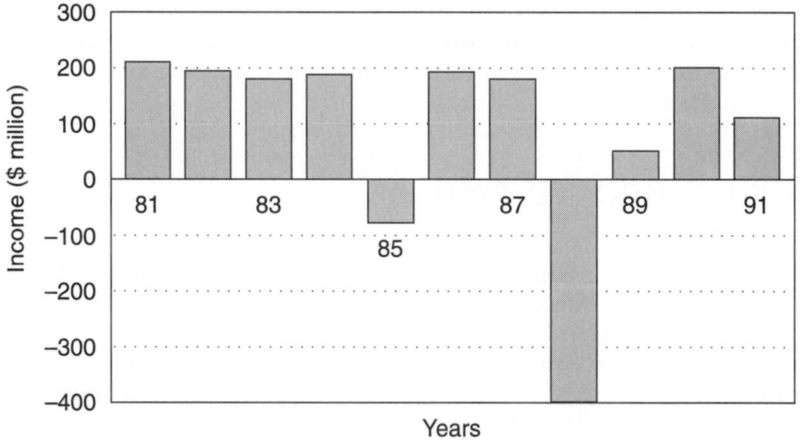

Source: Avon Products 1991 annual report.

opportunities, Avon is looking for new ways to give consumers greater access to its products. Avon estimates there are 10 million customers who currently do not have an Avon representative and would use an 800 number.

Additionally, the firm is considering an increase in the number of sales distribution centers now serving Avon sales representatives in the United States. These representatives pick up products at the centers, but consumers could buy directly there too. The concept has already proved viable in Mexico and Tokyo, where the centers have served as a showcase for products and an image enhancer to consumers.

Avon increased its U.S. ad budget to $11 million in 1992 and began running 15-second network television commercials and national print ads touting the options for ordering from the

Avon catalog through an 800 number, via fax, by mail, or through a traditional Avon sales representative.

Avon is working particularly hard to increase sales using direct mail. Since 1990, some Avon representatives have supplied the company with names of potential customers, who are then mailed catalogs. As of December 1991, about 11 percent of customers had responded to the personalized campaign, which is well above the average 2 to 3 percent response rate for direct-mail solicitations. Avon expects that direct mail will account for $300 to $500 million in sales within three to five years.

AVON'S CUSTOMERS

Avon sells primarily to women and secondarily to their families. Its product line appeals to both young and middle-aged consumers. Case Table 1.2 contains profiles of Avon's product-line users for some selected products. The table shows that Avon consumers are most likely to have upper-lower-class and lower-middle-class incomes.

CASE TABLE 1.2. Avon Products, Inc.: Selected User Demographics *(Women)**

	Perfume and Cologne	Face Creams and Lotions	Foundation Makeup	Mascara	Eye Shadow	Eye Liner
Age						
18–24	81	61	60	81	92	129
25–34	108	67	92	129	124	121
35–44	105	105	104	136	144	136
45–54	108	145	131	133	119	115
55–64	92	129	121	86	79	69
65 and over	101	115	101	24	30	22
Employment						
Full-time	102	100	100	116	127	124
Part-time	91	75	104	136	104	95
Not employed	100	105	99	77	73	78
Household income						
$60,000+	57	85	57	85	70	57
$50,000–$59,999	67	64	62	93	107	82
$35,000–$49,999	76	86	97	113	113	122
$25,000–$34,999	116	135	122	112	118	101
$15,000–$24,999	121	112	121	112	107	111
Less than $15,000	126	98	107	80	84	100
Marital status						
Single	84	56	54	85	89	99
Married	102	117	122	120	113	108

*Note: Index values are computed by dividing the proportion of women in a particular grouping by their proportion of the population. For example, if an age group has 20.2 percent of the products users and represents 18.3 percent of the population, the index value for the grouping is 110. Index values over 100 signify above-average usage, and index values below 100 signify below-average usage. However, values over 110 or under 90 are the most significant.

Source: Simmons Market Research Bureau, 1991.

CASE TABLE 1.3. Competitor Profiles: Selected User Demographics *(women)*

	Perfume and Cologne: Obsession	Face creams and lotions: Clinique	Foundation Makeup: Cover Girl	Mascara: Max Factor	Eye Shadow: Cover Girl	Eye Liner: Maybelline
Age						
18–24	173	140	162	155	197	144
25–34	131	124	125	120	144	135
35–44	117	106	92	111	106	115
45–54	73	104	80	82	62	88
55–64	67	67	87	93	51	70
65 and over	26	52	49	37	22	33
Employment						
Full-time	120	127	87	117	120	132
Part-time	103	121	106	94	114	82
Not employed	80	69	111	85	78	73
Household income						
$60,000+	130	233	86	136	89	103
$50,000–$59,999	88	146	92	95	105	85
$35,000–$49,999	109	101	110	111	131	85
$25,000–$34,999	110	93	109	96	96	131
$15,000–$24,999	111	79	107	103	103	139
Less than $15,000	66	36	90	75	77	64
Marital status						
Single	188	148	120	122	133	125
Married	87	97	96	104	99	93

Source: Simmons Market Research Bureau, 1991

One way to understand the demographics of Avon's customers is to compare the Avon customer profiles with those for selected competitors (see Case Table 1.3) and with those of heavy category users (see Case Table 1.4). Such comparisons show that some of Avon's competitors appeal much more to young consumers. For example, Obsession appeals mostly to younger consumers, while Avon's line of perfumes and colognes appeals to all ages (Case Table 1.2 versus Case Table 1.3). For mascara, Avon appeals more to those 25 to 54, while Max Factor's product line appeals more to those under 35 (Case Table 1.2 versus Case Table 1.3).

WHAT SHOULD AVON DO?

As Avon Products ponders distribution issues in more detail, it realizes that one major way it can expand its business activities is to provide more sales support to its representatives. Avon's management is thinking about various ways direct marketing might be used to enhance its direct sales force rather than just take sales from it. The idea would be to use one or more direct marketing tools to link Avon representatives with current and potential customers. To that end, Avon has established a database that stores information on where each of its direct sales

CASE TABLE 1.4. Heavy User Profiles: Selected User Demographics*
(Women)

	Perfume and Cologne	Face Creams and Lotions	Foundation Makeup	Mascara	Eye Shadow	Eye Liner
Age						
18–24	103	95	148	160	150	203
25–34	91	49	83	109	123	101
35–44	104	122	107	141	128	115
45–54	105	132	112	94	97	100
55–64	113	102	97	76	62	69
65 and over	91	124	70	20	29	24
Employment						
Full-time	116	90	125	147	141	139
Part-time	86	81	99	94	124	99
Not employed	87	113	76	55	55	61
Household income						
$60,000+	102	110	105	139	159	135
$50,000–$59,999	104	87	99	132	130	96
$35,000–$49,999	98	95	106	125	126	113
$25,000–$34,999	104	112	95	102	95	107
$15,000–$24,999	106	111	101	77	75	97
Less than $15,000	91	87	95	63	60	70
Marital status						
Single	113	88	120	136	128	168
Married	93	100	94	97	93	88

*Note:
P&C = more than 7 times per week.
FC&L = more than 14 times per week.
FM = more than 7 times per week.
M = more than 7 times per week.
ES = more than 7 times per week.
EL = more than 7 times per week.
Source: Simmons Market Research Bureau, 1991.

representatives lives. When Avon makes contacts with a consumer through its direct marketing efforts, it provides the closest representative with that person's address and phone number so that the representative can directly contact that person.

Avon is also concerned about the shifting nature of consumer demand, particularly because today's shopper is becoming increasingly value conscious. While customers have a taste for quality, they expect low prices too. In addition, a greater percentage of the women who buy cosmetics (many of whom are working) are insisting on convenience. That is good news for supermarkets and drugstores, which are making more and more sales of makeup and skin treatments.

What direct marketing efforts would you recommend to Avon? Who would be the target market? What range of products would be sold, and how would those products be offered? What other specific price, distribution, promotion, and product mix strategies and tactics would you propose and why?

CASE ONE
Avon Products, Inc.

ALBAUM, GERALD. "Current Status and Future Directions for Research on Direct Selling Channels." In *Direct Selling Channels,* ed. Burt Rosenbloom. New York: Haworth Press, 1992, pp. 95–117.

Avon Products, Inc. 1991 annual report.

"Avon Rings Millions of New Bells." *Sales & Marketing Management,* October 1992, p. 35.

"Avon Products." In *Contemporary Cases in Consumer Behavior,* ed. Roger D. Blackwell; W. Wayne Talarzyk; and James F. Engel. Chicago: Dryden Press, 1990, pp. 39–49.

HAGER, BRUCE. "Despite the Face-Lift, Avon Is Sagging." *Business Week,* December 2, 1991, pp. 101–2.

HEALY, DENIS F. "Avon Products, Inc.: For Whom the Bell Tolls." In *Consumer Behavior Dynamics: A Casebook,* ed. M. Wayne DeLozier. Columbus, OH: Charles E. Merrill, 1977, pp. 94–103.

Simmons Market Research Bureau, Inc., 1991.

WOTRUBA, THOMAS R., AND PRADEEN K. TYAGI. "Motivation to Become a Direct Salesperson and Its Relationship with Work Outcomes." In *Direct Selling Channels,* ed. Burt Rosenbloom. New York: Haworth Press, 1992, pp. 41–56.

ZELLNER, WENDY. "Mary Kay Is Singing 'I Feel Pretty,' " *Business Week,* December 2, 1991, p. 102.

ZELLNER, WENDY, AND BRUCE HAGER. "Dumpster Raids? That's Not Very Ladylike, Avon." *Business Week,* April 1, 1991, p. 32.

Case 2: Barney & Friends™

INTRODUCTION

This case is about the direct marketing opportunities, market segments, and strategies for selling products containing the very popular children's character called Barney. It deals with introducing a new Barney & Friends product as a sequel to the other highly successful Barney & Friends offerings. The new product is unique in that it is a computer software program—a CD-ROM coloring adventure that requires an IBM-compatible computer and a CD-ROM player. The list price will be $49.95, but when sold to a distributor, the price is $30.00. (The cost of goods per item is $12.00, and each buyer is expected to purchase only one.)

The television show *Barney & Friends* features eight multiethnic children from 7 to 14 years old who tra-la-la hither and thither about a rudimentary but bright school-yard set carpeted with fake grass, from which sprouts a big, brown, concrete tree complete with a tire swing. Inside the tire, or sometimes on top of the shellacked tree stump, rests the children's little stuffed mascot, the dinosaur doll named Barney.

In the TV show's straightforward, easily digestible episodes, Luci, Tina, Derek, Michael, Min, Shawn, Kathy, or Tosha might have a problem (a sharing dispute, stage fright before a recital, concerns about a "nontraditional" family, etc.), or maybe the children are just looking for fun on a rainy day. Either way, when they start pondering their predicament, and when they begin to use their imaginations, the Barney doll springs to life in a rainbow shower of computer-generated stars. With his beloved, adenoidal "Oh-ho-ho-ho," Barney, accompanied by Baby Bop (a squeaky-voiced, bow-wearing triceratops who makes frequent appearances), then jollies the kids with tunes they have heard a zillion times before, followed by jigs, hugs, a playful plan to action, and much make-believe.

Everything about Barney's television show is geared to young children. Adults rarely appear in Barney's school yard, and the repetition of songs and key words appeals to kids. It is almost as if the show were written by kids.

THE BARNEY EXPERIENCE

Every generation of youngsters has its own special "friend" to love and adore. The 1990s preschool children are no exception. The energetic, nurturing, and imaginative Barney, a purple-and-green *Tyrannosaurus rex,* has captured the adoration of preschoolers everywhere.

When the Public Broadcasting Service (PBS) added *Barney & Friends* to its programming lineup in 1992, no one could have anticipated the impact of that move. Today, *Barney & Friends* is the most watched children's program on PBS, with a weekly audience of about 14 million viewers.

In just three years, Barney's promoters released 18 home videos. During the same time, the Barney Fan Club grew to more than 700,000 members. Barney's first album, "Barney's Favorites, Vol. 1," sold through double platinum. Not surprisingly, PBS has extended broadcast rights for *Barney & Friends* through 1998.

Barney is successful because his show exudes warmth, simplicity, and the message that kids' concerns count. Barney appears, sings, dances, hugs, reassures, preaches a bit, and then he is gone. He never scolds or orders. He never tells the kids what to do.

BARNEY MANIA

Why do kids clamor for Barney videos; beg to watch Barney on TV; plead for Barney T-shirts, puppets, and books? And how come parents just don't understand? The answer to these questions lies in Barney's ability to charm and mesmerize his young audience and his inability to captivate adults. Nevertheless, Barney motivates the kids and the parents go along to make them happy.

Unlike *Sesame Street,* which charms grown-ups as well as kids with spoofs such as "Twin Beaks" and "Monsterpiece Theater," the *Barney & Friends* formula is unappetizing to many parents. But that is by design. Although their reactions to the show run from appreciation to mild astonishment to just plain disgust, parents one and all bow to their children's intense appreciation of that enigma called Barney.

Barney's public appearances rival those of a popular musical group in the enthusiasm and audiences they produce. A recent Barney appearance at 8:30 AM one Saturday in the biggest mall in Augusta, Georgia, tells the story. Even before the stores opened, the parking lot was crowded with Barney fans and their parents. The main event: a visitation by the big purple dinosaur of television fame. Inside the mall, a crowd estimated at 10,000 pushed toward the line of white plastic ribbon that separated Barney from his fans. The kids were absolutely crazy about Barney. They imitated his gestures, and those old enough to talk sang his songs. When Barney clapped, sang, and danced, they all did it along with him. After Barney took his leave and the good-byes died down, fans stampeded the J. C. Penney Barney boutique just across the mall. They emerged from the store one after another, with brand-new Barney and Baby Bop dolls.

CASE EXHIBIT 2.1. Barney Facts

- Anticipated total sales of Barney merchandise in 1993: $200 million.
- Number of Barney accessory boutiques in J. C. Penney stores: 625.
- Number of times the word *imagination* was used in one 30-minute *Barney & Friends* episode: 29.
- Number of people employed full-time to handle complaints about public appearances by unauthorized Barneys: 1
- Number of people attending Barney's first appearance in 1988: 600.
- Number of people at Barney's 1992 appearance in a Maryland mall: 36,000.
- Number of spots on Barney's back: 8
- Number of mall visits Barney has made since October 1992: 65.
- Barney's full height: 6 feet, 4 inches.
- Number of *Barney & Friends* viewers, per episode: 2,400,000.

Source: Adapted from Ann Reeks, "Barney *The* Dino-Star," *Parenting,* April 1993, pp. 88–93.

Although parents may not always be smiling about it, Barney mania clearly has them in its grip. But many parents still wonder what the attraction could possibly be. They wonder if there is something hypnotic, something subliminal, that reaches children and not adults. For many of these adults, their children's Barney adoration has made Barney bashing a popular pastime on park benches and in doctors' waiting rooms.

BARNEY MARKETING

The popularity of *Barney & Friends* has led to a marketing phenomenon, with videos, records, books, clothing, fan clubs, and recently even a special on NBC. Barney has his very own corner in the J. C. Penney stores, which contains Barney coloring books, Barney bedsheets, Barney belts, Barney nightlights, Barney suspenders, and even Barney underpants, with that large, grinning purple presence bringing up the rear.

Over 4 million videos and nearly 3 million plush Barneys and Baby Bops have been rung up at cash registers. During one Christmas season, J. C. Penney sold more than a million stuffed Barneys. Hasbro, which has a talking Barney, expects $75 million in retail sales, and Barney stuffed animals are expected to sell tens of millions of dollars' worth of business at retail.

The Barney & Friends video offer in Case Exhibit 2.2 (which appeared in *TV Guide*) illustrates how the elements of Barney's popularity are used to promote merchandise. The people who must purchase the product, the parents, tend to have negative feelings toward Barney, while the children who will want the videos love him. This creates an interesting marketing dilemma. To solve it, the ad emphasizes how much fun Barney is and how the videos train and educate children by stimulating their imagination. Barney is thus positioned as a teacher who educates children in numbers and the alphabet. The ad is targeted at parents, who will ultimately pay for the Barney video, if it is purchased. However, it is the children who will enjoy it.

CHILDREN, LEARNING, AND OTHER THINGS

Educators have long been captivated by the potential of television to support and supplement what children learn in school.[1] *Sesame Street,* which is the best known and perhaps most popular children's television show in history, was created to teach kids about letters and numbers, counting and vocabulary. Today, it is seen by almost half of America's 2- to 5-year-olds on a regular basis, and it is broadcast in more than 40 countries around the world. The designers of *Sesame Street* capitalize on the attention-grabbing power of fast-paced action, lively sound effects and music, and humorous puppet characters to foster basic academic skills.

Although *Sesame Street* facilitates school readiness skills, the rapid-paced, densely packed format on which it and other children's programs are based has not earned high marks in the area of imagination and creativity. *Barney & Friends* clearly outshines *Sesame Street* in that area. Nevertheless, in general, more television viewing at ages three and four is associated with less elaborate make-believe play in older preschoolers and lower creativity scores in elementary-school children. Studies of children and television have shown that in the area of facilitating young children's imaginative play, gains occurred only for children who watched slow-paced, nonviolent material with high continuity of storyline, and not for those who watched programs with rapid-paced, disconnected bits of information. In that sense, *Barney & Friends* is the ideal show for stimulating a young child's imagination. The studies suggest that television can have positive intellectual consequences as long as children's viewing is not excessive and programs are specially designed to take into account children's cognitive-developmental needs at their various stage of maturation.

NEW! as seen on TV!
Barney & Friends™ on video—yours at an irresistible price!
Special $9.99 offer
NOT AVAILABLE IN STORES!

Barney & Friends™ makes growing up a lot more fun!
This lovable, purple dinosaur makes growing up so much more fun as he gets boys and girls singing, dancing, playing, learning, and feeling good about themselves!
Just released! Not available in stores!
Now Time-Life has gathered the best of the hit BARNEY & FRIENDS programs, as seen on public television, into a brand new video series. So your children can enjoy their favorite dinosaur friend whenever they like, on the family VCR!
Each 30-minute video explores a subject of special importance to children—from making friends to keeping safe to starting school.
These widely acclaimed programs provide a rich television experience your youngsters can enjoy and benefit from...a nurturing experience based on creative imagination. And Barney will make such a hit in your home, your children will turn on these videos again and again!
First video just $9.99... plus bonus FREE GIFT!
Send for your first video, *Caring Means Sharing*, today. Enjoy it FREE for 10 days.
If you like, keep it for only $9.99, plus shipping and handling—and get a *Barney In Concert* audiocassette as a bonus gift! Your children will have a wonderful time singing along to the 21 tunes on this great music tape.
Additional videos will arrive, about one a month, with the same 10-day free preview, at the regular price of $14.99 plus shipping and handling. Keep only those you want. No commitment. No minimum number to buy. And you may cancel any time.
FREE PREVIEW! Order today.
Barney helps children understand feelings and gain confidence.
Barney mixes learning and fun into an irresistible alphabet soup.
Barney shows children how to have fun with numbers.
Barney introduces children to nature and examines ways we can care for our Earth.

Alongside the television, the new competitor for children's time is the personal computer. Today, computers are becoming a familiar fixture in many schools and homes, bringing a wide range of new entertainment and learning tools within easy reach of preschool through adolescent youngsters. Children generally prefer computers to television, perhaps because they combine the visual and auditory dynamism of television with an active role for the child. That is, computers are fun because children get to control the action and the progress of the storyline at their own pace. Television controls itself; it is a passive medium requiring little or no participation of any kind.

Computers have the potential to enrich a child's education and also to provide social benefits. Children as young as three like computer activities and can type in simple commands on a standard keyboard or use a mouse to select options on a screen. At the same time, children do not find the computer so captivating that it diverts them from other worthwhile play activities such as interacting with other children. Many preschool and elementary-school pupils use computers socially when small groups of children gathered around the machine take turns as well as help each other figure out the next steps.

In computer-assisted instruction, children acquire new knowledge and practice academic skills with the help of learning software specifically designed for their needs. The unique properties of many instructional programs make them effective, fun, and absorbing ways for children to learn. For example, pupils can begin at points that fit with their current level of mastery, and programs are often written to intervene when children's responses indicate that help is needed. Multimedia presentations that include combinations of text, graphics, videos,

animation, music, and voices capture children's attention and interest. While some programs provide drill and practice on basic academic skills, others involve gamelike activities that encourage a wide range of learning and thinking processes. A child may learn about how cars operate, how to find his or her way around in a strange place, or how to operate a small store. There tend to be significant gains in achievement when children use computers in school and at home.

Some educators refer to a concept called "knowledge acceleration" when describing the fact that children who work on computers at home learn more, and learn it faster, than children who do not use computers in their homes. The skills and knowledge gained by children who use home computers build on themselves and thus lead to the acquisition of more skills and knowledge. Children who use computers accelerate up the learning curve much more rapidly than their counterparts who do not have regular access to a computer.

THE BARNEY & FRIENDS CD-ROM

As noted previously, this case is about formulating a strategy for the introduction of a new Barney & Friends product. What direct marketing strategy would you recommend for the Barney & Friends CD-ROM offering? Your strategy should answer the following questions: How should the consumer market be segmented, and what segment(s) should be targeted? What are the direct marketing strategy alternatives for introducing the new Barney & Friends offering in the highly competitive children's entertainment market? What are the pros and cons of those direct marketing strategy alternatives, given the specific target segment(s) and direct marketing tools? How would those strategies operate? Which strategy alternative would be best?.

NOTES

1. Laura E. Berk, *Child Development,* 2nd ed, (Boston: Allyn & Bacon, 1991).
2. Ibid.

SOURCES

BERK, LAURA E. *Child Development,* 2nd ed. Boston: Allyn & Bacon, 1991.
DUDKO, MARY ANN, AND MARGIE LARSEN. *Barney's Hats.* Allen, TX: Barney Publishing, 1993.
HAYDEN, CHAUNCE. "Barney." *Steppin' Out,* March 30–April 5, 1994, pp. 22–23, 26, 28.
OVERBECK, JOY. "I Love You . . . You Hate Me?" *TV Guide,* April 23, 1994, pp. 30–32.
REEKS, ANN. "Barney *The* Dino-Star." *Parenting,* April 1993, pp. 88–93.
WEINER, STEWART. "Purple Passion." *TV Guide,* February 27, 1993, pp. 22–23.

Case 3: Deal-A-Meal USA[1]

INTRODUCTION

Success in the weight-loss and dieting industry is becoming increasingly difficult as the number of competitors grows and the intensity of competition becomes more ferocious. The competition is stimulating ongoing interest in losing weight and demand for related products by many segments of the population. Every year, more and more Americans become obese or just decide they are displeased with their weight. However, the vast majority who make the attempt to lose weight eventually put back on all that they lose and more. Millions of consumers are searching for the next great weight-loss scheme, but for most this search represents a fruitless journey replete with failures and reduced self-esteem.

Periodically, a dieting plan emerges from all the competition and becomes very popular or even institutionalized. Names like Jenny Craig and Nutri/System come readily to mind. However, if these plans really worked, they would quickly put themselves out of business. The reality is that weight loss is a lifestyle issue and not a one-time effort. The plans that appear to work best encourage regular exercise and an eating regimen that includes a significant reduction in the consumption of fatty foods. One of today's most successful weight-loss programs is offered by Deal-A-Meal USA.

DEAL-A-MEAL USA

Deal-A-Meal USA is a privately held firm that relies heavily on infomercials to market its product. Its main spokesperson and owner is Richard Simmons, the well-known perky exercise guru. The Deal-A-Meal plan, which includes exercise tapes and a dieting system, has sold millions of copies.

CASE EXHIBIT 3.1. Deal-A-Meal Revenues

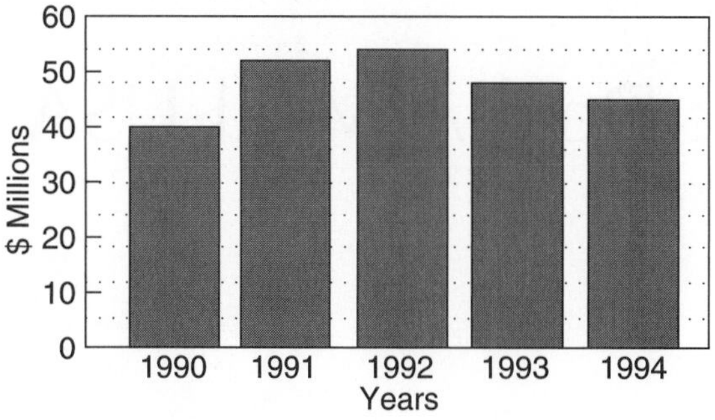

Source: Estimated from various sources.

Product Description

The Deal-A-Meal Life Plan has four parts:

1. The Deal-A-Meal Card System is a relatively small folder with diet cards that are moved from one side of a cardholder to the other depending on what the dieter eats. At the point when the requisite number of daily calories on the cards is transferred, the dieter stops eating. An audiotape and instruction manual for the Deal-a-Meal weight-loss plan comes with the diet cardholder.
2. The *Golden Edition Cookbook* contains low-calorie, low-fat, low-sodium recipes that the dieter can prepare.
3. The *Sweating to the Oldies 3* and *Stretching to the Classics* exercise videotapes instruct the dieter on how to perform regular, fun exercise routines that tone the body and reduce weight.
4. The *Project Me* motivational tapes are designed to encourage dieters to think positively and to feel good about themselves.

The entire system is usually priced at three payments of $29.95, for a total of $89.85. There is no lengthy commitment involved; it is a one-time purchase. Frequently, purchase incentives, such as free audiotapes, are offered.

Performance

Because Deal-A-Meal USA is privately held, its sales and income can only be estimated. Industry sources believe that Deal-A-Meal USA has steadily increased its revenues over the last several years, with 1994 income expected to reach $6 million on sales of $65 million (see Case Exhibits 3.1 and 3.2).

While Deal-A-Meal USA's offering has enjoyed much success, it has not produced any really new concepts beyond the core diet plan that started the whole venture in the early 1990s.

YOUR NEW JOB AT DEAL-A-MEAL USA

As a new employee at Deal-A-Meal USA, you are looking forward to your first meeting with the owner, Richard Simmons. You have seen him many times on television in half-hour infomercials and on the talk shows, but this will be your first face-to-face encounter. Richard is clearly a genius, a potentially intimidating person who is not only smart but also rich and very popular.

CASE EXHIBIT 3.2. Deal-A-Meal Net Income

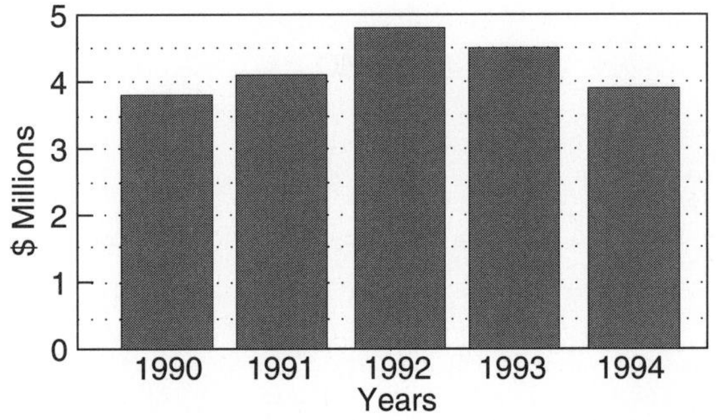

Source: Estimated from various sources.

Because he has been so successful with his Deal-A-Meal program, you are wondering what he might want from you in the way of a better understanding of the weight-loss and dieting market.

The Meeting with Richard

During the meeting with Richard, it becomes clear that he expects you to know a lot about marketing dieting and weight-loss products. He also keeps asking you questions about how consumers think and behave with respect to weight loss and dieting and about how friends and family influence a consumer's dieting and weight-loss goals. Richard's theories about why people are successful with the Deal-A-Meal USA program touch on everything from needs satisfaction to attitude change and the role of American culture in establishing standards of beauty.

Evidently, Richard wants a thoughtful understanding of the dieting and weight-loss business and its customers. You agree with him that certain specific areas need more consideration:

1. What consumer needs are being satisfied or not being satisfied by dieting and weight loss? How do these needs differ for men versus women?
2. What are the attitude and belief aspects of consumers' behavior in relation to dieting and weight loss?
3. What are the social and cultural influences that operate on consumer weight and dieting standards? How do these differ for men versus women?
4. For Deal-A-Meal USA, how does the program operate with respect to the aforementioned factors, and what marketing strategy alternatives exist?

At the end of the meeting, Richard asks you to draft a memo that answers these questions.

Back in Your Office

After the meeting, you return to your office to begin thinking about how to respond to Richard's request. You decide to review the file of memos written by your predecessor, David Robinson, before starting to write your own memo about the weight-loss and dieting industry. You find several relevant memos, and conclude that the ones written on June 23, 1994; August 12, 1994; and August 29, 1994 provide good summaries of the business issues that concern Richard. (See Case Exhibits 3.3, 3.4, and 3.5.)

MEMO

TO: Richard Simmons
FROM: David Robinson
SUBJECT: Weight-Loss and Dieting Industry Trends and Competition
DATE: June 23, 1994

As requested, this memo covers the competition and competitive structure of the weight-loss and dieting industry. Little published information exists on most companies, but there are highlights that should prove helpful.

One of every four Americans is dieting at any given time. Of those people, 97 percent cut down on high-calorie foods, 88 percent exercise, 29 percent skip meals, 12 percent crash-diet, and 4 percent use diet pills. How may of these dieters reach and maintain their weight loss? Unfortunately, not many, because otherwise the number of Americans on diets would steadily dwindle to nothing!

Approximately 34 million adults, or one-quarter of the population, are significantly overweight. Only one in five clients of a commercial weight-loss center stays with the program long enough to lose an appreciable amount of weight. It is estimated that up to 90 percent of all dieters who lose 25 or more pounds on a diet regain the weight they've lost over a two-year period, and only 1 in 50 manages to keep the weight off for seven years.

Nonetheless, dieting-industry revenues have grown rapidly. Meanwhile, weight-loss methods that do not promise a quick fix tend to do poorly with consumers. Health and fitness centers are having revenue declines and closings. Americans want quick results, and are attracted to companies promising rapid weight loss.

Annual revenues of commercial dieting centers grew by an average of 18 percent per year in the 1980s, reaching $2 billion in 1990. In 1991, however, revenues fell due to the recession and more competition from books, video plans, and do-it-yourself liquid regimens.

Many weight-loss centers are launching ambitious marketing and advertising campaigns. Some of the programs have raised questions in the medical community, partly due to the use of celebrities in weight-loss center advertisements.

Weight Watchers International creates a new food plan each year, making the program faster or easier to follow and giving the company yet another selling point. Weight Watchers targets its advertising to group-oriented women between the ages of 20 and 54 who have tried to lose weight in the past year. The fact that weight-loss centers make statements about health and fitness yet do not provide information on their track records is troubling to some people.

Nutri/System targets overweight adults and relies primarily on radio and newspaper ads. In place of the traditional celebrity endorsement, the company has built a force of 1,000 disk jockeys whom it supplies with Nutri/System food and services in exchange for daily on-air progress reports.

Dieting books and videos are enjoying a boom in sales. Millions of dollars are being spent on such diverse offerings as motivational tapes, fasting cookbooks, and comprehensive plans detailed in long and sometimes tedious books.

The following is a listing of the major business segments and competitors in the weight-loss and dieting industry:

Organized programs
Overeaters Anonymous
Take Off Pounds Sensibly (TOPS)

Enrollment programs
Diet Center
Jenny Craig
Nutri/System
Shapedown
Weight Watchers

Medically supervised diet programs
Health Management Resources
MediBase
Medifast
Optifast
Optitrim
United Weight Control Corporation
Weigh to Live

Weight-loss and diet books and videos
The Choose to Lose Diet (book)
The Executive Success Diet (book)
The Feel Full Diet (book)
The New American Diet (book)
Not Another Diet Book (book)
Deal-A-Meal USA (videos and books)
The Amazing Micro Diet (video and book)[2]

As you can see from this list, the business is divided into four major segments: organized programs, enrollment programs, medically supervised programs, and weight-loss and dieting books and videos.

Organized programs. Organized programs help people with eating disorders and/or weight problems to overcome their destructive behavior and to lose weight through strength of fellowship with people who have similar problems. These are not diet programs per se because they view overeating and being overweight as problems more complex than simply choosing what foods to eat. Through strength in numbers, in group support and compassion, members strive to achieve control over their eating, weight, and lives in general. Members may use any effective eating plan in tandem with group affiliation.

Enrollment programs. Enrollment plans are fee-for-service businesses designed to help people lose and maintain weight. While most of these programs offer support and counseling, they are limited by the realities of business: the counselors are paid employees and their time has a cost associated with it. Those counselors may be genuinely concerned about the dieter's plight, or they might just be doing their job, reciting from a memorized script without much feeling or interest. On the other hand, enrollment programs are comprehensive, offering a support system, nutritional counseling, a diet plan, and, in some cases, diet food that works in conjunction with the plan.

Medically supervised diet programs. Medically supervised diet programs are designed primarily for those whose obesity poses a health risk, such as diabetes

CASE EXHIBIT 3.3. Concluded

or heart disease. A number of programs require that participants be at least 20 percent above their ideal body weight before enrolling and going on a very-low-calorie diet. These programs operate under the supervision of a medical doctor—and for good reason, because rapid weight loss is highly stressful on the body and can produce severe side effects.

Weight-loss and dieting books and videos. Of all the available weight-loss plans, diet books and videos are by far the most popular and numerous. The selection includes a wide range of items. Some programs are complete plans addressing food, behavior, and exercise. Others address only one or two of those components but do so in an effective way and can thus become part of a successful weight-control program. These plans require a great amount of self-imposed structure, discipline, and motivation.

MEMO

TO: Richard Simmons
FROM: David Robinson
SUBJECT: Weight Loss and Dieting Industry Consumers
DATE: August 12, 1994

In response to your recent questions about consumers, I am writing this memo to summarize what we know about weight loss and dieting. I feel it's clear that we, and the weight-loss and diet industry in general, know very little about our customers. As you noted in our meeting, the current economic situation represents a big potential opportunity for Deal-A-Meal USA. Because our prices are lower than those of our competitors—that is, the organized programs, the enrollment programs, and medically supervised diet programs—consumers should be gravitating to us in large numbers. I know you want Deal-A-Meal USA's customers to succeed. One way to ensure that the purchasers of the Deal-A-Meal USA program lose weight is to understand why they tend to succeed or fail.

Some recent research on dieting suggests that people with lower weight loss expectations going into a dieting program have a better chance of keeping with the program. These people also receive greater support from family and friends, and have a more positive attitude about their chances for permanent weight loss. Program dropouts, on the other hand, seem to expect to fail. In other words, getting started is easy; staying motivated is not.

Most obesity experts agree that quick-fix diets promote a pattern of fasting and bingeing. They suspect that the so-called yo-yo syndrome may disturb the body's metabolism. There is some speculation that this could explain why chronic dieters find it ever more difficult to lose weight. Some experts believe that when dieters attempt to resume a normal eating pattern, not only are they bedeviled by all their old compulsive habits, but their body has lowered its metabolism in an attempt to conserve those precious calories. Studies have found that as soon as people lose significant weight, they begin to overproduce an enzyme called lipoprotein lipase, which helps restore fat cells shrunk by dieting. The heavier the person, the more enzymes were produced; this may be why people often regain lost weight quickly. This may also explain why chronic dieters have to struggle not only to lose weight but to maintain the loss.

CASE EXHIBIT 3.5.

MEMO

TO: Richard Simmons
FROM: David Robinson
SUBJECT: Deal-A-Meal Infomercial Analysis
DATE: August 29, 1994

I conducted an analysis of one of our 30-minute infomercials for the Deal-A-Meal USA program. In doing the analysis, I applied a communications and offer analysis format I find useful. It allows for a summarizing and itemizing of the creative strategy and offer we are making. I was able to define the benefits and reasons why in the television spot. The summary looks like this:

I. Creative Strategy
  A. Key selling concept (USP): Be in control of your weight
  B. Desired action: Purchase/order Deal-A-Meal package through 800 number
  C. Message strategy
    1. Primary target market—women 25–49, larger bodies
    2. Secondary target market—men 25–49, larger bodies
    3. Benefits
      a. Being in control
      b. Self-esteem
      c. Confidence
      d. Good feelings
      e. "A new you"
    4. Reasons why
      a. Do-it-yourself plan
      b. Testimonials
      c. Simple, safe, easy, fun
II. Offer Proposition
  A. Product description
  B. The four-step Deal-A-Meal Life Plan
    1. The Deal-A-Meal Card System: The audiotape and instruction manual (describing the Deal-A-Meal weight loss plan)
    2. The *Golden Edition Cookbook* (low-calorie, low-fat, low-sodium recipes)
    3. *Sweating to the Oldies 3* and *Stretching to the Classics* videotapes
    4. *Project Me* motivational tapes
      a. Price: 3 payments of $29.95 (Total = $89.85)
      b. Length of commitment: none
      c. Incentives: free with order two free audiotapes—*Take a Walk* and *Take a Hike*—plus $50 savings

When consumers buy products to satisfy needs, they are really buying the benefits they believe the products provide rather than the products per se. For example, consumers buy headache relief, not aspirin. ''Reasons why'' establish credibility. They can be linked to tangible attributes of the product, including materials, design, and the manufacturing process. In other words, product descriptions tend to be reasons why. Also, associations with a company or brand name are reasons why. Testimonials are powerful reasons why, too.

In proposing any changes to Deal-A-Meal's current marketing approach, you have three main concerns: (1) making maximum use of the available information on the weight-loss and dieting industry to appeal to the largest potential audience, (2) finding the right mix of Deal-A-Meal program elements and themes so as to appeal to those who have failed with other diets, and (3) keeping the program interesting to those who started but are still working on their weight problems.

The right product mix is also critical. Recent Deal-A-Meal offerings have included bigger packages of videotapes, books, and other items. There may also be an opportunity to mix in some higher ticket items with these more traditional products.

The real question for firms in this category centers on marketing issues: How can the firm develop and keep a differential advantage in a highly competitive and dynamic market, while maintaining sales growth and, above all, profitability?

What direct marketing strategies would you recommend for Deal-A-Meal USA? What specific price, distribution, promotion, and product elements would you propose and why? How would you deal with the growth of competition in the dieting and weight-loss market?

NOTE

1. Although Deal-A-Meal USA is an actual competitor in the dieting and weight-loss industry, the scenario and conversations in this case are fictional.

SOURCES

"The Allure Diet Survey." *Allure,* November 1991, pp. 146–49, 178–80.
BLODGET, BONNIE. "The Diet Biz." *Glamour,* January 1991, pp. 136–39, 175–76.
Deal-A-Meal promotional materials.
"Losing Weight." *Consumer Reports,* June 1993, pp. 347–57.
SCANLON, DERALEE. *Diets That Work.* Chicago: Contemporary Books, 1991.
SCHROEDER, MICHAEL. "The Diet Business Is Getting a Lot Skinnier." *Business Week,* June 24, 1991, pp. 132–34.

Case 4: Dell Computer

INTRODUCTION

The history of Dell Computer Corporation is about Michael S. Dell and his leadership in taking a new business from a storefront to a prominent position in the direct sales of personal computers (PCs). In 1984, Dell dropped out of college to devote all his energies to his PC parts business. In the beginning, he assembled and marketed IBM "clones" under the brand name PC's Limited. After one year, he was selling more than 1,000 computers per month. By the end of 1994, annual sales had reached $3.5 billion. (See Case Exhibits 4.1 and 4.2 for Dell Computer sales and profit information.)

All through the late 1980s and early 1990s, Dell Computer's marketing of PCs was competitive. The company prospered by taking orders over the phone and through the mail. It was a phenomenal success story until other PC makers, particularly rival Gateway 2000, flooded the direct channels and began a price war. Battered by the new competitors and problems with its product line, Dell Computer reported its first loss in 1993.

As a result, Dell Computer refocused its marketing effort. In 1994, Dell stopped selling its machines through retail outlets (mostly computer stores and superstores), which made up only 2 percent of 1993's $2.9 billion in sales, and concentrated on direct marketing—particularly targeted, product-focused mailings.

A Renewed Emphasis

Dell's renewed emphasis on direct marketing focused on two basic classes of customers: (1) the price-sensitive transactional customer who traditionally received direct mail and (2) the corporate customer who was usually serviced by Dell's sales representatives.

Dell's new catalog represented a value-oriented shift in strategy. Rather than using straightforward product descriptions, the new catalog put prices boldly in headlines, addressed leading-edge technology, and quoted testimonials from sources such as *Forbes* and *Personal Computing*. Fewer mailings and an emphasis on high-potential prospects resulted in 50 percent fewer catalogs in the mail and a tripling of response rates.

CASE EXHIBIT 4.1. Dell Computer Annual Sales

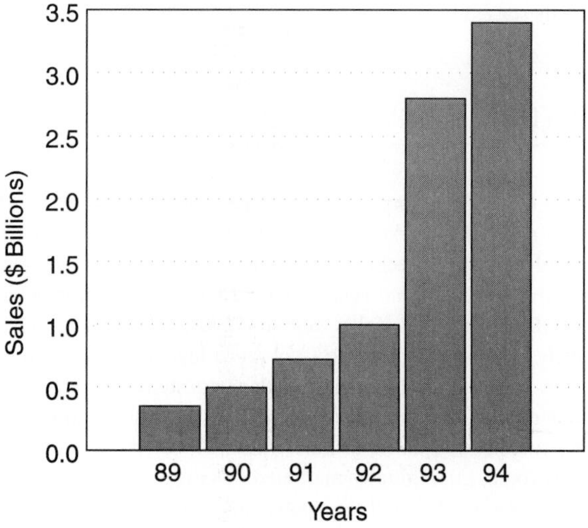

Source: Estimated from various sources.

CASE EXHIBIT 4.2. Dell Computer Net Income

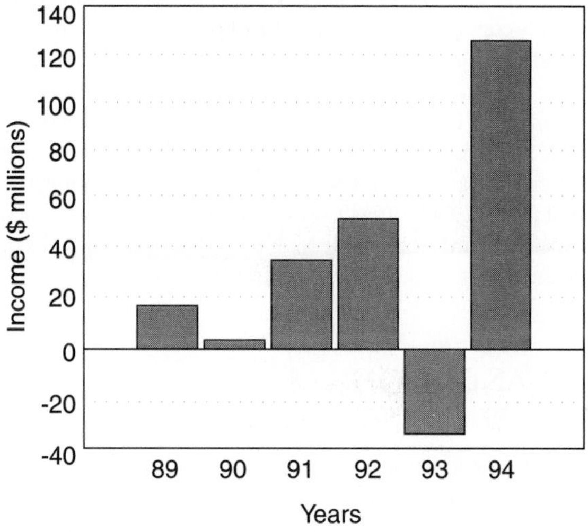

Source: Estimated from various sources.

Dell also switched gears for larger corporate accounts. Instead of receiving catalogs, this most profitable customer group received mailings centered on new-product introductions.

Meanwhile, Dell's direct-response print ads, which appear in PC magazines, portrayed the company as a price and technology leader. A typical ad promoted a single feature such as eight-hour batteries, with a price boldly tagged in red.

Dell also began investigating electronic direct channels such as interactive kiosks at Best Buy and Sam's, and online services such as Prodigy, CompuServe, and America Online.

However, some observers think Dell should go even further in other forms of media. They believe that Dell should take part of its direct-response budget and put it into broadcast television, infomercials, or cable.

DELL'S COMPETITIVE ADVANTAGE

The success of Dell Computer Corporation can be traced to Michael Dell's vision of a high-performance, low-priced PC marketed directly to end users. Dell computers are not designed to be the most powerful or the most technically advanced. Instead, they are intentionally designed to be of higher than average quality and very reliable. Likewise, Dell computers are not designed to be the lowest cost PCs available. Dell's key strategic concepts are "relatively high performance" and "relatively low price" combined to produce high value for buyers.

However, perhaps more important than its high performance-to-price ratio is the manner in which Dell Computer markets its products. Rather than marketing through one of the existing distribution channels such as traditional dealers, value-added resellers, or mass merchandisers, or by means of a sales force, Dell initially marketed its computers directly to end users through direct-response advertising in selected computer magazines. Later, it added telemarketing activities and, later still, a direct sales force. All products are distributed directly from the Dell factory to the end user by UPS or Federal Express. No intermediaries—that is, no wholesalers or retailers—were involved.

Generally, Dell PCs start at around $1,200 and range up to nearly $4,000. However, prices continue to drop while performance climbs. All but the lowest priced IBM-compatibles have a processor that is fast enough and powerful enough for most present-day needs; video and sound capabilities support most computer games; and Dell installs enough software for most serious work. Many models also include a fax/modem and introductory membership to an online service.

Each of Dell's computers is individually configured to the buyer's own specifications after the order is received. Therefore, there is no inventory of finished computers sitting in a warehouse, and each customer could theoretically own a unique computer. User support has always been given first priority. Dell offers a 30-day, no-questions-asked, money-back guarantee as well as free on-site servicing for a year and free technical support continually available through an 800 number.

COMPANY ORGANIZATION

Organizationally, Dell Computer consists of a domestic operation, Dell USA, and Dell International. Although the majority of the sales revenues are derived from the domestic operation, significant growth is occurring internationally in Canada, France, Germany, Sweden, and the United Kingdom.

The domestic sales organization (Dell USA) consists of four distinct entities: (1) commercial, (2) government and education, (3) field sales, and (4) direct sales. The commercial division focuses on *Fortune* 1000 firms and large privately held corporations. The government and education group markets Dell products to government entities and educational institutions. The field sales division markets Dell computers to selected value-added resellers and original equipment manufacturers. The direct sales division concentrates on medium and small businesses and the household market through direct-response advertising, mailouts, and telemarketing. The direct sales division accounts for approximately 40 percent of domestic revenues.

Dell's two major markets have very different needs and buying requirements. The household market consists of consumers using a computer for word processing, games, part-time businesses, and simple data processing. Businesses tend to want high-speed computers that are compatible with existing systems and that can be linked together to provide a variety of functions. Household consumers, on the other hand, are less concerned with computing power or system capability. However, a major concern of consumers is cost. In general, PCs sold to businesses tend to be on the high end of the price continuum and have higher margins, whereas PCs sold to households tend to be on the low end of the price continuum and have lower margins. The business market is also more heterogeneous than the household market. For instance, it consists of niches with very specialized performance needs and cost as a secondary concern (for example, scientific laboratories) as well as government entities whose purchase decisions are based primarily on price.

COMPUTER INDUSTRY TRENDS

Between 1981 and 1994, PC sales grew dramatically in the United States. The total number of PCs sold to businesses, government agencies, educational institutions, and households exceeded 50 million. During this period, dollar sales increased from $3 billion in 1981 to $56 billion in 1994.

However, after years of double-digit industry growth, the prospects are for a slowdown in PC sales. Direct sales in particular are expected to slow significantly because the traditional customers in this area are small businesses and individuals. Some analysts even go so far as to predict a shakeout in the industry.

The competitors range from well-known firms such as IBM, Compaq, and Apple to a couple hundred "no-name" firms, many of which consist of only one or two entrepreneurs assembling PCs in a garage or storefront location. It is common in the industry to refer to IBM, Apple, and Compaq as "tier 1" firms in terms of their sales. In 1994 IBM's PC sales totaled about $12 billion. Apple's were $10 billion, and Compaq's were $8 billion. Tier 2 competitors consist of firms such as Dell, CompuAdd, and Tandy. Tier 3 includes such firms as Advanced Logic Research (ALR), Zeos, and Amstrad, each with sales of up to $150 million annually.

Although tier 1 firms are well known and have high brand awareness, beyond this handful of firms there is relatively little brand awareness. For example, Dell is not well known except among individuals who subscribe to and/or read the major PC magazines (such as *PC Magazine, PC World,* and *Personal Computing*). With the exception of Apple, most manufacturers of PCs have adopted the "industry standard" set by IBM. Consequently, the vast majority of PCs are said to be "IBM-compatible" or, with a more negative connotation, "clones."

MARKETING CHANNELS

PC manufacturers use four primary channels to reach end users: dealers/value-added resellers, direct mail, mass merchandisers, and direct sales (see Case Exhibit 4.3). The two fastest-growing channels of distribution, direct mail and mass merchandisers, are each growing 30 to 40 percent a year, with direct mail currently accounting for a larger portion of the sales total than mass merchandisers. The seven leading PC hardware marketers are Gateway, Dell, Digital, Apple, CompuAdd, IBM, and Compaq (see Case Exhibit 4.4). Many PC marketers are less than 10 years old, and some are less than 5 years.

Retailers that specialize in niches and provide value-added services for specific markets are doing well. Likewise, retailers that compete primarily on a no-frills service strategy with low prices are doing well. Those retailers that are in the middle, however, which have neither the

CASE EXHIBIT 4.3. Market Share by Channel

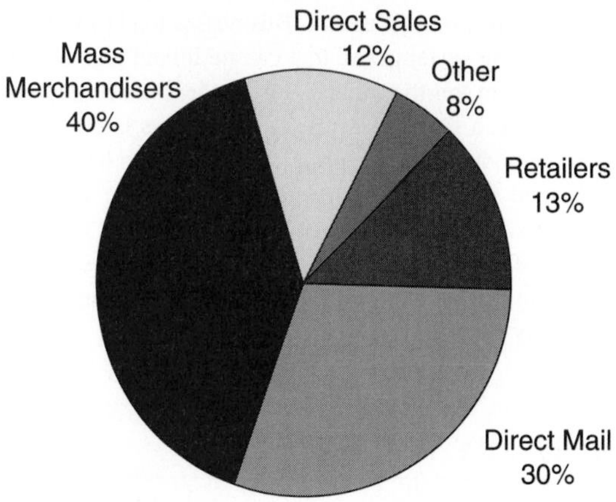

Source: Estimated from various sources.

CASE EXHIBIT 4.4. Leading Direct Computer Market Shares in 1993

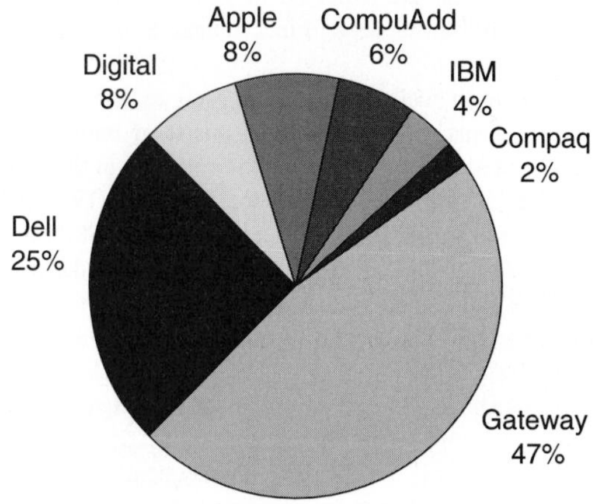

Source: Estimated from various sources.

lowest prices nor unique value-added service and support offerings, are no longer able to compete and have been leaving the marketplace.

Dealers/Value-Added Resellers

The traditional channel used to reach PC buyers is the storefront dealer. Dealers are retailers that focus on selling PCs and peripheral equipment to both the business and household markets. Some PC manufacturers, such as Compaq, tend to sell exclusively through dealers. There are major chains of dealers, such as Computerland. Generally, dealers operate out of facilities of 3,000 to 5,000 square feet and assume the marketing, servicing, and support functions for a manufacturer.

Manufacturer-owned outlets run by CompuAdd and Tandy (Radio Shack) market their computers in relatively small company-owned stores (5,000 square feet or less). This permits control over the distribution and selling process and an ability to feature the manufacturer's products without having to share space with competing brands. Also, the manufacturer does not have to rely on intermediaries for sales, servicing, and support functions.

Direct Mail

PC manufacturers marketing through direct mail typically use direct-response advertisements in computer magazines such as *PC Magazine* and *PC World;* direct mailings (catalogs, brochures, etc.); and both inbound and outbound telemarketing to reach prospects and communicate with customers. Firms selling through this channel traditionally have competed on the basis of price and have offered mainstream PCs. Manufacturers using this channel have tended to spend little on research and development. Instead, they have imitated others in their new-product development. This channel attracts the most competition of the four because of how easy it is to enter, given its low initial investment requirements. Unlike distribution through traditional dealers, which have a limited amount of shelf space available, entry into the direct-mail channel requires only a post office box number and/or a telephone number. The PC direct-mail market is growing at about 20 percent annually.

Mass Merchandisers

Until recently, relatively few PCs were sold through mass merchandisers. However, this distribution channel will become dominant in the near future, especially for the household market. The term *mass merchandisers* is a bit misleading because it covers a variety of different types of retailers. For example, this channel encompasses traditional retailers such as Sears, which sells IBM PCs. But it also includes discount stores such as CompUSA and Circuit City, which sell third-tier PC brands, often in a package including preloaded software and peripherals.

Superstores such as CompUSA and Circuit City typically range in size from 25,000 to 50,000 square feet and offer floor-to-ceiling merchandising of PCs and more than 5,000 different computer-related items. These stores operate on the principles of high volume, low prices, and low margins, with minimal service and support. These are retail environments that customers feel comfortable shopping in.

Some direct marketers argue that mass merchandisers will drain off only incremental shoppers, leaving the prime, more technology-savvy buyers where they always were—sticking with direct ordering based on print ads and reviews in PC magazines. But, if mass merchandisers keep capturing the growing consumer market, the effect may be to split the direct business into two branches: commodity products at the low end and sophisticated technology at the high end.

Direct Sales

The direct sales channel is typically used by PC manufacturers trying to reach large businesses and government agencies. It is a relatively expensive channel to operate in because of the costs associated with fielding and supporting a sales force. Its advantages are person-to-person selling and the ability to work closely with customers to solve problems. This channel is decreasing in importance as PCs become more user-friendly, prices decline, and businesses become more computer-literate.

DELL'S MARKETING EFFORT

As a PC manufacturer, Dell competes against both much larger companies, such as IBM and Compaq, and the aggressive low-cost, low-price competitors, such as Northgate and Zeos. Recently Dell was being squeezed from both sides by these firms. Dell has positioned itself as a price and performance leader. However, this positioning had been steadily eroded as a result of price cutting by rivals. Although Dell historically had a 10 to 15 percent price advantage over its more expensive competitors, this advantage has decreased to as little as 8 percent. Simultaneously, the price gap between Dell and its lower priced competitors has increased substantially, with these companies undercutting Dell by as much as 25 percent.

Dell's competitors have also substantially increased their expenditures for advertising and marketing communications, primarily in the form of direct-response print ads in the computer magazines. Although Dell has also increased its media expenditures, its share of spending for advertising and other promotion has declined substantially in recent years.

The direct-response print ads are used to build brand awareness, generate leads, and, often, sell products off the pages of newspapers like *USA Today* and the *Wall Street Journal* (for shorter promotions) and core PC magazines like *PC Week, PC Magazine, PC World* and *Computer Shopper* (for efforts with longer life cycles).

Frequently, the ads are product oriented, comparing Dell with other manufacturers and undercutting the competition's price and support services. Others welcome Compaq and IBM to the direct support fold, implying that these industry elephants are trying to build or emulate the Dell mousetrap. Dell frequently touts J. D. Power & Associates surveys, which have ranked the company number one in the category of end-user satisfaction. Dell's efforts are designed to appeal to second- and third-generation computer owners who are not intimidated by the technology.

The company's catalog *DellWare,* which was established in 1992, mails to 750,000 names six times a year plus special editions. The catalog was designed to encourage repeat purchases, broaden product penetration, and optimize lifetime value. Dell accepts advertising from the other vendors, which makes this catalog self-liquidating. The recent issue featured 100 pages of products and full-page, four-color ads for products from Intel, IBM, Lotus 1-2-3 for Windows, Xerox, Media Vision, Word Perfect, and others.

Orders move from telephone representatives to the manufacturing (or more accurately computer parts assembly) facility. Customers can pick from thousands of possible hardware combinations to satisfy their performance and features requirements. Dell preloads and configures a customer's software at the factory. Upon request, the company stocks third-party hardware and builds it into customers' systems during the assembly of the units. The computers are delivered directly to the customer and are ready to run as soon as they are pulled out of the box.

NEW DIRECTIONS FOR DELL

As Michael Dell begins pondering distribution issues in more detail, he focuses on developing a list of criteria to be taken into account when considering any new channel efforts or alternatives. However, if Dell does institute any new distribution approaches, there is the possibility of channel conflict and cannibalization: any distribution channel could simply divert sales from Dell's current channels with no incremental increase in unit sales. Also, costs and margin structures could potentially be affected by any changes in Dell's distribution strategy.

The alternatives include whether to use more direct mail or other existing marketing tools or to add such vehicles as infomercials and/or radio. What marketing strategies would you recommend to Dell for dealing with the competition and in preparing for the future? What does

Dell Computer Corporation need to do to ensure its differential advantage in the highly competitive and dynamic PC market? What specific distribution, price, promotion, and product mix would you propose and why?

SOURCES

"The Education of Michael Dell." *Business Week,* March 22, 1993, pp. 82–87.

BACHMAN, KATY. "Dell's New Plan." *Direct,* September 1994, pp. 1, 24–25.

BHARGAVA, SUNITA WADEKAR, AND STEPHANIE ANDERSON FOREST. "Computers by Mail: A Megabyte Business Boom." *Business Week,* May 11, 1992, pp. 93–94.

BURROWS, PETER. "The Computer Is in the Mail (Really)." *Business Week,* January 23, 1995, pp. 76–77.

________. "Beyond Rock Bottom." *Business Week,* March 14, 1994, pp. 80–81.

BURROWS, PETER, AND STEPHANIE ANDERSON FOREST. "Dell Computer Goes into the Shop." *Business Week,* July 12, 1993, pp. 138–140.

COLACECCHI, MARY BETH. "Sound Bytes," *Catalog Age,* June 1992, pp. 1, 27.

CYR, DIANE. "System Failure?" *Direct,* November 1993, pp. 1, 59–65.

"Dell Computer Corporation." In *Strategic Marketing Problems,* ed. Roger A. Kerin and Robert A. Peterson. Boston: Allyn & Bacon, 1993, pp. 427–38.

"Dell to Cease Retail Sales." *Direct Marketing,* September 1994, p. 7.

EGOL, LEN. "Mail Order Pivotal in PC Price War." *Direct,* September 1992, pp. 18–19.

Forest, Stephanie Anderson. "PC Slump? What PC Slump?" *Business Week,* July 1, 1991, pp. 66–67.

"How to Buy a Computer." *Consumer Reports,* November 1994, pp. 698–95.

KIRKPATRICK, DAVID. "What's Driving the New PC Shakeout?" *Fortune,* September 19, 1994, pp. 109–22.

MCGRAW, DAN. "The Kid Bytes Back." *U.S. News & World Report,* December 12, 1994, pp. 70–71.

NEAL, MOLLIE. "Dell Takes a Megabyte of the PC Market." *Direct Marketing,* May 1993, pp. 28–30, 79.

Case 5: Dial-A-Mattress

INTRODUCTION

Although it began as a store retailer, Dial-A-Mattress Corporation is the largest direct marketer of mattresses and other home furnishings in the United States today (see Case Exhibit 5.1). It carries Sealy, Simmons, Serta, and Somma; and just recently it began offering Spring Air as a private-label line. Dial-A-Mattress built its $65 million business almost exclusively from direct-response television. While the firm sells to a broad audience of buyers, its primary customers are women 25–44 with household incomes of more than $40,000 a year.

The television ads for Dial-A-Mattress invite interested prospects to phone 1-800-MATTRES ("Leave off the last S for Savings"). These 30-second spots are run on stations during the morning, afternoon, and late-evening hours. While the firm advertises that its merchandise can be bought for 60 percent less than at department store prices, the most important selling point is convenience: hassle-free delivery in two hours.

As the commercial airs and interested buyers pick up the phone, they reach one of 50 telemarketers who asks for the size mattress wanted (twin, regular, queen, or king), tells the caller the price, and determines when delivery can be made within a two-hour time frame. If the caller wants delivery immediately, the order is phoned to a roving driver. If delivery is requested for a later, specific, two-hour time slot, orders are accumulated and given to the appropriate driver attending the area of delivery during the two-hour slot requested. Some 30 percent of new orders come from referrals of satisfied customers.

In 1994, Dial-A-Mattress spent $10 million on direct marketing, some 80 percent of which was on direct-response television, 15 percent on direct-response radio, and 5 percent on direct mail. Sales are directly proportionate to the amount of advertising the company does. It can increase sales at any time of the year, month, or day simply by increasing the amount of advertising it does.

Competitive Pressure

The biggest threat to Dial-A-Mattress's success is competitive pressure. This keeps the firm moving and innovating to stay ahead of all the copycats such as Macy's 1-800-MACY-BEDS.

CASE EXHIBIT 5.1. Dial-A-Mattress Overview

Dial-A-Mattress is the nation's leading bedding telemarketing company. Founded in 1976, this privately owned firm has offices and a 62,000-square-foot warehouse located in Long Island City, New York.

Products: Beds/box springs/mattresses and some home furnishings.

Featuring: Sealy, Serta, and Simmons brands in 30 styles, at prices generally 60 percent lower than retail.

Volume: Sales in 1995 totaled $65 million. Sells approximately 400 units/day at an average price of $450. Inventory turns over 73 times/year.

Traffic: Approximately 35,000 inbound calls per week.

Employees: 180.

Trading Zones: New York, New Jersey, Southern Connecticut, Philadelphia, Boston, Chicago, San Francisco, San Jose, Los Angeles, Miami, and Washington, DC. Distribution by company-owned fleet in New York metro area. Network of 64 retailers covers distribution throughout the United States.

Advertising: Primarily TV (80 percent) and radio. Budget approximately 10 percent of gross revenues.

Principals: Napoleon Barragan, CEO and founder; Joe Vicens, executive vice president and general manager.

Source: Updated from "Barragan Family Sleeps Well at Night," *Direct Marketing,* October 1993, p. 56.

There are 13 others applying the 800 route in New York alone. This mattress idea has also clicked among retailers in other cities not associated with Dial-A-Mattress.

To stay ahead, Dial-A-Mattress intends to pioneer new media in marketing bedding and home furnishings. It has instructed its marketing and media people to seek out new distribution and communications channels and to experiment with evolving forms of media and technology.

Market Operations

Dial-A-Mattress has operations in 10 markets, though the company can deliver anywhere. The trading zones are New York, New Jersey, Pennsylvania, Massachusetts, Connecticut, Chicago, Maryland, Los Angeles, Washington, DC, and Florida. All these areas receive thorough broadcasting coverage with the firm's message.

Orders for other cities are faxed in minutes, with delivery time specified. In cities where there is no retail arrangement, the mattress is sent by Federal Express for next-day delivery at 10:30 AM. Dial-A-Mattress earns a 20 percent commission on each sale it forwards.

BRANCHING OUT

Dial-A-Mattress is looking to branch out from direct-response television into solo and cooperative direct mail and online services. For example, in 1995 it conducted a test in which 250,000 packages were sent to Chicago-area homes shortly before the Presidents' Day weekend. Chicago was chosen because the company had difficulty reaching prospects in that city by phone, even though Chicago customers have a higher conversion-to-sale rate than those in many other Dial-A-Mattress markets.

Going Online

Dial-A-Mattress also "put its toe in the water" with online marketing through contracts with CompuServe and Bloomberg. It earned its investment back five times on Bloomberg and twice on CompuServe. Dial-A-Mattress already has learned from its online experience. At first, its messages were detailed, but it found they did not sell. Someone using a keyboard does not want to spend so much time reading details on the screen. The messages now are simple, similar to Dial-A-Mattress's broadcast commercials, and they use printed-out coupons.

During the first months of 1994, 104 people purchased beds online from Dial-A-Mattress, with an average order of $557, which is higher than the company's overall average order size of $450. Cost per lead ranged from $2.60 to $5.75 and was competitive with television advertising.

Prodigy was added to the online list in 1995. Under the agreement, Dial-A-Mattress conducted a 90-day multimarket regional test to see what the impact of improved graphic interfaces might be on its business. Prodigy's advertising fee is higher than that of other online networks, but the company offers a different customer base and a different creative palette to test Dial-A-Mattress's sales message and approach.

Overall, customers from the online services tend to be almost exclusively male and more upscale than the remainder of Dial-A-Mattress's customer base. For example, customers from Bloomberg's online service earn $150,000 per year and are likely to work in finance, and 98 percent are male. Dial-A-Mattress suspects Prodigy customers would likely be similar, but it is not really sure. However, most home furnishings marketers, as sellers of high-ticket items, have been hampered in their online marketing efforts. Also, the online environment is a risky proposition for bedding products. The problem is that most mattress buyers are women, who are a minority of computer users.

Dial-A-Mattress is testing the Internet waters by launching not one but two sites on the global network. The company's Internet storefronts mirror its commercial online network; the storefronts feature e-mail connecting Dial-A-Mattress, customers, retailers, and manufacturers. The firm made its move on to the Internet because Dial-A-Mattress believes it is important to secure its own corporate name and to put the basic PC technology in place.

Infomercials, Print, and More

In other direct marketing developments, the company has arranged to have a two-minute segment produced for an infomercial test. The infomercial will be shown in New York, Chicago, and Los Angeles. It is designed to acquaint viewers with how the retailer does business and what can be expected upon dialing 1-800-MATTRES.

Direct-response print has been tried and, in the main, rejected because it does not have the immediacy the firm needs and the returns do not justify the costs. The firm is still also testing direct mail. For example, one mailing piece was a double postcard with a special offer time-linked with a six-week window. It included a dollar discount amount, which has historically worked better than percentages. These double postcards were chosen because the company could use them to offer customers a discount coupon they could give to the driver on delivery, which would later be attached to the invoice slip, enabling Dial-A-Mattress to know exactly to whom it was selling.

In conjunction with the direct mailings, Dial-A-Mattress is creating a predictive model from the data on the 500,000 customers it has accumulated. Recognizing the potential of this database, Dial-A-Mattress refined and analyzed the customer information with the objective of determining future customers and profiling the best markets for national expansion.

Dial-A-Mattress also got together with MasterValues, a co-op program developed by MasterCard, to promote its use as a customer's primary credit card. Under the arrangement, Dial-A-Mattress stuffers were inserted into MasterCard bills and included in Sunday newspaper freestanding inserts as part of a promotion for the World Cup soccer tournament. Dial-A-Mattress claims it got half a million dollars in incremental business.

However, it has not all been an easy effort for the retailer. Discussions with the Home Shopping Network and QVC have been complicated because of sales, customer service, and delivery issues that Dial-A-Mattress wants to handle on its own terms.

The company is keeping an open mind about other electronic marketing methods. Dial-A-Mattress is talking to US West about participation in its interactive television trial as well as several vendors of CD-ROM marketing programs. This is an experimental phase, and the company knows that not every new medium will ultimately prove out. But Dial-A-Mattress's challenge is to put its money where its mouth is and to work with online networks, new cable channels, CD-ROM producers, and home shopping networks and find the best results.

NAPOLEON BARRAGAN

Dial-A-Mattress was formed by Napoleon Barragan in the 1970s. The company took off in 1988 when it purchased a toll-free number. That year, with an advertising budget of $314,000, Dial-A-Mattress had $3.2 million in sales. The Equador-born entrepreneur got his big idea in 1976 when he saw an ad in the *New York Post* headlined "Dial-A-Steak." With business being just so-so, he needed a new approach. An idea flashed: Dial-A-Furniture? No, that wouldn't work. But what about mattresses? That might work. Despite the advice of well-meaning friends to forget the crazy idea, Barragan ran an ad in the *New York Daily News* headlined "Dial-A-Mattress," suggesting a telephone call to his regular business number. Three people called, and he was hooked, and on his way.

Barragan became a regular print advertiser until he became curious about television. He got someone to inexpensively produce a commercial, which ran in late-night slots. This, too, was encouraging. Volume picked up. Then, as he moved the commercial around to different time slots on cable stations, sales soared.

Dial-A-Mattress's sales rose to an estimated $65 million in 1994, up from about $41 million in 1993 (see Case Exhibit 5.2). Approximately 60 percent of sales are made with a credit card processed by the truck driver; 40 percent are cash transactions. The firm answers some 35,000 calls a day around the clock and sells some 400 units during that period. Profits on the company's income came to over $6 million in 1994 (see Case Exhibit 5.3).

NEW-PRODUCT DEVELOPMENT

In 1994, Dial-A-Mattress embarked on a private-label venture with Spring Air. The three-model Dial-A-Pedic line "fills in" the product lines the retailer already offers to cover all price points and features. The venture also introduces the Spring Air product by name into the Dial-A-Mattress lineup; the manufacturer's name appears on the Dial-A-Pedic label.

The Dial-A-Pedic line is not positioned as a low-end "house" brand; neither is it positioned at the top of the retailer's lineup, similar to the way Sears has positioned the Sears-O-Pedic, also manufactured by Spring Air. The three Dial-A-Pedic models range from low to medium in price, and they offer features that Dial-A-Mattress customers have requested.

For a long time, Dial-A-Mattress has been surveying its customers and talking to its bedding consultants and telephone salespeople and finding that in spite of all the products available, there still are certain gaps, in terms of both price points and construction of the bed.

One such gap, the surveys found, was the lack of a "seasonal" type of bed with silk on one side and wool on the other. Not surprisingly, the Diamond, Emerald, and Sapphire beds in the

CASE EXHIBIT 5.2. Dial-A-Mattress Sales

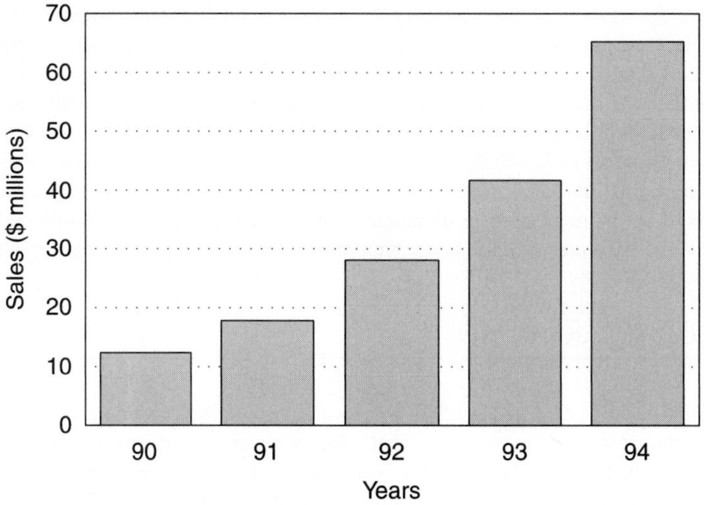

Source: Estimated from various sources.

CASE EXHIBIT 5.3. Dial-A-Mattress Income

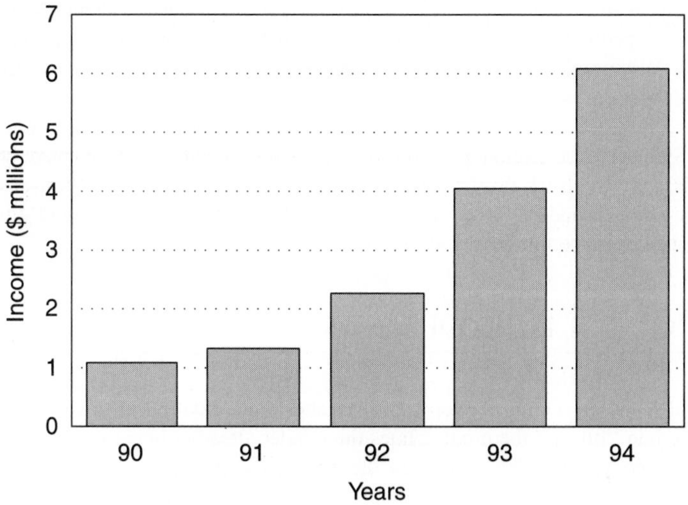

Source: Estimated from various sources.

Dial-A-Pedic line are comparable, though not identical, to Spring Air's flagship Back Supporter line. The Diamond model, marketed as Dial-A-Pedic's "bed for all seasons," is the Dial-A-Mattress version of Spring Air's Four Seasons bed; it also features silk on one side and wool on the other and has been a success nationwide. Similarities between the two lines are exactly what Spring Air and Dial-A-Mattress had in mind when they agreed on the joint venture. The Dial-A-Pedic line is not a "private" label in every sense of the word. It is really Dial-A-Pedic manufactured exclusively by Spring Air. Unlike other private labels, the Spring Air name is on the label. It is identified as the firm's, supported and warranted by Dial-A-Mattress.

What about product lines beyond mattresses? There is potential for related home furnishings, pillows and covers, drapes, and so on. There is already a modest catalog that is dropped off with the mattresses on deliveries now. What about going the whole way and including furniture? That possibility is not being overlooked.

Many of Dial-A-Mattress's ideas come from the reply cards dropped off at delivery time. Questions on the card include the following: What was your most important reason for buying? What part of the service did you like? What did you not like? What other products would you be interested in purchasing by telephone? The answers provide information that is invaluable in improving performance and, equally important, in deciding what to do next. Some of the best testimonials are recycled into commercials. Dial-A-Mattress's in-house television producer will go out with camera in hand and put the raves on tape, and then edit them for a commercial that may include two other raves.

MARKETING TO THE 1990s SHOPPER

Barragan's belief is that in order to be successful you have got to make it as easy as possible for consumers to be your customer. The firm's executives insist that it is the convenience of their method of selling and delivery that is the key element to their success. It is the service, more than the product, that keeps the sales ringing up: customers are getting what they want, when they want it, and without a lot of effort. Consumers want a simple way to buy their beds; that is why they come to Dial-A-Mattress. They can pick up the phone at any time of the day, before the stores open and after they close, and they can get fast delivery.

Getting the Order

Dial-A-Mattress is also successfully dealing with what could be its main obstacle to generating sales: consumer skepticism about buying beds "unseen." What Dial-A-Mattress really sells is the concept of ordering a bed in much the same manner as consumers would order a pizza. It is a new way of buying bedding in which the product really becomes secondary. Dial-A-Mattress sells the service first. In fact, the first thing new bedding consultants learn is how to overcome a customer who is skeptical or needs to see the bed. The key to this lies in the secondary product—the beds. The more knowledge the consultants have, the more confident they feel and the more credible they seem to the caller. What do they say when a customer says he or she needs to see the bed? They establish trust and then they make recommendations.

During new bedding consultants' four weeks of training they learn how to establish trust in the first 30 to 45 seconds of the call. They are taught to follow a tried-and-true formula for selling that consists of four questions:

- Are you using this product for every night or occasional use?
- Have you ever used our service before?
- Do you know how we work?
- Are you looking to buy top-of-the-line or middle-of-the-road?

The answers to these questions, coupled with the consultants' knowledge of different types of bedding, is what Dial-A-Mattress really sells when it gets consumers to order a bed.

This formula is used over and over again in rows of cubicles where salespeople wearing headsets spend six-hour shifts answering calls. While the average retail floor bedding sale takes at least 20 minutes, the average Dial-A-Mattress sale takes less than half that time. It is a much quicker sale, no doubt, and it is much more targeted to what the customer wants.

Delivering the Merchandise

Answering the calls is just one part of the sales process. Delivery is the other. Dial-A-Mattress contracts with small, independent trucking companies to make up their fleet of delivery trucks. They rent out the sides of the trucks, which are painted uniformly with the Dial-A-Mattress logo. These trucks are a powerful advertising tool. Three days each week a certain number of drivers are called in to run a convoy through key parts of the city. This rolling billboard generates calls every time.

Once a bed is ordered, regular delivery takes six hours and costs $20 to $30 depending on the area it is delivered to. About 10 to 15 customers a day take advantage of the company's optional two-hour delivery for an additional fee (on top of the regular delivery fee) of $100. Beds are sold on customer acceptance. Though orders go through three accuracy checkpoints before they are sent out, once in a while they are sent back.

There are various reasons for returns. It could be that the company pulled the wrong merchandise. Or the bedding consultant was wrong in the diagnostic process. But it could be that when the driver got to the house, he could not get the king-size bed up the steps. Then there is a tiny percentage that get damaged. A few beds are sent back because of "ego problems," which happens when a man sees a pink covering on the bed.

THE FUTURE

Consumer buying needs are changing very fast; more and more people want easy ways to shop. Barragan has capitalized on the burgeoning consumer demand for convenience. But, in its continuing quest for more sales and market share and in response to increasing competition, Dial-A-Mattress needs to develop marketing strategies that include direct marketing channels other than just direct-response television. Consider a direct marketing strategy for Dial-A-Mattress that addresses the following areas: How should the consumer market be segmented, and what segment(s) should be targeted? What are the direct marketing strategy alternatives for Dial-A-Mattress outside of its television offerings? What are the pros and cons of those direct marketing strategy alternatives, given their target segment(s) and direct marketing tools. Specifically, how would those strategies operate to expand the business operations of Dial-A-Mattress? Which strategy alternative you would recommend, and why?

SOURCES

"Barragan Family Sleeps Well at Night." *Direct Marketing,* October 1993, pp. 52–57.
FERN, DONNA. "The Uncommon Denominator." *Profit,* 1994, pp. 20–23.
GOLDBLUM, RISA. "Springing to the Top." *Direct,* October 1933, pp. 51–54.
ROBINSON, JULIA. "Dial-A-Mattress Uncovered." *Bedtimes,* September 1994, pp. 8, 31–33, 37–44, 47.

Case 6: Fidelity Investments

INTRODUCTION

When Edward Johnson founded Fidelity Investments in 1946, he had two simple ideas: to help people invest successfully and to offer them the tools they need to do so. Johnson was a strong individualist who admired independence in others. But when it came to investing, he observed that almost everyone needed some help.

These ideas are still the foundation of Fidelity Investments, the largest mutual fund management company in the United States, with $172 billion in assets under management in 1992. The firm believes that, given the right tools, individuals make their own best investment decisions. Fidelity says that its job is to give its customers the practical information they need. Fidelity representatives are trained to help investors ask questions and apply their own intelligence and common sense. They can then try to match the most appropriate investments to the individual customer's needs. And they do not have to worry about sales pressure because Fidelity believes that the investor will make smarter decisions without it.

When it comes to personal investing, Fidelity Investments knows that convenience is a necessity. Customers can do business the way that is easiest for them. They can visit Fidelity Investor Centers in more than 65 cities or phone a Fidelity representative at any hour of any day. Fidelity can even link the customer's personal computer directly to his or her Fidelity account. Fidelity strives to provide the level of service that sets the standard for other firms.

Fidelity is interested in new technology and innovation, especially when it can make investing easier and more efficient. But technology is not enough by itself. The firm stresses that, at Fidelity, it is people, using technology, who give the firm's customers every possible advantage and convenience.

In order to serve all its customers' financial needs, Fidelity wants to become a vast clearinghouse that sells both its own and other firms' financial products, from credit cards to insurance. It has also embarked on a new strategy to be a low-cost personal financial adviser, using its vast telephone and computer network to compete with the banks and brokers that traditionally have filled that role.

Investors come to Fidelity at all stages of life, and with different financial needs. Whatever their situation or goals are, Fidelity hopes to satisfy their investment needs through its family of mutual funds and offerings of individual securities.

People come to investing for their own reasons, with their own feelings and ideas about money. Often the decision to invest is prompted by some event such as a change of job, the birth of a child, or the death of a family member. It could also be something as simple as a news item about market trends or interest rates.

Risk and reward usually go together. In general, the higher an investment's potential for gain, the higher its risk. Lower-risk investments generally offer lower rewards. This is the classic trade-off faced by every investor, novice and experienced alike, and it forms the foundation for each investor's plans, expectations, and evaluations of performance.

Diversification is a way to moderate the risks associated with investing. Diversification means distributing money among several different investments in order to spread out the risk. The more diversified a portfolio, with its greater variety of investments, the less likely it is that the investor will be hurt by the poor performance of a single investment.

For long-term goals, consumers should choose stocks and growth funds. Historically, the stock market has been unpredictable in the short term, but over the long term, stocks have outperformed bond and money-market investments. Over the past 20 years, the S&P 500 (a group of 500 stocks) has averaged returns of approximately 11 percent each year (including reinvested dividends). That return outpaces corporate and government bonds, money-market investments, and the inflation rate. That is why, if investors have a sufficient time frame, they should consider investing at least a portion of their money in stock investments. Of course, their investment decisions will be affected not only by how soon they will need the money but also by their personal situation and tolerance for risk.

Investing regularly is a strategy that works over time. By investing the same dollar amount in a certain mutual fund or stock every month or every quarter, consumers can avoid buying all their shares at a market high, and take advantage of "dollar-cost averaging."

TYPES OF INVESTMENTS

Investment types are divided into three broad categories: growth, income, and money market. Each represents a different investment objective, with its own set of risks and rewards. To be well diversified, an investor's portfolio should include some combination of all three types. Within each category, these investments may include individual securities, mutual funds, or both. Ideally, diversification means that no matter what happens in the market, the consumer has at least one type of investment that will perform relatively well.

Money Market (Low Risk/Low Return)

Money-market investments are considered the lowest risk of all. While they do not offer the most potential for growth, they do provide regular interest or dividends, and they are designed to safeguard the investor's principal. Examples include money-market funds, federal and state tax-free money-market funds, certificates of deposit, and Treasury bills.

Money-market funds have a variety of uses. They can serve as a "safe haven" for money while it earns current interest rates, or they can add stability and balance to a growth-oriented portfolio. They can function as an interim investment while an investor is searching for the right growth or income opportunity. And, because many money-market funds offer check writing, some people use them as a reserve for cash or as an additional checking account.

Some money-market funds invest only in U.S. government securities for the additional margin of safety they provide. Other funds offer income that is free from federal taxes, and in some cases state and local taxes as well. Money-market funds are not insured or guaranteed by the U.S. government.

Income (Moderate Risk/Moderate Return)

Income investments, which include bonds and bond funds, pay regular dividend income. The values of income fund shares and individual bonds will change depending on market conditions, particularly changes in interest rates. As a trade-off for accepting these price fluctuations, income investments generally offer higher yields than money-market investments. Examples include individual bonds, global bond funds, corporate bond funds, federal and state tax-free bond funds, and government bond funds.

Growth (High Risk/High Return)

In the long run, growth investments such as stocks, and the mutual funds that invest in them, have the potential to outperform both income and money-market investments. While some stocks and growth funds offer regular income, in general the objective is to increase the value of an investment over time. Stock prices and growth fund share prices usually are subject to wider fluctuations than those of income or money-market investments. Examples of these instruments includes stocks, sector funds, international growth funds, growth funds, and growth and income funds.

Mutual funds pool investors' money and buy stocks, bonds, or money-market securities. As of January 1993, total mutual-fund assets in the United States were $1.6 trillion, compared to less than $50 billion in 1977. With these funds, individual investors get greater diversification, less risk, lower transaction costs, and far more professional management than they could achieve on their own.

The power of mutual funds is most obvious in their impact on the stock market. Over the 1990 through 1992 period, mutual funds put more than $300 billion into equities, giving a huge lift to stock prices. As funds increase in size, mutual-fund management firms such as Dreyfus, Fidelity Investments, and the Vanguard Group Inc. will increase their power over U.S. businesses. In the past few years, mutual funds have had a particularly strong influence on emerging growth companies. Mutual funds are also gaining ground on pension funds, which now control nearly twice as many financial assets as mutual funds.

FIDELITY INVESTMENTS

As the largest mutual-fund company in America, Fidelity Investments is also one of the biggest success stories in the industry. In 1991, the firm posted record revenues of $1.5 billion, up 16 percent from a year earlier, and record profits of $90 million, up 182 percent. Fidelity believes that the key to maintaining or even accelerating the company's growth is redefining its relationship with its customers. In the 1990s, investors want more guidance. By helping them solve specific problems, such as how to save enough for retirement or education, Fidelity will win more of their assets and handle more of their transactions.

Fidelity's products and customer service are the keys to its success. Fidelity's portfolio managers have at their disposal every necessary resource for investment decision making and research for their customers. Customers especially value the firm's full-service approach. Fidelity's philosophy of participant satisfaction has resulted in happy customers and increased business.

Fidelity Investments and its competitor Vanguard dominate the list of the top U.S. equity funds. Fidelity has 4 funds in the top 10, while Vanguard has 5. Fidelity's stock funds command 17.5 percent of all equity-fund assets.

As one of the most active stock-pickers around, Fidelity has turned in more than a decade's worth of good results. Investors have put ever-larger sums into Fidelity funds. Fidelity's reputation owes much to just one fund, the Magellan Equity Fund. Thanks to a run of inspired stock-picking, Magellan led the U.S. 10-year fund-performance rankings for most of the 1980s. The Magellan fund now has assets of $37 billion. Measured against suitable benchmarks, most Fidelity funds have turned in above-average performances.

But Fidelity's successes go far beyond Magellan. The average cumulative return for its diversified U.S. equity funds over the past 10 years is 407.7 percent. Excluding Magellan, the figure drops only slightly, to 403.5 percent. Among the companies managing the most equity fund assets, the closest to Fidelity is Twentieth Century Investors, with 375.7 percent. Although Fidelity's funds have trailed a few rivals in the past year, they have a commanding lead over the most recent three- and five-year periods.

FIDELITY INVESTMENT'S DIRECT-RESPONSE ADVERTISING

For all of Fidelity's investment savvy, technological prowess, and financial clout, the firm still depends on the willingness of investors to entrust it with their savings. Some attribute Fidelity's ability to continually attract new investors not to its stock-picking skills but to smart marketing, particularly its estimated $80 million advertising budget, which is the largest in the industry.

Fidelity is especially strong in direct-response print advertising. Its ads can be found in such publications as *Business Week, Forbes, Fortune,* and *U.S. News & World Report.*

Fidelity also makes heavy use of direct mail to solicit business and to keep in contact with its customers. If a consumer calls the telephone number in one of Fidelity's print ads, he or she will be sent a packet of information about the fund described in the ad.

Fidelity also offers a catalog of its investment offerings. This piece is extensive and provides detailed information about the firm and its individual offerings.

Although Fidelity funds are mainly sold directly to investors by phone and investor centers, the company's Fidelity Advisor funds are now sold by banks, brokerage firms, and financial planners.

DOING BUSINESS WITH FIDELITY

At Fidelity, customers can do business by phone, in person, by mail, or via their PC. They can choose whatever method is most convenient for them at the time. Thus, it's easy to open a new account, add to an existing one, or take money out of an account whenever it's needed. And customers can move money from one Fidelity fund to another with a single toll-free telephone call.

By Phone or in Person

Account balances, quotes, and transactions are just a touch-tone telephone call away. Fidelity provides access to customer automated information lines, which is the fastest way to get basic information. Customers can get mutual fund and stock quotes, account balances, and make exchanges all with privacy and security, and usually in half the time it takes to talk with a representative.

Fidelity Brokerage customers can use TouchTone Trader to place and review stock, option, and mutual fund orders, and get quotes and account balances. It is quick and easy, and the customer saves an additional 10 percent off Fidelity's already discounted brokerage commissions. Representatives are available 24 hours a day, 365 days a year, to help with choosing appropriate investments, opening an account, answering questions about a customer's account or statement, or discussing any of Fidelity's services.

Customers can make an appointment to review their investments in person with a Fidelity representative at an Investor Center. Fidelity representatives will review the customer's personal investment goals and objectives and assist him or her with any Fidelity investments or services. The customer can also stop by to pick up product information, sign up for a free educational Investor Seminar, open a new brokerage or mutual fund account, or make additional investments.

By Mail

Some customers may find doing business by mail the most convenient way to open their first Fidelity account, send additional investments, or request redemptions. Within 24 hours of receiving the customer's request for transactions, a confirmation statement will be on its way to the customer.

By Personal Computer

Customers can transfer money from their bank account to their Fidelity account electronically through "Fidelity Money Line." Fidelity Automatic Account Builder lets them use Money Line to invest $100 or more on a regular schedule. Fidelity On-line Xpress (FOX) is a comprehensive personal computer (PC) investment software package that gives Fidelity customers direct access to the financial markets through a PC. FOX enables customers to trade stocks, options, and mutual funds, obtain real-time quotes, monitor their Fidelity accounts, manage their portfolio, and perform research and analysis—all by using an IBM-compatible PC. Plus, they save an additional 10 percent off already discounted brokerage commissions.

FIDELITY INVESTMENT'S CUSTOMERS

Traditionally, investors have been successful white-collar professionals. However, there are new individual investors, including working women and younger baby boomers who are saving for their children's education, for retirement, or a first home. Former bank customers are also moving away from the low rates offered by bank CDs and passbook accounts. All these relative novices are purchasing stocks, bonds, and tax-exempt securities in a quest for high returns. Most are investing in equity funds (73 percent), while only 31 percent own fixed-income mutual funds.

FIDELITY INVESTMENT'S FUTURE

As the market leader in mutual funds, Fidelity faces challenges from a series of financially strong and sophisticated competitors. For example, with most firms offering easy investing with a mutual-fund family, investors can choose among a dozen or more funds, switch money from one to another by telephone, and track the progress of their holdings on a single quarterly statement.

Most major firms also offer customers the ability to choose among many types of funds. For example, all five of the big discount brokers, including Fidelity Investments, Charles

Schwab, Muriel Siebert, Waterhouse Securities, and Jack White, offer no-cost plans that let investors choose among as many as 300 no-load funds from 43 different fund companies as if they were all part of the same big family. To participate in any of the plans, all investors have to do is open a regular brokerage account at one of the firms. The account can be used to trade stocks and bonds as well as to hold mutual funds. While the firms' programs do have their differences, they are very similar in most respects.

Given this degree of similarly, Fidelity faces a marketing challenge in its quest to remain the market leader. It must use all the resources at its disposal in its effort to build and maintain a strong customer base and to attract new customers to its family of funds and other services. What direct marketing strategies would you recommend to Fidelity Investments for dealing with increasing levels of competition and in preparing for the future? What does Fidelity's mutual funds group need to do to ensure a differential advantage in the highly competitive and dynamic mutual fund investment market? What specific price, distribution, promotion, and product mix would you propose and why?

SOURCES

BEMOWSKI, KAREN. "The Secret to Fidelity's Success." *Quality Progress,* June 1993, pp. 25–28.

CHURBUCK, DAVID. "Watch Out, Citicorp." *Forbes,* September 16, 1991, pp. 38–40.

CLOWES, MICHAEL J. "Fidelity Wins 401(k) Sweepstakes." *Pensions & Investments,* August 3, 1992, p. 17.

EINHORN, BRUCE. "Fidelity Knows What It Likes: Lowbrow Art." *Business Week,* November 22, 1993, p. 74.

"Fidelity Changes Tack." *Economist,* August 8, 1992, pp. 67–68.

Fidelity Investments promotional materials.

"Fidelity Management Call Center Networks ACDs Nationwide." *Communications News,* September 1993, pp. 24–25.

"Fidelity, Vanguard Lead in Most-Used Funds." *Pensions & Investments,* February 8, 1993, pp. 17, 23.

GROVER, MARY BETH. "Betting on the House." *Forbes,* September 13, 1993, pp. 253–54.

KUTZ, KAREN. "Fidelity Investments: More Than Just Mutual Funds." *Pension World,* December 1988, pp. 38–40.

LADERMAN, JEFFREY M. "The Power of Mutual Funds." *Business Week,* January 18, 1993, pp. 62–68.

MAHAR, MAGGIE. "The New Investors." *Barron's,* August 30, 1993, pp. 8–9.

O'CONNELL, VANESSA. "A Great Way to Shop for Funds." *Money,* February 1994, pp. 150–56.

SIMMERMAN, SCOTT J. "Achieving Service Quality Improvements." *Quality Progress,* November 1993, pp. 47–50.

SMITH, GEOFFREY. "Inside Fidelity." *Business Week,* October 10, 1994, pp. 88–96.

________. "What's Behind Fidelity's Riveting Results." *Business Week,* November 22, 1993, pp. 114–15.

________. "Fidelity Jumps Feet First into the Fray." *Business Week,* May 25, 1992, pp. 104–6.

WEISEND, TOM. "Mutual Opportunity." *Adweek,* January 31, 1994, pp. 1, 7.

Case 7: The Franklin Mint

INTRODUCTION

In 1993, the sales of collectibles in the United States totaled about $1.8 billion, up some 33 percent from 1989. The most popular product lines in this category are dolls, plates, and figurines. However, collectibles are becoming much more diverse, with major offerings from nearly all markets, including jewelry.

Spending on advertising for collectibles has grown also. The industry spent about $500 million in 1993. The category helped many women's magazines during the recession. Instead of cutting back, as so many magazine advertisers did in those years, collectible marketers started investing more.

The direct-response end of the collectible industry is made up of five major players: the Franklin Mint, the Danbury Mint, the Bradford Exchange, Lenox, and Stanhome (see Case Table 7.1). The Franklin Mint leads the category with about $610 million in 1993 sales, which is significantly up from about $490 million in 1989 (see Case Exhibit 7.1). Overall, the Franklin Mint spent about $100 million on advertising. One of the largest competitors of the Franklin Mint is the Danbury Mint, whose revenues increased from $25 million a year in the mid-1970s to more than $325 million in 1993. The Danbury Mint copies everything that the Franklin Mint produces but claims to do it better, quicker, and in a much cheaper way. The Bradford Exchange, another major Franklin Mint competitor, makes and sells collector plates decorated with popular themes. Bradford's 1993 revenues were $280 million. In its high-pressure advertisements and mail-order promotions, Bradford sells its plates as investment items.

THE FRANKLIN MINT

The Franklin Mint is a subsidiary of Roll International Corporation, a privately held diversified corporation with a network of luxury products and services. Roll International was ranked in the *Forbes* 1993 listing of the top 400 privately held companies in the United States.

CASE TABLE 7.1. Major Competitors and Estimated 1993 Sales in the Collectibles Market*

Firm	1993 Sales in Millions
The Franklin Mint	$610
The Danbury Mint	325
The Bradford Exchange	280
Lenox	165
Stanhome	111

*Note: Only firm sales from collectibles are listed.
Source: Estimated from various sources.

CASE EXHIBIT 7.1. Franklin Mint Sales

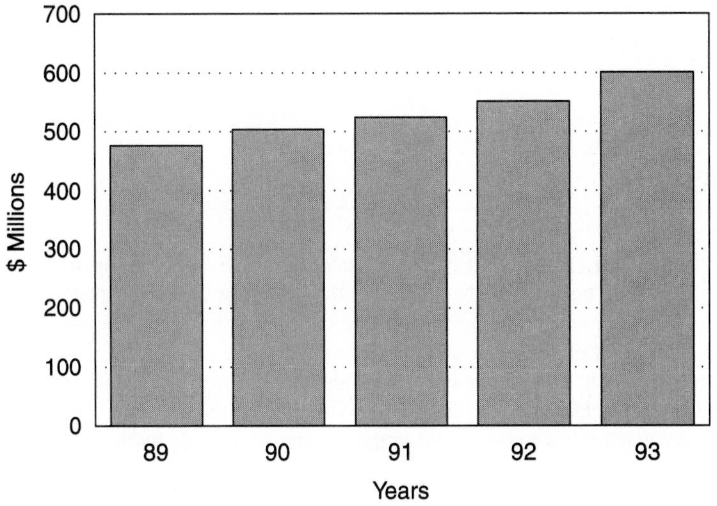

Source: Estimated from various sources.

The Franklin Mint operates in 20 countries on four continents, with more than 4,000 employees worldwide; 1,500 are based in Pennsylvania. Stewart and Lynda Resnick, co-owners of Roll International, serve as the Franklin Mint's chairperson and vice chairperson, respectively. The president of the Mint is Tom Durovsik.

The people who work at the Franklin Mint are on the cutting edge of their professions. Their talent and experience are given free rein, and their inquisitive minds are given every opportunity to explore new ideas, new horizons. This atmosphere attracts men and women of skill and dedication. The Franklin Mint's creative staff includes many fine advertising professionals—artists, copywriters, and photographers who are masters at communicating not just the nature of a new product but its importance as well.

All of the Franklin Mint's products are marketed and distributed directly and exclusively by the Franklin Mint. In a 1993 listing of the top 100 brand advertisers, the Franklin Mint ranked 46th in advertising spending.

The Franklin Mint works closely with world-renowned museums, associations, companies, and individuals, all of which sponsor and authenticate the company's products. Among the more than 300 organizations affiliated with the Mint are the Vatican, the Louvre and the Prado museums, the National Wildlife Federation, the World Wildlife Fund, Paramount, Metro-Goldwyn-Mayer, the Walt Disney Company, McDonald's, and Coca-Cola.

The Mint is the world's leading creator of fine-quality collectibles and personal luxury products and one of the world's largest direct-response marketers. It brings works of artistic beauty and historical significance to about 10 million collectors around the globe. The Mint creates originally designed, upscale home decor and luxury products, in addition to its treasured collectibles. Full-service in-house design studios are found in the firm's U.S. headquarters and in its London office. It claims that its mission is to offer works of beauty in a diverse range of artistic media and genres that can be displayed and enjoyed today, and passed on with pride to future generations.

The Mint's major product lines include sculpture, Franklin Mint Heirloom Dolls (porcelain collector dolls), fashion and traditional jewelry, Franklin Mint Precision Models (production die-cast car, truck, and motorcycle replicas), home decor accessories, collector plates, numismatics, and historic and artistic arms reproductions. All products are marketed and distributed directly and exclusively by the Mint.

The Mint reaches people in their own homes with personally addressed announcements delivered right to their doors; with full-color presentations in the most prestigious publications; on national television; and with the most widely circulated collector's magazine in the world today: *The Franklin Mint Almanac,* with more than a million readers of every issue.

The Franklin Mint's range of products is unmatched by competitors. The Mint is involved in arts as diverse as bookbinding, crystal sculpture, minting, enameling, engraving, dollmaking, woodcarving, cabinetry, clockmaking, and revitalizing. Much of the Franklin Mint's work involves the creation of commemorative art for governments around the world, major museums, and prestigious organizations on six continents.

CONSUMERS OF COLLECTIBLES

Buyers of consumer collectibles are primarily women ages 30 to 60 with above-average incomes. These customers believe that the joy of art collecting is not just possessing the object but also knowing about the object and sharing that knowledge. This becomes a form of self-education and a way of socializing.

THE FRANKLIN MINT MARKETING EFFORTS

Direct response is the Franklin Mint's main marketing tool. It offers items that, in conjunction with a sponsor's already fine name, creates interest among collectors. A typical offering includes a product backed by the name of the Franklin Mint, along with its sponsor's official issue acknowledgment. Installment terms are available to customers in order to make an offer more obtainable. The Franklin Mint's ads emphasize that its items are made of quality components, hand-painted with gold, trimmed in the finest lace, or limited in quantity (to stimulate sales).

Half of the Franklin Mint's customer base of about 10 million is in the United States, and the other half is located in other countries.

Case Table 7.2 shows a breakdown of the overall 1992 advertising expenditures of Roll International, the parent company of the Franklin Mint, Teleflora Flower Delivery, and Paramount Farms. An estimated 90 percent of those expenditures are for the Franklin Mint.

Direct-Response Print

The Franklin Mint is especially strong in direct-response print advertising. Its ads can be found in such publications as *TV Guide, Parade Magazine, McCall's,* and others. Case Exhibit 7.2 provides examples.

CASE TABLE 7.2. Roll International 1992 U.S. Advertising Expenditures*

Media	1993 Expenditures (in Millions)
Magazine	$ 40,537
Sunday magazine	62,555
Newspaper	3,131
National newspaper	28
Outdoor	2
Spot TV	9
Network radio	169
Total	106,431

*Note: Figures show spending for all Roll International divisions.
Source: Advertising Age, September 29, 1993, p. 59.

Direct-Response Television and Radio

The Franklin Mint also uses direct-response television and radio advertising for selected items in its product line.

Direct Mail

Direct mail also plays a prominent role in the Mint's marketing activities. Once on the firm's mailing list, consumers receive colorful, well-designed catalogs.

THE FRANKLIN MINT'S FUTURE

In considering the Franklin Mint's current marketing approach, there are two areas to focus on: (1) the mix of the Franklin Mint's program elements and themes and how they appeal to those who already own collectibles and, perhaps, to those who do not have any collectibles and (2) the product line and how it is kept interesting to those who are exposed to the Franklin Mint's advertising. The right product mix is critical. Recent Franklin Mint offerings show a proliferation of items and price points.

The critical questions for the Franklin Mint, and its competitors, revolve around direct marketing issues: how to develop and keep a differential advantage in a highly competitive and dynamic market, while maintaining sales growth and, above all, profitability. With the changing nature of the collectibles industry, increased competition, and the fickle nature of customer preferences, the Franklin Mint faces many challenges.

Consumer buying needs are changing very fast, as are the ways people want to shop. The Franklin Mint has capitalized on the burgeoning consumer demand for collectibles, but, in its continuing quest for more sales and market share and in response to increasing competition, the Mint needs to develop new direct marketing strategies that include a more varied set of approaches. The Mint must address the following questions: How should the consumer market be segmented, and what segment(s) should be targeted? What are the direct marketing strategy alternatives for the Mint? What are the pros and cons of those direct marketing strategy alternatives, given the target segment(s) and direct marketing tools? Specifically how would these strategies operate to expand the business operations of the Mint? Which strategy alternative is best, and why?

CASE EXHIBIT 7.2. Sample Franklin Mint Advertising

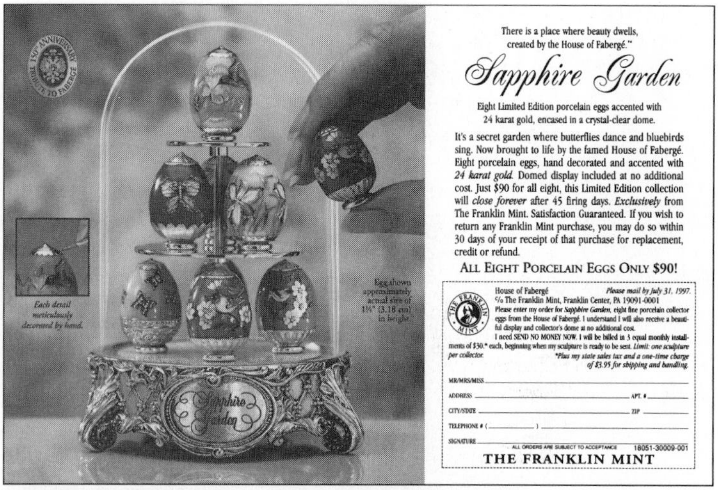

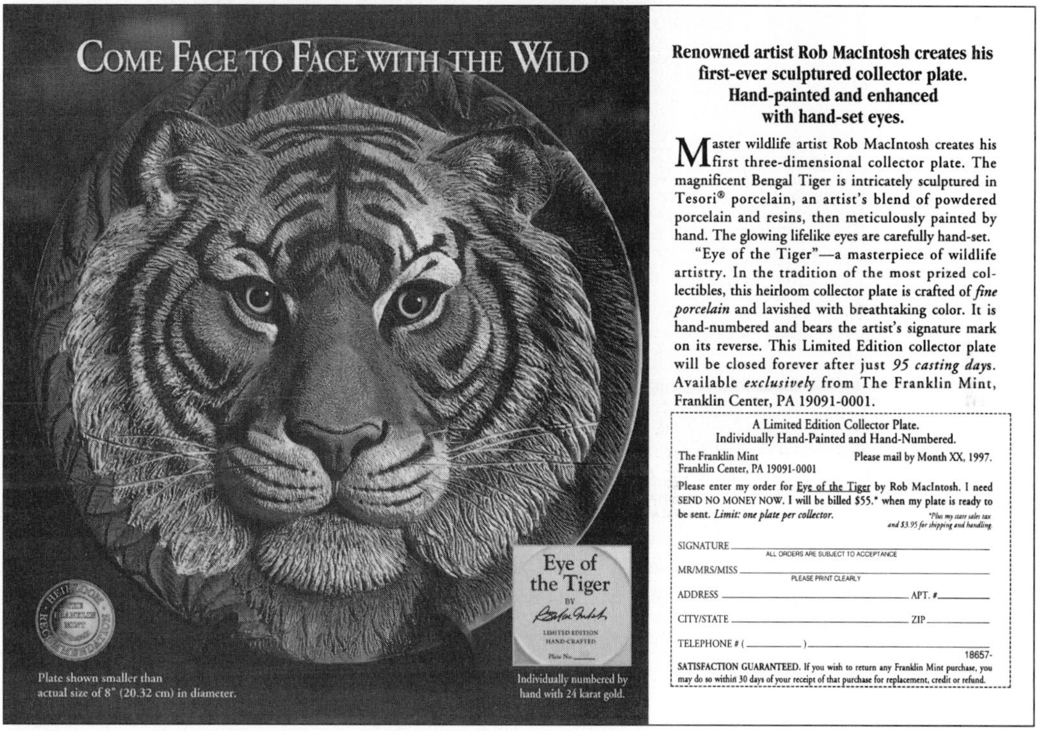

NEXT STEPS FOR THE FRANKLIN MINT

The Mint is concerned about the shifting nature of consumer demand, particularly because today's shopper is becoming increasingly value conscious. While customers have a taste for quality, they expect low prices too. In addition, the level of competition is increasing daily. What

CASE EXHIBIT 7.2. *Continued*

direct marketing efforts would you recommend to the Mint? Who would be the target market? What range of products would be sold, and how would those products be offered? What other specific price, distribution, promotion, and product mix strategies and tactics would you propose, and why?

SOURCES

Advertising Age, September 29, 1993, p. 59.
Leading National Advertisers, 1992.
The Franklin Mint 1993 annual report.

Case 8: The Home Shopping Network[1]

INTRODUCTION

In the summer of 1995, the Home Shopping Network (HSN) convened a senior management team to assess the impact that emerging competition from new television shopping channels would have on the future of the firm. This team of HSN's best planners and operations managers, dubbed the "S-Team," was instructed to pay particular attention to the expected nature of shopping in the next 10 to 20 years and strategies for reacting to any forecasts of changes that would seriously affect HSN.

The S-Team worked for several months and produced a list of scenarios, which top HSN management reviewed and ranked according to whether the scenario posed a major threat to HSN's future. High on that list was a scenario in which the amount of competition would increase significantly on new and existing broadcast and cable channels.

Perhaps early in the next century, millions of people will shop interactively: calling up products on their television screens, examining items via remote control, trying out features, even fitting clothes onto electronic mannequins that match the viewer's size and shape. All that is very unlike television shopping today, which is not very interactive. Today, when viewers see an item on the screen, they must still call a live operator or automated order-taking system, place an order, and wait for delivery.

Television shoppers of the future may be treated to a bounty of products, from underwear to sofa beds. Several major retailers, including Macy's and Nordstrom, have already announced plans for televised shopping services. However, the fare of most televised-shopping channels today is the same as it has been for years: collectibles, clothing, electronics, housewares, and jewelry, jewelry, and jewelry.

A Changing Industry

Televised shopping has already changed over the last 15 years. When HSN, the first television retailer, started in Florida in 1977, it mainly sold factory overruns and discontinued items. Now, it and QVC, the other major home shopping network, operate more like traditional retailers and offer many of the same types of products and service policies. Both networks have liberal return policies, including up to 30 days after the buyer receives the item, and money-back guarantees. Both accept most major credit cards and their own cards. They also offer installment plans for more expensive purchases.

Like other merchants, these shopping networks try to hook consumers by offering exclusive lines of merchandise. If you yearn for Vanna White's shoes or covet Ivana Trump's sweaters, you will have to buy them from HSN. QVC sells private-label fashions by designers Susan Graver and Randolph Duke. Aside from their appeal to viewers, another reason that exclusive lines and private labels are so popular with television retailers is that viewers cannot comparison shop.

Just like conventional retailers, HSN and QVC are striving hard to reach new consumers. QVC's second channel, Q2, targets a younger, fitter, more sophisticated audience. On its main channel, QVC constantly experiments with new products designed to raise viewer interest. These range from Star Trek memorabilia to Barbara Streisand concert souvenirs. HSN now produces three television shows. Home Shopping Club 1 and Home Shopping Club 2 offer the same mix of merchandise but at different times. Its third new show, Spree, offers leftovers and goods in quantities too small to sell on the other channels. HSN also has printed catalogs and walk-in close-out centers.

These formulas must be working; the two largest networks alone sell nearly \$2.5 billion worth of merchandise a year. Overall, by the end of 1994, industry home shopping sales were about \$3 billion, with HSN accounting for about 47 percent of that amount. Case Exhibits 8.1 and 8.2 show that HSN's sales revenue reached \$1.2 billion in 1994, of which over \$60 million was net income. Of the estimated 5 million HSN member households, 85 percent of the members are female, with an average age of 35 to 54.

Hundreds of Channels

Many experts are talking about a future with hundreds of channels in every home. Not only will this proliferation of channels change viewer habits, it also presents reasons why televised shopping will become a dominant direct marketing medium.

What kind of programming would fill up a system with hundreds of channels? It is clear that broad-based, advertiser-supported programming will only be a small part of it. Cable systems will carry many services, such as banking, pay-per-view offerings, and home shopping. As television audiences become fragmented, there will be more opportunities for shopping channels to target smaller and smaller groups of consumers. Television schedules and channels will become obsolete as empowered consumers use menu-driven screens to decide both what and when they want to watch. This large-channel cable universe will also open much more time for direct-response advertisers, infomercials, and interactive home shopping channels.

However, not everyone believes the universe of home shopping viewers can be expanded. Some believe that there is a certain small segment of the population to which this marketing approach is very entertaining, and HSN and QVC have pretty much tapped them out. They are skeptical that a more entertaining approach will draw new shoppers. Rather, they speculate that a world with hundreds of channels could allow the repeated broadcasting of a very defined segment of merchandise. Channel 440 might be upscale menswear. Channel 323 could be camping equipment. Taped segments could be changed weekly.

Nevertheless, the scenario about expanding competition based on changes in technology is of particular concern to HSN because it could have a major influence on all aspects of retailing in America, directly affecting the nature of consumer demand for stores, catalogs, and televised shopping. The consumer lifestyles serviced by these retailers represent product and service consumption patterns, and as technology changes, so too will purchasing patterns.

Home shopping has to overcome two obstacles before it can expand its reach. Limited product selection is the first barrier. There are people with above-average income levels who are interested in home shopping, but they are not seeing what they want to buy on existing channels.

CASE EXHIBIT 8.1. HSN Annual Sales

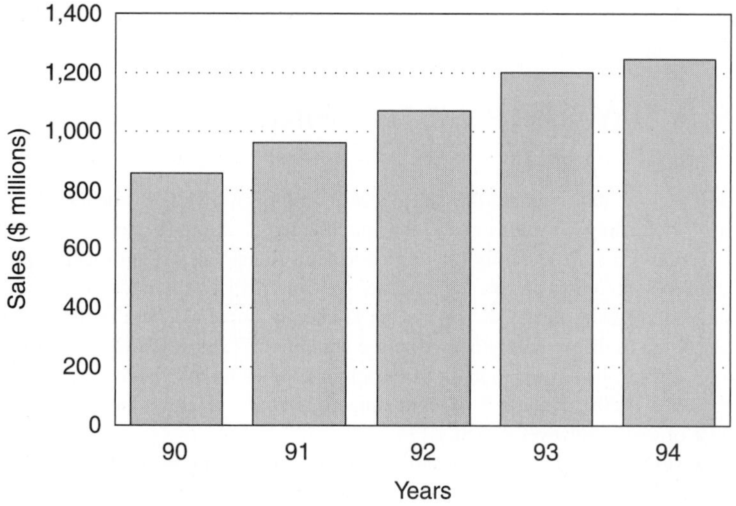

Source: Estimated from various sources.

CASE EXHIBIT 8.2. HSN Annual Income

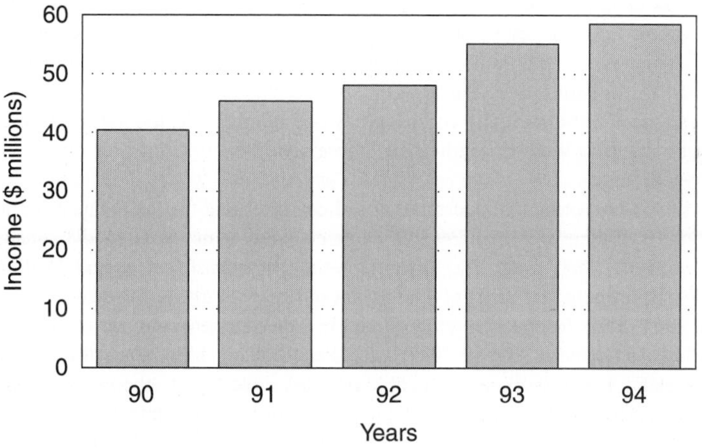

Source: Estimated from various sources.

By providing varied and more selective merchandise across multiple channels, the shopping networks can increase penetration in more consumer markets. Consumer impatience is the second barrier; most people do not sit for hours in front of the television to shop. An answer is interactive shopping that gives consumers instant access to specific merchandise.

The Report

After receiving the approved list of scenarios from HSN's top management, the S-Team set about expanding on each one by developing an in-depth analysis of the threat, its current manifestations, and a description of attempts by HSN and competitors to deal with similar events. Below is a summary of what the S-Team wrote about the scenario involving increased competition, the changing nature of shopping, and shopping-related technologies.

THE EARLY DAYS OF HOME SHOPPING TV

In television's early days, about the only direct selling was for a kitchen device called Veg-o-Matic. According to the fast-talking pitchmen, it would perform any number of miraculous operations such as deftly making paper-thin tomato slices, corrugating potatoes for French frying, or shredding carrots to be squeezed for fresh carrot juice. Unfortunately, the Veg-o-Matic did not work nearly as well in the kitchen at home as it did in the one on TV.

But a new era in direct sales emerged in the summer of 1985 when HSN, which started as a radio merchandiser, began a national live program over cable television stations, 24 hours a day. In the early 1980s, a number of companies attempted to enter the televised shopping market. Most of them, however, failed.

The new HSN was a prototype for today's shows. The selling techniques resembled those used by carnival barkers rather than normal television commercials, including hosts with names like Budget Bob. They endlessly pushed such glitzy merchandise as $13.95 Taiwanese cubic zirconium "diamond" earrings and Milanese 18-karat gold necklaces. These products became household items in the United States and came to symbolize the early days of home shopping.

In the 1980s, earrings accounted for one-fifth of HSN sales, and gold chains sold so well that the network claimed to be the nation's largest importer of that quality of gold. Other popular items were rabbit fur coats, close-out Christmas ornaments (sold in January), and a $129 cat scratcher. Customers were high-pressured and told that they had only 10 minutes to take advantage of "the opportunity of a lifetime."

Viewers placed their orders by calling a toll-free number and joining the Home Shopping Club. Most transactions were by credit card. There were also drawings for prizes or "cash" to buy displayed products.

Given such a hot, profitable operation, it did not take long for the competition to move in. By the end of 1986, there were five 24-hour cable channels with a combined audience of nearly 40 million viewers. There were also seven part-time broadcast, cable, and satellite channels claiming 87 million potential viewers. Noting these figures, large U.S. retailers jumped on the bandwagon early. Sears Roebuck announced late in 1986 that it would sell products on QVC to some 8 million subscribers. And in 1987, J. C. Penney Co., the nation's third largest general merchandise chain, began working on a cable network advertising scheme that enabled buyers to push telephone buttons to order merchandise displayed on their television screens.

By 1989, there were three major competitors in the home shopping business; QVC Network, CVN, and HSN. But in mid-1989, HSN posted its first quarterly loss since it went public in 1986. Company representatives attributed this decline to higher administrative costs and fees from a legal squabble with the GTE corporation.

Spurred by this reverse in fortunes, HSN altered its overall marketing strategy. While QVC continued to offer more sophisticated selling techniques and products, HSN continued the hucksterish carnival approach that accounted for its double- and triple-digit sales gains over the past several years. CVN also followed this technique, but in a less aggressive mode. But there were signs that the segment of middle-aged, middle-income women who responded to this approach was becoming saturated with the jewelry and collectible products that formed the core of HSN's merchandising. Realizing that it needed to penetrate other types of homes, HSN began to feature such items as VCRs, CD players, and computers. But the demand just was not there, and the network pulled the new items off after only a few weeks.

CASE EXHIBIT 8.3. 1994 Home Shopping Channel Market Shares

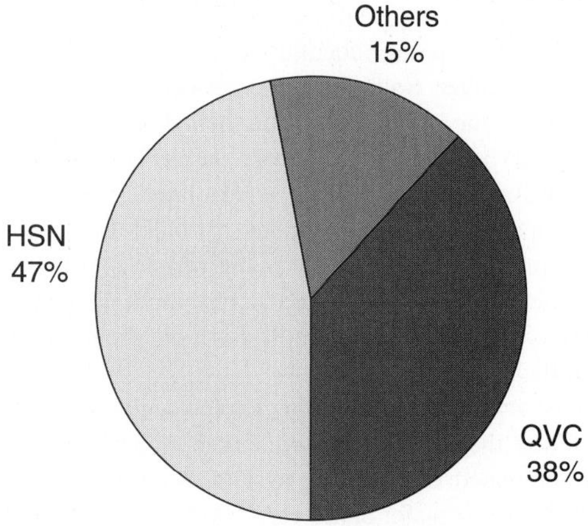

Source: Estimated from various sources.

QVC used a more highly refined approach that attracted a number of different market segments rather than the single group HSN was courting. Instead of offering the endless chain of unrelated products, QVC separated its programming into individual blocks. For example, one hour featured home furnishings; another showed toys; and a third, clothing. Periodically, future segments were flashed on the screen, and product times were listed in some cable guides. The presentations were more low-key. Instead of the pushy promoter, a host or hostess seated comfortably in a living room or a kitchen gave demonstrations of products or showed the quality features of, say, a lamp. Often, the segments featured short talks about how products might be used. In one of these, a camcorder was shown filming valuable possessions for insurance purposes.

By the beginning of 1995, almost 14 years after television home shopping first appeared, the industry settled into a stable pattern. Retailers discarded their early fears that this form of selling would cut deeply into store shopping. The dollar value of shop-at-home television amounted to roughly $3 billion, a small fraction of total retail sales. Most television shopping shows ran on cable, appealed to limited audiences, and pushed low-priced, bargain-basement goods. HSN and QVC still dominated the medium (see Case Exhibit 8.3).

THE SHOPPING EXPERIENCE

For viewers tuning in for the first time, what is most striking about television shopping is the seemingly endless parade of jewelry. In fact, jewelry makes up about 41 percent of all merchandise sold on home shopping television. One reason is that it is often an impulse buy. Another is that it shows up well on the screen. And finally, it can yield higher profits than many other types of goods. Aside from jewelry, hot products include clothing, small appliances, bedding, and collectibles.

Television shopping also offers an element of entertainment, supplied by the show's affable, accessible hosts. Not only can they point out all the details of a product, but they are also quite willing to share their private lives, from their latest vacations to the results of their pregnancy sonograms.

Testimonials from viewers are another big part of the television sell. The shopping channels maintain that all testimonials are unsolicited and spontaneous. When people call from Arkansas or Washington with good things to say, that helps sell the product.

Throughout the television-shopping subculture runs a sense of urgency designed to turn the casual watcher into an eager buyer. Sometimes the networks show time clocks on the screen. That suggests to viewers that time is running out on their opportunity to buy. In fact, the timers merely indicate how long the product will be shown on air. Unless the host says it is sold out, it will probably still be available hours, days, or weeks later.

Both HSN and QVC monitor sales by computer, virtually as they happen. While an item is being shown, the show's producer can see how many people are buying, which sizes are still available, and how busy the operators are. If a product is bombing, the producer will tell the host to end the segment and move on to the next item. If it is a hit, the host may extend the pitch until interest wanes or the product sells out.

For consumers, the basic television-shopping experience is much the same as buying from a mail-order catalog. When they call a toll-free number they are connected with a human order-taker or with an automated order-taking system. Most home shopping channels accept personal checks, money orders, or major credit cards. After customers place their order, they get an estimated delivery date and an order number.

It is difficult to generalize about whether home shopping channels give good value because they sell so many items. QVC, for instance, sells some 6,000 different products a month. What's more, comparison shopping is not easy, even with brand-name goods.

CONSUMER DYNAMICS

Television shoppers tend to be regulars. Of the roughly 100,000 new customers QVC signs on monthly, the company says 60 percent become repeat purchasers, with the average customer spending about $45. HSN has a 6 percent response rate from its potential audience, considerably better than the 2.5 percent average for other direct-response media.

The quick acceptance of this new form of direct selling is not too surprising considering that in 7 out of 10 homes in the United States there are no adults present during the day to go shopping. In these two-income households, teenaged children often buy much of the family food and other convenience goods. When the adults get home, they may be too weary or may not have enough time to shop for other goods. This is one reason why the catalog industry has expanded. As a logical extension to catalogs, television selling adds color, movement, sound, and entertainment to make both the process and the products exciting.

Shopper Demographics

Overall, television shoppers are younger and more active than many observers of the retail industry might think (see Case Table 8.1). Almost half of this group are 25 to 44 years old. Furthermore, the television shopper is more likely to enjoy amusement parks, night clubs, snow skiing, gambling resorts, photography, and eating out, while the market average consumer is more likely to enjoy sedentary activities such as reading, listening to music, and watching television.

Forty-three percent of television shoppers are married, and 8 percent are widowed. But the more surprising statistic is that television shoppers exceed the market average in the "single, never married" classification, some 27 percent of television shoppers. By occupation, the largest television shopper group is made up of professionals and managers, 13 percent and 11 percent, respectively. More than 34 percent of television shoppers graduated from high school, compared to 31 percent of the market average. And more than 27 percent of television shoppers have completed one to three years of college, which is slightly below the 30 percent of the market average.

CASE TABLE 8.1. Comparison of Television Shoppers and Average Consumers*

DEMOGRAPHIC COMPARISON OF TV SHOPPERS AND THE MARKET AVERAGE

	Percentage of TV-Shopper Market	Percentage of Market Average
Married	44	49
Widowed	8	8
Single never married	27	25
25 to 34 years old	26	24
35 to 44 years old	22	21
65 and over	11	16
Professional	13	18
Manager in a business	11	12
Factory worker/laborer/driver	12	9
Homemaker	11	9
Salesperson	10	8
Retired	12	16

ETHNIC PROFILE OF TV SHOPPERS AND THE MARKET AVERAGE

	Percentage of TV-Shopper Market	Percentage of Market Average
White	55	72
Black	20	14
Hispanic	17	8

*Note: Figures have been rounded.
Source: Harvey D. Braun, "Guess Who's Watching?" *Direct Marketing,* July 1993, p. 22.

The average household income of television shoppers is $34,900, compared to $38,000 of the market average. Consumers in the lower income categories, below $30,000, are more likely than market average consumers to be television shoppers. But the percentages are very close at the highest income levels. While 9 percent of consumers in the market average earn more than $75,000 a year, 8 percent of television shoppers earn that much. In other words, television shopping appeals to consumers at the upper as well as lower ends of the income scale.

More than half (55 percent) of all television shoppers are white, considerably lower than the percentage of whites in the market average, some 72 percent. Blacks and Hispanics are the next two largest ethnic groups among television shoppers, both exceeding their percentage representation in the market average. That is, while 14 percent of the market average is black, 20 percent is black. While 8 percent of the market average is Hispanic, Hispanics comprise 17 percent of the television-shopper market.

Television shoppers are more likely—often much more likely—to own and use home technology than are consumers in the market average. This fact is true of not only television-related items such as remote controls and VCRs but also of compact disc players, home computers, and cellular phones.

Television shoppers spend 37 minutes more per day, some 207 compared to 170, in front of the tube. And they spend 21 minutes more per day listening to the radio. Furthermore, a much smaller percentage of television shoppers cite reading as a favorite activity, yet these consumers spend as much time as the average consumer reading the newspapers each day.

Shopping ranks third as a leisure-time activity for both consumer groups, and television shoppers are significantly more likely to enjoy shopping than the market average.

How to Reach Them

Television shoppers can be reached through the telephone and mail, being far more likely than the market average to listen to sales solicitations on the phone and to read mail advertisements. More than 27 percent of television shoppers will listen to half or more of a telephone sales solicitation, in contrast to just 13 percent of the market average. Similarly, while more than 50 percent of television shoppers will read half or more of mail advertisements, less than 40 percent of the market average will read that much. Regular television shoppers are far more likely than market average consumers to buy from catalogs and direct mail. More than 44 percent of all television shoppers buy from catalogs or direct mail, as opposed to just under 12 percent in the market average.

The Consumer Segments

Case Exhibit 8.4 shows the five television shopper segments in the United States:

1. *Personal shoppers* (31 percent) are the largest group of frequent home shopping channel item buyers. They attach major importance to product value, the demonstration of product features, recommendations made for merchandise, conversations among and with the hosts, and the personality aspects of the programming. Merchandise variety and the recreational aspects of the shopping experience play smaller roles in their buyer behavior.
2. *Reliant shoppers* (24 percent) are mainly interested in product value, demonstrations, confidence in recommendations, and the channel personalities. The product variety, conversation, and convenience influences explain less of their buyer behavior and the recreational dimension has no role.

CASE EXHIBIT 8.4. Home Shopping Channel Customer Segment Membership
(Purchased twice in last three months)

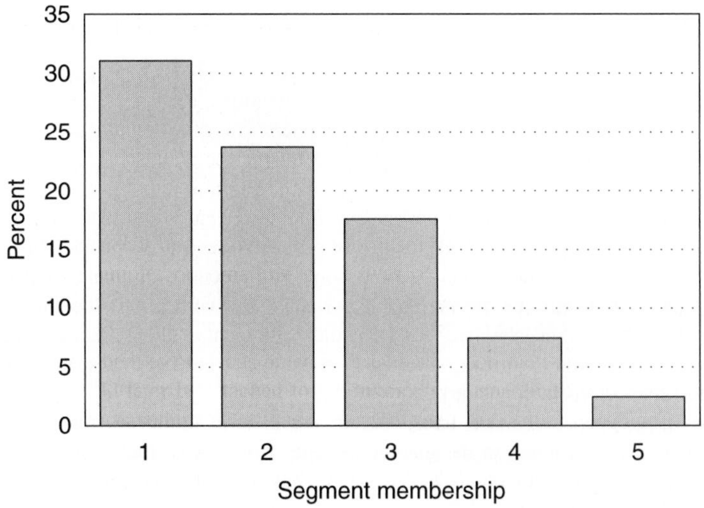

Where: 1 = Personal shoppers
2 = Reliant shoppers
3 = Entertainment shoppers
4 = Recreational shoppers
5 = Social shoppers

Source: William J. McDonald, "Home Shopping Channel Customer Segments: A Cross-Cultural Perspective," *Journal of Direct Marketing* 9 (Autumn 1995), p. 60.

3. *Entertainment shoppers* (18 percent) attach importance to product value, demonstrations, confidence in recommendations, the recreational aspects of the shopping, and conversations during the shows. The channel personalities are also important. Less importance is attached to merchandise variety and convenience.
4. *Recreational shoppers* (8 percent) are described by their interest in product value, demonstrations, recreation, and conversation. They attach less importance to variety, confidence in recommendations, and convenience.
5. *Social shoppers* (3 percent) are oriented to conversation and personalities. All the other categories are of lesser importance to this final segment. Some 16 percent of home shoppers do not fit into any of the five shopper segments.

EMERGING COMPETITION

Until recently, most major retailers resolutely shunned television shopping. Not anymore. Suddenly a stampede of department-store chains, specialty outlets, catalog retailers, and mass merchants is reexamining home shopping. Some now plan to sell their wares on the existing channels, such as QVC and HSN. In fact, home shopping passed a milestone of sorts, when Saks Fifth Avenue went on QVC twice with items from its Real Clothes private-label collection. Saks racked up more than $1 million in sales. Plenty of others will follow Saks's lead, including those interested in selling lifestyle-related items, health care products, videos, and recorded music. Other retailers are hoping to launch their own full-time shopping channels, and still others are laying plans for high-tech interactive services. Then there are those spending big on infomercials that air on cable and broadcast television.

Already, the store and catalog retailers are invading HSN's sales channel. Cataloger Lands' End is exploring possible approaches to interactive catalog shopping, as is retailer Sears. Dayton Hudson Department Stores has tested a 30-minute infomercial for bedding and one-way interactive television home shopping. One of the most ambitious television home shopping ventures that has emerged so far is TV Macy's, a 24-hour shopping channel dedicated entirely to Macy's merchandise.

Both Catalog 1, HSN's new offering, and TV Macy's are aiming for a more upscale customer than the average QVC buyer, who has a household income near $40,000. But QVC, too, is moving uptown with its Q2. Pitched as an electronic specialty store, Q2 aims to capture a younger and more active audience that formerly may have shied away from television home shopping channels.

ALTERNATIVE COURSES OF ACTION FOR HSN

After reading the S-Team's report, senior HSN management wanted specific marketing strategies to address each scenario about the future of retailing, particularly the one about America's expanding access to shopping alternatives. They instructed the S-Team to develop direct marketing approaches that were consistent with the firm's need to deliver a solid return on investment to its shareholders, while at the same time investing in HSN's future growth.

In providing direction to the S-Team, HSN's upper management had several concerns that new direct marketing alternatives should specifically address: What should HSN's target customer be? What is the right product mix for that customer? What changes are needed in HSN's merchandise to address existing and new customer targets? Can HSN appeal to new customers without losing its traditional customer base? What are the potential customer confusions over what HSN represents?

In its continuing quest for more sales and market share and in response to increasing competition on the television home shopping front, HSN needs to develop strategies that support and enhance its shopping channel offerings.

Recommend a direct marketing strategy for HSN that addresses the following areas: How should the consumer market be segmented, and what segment(s) should be targeted? What strategy alternatives are there for HSN within and outside of its television channel offerings? What are the pros and cons of those marketing strategy alternatives, given the target segment(s) and direct marketing tools available to HSN, and how would those strategies operate to expand the business operations of the HSN? Which strategy alternatives should the S-Team recommend, and why?

NOTE

1. Although the Home Shopping Network is an actual competitor in the shop-from-home industry, the specifics of this case are fictional.

SOURCES

Bauman, Risa. "A New Dawn for Home Shopping." *Direct,* January 1993, pp. 1, 16.

Braun, Harvey D. "Guess Who's Watching?" *Direct Marketing,* July 1993, pp. 21–23.

Cohen, Warren. "Purchasing Power." *U.S. News & World Report,* January 31, 1994, pp. 56–59.

Darian, Jean C. "In-Home Shopping: Are There Consumer Segments?" *Journal of Retailing* 63 (Summer 1987), pp. 163–86.

Davis, Riccardo A. "Home Shopping Moves to Radio." *Advertising Age,* January 17, 1994, p. 27.

———. "QVC Clicks for Kodak Cameras." *Advertising Age,* January 17, 1994, p. 17.

Drucker, Mindy. "At the Top of Its Game." *Target Marketing* 17, no. 3 (March 1994), pp. 17–22.

Fitzgerald, Kate. "Home Shopping Comes Up Short." *Advertising Age,* March 21, 1994, p. M1–14.

Goldblum, Risa. "Home Shopping Blazes New Upscale Trails." *Direct,* November 20, 1993, pp. 20–21.

James, E. Lincoln, and Isbella C. M. Cunningham. "A Profile of Direct Marketing Television Shoppers." *Journal of Direct Marketing* 4 (Autumn 1987), pp. 12–23.

Lang, Curtis. "The Future of Home Shopping?" *Advertising Age,* February 28, 1994, pp. 19, 22.

McDonald, William J. "Home Shopping Channel Customer Segments: A Cross-Cultural Perspective." *Journal of Direct Marketing* 9 (Autumn 1995), pp. 57–67.

Roberts, Mary Lou, and Paul D. Berger. *Direct Marketing Management.* Englewood Cliffs, NJ: Prentice Hall, 1989.

Rubel, Chad. "Home Shopping Targets Younger Audience." *Marketing News,* July 17, 1995, pp. 13, 26.

"Shopping by Television." *Consumer Reports,* January 1995, pp. 8–12.

Zinn, Laura, and Antonio N. Fins. "Home Shoppers Keep Tuning In—But Investors Are Turned Off." *Business Week,* October 22, 1990, pp. 70–72.

Zinn, Laura, et al. "Retailing Will Never Be the Same." *Business Week,* July 26, 1993, pp. 54–60.

Case 9: id Software, Inc.

INTRODUCTION

Some observers consider America's current crop of video games the precursor to a whole new entertainment medium where the line between illusions and reality becomes blurred and where movies, games, and other forms of entertainment, such as television, merge into a virtual world. The signs of this revolution are all around us. A vision of how it will develop is available to those who follow the progress of computer technology, software innovations, and the evolution of personal computer (PC) games.

However, this revolution is still in its beginning stages. The PC is only a little over a decade old. PC-based computer games are just now beginning to appear lifelike. The media that will eventually merge to produce the new entertainment forms hold separate turfs that are aggressively protected. Mass-market games such as those that come from Nintendo and Atari are popular, but they rely on the weak computing power of cheap home-oriented units. Some games are available over online services, but those offerings are crippled by slow telephone transmission rates.

The real power for running games lies in the PC. Its processing speed, storage capacity, and graphics make it the clear winner in the current game-delivery competition. However, there is a real cost issue. Most PC games require a state-of-the-art machine (with many accessories) to perform at their maximum. In other words, a consumer needs a $3,000 to $3,500 fully equipped machine to play a $50 game.

Nevertheless, the PC game makers deserve credit for constantly pushing the game frontier. Over the last 10 years, small entrepreneurial companies have contributed to the birth of an entire industry, complete with magazines, clubs, and conventions. And, game playing has moved to near the top of the list of PC uses.

One pioneer in the PC games industry has been id Software, Inc. (The letters in the name *id* are never capitalized.) Over the last several years, this firm has produced some of the most innovative and groundbreaking games available on the market. However, as the industry changes, id faces challenges, particularly those coming from new technologies and increased competition.

A HISTORY OF VIDEO GAMES

A video game is a contest between a player and a computer-designed program on a machine equipped with a video screen and a joystick or buttons that control the game's action. The machine may be designed to play one game, as are those in video-game arcades, or many games, as are game consoles and home computers. The latter use different videotape game cartridges and software programs, respectively.

The first video games were created on mainframe computers by engineers and computer programmers in the late 1950s and early 1960s. The games traveled via a kind of programmers' network from one computer research center to another. Games such as Star Trek and Space Wars were played whenever there was spare computer time, usually in the middle of the night. These first games were essentially verbal—that is, the graphics, if there were any, were limited and the computer was programmed to respond primarily in words to each of the choices made by the player.

As games proliferated, they gained color and complexity and adopted the basic theme that most of them still exhibit: the violent annihilation of an enemy (a spaceship, an alien, or a man-eating crocodile) by means of one's skill at moving a lever or pushing a button (representing a gun, a bomb, an arrow, or an unidentified explosive).

Increasingly, these games are becoming more sophisticated, more difficult, and no longer dependent on elapsed time. Unlike arcade games, where a coin pays for a set number of minutes, some computer games can go on for many hours. Graphics have improved to the point where the games resemble movies, amazing to players used to the rough, jagged visuals of past games. Many new games also include complicated sounds and music. These sophisticated video games have the potential for offering an almost limitless array of exotic worlds and fantastic situations.

There are those who feel that in order to play, one must accept the values implicit in these interactive games, which, like the often-condemned fantasy game Dungeons and Dragons, may involve extremely violent or aberrant events and characters. Other types of games, especially those that use simulation (see the description in the next section), are simply highly imaginative tests of intelligence and skill.

TYPES OF PC GAMES

For the PC, there are seven major classes of games. Each represents a distinctive playing mode that places specific demands on the player. *Adventure games* involve roaming around, finding things, and solving clues and puzzles. In *role-playing games* the player takes the role of a character in a plot. Usually, the game player sees the action through the eyes of the person he or she portrays. *Simulation games* may be the most popular type of PC game. They tend to be action-oriented games of skill and strategy where the player is flying a plane, driving a race car, or piloting a helicopter. The emphasis is on combat and destruction, with the consequence of failure being death. One highly rated such game is X-Wing from LucasArts, an excellent Star Wars simulation where the player serves as a pilot for rebel fighters against the Empire. The newly released Rebel Assault, one of the best simulation on the market, sold out at CompUSA in two days. *Strategy games* are much more methodical and less action-oriented than simulations. In such games, players must develop a plan and execute it methodically to accumulate enough successes to win the game. Strategy games are much slower and less arcadelike than simulation games. It takes a dedicated player to find the energy for a game that literally takes days to finish. Currently, the second most highly rated such game is Dune II from Virgin. Dune II is patterned after the movie of the same name. *War games* involve strategy-oriented plots in which the game player manipulates armies on battlefields. These games either recreate historical situations or present the player with new scenarios. *Action games* tend to be arcadelike in their play. Players are either shooting or running or dying during the process of trying to defeat an enemy. Some of these games are not violent, but the premise of the majority is kill or be killed. The number one game in this category is id Software's DOOM. *Sports games* are, as might be expected, games that simulate sporting activities. The most highly rated such game is a golf simulation. Others include football, baseball, and tennis.

THE PC GAMES INDUSTRY

A recent directory of PC game firms printed in a magazine dedicated to this type of entertainment listed 50 companies involved in software development, marketing, and online services. While that sounds like a lot, only a few are dominant players in the market. Because most are private companies, information about sales and profits or market growth and market share is virtually nonexistent. However, a few names appear repeatedly on the list of top 100 games as identified by the readers of *Computer Gaming World* in its readers' poll. LucasArts excels in adventure games and simulation games; ElectronicArts at adventure games, simulation games, strategy games, and sports games; Spectrum HoloByte at simulation games and action games; Origin at role-playing games and action games; and MicroProse at simulation games, adventure games, and strategy games.

Individual games become popular because of plots, graphics, and playability. Games are advertised in gaming magazines only because the sales volume involved is specialized and relatively small. Both packaging and store displays in such locations as CompUSA play an important role in sales, as do reviews in the gaming magazines. Game producers must continually come out with new titles and, to a lesser extent, upgrades of existing games. The PC technology used to play these games is moving very quickly. Only games that make use of the power of the new computer models can expect to do well.

MAJOR PC GAME COMPETITORS

The PC game industry is unique in that much of its most formidable competition is just on the horizon. While other PC game makers and makers of games for non-PCs have always been threats to any given firm in this industry, online networks and cable-related products that do not require a PC are probably the greatest long-term concern for most PC game firms.

The most immediate phenomenon of concern to PC game makers should be the alliances of PC game and movie industry firms. LucasArts is a prime example. Because the firm owns all the rights to the *Star Wars* films, it is able to create PC games that have stunning visual effects and highly popular plots. But firms like LucasArts are also master game producers for original titles not based on movies. The special effects and other related cinematic skills of the movie-industry people are emerging as a formidable force in PC games.

id SOFTWARE, INC.

id Software is located by the side of a Dallas expressway in a large box of a building. There, in a modest office on an upper floor, the firm has created intensely violent action games—particularly Wolfenstein 3D and DOOM—that have had a significant impact on computer gaming. Stepping into the firm's modest offices, one can see how democratically, and often anarchistically, 10 people run a very lucrative operation.

id's games are hugely successful, as is its unconventional shareware marketing approach. This involves distributing a playable version of a program for free on bulletin boards and locations on the Internet. If the user likes the shareware program, he or she can order more episodes to play. Recently, id also used direct-response ads in many of the popular PC game magazines to sell its software in cooperation with a game software publisher (see Case Exhibit 9.1). It distributed the commercial version of its popular Wolfenstein 3D as Spear of Destiny in retail outlets using a game publisher that handled all aspects of the store distribution process.

id CEO Jay Wilbur manages the overall operations of the firm. He oversees an office with a spartan reception area and a shelf packed with awards; offices for the programmers, technical support personnel, and artists; a storage room and kitchen occupied by a Foosball table; and an entire pallet of caffeinated drinks, a large box of chips, and a refrigerator filled with ice cream treats. Roughly at the center of the space is a "living-room" area with couches and a pool table.

At any hour, game play among the employees can get intense. Office small talk is frequently cut short by screams and sounds. But these noises are merely coming from programmer John Romero and program tester Shawn Green, who engage in many daily network DOOM sessions. The level of competition is vicious. Nearly four months after the release of DOOM (December 1993), id is still obsessed with its highly successful creation. It set out to create great games, and it is convinced it did.

The major participants at id are John Carmack, the 23-year-old programming whiz and the man behind the core id technology; 26-year-old John Romero, tools programmer, level designer, and the best DOOM player in the world; Sandy Petersen, a long-time paper-game and

CASE EXHIBIT 9.1. Direct-Response Ads for id Software's Games

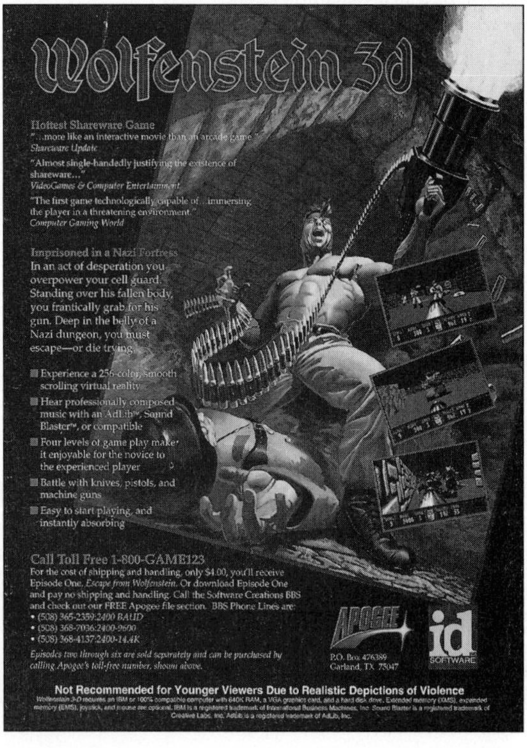

computer-game designer who did the majority of the program episode design for DOOM; Kevin Cloud, a soft-spoken southern gentleman of 26 years and one of two id artists; and, finally, Jay Wilbur, the 33-year-old who handles operations and manages the finances.

id: The Beginning

id Software is basically a collection of programmers from a company called SoftDisk. SoftDisk puts out a monthly disk of arcade games, and, in 1989, Romero, Wilbur, Cloud, and Adrian Carmack were part of the game development group there.

In 1990, Romero began to get fan mail for one of the arcade games his group had programmed. He failed to recognize, however, that though the names on the letters were different, the address was the same. He eventually made a connection while reading about a piece of shareware in a computer magazine.

Scott Miller, head of Apogee Software, had written all of the letters, each with a different variation on his name, knowing that all of the mail at SoftDisk was screened. He could not contact Romero directly about working for him, so he wrote the letters as if he were a fan.

Romero at last called Miller, and ideas were thrown about. In December of 1990, a group of programmers at SoftDisk proposed Commander Keen to Miller. They began moonlighting, programming Keen out of the bedroom of a lake house.

Commander Keen sold very well for a shareware game, and when Romero, John Carmack, and Adrian Carmack (no relation) got their first check from Apogee, they decided to leave and

CASE EXHIBIT 9.1. Direct-Response Ads for id Software's Games—*Continued*

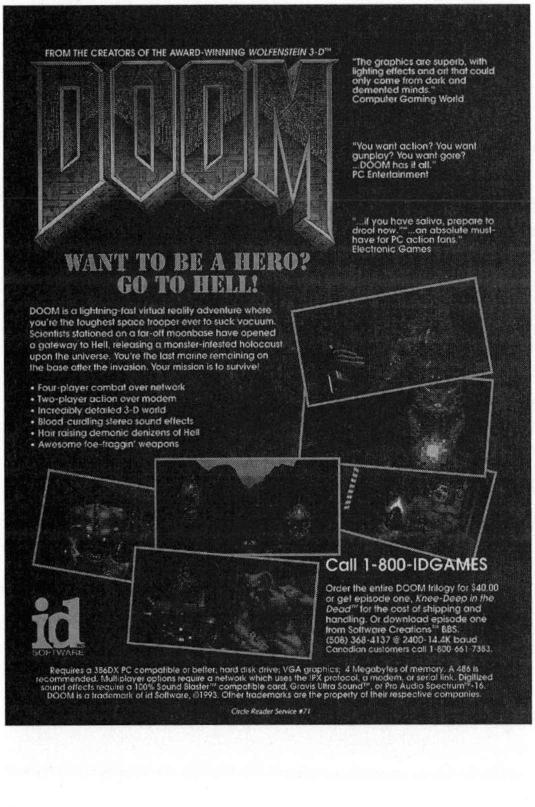

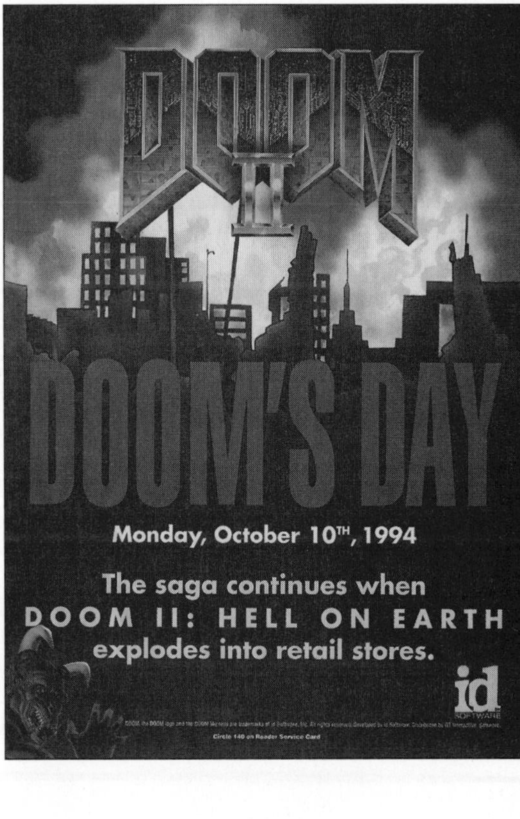

form their own company. The original name was IFD Software, or Ideas From the Deep, but it was later shortened to ID, which originally stood for In Demand. Not pleased with In Demand, someone suggested the connection with the Freudian term *id.*

After a hard winter of programming the remainder of the Commander Keen series, the group moved to its current location. The new company hired Jay Wilbur and Kevin Cloud from SoftDisk and began working on Wolfenstein 3D, which followed a Carmack project called Catacombs 3D. The group wanted to fold the knowledge it had gleaned from Catacombs 3D into a fast-action 3D game called It's Green and Pissed, in which the player would hunt mutants in a biological-research lab. They frequently reminisced about an old Apple II game called Castle Wolfenstein and decided that the premise of this classic (a captured U.S. soldier trying to escape from a Nazi fortress) would make for a great game in 3D. They hunted down the original designer, Silas Warner, only to find that he had sold the rights. The rights trail led through three or four long-dead companies, finally ending with a guy selling the original game out of his basement. The copyright on the game had long since lapsed, so they applied for the copyright themselves.

When Wolfenstein 3D was released, the overwhelmingly positive reaction was unexpected. The tremendous 3D environment amazed people who had come to expect a certain level of production value in shareware games. They could not believe it was shareware. The game logged 150,000 registrations as shareware, and sold 150,000 copies in retail stores under the name Spear of Destiny. id estimates worldwide shareware distribution at over 1 million.

About this time, the ideas for DOOM began to develop. As DOOM progressed, word of its wonders began to spread through the press and the online networks. Anticipation in the gaming community reached a fever pitch when the company announced a December 1993 release.

Despite the success of its games, id continues to surprise the market by sticking with shareware distribution. However, there are advantages to marketing via shareware, not the least of which is a healthy profit margin. id also likes the fact that people can try out its games before they buy them, and it likes being able to distribute its games immediately after they are finished. id especially enjoys not having to deal with marketing and retail pressures.

DOOM II

In the meantime, id is working on the sequel to DOOM—DOOM II: Hell on Earth. At the end of DOOM, the marine escapes the Pit of Hell, along with a couple of friendly demons. In DOOM II, the marine returns to an Earth city to find that it is overrun by nasties.

DOOM II uses the same engine (the program that drives the game and gives it its appearance) as the original, but offers 27 to 30 new levels (areas or settings where the game play occurs) populated by six new evil creatures. id wants to please players who have played all of the shareware. It plans to include the first version of DOOM so that if people find DOOM II too tough, they can go back and train on that.

The new cast of characters for DOOM II is interesting and deadly. In the Junior Badguy division are a chaingun-wielding sergeant, the Hell Knight (a junior version of the Baron of Hell), and a new Cacodemon that shoots Lost Souls (screaming heads) out of its mouth. In the heavyweight division are a skeleton that shoots guided fireballs that will track the player, an obese villain with plasma launchers for arms, and the ArchVile. The ArchVile is a truly hideous thing that attacks by conjuring hell fire from the ground.

As if the creatures were not nasty enough, the level designs are downright devious. id learned a lot about designing levels in DOOM, and it put what it learned to use in DOOM II. Apparently, what id learned was how to put the player in more perilous predicaments. Each new level has a few very sticky moments. In a particularly hairy scenario, the player is locked inside

CASE TABLE 9.1. Uses of Personal Computers: At Home and at Work
(Respondents are all adults)

Purposes	At Home or at Work (%)	Own at Home (%)	Use at Work (%)
Accounting	8.8	4.4	5.7
Business analysis/forecasting	4.5	1.4	3.4
Computer games	8.1	7.4	1.1
Desktop publishing	3.8	2.2	2.2
Education	6.3	4.8	2.0
Filing/database management	8.3	3.5	6.0
Graphics/presentation	4.5	1.9	3.1
Personal networking/electronic mail	2.2	0.7	1.7
Programming	4.8	3.1	2.6
Online information retrieval	3.9	1.0	3.2
Word processing	14.3	8.8	9.2

Source: Simmons Market Research Bureau, Inc., 1991.

a small arena with both a Cyberdemon and the Mastermind Spider—the end-level creatures from the registered version of DOOM. The player enters this arena with little in the way of weapons, and the creatures immediately turn their tremendous firepower on him. If he hesitates, he is gone. The key is to run around the arena, frantically dodging rockets and machine-gun spray, and to try to get the two creatures to fight each other. Once they are going at it, the player must creep up on the platform where they are battling and inch his way around them to get to a lever that opens up the exit door.

PC GAME CUSTOMERS

PC games are primarily an at-home activity, although play at work is also popular (see Case Table 9.1). In fact, next to word processing, game playing is the most popular use of PCs at home. Case Table 9.2 shows that those who own a PC and use it for games have distinctive demographics. Generally, they are male, middle-aged, married, upper-income, and parents of children over the age of six. Most likely, the children are playing the games, but the themes and content of a large number of PC games is clearly adult oriented. Most eight-year-olds, for example, could never understand or play many of the strategy games. Unofficial estimates are that better than half of the PC games market is based on adult players, and more than 90 percent of the time adults are the game buyers.

HOLLYWOOD AND SILICON VALLEY JOIN FORCES

The movie industry has made the disturbing discovery that it is losing some of its best customers in the 13- to 25-year-old age group to video and computer games. The games market totaled an estimated $7 billion in 1993, far exceeding the approximately $5.3 billion Americans spent on movie tickets. A blockbuster video game can earn more than $500 million, a figure only blockbuster movies can match.

CASE TABLE 9.2. Personal Computer: Ownership, Games Usage, and Joystick/Paddle Ownership
(Respondents are all adults)

	Own Home Personal Computer (%)	Index	Use for Games (%)	Index	Own Joystick/ Paddles (%)	Index
Total	21.4	100	7.4	100	4.9	100
Gender						
Male	22.7	106	7.9	102	5.4	109
Female	20.2	94	6.9	94	4.5	92
Age						
18–24	19.7	92	7.4	101	4.5	92
25–34	21.8	102	7.0	95	4.2	85
35–44	28.9	135	12.8	173	9.0	183
45–54	24.3	113	8.5	115	6.5	131
55–64	19.6	92	4.7	64	3.0	60
65 and older	11.5	54	1.8	25	1.3	25
Marital status						
Single	20.9	97	6.3	85	3.7	75
Married	24.1	113	9.1	124	6.3	127
Divorced	13.4	62	3.0	41	2.1	43
Parents	26.7	125	11.9	161	8.4	170
Region						
Northeast	20.7	97	8.2	111	5.5	111
Midwest	22.1	103	8.1	109	5.8	118
South	20.1	94	6.0	81	4.0	80
West	23.5	110	8.1	110	5.0	101
Income						
$75+	32.5	152	13.2	179	8.1	164
$60+	30.7	143	12.8	173	7.8	158
$50+	30.3	141	12.3	167	7.4	149
$40+	29.6	138	12.0	162	7.2	145
$30+	27.8	130	10.8	147	6.7	136
$30–$39	22.7	106	7.7	104	5.4	109
$20–$29	17.1	80	4.4	59	3.4	69
$10–$19	10.8	51	2.5	33	2.3	47
Less than $10	11.3	53	1.7	23	2.1	43
Presence of children						
Under 2 years	20.6	96	7.7	105	4.3	88
2–5	22.9	107	8.0	108	4.9	98
6–11	26.6	124	12.0	162	9.0	182
12–17	29.6	138	13.9	188	10.4	210

Note: Index values above are computed by dividing the proportion in a particular grouping by their proportion of the population. For example, if an age group has 20.2% of the product's users and represents 18.3% of the population, the index value for the grouping is 110. Index values over 100 signify above average usage and index values below 100 signify below average usage. However, values over 110 or under 90 are the most significant.
Source: Simmons Market Research Bureau, Inc., 1991.

Those kinds of numbers have opened a lot of eyes in the movie industry. Producers, directors, actors, agents, writers, and cinematographers are scrambling to jump aboard the games bandwagon. They hope to use their skills and savvy to stretch the creative boundaries of computer games and bring a new sophistication to interactive entertainment.

Their arrival promises to change the very nature of the business, transforming high-end computer games from the special province of a small number of devoted fans to the mass-market toy for the middle class. Right now there is a big gap between what makes a good game and what makes a good movie, but that isn't going to be the case for long.

In 1993, LucasArts released *Indiana Jones and the Fate of Atlantis,* not as a movie but as a CD-ROM title for PCs. The disc—with 40 computer characters, numerous alternative outcomes, crisp sound, and more than 8,000 spoken lines—allows the player to change the story with every move. Technicians at the firm also rendered the three-dimensional intergalactic villains and pockmarked asteroids of the *Star Wars*–based game Rebel Assault.

Before movies and games can converge successfully, three things have to happen. First, the technology must continue to improve to the point where PC games can rival the look and feel of television, if not of theatrical movies. To eyes accustomed to the 30-frames-a-second speed of television, 15 frames a second on the computer screen can appear unsophisticated. Improving the technology is the job of the Silicon Valley contingent, which is making rapid progress. Next, game makers must raise their production values to similar levels. That is where the Hollywood directors, cinematographers, lighting technicians, grips, production assistants, and other specialists come in. And the results of their expertise are already showing up on computer screens. Finally, and most important, Hollywood writers and performers must transfer their storytelling and character-building talents to this new medium. Traditionally, computer games have focused on a few themes—such as fantasy worlds, flight simulators, and sports—that appeal to a relatively narrow audience. Hollywood storytellers hope to draw new customers by expanding the range of topics to include the whole range of human experience.

GAME PLAYER TRENDS

To industry executives, predicting the future of gaming is not an insignificant task because it means survival for their companies. It is not only possible but also common for individual companies to flounder while the field in which they operate prospers. Companies in the PC game industry fail because they lose touch with the public's desires. If they don't produce the games consumers want to buy, sales plummet. On the bright side, as formerly successful game makers disappear, new ones appear.

So PC gaming people talk about trends. They talk about how gamers are getting older. Without losing appeal for teenagers and grade schoolers, games now attract a high school, college, and adult audience. The PC gaming segment has always skewed older, but now the mass market is going that way, too. The average Sega Genesis owner is 18—and the typical Sega CD gamer is 24. Action, adventure, role playing, and strategy games are the rising categories.

Games are becoming more segmented by age-specific demographics, with more children's titles and more entertainment products with mature content. The playing environment is also changing. High-end gaming is coming out of the den, away from the computer workstation, and into America's living rooms. Computer gaming will remain viable for many years, but it would not expand much, at least not along traditional lines. That's because the last decade has proved that the number of people who want to sit at a desk, stare at a small screen, and play solitaire electronic games is limited. It would be foolish not to notice that 10 to 20 times as many people play video games that are connected to a television set. Multimedia is about capturing the mass market and make interactive electronic entertainment as important as the VCR. Ten years ago, 100,000 was a good sale for a computer game, and the same total would gladden almost every software publisher's heart today. That would not change in the next few years, either.

Games must get even more intuitive and easy to learn to appeal to the living-room audience. Simple rules, clear-cut goals, and point-and-click interfaces figure to gain at the expense of keyboard order entry and tiered menus. Written documentation is an insurmountable hurdle for some, so interactive tutorials will supplement the written instructions.

Multiplayer contests will contribute much greater sales years from now; bringing the hardware into the room where families congregate works against extended solitaire play. The popularity of head-to-head competition and multiplayer games will explode. People want to play games, not watch them, no matter how fantastic the art and music.

The hardest factor to evaluate is the potential impact of telecommunications. This is such a powerful force that the net result of many expected effects is tough to judge in advance. Downloading games over a cable wire will soon be an everyday fact for subscribers of planned Sega and Sony networks. These games will have to play well on a standard television set. That means less on-screen text, which would hurt games that require a lot of explanation and commentary during play. It would also militate against game systems that offer a list of menu choices. In the short run, however, online networks are expanding at an incredible rate. Prodigy recently signed up its 2 millionth user, and America Online doubled to 600,000 subscribers in just 12 months.

The last factor is harder to pin down than any of the others: fashion. Game categories, graphic styles, and so forth go in and out of style like clothing and cars. Right now, fighting games are the hottest ticket, but that craze looks like it is going into its final phase. The games have settled into a rut that keeps hard-core fans happy, but converts few.

id SOFTWARE'S FUTURE

With the changing nature of the games industry and evolving customer preferences, id Software faces serious potential challenges. The firm is one of many game producers, most of which have many times its resources. id has distinguished itself in a particular niche of the gaming market. But the entry of major entertainment conglomerates may present a problem, as does the limited size of the current PC games market. Thus, the future appears to hold both threats and opportunities. All this implies that id Software may need new marketing strategies to prosper in the future. Direct marketing approaches appear to hold the greatest promise. The questions are about which strategies to use and what tools to apply.

id Software's immediate problem is the decision on how to market DOOM II. As noted previously, the firm's first product offerings were initially distributed as shareware, with later products distributed either as shareware or with the aid of a game publishing company. Direct-response print advertising has played an important role in id's recent successes.

What direct marketing plan would you recommend for DOOM II? How would you justify that plan in terms of the problems, opportunities, and threats faced by id Software?

This case describes the strategy used for the original DOOM. What direct marketing strategy would you recommend for DOOM II? How should the consumer market be segmented, and what segment(s) should be targeted? What are the direct marketing strategy alternatives for introducing DOOM II in the highly competitive game market? What are the pros and cons of those direct marketing strategy alternatives, given the specific target segment(s) and direct marketing tools? How would those strategies operate to sell DOOM II? Which strategy alternative would you recommend?

DALY, JAMES. "The Hollywood Connection." *Electronic Entertainment,* February 1994, pp. 41–51.

id Software promotional materials and public relations releases.

KATZ, ARNIE. "Nothing Is Constant Except Change . . ." *Computer Game Review,* March 1994, p. 60.

LOMBARDI, CHRIS. "To Hell and Back Again." *Computer Gaming World,* July 1994, pp. 20–24.

Simmons Market Research Bureau, Inc., 1991.

The Software Toolworks Multimedia Encyclopedia. Danbury, CT: Grolier Electronic Publishing, 1992.

WALKER, BRYAN. "id's Software's DOOM." *Computer Gaming World,* March 1994, pp. 38–39.

Case 10: NordicTrack

THE CML GROUP

The CML Group is a holding company with subsidiaries that design, manufacture, and market high-quality aerobic and anaerobic exercise equipment; operate speciality retail stores offering nature-related items, including nature videos, minerals, and educational toys; market garden tools, plants, and accessories; and operate men's clothing stores offering tailored suits, sport coats, trousers, shirts, and ties.

Since its inception in 1969, the CML Group has grown from $1 million in retail sales to $645.5 million for fiscal 1993 (see Case Exhibit 10.1). CML's growth has come from acquiring retail companies such as Carroll Reed, Britches of Georgetowne, and NordicTrack and encouraging their growth. CML bases its choice of acquisition targets on whether the company under consideration targets the same group of consumers as CML: affluent, active, sports-minded people interested in quality products. In addition, CML allows the companies it acquires to maintain their identities while providing an opportunity for further growth that otherwise would not have been possible.

The CML Group had record profits of $58 million in 1993 (see Case Exhibit 10.2). Business expansion was significant, particularly by NordicTrack (CML's home fitness equipment division), and relatively new acquisitions such as the Nature Company (CML's environmental gifts division), and Britches of Georgetowne (CML's men's and women's retail apparel division). Earnings and in-stock performance are improving as CML focuses growth on those three companies.

Charles M. Leighton and G. Robert Tod founded CML Group Inc. with $40,000 of their own money and $2 million that they raised from other sources. Their strategy was to buy steady businesses with sales targeted to the 35-to-55-year-old consumer group. CML's first acquisition was Boston Whaler Inc., a builder of quality small boats. Other purchases included Carroll Reed (a direct-mail seller of women's clothing) and Mason & Sullivan (a company that sells do-it-yourself clock kits through the mail). CML operates on a earn-out system for its purchases under which the seller is given a small amount of cash up front then is left to run the firm for

CASE EXHIBIT 10.1. CML Group Sales

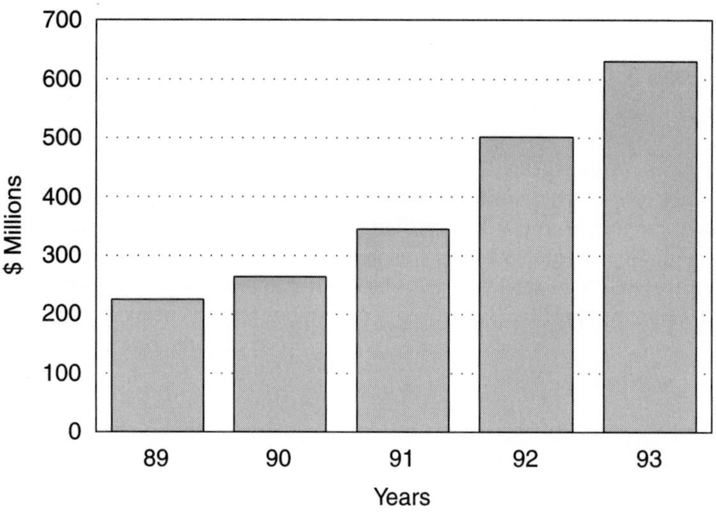

Source: Estimated from various sources.

CASE EXHIBIT 10.2. CML Group Net Income

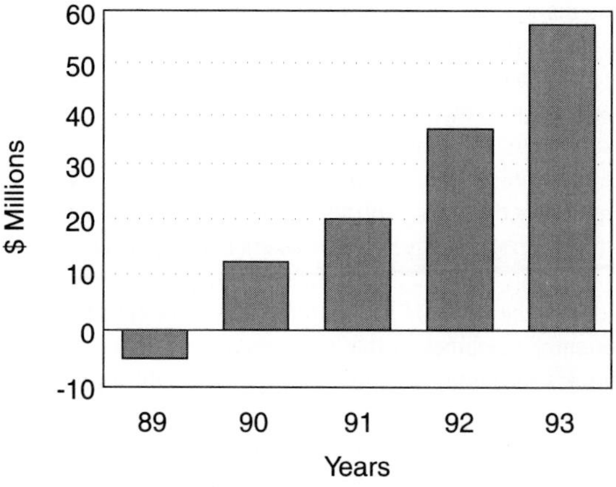

Source: Estimated from various sources.

CML, with the ultimate payout coming after five years, depending on profits. This encourages the management of new acquisitions to be as creative with their product lines and marketing plans as they were when the companies were begun.

This approach, encouraging the creativity of management and leaving the strategy of expansion with the parent company, has helped two of its acquisitions, NordicTrack and the Nature Company, achieve remarkable growth. These two companies are primarily responsible for CML's financial success.

In 1992, NordicTrack opened 15 stores, and another 25 in 1993, according to the company's 1992 report. The Nature Company opened 20 stores in 1992 and another 23 in 1993. To fuel this retail expansion, CML leveraged \$57.5 million in 1992 through a debenture sale.

Part of CML's retail strategy also includes the troubled gardening catalog Smith & Hawken, which operates as an affiliate of the Nature Company. Smith & Hawken, which publishes gardening and furniture catalogs, had 1992 revenue of about \$50 million. The gardening/furniture segment of the business is estimated at 80 percent of that total.

Overall, CML's direct-response and mail-order sales in 1993 increased by \$68.8 million, or 31.5 percent, over the prior year to \$287.1 million. The percentage of total sales derived from direct response and mail order increased from 41.5 percent in 1991 to 44.1 percent in 1992 to 44.5 percent in 1993. The increase in direct-response and mail-order sales was primarily attributable to higher direct-response sales at NordicTrack and mail-order sales at Smith & Hawken.

THE HOME EXERCISE MARKET

Despite all the attention given to jogging, aerobics, and Jane Fonda, health experts say Americans are fatter and lazier today than they were two decades ago when the fitness frenzy first began. An aging population is largely to blame. The bright spot in the fitness industry has been indoor exercisers, thanks to heavy promotion of two additions to the home gymnasium, particularly cross-country skiing machines and step-exercisers.

The home fitness market has grown around 10 percent a year for the past five years. Sales in 1993 rose an estimated 6 percent, to around \$2.4 billion at retail. This growth has been partly fueled by a growing phenomenon—health club dropouts. They are the people who as 20- and 30-somethings helped pump up the health club craze 10 years ago.

Of the 150 or so makers of home exercise equipment, roughly one-third have entered the business within the past five years. The new competition in this market is turning exercise equipment into a commodity business, with few companies making much money. To distinguish their products from the others, the equipment makers spend big money on advertising, design, and technology.

The company doing the best in this home fitness market is CML's NordicTrack. The appeal of its cross-country machines is that they exercise the whole body rather than just the lower half. NordicTrack's machines are also said to do the job better than any of their cheaper imitators.

As of 1994, 55 percent of United States households owned one or more pieces of exercise equipment, and 43 percent of families were considering expanding their workout gear in the coming year. In fact, 50 percent of those who already own some equipment intend to buy, while only 34 percent of first-time buyers were considering a purchase. Topping the list of products they intended to buy in the coming year were treadmills and NordicTrack. Rowing machines and weights and barbells did not figure largely in these future buying plans.

According to Case Table 10.1, the most popular form of exercise is fitness walking, with stationary biking and jogging second and third, respectively. Case Table 10.2 shows that 18 percent of the adult population exercised at home in the last 12 months. However, home exercise is more of an upper-income, young (under 44), single person's activity. Case Tables 10.3 and 10.4 reinforce the idea that exercise, regardless of its form, is a younger person's activity, and more a male than female activity.

CASE TABLE 10.1. Exercise Participation
(Respondents are all adults)

	Free Weights	Weight Training Machines	Stationary Bicycling	Stair Machine	Aerobics	Fitness Walking	Jogging	Distance Running
Participated in last 12 months (percent)								
Yes	4.7	3.6	9.2	3.0	6.5	23.2	7.0	2.3
No	95.3	96.4	90.8	97.0	93.5	76.8	93.0	97.7
Total	100.0	100.0	100.0	100.0	100.0	100.0	100.0	100.0
Frequency in last 12 months (number of times)								
1–4	0.3	0.2	0.9	0.5	0.7	1.5	0.9	0.3
5–9	0.4	0.3	1.1	0.2	0.4	2.1	0.9	0.3
10–19	0.8	0.5	1.5	0.6	1.2	3.3	1.2	0.3
20–39	0.7	0.8	1.8	0.7	1.3	3.7	1.2	0.5
40–59	0.6	0.5	0.9	0.3	0.9	2.9	0.5	0.2
60–79	0.4	0.3	0.6	0.3	0.5	1.6	0.3	0.0
80–99	0.4	0.2	0.4	0.1	0.4	1.3	0.4	0.2
100–149	0.4	0.3	0.6	0.1	0.4	2.4	0.8	0.3
150 or more	0.7	0.5	1.4	0.3	0.7	4.4	0.8	0.3
Total	4.7	3.6	9.2	3.1	6.5	23.2	7.0	2.4

Source: Simmons Market Research Bureau, Inc., 1991.

NORDICTRACK

Eighteen years ago NordicTrack introduced the first cross-country ski exerciser and started a fitness revolution. Since then, 2 million people have achieved improved overall health with this remarkable machine. In the process, NordicTrack has become the fitness leader in quality and innovation.

As shown in Case Exhibit 10.3, NordicTrack net sales rose from $266.8 million in 1992 to $377.8 million in 1993, a 41.6 percent increase. Retail store and kiosk sales increased $54.2 million, or 85.2 percent, to $117.8 million in 1993, compared to $63.6 million in 1992. Direct-response and mail-order sales increased $56.8 million, or 28 percent, to $260 million in 1993, up from $203.2 million in 1992. The increase in retail sales was due to the opening of 29 retail stores (26.7 percent increase in comparable store sales).

During 1993, NordicTrack accounted for approximately 58.5 percent and 91.6 percent of the CML Group's consolidated sales and operating income before corporate expenses, respectively. In 1992, approximately 54 percent of CML's consolidated sales and approximately 90.5 percent of its consolidated operating income before corporate expenses and restructuring charges came from NordicTrack. NordicTrack's sales strength is attributable to the continued growth of NordicTrack's classic cross-country ski line—"The World's Best Aerobic Exerciser"—and the success of several new products, including NordicFlex Gold and the Aerobic Cross-Trainer, as well as its aggressive retail store expansion.

While CML was pleased with NordicTrack's financial achievements, it believes that 1993 operational enhancements established a foundation for NordicTrack's long-term growth plans. During 1993, NordicTrack doubled its manufacturing capacity; improved its manufacturing efficiencies; developed an array of exciting, fun, and unique fitness products; broadened its retail operations; and established telemarketing facilities in the United Kingdom and Germany.

CASE TABLE 10.2. Physical Fitness Participation Location in the Last 12 Months
(Respondents are all adults)

	At Private Club (%)	Index	At Home (%)	Index	At Other Facilities (%)	Index
Total	4.5	100	18.0	100	5.6	100
Gender						
Male	0.5	99	16.1	89	5.1	92
Female	4.6	101	19.8	110	6.0	108
Age						
18–24	6.6	147	20.2	112	7.1	127
25–34	5.3	118	20.4	113	6.5	115
35–44	5.2	114	21.3	118	6.8	122
45–54	4.1	90	18.5	102	5.2	93
55–64	3.7	82	15.3	85	4.5	80
65 and older	1.6	35	9.9	55	2.5	45
Marital status						
Single	6.5	144	20.8	115	6.6	118
Married	4.0	88	18.2	101	5.4	96
Divorced	3.9	86	14.2	79	5.1	92
Parents	3.9	86	19.7	109	6.3	113
Region						
Northeast	3.9	87	16.6	92	4.3	77
Midwest	5.1	112	21.2	118	5.5	99
South	3.4	74	15.5	86	5.2	92
West	6.4	142	19.9	110	7.8	139
Income						
$75+	7.3	161	24.0	133	7.3	129
$60+	7.3	163	23.1	128	6.9	124
$50+	6.6	147	22.3	124	6.7	119
$40+	6.5	144	21.8	121	6.4	115
$30+	6.0	133	21.2	117	6.5	117
$30–$39	4.6	101	19.5	108	6.8	121
$20–$29	3.9	86	17.0	95	6.5	115
$10–$19	2.6	58	14.6	81	3.9	69
Less than $10	0.7	15	8.5	47	2.0	36
Presence of children						
Under 2 years	4.1	92	18.0	100	5.1	91
2–5	3.6	79	17.4	96	6.4	115
6–11	3.4	76	18.6	103	6.0	106
12–17	3.9	86	19.8	107	5.8	103

Note: Index values above are computed by dividing the proportion in a particular grouping by their proportion of the population. For example, if an age group has 20.2% of the product's users and represents 18.3% of the population, the index value for the grouping is 110. Index values over 100 signify above average usage and index values below 100 signify below average usage. However, values over 110 or under 90 are the most significant.
Source: Simmons Market Research Bureau, Inc., 1991.

CASE TABLE 10.3. Physical Fitness Participation Type in the Last 12 Months
(Respondents are all adults)

	Stationary Bicycling (%)	Index	Stair Machine (%)	Index	Aerobics (%)	Index
Total			3.0	100		
Gender						
Male	0.5	100	3.0	100	0.5	109
Female	0.5	97	3.0	100	0.5	92
Age						
18–24	0.2	116	4.7	155	0.2	177
25–34	0.3	114	3.8	126	0.3	124
35–44	0.2	109	3.5	115	0.2	117
45–54	0.1	99	3.1	102	0.1	80
55–64	0.1	83	1.7	57	0.1	51
65 and older	0.1	65	0.6	21	0.0	26
Marital status						
Single	0.3	120	4.6	153	0.4	170
Married	0.6	94	2.3	77	0.5	79
Divorced	0.2	95	3.4	112	0.2	86
Parents	0.4	107	2.7	88	0.4	107
Region						
Northeast	0.1	52	2.4	81	0.1	38
Midwest	0.3	130	3.2	105	0.3	116
South	0.4	108	2.3	76	0.3	98
West	0.2	102	4.7	155	0.3	148
Income						
$75+	0.1	123	5.2	173	0.1	111
$60+	0.3	127	5.0	166	0.2	119
$50+	0.4	121	4.9	161	0.3	118
$40+	0.5	114	4.6	152	0.5	121
$30+	0.6	114	4.2	140	0.7	116
$30–$39	0.2	113	3.2	107	0.2	103
$20–$29	0.1	88	2.5	81	0.2	92
$10–$19	0.2	93	1.0	35	0.1	78
Less than $10	0.1	56	0.7	22	0.1	61
Presence of children						
Under 2 years	0.1	99	1.8	60	0.1	112
2–5	0.1	95	2.2	73	0.2	109
6–11	0.2	102	3.0	98	0.2	105
12–17	0.2	118	2.4	80	0.2	115

Note: Index values above are computed by dividing the proportion in a particular grouping by their proportion of the population. For example, if an age group has 20.2% of the product's users and represents 18.3% of the population, the index value for the grouping is 110. Index values over 100 signify above average usage and index values below 100 signify below average usage. However, values over 110 or under 90 are the most significant.
Source: Simmons Market Research Bureau, Inc., 1991.

CASE TABLE 10.4. Physical Fitness Participation Type in the Last 12 Months

(Respondents are all adults)

	Fitness Walking (%)	Index	Jogging/ Running (%)	Index	Distance Running (%)	Index
Total	23.2	100	7.0	100	2.3	100
Gender						
Male	18.2	78	8.1	116	2.8	118
Female	27.9	120	6.0	86	2.0	84
Age						
18–24	21.1	91	11.5	164	3.4	146
25–34	22.0	95	9.2	131	2.9	124
35–44	26.6	115	7.4	105	2.7	115
45–54	26.6	115	5.6	80	1.7	73
55–64	25.0	108	4.2	60	1.6	69
65 and older	18.4	79	2.5	35	1.2	49
Marital status						
Single	21.3	92	11.3	161	2.9	125
Married	25.6	110	6.1	87	2.2	95
Divorced	17.7	76	4.9	70	2.0	85
Parents	23.3	100	7.2	103	2.6	111
Region						
Northeast	20.1	86	5.2	75	1.9	80
Midwest	29.0	125	7.9	113	2.0	85
South	20.4	88	6.1	86	2.0	85
West	24.4	105	9.4	134	3.9	165
Income						
$75+	33.3	143	8.7	124	2.3	98
$60+	31.7	137	9.4	134	2.3	99
$50+	30.4	131	9.0	128	2.5	105
$40+	29.9	128	8.9	127	2.6	110
$30+	28.1	121	8.5	122	2.5	105
$30–$39	23.4	101	7.6	108	2.2	93
$20–$29	21.4	92	6.0	86	3.0	129
$10–$19	18.0	77	5.2	74	2.1	90
Less than $10	8.6	37	3.3	47	1.0	45
Presence of children						
Under 2 years	21.0	90	9.0	129	3.0	127
2–5	19.1	82	6.9	99	2.3	100
6–11	18.1	97	7.0	100	2.6	112
12–17	18.7	101	7.0	99	2.4	104

Note: Index values are above computed by dividing the proportion in a particular grouping by their proportion of the population. For example, if an age group has 20.2% of the product's users and represents 18.3% of the population, the index value for the grouping is 110. Index values over 100 signify above average usage and index values below 100 signify below average usage. However, values over 110 or under 90 are the most significant.
Source: Simmons Market Research Bureau, Inc., 1991.

CASE EXHIBIT 10.3. NordicTrack Sales

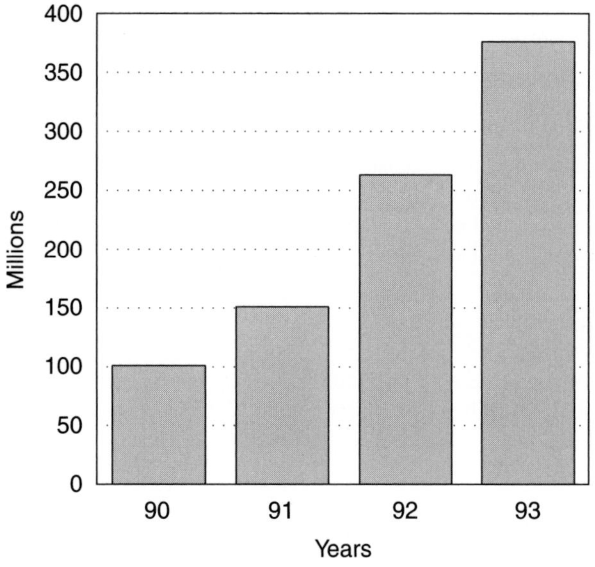

Source: Estimated from various sources.

Additionally, NordicTrack refined its organization structure to support its rapid expansion while at the same time maintaining a creative, innovative, can-do culture.

NORDICTRACK MARKETING STRATEGY

NordicTrack's marketing strategy places heavy emphasis on the 25-to-54-year-old consumer group, particularly affluent, active, sports-minded people interested in quality home exercise products. The firm's ability to continually attract new customers is frequently attributed to its smart marketing. With a multimillion-dollar budget for all forms of direct marketing, the NordicTrack has deftly used strong appeals to fitness and self-esteem to push its line of equipment.

Direct-Response Print

NordicTrack is especially strong in direct-response print advertising. Its ads can be found in such publications as *Business Week, Forbes, Fortune,* and *U.S. News & World Report.* Just by calling a phone number, prospects can order a brochure and/or a videotape.

Direct Mail

Direct mail also plays an important role in NordicTrack's marketing activities. Once on the firm's mailing list, consumers receive a constant barrage of offers.

Direct-Response Television Commercials

NordicTrack places numerous 30- and 60-second commercials on cable channels to keep consumer awareness of its product line high.

Infomercials

In 1992, a 30-minute infomercial campaign by NordicTrack led to a 19 percent increase in sales of cross-country ski simulators. However, as of 1994, the infomercial competition for home fitness equipment dollars had become so pervasive in the arena that the product area accounted for 40 percent of infomercial sales.

Telemarketing

NordicTrack uses its free videotape and brochure inquiries to generate leads for its telemarketing efforts. It then follows each prospect through three or more outbound telemarketing and direct-mail efforts.

REASONS FOR BUYING A NORDICTRACK MACHINE

NordicTrack says that customers can achieve a lifetime of health and fitness benefits from investing in a NordicTrack machine. These machines enrich their users' health and enhance their life. According to NordicTrack, when you take care of your health, you take care of every aspect of your life, including your looks, your mood, your energy, your relationships, and your job. Good health is an essential ingredient for a happy, productive life.

NordicTrack believes that the best way to ensure good health is to maintain fitness (proper body weight, firm muscle tone, and a strong cardiovascular system) through regular aerobic exercise. A NordicTrack machine is described as the most effective aerobic exercise machine available. Today, over 1 million people own a NordicTrack. The following list elaborates on some of the reasons for buying a NordicTrack machine the company stresses in its advertising:

1. *Weight loss.* NordicTrack helps take off body fat and keep it off by burning more calories in less time than any other exercise machine.
2. *Cardiovascular fitness.* By incorporating resistance and using a standing, total-body motion, a NordicTrack workout makes it easy to reach and maintain a target heart rate. Using a NordicTrack regularly makes the heart more efficient at transferring oxygen, nutrients, and other life-sustaining substances to the body's cells and organs.
3. *Increased energy.* People who exercise regularly have more stamina and a higher level of energy. NordicTrack provides an efficient total-body workout to effectively increase one's energy.
4. *Stress control.* By working all the major muscles, NordicTrack relaxes the entire body and relieves pent-up tension.
5. *Total fitness.* NordicTrack is the ideal total-body trainer. It tones and conditions the entire body as well as enjoy a long list of health benefits. It raises the user's heart rate to a target zone and keeps it there.

According to NordicTrack, when dieting, the body fights to maintain its normal percentage of body fat, or set point. Metabolism decreases and appetite increases, which can make the dieter lethargic and hungry. But it does not make the dieter thinner. Most of the weight lost during dieting is due to water loss. If the dieter does lose a little fat, it is likely to return as soon as the dieter starts eating normally.

The only sure way to keep weight off is to lower the body's set point. And the only way to do that is through aerobic exercise. NordicTrack says that its exerciser provides the most efficient and effective form of aerobic exercise by exercising the body's major muscle groups: arms, legs, buttocks, shoulders, and stomach. By doing so, it burns more calories in less time than many other exercise machines—over 1,100 per hour.

By providing the body with a complete cardiovascular workout, a NordicTrack workout increases the maximum rate at which the body utilizes oxygen, which often leads to improvement in lung capacity, heart condition, and circulation. NordicTrack lowers the heart rate through cardiovascular conditioning, and dissipates chemicals that cause discomfort and disease.

With NordicTrack, buyers can get in shape with as little as one hour of exercise per week—that is, a 20-minute session, three times a week. And this can be done in the comfort and the convenience of one's own home.

NordicTrack positions itself as the ideal total-body trainer. Unlike other machines which only exercise the muscles of the lower body, a NordicTrack machine exercises all the major muscle groups in both the upper and lower body. So people can tone and condition their entire body. Plus, a NordicTrack machine offers adjustable tension on both the upper- and lower-body exercisers so people can design a workout that concentrates on the areas they need to exercise and challenges them at the level they desire. The patented flywheel and one-way clutch mechanism provide a smooth, nonjarring motion that won't stress the joints and cause injury.

NORDICTRACK'S FUTURE

In considering NordicTrack's current marketing approach, there are three areas to focus on: (1) the firm's use of information on the home exercise equipment market (and consumers) to appeal to the largest potential audience; (2) the mix of NordicTrack's program elements and themes and how they appeal to those who don't have a home exercise machine or those who own one that they do not use; and (3) the product line and how it is kept interesting to those who are exposed to NordicTrack's appeals via print ads, direct-response television ads, infomercials, and so on. The right product mix is critical. Recent NordicTrack offerings show a proliferation of models and price points.

The critical questions for NordicTrack, and its competitors, revolve around both marketing and technology issues: how to develop and keep a differential advantage in a highly competitive and dynamic market, while maintaining sales growth and, above all, profitability. With the changing nature of the fitness equipment industry, increased competition, and the fickle nature of customer preferences, NordicTrack faces many challenges.

In its continuing quest for more sales and market share, NordicTrack regularly produces new models and innovations on old models. The firm's newest idea is a "different kind of total body fitness machine" that operates like a combination treadmill and upper-body exerciser. That product is called the WalkFit. The WalkFit user walks on a treadmill while holding a metal rod in each hand, alternatively pushing one arm ahead of the other. This nonmotorized exercise machine is unique in its ability to tone the entire body.

NordicTrack needs to formulate a direct strategy for its introduction of the WalkFit product. Recommend a direct marketing strategy for the WalkFit. In the process, address the following areas: How should the consumer market be segmented and what segment(s) should be targeted? What are the direct marketing strategy alternatives for introducing WalkFit in the highly competitive home exercise equipment market? What are the pros and cons of those strategy alternatives, given the target segment(s) and direct marketing tools? How would those strategies operate to sell the WalkFit? Which strategy alternative would you recommend, and why?

ANGRIST, STANLEY W. "It's All in the Earn-Out." *Forbes,* April 25, 1988, pp. 52, 54.

CML Group 1993 annual report.

"The Fitness Industry: Snow Motion." *Economist,* March 27, 1993, pp. 71–72.

KIRKPATRICK, MICHAEL. "Mission: Create." *New England Business,* April 1991, pp. 22–26, 79.

LASEK, ALICIA. "Infomercials Help Shape Home Fitness." *Advertising Age,* January 10, 1994, pp. S–6.

LEVINE, JOSHUA. "Fancy Coatracks." *Forbes,* February 15, 1993, pp. 112, 114.

MCEVOY, CHRISTOPHER. "NordicTrack Rolls Out New Store Concepts." *Sporting Goods Business,* July 1994, p. 24.

MCLAUGHLIN, MARK. "In Successful Acquisition Strategy, CML Asks about Lifestyles before It Acts." *New England Business,* March 21, 1988, pp. 74–76.

NordicTrack Promotional materials, 1993–1994.

POIRIER, MARK. "CML Switches Tracks." *Catalog Age,* March 1993, pp. 1, 55.

REDA, SUSAN. "Exercise Equipment Ranks High on Shopping Lists." *Stores,* July 1994, pp. 44–46.

Simmons Market Research Bureau, 1991.

Company Index

Subject Index

CREDITS

Cover photographs: Bose Corporation; The Direct Marketing Association Web Site, designed by Grey Direct & Marketing; Photograph provided courtesy of Dell Computer Corporation. Copyright August 1997 Dell Computer Corporation. All Rights Reserved; Home Shopping Network, Inc.; The Franklin Mint **Interior photographs:** *page 4:* © 1-800-FLOWERS; *page 15:* Lens Express, Inc.; *page 16-18:* The Bradford Exchange; *page 24:* History Book Club; *page 25:* Franklin Templeton Distributors, Inc.; *page 26:* Reprinted from COMPUTER LIFE Copyright © 1997 Ziff-Davis Publishing; *page 27, 28:* Reprinted from PC MAGAZINE Copyright © 1997 Ziff-Davis Publishing; *page 38:* Lands End; *page 75:* Mary Kay Inc.; *page 88:* The Direct Marketing Association; *page 100:* Cahners Reprint Services; *page 122:* Compilers Plus; *page 135:* The Sharper Image; *page 153:* The Franklin Mint; *page 202:* Blands Farms; *page 205:* Linen & Lace Inc.; *page 212:* Courtesy of Victoria's Secret Catalog. All Rights Reserved; *page 213:* Art © Rick Meyerowitz; *page 218:* Courtesy of JC Whitney—Everything Automotive; *page 228:* Designed by Janice St. George, Graphic Designer, DeltaPoint; *page 265:* VW Dealers "Exotic"/BMP DDB Needham, London, Tony Davidson, Nick Gill and Mike Rudman; *page 266:* AT&T; *page 297:* Courtesy of Fingerhut; *page 298:* NRI Schools; *page 301:* The Franklin Mint; *page 303:* © 1996 Hyperion Software Operations Inc. TM & © Marvel Characters, Inc. All Rights Reserved; *page 306:* Learning International; *page 308:* Used with permission of Doubleday Direct, Inc. MYSTERY GUILD is a registered trademark of Doubleday Direct, Inc.; *page 329:* DCI, Andover MA; *page 333:* Viking Office Products; *page 335:* Reprinted permission of Sales & Marketing; *page 336:* Photo provided courtesy of Proxima Corporation; *page 337:* Reprinted permission of Sales & Marketing; *page 357:* Courtesy IBM; *page 358:* M & C Saatchi for British Airways; *page 450, 451:* Lyrick Studios; *page 487, 8:* Franklin Mint; *page 502, 3:* QUAKE 2™ © Id Software, Inc. 1997 All Rights Reserved. *QUAKE 2™* is a trademark of Id Software, Inc. **Additional textual material:** *Chapter 1:* "Competitor Profiles," Simmons Market Research Bureau, 1991; "Heavy User Profiles," Simmons Market Research Bureau, 1991; "Avon Products, Inc. Selected User Demographics," Simmons Market Research Bureau, 1991; "Avon Products Worldwide Net Sales," AVON PRODUCTS 1991 ANNUAL REPORT; "Avon Products Worldwide Net Income," AVON PRODUCTS 1991 ANNUAL REPORT; "Uses of Personal Computers: At Home and At Work," Simmons Market Research Bureau, 1991; "Personal Computer" Own, Games, Usage, and Joystick/Paddles," Simmons Market Research Bureau, 1991; "The Weight-Control Diets Business Segments" Reprinted from "Diets That Work," by Deralee Scanlon, 1991. Used with permission of NTC/Contemporary Publishing Company; "Roll International 1992 U.S. Advertising Expenditures" Reprinted with permission from the Sept. 29, 1993 issue of Advertising Age. Copyright, Crain Communications Inc. 1993; "Demographic Comparison of TV Shoppers and the Market Average," Source: "Guess Who's Watching?" by Harvey D. Braun, DIRECT MARKETING, July 1993, p. 22; "Home Shopping Channel Customer Segments: A Cross-Cultural Perspective," by William J. McDonald, JOURNAL OF DIRECT MARKETING, Copyright © 1995 by John Wiley & Sons, Inc. Reprinted by permission of John Wiley & Sons, Inc.; "Top Five Bread Market Share Rankings," Simmons Market Research Bureau, 1991; Adapted from "The Art of Relationship Management," by Harold M. Brierley, DIRECT MARKETING, May 1994, pp. 25-26; Adapted from "1-800-Flowers Blossoms As Premier Marketing Utility," by Henry R. Hoke, DIRECT MARKETING, March 1993, pp. 28-30; "Total Amount Spent on Merchandise & Services Ordered by Mail or Phone," 1996 STATISTICAL FACT BOOK, Direct Marketing Association, as adapted from "Study of Media and Markets, 1992, 1993, AND 1994"; "Items Ordered by Mail or Phone in Last 12 Months," 1996 STATISTICAL FACT BOOK, Direct Marketing Association, as adapted from "Study of Media and Markets, 1993 and 1994"; "Value of U.S. DM Driven by Medium and Market," 1996 STATISTICAL FACT BOOK, p. 325; "Lands' End Sales, 1991-1995," and "Lands' End Income, 1991-1995," LANDS' END 1995 ANNUAL REPORT; *Chapter 2:* "Strategic Planning: An Overview," by Dick Shaver, in THE DIRECT MARKETING HANDBOOK, 2nd ed., ed. by Ed Nash, McGraw-Hill, 1992, pp. 25; *Chapter 3:* CONSUMER BEHAVIOR, 4th ed., by Leon G. Schiffman and Leslie Larzar Kanuk, Prentice Hall, 1991, p. 29. Reprinted by permission of Prentice-Hall, Inc. Upper Saddle, NJ; MARKET SEGMENTATION, 2nd ed., by Art Weinstein. Probus Publishing, 1994, p. 91-93; *Chapter 5:* Shaw, Robert and Merlin Stone, DATABASE MARKETING AND STRATEGY IMPLEMENTATION, Wiley & Sons, 1990; "The

Percentage of Direct Marketing Budgets Allocated to Database Development and Maintenance," DIRECT MAGAZINE, FORCAST SURVEY, 1994; "The Types of Databases that Direct Marketers Maintain," DIRECT MAGAZINE, FORCAST SURVEY, 1994; Shaw, Robert and Merlin Stone, DATABASE MARKETING AND STRATEGY IMPLEMENTATION, New York: Wiley & Sons, 1990, pp. 4-6; "List Industry Overview," by Arnold Fishman, DIRECT MARKETING, August 1992, pp. 23-24. *Chapter 6:* List Broker Services," 1996 STATISTICAL FACT BOOK; Adapted from DMA Circulation Council List Broker Quick Study, 1995; "List Industry Overview," by Arnold Fishman, DIRECT MARKETING, August 1992, p. 24. Adapted from "List Industry Overview," by Arnold Fishman, JOURNAL OF DIRECT MARKETING, Copyright © 1992 John Wiley & Sons, Inc. Reprinted by permission of John Wiley & Sons, Inc. *Chapter 7:* DIRECT MARKETING MANAGEMENT, by Mary Lou Roberts and Paul D. Berger, Prentice Hall, 1989, p. 70. Reprinted by permission of Prentice-Hall, Inc. Upper Saddle, NJ; *Chapter 9:* Adapted from "Casinos Gamble on Direct Mail," by Murray Raphel, DIRECT MARKETING, February 1992, pp. 32-34; Reprinted from "The United States Mail Order Industry," by Maxwell Scoge, 1994. Used with permission of NTC/Contemporary Publishing Company; Adapted from "Scott Paper Company Achieves Growth With Innovative Marketing Campaign," by Edward D. Pasternack, DIRECT MARKETING, May 1996, pp. 56-57; Direct mailing letter courtesy of National Audobon Society; Ethics Department, DMA, Inc. 1111 19th Street N.W. Suite 1100, Washington, D.C. 20036-3603. *Chapter 10:* "Catalog Sales," by Jo-Von Tucker, THE DIRECT MARKETING HANDBOOK, ed. by Edward L. Nash, McGraw-Hill, 1984; "Consumer Preference Structure Analysis," by William J. McDonald, JOURNAL OF DIRECT MARKETING, Copyright © 1993 by John Wiley & Sons, Inc. Reprinted by permission of John Wiley & Sons, Inc.; Adapted and reprinted from "How to Create Successful Catalogs," by Maxwell Scoge, 1988. Used with permission of NTC/Contemporary Publishing Company; Adapted from "Effective Use of Marketing Databases For Catalog Companies," by Cary Stronach, DIRECT MARKETING, April 1996, pp. 48-50; Adapted from "Catalog Age 100," CATALOG AGE, August 1996, pp. 1, 62-68, 72-74. *Chapter 11:* Adapted from "Telemarketing and the Law," by Mag Gorrlieb, DIRECT MARKETING, February 1994, pp. 22-23; Adapted from STARTUP TELEMARKETING, by Stanley Leo Fidel, Wiley & Sons, 1987, pp. 227-243; Source: Ethics Committee, Direct Marketing Association, Inc., Washington, DC. *Chapter 12:* Ethics Committee, DMA, Inc. Washington, DC; Adapted from "The Crying Mechanics," DIRECT MARKETING, November 1991, p. 29. *Chapter 13:* Roberts, Mary Lou and Paul D. Berger, DIRECT MARKETING MANAGEMENT, Prentice Hall, 1989, pp. 376-7. Reprinted and adapted by permission of Prentice-Hall, Inc. Upper Saddle, NJ; "Radio," ADVERTISING AGE, May 9, 1994, p. 41. Reprinted with permission from the May 9, 1994 issue of Advertising Age. Copyright, Crain Communications Inc., 1993; "Radio Listening by Gender and Station Format," Simmons Market Research Bureau, STUDY OF MEDIA AND MARKETS, 1994; Reprint from "Eicoff On Broadcast Direct Marketing," by Al Eicoff, 1988. Used with permission of NTC/Contemporary Publishing Company. *Chapter 14: page 302:* Sports Illustrated's "Advertising Rate Card"; *page 305:* "SALES AND MARKETING MANAGEMENT magazine SRDS rate information," SALES AND MARKETING MANAGEMENT; *page 306:* "New York Times Advertising Rate Card, NYT; "New York Times Book Review" newspaper advertising, NYT; Roberts, Mary Lou and Paul D. Berger, DIRECT MARKETING MANAGEMENT, Prentice Hall, 1989, pp. 349-50. Reprinted by permission of Prentice Hall, Inc. Upper Saddle, NJ; "Print Space Advertising Expenditures: 1994 vs. 1993," from DMA's 1996 STATISTICAL FACT BOOK. Source: Leading National Advertisers, Competitive Media Reporting, 1995; "Direct Marketing Association Guidelines for the Acceptance of Print Mail Order Advertising," Ethics Committee, DMA. *Chapter 15:* "Business-to-Business Direct Marketing Advertising Trends," DMA 1996 STATISTICAL FACT BOOK, 1996, p. 321. *Chapter 19:* "Customer Service Handled by a Service Bureau vs. In-House," DMA CONSUMER MAGAZINE CUSTOMER SERVICE SURVEY, 1995; "Fulfillment Centers," mediaweek infomercial 95, 1995, pp. 43-47 © 1995 ASM Communications, Inc. Used with permission from Mediaweek magazine; "Fulfillment Software," adapted from "Mail Order Fulfillment (Part I)," DIRECT MARKETING, v56, n2, June 1993, pp. 27-28; *Chapter 20:* "The New Interactive Marketing Opportunities," by Robert McKim, DIRECT MARKETING, September 1993, pp. 30-31 & 67.